A Dictionary of

Media and Communication

FIRST EDITION

DANIEL CHANDLER
and
ROD MUNDAY

OXFORD
UNIVERSITY PRESS

OXFORD
UNIVERSITY PRESS

Great Clarendon Street, Oxford OX2 6DP

Oxford University Press is a department of the University of Oxford.
It furthers the University's objective of excellence in research, scholarship,
and education by publishing worldwide in

Oxford New York

Auckland Cape Town Dar es Salaam Hong Kong Karachi
Kuala Lumpur Madrid Melbourne Mexico City Nairobi
New Delhi Shanghai Taipei Toronto

With offices in

Argentina Austria Brazil Chile Czech Republic France Greece
Guatemala Hungary Italy Japan Poland Portugal Singapore
South Korea Switzerland Thailand Turkey Ukraine Vietnam

Oxford is a registered trade mark of Oxford University Press
in the UK and in certain other countries

Published in the United States
by Oxford University Press Inc., New York

© Oxford University Press 2011

The moral rights of the authors have been asserted

Database right Oxford University Press (maker)

First published 2011

British Library Cataloguing in Publication Data
Data available

Library of Congress Cataloging in Publication Data
Data available

Typeset by SPI Publisher Services, Pondicherry, India
Printed in Great Britain
on acid-free paper by
Clays Ltd., St Ives plc

ISBN 978-0-19-956875-8

10 9 8 7 6 5 4 3 2 1

Contents

'Only connect...'
E. M. Forster

Preface

This dictionary defines nearly 2300 terms, and is thus one of the most comprehensive one-volume reference sources on its topic. However, every dictionary is unavoidably selective. Detailed comparison of the coverage of similar dictionaries, noting omissions, reveals implicit, and no doubt often unconscious, editorial policies. In the interests of transparency, we endeavour to make our own editorial policy explicit here, but readers are invited to compare the volume with its competitors.

First and foremost, we wanted this volume to be an authoritative starting-point for framing terms of reference in academic enterprises within the field, ranging from student essays to research projects. Students regularly resort to the web for definitions of key terms, and these are not always the most appropriate ones for their assignments. The adequacy of definitions depends on their framing within relevant contexts: in this book, entries include definitions of different senses related to relevant discourses (e.g. semiotics, sociology, or film-making), including significant connotations. Subject dictionaries sometimes resemble encyclopaedias or even textbooks arranged in alphabetical order of concepts. While some editorial gloss is expected in such works, we sought to produce a dictionary offering concise definitions of terms in usages relevant to the mass media and to interpersonal communication (both verbal and nonverbal). Based on an initial list of over 11 000 terms garnered from existing dictionaries, encyclopaedias, glossaries, and the indexes of academic textbooks in this field, our final selection consists primarily of those that are most regularly used (and misused) in the academic study of media and communication, and also some of the key technical terms familiar to practitioners in occupations attracting students of these topics. These terms cover a broad range of media, including TV, radio, film, telecommunications, print media, and the internet, and cross-media modes including advertising, journalism, and design. They are drawn from a wide range of disciplines including sociology, psychology, linguistics, literary theory, cultural studies, philosophy, history, art, marketing, and political theory, though we bore in mind the existence of sister dictionaries within the same series. No doubt every subject dictionary represents a particular concern with certain aspects of its field, and we were conscious of ensuring adequate coverage of certain topics under-represented in rival sources, such as perception, visual culture, the philosophy of mediatedness, new media, and videogaming. The terms selected represent a range of academic paradigms within the fields of media and communication, including both the social sciences and the humanities (and even a few relevant aspects of science and technology). The dictionary also straddles several major conceptual divides, covering issues of reception and production as well as textual analysis, qualitative and quantitative research, theory, and practice. Although this is not a historical dictionary, we have not confined ourselves to contemporary discourses but have included terms associated with previous decades of theory and research, so as to assist readers of classic works. We have excluded highly specialist terms which lack general currency in the field. We chose not to include entries for terms in everyday usage which are adequately defined in the *Concise Oxford English Dictionary*, though we do include many common terms which have currency and special significance in academic discourse on these topics but which are often undefined and taken for granted (such as style). Nor have we included biographical entries, though we do include a few of the most common 'isms' derived from influential figures (McLuhanism, Leavisite, Reithianism), and we have included as an appendix some minimal biographical notes for those mentioned in several entries. There are also no entries for organizations (e.g. BBC), proprietary brands (e.g. Facebook), or national statutes (e.g. Broadcasting Acts). However, some names, organizations, laws, and brands do appear within entries under related concepts.

In seeking to make the text as reader-friendly as possible, and to help readers to make connections between different discourses, we have included extensive cross-referencing to related terms (*see* . . . , *see also* . . . , *compare* . . .). After careful consideration we chose not to highlight any particular terms as 'key terms', since each of the many specialisms within the fields covered has its own frame of reference and core concepts. Indeed, we hope that one of the contributions of the present work will be helping to enable those in the field who 'speak different languages' to communicate more effectively with each other.

We thank colleagues who have offered specific suggestions, including Martin Barker, Richard Fallows, and Tom O'Malley at Aberystwyth University, Joshua Meyrowitz at the University of New Hampshire, and David Klafkowski, technical director of The Farm post-production; however, they are not implicated in our final editorial decisions. We welcome readers' suggestions for any future edition, which should be directed to our publisher.

Daniel Chandler and Rod Munday
Aberystwyth, May 2010

aberrant decoding Making sense of a *message or *text in terms of a different *code from the one used to encode it (Eco). This can be the basis for cultural misunderstandings: for example, the hand gesture made by joining the thumb and forefinger into a circle signifies 'OK' in the UK and the USA but in France it signifies 'worthless' or 'zero' and in Brazil it is an obscene gesture. *See also* ENCODING/DECODING MODEL; PREFERRED READING.

above-the-fold *Compare* BELOW-THE-FOLD. **1.** (print journalism) The top half of a newspaper, visible when folded in a vendor's rack—the place occupied by the *masthead and main headline. **2.** (web design) The area of a webpage visible without *scrolling—where the most important content goes.

(((⊕))) SEE WEB LINKS
• Blasting the myth of the fold

above-the-line **1.** A business model for creating mainstream *advertising, distributing it through *mass-media *channels, and charging clients a commission. This model is predicated on the logic of mass communication where one advertisement reaches millions of consumers simultaneously. However, it is being challenged by the rise of digital broadcasting and the *internet which have led to a more fragmented media audience. *See also* AUDIENCE FRAGMENTATION; DIGITAL TRANSMISSION; *compare* BELOW-THE-LINE. **2.** (film-making and television) Expenditure prior to filming, including the salaries of those on individual contracts.

absent presence **1.** In *poststructuralist theory, a concept most closely associated with Derrida, for whom it refers to the mythical status of the supposed hub of any system of ideas (*see also* DECONSTRUCTION; DIFFÉRANCE; TRANSCENDENT SIGNIFIED). This derives from the point voiced by Socrates in Plato's *Phaedrus* (*c.*370 BC) that the absence of the writer from a (circulated) text leaves it open to misinterpretation, in contrast to *presence in *face-to-face interaction (*see also* PHONOCENTRISM). This is in fact a feature of all *mediated communication, where the participants are spatially and/or temporally separated. **2.** The *structuralist notion of (present) *signifiers referring to (absent) *signifieds, which is also a *design feature of language (*see also* DISPLACEMENT), and of all *representation. **3.** The mass-mediated presence of onscreen personalities and events which can generate the illusion of almost immediate presence or even (particularly with television) *parasocial interaction. **4.** Some important and relevant term, concept, factor, question, or issue that is 'conspicuous by its absence' in a *discourse ('the elephant in the room' phenomenon). The avoidance involved is often based on embarrassment or social taboo (e.g. in the case of disability). **5.** The *symbolic

erasure of a particular sociocultural group (e.g. females, gay people, or ethnic minorities) in a *text, *genre, or *medium, or in a particular social context.
6. The discernible influence of a particular individual on some social or textual practice even when they are not present (especially when they are no longer alive), e.g. in film, when one discerns the absent presence of Hitchcock in the style of a contemporary thriller.

absent signifier 1. A particular feature which is perceived as missing from a *representation in any medium, especially where it is 'notable by its absence', breaching *expectations. *See also* COMMUTATION TEST; DECONSTRUCTION; PARADIGM; MARKEDNESS. **2.** A *medium, tool, or *representational code which is *phenomenologically *transparent. *See also* IMAGINARY SIGNIFIER.

Academy aperture Named after the Academy of Motion Pictures Arts and Sciences, this is the standard size of the 35-mm aperture plate of film projectors and printers. It produces an *aspect ratio (expressed as 1.33:1 or 4:3) which is associated with Hollywood films of the 1930s and 1940s and with television programmes from the 1950s to the 1990s.

(()) SEE WEB LINKS
• Aspect ratios

access 1. **(accessibility)** General availability for use: e.g. the percentage of a given population owning or having access to a communications medium/technology. This was a key issue for Cooley in 1909; policy-makers have argued that *public service broadcasting or the *internet should be universally available (*see* REITHIANISM). Both social factors and the *affordances or *biases of particular *communication technologies can have implications for access. *See also* CIRCULATION; DIFFUSION; DIGITAL DIVIDE; GLOBAL VILLAGE; PRIMARY AND SECONDARY DEFINERS; REACH. **2. (accessibility)** The availability of *information. *See* INFORMATION FLOW. **3. (access television)** In pay-TV, a special timeslot or *channel devoted to non-commercial use. *See also* COMMUNITY BROADCASTING. **4. (accessibility)** (*semiotics) The extent to which the *codes employed in *texts and communicative practices are available to those interpreting them. *See also* ABERRANT DECODING; BROADCAST CODES; ENCODING/DECODING MODEL; INTERPRETIVE REPERTOIRE; NARROWCAST CODES; SYMBOLIC CAPITAL. **5.** *v.* To extract *data from a computer.

accommodation 1. (*optics) The process where the eye changes focus to keep near or distant objects clearly in view. **2. (communication accommodation theory, CAT)** In *interpersonal communication, the conscious or unconscious modification of verbal and/or nonverbal features to be more like those of others present (*see also* POSTURAL ECHO). In *linguistics, **accommodation theory** postulates that people adjust their speaking styles in order to fit in with others. **3.** (sociology) The efforts made by immigrants to conform publicly to the *norms of a host culture (while actively resisting becoming assimilated to its *values). **4.** (psychology) For Piaget, the process of modifying our existing *knowledge or *schemata in order to integrate new *information. *Compare* ASSIMILATION.

account handler In *advertising and web design agencies, the person who acts as the intermediary between the *agency and the client, whose job is to interpret the client's brief and manage the process of its realization.

acoustic flow In *speech perception, the stream of vocal sounds in which a listener competent in that spoken language is able to identify words.

action code *See* PROIARETIC CODE.

action theory *See* INTERACTION.

active audience theory The view (particularly associated with *mass-media usage) that the audiences are not merely passive receptacles for imposed *meanings (*see* HYPODERMIC MODEL) but rather individual audience members who are actively (albeit often unconsciously) involved—both cognitively and emotionally—in making sense of texts. This active involvement has several interrelated dimensions: *perception, *comprehension, *interpretation, *evaluation, and response. Proponents of active audience theory claim that scholars cannot assume that the meaning of a text is fixed in advance of its reception because meaning is the product of a negotiation between the audience and the text in a particular *context of reception. They argue that people use the media for their own *purposes (*see* USES AND GRATIFICATIONS). *See also* BEHOLDER'S SHARE; CONSTRUCTIVISM; ENCODING/ DECODING MODEL; RECEPTION MODEL; *compare* CULTURAL POPULISM; EFFECTS TRADITION.

active picture The television picture visible to the viewer, as distinct from the parts of the image at the top and bottom of the screen visible only to the television engineers. *See* VERTICAL INTERVAL.

((⊕)) SEE WEB LINKS
• Television active picture sizes

actuality 1. Film of real people going about their everyday lives rather than of actors playing roles (often as segments incorporated into fictional or fictionalized narrative films in order to add *realism). 2. [French *actualité*] An early *film genre that featured short accounts of non-fictional subjects in the form of travelogues or newsreels. 3. (philosophy) That which is present at a particular place and time, and is accessible to the senses—as opposed to that which is falsified, fabricated, or that exists only in its potentiality.

actual sound *See* NATURAL SOUND.

ad *See* ADVERTISEMENT.

adaptors In *nonverbal communication, acts involving physical manipulation that serve to manage stress or tension. These include **self-adaptors** (*see* SELF-TOUCH); **alter-adaptors** (adaptations to others), including protective arm movements and arm-folding; and **object adaptors,** such as tapping a pencil on a table. One of five types of nonverbal acts according to Ekman and Wallace Friesen (the others being *affect displays, *emblems, *illustrators, and *regulators).

ADC *See* DECODER.

addition 1. One of the four logical ways in which *perception, *memory, or *representation can transform an experience that is ostensibly merely reproduced. Addition involves adding one or more elements which were not identifiably part of the original source material. For example, in eyewitness testimony, we might innocently recall a particular observation or *event which would normally be part of a similar situation but which did not occur on the particular occasion in question. *See also* DELETION; LEVELLING AND SHARPENING; SELECTIVE PERCEPTION; SELECTIVE RECALL; SUBSTITUTION; TRANSFORMATION; TRANSPOSITION. 2. In *rhetoric, *adjectio*, one of Quintilian's four types of rhetorical *figures of speech involving deviation (*mutatio*): in this case, the addition of elements.

additive colour A process of generating colours by combining red, green, and blue *light that is used in film, photography, stage-lighting, and graphic design. Mixing the *primary colours of red and green produces the secondary colour yellow, similarly, green and blue produce cyan, and blue and red produce magenta. The more that colours in light are mixed together, the lighter they become. Mixing every colour produces white light. *See also* COLOUR; RGB; *compare* SUBTRACTIVE COLOUR.

addresser and addressee 1. Alternative terms to *sender and *receiver originated by Bühler and employed in *Jakobson's model of communication. *See also* ENCODER. 2. Roles implied within a *text and/or inferred by readers: **addresser** refers to an authorial *persona, while **addressee** refers to an *ideal reader.

adjacency pairs In *conversation analysis, two successive *utterances where the second (e.g. an answer) is required by the first (e.g. a question). *Compare* INTERCHANGE.

ADR (Automatic Dialogue Replacement) A process in audio *post-production where an actor records lines of dialogue in synchrony with a character's onscreen lip movements.

ad retention (retention, retention level, adstock) (*market research) The percentage of consumers who recall a specific *advertisement or *brand even after exposure to the *advertising has ceased. Advertisements thus have a residual 'half-life'. *See also* ADVERTISING EFFECTIVENESS; AIDED RECALL; FORGETTING RATE; MESSAGE DECAY; WEAROUT.

adventure games *See* INTERACTIVE FICTION.

adversarial journalism A model of reporting in which the journalist's role involves adopting a stance of opposition and a combative style in order to expose perceived wrongdoings. This style is sometimes criticized as being aggressively antagonistic or cynically divisive. *See also* AGONISTIC STYLE; FOURTH ESTATE; WATCHDOG; *compare* ADVOCACY JOURNALISM; INVESTIGATIVE JOURNALISM.

advertisement (ad, advert) An *attention-grabbing presentation in any medium which typically serves the *marketing function of persuading consumers to purchase a product or service but which may also function to raise or maintain awareness of a brand and of the distinctive *values with which it seeks to be allied

(part of the way a brand is positioned against its rivals: *see* BRAND POSITIONING).
In terms of *communicative functions, although the advertisement is primarily a
persuasive *genre, ads are not limited to commercial purposes (e.g. political ads);
they may also be *informational (notably in advertisements from public bodies) and
in the context of the *clutter of competing claims for *attention, they often seek to be
entertaining. *See also* ABOVE-THE-LINE; ADVERTISING APPEALS; ADVERTISING
FORMATS; COMMERCIAL.

advertising 1. The process and means by which products, services, ideas, and
*brands are promoted through *mass-media messages with the intent to influence
audience behaviour, awareness, and/or attitudes. *See also* ABOVE-THE-LINE;
ADVERTISEMENT; ADVERTISING AGENCY; ADVERTISING CAMPAIGN; ADVERTISING
EFFECTIVENESS; ELABORATION LIKELIHOOD MODEL; MARKETING COMMUNICATIONS;
compare PUBLIC RELATIONS. 2. The manipulative generation of 'false needs'
which can be met by *consumption—the stance of Vance Packard, an American
journalist (1914–96)—and which promotes capitalist *values. *See also* CONSPICUOUS
CONSUMPTION. 3. The business of linking specific *commodities or *brands to
existing *values among *target audiences, producing new commodity *signs.
See also MEANING TRANSFER. 4. The shaping of lucrative *target audiences around
which commercial *mass-media content is planned. *See also* PUBLICITY MODEL.
5. A cultural currency of *lifestyle *imagery reflecting dominant social values upon
which consumers draw in the construction of *personal identities. *See also*
BRICOLAGE; CONVERSATIONAL CURRENCY; USES AND GRATIFICATIONS.

(⊕) SEE WEB LINKS

• History of Advertising Trust

advertising agency (agency) In *advertising, *public relations, and web
design, a company that provides advertising services for paying clients: e.g. Abbott
Mead Vickers BBDO. *See also* ABOVE-THE-LINE; ACCOUNT HANDLER; ADVERTISING
CAMPAIGN; ART DIRECTOR; COPYWRITER; CREATIVE BRIEF; CREATIVES; FULL-SERVICE
AGENCY; MEDIA BUYING; MEDIA PLANNING.

advertising appeals The rhetorical modes of *persuasion underlying the
implicit psychology of advertisements. Distinctive appeals contribute to *brand
positioning. For analytical purposes, ad appeals are often broadly categorized as
*rational (e.g. value for money) or *emotional (e.g. 'you deserve it'). This basic
choice of 'routes' can be related to the *Elaboration Likelihood Model of
persuasion in which the focus is either on *argument and *information or on 'the
peripheral route' (the subtleties of *connotation, *symbolism and so on).
Appeals may also be *positive or *negative, or related to hierarchical systems
such as *Maslow's hierarchy of needs. *Advertising campaigns are designed
around particular appeals—often encapsulated in a product slogan. *See also*
ADVERTISING FORMATS; APPEAL; EGO APPEALS; FEAR APPEALS; GUILT APPEALS;
NOVELTY APPEALS; PRICE APPEALS; SOCIAL ACCEPTANCE APPEALS; UTILITARIAN
APPEALS.

advertising campaign A series of advertisements for a product, service or
*brand based around a single *theme. Campaigns are carefully planned as part of an

integrated *marketing communication strategy to appear across different media over the same period so as to reach and influence a specific *target audience as effectively as possible.

advertising codes 1. Formal, published ethical codes of professional practice within the *advertising industry. 2. In *semiotics, *conventions of *form and/or *content regularly employed within advertisements. *See also* ADVERTISING FORMATS; CODES.

advertising copy The verbal (spoken or written) text in an *advertisement, which is the responsibility of a *copywriter.

advertising cultures (commercial cultures) The occupational contexts in which *advertising is practised and the prevailing practices, *value systems, and professional discourses within the advertising industry and *advertising agencies. *Compare* PROMOTIONAL CULTURE.

advertising discourse 1. In *linguistics and *discourse analysis, the ways in which different forms of language and various linguistic (and sometimes also visual and aural) techniques—are deployed within the advertising *genre, within individual ads or *advertising campaigns and/or more broadly in the *advertising industry or in particular contexts within it. *See also* ADVERTISING APPEALS; ADVERTISING CODES; ADVERTISING FORMATS. 2. In Foucauldian cultural theory and in *semiotics, a particular 'regime of truth'—the world of advertising *myths—which commentators seek to identify and deconstruct.

advertising effectiveness Whether, and to what extent, advertisements or *advertising campaigns achieve their *marketing goals (most importantly the effectiveness with which they reach and influence their specific *target market in the desired ways). Measures for assessing ad effectiveness include *ad retention and *aided recall. Within advertising agencies, an issue often seen as in tension with advertising creativity in the motivations of some *agency staff; this is reflected in and reinforced by the separate awards that exist in advertising for effectiveness and creativity. *See also* COPY TESTING; EFFECTIVE FREQUENCY; EFFECTIVE REACH; FORGETTING RATE; MESSAGE DECAY; RATINGS; REACH; WEAROUT.

advertising formats 1. Widespread *conventions of *form and/or *content that can be discerned in ads within a particular *medium. Three key elements in ad formats are product, person, and *setting. On television, the traditional format for selling domestic products to women is known within the industry as 2CK, or euphemistically as 'two women in the kitchen'. Another way of categorizing formats identifies the primary focus of the ad: e.g. on product *information, on *symbolism, or on user gratifications (*see also* ADVERTISING APPEALS; DEMASSIFICATION; LIFESTYLE FORMAT; PERSONALIZED FORMAT; PRODUCT-INFORMATION FORMAT; PRODUCT-SYMBOL FORMAT). In *semiotics, the identification and analysis of such formats is part of the broader study of *advertising codes and *conventions. 2. In the buying of media space by advertisers, differentially priced options: e.g. in print publications, specific formats offered to advertisers by a magazine or *newspaper— such as full-page, half-page and so on. *See also* MEDIA BUYING.

advertorial A portmanteau term (*advertisement* + *editorial*). Material in a *newspaper or magazine that has been constructed to look very similar to journalistic articles in the same publication but which is intended to raise awareness of a product or service and to imply endorsement by the magazine. Typically, advertorials are paid for by an *advertising agency but produced by the staff who work for the publication in which they are placed.

advocacy journalism A style of journalism that actively campaigns for a certain cause or adopts a particular perspective, sometimes derogatively contrasted with a journalistic ideal of *impartiality and *objectivity.

aerial perspective (atmospheric perspective) A *depth cue in the *visual perception of the world and a *pictorial depth cue and representational *convention in which objects appear less distinct (with less contrast) the further away they are. They also become less *saturated in colour and more like the *background colour (usually blue). *See also* PERSPECTIVE.

aerial shot *See* HIGH-ANGLE SHOT.

aesthetic codes In the discourse of *semiotics, recurrent features of *form and *style within the various expressive arts (poetry, drama, painting, sculpture, music, etc.) or *expressive and *poetic functions (sometimes termed **aesthetic functions**) which may be evoked within any kind of *text. These tend to celebrate *connotation and diversity of *interpretation in contrast to logical or scientific *codes which seek to suppress these *values. *See also* COMMUNICATIVE FUNCTIONS.

aesthetic distance (psychical distance, distance) 1. In literary and aesthetic theory, a psychological relationship between an audience and an artwork reflecting a certain degree of disinterest, or critical detachment from it. Some critics (influenced by Kant) have regarded **distancing** (or **distanciation**) as necessary in order to *background subjective emotional responses and to cultivate an approach thought to be appropriate for an aesthetic construct as opposed to everyday experience. This is consonant with the *formalist technique of *defamiliarization. 2. A similar detachment on the part of the creator of the work. 3. **(Brechtian distance)** The manipulation of audience detachment and involvement by the creator of an artwork (*see also* BRECHTIAN ALIENATION). This is reflected in signs of *constructedness in any kind of *text. *See also* REFLEXIVITY. 4. In *reception theory, the difference between how a work was regarded from the *horizon of expectations of contemporary commentators at the time of its creation and how it is viewed at the current time (Jauss).

aesthetic function *See* POETIC FUNCTION.

aestheticization 1. An alleged social trend which involves an increasing personal concern with visual displays and/or a growing role for public *spectacle in *everyday life; typically a pejorative term. *See also* VISUAL IMPERATIVE. 2. A process where a set of *values defined by ethics and based on principles and truth is replaced with a set of values defined by *aesthetics and based on feelings and *appearances.

aesthetics *See also* MEDIA AESTHETICS. 1. The philosophical study of the nature of art and the arts (e.g. what is art and what is its value?), of works of art in any medium, of the nature of beauty (in nature as well as art), of aesthetic experience and pleasure, and of theories of *taste and criticism. 2. Formal compositional or stylistic aspects of a *production in any medium as distinct from its *content or what it may depict or represent. 3. In design and *advertising contexts, what are typically thought of as 'artistic' or 'creative' aspects of design (e.g. the 'look' of a product)—stylistic rather than technically functional features.

affect 1. *v.* To have an effect on ('it affected me'). 2. *n.* The subjective or evaluative dimension in human experience (*see also* EVALUATION; SUBJECTIVITY). (psychology) *Emotion or feeling, mood, or desire which may be reflected nonverbally in *affect displays. Psychology has sometimes been divided into the domains of affect, behaviour, and *cognition, but affect leaks into all human behaviour and cognition.

affect blends *Facial expressions revealing two or more *emotions simultaneously.

affect displays (emotional expressions) In *nonverbal communication, *facial expressions in particular, but also *gestures, *postures, or other body movements demonstrating *emotion. One of five types of nonverbal acts according to Ekman and Wallace Friesen (the others being *adaptors, *emblems, *illustrators, and *regulators). **Display rules** are culturally variable; however, affect displays are not necessarily intentional.

affective communication A *communicative function involving the expression of *emotions to another person, in particular contrast to *instrumental communication. This is a key factor in *nonverbal communication and is frequently regarded as a primarily nonverbal function which is hampered by *cuelessness. *Compare* EXPRESSIVE COMMUNICATION.

affective fallacy A tendency to relate the *meaning of a *text to its readers' *interpretations, which is criticized as a form of *relativism by those literary theorists who claim that meaning resides primarily within the text (*see also* LITERALISM). Few contemporary theorists regard this as a 'fallacy' since most accord due importance to the reader's *purposes. *Compare* INTENTIONAL FALLACY.

affective language *See* EXPRESSIVE COMMUNICATION.

affective meaning *Compare* IDEATIONAL MEANING. 1. **(expressive meaning)** The personal feelings expressed by a speaker or writer. 2. **(attitudinal meaning)** The personal feelings, *attitudes, or *values of an author or speaker inferred from their words and/or *nonverbal behaviour. 3. The subjective feelings aroused in audiences or readers by a *text in any medium (*see also* CATHARSIS), or by particular words (which may be 'emotive'). The *evaluation of texts on this basis was condemned by Wimsatt and Beardsley as the *affective fallacy. 4. Sometimes synonymous with *connotation.

affective stylistics *See* READER-RESPONSE THEORY.

affiliation *See also* EXTRAVERSION. 1. (social psychology) *Liking, or the
degree to which one individual likes another. According to Argyle, this is the
most important dimension of *attitudes towards other people. This is expressed
in **affiliative behaviour** in *verbal communication generally through greater
self-disclosure (*see* DISCLOSURE), in *speech communication also through warm
and soft tones of voice and/or higher vocal *pitch, and additionally in *face-to-face
interaction through nonverbal *cues such as closer *proximity, forward leaning,
more *gaze and *eye contact, more smiling, nodding, *open (and relaxed) postures,
greater touch, *tie signs, and *postural echo. 2. **Affiliative motivation** (also
affiliation need). A human social *need* for close relationships with other people
and for approval from them, especially those of a similar age and circumstances.
Social psychologists have reported that women tend to have stronger affiliative
needs than men.

affordances (affordances and constraints) The different kinds of benefits and
restrictions that a particular *medium, tool, *technology, or technique involves.
James Gibson introduced the term affordances (which for him also implied
constraints) in order to describe the interrelationship between an animal and its
environment. Just as particular environment is conducive to certain kinds of life,
so a particular medium is conducive to certain kinds of communication (due to
its technical properties and the uses to which it is put): for example, the telephone
affords simultaneous *interpersonal communication at a distance, but constrains
that communication to voice only. *See also* MEDIA ENVIRONMENT; MEDIUM THEORY.

after-image 1. A ghost image that appears in a person's vision after fixing their
gaze upon an area of flat colour (such as a red triangle) for thirty seconds or more.
It is caused by the eye's photoreceptors losing sensitivity to high contrast images
that remain stationary in vision. **Hering after-images** are paler than the stimulus;
Perkinje after-images are a *complementary colour. 2. A phenomenon also known
as **iconic memory** that forms the basis for the concept of the *persistence of vision.
The after-image described in this context is conceived of as a frozen instant of reality
that remains stationary on the retina for a brief period before decaying. Identified by
George Sperling (b. 1934), an American psychologist. *See also* PHI PHENOMENON.

age cohort A group of people born in the same generation. In *marketing and
popular cultural history, distinctive labels are often retrospectively applied to
distinguish the differing *values and *lifestyles of successive generations (such
as *baby boomers, *generation X, *generation Y). *Compare* PEER GROUP.

agency 1. (sociology) A central thematic opposition with *structure representing
the scope for human freedom of action—versus the ways in which actions may be
determined by *social structures. *See also* DETERMINISM; ETHNOMETHODOLOGY;
PHENOMENOLOGY; SYMBOLIC INTERACTIONISM. 2. (advertising) *See* ADVERTISING
AGENCY. 3. (news) *See* NEWS AGENCY.

agenda setting A situation where critics perceive inexplicit political motives
(or an institutional tendency to overlook underprivileged perspectives) to lie behind
the choice of topics covered (e.g. in news, current affairs, and *documentaries),
their relative importance (inferred from sequence and/or the relative amounts of

space or time devoted to them), how they are presented, and what issues are backgrounded or excluded (*see also* SELECTIVE REPRESENTATION). Media agendas are often set by 'authoritative sources' in government and industry upon which news organizations rely. The primary concern is that those in power thus call attention to issues that suit their agendas and distract attention from those that undermine them. It is usually argued that this influences or determines the terms and scope of public debate—not by telling people what to think but by telling them what to think *about* and influencing the *salience for them of particular issues. *See also* FRAMING; NEWSWORTHINESS.

agent *See* SUBJECT.

agon [Greek 'contest'] Games of *competition; one of four game categories introduced by Caillois. *See also* ALEA; ILINX; MIMICRY.

agonistic style A type of oratory taking the form of an interactive exchange between persons that is characterized as a verbal duel or contest of wits. Ong characterizes *oral cultures as having an agonistic style in comparison with literary cultures.

ahistorical A critical adjective applied to a theory or a research claim that is not anchored in a specific historical *context or that does not account for change over time. *See also* HISTORICITY.

aided recall In *market research, a technique to determine how well an advertisement is recalled by a subject prompted with hints or clues. In contrast, **unaided recall** elicits subjects' recollections of a specific ad without prompting: for example, by asking them to recall any ads to which they had been exposed within the last 24 hours. *See also* AD RETENTION.

airbrushing 1. Altering the appearance of a photograph using paints or dyes which were often applied to photographic prints with an airbrush. Airbrushing was routinely used to remove unwanted blemishes in fashion magazine shoots, hence the *connotation of presenting an unattainable idealized image. In Stalin's Russia, officials were removed from photographs altogether and thus airbrushed from history. 2. Loosely, any photographic alterations, including those done digitally. *Compare* PHOTOSHOPPING.

alea [Latin 'die,' as in a six-sided cube marked with numbers] Games of chance: one of four game categories introduced by Caillois. *See also* AGON; ILINX; MIMICRY.

aliasing 1. The rendering of curves or diagonal lines in a television or digital image as a series of steps. Aliasing is an *artefact of the process of *rasterization in television and *quantization in *digital media. At lower *resolutions, the 'blocky' nature of electronic pictures begins to manifest in the form of jagged lines around diagonals and circles. *Compare* ANTI-ALIASING. 2. In digital audio, a characteristic distortion caused by a low sample rate, which is unable to approximate higher frequencies.

(((⊕))) SEE WEB LINKS

• Digital audio aliasing

alienation effect (Brechtian alienation, distanciation) A theatrical
technique intended to remind audiences that the drama is a *performance, the
characters are actors, and the *events are taking place on a stage. For example, an
actor may suddenly break out of character and speak to the audience as themselves.
Brecht believed it was important for audiences to maintain a sense of critical
distance and not to get swept up in the drama. This runs counter to the goal
of audience involvement in the *classic realist text. *See also* HIGH AND LOW
INVOLVEMENT; *compare* AESTHETIC DISTANCE; DEFAMILIARIZATION; SUSPENSION
OF DISBELIEF.

alignment 1. (*semiotics) The relation of one pair of culturally widespread
oppositional concepts (such as male/female) to another pair (such as mind/
body)—reflected in the thematic structure of texts and/or cultural practices as
revealed by *structural analysis. Lévi-Strauss illustrated a human tendency to relate
such *oppositions to each other by *analogical thinking. If we imagine commonly
paired oppositions as a horizontal dimension, then associating such pairs with
each other generates vertical relationships also—forming a conceptual basis for
cultural *codes and *myths. An *advertising campaign launched in 2005 for the
washing powder Persil in the UK was 'dirt is good'. This provocative inversion of
the Christian folklore that 'cleanliness is next to godliness' can be seen as part
of a deliberate strategy of conceptual realignment which has a distinctly
Lévi-Straussean flavour. 2. In document design, the layout of the text on the page
or onscreen—left- or right-alignment referring to which side of a textual block is
uniformly aligned with a margin on that side (the other side being consequently
'ragged').

allegory of the cave A story told by Plato in Book VII of *The Republic* to
illustrate the superiority of *information derived from reason to that derived from
the senses. The allegory takes the form of a dialogue between the philosopher
Socrates and Plato's older brother Glaucon. Socrates likens people who rely on their
senses to a group of prisoners who have spent their entire lives chained inside a
cave facing the blank back wall and unable to turn around. All they see before them
are the shadows projected onto the wall by things passing in front of the cave
entrance. These shadows of things are their only reality. In contrast, experiencing
reason is likened to a prisoner escaping the cave into the full sensory richness of the
world outside. The shadows on the wall are often used as a *metaphor for the
cinema (Baudry); the film *The Matrix* (1999) and its sequels can be seen as a
cinematic variation.

(((⬦))) SEE WEB LINKS

• Book VII of Plato's *Republic*

allusion An indirect reference within a *text or *utterance to a person, place,
*event, or another text or utterance. This either presupposes that such references
will be generally recognized or favours a particular *target audience (e.g. a classical
allusion for the well-educated, an in-joke for friends, or an allusion to *popular
culture for a youth audience).

alphabet 1. A particular sequential arrangement of a set of letters or other graphic *symbols used to write a *language in which these *graphemes are used to represent the basic speech sounds or *phonemes. 2. A *writing system based on symbols representing consonants and vowels.

alphanumeric A portmanteau word (*alphabetical* + *numerical*). An **alphanumeric character** is a number, letter, or other conventional written symbol. *See also* ASCII; FIELD.

alterity 1. In *postmodern, *poststructuralist cultural theory, **otherness** or a radical sense of *difference. *See also* OTHER. 2. In existentialist *discourse, a sense of alienation or separation from other people.

alternate reality game (ARG) A game that can take place in both physical locations and online, utilizing a variety of media such as websites and *mobile phones.

(⊕) SEE WEB LINKS

• Kubrick's strange afterlife

alternative media 1. **(community, alternative, underground media, press)** Non-mainstream media forms such as graffiti, street theatre, *fanzines, pamphlets, and community newsletters—especially when used by minority groups for campaigning on particular issues. 2. **(radical media, press)** *Newspapers, magazines, *radio stations, or online media which are not corporately owned and which circulate political messages felt to be under-represented in 'mainstream media' (seen as geared towards maximizing profits and supporting a 'free-trade' agenda). 3. **(alternative)** A *marketing category—particularly associated with cinema, music, and writing—that defines its product as being other than mainstream—either because its form is more challenging, or it expresses non-conformist values, or both.

always-already given 1. **(givenness)** Broadly, in cultural theory, a key abstract concept that is taken for granted as an essential starting-point for any *theory—often inexplicit but nevertheless the philosophical foundation on which subsequent theorizing is built (*see also* FOUNDATIONALISM). For instance, *structuralists give priority and determining power to *language—which pre-exists all individuals and determines the consciousness of human subjects. 2. In *Marxist theory, a term coined by Althusser [French *toujours-déjà-donné*] and used by those influenced by his inflection of *Marxism. For him, it referred to the way in which *ideology is a determining force shaping consciousness. He claimed that an individual is always-already a *subject, because their *gender identity, their place in a family, and their *roles and responsibilities as 'free citizens' are *ideologically determined even before they are born. *See also* CULTURAL DETERMINISM; IDEOLOGICAL STATE APPARATUS. 3. In *phenomenology, the irreducible essence of a thing. Phenomenologists claim that *being* is always-already given: i.e. that thought (in the form of an awareness of our being) comes before language. Husserl argued that the study of that which was already given was a method of bypassing metaphysics by focusing on the essence of things rather than on ideas about them. **4.** The *ontological *foundationalism that Derrida criticized as being at the heart of all metaphysics. *See also* DECONSTRUCTION; TRANSCENDENT SIGNIFIED.

ambient advertising Commercial messages embedded in the environment: e.g. on hoardings.

((⊕)) **SEE WEB LINKS**
• Creative advertisements

ambient light In photography and 3D graphics, indirect light that does not emanate from a discernible source but is reflected and refracted by surfaces and diffused in the atmosphere.

ambient optical array James Gibson's term for the patterning of light and shade that constitutes a perceiver's immediate sensory environment. *See also* FIELD.

ambiguity *See also* TOLERANCE OF AMBIGUITY; *compare* POLYSEMY. **1.** The quality of being open to more than one *interpretation (regardless of any intent). **2.** Where *meaning or intent is not immediately apparent or is indeterminable (*see* INDETERMINACY). Where the ambiguity is noticed by an audience (e.g. 'This door is alarmed'), the *preferred meaning may be inferred by drawing on relevant *social knowledge (in particular contextual cues) and *textual codes. **3.** In *instrumental communication a pejorative term identifying a communicative fault; in literary and aesthetic contexts (where this may also be called **plurisignation**), a richness of *connotations that may be positively valued as a source of divergent *interpretations.

((⊕)) **SEE WEB LINKS**
• Ambiguity as an aesthetic principle

amplification of deviance A version of *labelling theory explaining *moral panics in terms of a negative *feedback loop that spirals out of control when the strength of social condemnation of a criminal act leads to more reported instances of that act (or apparently similar acts) which leads to more condemnation, and yet more instances. Although the phenomenon is a social one, the *mass media are often blamed for increasing the power and range of the amplification effect, creating a *moral panic.

amplitude modulation (AM) A method of *encoding *information into the wave of a carrier signal by increasing and decreasing its height but not altering its length. The height of wave (**amplitude**) is measured as the distance between its peak and trough.

AM radio *Analogue radio stations that broadcast using *amplitude modulation, typically at frequencies between 530 and 1600 KHz, which includes medium and long wave bands. AM radio has a large range because it does not rely on the *transmitter being in the line of sight of the *receiver but it is prone to electrical interference. *See also* RADIO WAVES.

analepsis *See* FLASHBACK.

analogical thinking 1. (analogical reasoning, metaphorical thinking)
Generating ideas through making analogies between different phenomena.
2. According to Lévi-Strauss, the way that people make connections between the
fundamental *binary oppositions that they encounter in their everyday lives,
perceiving metaphorical resemblances between paired categories (notably 'similar
differences' connecting more concrete with more abstract *oppositions). For
example, raw is to cooked as nature is to culture: in *structuralist shorthand, 'raw :
cooked :: nature : culture'. *See also* ALIGNMENT. Oppositions like these are argued to
be the basis for universal *myths that cut across cultural distinctions and contexts.

analogic communication 1. *Meaning 'given off' (Goffman) through *body
language. Such communication is typically unintentional, and unavoidably 'gives us
away', revealing such things as our moods, *attitudes, intentions, and truthfulness—
or otherwise. *See also* LEAKAGE. 2. Any communication through *modalities based
on graded relationships on a continuum (not only *body language, but also
*paralinguistic features and pictures) rather than being based on discrete elements
such as words. *See also* MEDIA FORMS; *compare* DIGITAL. 3. In some contexts (e.g.
therapy), an emphasis on *process rather than on *content—on *how* people are
saying things rather than on *what* they say.

analogue *See also* ANALOGUE TRANSMISSION. 1. A *modality based on graded
relationships on a continuum: e.g. *body language, paralinguistic *cues, *emotions,
pictures, and photographs (regardless of whether they were produced using digital
technology) rather than on discrete, recombinable elements (as in verbal language
and mathematics). *Analogical communication can signify infinite subtleties which
seem 'beyond words'. On the other hand, analogue modes lack the syntactic
complexity or semantic precision that is achievable with *digital modes (notably
with verbal language). 2. A process whereby the physical properties of one medium
are transferred to another in an analogous physical form. For example, in sound
reproduction minute pressure differences in the air which the ear perceives as
sounds are captured by the pressure-sensitive diaphragm of a microphone and
converted into an electrical *signal which is modulated to match them exactly.

analogue-to-digital converter *See* DECODER.

analogue transmission A method of sending *information over long distances
by encoding it as an analogue *signal. This involves modulating a continuous beam
of charged *electromagnetic particles (most commonly *radio waves but also
microwaves and visible light sent through fibre-optic cables). Analogue signals are
so called because they are modulated in ways that are directly proportional
(analogous) to changes in the source material they encode, and their modulations
consist of smooth transitions between states (slopes) rather than the abrupt changes
(steps) which are characteristic of *digital signals. There are three main
disadvantages of analogue transmission systems as compared with *digital
transmission: firstly, analogue processes encode both wanted and unwanted
information (or *noise) into the signal itself, so analogue transmission suffers from
artefacts such as audio 'hiss' and picture 'snow'. Secondly, analogue signals are
continuous temporal segments which are transmitted in *real time: consequently

the frequency occupied by a particular analogue signal which is regularly sent has to be allocated in advance for that single purpose. In the case of radio, television, and mobile phones, this allocation relates to the licensing of specific frequency bands (or channels) within the *electromagnetic spectrum. Thirdly, analogue signals cannot be *compressed: consequently media that encode a large amount of information (such as television) require a correspondingly large amount of signal *bandwidth. *See also* SPECTRUM SCARCITY; TRANSMITTER.

analogy A comparison between two different things based upon some *similarity, in the interests of clarification or explanation. Typically the illustration of an unfamiliar or abstract concept by comparison to a more familiar or concrete one. Rhetorically these may be expressed in the form of *metaphors or *similes. *Compare* ANALOGICAL THINKING.

anamorphic image An image that appears distorted or even unrecognizable unless viewed from a particular point or with a correcting mirror or lens. A mild everyday example is the elongated image of a bicycle on a road surface (indicating a cycleway). **Anamorphosis** is the process involved.

anamorphic process (film) A technique for producing *widescreen images using two distorting lenses: one in the camera that squeezes the horizontal axis of image as it is being filmed; the other in the projector that expands it as the film is being projected. This technique allowed for widescreen films to be shot cheaply using standard 35-mm equipment. Standard definition 16:9 television uses a *digital anamorphic process rather than a lens.

anaphora (*adj.* **anaphoric**) 1. In *rhetoric and poetry, emphasis created through the repetition of an initial word or phrase. For example, the phrase 'let freedom ring' from the 'I have a dream' speech of Martin Luther King Jr. 2. (linguistics) An element of referral in a sentence that links it with a *referent identified earlier. Most commonly a pronoun performs this function: for example, 'Jane was happy: *she* passed the test'. In **zero anaphora** the element of referral is omitted entirely: for example, in a recipe you might be asked to 'dice the carrot and simmer for 5 minutes'. *See also* ELLIPSIS.

anchor In US television and radio (especially newscasts) the main presenter and coordinator of a *live broadcast.

anchorage (*semiotics) A function whereby linguistic elements in a text (such as a caption) constrain the *preferred readings of an image (Barthes). Conversely, the illustrative use of an image can anchor an ambiguous verbal text.

animal communication (zoosemiotics) 1. The various nonverbal strategies of signalling and *information exchange used by animal species. The types of animal communication include vocal calls, visual displays, body movement, the use of territory, and chemical *signals. 2. The study of such communication.

animation A film-making technique that traditionally involved photographing a series of drawings or inanimate objects, adjusting them each time a new photograph is taken so that they appear to move when the film is run through a projector. In **cell animation,** individual characters are painted and the animator draws onto sheets of clear acetate (or cells), the transparency of which allows multiple elements to be combined and photographed over the same background drawings. Until the rise of computer animation, this technique was used extensively in the creation of cartoon films. Each element in a complex scene could be drawn by a different artist in a *production-line process. **Stop-motion animation** is the technique of photographing three-dimensional models and moving them frame-by-frame: as seen in films such as *Jason and the Argonauts* (1963). **Computer animation** combines individual frames that are digitally created in the computer or captured using software tools. Animating on a computer allows for the complex mathematics involved in such effects as *motion parallax and *depth of field to be routinely incorporated into the *mise-en-scène of cartoon films. In addition, realistic-looking images can be created using sophisticated texture-mapping, image-tracking, and lighting—which has led to computer animation being incorporated in live-action films such as *Jurassic Park* (1993).

announcement lists *See* ELECTRONIC MAILING LISTS.

anomalous motion or movement *See* APPARENT MOTION.

anonymity [Greek 'nameless'] A state where a person's name or other identifying characteristics are not known. A characteristic of *internet communication of the kind that takes place in online forums such as *chatrooms or *bulletin boards, or in *virtual worlds. *See also* DISCLOSURE.

antagonist The main character opposing the *protagonist in a drama or narrative. Often a cruel or evil villain, but where the protagonist is a cruel or evil *anti-hero, the antagonist may have admirable qualities.

anti-ads A genre of advertisements that emerged in the 1980s and drew attention to discrepancies between *advertising and reality. Although anti-ads were created by commercial companies to sell products, they did so by being critical of traditional advertising techniques: targeting *savvy consumers using gritty visuals, no-nonsense *voiceovers, or by deconstructing other advertising styles through parody. *See also* CULTURE JAMMING; SUBVERTISING.

anti-aliasing In computer graphics, *typography, and television, a method of smoothing-out the jagged appearance of diagonal or curved lines by blurring their edges. *See also* ALIASING.

anticlimax (*adj.* **anticlimactic**) In *drama and *narratives, an *event or revelation that either does not live up to *expectations, or diminishes the impact of what has gone before. The shift in tone signalled by an anticlimax can be used deliberately: for comic or ironic effect, as is the case when Indiana Jones nonchalantly shoots a sword-wielding adversary in *Raiders of the Lost Ark* (1981), or to heighten the shock value of a scare in a horror film: for example, in the final scene in *Carrie* (1976). Sometimes this effect is termed **bathetic**.

anticlimax order *See* CLIMAX.

anti-hero A central character in a *narrative or *drama who lacks the admirable qualities of fortitude, courage, honesty, and decency that are usually possessed by traditional heroes. Examples include Alex in *A Clockwork Orange* (novel 1962; film 1971). Note that the anti-hero is not the *antagonist or villain.

aperture An opening; an adjustable hole behind a lens, through which light passes in a *camera or projector.

API *See* APPLICATION PROGRAMMING INTERFACE.

aporia (*adj.* **aporetic**) 1. In literary theory, an *ambiguity that makes *meaning undecidable. *See also* INDETERMINACY. *Deconstruction can be seen as the identification of aporia—deep *contradictions arising from the inadequacy of *binary oppositions and that lead to the unravelling of a text. 2. In *rhetoric, the deliberate expression of doubt or uncertainty by an author or speaker (e.g. Hamlet's 'To be or not to be' soliloquy). 3. Originally in philosophy, the perplexity induced by *propositions that seem plausible taken separately but which are logically inconsistent when taken together. 4. In *videogame theory, Aarseth's term for an obstacle that prevents the player from completing a game and that can only be overcome with effort. *See also* ERGODIC.

apparatus 1. As in **state apparatus** (Marxist theory) *See* IDEOLOGICAL STATE APPARATUS. 2. As in **apparatus theory** (film theory) *See* CINEMATIC APPARATUS.

apparent motion (**illusory** or **anomalous motion** or **movement**) A sensation of movement in a context where neither the observer nor the stimulus are physically moving. **Real motion** is the continuous physical displacement of an object from one location to another. In apparent motion the movement is caused by a perceptual illusion: for example, moving pictures in the cinema are actually a series of rapidly photographed still images shown in quick succession. Shimmering anomalous 'motion illusions', such as those produced by the Japanese psychologist Akiyoshi Kitaoka (b. 1961) are variously attributed to blending *after-images, colour and brightness contrasts, eye movement (*see* SACCADE), neural fatigue, and peripheral drift (*see* PERIPHERAL VISION); such illusions are most striking on the printed page, where the viewer knows that they are not actually animated. *See also* BETA MOVEMENT; PHI PHENOMENON.

appeal 1. A persuasive strategy employed in a *message. *See* ADVERTISING APPEALS; EGO APPEALS; FEAR APPEALS; GUILT APPEALS; SOCIAL ACCEPTANCE APPEALS. 2. (**audience appeal**) (television and radio) A loose reference to the predicted popularity of a programme invoked in commissioning and scheduling. Audience appeal is often used as a justification by the makers of popular television programmes criticized by highbrow critics as targeting the 'lowest common denominator'. 3. (**charity appeal**) A short radio or television spot or campaign asking for donations for a particular cause.

appearance 1. The way something seems on the surface, as opposed to some underlying reality. 2. In *nonverbal communication, the way someone looks to an observer (e.g. *body type, style of dress)—a key feature of initial *impression formation and visual *stereotyping.

appellation *See* INTERPELLATION.

appellative function *See* CONATIVE FUNCTION.

application programming interface (API) A software tool on computers and the internet which performs a particular computational function (such as accessing memory or graphics). APIs act as 'building blocks' allowing software developers to create new applications without having to code every function from scratch. *See also* MASHUP.

appreciation index *See* RATINGS.

appropriation 1. **(cultural appropriation)** The adoption by one cultural group of some of the *cultural forms of a different cultural group (including *subcultures). For instance, 'metrosexual' fashions can be seen as a cultural appropriation of gay culture by heterosexual men. 2. (*advertising) A 'cannibalistic' process drawing on widespread cultural and subcultural *imagery and recontextualizing this in advertisements for *target audiences for whom such imagery may be particularly meaningful. For example, the imagery associated with existing representations of nostalgia, *feminism, and homosexuality has been widely appropriated in this way, as have celebrities and stylistic fashions. In semiotic terms, this is the appropriation of *signifiers and their *recontextualization in advertisements, where they acquire new *signifieds and thus become new *signs. *See also* MEANING TRANSFER; METAPHOR; *compare* CONDENSATION. 3. *See* MASHUP.

apps *See* SOFTWARE.

arbitrariness (not to be confused with randomness) 1. In classical Greek philosophy, the issue of whether there was a natural connection between words and what they represent or whether the relation between them was merely a matter of *convention. *See also* CONVENTIONALITY. 2. For Saussure, a fundamental principle referring to the purely conventional nature of the relationship between the *signifier and the *signified in the *sign—at least in linguistic signs (words). The word 'apple' (whether spoken or written) does not resemble an apple, and speakers of different languages refer to it by other names. 3. For Hockett, this same quality was a fundamental *design feature of human language that contributed to its power and flexibility, in this case a feature shared with the communication systems of other primates. 4. In *structuralist semiotics, a principle that all signs (not just linguistic ones) are to some extent arbitrary and conventional (and thus subject to *ideological manipulation)—a notion that has been applied to the *mass media, for instance. *See also* CONVENTIONALITY; MOTIVATION. 5. For Peirce, the degree of arbitrariness involved in different kinds of signs. *See* RELATIVE ARBITRARINESS.

ARC *See* ASPECT-RATIO CONVERSION.

archaic forms *See* RESIDUAL FORMS.

archetype 1. An idealized *model of a typical example of some category. 2. In Jung's *psychoanalytic theory, a recurrent and universal *symbolic image found in the 'collective unconscious' of humankind, such as the 'great mother'. 3. A *motif (such as a *symbol, stock character, or *scenario) widely encountered in mythology, folklore, dreams, literary works, or art.

archive (library footage) 1. Film or television *footage that is sourced from a film or video library. 2. **(archive quality)** A general term used by video engineers to describe poor-quality library footage.

arcing *See* ASPECT-RATIO CONVERSION.

ARG *See* ALTERNATE REALITY GAME.

argument 1. In modern *rhetoric, *discourse that is intended to convince an audience. One of the four rhetorical modes of discourse identified by Brooks and Warren as fulfilling basic human *communicative purposes (*compare* DESCRIPTION; EXPOSITION; NARRATION). They distinguish between argument (using *rational appeals) and *persuasion (using *emotional appeals), suggesting that persuasion is almost a fifth type. 2. (logic) One of the three components of rational thought, along with terms and *propositions.

arousal A state of heightened alertness or preparedness to act reflected in physiological signs such as: increased heart rate, blood pressure, respiration, and skin conductance; pupil dilation; higher blinking rate and vocal *pitch; and speech hesitations. Arousal can reflect *emotions which are positive (e.g. liking, love, or relief) or negative (e.g. dislike, anger, embarrassment, or anxiety). In *nonverbal communication research, mutual gaze (*see* EYE CONTACT) has been found to be physiologically arousing and *gaze aversion functions to reduce arousal. Discrepant signs of arousal are widely cited as indicators of deception (*see also* LEAKAGE). *Mass-media *effects researchers often refer to the role of arousal in relation to onscreen violence. According one theory, those already in a state of high arousal (which may itself have been influenced by TV viewing) are more likely to engage in aggressive behaviour in response to watching a violent incident on TV than are others. Berkowitz found that if viewers of a violent film were made angry or frustrated before they watched it, they expressed more aggression than those who were not already angry or frustrated. However, *heavy viewers tend to be less emotionally aroused by violent TV itself than do light viewers.

art director In *advertising agencies, a person involved in the creative *production of ads who deals mainly with the visual images. *See also* CREATIVES.

artefact (artifact) 1. **(cultural artefact)** An object made by a human being. 2. **(methodological artefact)** In research, a phenomenon generated by the investigative procedure itself. 3. In film or video engineering, the manifestation of a fault in any given medium: for example, scratches on a film, crackle heard on the radio, *dropout on videotape. *Compare* NOISE.

articulation 1. In *oral communication, control of the voice so as to produce clear and distinct sounds in speech. 2. (*semiotics) Structural levels within semiotic *codes—which are divisible into those with **single articulation, double articulation,** or which are **unarticulated**. A semiotic code which has **double articulation** (as in the case of verbal language) can be analysed into two abstract structural levels: a higher level called the level of **first articulation** and a lower level—the level of **second articulation**. At the level of first articulation the system consists of the smallest meaningful units available (e.g. *morphemes or words in a language). These meaningful units are complete *signs, each consisting of a *signifier and a *signified. At the level of second articulation, a semiotic code is divisible into minimal functional units which lack meaning in themselves (e.g. *phonemes in speech or *graphemes in writing). They are not signs in themselves (the code must have a first level of articulation for these lower units to be combined into meaningful signs). If a code cannot be decomposed into minimal re-usable elements which are in themselves non-meaningful then the code lacks the double articulation found in verbal language. No-one has been able to identify any basic, recurrent, and rearrangeable non-meaningful units into which paintings, photographs, or films could be wholly decomposed and thus such media are said to lack double articulation. In *linguistics, the use of the term articulation in the structural sense is largely abandoned, and double articulation is referred to as **duality of patterning**. In his list of the *design features of human language, Hockett listed this as a feature not shared with the communication systems of any other species. 3. Structural relationships between elements of a social *formation. *See also* BASE AND SUPERSTRUCTURE; RELATIVE AUTONOMY. 4. Broadly, in *cultural studies, the intersection of different facets of *social identity (such as *gender, *ethnicity, *class, and age) at a particular moment.

(((()))) SEE WEB LINKS

• Articulation

ASCII (American Standard Code for Information Interchange) A protocol consisting of 95 *alphanumeric characters and 33 control codes that allows documents to be read and manipulated across different computer systems and programs.

ASL In the online parlance that grew up around *Internet Relay Chat (IRC), an acronym standing for Age, Sex, Location—a request (normally terminated with a question-mark) for the other party in a text-based chat to provide this initial screening information (which would not require an explicit request in *face-to-face interaction).

asocial *adj.* 1. The absence of a social dimension in a *theory. 2. An individual trait of avoiding social *interactions or of lacking social sensitivity.

aspect ratio A standardized relationship between the width and height of an *image. Film aspect ratios include 1.33:1 (also known as Academy ratio until the 1950s), 2.35:1 (the *anamorphic format Cinemascope) 1.85:1 and 1.66:1 which are both non-anamorphic formats. Television at first adopted the Academy ratio, but since the 1990s *widescreen sets of 1.77:1 (more commonly expressed as 16:9) have become the norm. *See also* ASPECT RATIO CONVERSION; LETTERBOX FORMAT; PILLARBOX FORMAT.

aspect-ratio conversion (ARC) In television *post-production, 'arcing' typically involves *cropping, 'letterboxing', or stretching the picture to accommodate different screen formats. Each process has advantages and disadvantages. For example, when arcing 4:3 images for a 16:9 screen: cropping allows the image to fill the screen but twenty-five percent of the original picture is lost; masking preserves the original image but the areas at the top and bottom of the screen are left blank; stretching makes use of the entire screen and preserves the picture but distorts the image. *See also* ASPECT RATIO; LETTERBOX FORMAT; PAN AND SCAN; PILLARBOX FORMAT.

🌐 **SEE WEB LINKS**
• Digital widescreen TV

assemble editing A method of linear video *editing which records control *track information along with picture, audio, and *timecode. Assemble editing does not require a striped tape (*see* STRIPING) but the *shots must be joined together in chronological sequence or there will be picture disturbances.

assimilation A psychological tendency to interpret new experience in a manner consistent with existing concepts or *knowledge; *compare* ACCOMMODATION. It includes the influence on *perception of habits, interests, and sentiments, a concept introduced by Allport and Leo Postman in 1945 (*see also* LEVELLING AND SHARPENING). Assimilation by *condensation involves fusing several details into one. Assimilation to *expectation involves transforming details into what one's habits of thought suggest they usually are. Assimilation to linguistic habits involves fitting phenomena into the familiar frameworks of conventional verbal categories (*see also* CATEGORIZATION). Assimilation to interest involves giving primary attention to details which reflect one's occupational interests or roles. Assimilation to prejudice may simply involve assimilation to *expectation or to linguistic categories, but it may also involve deep emotional assimilation to hostility based on racial, *class, or personal prejudices. *See also* ADDITION; DELETION; SUBSTITUTION; TRANSFORMATION; TRANSPOSITION.

associative editing (**associational** or **relational editing**) (film or video) The *juxtaposition of two contrasting images which can be interpreted as having an analogous thematic meaning: for example, a *shot of a passionate kiss followed by a shot of fireworks exploding signifies explosive passion. *Compare* DIALECTICAL MONTAGE; KULESHOV EFFECT.

asymmetrical relationships (**asymmetrical roles**) *See also* COMMUNICATION NETWORK; RELATIONAL COMMUNICATION; SOCIAL NETWORKS. **1.** In communication, unequal *status or *power relations between participants, whose *roles are termed superior (or superordinate) and subordinate. *Expectations and behaviour are largely non-reciprocal (in contrast to *symmetrical relationships). This may be reflected in the initiation, termination, direction, amount, form, or style of the communication that takes place. For instance, in hospitals, a doctor is more likely to touch a nurse than vice versa (Goffman). **2.** More broadly, communicational arrangements on occasions when there is unequal *access to *information on the part of the *sender and the *receiver, in which these roles are not reversible, and in which there is no *feedback, such as when someone is eavesdropping or spying on another person. *See also* ONE-WAY COMMUNICATION.

asynchronous communication A communication exchange that does not take place at the same time for its participants. Any communication where responses are significantly delayed is considered to be asynchronous. Some forms of communications media render communication more asynchronous than others: for instance, communication through the printed word is asynchronous whereas telephone conversations are synchronous. *Compare* SYNCHRONOUS COMMUNICATION.

asynchronous sound (audiovisual media) *Compare* SYNCHRONOUS SOUND. 1. Diegetic sound that is heard prior to the depiction of the action that produces it or that continues after that action is no longer onscreen. *See* DIEGESIS; SOUND BRIDGE. 2. A technical fault in which the sound is unintentionally out of sync with the screen image. 3. Intentional background sounds not directly related to onscreen actions.

asyndeton *See* DELETION.

atmospheric perspective *See* AERIAL PERSPECTIVE.

attention The process of selecting what is attended to and what we become conscious of in the welter of *sensory data received simultaneously, so as to make efficient use of limited processing capacity. Current theories suggest that sensory data undergoes an initial process of pattern analysis and then a 'filter' mechanism blocks some of the results from consciousness (as when we realize that we have driven for a while without awareness); and/or a perceptual *bias (or *perceptual set) makes us aware of what might be expected based on *context, probability, recent experience, and importance to the individual. While relevance to current concerns is one key reason for features in a perceptual field 'standing out' for individuals, another is that, all things being equal, our attention is drawn to intense stimuli such as bright lights, loud noises, saturated colours, and rapid motion (*see also* SALIENCE). *See also* SELECTIVE ATTENTION.

attitude measurement Any attempt to survey and measure people's *attitudes in relation to a *topic, whether by academic social scientists, *market researchers, *media industry researchers, or *public opinion pollsters. Attitude *surveys typically take the form of *questionnaires asking people to agree or disagree with a series of statements and to express the strength of their opinion (*see* LIKERT SCALE), though Osgood's *Semantic Differential scale is more open-ended. The drawbacks of attitude surveys include the issue that not everyone will have well-developed attitudes to the topic and that they have not been found to be reliable predictors of behaviour.

attitudes 1. Long-term **beliefs** (or systems of beliefs) that reflect deeper *values, may be expressed as opinions and may or may not be reflected in a tendency to behave in accord with these (e.g. as reflected in *nonverbal behaviour). Some social scientists regard attitudes as predictive of behaviour; others argue that they can only be inferred from behaviour. They are traditionally identified as having *cognitive, affective, and behavioural components. Deeply-held beliefs include prejudices and may be regarded as key features of personality but attitudes may be positive,

negative, or neutral. **Interpersonal attitudes** are attitudes towards others (including
*liking and disliking, friendliness and hostility). 2. For Schutz, frames of mind. *See*
CRITICAL ATTITUDE; NATURAL ATTITUDE.

attitude scale *See* LIKERT SCALE.

attitudinal effects *Compare* BEHAVIOURAL EFFECTS; COGNITIVE EFFECTS.
1. Any changes in the *attitudes of individuals or groups attributed to specific
causes. 2. In relation to the *mass media, influences of the use of particular media
on the attitudes of users—one focus of academic media research within the *effects
tradition. *Cultivation theory, for instance, emphasizes attitudinal effects of
television viewing on viewers rather than *behavioural effects. Heavy watching of
television is seen as 'cultivating' attitudes which are more consistent with the world
of television programmes than with the everyday world.

attitudinal meaning *See* AFFECTIVE MEANING.

audience 1. The *receiver(s) of a *message. 2. Those viewing and/or listening to
broadcast media—radio and/or television **(mass-media audience)**—or to a
particular station, channel, programme, series, or advertisement (*see also* RATINGS).
Note that the plural term **audiences** in relation to the *mass media sometimes
alludes to *audience fragmentation. 3. The assembled spectators or listeners at a
public *event, such as a film at a cinema, or a *live *performance such as a play at a
theatre—or the studio audience for a broadcast programme. *See also* FILM
AUDIENCE. 4. The *readership of a book or of a *newspaper or magazine. *See also*
AUDITED CIRCULATION. 5. The group at whom a product, service, advertisement, or
*advertising campaign is directed—also *target audience. *See also* DUAL AUDIENCE;
MINORITY AUDIENCES; NICHE AUDIENCE; PRIMARY AUDIENCE; SECONDARY AUDIENCE.
6. A broad **reception** concept employed by researchers (both academic and within
the *media industry) involved in the analysis of patterns of *mass-media usage and
responses to *productions and *performances. *See also* AUDIENCE FLOW; AUDIENCE
MEASUREMENT; AUDIENCE RESEARCH; AUDIENCE STUDIES; CUMULATIVE AUDIENCE;
INHERITED AUDIENCE. 7. A core concept in *rhetoric, in which writers and speakers
are urged to 'consider the audience'. *See* RECEIVER-ORIENTED COMMUNICATION.
8. A polemical construct in public debate in relation to the *mass media, in which
'the audience' is represented as an undifferentiated mass—often also being seen as
passively manipulated by the media (*see also* EFFECTS TRADITION; FRANKFURT
SCHOOL; HYPODERMIC MODEL; MANIPULATIVE MODEL; MASS AUDIENCE). This view
ignores *segmentation, *audience fragmentation, and the diversity of responses to
media output. *See* ACTIVE AUDIENCE THEORY; BEHOLDER'S SHARE; NOMADIC
AUDIENCES; RECEPTION MODEL. 9. In *active audience theory, readers, viewers, or
listeners as determinants of the *meaning of texts.

audience determinism *Compare* AUTHORIAL DETERMINISM; TEXTUAL
DETERMINISM. 1. In relation to the *interpretation of *texts that are separated from
their authors (e.g. published books and broadcasts), the notion that the last word
rests with the *readership, since, as Socrates notes in Plato's *Phaedrus* (*c.*370 BC),
the author cannot answer back. Ultimately, then, readers rather than authors
determine the *meaning of texts. However, texts cannot mean whatever we want

them to mean—a reader needs textual evidence and support from an *interpretive community for their interpretation to be taken seriously. 2. An extreme *social determinist position relating to the *decoding of texts which reduces individual decodings to a direct consequence of social *class position. A more moderate stance is that *access to different *codes is influenced by social position and that this might influence how texts are interpreted (Morley). 3. With regard to the *mass media, the voluntarist stance opposed to *media determinism, whereby instead of media being presented as doing things to people the emphasis is on people doing things with media. *See also* USES AND GRATIFICATIONS.

audience effects 1. (psychology) The influence on *performance of the presence of an audience. This applies both to public performances and to everyday behaviour in *synchronous communication, especially in *face-to-face interaction. *Compare* HAWTHORNE EFFECT. 2. In discourse within the *effects tradition, consequential influences of *mass-media use on individuals or groups. *See* EFFECTS.

audience factors 1. In models of communication or *persuasion, specific *variables associated with the audience (e.g. education) that research has identified as among those that can affect the effectiveness (e.g. the persuasiveness) of a *message. In the *Yale model these are normally called *receiver factors. 2. In market research, all relevant factors relating to the *target audience. 3. In *audience research (both by academics and *media industry researchers), audience variables (e.g. *demographic factors) that are identified by researchers and used to analyse patterns of media use and responses to *productions. 4. In technical writing, one of the key factors that writers are advised to bear in mind from the outset: for whom are they writing?

audience flow 1. The carry-over of audience members from one radio or television programme to another or from one time period to another. This is used strategically by television companies to plan schedules and boost ratings. 2. The changing pattern of audiences for a particular television channel or radio station throughout the day.

audience fragmentation 1. The break-up and dispersal of the *mass-media audience since the shift to *digital media that began in the later 1980s. *See also* DEMASSIFICATION; NARROWCASTING; *compare* HOMOGENIZATION; MASS AUDIENCE. 2. Especially in relation to television, the idea that multiple channels have led to a loss of widely-shared experiences of the same programmes (a potential threat to social *cohesion). This view may underestimate the appeal of core, mainstream content.

audience measurement Primarily applied to *quantitative research into audience size and *demographics for particular broadcasting media, individual channels, stations, or programmes, or for particular *newspapers or magazines. Typically undertaken by independent, industry-wide bodies. *See also* AUDIENCE SHARE; AUDITED CIRCULATION; PEOPLEMETER; RATINGS; REACH; TELEVISION VIEWING PATTERNS.

audience needs *See* MASLOW'S HIERARCHY OF NEEDS; MOTIVATION; PERSONAL FUNCTIONS; USES AND GRATIFICATIONS.

audience-oriented theory or criticism *See* READER-RESPONSE THEORY.

audience participation 1. Any active involvement of audience members in a live public performance, whether or not planned as part of the performance. 2. The involvement of audience members in a broadcast programme—primarily involving either: a studio audience (for instance, asking questions or providing contestants in game shows); phone-ins; or, in *interactive television, making choices by button-pressing. *See also* HIGH AND LOW INVOLVEMENT.

audience research 1. Broadly, empirical studies of *mass-media usage undertaken by academics (*see also* AUDIENCE STUDIES) or those in the *media industry (*see also* AUDIENCE MEASUREMENT; USES AND GRATIFICATIONS)—though the functions and research methods often differ considerably. Such research may be *quantitative or *qualitative. 2. *Market research into a *target audience.

(()) SEE WEB LINKS

• *Lord of the Rings*: film audience research

audience share (share) In *media industry research, the percentage of all households tuned to a particular radio station/TV channel or programme at a particular time. A programme's share is affected by factors such as competing programmes. *Compare* RATINGS; REACH.

audience studies Usually academic (rather than *media industry) research into culturally significant aspects of the use of particular *mass media (e.g. the domestic politics of television use) or into relationships between media *texts or *genres and their interpreters. They tend to be primarily *qualitative and may also be *ethnographic. *Compare* AUDIENCE RESEARCH.

audited circulation Industry-standard figures for the average number of copies of each issue of a particular *newspaper or magazine in circulation. The actual *readership is likely to be larger. These figures are independently verified to provide reliable data for *media buyers in *advertising. *Demographic data has not traditionally been an integral element of such audits but is increasingly being made available to advertisers (and thus more in accord with other mass media). The process of verification is overseen in the UK and the USA by the Audit Bureau of Circulations (ABC)—an independent body paid for by media owners.

auditory perception (sound perception) (psychology) The recognition, discrimination, and *interpretation of sounds, including: frequency, *pitch, timbre, loudness, speech, and music, together with sound localization, temporal analysis, and the *perceptual organization of auditory phenomena. Also a designation for this field of study in the psychology of perception and of hearing. *See also* COCKTAIL PARTY EFFECT; SPEECH PERCEPTION; SPEECH RECOGNITION.

auditory perspective *See* SOUND PERSPECTIVE.

auditory phonetics The study of the *perception of speech sounds.

augmented reality Vision technologies that superimpose a computer-generated object on an image of a real-world scene.

aura According to Benjamin (1936), the distinctive singularity of an original work of art, the potency of which he attributed to its *authenticity, *presence, uniqueness, and historical *context. He argued that *mechanical reproductions of artworks had none of the aura of the originals (although he saw radical potential in photography and film).

aural/oral channel The physical, sensory, and physiological medium or mode through which one hears (aural) and produces sound (oral). A *design feature of human *language (labelled by Hockett the **vocal/auditory channel**): in this case one that is not unique to human beings but which is found in the communication systems of other species.

aural perspective *See* SOUND PERSPECTIVE.

auteur theory A perspective on cinema in which the *director is seen as the author of a film, which is seen as an artwork reflecting their distinctive personality, vision, point of view, and aesthetic style. This theory looks at a particular director's **oeuvre**, or all the films they made in their career, for evidence of similar thematic concerns, *iconography, *mise-en-scène, technique, and/or stylistic choices. Auteur theory originated in French film criticism in the 1950s and was seen as a way to counter the dominant opinion held at the time that films (particularly those of the Hollywood studio system) were industrially produced *entertainments rather than art. **Auteurism** has been criticized for its romantic individualism, *authorial determinism, and general disregard for sociological, economic, technological, and audience factors in film-making.

authenticity 1. In relation to human character, the quality of being genuine or 'true to oneself'. 2. The issue of whether an *artefact (especially an artwork) is a genuine original rather than a copy or an imitation (*see also* AURA) and/or whether it is in fact the work of the person who seems to be (or who is claimed to be) its maker (**authentication** being a formal process of establishing the authenticity of works of art). 3. A quality sometimes attributed to *artefacts that are handmade or traditional, simple and uncomplicated, homely rather than sophisticated. 4. A quality sometimes associated with a style of communication that is simple, honest, transparent, without hype or *spin, meaningful and not superficial and/or personal rather than faceless. 5. (*marketing) An *emotional appeal to nostalgia that seeks to associate a brand with uncomplicated, traditional *values and methods, history and heritage, and a rejection of hype and artificiality in favour of the natural. Also reflected in the use in advertisements of 'real' (ordinary) people rather than perfect models. 6. In the romantic philosophy of Rousseau, the true, natural self, which he regarded as essentially good but corrupted by society. In existential philosophy, not an essential state but a process towards a goal. For the Danish philosopher Søren Kierkegaard (1813–55), the personally chosen self as opposed to one's imposed public identity; for Heidegger, a movement towards one's individual being-in-the-world as distinct from the dehumanized inauthenticity of one's public or *social identity; for Sartre, true being, which involved choosing our own path, not behaving according to imposed roles and avoiding self-deception or 'bad faith'. Adorno later criticized all this as 'the jargon of authenticity'.

author 1. The title given to the creator of a *text in any *medium—although traditionally associated with the writer of a literary work. 2. The romantic notion of an individual artistic voice that brings unity to a work either explicitly or implicitly. In the former sense the **authorial voice** is a typical feature of 19th-century literature (e.g. Charles Dickens). The validity of this definition has been called into question, notably by Barthes (who proclaimed 'the death of the author'). 3. A culturally-privileged term for a writer of conventionally-published books—sometimes reserved for literary work and 'high culture' rather than popular published writing. 4. Legally, the creator of any *copyright work. 5. **(implied author)** The authorial *persona inferred from a text by its readers, as distinct from the actual author or the *narrator. The term 'implied author' was coined by Booth.

authorial determinism The notion that *author is the creator of a text and as such is the sole arbiter of its *meaning. For the limitations of this view, *see* AUTHORIAL INTENTION.

authorial intention A position that argues that the creator of a text possesses a privileged understanding of its *meaning and that consequently any *interpretation that contradicts this understanding must defer to the author's intentions. This position has been criticized for its assumption that authors can ever be fully conscious of the meaning of what they produce and for ignoring or underplaying the contribution that the purposes of readers make to the understanding of a text. *See also* AUDIENCE DETERMINISM; INTENTIONAL FALLACY.

authorial voice *See* AUTHOR.

Automatic Dialogue Replacement *See* ADR.

avatar [Sanskrit *avatara*, 'descent'—the human form Hindu deities take when they appear on earth] 1. A computer-generated 'puppet' that acts as an interface between a user and a virtual environment and/or as a visual representation of that user online. 2. **(icon)** A photograph or personalized visual representation that identifies the author of a *message in an online public forum.

axis of action *See* CROSSING THE LINE.

baby boomers The generation born between the end of the Second World War in 1945 and before mass introduction of the birth control pill in 1964. Strictly speaking the term actually applies to the USA, since in the UK the birth-rate actually fell in the same period. Baby boomers are sometimes divided into **leading edge** (1946–55) and **trailing edge** (1956–64). As a demographic, baby boomers are characterized as more ethnically diverse, wealthier, and better educated than their forebears. They also had fewer children and higher rates of divorce and remarriage. *See also* DEMOGRAPHIC VARIABLES.

back-channel In *nonverbal communication, *feedback signals from an audience to a speaker—usually functioning as small reinforcements that increase the rate of *production of whatever was reinforced, but also used as cues in conversation *turn-taking. The main back-channels are *head nods, short *vocalizations (e.g. 'uh-huh', 'mm-hmm', 'yeah'), glances, and *facial expressions (e.g. smiles). The absence of back-channel signals is usually interpreted as a negative audience reaction (Argyle). Providing such feedback is called **back-channeling**. The conventions vary greatly from culture to culture.

background 1. In visual images which involve the *representation of spatial depth, the depicted area that appears to be farthest from the viewer. One of the three *zones of recession lying behind the *picture plane in the visual representation of depth. The term was originally applied to paintings, but it can also be applied to photographs. *See also* PICTORIAL DEPTH CUES; *compare* FOREGROUND; MIDDLE DISTANCE. 2. In a *narrative, the *setting.

backgrounding *See* FOREGROUNDING.

back stage 1. In the theatre, an area behind the stage or performance space that is not visible to the audience. 2. **(back region)** Goffman's *metaphor for a private place where a person does not have to keep up *appearances. He likens a person's public *persona to a *performance. **Front stage** (or **front region**) areas are places where a person is performing under the scrutiny of others and backstage areas are private spaces where a person can either relax or rehearse future performance strategies: for example, in a restaurant the kitchen is the backstage area where the staff can drop the veneer of politeness. *See also* DRAMATURGY; PUBLIC AND PRIVATE SPHERES.

((⊕)) SEE WEB LINKS

• Erving Goffman archives

back-story 1. In fictional *narratives (in print, on stage or on screen), the untold story of significant *events leading up to the situation at the outset of the narrative. 2. (journalism) Either fuller details of the story behind the headlines and the short bulletins, or 'behind-the-scenes' information and updates released by a news organization regarding how its reporters have been investigating a story. 3. A brief *montage (sometimes with a *voiceover) at the start of an *episode of a television *serial (or at the start of a sequel) summarizing events from the story so far—primarily in case the viewer had missed an episode or only just started watching the serial. 4. A prequel.

backward integration *See* VERTICAL INTEGRATION.

balance 1. In the *mass media (more particularly the broadcast media, and especially in *public service broadcasting), an ideal of *impartiality, fairness, and representativeness reflected in editorial and journalistic policies such as: covering a broad spectrum of subjects; offering a wide range of different (and often opposing) views on controversial subjects; avoiding *bias by giving equal weight to conflicting viewpoints and being fair to all sides. Even-handedness includes offering a 'right of reply'. The 'avoidance of imbalance' applies to the content of individual programmes, to the overall coverage of a topic, to individual journalists and presenters (who should never take sides), and to programming in general (*see* BALANCED PROGRAMMING). In news journalism, balance is closely aligned with a goal of *objectivity. Where different viewpoints are fairly easily identifiable (as with different political parties) balance may be sought through an equal (or at least equitable) allocation of airtime (or column inches) to each of the parties. However, only rarely can *arguments be fairly represented as having 'two sides' with tidily opposing points of view, and opinions can seldom be reduced to a single 'spectrum'. *See also* POLITICAL BIAS. 2. In aesthetic contexts, a subjective dimension of composition referring to a sense of equilibrium in the relative 'weights' of its elements. A work could be judged 'one-sided' if the main areas of interest were on one side only. *See also* HEMISPHERIC LATERALIZATION; READING DIRECTION.

balanced programming In television and radio scheduling, a policy of offering diverse content consisting of *information, *entertainment, and *educational material that caters for a broad spectrum of *tastes and opinions, including those of minorities. It also includes issues of timing, seeking to avoid the imbalances created when *peak time viewing is dominated by programmes aimed at the 'lowest common denominator'. The provision of balanced programming is a condition of many *public service broadcasting mandates. The rationale behind this is that balanced programming provides for a plurality of views and ensures that there is equal *access to *information across the population. However, some public service broadcasters have been criticized as interpreting this as a licence to give the public what it 'needs' (in terms of highbrow programming), rather than what it wants. *See also* MARKET MODEL.

bandwidth 1. A technical measure of the frequency range of a *signal or the data capacity of a *channel, which is commonly conceptualized as a limited commodity, the scarcity of which determines the conditions that technologies like radio, television, and the *internet operate. *See* SPECTRUM SCARCITY. 2. In the transmission of a communications signal, **analogue bandwidth** is the measure of the width of a carrier signal that is taken at the halfway point between the peak and trough of the signal wave. This is more commonly expressed as a frequency (e.g. 50 Hz), or the numbers of waves that can be counted in a second. 3. (computing) The amount of data that can be transmitted across a network. Digital bandwidth is not properly bandwidth at all but the colloquial name given to **baud rate**, which is measured in bytes per second (bps).

banner advert 1. On the *World Wide Web, a small advertisement with a banner-like width-to-height ratio that links to an advertiser's website. 2. An advertisement running across the top or bottom of a printed page.

base and superstructure In classical *Marxist theory, a *model or *metaphor representing *social structure and social change, in which economics (more specifically the mode of *production) is the structural base and material foundation of society and the driving force behind social change, while *culture (including politics, art, and philosophy) is a dependent **superstructure**. In capitalist societies, private ownership of the means of *production determines social *class relations. Furthermore, such relations determine consciousness. In contrast to this kind of *structural determinism, Gramscian neo-Marxist theory allowed more scope for human *agency. *See also* ARTICULATION; ECONOMISM; OVERDETERMINATION; *compare* CULTURAL MATERIALISM; RELATIVE AUTONOMY.

baseband *See* DIGITAL TRANSMISSION.

bathos *See* ANTICLIMAX.

baton (baton signal, baton movement) A *gesture that accompanies speech and functions to emphasize particular points being made (sometimes regardless of whether the other party can see it). A baton is a type of *illustrator giving visual form to the rhythms of thought: stressing and orchestrating speech. Usually referring to movements of the arms and hands, but sometimes also to other bodily movements that fulfil the same function.

baud rate *See* BANDWIDTH.

BBS *See* BULLETIN BOARDS.

BCU *See* BIG CLOSE-UP.

behavioural effects *Compare* ATTITUDINAL EFFECTS; COGNITIVE EFFECTS. 1. Any changes in the behaviour of individuals or groups attributed to specific causes. 2. In relation to the *mass media, influences of the use of particular media (or particular kinds of media *content) on the behaviour of users—one focus of academic media research within the *effects tradition. Antisocial behaviour has been the focus for much of the research in this area: specifically the attempt to find evidence for causal connections between the viewing of violence in the mass media and increased aggression or violent behaviour. *See* VIOLENCE DEBATE.

behaviourism A doctrine in psychology that rejects theories based on *inferences about internal psychological processes—focusing instead on observable and quantifiable behaviour and on the role of environmental factors (*see* CONDITIONING). Critics accuse it of being reductionist and dehumanizing in its bracketing-out of human *subjectivity. In media research, behaviourism has been influential in the effects tradition.

beholder's share Gombrich's term for what viewers bring to pictures in order to make sense of them. He referred in particular to the need to draw upon 'prior knowledge of possibilities' in order 'to separate the *code from the *message'. Where representational images depict what is familiar from *social knowledge and employ familiar *textual codes, viewers tend to be unaware of the contribution they are making to the process of *representation. *See also* PICTURE PERCEPTION.

beliefs *See* ATTITUDES.

below-the-fold *Compare* ABOVE-THE-FOLD. 1. The bottom half of a *newspaper page (particularly the front page). 2. The part of a webpage that can be seen only by *scrolling down.

below-the-line 1. *Marketing through sales promotions that typically do not involve *mass-media *advertising (e.g. email, direct mail). 2. Advertising for which no commission is paid to an *agency. 3. (film-making and television) A usually fixed *production budget excluding the costs of the 'creative' talent.

Berliner format A *newspaper format slightly taller than the *tabloid and shorter and narrower than the *broadsheet. In the UK, *The Guardian* has used this format since late 2005.

beta movement A kind of *apparent motion seen, for example, when two lights stationed at different positions are flashed on and off alternately at intervals of between 30 and 60 Hz, which produces a realistic sensation of the light moving from one position to the other. Beta movement and the *phi phenomenon have supplanted the *persistence of vision theory as the most plausible explanation of how motion pictures appear to move.

bias 1. Broadly, the conscious or unconscious *interpretation or *representation of a phenomenon in a way that (normally recurrently) favours (or is perceived by others as favouring) one particular point of view rather than another. *See also* LOADED LANGUAGE; LOGOCENTRISM; MARKEDNESS; OBJECTIVITY; OBSERVER BIAS; PHONOCENTRISM; SELF-SERVING BIAS; SUBJECTIVITY; UNCONSCIOUS BIAS; VISUALISM. 2. A conscious or unconscious *attitude towards an individual or group that can be interpreted as a (positive or negative) prejudice and that may be manifested in behaviour as discrimination; or in *representation, the evaluative loading of *description or depiction so that connotative meanings become definitive characteristics: for example, in *stereotyping. While many insist that there can be no denotation without *connotation, such loading is often potentially reducible where this is deemed desirable. *See also* ETHNOCENTRISM; EUROCENTRISM; GENDER BIAS; HETERONORMATIVITY; HETEROSEXISM; HOMOPHOBIA; INSTITUTIONAL BIAS; LOOKISM; MALE NORM; RACISM; SEXISM; SYMBOLIC ERASURE. 3. **(perceptual bias)**

The unconscious selectivity of *attention that is an intrinsic feature of *percep[tion]. Many theorists argue that perception and *interpretation (or *evaluation) are inseparable (*see also* ASSIMILATION; FRAME OF REFERENCE; FRAMING; HALO EFF[ECT]; NONVERBAL BIAS; PERCEPTUAL CODES; PERCEPTUAL SET; RECEIVER SELECTIVITY; SALIENCE; SELECTIVE DISTORTION; SELECTIVE EXPOSURE; SELECTIVE INFLUENCE[;] SELECTIVE PERCEPTION). *Memory also involves *unconscious bias: *see also* SELECTIVE RECALL; SELECTIVE RETENTION. **4. (journalistic** or **news bias)** In journalism, a personal or institutional stance that is perceived to be reflected in *factual reporting (e.g. a news report, overall news coverage of a topic, an interview, or a *documentary)—especially in its apparent pattern of selectivity; a professional lapse in the journalistic goals of *impartiality, *objectivity and/or *balance (regardless of intention). *See also* AGENDA SETTING; GLASGOW MEDIA GROUP; HIDDEN AGENDA; IDEOLOGICAL BIAS; INSTITUTIONAL BIAS; INTERVIEWER BIAS; MANUFACTURE OF CONSENT; METROPOLITAN BIAS; NEWS VALUES; POLITICAL BIAS; SPIN. **5. (technological bias)** In 1979, Neil Postman argued that every *medium 'contains an *ideological bias'. He added that the symbolic *forms in which *information is encoded gives different media intellectual and emotional biases, the accessibility and speed of their information gives them *political biases, their physical form gives them sensory biases, the conditions in which we attend to them give them social biases; and their technical and economic structure give them *content biases. Where such views ignore the social framework of technology, this is a form of *technological determinism; furthermore, the *functions of technologies can always be overridden by the *purposes of their users. *Compare* AFFORDANCES; NEUTRALITY. **6.** In sound recording, the addition of an inaudible high-frequency *signal that increases the quality of the audio. Recording a raw audio signal to electromagnetic tapes produces a lot of distortion at low frequencies. Bias has the effect of boosting the whole signal so that this effect is counteracted.

big close-up (BCU, extreme close-up, ECU, XCU) In photography, film, and television, a standard *shot size which shows a detail of a *foreground subject filling the entirety of the screen. A BCU of a person would show their face from forehead to chin. This mimics the extreme *proximity of the *intimate zone in *face-to-face interaction. Where the shot is of a face the shot appears interrogatory and the viewer's attention is focused on the feelings or reactions of the person depicted. In *semiotic terms, such unusual shots are *marked. *See also* CLOSE-UP.

bi-media journalism The practice of journalists submitting two versions of the same story, one tailored for radio and the other for television news. This was introduced as part of efficiency drives within the BBC in the 1990s; it was criticized for not taking account of fundamental differences between media. Bi-media journalism challenged the culture of media specialization and began a trend towards multiskilling, where news reporters and camera-persons do the jobs of sound recordists and editors.

binarism **1.** The *ontological division of a domain into two discrete categories or polarities, e.g. mind/body or active/passive. *See also* BINARY OPPOSITION. **2.** A loaded term applied by critics to what they regard as the obsessive *dualism of *structuralists such as Lévi-Strauss and Jakobson.

binary (binary code) A base-two number system consisting only of zeros and ones. Binary numbers are used in computing because they can be mapped onto the 'on' and 'off' positions of a switch.

binary opposition (*semiotics) A pair of mutually-exclusive *signifiers in a *paradigm set representing categories which are logically opposed and which together define a complete *universe of discourse: for example, alive or dead. In such *oppositions each term necessarily implies its opposite and there is no middle ground. *See also* ALIGNMENT; ANALOGICAL THINKING; BINARISM; CONTRADICTION; DECONSTRUCTION; DUALISM; GENDER; GREAT DIVIDE THEORIES; MARKEDNESS; MYTH; OTHER; PARADIGM; SEMIOTIC SQUARE; STRUCTURALISM; STRUCTURE; UNIVERSALISM; VALORIZATION.

binocular disparity *See* RETINAL DISPARITY.

binocular vision Sight based on the simultaneous use of both eyes. Human vision is binocular: we see with two forward-facing eyes with widely overlapping *fields of view. The integration of information from two slightly different angles offers two **binocular cues** for *depth perception: ocular *convergence (the turning inward of the lines of sight toward each other) and **stereopsis** (based on *retinal disparity).

biological determinism *See also* DETERMINISM. 1. (genetic determinism) The idea that an individual's personality or behaviour is caused by their particular genetic endowment, rather than by social or cultural factors—by nature rather than nurture. 2. The stance that males are the naturally dominant sex by virtue of anatomy and genetics or that women are naturally carers by virtue of their reproductive capabilities. 3. Often used synonymously with *biological essentialism; however, the focus of determinism is on *causes* rather than *essences*.

biological essentialism The belief that 'human nature', an individual's personality, or some specific quality (such as intelligence, creativity, homosexuality, *masculinity, *femininity, or a male propensity to aggression) is an innate and natural 'essence' (rather than a product of circumstances, upbringing, and culture). The concept is typically invoked where there is a focus on *difference, as where females are seen as essentially different from males: *see* GENDER ESSENTIALISM. The term has often been used pejoratively by *constructionists; it is also often used synonymously with *biological determinism. *See also* ESSENTIALISM; *compare* STRATEGIC ESSENTIALISM.

Birmingham school *See* CULTURAL STUDIES.

bit A 'binary digit': either zero or one. The smallest unit of *information handled by a computer, where bits are grouped into *bytes.

BITC *See* BURNT-IN TIMECODE.

bitmap graphics *See* RASTER GRAPHICS.

bit torrent (computing) A *file-sharing protocol for large amounts of *data. *See also* COPYRIGHT; PEER-TO-PEER.

blacking *See* STRIPING.

black propaganda *See* DISINFORMATION.

bleed 1. *n.* An image that extends to one or more edges of a printed page. 2. *v.* To print something so that trimming cuts off the edges of a printed area. 3. *n.* and *v.* In *printing, (usually unintended) leaking of colour into surrounding areas of the paper. 4. *n.* and *v.* In *analogue television engineering, soft or displaced colours caused by technical mismatches between the colour *signal and the main picture signal.

blind spot 1. (*optics) An area of absence in the visual *field where the optic nerve joins the sheet of photoreceptors covering the back of each eye. The blind spot is not perceived as a gap because the brain fills in the hole with the surrounding visual information. 2. An area that does not receive radio reception. 3. A blocked area in someone's field of vision. 4. A *metaphor for an area in which someone lacks understanding or is biased.

blocking 1. In broadcast programme scheduling, creating a sequence of related programmes in order to retain the audience. 2. In theatre and film *production, choreographing the movements of cameras or performers in the rehearsal of a particular scene. 3. In interactive online environments, a technical method of preventing specific users from contacting you. 4. Restricting the *access of specific users to certain online material.

blog An individual or shared online journal with entries dated and displayed in reverse chronology, and an option for readers to add their comments. Blogs can also take the form of topic-driven articles or links to other online content. The more serious blogs have been seen by some as a form of *citizen journalism. **Blogger,** a person who writes a blog; **blogging,** producing a blog.

blogosphere The *virtual community of bloggers.

blue screen *See* GREEN SCREEN.

bodily communication *See* NONVERBAL COMMUNICATION.

body 1. Human physical form and physicality, the *representation and social shaping of which has become a key focus of study in *cultural studies. 2. **(body copy)** In journalism and *advertising, the main part of an article or advertisement, not including any headlines, subheads, *call-outs, illustrations, captions, and so on. 3. The part of a webpage that appears within the frame of a *browser. 4. The part of an *email containing the *message. 5. (*typography) The **main body** is the part of lowercase letters apart from any 'ascenders' or 'descenders'; **body size** is the length from the top of the highest ascender to the bottom of the lowest descender. 6. In text design, the **body text** is the main body of the text, as distinct from the *display text: *compare* BODY TYPE.

body-ism *See* FACE-ISM.

body language Bodily *nonverbal communication (conscious or unconscious) through movement, *posture, *gesture, *facial expression, and so on. Theorists have questioned the extent to which it is useful to think of *nonverbal behaviour as reducible to a kind of *language (though *see* KINESICS).

body movement *See* KINESICS.

body politics 1. An ideological struggle between individuals, groups, and social *institutions over control of the human body. 2. Institutionalized social practices and policies through which the human body is regulated. 3. The active struggle of socially disadvantaged groups against the social forces regulating the use and *representation of their bodies, originally associated primarily with *feminism (notably in association with rape, sexual abuse, violence, and abortion). A form or aspect of *identity politics. 4. The ways in which *power may be communicated through *nonverbal communication, particularly the power of men over women (a concept discussed by Henley in her book *Body Politics*). 5. The attribution of social characteristics to individuals or groups on the basis of bodily features. *See also* RACIAL STEREOTYPING. 6. Controversies in the visual *representation of the body, particularly over visual *stereotyping. *See also* FACE-ISM; FRAGMENTATION; OBJECTIFICATION.

body type 1. Typologies of human physical shape, the most influential being the three somatotypes: ectomorphic (slim), mesomorphic (the dominant Western ideal), and endomorphic (rotund)—a typology created in 1954 by William H. Sheldon (1898–1977), an American psychologist who sought also to relate these to different temperaments. Often linked to cultural *stereotypes. 2. In *printing and in webpages, the *typeface used in the *body text (the main typeface used)—often as distinct from the *display type.

bold face A heavier form of the standard version of a *typeface, having thicker strokes.

book 1. *n.* Any substantial written text (whether printed or not). 2. A collection of printed pages bound together, defined by UNESCO as having more than 49 pages. 3. The **codex** form: originally a collection of leaves bound along one edge. This form eventually prevailed over the roll or scroll: its primary advantage being that pages could be numbered and indexed, assisting information retrieval. 4. A substantial text stored in digital form and displayed on a screen: *see* E-BOOK.

(⊕) SEE WEB LINKS
• UNESCO book definition

bookmark A menu option in web *browsers that enable the storage, display, and retrieval of the *URLs of selected webpages.

Boolean operators Logical operations or relations (notably AND, NOT, OR) used in *database searches. A search for "media OR communication" would produce more results than "media AND communication". Also used in computer programming.

bottom-up communication *See* UPWARD COMMUNICATION.

bottom-up processing A mode of *perception (or a phase in the *perceptual cycle) which is **data-driven** rather than hypothesis-led. It is driven by salient *sensory data that may modify one's current *hypotheses or *schemata, changing subsequent *expectations. This is the dominant mode when you realize that you have misrecognized someone: some of the data doesn't fit the previous hypothesis. Also, an analogous mode of inductive *inference. *Compare* TOP-DOWN PROCESSING.

boutique *See* FULL-SERVICE AGENCY.

bracketing the referent The deliberate exclusion from a formal *communication model of any direct reference to an object, idea, or *event in the world. Saussure's model of the *sign brackets the *referent—consequently critics have seen it as an *idealist model. His focus was on the meaning generated from relations within the (language) system: *see also* RELATIONAL MODEL.

brand 1. **(brand name)** The distinctive name, *logo, trademark, or design (or a combination of these) that signifies a particular company, product, or service. 2. That which is signified by a brand name: the characteristics (both physical and *connotational) associated with a particular company, product, or service that distinguish it from others.·

brand awareness 1. Consumer familiarity with a particular company, product, or service and/or the extent of this familiarity. 2. A measure of the target consumers' recall of a particular *brand: *see* AIDED RECALL.

brand image Impressions of a company, product, or service that various groups of consumers have—not necessarily just those of its *target audience.

branding The *marketing processes by which a company, product, or service acquires a distinctive identity in the minds of consumers—becoming associated with particular *values, *lifestyles, and *meanings.

brand personality 1. A set of human characteristics associated by consumers with a company, product, or service. 2. A specific personification of a company, product, or service: for instance, elicited for *market research in a *focus group. 3. The kind of people and *lifestyles with whom consumers associate the use of a product or service.

brand positioning 1. Consumer perceptions of the place occupied by a company, product, or service within a given market, measured across a range of criteria and compared with its rivals. 2. A conceptual mapping of the position of a product or service in relation to its rivals in terms of key factors (e.g. target audiences and *connotations). 3. *Marketing initiatives that seek to influence consumer perceptions of the relation of the company and its products or services to its competitors.

breaching experiments *See* ETHNOMETHODOLOGY.

break bumper A brief transition element placed between a television or radio programme and a commercial break. In television, the duration of a break bumper is usually 3–10 seconds; it takes the form of a graphic, animation, or short clip.

breaking frame *See* FRAMING.

breaking news An especially dramatic or significant *event that is reported live as part of a news bulletin rather than appearing in the standard form of a pre-edited report.

Brechtian alienation *See* ALIENATION EFFECT.

Brechtian distance *See* AESTHETIC DISTANCE.

bricolage The *appropriation of pre-existing materials that are ready-to-hand to create something new (Lévi-Strauss). This creation both reflects and constructs the **bricoleur**'s identity. The term is widely used to refer to the *intertextual authorial practice of adopting and adapting fragments from other texts and to the ways in which consumers make use of commercial products and/or their *advertising for their own purposes, making them their own by giving them new meanings. The American sociologist Sherry Turkle (b.1948) uses the term to refer to the way people use objects to think with. *See also* JUXTAPOSITION; RECONTEXTUALIZATION; *compare* COUNTERBRICOLAGE.

brightness A subjective, psychological dimension of *colour experience related to the apparent amount or intensity of light emitted by an object. One of the three major psychological dimensions of colour, the others being *hue and *saturation. It corresponds to the physical dimension of *luminance. *See also* BRIGHTNESS CONSTANCY.

brightness constancy (lightness constancy) A psychological mechanism that stabilizes relative shifts in the *brightness of things. Light changes continuously and transforms *appearances, but we rarely notice this. A white tee-shirt looks white whether it is brightly or dimly lit even though the *wavelength of light reaching the retina is different. *See also* PERCEPTUAL CONSTANCIES.

broadband 1. **(broadband internet access)** A continuous high-bandwidth *internet connection offering data rates of 128 kbps and above. 2. In data transmission, a *medium with the capacity to carry more than one channel simultaneously. 3. (*telecommunications) Using *signals across a wide range of frequencies.

broadcast codes *Conventions of *form and *content tailored to a *mass audience and widely employed in popular media forms (not restricted to the *broadcasting media). In contrast to *narrowcast codes, they are simpler— employing standardized conventions and 'formulas' in a repetitive and predictable way that tends to generate clichés and *stereotypes. They are associated with *entertainment rather than *aesthetics. These codes are learned informally through experience rather than deliberately or institutionally. Following Bernstein, they are controversially described by Fiske as *restricted codes. *See also* OVERCODING.

broadcasting *v.* 1. Communicating to a *mass audience. 2. Transmitting by radio or television. A method of *distribution for television and radio *signals via a network of a few powerful radio *transmitters that operate in the very high (VHF) and ultra high (UHF) frequency bands of the *electromagnetic spectrum, and send a signal that is picked up by many less powerful *receivers (televisions and radios) located mainly in homes. Broadcasting can be subdivided into *terrestrial broadcasting and satellite broadcasting. *See also* DIGITAL TRANSMISSION.

broadcast journalism News and current affairs reporting for the broadcast industries (radio and television). *See also* BI-MEDIA JOURNALISM.

broadcast quality A standard set of criteria by which television engineers judge whether a programme is technically fit or unfit to be broadcast. These include, on tape-based formats, the picture and audio quality, the existence and the correct type of *timecode, the presence of a line-up signal (bars and tone) and the amount of black and silence between it and the programme: in the UK, many of these criteria are set by the European Broadcast Union (EBU).

broadsheet 1. The largest *newspaper page format, with long tall pages. In the UK *The Daily Telegraph/Sunday Telegraph, The Sunday Times*, and the *Financial Times* are broadsheets. *Compare* BERLINER FORMAT; TABLOID. 2. In the UK, all of the **quality press** were once broadsheets, and both terms are used to refer to newspapers targeting an elite audience of generally middle-class readers. Their editorial and presentational style is characterized by serious and erudite journalism with an emphasis on politics and economics. They have longer articles and a higher text-to-picture ratio than the more *downmarket *redtops, although the latter contrast is less dramatic since *tabloidization. 3. An advertisement or pamphlet printed on one side of an unfolded sheet of paper.

brown goods A category of electrical consumer goods. A reference to early TVs, radios, and radiograms in wooden, wood-coloured plastic, or bakelite cases. They are all essentially *entertainment products, including: TVs, *camcorders, sound systems, and DVD players. These are now sold in a variety of colours, and the term is old-fashioned, but the concept persists. In contrast to *white goods, they have traditionally been marketed to males with a primary focus on technical specifications. *See also* GENDERED TECHNOLOGIES.

browser Computer software enabling users to view webpages on the *internet.

browsing A characterization of a user's activity on the World Wide Web connoting a 'high breadth, low depth' style of engagement. *See also* FLÂNEUR; SURFING.

bug *See* IDENT.

bulletin boards Software that enables *asynchronous communication among groups of people on the *internet in the form of *messages to which multiple persons can reply. These replies form lists or *threads. A **bulletin board system (BBS)** enables users to log on to a *computer network and to exchange *data. *See also* NEWSGROUP.

burnt-in timecode (BITC) A *timecode display superimposed on a video image. *Compare* VERTICAL INTERVAL TIMECODE.

burst campaign (*advertising) A campaign in which media expenditure is compressed into a series of brief periods, with relatively long gaps in between, in contrast to *drip campaigns. This strategy is often used to increase *brand awareness and audience *reach.

burying 1. (journalism) The knowing suppression of a story by relegating it to a less prominent position—not through lack of *newsworthiness but because of pressure from outside parties. 2. (PR) The tactic of releasing a potentially damaging story on a busy news day.

byline (journalism) The name (and often staff position) of the writer which typically appears immediately underneath the title of a *newspaper story or magazine article (sometimes after the word 'by').

byte A unit of *information and computer storage consisting of eight *bits. One byte can represent a single *alphanumeric character. *See* ASCII.

CA *See* CONVERSATION ANALYSIS.

cable network In the US, a colloquial name for a television channel that is distributed via cable rather than being transmitted.

cable television A television broadcasting system that is delivered to homes via a network using coaxial or fibre-optic cables rather than being transmitted through the air.

calligraphy 1. Decorative handwritten lettering. 2. The art of fine handwriting. 3. **Calligraphic type**: any *typefaces designed to resemble handwriting.

call-out In the layout of a printed page (typically in a magazine article), a quotation lifted from the body of the text that is reprinted larger or in *bold face and strategically placed on the page to attract the *attention and interest of the reader.

camcorder A portmanteau word (*camera + recorder*). A small portable video-camera and video-recorder combined as a single unit.

camera 1. Any equipment used to photographically record images. The name for a number of devices that use lenses and *apertures to photograph either a single still image or a series of still images captured in rapid succession (a movie). These images can be recorded either chemically, by being preserved in a light-sensitive coating applied to *film, or as electrical voltages stored on magnetic tape, encoded in either digital or analogue form. *See also* INDEXICAL. 2. **(camera operator)** A non-sexist variation on **cameraman**, the *production credit given to the person who operates the camera in the film and television industries.

camera angle Any tilted position representing a significant deviation from the horizontal default (in *semiotic terms, 'unmarked') position of a level shot (in which the lens points in a direction parallel to the ground). *See* DUTCH ANGLE; HIGH-ANGLE SHOT; LOW-ANGLE SHOT.

camera lucida [Latin 'light chamber'] An optical device for reflecting an image of a three-dimensional scene onto a flat surface where it can be traced by hand. There are two forms of this device—using either a prism or a half-silvered mirror. Adjusting the relative distances enlarges or reduces the image.

camera movement *See* PANNING; PED-UP OR -DOWN; TRACKING.

camera obscura [Latin 'dark chamber'] **1.** An optical device for projecting an image of a three-dimensional scene onto a surface which, in its simplest form, consists of a darkened box with a small *aperture through which light passes, forming an inverted image of the scene on the facing side. Lenses and mirrors can be also be used to re-invert, brighten, and sharpen the image. The camera obscura is a precursor to *photography and works on the same principle as a pinhole camera. **2.** A small building with an angled mirror in the roof that projects an image of the surrounding landscape onto a horizontal viewing surface inside.

camera operator *See* CAMERA.

camerawork *See also* APERTURE; CINEMATOGRAPHY; CRASH ZOOM; CROPPING; EXPOSURE; GENDERED CAMERAWORK; HEADROOM; OBJECTIVE CAMERAWORK; SUBJECTIVE CAMERAWORK. **1.** The art, craft, and techniques of using any kind of camera. **2.** A generic term for all the techniques used by camera operators to film moving images. **3.** Sometimes used to distinguish what is done 'in camera' from what may be done afterwards in *post-production. It includes *framing, camera position, *camera angle, *shot size, lens choice, focus (*see* DEEP FOCUS; DEPTH OF FIELD), *zooming, and *camera movement.

canon (*adj.* **canonical**) **1.** In music, film, art, and especially literature, an elitist conception of an exemplary body of classic works—usually closely identified with a traditional conception of the cultural heritage of a particular country or language (such as 'great works' of English literature) or regarded as characterizing a particular historical era (e.g. Renaissance art). Study of the canon traditionally formed the basis for the curricula for the teaching of many humanities subjects. Heavily criticized by *Marxist, *feminist, *postcolonial, and *queer theorists for being almost exclusively the work of **dead white** (European) **males**. **2.** Books of Holy Scripture officially endorsed by religious authorities as genuine or of divine inspiration, other contemporary contenders being relegated to the Apocrypha. **3.** A body of writings regarded by specialists as authentic and genuine in their shared authorship: e.g. the Shakespeare canon.

canted shot (**canting, oblique angle, Dutch angle**) An oblique or 'crooked' shot in which the camera is angled clockwise or anticlockwise (*see also* DIAGONALITY). In *semiotic terms, a *marked shot connoting disorientation. *See also* DUTCH ANGLE; *compare* ROLL.

captionless master (**titleless master, clean version**) A final version of a film or television programme recorded without any titles and captions which is used to make foreign language versions or for re-edits. *See also* M&E.

carrier signal *See* ANALOGUE.

Cartesian dualism The mind-body *dualism of the French philosopher Réne Descartes (1596–1650) that views human beings as a combination of two distinct substances: a non-corporeal mind and a corporeal body, which nevertheless interact causally. Descartes presented the subject as an autonomous individual with an *ontological status *prior to* *social structures (a notion rejected by *structuralist and *poststructuralist theorists). He established the enduring assumption of the independence of the knower from the known (*see also* OBJECTIVITY). Cartesian dualism also underpins a host of associated and aligned dichotomies: reason–emotion, male–female, true–false, fact–fiction, public–private, self–other, and human–animal. Many *feminists regard it as an ontological framework that endorses patriarchy.

cartoon violence 1. Heavily stylized comic displays of aggression in which the perpetrators suffer every kind of abuse without being harmed. 2. A pejorative term for any stylized action sequence in live-action performance media that emphasizes the *spectacle of violence while de-emphasizing its consequences. 3. An issue in the *violence debate that highlights the importance of the degree of *perceived reality in children's responses to violence in the media.

CAT (communication accommodation theory) *See* ACCOMMODATION.

catastrophe *See* FREYTAG'S PYRAMID.

categorization 1. Classifying things: dividing them into groups according to shared characteristics and labelling these. **Taxonomy** is the name given to the activity of systematic categorization (e.g. taxonomies of *genre and of *communicative functions). Categorization differs between *languages (*see also* SAPIR-WHORF HYPOTHESIS). In the *representation of people, categorization generates *stereotypes. 2. In *perception, the automatic and unconscious mental process of classifying *sensory data. *See also* SCHEMATA. 3. (philosophy) Seeking fundamental divisions of reality into types (*see also* ONTOLOGY). Aristotle divided reality into ten categories: substance, quantity, quality, relation, action, affection, place, time, position, and state. Kant arrived at four: quantity, quality, relation, and modality. Peirce used three as the basis of his *semiotics: firstness (undifferentiated quality), secondness (blind force), and thirdness (mediation).

catharsis 1. In Aristotle's conception, a cleansing of *emotions experienced by the audience at the end of a tragedy. The most common interpretation of this is that audience emotions are purged through their *identification with the hero and their tragic downfall. Another is that audiences are so involved in their feelings of fear or pity for the hero that they forget their own troubles. 2. A therapeutic treatment of hysteria devised by Freud and the Austrian physician Josef Breuer (1842–1925) involving the discharge of emotion by patients through the release of repressed thoughts into consciousness. 3. **(cathartic hypothesis)** As applied to violent media, the theory that experiencing vicarious acts of violence acts as a 'safety valve'—defusing latent aggression or decreasing levels of *arousal, leaving viewers less prone to aggressive behaviour. *See also* VIOLENCE DEBATE.

(((⊕))) SEE WEB LINKS

• Catharsis

causation (causality, causal relationship) The relationship between cause and *effect: the central issue in media and communication research within the *effects tradition. Deterministic theories (*see* DETERMINISM) focus on a **monocausal relationship,** whereby one factor is singled out as a *necessary or even *sufficient condition. However, such *reductionist explanations are widely regarded as inapplicable to the complexity of human behaviour, where multiple factors are normally involved. A key issue is the **direction of relationship**. For instance, if heavy viewers of television violence are more likely to be aggressive than lighter viewers, this could be because they are more likely to watch such material rather than because it made them aggressive. *Correlation is not adequate evidence of causation.

CC See CLOSED-CAPTIONING.

CCD See DIGITAL.

CCTV (closed-circuit television). Broadly, a video surveillance technology consisting of a camera or cameras directly linked to centralized monitoring or recorded devices, rather than being part of an 'open' broadcast system.

CD See COMPACT DISC.

CDA See CRITICAL DISCOURSE ANALYSIS.

CD-ROM (compact disc read-only memory). **1**. A standardized format introduced in 1983 that used CDs to store up to 700 MB of computer data which can be accessed but not altered or erased. **2**. In the 1990s an *entertainment medium particularly associated with *multimedia applications like *videogames and educational tools.

celebrity culture An industry emerging in the late 1990s that treats celebrities as *commodities—including television programmes such as *Big Brother* and *Pop Idol* that 'manufacture' celebrities who are 'famous for being famous' and whose lives become the subject of celebrity journalism. Linked by some commentators to a shift towards the *sign economies of late capitalism.

cellular radio system A *full-duplex, *digital, or *analogue telephone transmission system which uses radio frequencies. Rather than having powerful *transmitters covering a given region, it is divided up into smaller areas or cells which can be covered by less powerful transmitters. The cells are linked together to form a *network controlled by a centralized Mobile Telephone Switching Office (MTSO) which ensures that every time a *mobile phone moves in or out of the range of a given cell, the call is switched over to an adjacent cell.

celluloid **1**. A generic name for the clear plastic used to make film—which in the early days of cinema was derived from cellulose. **2**. A *metonym for film or the cinema.

censorship **1**. Any regime or context in which the content of what is publically expressed, exhibited, published, broadcast, or otherwise distributed is regulated or in which the circulation of *information is controlled. The official grounds for such control at a national level are variously political (e.g. national security), moral (e.g. likelihood of causing offence or moral harm, especially in relation to issues of obscenity), social (e.g. whether violent content might have harmful effects on behaviour), or religious (e.g. blasphemy, heresy). Some rulings may be merely to avoid embarrassment (especially for governments). **2.** A regulatory system for vetting, *editing, and prohibiting particular forms of public expression, presided over by a **censor**: an official given a mandate by a governmental, legislative, or commercial body to review specific kinds of material according to pre-defined criteria. Criteria relating to public *attitudes—notably on issues of 'taste and decency'—can quickly become out-of-step. **3.** The practice and process of suppression or any particular instance of this. This may involve the partial or total suppression of any text or the entire output of an individual or organization on a limited or permanent basis. **4. Self-censorship** is self-regulation by an individual author or publisher, or by 'the industry'. *Media industries frequently remind their members that if they do not regulate themselves they will be regulated by the state. Self-censorship on the individual level includes the internal regulation of what one decides to express publically, often attributable to *conformism. **5.** In Freudian *psychoanalytical theory, the suppression of unconscious desires that is reflected in the oblique *symbolism of dreams: *see* DISPLACEMENT.

central route In the *Elaboration Likelihood Model (Petty and Cacioppo), a strategy of *attitude change based on *argument (in which the focus is on explicit message *content). This kind of approach requires considerable *cognitive effort or *elaboration on the part of the *receiver. However, if the message is convincing and elaboration occurs, long-term attitude change is more likely than with the alternative strategy of the *peripheral route.

cerebral dominance *See* HEMISPHERIC LATERALIZATION.

certification The classification of films, *DVDs, and *videogames by an official ratings board according to their perceived suitability for audiences—primarily by minimum age. In the UK, such classification firstly checks issues of legality (e.g. relating to obscenity, *racism, or cruelty to animals). Secondly, it assesses the likelihood of harmful consequences (moral harm or anti-social behaviour). Thirdly, it makes judgements about public acceptability (predicting what might cause widespread offence). Key issues include the depiction of sexual activity or violence (*see* VIOLENCE DEBATE), 'bad language', or whatever might frighten or disturb young viewers. Since certification can be denied and *distribution consequentially be made illegal (e.g. in the UK) or where most movie chains would not show an unrated domestic film (e.g. in the USA), certification is a form of *censorship. In the USA the process of official certification is known as the motion picture **rating system**.

CGI 1. Computer graphics: *see* COMPUTER-GENERATED IMAGERY. **2. Common Gateway Interface**: a standard defining the interface between a web server and an application such as a *database program. CGI programs are commonly used for processing the forms found on webpages.

channel 1. Often used broadly to refer to the ways in which the *message reaches the *receiver, to any *medium of communication, or to anything conceptualized as a conduit for *information (*see* CONDUIT METAPHOR): that which carries the *message. **2.** (*semiotics) A sensory mode utilized by a *medium (e.g. visual, auditory, *haptic). The sensory bias of the channel limits the *codes for which it is suitable. **3.** The physical and/or technical system carrying a transmitted *signal (e.g. a telephone cable or radio waves)—as in *Shannon and Weaver's model of communication. **4.** A band of frequencies within the *electromagnetic spectrum assigned to a particular radio or television station or mobile phone company. Dividing the electromagnetic spectrum into channels was a direct consequence of the technical requirements of *analogue transmission systems. Although no longer a requirement of digital systems the fact that powerful socioeconomic institutional practices have developed around this model ensures its continuation at least for the foreseeable future. **5.** A *metonym widely used in the UK for a television station (the latter term tending to be confined to radio). **6.** A television or radio station packaged and marketed as a brand: *see* CHANNEL BRANDING.

channel branding The *marketing endeavour to establish a strong and distinctive audiovisual, stylistic, and content identity for a particular radio or television channel (primarily through on-air promotion) in order to attract more viewers from the *target audience and to develop and maintain *brand loyalty. *See also* IDENTS.

channel factors (medium factors) In *models of communication or *persuasion, specific *variables associated with the *channel or *medium that can influence the effectiveness of the *message. This includes media type (e.g. TV, radio, *newspapers, face-to-face communication), verbal versus *nonverbal communication, and so on. Communicators need to consider whether research has shown that the channel/medium suits the intended *communicative function and whether the *target audience will regard its choice as appropriate. *See also* YALE MODEL.

channel hopping (channel surfing) A practice found among television viewers involving recurrent periods of rapid switching from channel to channel using the remote control—often during breaks in the programme they were originally watching and typically in search of more stimulating material. The practice tends to be associated more with men than with women. *See also* FLÂNEUR; ZAPPING.

charge-coupled device *See* DIGITAL.

chatroom A web-based meeting-place for people with shared interests to communicate *synchronously (primarily through typing but sometimes also through voice and/or *webcams).

chat show (talk show) A radio or television programme (and *genre) with a 'host' (typically a well-known 'personality'), conducted in a conversational style and including such features as interviews and phone-ins.

chequebook journalism Pejorative term for the controversial journalistic practice of paying a source for information (often for an exclusive story).

chiaroscuro **1.** In painting and drawing, the use of light and dark to create a three-dimensional effect and/or as a compositional technique (particularly when these are strongly contrasted). **2.** In photography and film, a style of lighting that creates deep shadows and contrasts.

chroma See CHROMINANCE.

chroma key (colour separation overlay) A video *post-production and graphical technique in which one *colour in a *shot or image is removed or made transparent ('keyed out') and replaced by a different background: e.g. the weather-map that appears to be behind the forecaster on television. *See also* GREEN SCREEN; TRAVELLING MATTE.

chrominance (chroma) 1. In *colour theory, an aspect of the perceived intensity of a colour referring to the colourfulness of a stimulus relative to the brightness of another stimulus that appears white under similar viewing conditions. **Chromatic colours** are all those other than black, white, and grey. *See also* SATURATION. 2. In television transmission, the part of the signal (sub-carrier) containing information on colour *hue and *saturation. 3. A measure of the intensity of a particular *colour on a television screen in relation to a standard colour of equal *luminance.

chronemics The study of the communicative role of time in *nonverbal behaviour (e.g. pauses, punctuality). The use of time is highly culturally variable.

chunking 1. Organizing items into manageable units (e.g. in *information design or learning). The psychologist Miller argued that the human mind can deal with about seven items at one time. *See also* SIGNPOSTING. 2. (psychology) The recoding of information to maximize the efficient use of short-term *memory.

(⊕) SEE WEB LINKS

• The magical number seven

cinema 1. A building in which films are shown, containing at least one auditorium in which an audience watches together. 2. Films produced for viewing by the general public. 3. The industry involved in the *production, *distribution, and exhibition of films. 4. A *metonym for the art of film-making: *compare* FILM.

cinema audience See FILM AUDIENCE.

cinematic *adj.* 1. Anything that pertains to the medium of film. 2. A certain quality associated with feature films which is also reproduced in television programmes and pop videos which have high *production values.

cinematic apparatus (apparatus theory) In the *Marxist and *psychoanalytic traditions of *film theory (e.g. Baudry), the whole system of cinematic technologies and practices that not only produces films but also constructs film *spectators—both being seen as *ideological processes concealed by cinematic illusion. *See also* SUTURE; *compare* IDEOLOGICAL STATE APPARATUS.

cinematography The art and techniques of film photography (including lighting). The work of the cinematographer.

cinéma vérité [French 'cinema truth'] Style of *documentary film-making, developed in the 1960s by Jean Rouch (1917–2004), a French film-maker and anthropologist, featuring ordinary people answering probing questions from the film-maker about their experiences. An undramatized and non-narrative form, filmed using a hand-held camera.

circuit of communication Stuart Hall's *encoding/decoding model of *mass communication (1980), in which the traditional linear model of sender–message–receiver (*see* TRANSMISSION MODELS), rendered in the context of mass communication as a loop involving *production–*distribution–(re)production, was broken down into several linked but distinctive 'moments': *production, *circulation, *distribution/*consumption, and *(cultural) reproduction. *See also* ENCODING/DECODING MODEL; HEGEMONIC READING; NEGOTIATED READING; OPPOSITIONAL READING; PREFERRED READING.

circuit of culture A model of the central practices which produce *culture, devised by Stuart Hall and others in 1997. Defining culture as being about 'shared meanings', this circular model presents *representation, *identity, *production, *consumption, and *regulation as wholly interrelated. Each of these linked 'moments' contributes to the *production of *meaning.

circulation 1. The *distribution of a publication (particularly *newspapers and magazines). 2. The number of copies sold of a single issue of a magazine or newspaper (*see* AUDITED CIRCULATION). The actual *readership may be larger. 3. The scale of public availability of something. *See* ACCESS. 4. The extent of awareness of a particular idea. 5. In *Marxist theory, the sphere of the *exchange of goods and services, as distinct from the sphere of *production.

citizen journalism The reporting and dissemination of *news and *information independently of conventional news *institutions by individuals who are not professional journalists. *See also* ALTERNATIVE MEDIA; BLOG.

civil inattention In social *interaction, the practice of giving some minimal acknowledgement of the presence of a stranger (e.g. a slight, fleeting smile) followed by an avoidance of further *eye contact (Goffman). *See also* GAZE; INTERACTION RITUALS.

class 1. In common usage, a hierarchical distinction between people in society according to distinct basic structural levels: upper, middle (sometimes subdivided into upper-middle and lower-middle), and lower (or working class). 2. A social category identifying an individual's relative position in a society. Class is typically conceived as a pyramid in relation to wealth, *power, occupation, and/or *status. 3. **(class identity)** For Marx, one's relationship to the means of *production: those with control over such a means were capitalists or the bourgeoisie; those with only their labour power were the working class or proletariat. 4. For Weber, social positioning reflecting differences in 'market capacity' and consequently in 'life chances' (opportunities). The sources of market capacity include capital, skill, and education. He stressed that class has no necessary relation to social *status. 5. **Social class** or **social grade**: an occupational classification system particularly associated with *market research, where the primary concern has traditionally been with income and spending power. In the UK: **A** (higher managerial, administrative, or professional; **B** (intermediate managerial, administrative, or professional; **C1**

(supervisory, clerical, junior managerial, administrative, or professional); **C2** (skilled manual worker); **D** (semi-skilled and unskilled manual worker); **E** (state pensioner, casual worker, the unemployed). **6.** In sociology and *cultural studies, a combination of various factors such as education, occupation, status, *taste, *lifestyle, and *values—especially in relation to *social identity and as inflected by *gender, *race, and age.

classical economics *See* POLITICAL ECONOMY.

classical Hollywood cinema **1.** Films produced by the major Hollywood studios in what many refer to as the 'golden age' of Hollywood from the 1930s until the early 1950s. **2.** Conventions of *narrative, *camerawork, and *editing employed in these films and their continuing use and influence as the dominant (though increasingly flouted) film conventions in cinema and television. In particular, the *convention or *code of invisible or *continuity editing. More broadly a style that *foregrounds the narrative and backgrounds the processes of construction involved in making a film: *see also* CLASSIC REALIST TEXT; NATURALISM. **3.** Specifically, the *classical narrative structure employed in these films. **4.** The *studio system that produced these films, which had largely disappeared by the early 1960s.

classical narrative structure A traditional three-part framework for the course of *events in a *narrative, usually traced back to Aristotle's *Poetics* (*c.*335 BCE). Typically characterized as equilibrium–disruption–equilibrium (or balance–imbalance–balance)—a chain of events corresponding to the beginning, middle, and end of a story. The **Three Act Structure** commonly employed in writing for stage and screen, sometimes referred to as: *exposition, complication (or *conflict), and resolution or *dénouement (the latter sometimes being subdivided into *climax, fall, and *closure). Such homeostatic structures may serve psychological functions for individuals and/or broader social functions, such as resolving tensions. This is the basic formula for mainstream *classical Hollywood movies in which the storyline is given priority over everything else. *See also* HERMENEUTIC CODE; NARRATIVE.

classicism **1.** The classical aesthetic ideals of simplicity, form, order, harmony, balance, clarity, decorum, restraint, serenity, unity, and proportion—together with an emphasis on reason. The term is not limited in its application to art of the classical period. As an adherence to artistic rules, the antithesis of *romanticism's emphasis on individual creative expression. **2.** Art or literature echoing elements of the styles of ancient Greece or Rome.

classic realist text A *modernist text that is orchestrated to effect *closure (*see also* NARRATIVE CLOSURE; OPEN AND CLOSED TEXTS; READERLY), in which *contradictions are suppressed and the reader is encouraged to adopt a position from which everything seems 'obvious' (a form of '*false consciousness'). Such texts seek to obscure their own *constructedness (*see also* NATURALISM; NATURALIZATION). The term was introduced by MacCabe. **Classical realism** was the dominant style of *classical Hollywood cinema and it remains dominant in mainstream television and film.

class stereotypes The caricature of members of one *class by those of another (either mentally or in public *representations). Negative class *stereotypes abound: the working classes are frequently portrayed as lazy and feckless, the middle classes as obsessed with 'keeping up with the Joneses', and the upper classes as aloof and condescending.

clean version *See* CAPTIONLESS MASTER.

cliffhanger An unresolved ending to a part of a serialized novel or *drama intended to leave the audience eager to know what happens next.

climax 1. A moment in a *narrative when the *conflict and tension peak for the audience. Often synonymous with *crisis. 2. The third phase of dramatic structure in *Freytag's pyramid. 3. **Climax order**: a sequential *argument in which the last point is the most important and forceful (the opposite being **anticlimax order**). 4. In *rhetoric, successive phrases building upon a previous one: e.g. Martin Luther King Jr.'s cumulative use of 'I have a dream'.

cloak theory The neoclassical idea of *language as simply the dress of thought, based on the assumption that the same thought can be expressed in a variety of ways **(linguistic dualism)**. Linguistic *universalists argue that we can say whatever we want to say in any language, and that whatever we say in one language can always be translated into another (*see also* TRANSLATABILITY). This is the basis for the most common refutation of the *Sapir-Whorf hypothesis. *Compare* MOULD THEORY.

closed captioning (CC) (television) A system that encodes subtitling information for the hearing-impaired into the *vertical interval of a broadcast television *signal which appears as superimposed text at the bottom of the screen. Programmes with such text are **closed-captioned**.

closed-circuit television *See* CCTV.

closed forms The kinds of *narratives that are self-contained and have a sense of structural (and arguably *ideological) *closure. The British cultural theorist Anthony Easthope (1939–99) argues that the masculine ego favours such forms: 'masculine' narrative form favours action over dialogue and avoids *indeterminacy to arrive at resolution; it is linear and goal-oriented. *See also* NARRATIVE CLOSURE; OPEN AND CLOSED TEXTS; *compare* OPEN FORMS.

closed posture A typically unconscious bodily *posture in which the body tends towards being closed in on itself—with arms and legs close to the body or crossed. In very closed postures the head is also lowered and the body is huddled in something approaching 'the foetal position'. Depending on *context, in social *interaction closed postures are variously interpreted as defensive, as signifying disagreement, and/or as discouraging interaction. When women sit with a closed body posture, with their arms close to the body and a minimal angle between the upper legs, this is sometimes interpreted by *feminist theorists as a *performance of feminine submission. *Compare* OPEN POSTURE.

closed questions (closed-ended questions) *Compare* OPEN-ENDED QUESTION. 1. In *survey *questionnaires, questions for which the alternative answers are limited and specified (usually involving ticking boxes). The great advantage to the researchers is that these are easy to quantify (*see* QUANTITATIVE RESEARCH); the primary disadvantage is that they impose a rigid framework which is not that of the *respondents. 2. In conversations or interviews, questions that are likely to lead to short answers such as 'Yes' or 'No' (either through design or ineptitude). Closed questions control and limit *information flow.

closed text *See* OPEN AND CLOSED TEXTS.

closeness 1. (psychological) *See* PSYCHOLOGICAL DISTANCE. 2. (physical) *See* PROXIMITY.

close-up (CU) In photography, film, and television, a standard *shot size which shows a *foreground subject that fills the screen. A CU of a person would show their face and shoulders, cutting off the top of their head. This mimics the *intimate zone in *face-to-face interaction, draws attention to *facial expression, and abstracts the subject from the *context. *See also* BIG CLOSE-UP; MCU.

closure 1. A satisfying sense of completion or completeness. 2. A defining feature of a *narrative that resolves all of the issues in a 'proper ending'. *See* NARRATIVE CLOSURE. 3. The processes by which a text is brought to a conclusion or structured to feel complete. 4. **(structural closure)** The extent to which a narrative form is linear, self-contained, and leads to a final resolution. Narrative forms characterized by closed structures are often perceived as having masculine *connotations: *see* CLOSED FORMS. 5. **(ideological closure)** the authorial strategies employed to constrain the *interpretation of a text by its audiences. An illusion of completeness amounts to an attempt to prevent the reader from butting in (*see also* UNIVOCALITY). It suggests that 'the matter is closed'—that the text is 'finished'. Seamlessness and sequential structures reinforce an impression of the ground having been covered, of all the questions having been answered, of nothing important having been left out. Closure implies mastery of the material through its control of form. However, no text can say everything that could be said; there is no first or last word on any subject. *Ideological closure can be aligned with structural closure. *See also* OPEN AND CLOSED TEXTS; PREFERRED READING. 6. A property associated with the conservatism of *classical realist texts which some modern literary narratives avoid, preferring anti-closure. *See also* OPEN FORMS. 7. The reduction of a text by a reader to a single *interpretation (a pejorative term in literary theory). 8. In *gestalt psychology, a standardizing tendency in *perception and recall to add that which would normally be there but was missing: e.g. in *visual perception we routinely mentally fill in the gaps in broken outlines. *See also* GESTALT LAWS. 9. In psychology, an individual trait reflecting aversion to uncertainty. *See* TOLERANCE OF AMBIGUITY.

cluster analysis A computer-aided statistical method of identifying groupings of closely-associated patterns in *data. For instance, as applied by Livingstone to questionnaire responses, identifying four different groups of soap opera viewers in relation to degrees of *romanticism or cynicism in their *evaluations of characters.

clutter 1. In *advertising, the *co-presence of a large number of individual commercial messages in any medium competing for the consumer's *attention. 2. Pejorative term for the general proliferation of *non-programme material on television. 3. In *communication design, any unnecessary elements distracting attention from the main focus or *message (e.g. gratuitous sound effects on a webpage). *See also* WHITE SPACE.

CMC *See* COMPUTER-MEDIATED COMMUNICATION.

coaction A minimal mode of *interpersonal relations in which *co-present individuals are engaged separately in tasks and in which interpersonal *interaction is not required but in which the presence of others may have an influence on behaviour. *See also* HAWTHORNE EFFECT; *compare* COMPETITION; COOPERATION.

cocktail party effect (cocktail party phenomenon) In *speech perception, a feature of *selective attention enabling a listener to isolate and focus upon a single conversation from among several simultaneous conversations competing for *attention. The concept was noted by the British cognitive scientist Colin Cherry (1914–79).

code 1. *n.* In *communication theory, any system of *signals used to send *messages (*see also* ENCODING/DECODING MODEL). The transformational rules for converting a message from one form (or *modelling system) into another and back again: *see also* ALPHABET; MORSE CODE; TRANSFORMATION. 2. *n.* (*semiotics) A communication system based on rules or conventions of meaning-making assumed to be shared and understood by its intended users (e.g. a shared *language or the traffic-light system). Semiotic codes are procedural systems for correlating *signifiers and *signifieds in certain semantic domains. Codes provide a framework within which *signs make sense: they are normative interpretive devices which are used by *interpretive communities. In *Jakobson's model of communication, messages only make sense in relation to relevant codes and *contexts. Codes can be broadly divided into *social codes, *textual codes, and *interpretive codes. Some codes are fairly explicit (as with *Morse code and traffic lights); others (dubbed *hermeneutics by Guiraud) are much looser (as with the nonverbal signals for conversational *turn-taking). Within a code there may also be *subcodes: such as stylistic and personal subcodes or *idiolects: *see also* CODES OF LOOKING. 3. *n.* In common usage, a representational system used to hide messages from anyone unfamiliar with the system; also, any message hidden in this way; *v.* the process involved. 4. *n.* The symbol systems used in computer programming and mark-up languages, and any sequence of such symbols used in a particular application. Also, a particular computer language in which a program is written. *See also* BINARY; HTML; SCRIPT. 5. *n.* In social science research, a system used to classify *data; *v. see* CODING. 6. *n.* In loose usage in *sociolinguistics, a *language, *dialect, or language variety, whether spoken or written. *See also* CODE-SWITCHING; ELABORATED CODE; RESTRICTED CODE; *compare* REGISTER. 7. *n.* Formal (often official) rules and guidelines for some cultural practice. *See* ADVERTISING CODES; CODES OF PRACTICE; DRESS CODES; HAYS CODE.

codec A portmanteau term (*coder* + *decoder*). In *telecommunications and computer-based audio and video, software applications or hardware devices that convert *analogue-encoded *signals to *digital form or that apply different *compression algorithms to digital signals.

codes of looking Culturally variable *social norms, *conventions, and taboos regarding those at whom we may look and the nature and duration of that look (*see* GAZE; GLANCE), including whether or not we may make *eye contact. Some of these codes reflect *status differences.

codes of practice Formally-defined professional rules of conduct, either widely agreed within an industry or legally binding, the breach of which may lead to sanctions against offenders. In the UK there are multiple codes of conduct for all of the media and *advertising industries. *See also* ADVERTISING CODE.

code-switching 1. (*sociolinguistics) Bilingual speakers shifting from one language to another. 2. More rarely, monolingual speakers switching between *discourse types. 3. (*semiotics) Switching between *subcodes in any *sign system.

codex *See* BOOK.

codification A historical social process whereby the conventions of a particular *code (e.g. for a *genre) become widely established (Guiraud). *See also* EMERGENT CODE.

coding 1. The formal process of classifying *data according to standardized categories in order to facilitate the identification of patterns. Typically associated with *quantitative research (e.g. *survey research and *content analysis) but also used for the analysis of *qualitative data. 2. The process of computer programming, scripting, and/or webpage mark-up. 3. Sometimes a synonym for *encoding.

cognition (cognitive processes) *See also* SOCIAL COGNITION. 1. Broadly, thinking or mental processes, whether conscious or unconscious. A term originally distinguishing rational from emotional and impulse-driven mental processes. 2. In psychology and cognitive science, the psychological processes involved in mental *information processing. This includes *perception, *attention, learning, *memory, *language, thinking, decision-making, and problem-solving. *See also* SCHEMA THEORY; VISUAL INFORMATION PROCESSING. 3. A field of study for those in cognitive psychology, *psycholinguistics, artificial intelligence, and cognitive neuropsychology.

cognitive dissonance (dissonance theory) Psychological conflict arising from inconsistencies between one's ideas, *attitudes, beliefs, and practices (e.g. believing that smoking cigarettes is bad for your health but continuing to smoke regularly). According to **cognitive consistency theory** this leads to **dissonance reduction** (an attempt to reduce the cognitive inconsistencies), so conflicted smokers might try to convince themselves that they were more likely to die in a car crash than from smoking-induced cancer. This theory derives from the American psychologist Leon Festinger (1918–89).

cognitive effects 1. Any changes in the thinking of individuals or groups attributed to specific causes. 2. In relation to the *mass media, influences of the use of particular media on the mental processes of users—one focus of academic media research within the *effects tradition. Gavriel Salomon (born 1938), an Israeli psychologist, argued that media differ in how much cognitive *elaboration they involve and in the kinds of mental processes they call on. *See also* ELABORATION LIKELIHOOD MODEL.

cognitive film theory *Hypotheses about the (unconscious) mental processes involved in making sense of film and television *codes and *conventions (not to be confused with *psychoanalytic theory). Cognitive film theorists have argued that the *comprehension of films depends more on *inference than on the *decoding emphasized in *structuralism. *Spectators frame and resolve hypotheses about the *narrative enigmas they encounter (*see also* HERMENEUTIC CODE). *See also* CONSTRUCTIVISM; *compare* RELEVANCE THEORY.

cognitive meaning *See* IDEATIONAL MEANING.

cognitive style An individual's characteristic way of thinking and perceiving. A popular measure of cognitive style is the Myers-Briggs Type Indicator (MBTI). *See also* CONVERGENCE; FIELD DEPENDENCE AND INDEPENDENCE; LEVELLING AND SHARPENING; REFLECTIVITY–IMPULSIVITY; TOLERANCE OF AMBIGUITY.

coherence *Compare* COHESION. 1. A quality of *discourse that makes sense: i.e. that is logical, clear, well-formed, unified, and consistently relevant to its topic. 2. In *discourse analysis and *stylistics, how a *text is held together by an underlying development of *propositions, a concept introduced by the British linguist Henry G. Widdowson (b.1935).

cohesion 1. In *discourse analysis and *stylistics, how a *text is connected together linguistically (phonologically, grammatically, lexically, semantically); its internal structure. **Cohesive ties** include conjunctions, pronouns, *anaphora, repetition, *ellipsis, and alliteration: *compare* COHERENCE. 2. **(social cohesion)** In sociology, social policy, and political science, the extent to which society holds together as a whole: the issue of social order. It concerns the nature and strength of social ties, *social networks, *consensus, cultural *integration, prosocial *values, and a sense of community. There is a debate over whether society is becoming more cohesive or whether the public sphere is being eroded by such factors as individualism and a relative increase in *weak ties (*see also* PUBLIC AND PRIVATE SPHERES). This is related to the extent to which a culture is *collectivistic or *individualistic and to the degree of cultural homogeneity or diversity within a society. An emphasis on cohesion and consensus tends to be associated with a *functionalist perspective and *conflict theorists stress that conflict and *contradictions are inherent in society. 3. **(group cohesion)** The extent and nature of social ties and relations, and of trust and *reciprocity, within a group.

cohort *See* AGE COHORT.

collage *See* MONTAGE.

collectivistic cultures Cultures in which there tends to be more emphasis on
*norms, social position and relationships, group *cohesion, *cooperation, and
social harmony than on *personal identity, individual autonomy, and
competitiveness: e.g. cultures in much of Asia, Africa and Latin America (Hofstede).
Such societies tend to have a strong sense of family, community, and tradition.
Collectivistic cultures tend also to be high *power distance cultures. *See also*
HIGH-CONTEXT; INTERCULTURAL COMMUNICATION; RELATIONAL COMMUNICATION;
ROLE-ORIENTED COMMUNICATION; *compare* INDIVIDUALISTIC CULTURES.

collocation 1. In *linguistics (lexicology), the recurrent and predictable
*co-presence of individual words in conventional usage: as in idioms such as 'neat
and tidy' (Firth). Words routinely found closely together are said to belong to the
same **lexical set**. 2. The process by which a word generates *connotations through
its co-occurrence with other words. The connotations of the word 'pretty' generated
by its association with terms associated with femininity make it *marked when
applied to a boy as opposed to a girl. 3. The *juxtaposition of items according to
some system.

colonial discourse analysis *See* POSTCOLONIALISM.

colour 1. In common usage, a spectrum of visible *hues that we routinely divide
into discrete categories to which we assign conventional labels such as red, green,
and blue. In the *natural attitude, a feature regarded as a property of objects, which
can signify in relation to relevant *codes and *contexts. In the *textual analysis of
visual media, a *formal feature which in *semiotics is a *paradigm (*see also*
COMMUTATION TEST). Quite apart from individual colour preferences, colours can
be perceived as warm or cool (*see* COLOUR TEMPERATURE), generate cultural
*connotations (*see also* BROWN GOODS; GENDERING; WHITE GOODS), or function
symbolically (*see* COLOUR SYMBOLISM). 2. (physics) The radiant energy of
*wavelengths of light within the narrow band of the *electromagnetic spectrum that
is visible to the naked eye in human beings with normal vision. To the physicist,
colour is just light—it is not a property of objects. The colour we perceive is affected
by the relative **reflectance** of a surface. When all visible wavelengths are reflected off
an object, we detect white; when they are all absorbed, we detect black; when all but
one are absorbed, we detect that wavelength. The three major physical properties
of light on which colour vision depends are: *wavelength, *spectral purity, and
*luminance. 3. In biological (psychophysical and physiological) terms, a visual
sensation generated by the radiant energy of wavelengths of light as detected by the
millions of **cones,** which are the visual receptor cells in the retina that are sensitive
to colour. From this perspective the colour we see depends on both the physical
properties of light and the biological property of the human eye and is a
consequence of the unequal stimulus of the three types of cones: *see* RGB. 4. In the
psychology of *perception, a perceptual response to *sensory data that generates
qualities such as redness or greyness. Colour is a subjective construction of the
mind: there are no colours in the outside world; objects do not have colours of their
own. However, colour is a psychological reality: colours are meaningful to us; we

perceive objects as having colours. The three major psychological dimensions of what we perceive as colours are *hue, *saturation, and *brightness. *See also* COLOUR CONSTANCY. **5. (local colour)** (art) The (apparent) colour of an object as seen in plain daylight: *see also* COLOUR CONSTANCY. **6.** In colour theory, visual data variously decomposed into constituent factors according to the **colour appearance** model employed. In computer graphics, photography, and video *post-production, the most common terms are *hue, *saturation, and *lightness; other terms include *luminance and *brightness. *See also* ADDITIVE COLOUR; SUBTRACTIVE COLOUR. **7.** (philosophy) Often classified as a secondary quality of material objects (whereas shape, size, and weight are primary and intrinsic qualities). Philosophy has not yet produced a satisfactory theory combining the subjective and objective aspects of colour.

colour balance (photography) The subjective *evaluation of a lack or predominance of particular colours in an image or print compared to what the photographer saw (or would expect to see) with the naked eye.

colour blindness A physical inability to distinguish some colours even under bright illumination due to a shortage of the cones in the retina that are sensitive to a particular range of *wavelengths. *See also* RGB.

colour constancy A psychological mechanism that stabilizes relative shifts in the apparent *colour of things. To achieve colour constancy, the brain 'discounts the illuminant', argued the German physicist Hermann von Helmholtz (1821–94). We adapt to the illuminant and perceive surfaces as having constant colours rather than purely in relation to *wavelengths of light. *See also* PERCEPTUAL CONSTANCIES.

colour correction 1. The reduction of chromatic aberrations in any optical system. 2. *Editing an image to adjust the *colour balance: *see also* GRADING.

colour depth In digital images and displays, the number of *bits of information contained in a single *pixel. Examples of standardized colour depths include 8-bit, which is equivalent to a 'greyscale' or 256-colour image, and 24-bit, which is equivalent to a so-called 'true colour' image, having the capacity to represent 16 777 216 distinct colours. Greater colour depth combined with higher image *resolutions produces better quality images.

colourist (grader) In video and film *post-production, the person who grades film or video *footage. This is a separate task to operating a *telecine, although the colourist, or an assistant, typically does both. *See also* GRADING.

colour separation overlay See CHROMA KEY.

colour symbolism The deliberate use of *colour to represent some abstract concept, typically according to some shared *code or *convention within a *culture, *subculture, or religion. In symbolic colour codes in many cultures, black is a negative *signifier and white a positive one, but it all depends on code and *context. What may be signified by particular colours is culturally variable. Colour symbolism is normally distinguished from less formalized colour *connotations.

colour temperature 1. The warmth of colour as measured on the Kelvin scale, based on the fact that a blue flame burns hotter than a red flame. Warm or reddish colours are counter-intuitively relatively cool (around 2 000 K) while cold or bluish colours are relatively warm (around 5 400 K). In photography, a technical way of identifying colour differences based on the temperature at which an inert substance glows a particular colour. 2. The relative warmth or coolness subjectively ascribed to particular *hues. **Warm colours** typically include *red, yellow, and orange. These tend to be perceived as *salient: as 'advancing' figure (*see* FIGURE AND GROUND). This is generally assisted by high *saturation and greater *luminance. **Cool colours** typically include blue, green, and purple. These tend to be perceived as receding or as *ground. This is generally assisted by low saturation and lower luminance. This dimension of colour *perception applies quite widely cross-culturally.

colour timing A laboratory-based process that uses chemicals and *exposure times to adjust the *colour balance of motion picture films. *Compare* GRADING.

column inches In *newspapers, a unit of space that is one column wide by one inch high. Used as a guide for reporters as to how much copy is required (approximately 25–35 words per inch) or for calculating *advertising charges. Also used as a *metonym for the relative importance of news stories.

combination, axis of A *structuralist term for the 'horizontal' axis in the analysis of a textual structure: the plane of the *syntagm (Jakobson). *Compare* SELECTION, AXIS OF.

comedy 1. Any humorous *discourse designed to entertain and amuse an audience. 2. A *genre of *drama or any literary work designed to amuse, appealing to the audience's sense of superiority over the characters depicted, and ending happily for the leading characters: in this sense, a form *ideologically endorsing social *integration (*compare* TRAGEDY). One of the four main *literary genres according to Frye. 3. A *television genre in which the main subgenres are situation comedies (or sitcoms) and political *satire. 4. A *film genre that includes subgenres such as black comedy, satire, screwball comedy, farce, and slapstick.

commercial (TV ad, advert) A non-programme *television genre or message, the *function of which is primarily persuasive, being to advertise a product, service, brand, or political campaign. The form is strongly tailored to establishing a *preferred reading and to *positioning the *target audience. *See also* INFOMERCIALS.

commercial cultures *See* ADVERTISING CULTURES.

commercialization 1. A typically pejorative reference to the subordination of education, public space, news, and the *internet to commercial interests. 2. The increasing pressures of commercial competition faced by public *institutions or not-for-profit organizations in certain sectors, including the media. In the UK, applied to the gradual process experienced by the BBC since it ceased to be a monopoly in the 1950s.

commercial model *See* MARKET MODEL.

commercial radio and television Radio stations and television channels partly funded by *advertising.

commodification (commoditization) *See also* PRIVATIZATION OF INFORMATION. 1. (*Marxist theory) The *production of goods or services for 'exchange' via a market as opposed to simply for the producer's own use. This converts **use values** into **exchange values** and characterizes the production relations of the market as opposed to a subsistence economy. Commodification is often regarded as subordinating real needs to manufactured desires in its pursuit of profit. Adorno, for instance, saw commodification as producing standardized products for passive *consumption. *See also* COMMODITY FETISHISM. 2. The process of becoming a *commodity.

commodification of information *See* PRIVATIZATION OF INFORMATION.

commodity 1. Loosely, any product that can be bought or sold. 2. (economics) A raw material or primary product. 3. (*marketing) A basic product with no significant differences from others of the same type, which is therefore generally sold on price. 4. (*Marxism) An object having a **use value** if it satisfies a human need and an **exchange value** if it can be exchanged for other commodities. Its exchange value is determined by the amount of labour required to produce it. For the *critical theorists of the *Frankfurt school, the use value of the *mass media and *popular culture is the *ideological *diversion function.

commodity fetishism (*Marxist theory) The qualities attributed to objects in the market that distinguish their exchange-values from their use-values (*see* COMMODITY). Commodity fetishism is seen as characteristic of capitalist society, where the object becomes a fetish—a substitute for the *social relations that it supplants. Its origin in exploitation is thus obscured. *See also* COMMODIFICATION; FETISHISM; REIFICATION.

common fate In the *gestalt laws of *perception, a perceptual bias (*see* ATTENTION) that tends to treat features in a visual stimulus that move in unison as being part of the same entity. This principle works best in the recognition of the movement of familiar objects or living beings, especially humans. In 1975 Gunnar Johansson (b.1911), a Swedish psychologist, attached lights to the joints of a black-clad actor and filmed him as he moved across a darkened room. When he was stationary no pattern could be seen in the lights but as soon as he moved it was easy to identify the pattern as a moving human figure.

Common Gateway Interface *See* CGI.

common sense *See also* CONVERSATIONAL CURRENCY; CULTURAL CODE; CULTURAL LITERACY; FOLK PSYCHOLOGY; IMAGINED COMMUNITY; SOCIAL UTILITY FUNCTION; TACIT KNOWLEDGE. 1. A positively-valued quality in individuals who are deemed sensible, 'down-to-earth', and of sound judgement in practical matters. 2. The most widespread *values, *attitudes, and beliefs about the world within a culture, acquired in *socialization, assumed to be universal, and taken-for-granted in *everyday life—even if this conflicts with what has been empirically established. Typically associated with the idea that whatever is deemed to be common sense is self-evidently true and does not need to be studied or analysed (*see also* ETHNOMETHODOLOGY). The *conduit metaphor, for instance, reflects common-sense notions of what *communication is: *see also* NATURAL ATTITUDE. **3.** For Gramsci, the incoherent, conformist, and unexamined beliefs of the masses established and naturalized by the acceptance of ruling-class attitudes and interests and which serve to maintain hegemonic structures. Thus, according to common sense, the *status quo—the way things are—is the way things should be. For Gramsci, it was the task of intellectuals to challenge such beliefs. This was a neo-Marxist re-evaluation of the role of *culture, consciousness, and *ideology rather than that of political and economic structures. **4.** For Barthes, who used the term **doxa,** common sense was a series of *myths generated by *ideological forces. These serve to ensure that certain familiar assumptions and values are taken for granted and unquestioned by most members of the culture, and seem entirely natural, normal, and self-evident (*see also* NATURALIZATION). Such myths are powerful since they seem to 'go without saying' and appear not to need to be deciphered or demystified. Common sense does involve incoherences, ambiguities, paradoxes, *contradictions, and omissions; the role of *ideology is to suppress these in the interests of dominant groups. **5.** (*semiotics) Widespread assumptions embedded in *codes that have become naturalized within a culture and that the semiotician seeks to denaturalize and make explicit: *see also* DENATURALIZATION. **6.** **(common sense realism, naïve realism)** (philosophy) The doctrine that there is an external, material world that we perceive directly, that it exists whether we perceive it or not, and that what we perceive is the way things are. Associated with a hostility to complex theories; potentially misleading since common sense tells us many things that have been proven to be false.

communication [Latin *communicare* 'to share'] **1.** Most broadly, a process of *interaction through *messages or *signals among or within humans, animals, machines, or plants (*see* COMMUNICATION MODELS). In the *common-sense understanding of human communication, the transmission of *messages or *information from a *sender to a *receiver (*see also* CONDUIT METAPHOR; TRANSMISSION MODELS). However, this simplistic model of *informational communication takes no account of the roles played by such factors as *codes, *context, *medium, *communicative functions, or *communicative relationships. Other models focus, in various ways, on the *production of *meaning. The term can refer to direct *face-to-face interaction or *mediated communication, to *interpersonal or *mass communication, which may be *intentional or *unintentional, *synchronous or *asynchronous, based on *symmetrical or *asymmetrical relationships, verbal or *nonverbal, and may employ any *channel— though these are primarily visual, auditory, or tactile. *See also* AURAL/ORAL CHANNEL; COMPUTER-MEDIATED COMMUNICATION; VISUAL COMMUNICATION. **2.** A product of such a process (loosely, 'a communication'): a *message, an *utterance, a *sign, or a *text: *see also* COMMUNICATIONS. **3.** In the study of human communication, an umbrella concept embracing *mass communication, interpersonal *interaction, and *intrapersonal communication. The only academic approach primarily concerned with communication in all of its modes is *semiotics (*see also* SEMIOSIS); however, human communication is a key concept in several disciplines and subdisciplines of the social sciences, including *linguistics, *sociolinguistics, *psycholinguistics, social psychology, anthropology, and sociology (*see also* SYMBOLIC INTERACTIONISM). For Bateson, 'all culture is communication' (*see also* SAPIR-WHORF HYPOTHESIS). It is a basic form of social behaviour and the primary means of social organization. The American philosopher John Dewey (1859–1952) writes that 'society . . . may be fairly said to exist . . . *in* communication,' and Habermas sees communication as the foundation of democracy. Communication departments arose in the United States in the 1950s. *See also* COMMUNICATION SCIENCE; COMMUNICATION STUDIES; COMMUNICATION THEORY; *compare* COMMUNICATIONS. **4.** In *advertising and other forms of *sender-oriented communication concerned with *effects and effectiveness, often reductively conceptualized as *persuasion: *see also* ELABORATION LIKELIHOOD MODEL; HYPODERMIC MODEL; TWO-STEP FLOW; YALE MODEL. **5.** Collectively, the systems that physically transport people, goods, and messages in material form from place to place: *see also* COMMUNICATIONS.

communication accommodation theory *See* ACCOMMODATION.

communication competence (*interpersonal communication) Not to be confused with *communicative competence. **1.** The ability to choose a communication strategy that is appropriate and effective in a given situation or *context. **2.** The degree to which a communicator's goals are achieved through effective and appropriate *interaction: a *sender-oriented approach: *see also* SENDER SKILLS. **3.** The ability to communicate effectively with people of different backgrounds and cultures (a *receiver-oriented approach). This includes being responsive to the social and linguistic characteristics of particular audiences.

communication design An emergent field of disparate specialisms sharing a common concern for matching design features and media to different *target audiences, *contexts, and *functions. It spans such areas as: *advertising, brand management, document design, graphic design, *information architecture, *information design, *infographics, instructional design, *marketing communication, *marketing semiotics, *media aesthetics, *psychographics, technical writing, *typography, *visual communication, *visual rhetoric, and website design. It also draws on *communication research and *market research.

communication game An approach to *interpersonal communication based on the metaphor of a game, with *roles, rules, and goals. This approach emphasizes: shared *conventions and *expectations concerning social roles and appropriate *communication styles, taking into account both formal and situational *contexts; mutually *receiver-oriented strategies; a range of *communicative functions including establishing the *relationship between the participants; the collaborative definition of interactional purpose and the mutual construction of social reality within the exchange. The concept is associated with the American psychologist E. Tory Higgins (b.1946). *Compare* CONSTITUTIVE MODELS; INTERACTIONAL MODEL; RELATIONAL MODEL; SYMBOLIC INTERACTIONISM.

communicationism Pejorative term for reducing complex issues to matters of *communication (narrowly conceived): a form of *reductionism.

communication models 1. Formal specifications of elements and relations, or underlying *metaphors, which represent *interaction through *messages. 2. Models of interpersonal *interaction. While there are countless forms, the salient features of most are outlined in these five broad types: *transmission models, *encoding/ decoding models, *interaction models, *relational models, *constitutive models: *see also* INTERPERSONAL COMMUNICATION. 3. Any of the various conceptualizations of the *production and reception of *mass media content, or of core media functions. *See* DOMINANCE MODEL; ELABORATION LIKELIHOOD MODEL; ENCODING/ DECODING MODEL; HYPODERMIC MODEL; MANIPULATIVE MODEL; MARKET MODEL; MASS COMMUNICATION; PLURALIST MODEL; PUBLICITY MODEL; RECEPTION MODEL; REGULATORY MODELS; RITUAL MODEL; TWO-STEP FLOW.

communication network A system of interactional *channels linking **nodes** (normally individual people, but also applicable to non-human elements) within a particular system (e.g. a group, an organization, or a *computer network), and enabling the flow of *information or *messages between them. Such systems have distinctive structural patterns of relations. Within communication networks, a *dyad is a pair of nodes, a key property of these being the extent of *reciprocity (*see also* ASYMMETRICAL RELATIONSHIPS). The relative centrality of individuals within communication networks tends to reflect *power. *See also* GROUP COMMUNICATION; NETWORK; NETWORK SOCIETY; SOCIAL NETWORKS; SYSTEMS THEORY.

communications 1. Loosely, *messages, *utterances, *signs, or *texts. 2. Sometimes distinguished from *communication as the material *institutions and practices of communication media, including the *mass media and *telecommunications; often also including *writing and *printing, and sometimes even speech, nonverbal *interaction, and/or (especially in historical accounts) transportation systems.

communication science An influential social scientific approach to the study of both *mass and *interpersonal communication, originating in the USA in the 1950s. It draws primarily on psychology, sociology, and political science and tends to be based on *quantitative research using *experiments and *surveys. At the heart of the *effects tradition, it is particularly associated with the study of *sender-oriented issues (e.g. effectiveness and persuasive strategies), and of technical and practical problems in communication. *See also* YALE MODEL.

communications satellites Electronic devices orbiting the Earth to provide *telecommunications (e.g. for telephony and *broadcasting). *See also* SATELLITE BROADCASTING.

communication studies An umbrella term for a field of study dealing with all aspects of *communication (including both *interpersonal and *mass communication). The term often indicates a distinction from the *positivism and *sender-orientation of *communication science. *Compare* MEDIA STUDIES.

communication style *Compare* CONVERSATIONAL STYLES. 1. The habitual mode of *interaction of an individual, variously typified (usually in the context of communication skills training and often in relation to personality types). For example: aggressive, passive-aggressive, passive, or assertive. 2. Modes of communication stereotypically associated with *gender, in which a masculine communication style is seen as *instrumental, *functional, and/or *task-oriented, and a feminine style as *expressive, social/relational, and/or *person-oriented: *see also* DIFFERENCE MODEL. 3. A dominant mode of *interaction within a particular *culture: *see* HIGH-CONTEXT; LOW-CONTEXT. 4. Individual verbal or nonverbal behaviour functioning as a *metamessage indicating how the *message *content is to be understood or an *attitude towards it (e.g. indicating *irony or a joke). 5. Lull's term for a recurrent style of *interaction within a family: *see* CONCEPT-ORIENTED COMMUNICATION; SOCIO-ORIENTED COMMUNICATION. 6. Institutional and managerial modes of human *interaction: *see also* DOWNWARD COMMUNICATION; UPWARD COMMUNICATION.

communication technologies 1. Equipment (and associated techniques) directly used to enable *interpersonal communication (both *synchronous and *asynchronous); and/or the *mass media. This is not quite synonymous with 'the means of communication' or even 'the media of communication'. The term 'communication technology' excludes *language in general or speech in particular (even though in some contexts either may be referred to as a *medium), since these are not construed as *technologies (*see also* PHONOCENTRISM). However, the term does include technologies enabling *mediated *speech communication (such as the telephone). It technically incorporates *writing, since that involves the use of tools, and the means by which writing is circulated (such as books—even prior to *printing). However, for literate people, writing has become such a *transparent medium that few are aware of it as a *technology. The term can also include the media utilized in *visual communication (though once again, this is not conventional usage). In 1909, Cooley noted that a communication medium could be assessed in terms of four key features that we may nowadays term *affordances: expressiveness or 'the range of ideas and feelings it is competent to carry'; permanence or 'the overcoming of time'; swiftness or 'the overcoming of space'; and diffusion or '*access to all classes of men'. 2. In references to *Information and Communication Technologies, the latter are conventionally regarded as consisting of *telecommunications and network technologies.

(()) SEE WEB LINKS

• *History of Communication Media*: Friedrich Kittler

communication theory 1. Any *theories about the nature of communication (particularly *interpersonal communication, and including *nonverbal communication). Major frameworks include: *rhetoric, *semiotics, *phenomenology, *cybernetics, social psychology, sociocultural theory, and *critical theory. 2. **(communicology)** More narrowly, theories about human communication arising from social science (including *communication science). 3. A synonym for mathematically-based *information theory.

communicative action Human social *interaction based on reaching a *consensus with others through unconstrained discussion and a search for understanding—in contrast to instrumental action (Habermas).

communicative competence A speaker's *knowledge of *sociolinguistic rules, *norms, and *conventions for a particular *language. The concept derives from Hymes. It is broader than Chomsky's purely grammatical notion of *linguistic competence, including, for instance, knowledge of *genres, media, and appropriateness. Not to be confused with *communication competence.

communicative functions 1. Ways of classifying acts of communication or uses of a *medium of communication either from the perspective of individuals—*personal functions—or from that of society—*social functions (*see also* MEDIA FUNCTIONS). *Jakobson's model, which listed six basic functions, originated as a model of *linguistic functions in the context of *interpersonal communication; others have proposed various functions of mass *media functions. Four primary functions of communication (often listed as *communicative purposes) are the *information function, the *education function, the *entertainment function, and the *persuasive function. 2. Generic objectives in *complementary relationships: *see* COMMUNICATIVE RELATIONSHIPS.

communicative intent *See* AUTHORIAL INTENTION.

communicative presumption According to *speech act theorists, a basic and universal assumption that underlying any speech act is an intention—at the very least an intention to communicate but also a more specific and recognizable communicative intent (which others have called a *preferred reading). However, note that *unintentional communication is possible: e.g. through nonverbal *leakage.

communicative purposes The primary goals and intentions of those involved in acts of communication on a given occasion. Some theorists suggest basic generic purposes as an analytic convenience (these are often reflected in lists of *communicative functions). Schramm lists four: to inform, to teach, to persuade, and to entertain. So do Brooks and Warren: to inform (*see* EXPOSITION), to persuade (*see* ARGUMENT; PERSUASION), to describe (*see* DESCRIPTION), and to narrate (*see* NARRATION). The Survey of English Usage also lists four categories of printed texts: informative, instructional, persuasive, and imaginative. Purposes often combine and blend, and of course many communicative purposes fall outside such frameworks; in casual encounters responses tend to be reactive.

communicative relationships 1. In *interpersonal communication, the relations between participants. These may precede the *interaction as social *roles or established *power relations and/or be established or modified (at least temporarily) by it (*see also* RELATIONAL COMMUNICATION). Conventionalized *complementary relationships involve normative objectives: e.g. to inform/to understand; to teach/to learn; to persuade/to decide; to entertain/to enjoy. Schramm argued that in familiar social *scenarios, these relationships amount to an informal *contract. *Communicative purposes do not always match *expectations, are seldom unidimensional, and can be subject to dynamic shifts. *See also* MODE OF ADDRESS; RELATIONAL MODEL. 2. In relation to the readership of *texts in any *medium, *see* TEXT-READER RELATIONS.

communicative turn *See* LINGUISTIC TURN.

communicator 1. Any active *participant in acts of communication. 2. In *sender-oriented theories, a synonym for *sender (rather than a term applied to both sender and *receiver). 3. Sometimes distinguished from the sender and referring to those who both produce message *content and communicate with the audience: e.g. news journalists or *copywriters in ads. Those who have minimal control over the content, such as celebrities who endorse products, are termed **pseudo-communicators**.

communicator characteristics *See* SOURCE FACTORS.

communicology *See* COMMUNICATION THEORY.

communities of interest *See* EPISTEMIC COMMUNITY.

community broadcasting Public access television and radio stations serving a small area, run by and for local people. They can be financed by commercial, non-profit, or government organizations but are subject to a host country's broadcasting *regulations. Typically these stations exist on cable. Equipment is provided and local people are trained how to use it.

community media or press *See* ALTERNATIVE MEDIA.

commutation test (*semiotics) A *structuralist analytical technique used in the *paradigmatic analysis of a *text to determine whether a change on the level of the *signifier leads to a change on the level of the *signified. To apply this test a particular signifier in a *text is selected. Then meaningful alternatives taken from the same paradigm set are considered. For instance, one might consider changing a *colour, a *typeface or, in photography, a *shot-size (such as a *close-up instead of a *mid-shot). The effects of each *substitution are assessed in terms of how this might affect the sense made of the *sign. *See also* ABSENT SIGNIFIER; MARKEDNESS.

compact disc (CD) An optical disc used to store digital audio recordings. A standard format for commercial music, introduced in 1982. *See also* CD-ROM.

competence 1. The ability to do something satisfactorily. 2. **(system of knowledge, I-language)** (*linguistics) A person's *tacit knowledge of the grammatical rules of speech in their first language, as distinct from their linguistic *performance (Chomsky). *Compare* COMMUNICATIVE COMPETENCE. 3. Communicative (Hymes): *see* COMMUNICATIVE COMPETENCE. 4. In interpersonal communication: *see* COMMUNICATION COMPETENCE. 5. (*ethnomethodology) The *tacit knowledge of social actors regarding *interaction in social *contexts.

competition 1. A mode of *interpersonal relations in which *co-present individuals are motivated as rivals in separately achieving the same goal, each striving to outdo the other. *See also* AGON; *compare* COACTION; COOPERATION. 2. The cultural *value of personal success particularly favoured in *individualistic cultures. 3. (economics) A market in which consumers have a choice of producers for a given type of product (unlike a *monopoly)—potentially keeping prices in check. Such 'free markets' are central in capitalist *discourse. *See* MARKET MODEL. 4. Market rivalry, typically in relation to the *four Ps. 5. (*marketing) Rival companies, products, or services within the same market sector.

complementarity In Greimas's *semiotic square, the relationship between an 'assertion' (e.g. beautiful) and its non-negation (not ugly) and between its negation (ugly) and non-assertion (not beautiful). *Compare* CONTRADICTION; CONTRARIETY.

complementary colours (complementaries) *Hues that are directly opposite from each other on a colour wheel and thus extreme contrasts. In *subtractive colour systems, red is opposite green, blue is opposite orange, and yellow is opposite violet. In *additive colour systems, red is opposite cyan, green is opposite magenta, and blue is opposite yellow.

complementary relationships Interactional partnerships in a *dyad based on unequal *status or *power and employing *communication styles that reflect this. One partner is dominant or active and the other is subordinate or passive (Watzlawick stresses that this is not about strength and weakness and no evaluative judgement is implied). Such relationships are often a correlate of the sociocultural *context: e.g. parent/child, teacher/student, doctor/patient, or employer/employee, though they can also be idiosyncratic. They are characterized by non-competitive *interaction based on maintaining differences. Behaviour is complementary: e.g., one person controls and the other submits. *See also* POWER RELATIONS; RELATIONAL COMMUNICATION.

compliance *See* CONFORMITY.

complication *See* CLASSICAL NARRATIVE STRUCTURE.

component video An *analogue video format that encodes video into a *luminance or Y channel and two *chrominance channels of blue (B-Y) and red (R-Y). Green is not encoded because it can be inferred from the information in the other two colours. The advantage of component video over *composite is that it has twice as much colour information. It is particularly associated with the domestic S-VHS and professional Beta SP formats. *Compare* COMPOSITE VIDEO.

composite video An *analogue video format that consists of *colour information 'piggybacked' onto a black-and-white transmission *signal. The format is a legacy of when colour television was first developed to be compatible with the existing black-and-white technology. Colour television systems (*NTSC in the US, and *PAL in the UK) transmit colour information in the form of a sub-carrier signal along with the main black-and-white picture and sound information. *Compare* COMPONENT VIDEO.

comprehension 1. Broadly, the mental processes involved in making sense of any communication. 2. **(literal comprehension)** Ascribing plausible *meanings to message elements and understanding their *denotation. *See also* LITERAL MEANING. 3. **(inferential comprehension)** Constructing an *interpretation of a *message. Inferring the *preferred meaning by 'going beyond the information given' (Bruner). *See also* INFERENCE. Decoding a message with appropriate reference to *textual and social codes or *schemata, and to *context. 4. For most theorists, a function of a

higher order than the perceptual level (hearing, seeing etc.); others insist that
*interpretation cannot be tidily separated from *perception or that interpretation
may also guide perception. 5. In some models this includes the higher order skills
of *evaluation (e.g. character evaluation and *modality judgements) and
appreciation (including awareness of *connotations). 6. The understanding
resulting from such processes.

compression *See also* TIME-SPACE COMPRESSION. 1. In *digital media, a range of
technologies that reduce the number of *bits needed (for example, to represent the
image) and therefore the storage and transmission costs. In relation to digital
images and audio, compression can either be **lossless,** where there are not
perceivable *artefacts resulting from the process, or **lossy** where compression
artefacts can be perceived. A common method of image compression involves
identifying areas of *redundancy by examining small squares of an image and
averaging out the *colour values of each square. *See also* JPEG; MP3. 2. In *analogue
and digital audio, technologies that reduce the dynamic range of an audio *signal
but preserve its overall loudness.

compulsory heterosexuality *See* HETERONORMATIVITY.

computer conferencing *See* VIDEOCONFERENCING.

computer game *See* VIDEOGAME.

computer-generated imagery (CGI) The use of 3D computer graphics for
*special effects in films, television programmes, and commercials.

computer literacy 1. *Knowledge, understanding, and experience of
computers and their uses. 2. Particular skills and levels of competence in using
computers and specific applications.

computer-mediated communication (CMC) Any communication in which
users interact via the direct use of a computer. This is primarily *online
communication: whether *synchronous (e.g. *chat rooms, *instant messaging,
*virtual worlds, or *webcams) or *asynchronous (e.g. electronic *bulletin boards,
*email, or *newsgroups). However, it can also include human-computer dialogues,
as in the case of the *Turing test, and also Joseph Weizenbaum's *Eliza* program
(1966), which simulates a psychotherapist.

((⊕)) SEE WEB LINKS

• *Journal of Computer-Mediated Communication*

computer network (network) A system of linking two or more
computing devices together for the purpose of sharing *data. Networks can be
classified in various ways: according to hardware or software, e.g. fibre optic
cable, Ethernet, wireless (*WiFi); by geographical range, e.g. Local Area
Network (LAN), Wide Area Network (WAN); or by relationships, e.g. client/server,
*peer-to-peer.

conative function (for Bühler, the **appellative function**) A *function of
*language or, more generally, communication, that is focused on, and concerned

with influencing the behaviour of, the *addressee, and thus concerned with *persuasion. A key function in *Jakobson's model. *See also* COMMUNICATIVE FUNCTION; LINGUISTIC FUNCTIONS.

concealment error (television) Digital *dropout that is caused by some break in the code for which error-correcting software cannot compensate.

concept-oriented communication A style of family communication and media use that involves: an emphasis on presenting and discussing ideas; children being encouraged to express ideas and challenge others' beliefs; children being exposed to more than one side of controversial issues and encouraged to discuss controversies with adults; relatively low TV use; considerable parental control exercised over TV viewing; *mass media used mainly for news and not much for 'escape' (Lull). *Compare* SOCIO-ORIENTED COMMUNICATION.

conceptually-driven processing *See* TOP-DOWN PROCESSING.

conceptual meaning *See* IDEATIONAL MEANING.

condensation In *psychoanalytical theory, a concept introduced by Freud for the *interpretation of dreams: emotionally-charged ideas (*latent meaning) are attached to a more neutral image (*manifest content), creating a *symbol which is a fusion of these. Lacan, for whom the unconscious is structured like a *language, makes an analogy with *metaphor. *See also* DREAM-WORK; OVERDETERMINATION; *compare* DISPLACEMENT.

conditioning 1. A process of learning in which behaviour is shaped by recurrent environmental stimuli: *compare* MODELLING. 2. A deliberate and systematic attempt to modify behaviour. There are two forms. Firstly, **classical** or **Pavlovian conditioning**: a form of associative learning in which the repeated association of an arbitrary stimulus with another one already associated with some reflex response eventually leads to it generating the same reflex. This concept is that of the Russian physiologist Ivan Pavlov (1849–1936). Secondly, **operant** or **instrumental conditioning**: the control of behaviour through the manipulation of its consequences, devised by the American psychologist B. F. Skinner (1904–90). The frequency of a desired response is controlled through rewards or **reinforcement**. *See also* BEHAVIOURISM.

conduit metaphor A *metaphor underlying everyday references to communication, identified in 1979 by Michael Reddy, an American linguist, reflecting the notions that: *language functions like a conduit transferring thoughts from one individual to another; writers and speakers insert their thoughts or feelings into words; words act as containers conveying thoughts and feelings to others; listeners and readers extract the thoughts and feelings from such words. This is reflected in usages such as 'conveying ideas', 'transferring meaning', 'getting thoughts across', 'transmitting information', and 'delivering the curriculum'. Our implicit, *common sense *model of communication is thus a *transmission model, and is subject to all of the limitations of such models.

cones *See* COLOUR.

conferencing *See* VIDEOCONFERENCING.

conflict 1. **(psychological conflict)** (psychology) Conscious or unconscious tensions within the mind of an individual (*compare* COGNITIVE DISSONANCE). In *psychoanalytical theory, **psychical conflict** reflects contradictory impulses. 2. **(social conflict)** Tensions between individuals or groups in a society. 3. **(international conflict)** Tensions or overt struggle between nation states. 4. **(dramatic conflict)** In literary theory, tension between characters or forces around which the plot of a *narrative revolves. This includes internal or **psychological conflict,** and conflict between a character and society or the environment. 5. (sociology) **Conflict theory** refers to theories that evolved in the 1960s in reaction to structural *functionalism. Drawing variously on Weber, Marx, and Simmel, these stressed economic and political interests leading to *competition and conflict over *power. Social order involves coercion rather than *consensus, and conflict underlies social change. *Pluralists also note that conflict and *contradictions are inherent in society.

conform *n.* In television *post-production, an intermediate *editing stage (coming after an *offline edit and before an *online edit) where a low-quality sequence is recreated at a higher quality *resolution, according to a set of instructions contained in a *timeline or *edit decision list. This *edit is called a conform because the high-quality sequence must exactly match (or conform to) the low-quality one. While many *rushes tapes may have been shot and used in the offline edit, the conform only uses the *footage that is referenced in the final sequence.

conformity (conformism) A tendency to accept or act in accordance with dominant social *conventions and *norms or the opinions, *expectations, or behaviour of a majority, e.g. in experiments by the American psychologist Solomon Asch (1907–96), where some subjects gave the same answers to questions that they heard others supply even when the subjects knew these to be incorrect. As distinct from **compliance,** which tends to be associated with obedience to authority, as in the famous experiments by the American psychologist Stanley Milgram (1933–84). *See also* INTERNALIZATION.

connectivity 1. The extent to which an electronic device can be linked with other electronic devices (e.g. a computer with *USB and *WiFi has more connectivity than one with just USB). 2. An evaluative criterion of the quality of an *internet connection based on the capacity of the *channel: for example, *broadband users are said to have greater connectivity than dial-up users.

connotation (connotative meaning) *See also* SURPLUS MEANING; *compare* DENOTATION 1. In *linguistics and literary theory, a 'secondary' (often emotional) meaning (or a range of associations) evoked by a word beyond its explicit *denotation or dictionary meaning. Such meanings may be implied by the writer or speaker and/or inferred by the reader or listener. More broadly in the arts the same process generated by an image, sound, gesture etc. A photograph of a tree denotes what it depicts—for instance, an old oak tree—but the same image could also connote Englishness for an English viewer. 2. (*semiotics) The process by which sociocultural associations are produced as a reader *decodes a *sign or *text in any medium in a particular *context (some theorists also include purely personal associations). For Barthes, connotation was a second (but not secondary) *order of signification which uses the denotative sign (*signifier and *signified) as its signifier and attaches to it an additional signified. In this framework connotation is a sign which derives from the signifier of a denotative sign (so denotation leads to a chain of connotations).

consciousness industry *Institutions and agencies, primarily the *mass media, which the German writer Hans Magnus Enzensberger (b.1929) argued were involved in the *cultural reproduction of human consciousness as a social product in the interests of economic and political elites. According to this perspective, the ruling class seeks to control the content and output of the media in order to naturalize the *status quo in the consciousness of subordinate classes. *See also* MEDIA HEGEMONY; *compare* CULTURAL INDUSTRY.

consensus 1. General agreement about some issue within a group or in *public opinion: *compare* DISSENSUS. 2. Shared ideas, *norms, and *values in a society (for *functionalists, particularly Parsons, the basis of social order and social *integration). These values are perpetuated through *socialization. 3. (*Marxist theory) An *ideological concept used to perpetuate the *status quo by masking the extent of social *conflict.

consensus function (correlation function) From a *functionalist perspective on society, the persuasive role played by social communication and the *mass media in developing a social *consensus, correlating the component parts of society. A key *social function (as distinct from *personal function) of such communication. For Lasswell in 1948 this was one of the three key functions of social communication (the others being the *surveillance function and the *socialization function). *See also* MEDIA FUNCTIONS.

consent form In academic research, photography, and broadcasting, a printed sheet given to individuals, the signing of which serves as legal evidence of *informed consent to being photographed, filmed, recorded, or otherwise involved in a study or broadcast.

console 1. **(game console, videogame console)** An electronic device (such as the Sony PlayStations and Nintendo Wii) used with a display device (a television or a monitor) to control *entertainment software such as *videogames. 2. **(handheld game console)** A portable electronic entertainment device with a built-in screen, controls, and speakers (e.g. Nintendo DS).

conspicuous consumption Extravagant spending on goods or services primarily as a mark of social *status. Veblen coined the term in 1899 to refer to the behaviour of the *nouveau riche*.

(((•))) SEE WEB LINKS

• Veblen on conspicuous consumption

constitution of the subject   In Althusserian *Marxist and *structuralist theory more generally, a process in which the pre-given structures of *social relations construct *roles that define the *subjectivity of individuals who inhabit them. *See also* INTERPELLATION; SUBJECT.

constitutive models   *Communication models in which *meanings are reflexively constructed, maintained, or negotiated in the act of communicating (rather than pre-established, as implied in linear *transmission models). Communication is seen as a social practice that transforms not only our thoughts and feelings, but also our *identities, our *social relations, our framings of reality, and our social *institutions. This is a key concept in *ethnomethodology, where it is referred to as *reflexivity. The American communication theorist Robert T. Craig (b.1947) argues that in the constitutive view communication is a primary phenomenon shaping other social processes (psychological, sociological, cultural, and so on) rather than a secondary one explicable in terms of antecedent factors. Furthermore, it can be seen as a metamodel for communication, enabling theorists to frame other models as differentially constituting particular processes and reflecting different theoretical purposes. *See also* COMMUNICATION GAME; CONSTRUCTIONISM; MEANING-ORIENTED COMMUNICATION; RELATIONAL MODEL; SYMBOLIC INTERACTIONISM; *compare* INTERACTION MODEL; RECURSIVE COMMUNICATION THEORY.

constraint   1. (media theory) *See* AFFORDANCES. 2. (semiotics) *See* MOTIVATION.

constructedness   The status of a *text (in any *medium) as something created, authored, composed, *framed, *mediated, and/or edited rather than being an unmediated *slice of life or a window on the world (*see* MAGIC WINDOW). A basic criterion involved in *modality judgements about the reality status of texts. In *realist texts constructedness is disguised, but viewers of television and film from 8-years-old (in some cases even younger) can recognize methods of media *production and the use of certain *formal features (e.g. filmic *cuts), can distinguish fantasy from reality, and make distinctions between actors and the characters they play.

constructionism (social constructionism, constructivism)   A philosophical (specifically *epistemological) stance in *phenomenological sociology in which social realities are seen as the product of sociohistorically situated practices rather than objective *facts (*compare* OBJECTIVISM). Similarly, *social identities are seen as constructed rather than pre-given: making social constructionism an anti-*essentialist stance as well as anti-positivist one. In contrast to *realists, constructionists argue that reality is not wholly external to and independent of how we conceptualize the world: our *sign systems (especially *language) play a major part in the *construction of social reality*, which cannot be separated from the sign systems in which it is framed. Although a constructionist stance does not necessarily entail a denial of the existence of physical reality, some inflections emphasize more radically the *social construction of reality*: for instance, *perception itself involves *codes (*see also* PERCEPTUAL CODES), and what count as objects, their properties, and their relations vary from language to language (*see also* LINGUISTIC

RELATIVISM; ONTOLOGY; SAPIR-WHORF HYPOTHESIS). Constructionism can be seen as offering an alternative to the *binarism involved in polarizing the issue into the *objectivism of naive *realism versus the radical *subjectivism of *idealism (*see also* INTERSUBJECTIVITY). Social constructionists differ from extreme subjectivists in insisting that realities are not limitless and unique to (or definable by) the individual; rather, they are the product of social definitions and as such far from equal in status. Realities are contested, and textual *representations (and *theories) are thus *sites of struggle. Realists often criticize constructionism as extreme *relativism or *conventionalism—a position from which constructionists frequently distance themselves. *See also* INTERPRETIVISM; LABELLING THEORY; PHENOMENOLOGY; SYMBOLIC INTERACTIONISM; *compare* CONSTRUCTIVISM.

construction of reality *See* CONSTRUCTIONISM; REALITY CONSTRUCTION.

constructivism 1. **(genetic epistemology)** Originally, a psychological focus on the development of the mental structures of individuals over time (Piaget). *See also* ACCOMMODATION; ASSIMILATION. 2. More broadly, the individual's psychological *interpretation or construction of *meaning. According to this perspective, individuals play a very active (albeit typically unconscious) role in making sense of the everyday world around them: in *perception, through *selective attention, for instance; and in making sense of texts, in *comprehension, *interpretation, and both cognitive and emotional responses. *See also* ACTIVE AUDIENCE THEORY; SCHEMA THEORY. 3. (social psychology) Stances emphasizing theory-driven processes in *social perception (*see* TOP-DOWN PROCESSING), as opposed to structuralist theories, which emphasize data-driven processes (*see* BOTTOM-UP PROCESSING). 4. (*film theory) An approach associated with Bordwell that addresses the formal conditions under which *spectators comprehend a film by focusing on their *cognitive (rather than emotional) operations: for instance, through the use of *schemata. Spectators construct an *interpretation by making a series of *inferences. The film provides cues in the forms of *representations that trigger or constrain these inferences: *see also* COGNITIVE FILM THEORY. 5. (sociology) Often a synonym for *constructionism.

consumer 1. A person who eats or uses something. 2. The ultimate user of a product or service (not necessarily the purchaser). 3. In relation to media use, synonymous with *user.

consumer behaviour 1. The processes involved in the purchase and use of products or services by individuals or particular demographic groups. For example, why people buy a particular product, their decision-making processes, or the desires and needs that products address. *See also* MASLOW'S HIERARCHY OF NEEDS. 2. The study of these processes in *market research or by academics.

consumer culture (consumer society, consumerization) *See also* ADVERTISING CULTURES; TASTE. 1. A pejorative reference to modern Western society in terms of its domination by the *marketing and *consumption of goods and services (*see also* PROMOTIONAL CULTURE). **Anti-consumerists** characterize its *materialism as the reduction of personal fulfilment to consumption, criticize its superficiality, or see it in terms of cultural manipulation. *See also* AESTHETICIZATION; COMMODIFICATION; COMMODITY FETISHISM; CONSPICUOUS

CONSUMPTION; FRANKFURT SCHOOL; MANIPULATIVE MODEL; MASS CULTURE. 2. A society in which patterns of consumption are a key basis for *status differentiation, *personal identities, and pleasure: *see also* LIFESTYLE; POST-FORDISM; SEGMENTATION. 3. A reference to the site within which the active, *savvy consumer subversively subordinates commodities and advertisements to their own purposes, especially in the construction of *social identity. In this framing, the *form (*advertising, packaging) can be at least as important as the content. Neo-liberals also welcome competitive pricing and 'consumer sovereignty', seeing consumers as pushing for higher quality products, and green consumerism as leading to products that are more ethically-sourced and sustainable. *See also* ACTIVE AUDIENCE THEORY; BRICOLAGE; *compare* CULTURAL POPULISM. 4. The cultural *contexts, practices, *institutions, and *discourses involved in *marketing and/or consumption, and also their academic study.

consumer group *See* REFERENCE GROUP.

consumerism 1. A synonym for consumerization: *see* CONSUMER CULTURE; POST-FORDISM. 2. **(consumer movement)** The consumer rights movement.

consumerization *See* CONSUMER CULTURE.

consumer needs *See* MASLOW'S HIERARCHY OF NEEDS.

consumer society *See* CONSUMER CULTURE.

consumption Using products, services, or *mass-media content in order to satisfy desires and real or imagined needs. Typically paired with *production, the term is sometimes used pejoratively by cultural *elitists and *critical theorists, implying manipulation and/or passivity. *See also* CONSPICUOUS CONSUMPTION; CONSUMER CULTURE; CONSUMERISM; FRANKFURT SCHOOL; LEAVISITE; MASLOW'S HIERARCHY OF NEEDS; MASS CONSUMPTION; MASS CULTURE; *compare* ACTIVE AUDIENCE THEORY.

contact 1. *n.* In *Jakobson's model of linguistic communication, the physical *channel together with the psychological connection between the *addresser and addressee. In his list of *functions, *orientation towards this factor is the *phatic function. 2. *n.* (journalism) A person who provides information for a story. 3. *n.* and *v.* Touch: *see* HAPTICS. 4. *v.* To initiate a communication with someone.

contagion effect 1. The concept that heavy media coverage of certain phenomena (typically criminal or violent acts but also fads) will lead to imitation or create a craze. 2. **Social or behavioural contagion**. The spread of behaviour, *attitudes, or beliefs through *conformity and imitation.

content 1. The *subject matter of a *text or *message, as distinct from its *form or *style. *Informational texts tend to foreground content (in contrast to aesthetic texts). Content can only be separated from form for analytical purposes. The idea that content (or thought) precedes form has often been criticized; from a *structuralist perspective there is no content before form: *see also* CLOAK THEORY; MOULD THEORY. 2. What is denoted, depicted, or otherwise represented: *see also* DENOTATION; REFERENTIALITY; REPRESENTATION. 3. **(informational content)** The *information in a message. In *information theory this is based on the predictability of letters or digits in a sequence. **4.** The *meaning of a message. This kind of definition reductively equates meaning with message, implying that meaning can be 'extracted' without an active process of *interpretation. However, what is meant is invariably more than what is said, and interpreters have to 'go beyond the information given' (Bruner). **5.** *Propositional meaning. **6.** The *explicit, *manifest, or *literal meaning of a message: *see also* MANIFEST CONTENT. **7.** In the *conduit metaphor, ideas, thoughts, or feelings that we tend to talk about as if they were 'contained' in words.

content analysis A primarily *quantitative type of formal *textual analysis involving the systematic *categorization and counting of recurrent elements in the *form or *content of *texts (*see also* CODING). It has been widely employed in the study of *bias and *balance in news coverage (*see also* GLASGOW MEDIA GROUP). Yet, just because an item occurs frequently in a text does not establish its *significance. A rare occurrence may be more important than a frequent one. Indeed, what is most significant may be what is absent. Researchers often combine this technique with other approaches, such as *semiotic analysis (in particular the concept of *markedness).

content message A primarily *informational message, typically intended to be *explicit, *literal, and unambiguous and reflecting an instrumental *communication style. *See also* INFORMATIONAL COMMUNICATION; INSTRUMENTAL COMMUNICATION; *compare* RELATIONAL MESSAGE.

content provider An organization (such as a *mass media company) that provides materials for websites, *television networks, *mobile phone companies, etc. in the form of television programmes, audio, video or print news packages, etc. This is then packaged by the buyer to target the audience they are hoping to attract: in the case of a television network, for example, by creating trailers and other marketing materials which rebrands the content so that it is perceived to be part of the network's output.

content words *See* GRAMMATICAL WORDS.

context **1.** Most broadly, any *frame of reference or framework within which something is perceived, produced, consumed, communicated, interpreted, or otherwise experienced, or which is seen as relevant to the *description or analysis of any phenomenon. *Contextualism emphasizes such factors; failing to account for them may be criticized as *decontextualization. However, *deconstructionists remind us that, as *frames of reference, contexts are not fragments of an objective reality. *See also* CONTEXT FACTORS; CONTEXTUAL EXPECTATIONS; CONTEXTUALIZATION; INDEXICAL; SITUATEDNESS. **2.** (**social context**) The social environment within which some phenomenon occurs: either the **micro-context** of the immediate social situation, or the **macro-context** of the broad social, cultural, historical, political, and/or economic circumstances and conditions (including *social structure, *roles, and *social relations). Accounts that neglect such factors may be criticized as *asocial; overplaying them may be called *sociologism: *see also* SOCIAL SITUATION. **3.** (**situational context**) The immediate physical and social *setting and circumstances within which some phenomenon occurs, which may include relevant roles and tasks and how the participants themselves situate the phenomenon: *see also* CONTEXT OF RECEPTION; CONTEXT OF SITUATION; CONTEXT OF USE; SOCIAL SITUATION. 4. **(cultural context)** Factors relating to *ethnic or *subcultural backgrounds and associated environments and practices which may influence *perception, *communication, *interpretation, and/or media use. Over-emphasis on such factors may be criticized as *relativism. *See also* CONTEXT OF SITUATION; HIGH-CONTACT CULTURES; LOW-CONTACT CULTURES; READING DIRECTION. 5. **(historical context)** Historical *events, movements, processes, and/or forces seen as of explanatory relevance in the *description and analysis of a social phenomenon. Ignoring such contexts may be criticized as *ahistorical; overplaying them may be called *historicism. 6. **(psychological** or **perceptual context)** The *frame of reference that individuals bring to an experience and that guides their *expectations. These include: their *attitudes and *values; the *knowledge and experience on which they draw in the form of active *schemata such as *social schemata and *textual schemata; their interests, recent experiences, current *purposes, and needs, which may generate *unconscious biases (as in *perceptual set); their *cognitive styles, and so on. Overplaying such factors may be criticized as *psychologism. 7. **(task-context)** The specific task in which participants are engaged, and the *roles associated with it, including the ways in which they individually and collectively interpret these. 8. **(formal context)** Relationships between *formal features (such as lines, *colours, and shapes) that may influence the *perception or *interpretation of any element (*see also* GESTALT LAWS). The apparent size or *brightness of shapes, for instance, can be dramatically affected by their *proximity to other shapes. Formal relations are not only spatial but also temporal: the sequence of consecutively encountered items affects the sense that we make of each one (*see also* CONTIGUITY; JUXTAPOSITION; SEQUENCE; SPATIAL RELATIONS; SYNTAGM). Overplaying formal factors may be criticized as *formalism: *see also* FORMAL ANALYSIS. 9. **(linguistic context)** Any linguistic factors which act as cues in the recognition of meaningful units in an *utterance or written text, notably: semantic context, syntactic context, phonetic context, and logographic context. For extralinguistic reference, *see* DEIXIS. 10. A key element in *Jakobson's model of (linguistic) communication, in which making sense of a message is dependent on a shared understanding of context (as well as a shared *code). In this sense, the context is the *referent: what the *message is about. Jakobson declared that 'It is not enough to know the code in order to grasp the message . . . you need to know the context'. However, the normative dependence of meaning on context is culturally variable. *See* ELABORATED CODE; HIGH-CONTEXT; LOW-CONTEXT; RESTRICTED CODE. 11. In general *semiotic usage, an *indexical dimension.

context factors In *models of communication or *persuasion, specific *variables associated with a specific *context of reception that research has identified as among those that can affect the effectiveness of the message. Where and in what circumstances is the message likely to be received, and how might this impact on its effectiveness? *See also* YALE MODEL.

context of reception The social *setting within which an audience encounters a *text in any *medium. For instance, the **viewing context** of a film could involve viewing with friends at the cinema, viewing a broadcast of the film on television at home with the family or alone in a hotel on DVD. These are quite different viewing experiences which may involve different viewing styles (*see also* TELEVISION VIEWING STYLES). Within a family context at home, the viewing experience becomes part of domestic politics and the *performance of *identity.

context of situation *See also* RELEVANCE THEORY. 1. Malinowski coined this phrase in 1923 to refer to the cultural *context of use in which an *utterance was located; furthermore, 'the whole way of life' (cultural context) had to be borne in mind in interpreting an utterance. 2. For Firth, all of the circumstances in which a spoken utterance occurs that are relevant in making sense of it. He emphasized that *meaning is context-dependent: *see also* SOCIAL SITUATION. 3. For Halliday, *extralinguistic circumstances of use that influence the linguistic form of an utterance: not only the social and physical *setting, but also such factors as *social relationships, the nature of the *medium, the task, and the *topic. He proposed that there is a systematic relationship between 'typical' situations and the types of language employed within them (*see also* REGISTER).

context of use 1. In the discourse of user-centred design, the circumstances in which a utilitarian product will be used, the tasks for which it will be used, and the ways in which its users will use it—*usability factors to which such design assigns a high priority. 2. Sometimes a synonym for *context of situation. 3. The other words together with which a given word is used: *see* COLLOCATION.

contextual communication *See* HIGH-CONTEXT.

contextual expectations What *textual or *social schemata lead us to predict in textual or social *scenarios. While this can be useful in guiding our *interpretations and managing our behaviour, it can also lead to *selective perception or recall when our *expectations override some of the actual details.

contextualism 1. (philosophy) The position that actions or *utterances can only be understood relative to the *context in which they occurred (often criticized as *relativism). 2. An emphasis on the importance of particular contextual and situational factors (rather than general 'laws') in the explanation of social, psychological, and historical *events. 3. In *aesthetics and literary theory, the view that a work can only be understood in relation to the sociohistorical circumstances of its *production, aesthetic movements at the time, or the creator's life and work, rather than solely on the basis of formal criteria, as was Kant's position. *Compare* HERMENEUTICS.

contextualization *Framing *texts or *events within broader *contexts for the purpose of *interpretation and analysis. Sociological critiques have argued that news reports fail to offer adequate explanatory contextualization for reported events. *See also* DECONTEXTUALIZATION; RECONTEXTUALIZATION.

contextual meaning The bearing of situational, social, and/or interpersonal factors on the *interpretation of a message or an action. In linguistic usage, this usually refers to *extralinguistic factors (*see also* CONTEXT OF SITUATION), but it can also refer to a textual *context: a higher level of linguistic structure (e.g. the context of a sentence within a *discourse). Many contemporary theorists argue that there is no meaning without context (*see* CONTEXTUALISM). *See also* HIGH-CONTEXT.

contiguity 1. Broadly, the condition in which things are next to each other: adjoining, touching, or sharing a border: *see also* CO-PRESENCE; JUXTAPOSITION. 2. (*semiotics) The condition in which something is in some sense part of (or part of the same domain as) something else. Contiguity may be causal, cultural, spatial, temporal, physical, conceptual, formal, or structural. For instance, at the level of the *signified, *metonymy is said to be based on contiguity—in contrast to *metaphor (which involves *transposition from one domain to another) since metonyms stand for things to which they are regarded as 'belonging' (in some *ontological framework): metonymy may thus seem more 'realistic' than metaphor. At the level of the signifier, *syntagms, unlike *paradigms, are based on formal contiguity (adjacency within the same text).

contingency (philosophy) The issue of *propositions lacking necessary truth or falsity, or the extent to which their validity is dependent on conditions ('contingent on'). *See also* DETERMINISM.

continuity editing (invisible editing) In film and video *post-production, a technique of removing moments of *redundancy in a moving image while still presenting the illusion of the continuous passing of time. This is achieved in three main ways: firstly, by cutting to a different *shot, as in a *shot/reverse-shot; secondly, by a *match cut; thirdly, by using a *cutaway. Continuity editing is a practice that focuses on narrative continuity and that evolved and became ubiquitous in the realist feature films developed in Hollywood. It is still the dominant convention in mainstream film and television. *Cuts are intended to be unobtrusive except for special dramatic shots. *Content is *foregrounded and *form and *style are backgrounded. Invisible editing is intended to support rather than dominate the *narrative: the story and the behaviour of its characters are intended to be the centre of attention. The technique gives the impression that the edits are always motivated by the *events in the 'reality', that the camera is simply recording the action rather than being operated out of a desire to tell a story in a particular way. The seamlessness convinces us of its *realism, but its devices include: *motivated cuts; *match cuts (rather than *jump cuts); the *180-degree rule; *establishing shots; the *sound bridge, and so on. Together, these devices constitute a system of related *conventions. The editing is not truly invisible but the conventions and the system have become so familiar to visual literates that they no longer consciously notice them: indeed, they feel 'natural' rather than merely conventional. From the practitioner's point of view, the main limitation of continuity editing is that in order to make cuts invisible, interesting *footage sometimes has to be rejected simply because it cannot be edited seamlessly into a *sequence. *See also* EYELINE MATCH; *compare* JUMP CUT.

continuity theories *See* GREAT DIVIDE THEORIES.

contract 1. **(legal contract)** A written or oral agreement intended to be legally binding. 2. **(language contract)** The non-negotiable linguistic system into which one is born (Saussure). From the point of view of individual language-users, *language is a 'given': we don't create the system for ourselves. 3. **(social contract)** In **social contract theory**, a tacit collective agreement by the members of society to accept the regulatory authority of the state in return for its maintenance of social order (the terms of this hypothetical contract are couched differently by different political theorists). 4. **(communication contract)** Normative *expectations for *social relationships in familiar *scenarios of interpersonal *interaction (Schramm). For instance, in asking for road directions the asker expects either simple directions or the admission of a lack of local *knowledge while the person replying expects the asker to listen carefully and to thank them afterwards. *See also* RELATIONAL COMMUNICATION; RELATIONAL MODEL. 5. **(narrative contract)** The relation between a *narrator and the intended audience. For relations between texts (in any medium) and their audiences *see* TEXT-READER RELATIONS.

contradiction 1. A logical flaw in an *argument involving the *co-presence of statements which are incompatible opposites. 2. In Greimas's *semiotic square, the relationship between an 'assertion' (e.g. beautiful) and its non-assertion (not beautiful) and between its negation (ugly) and its non-negation (not ugly). *Compare* COMPLEMENTARITY; CONTRARIETY. 3. A dynamic tension between opposing forces or groups. In *Marxist theory, the basis of social change. *See also* CONFLICT; IDEOLOGICAL ANALYSIS; *compare* COHESION. 4. In *structuralist theory, a tension between *binary oppositions which *myth seeks to resolve. 5. In *poststructuralist theory, a destabilizing and irresolvable tension between oppositional concepts: *see also* APORIA; DECONSTRUCTION.

contrariety In Greimas's *semiotic square, the relationship between an 'assertion' (e.g. beautiful) and its negation (ugly) and between its non-negation (not ugly) and its non-assertion (not beautiful). *Compare* COMPLEMENTARITY; CONTRADICTION.

control *See* MEDIA CONTROLS.

control group *See* EXPERIMENT.

control track A 'sync pulse' that synchronizes the video and audio information (modulating to 50 Hz in *PAL and 60 Hz in *NTSC) which is recorded onto *videotape in the form of a linear audio *track.

convenience sample A sample of participants in research selected not for their representativeness but for their accessibility.

convention 1. **(social convention)** An established understanding, standard practice, rule, or *expectation widely shared by members of a *culture or *subculture: often implicit, taken for granted, and experienced as natural. *See also* COMMON SENSE; CONFORMITY; CULTURE; GENDER; NATURALIZATION; NORM; SCENARIO; SOCIAL CODES; SOCIAL SCHEMATA. 2. **(textual convention)** A well-established feature of *content, *form, and/or *style of *text in any *medium, widely understood by the intended audiences (e.g., in film and television, *continuity editing). Textual conventions in the *mass media can sometimes be formulaic (*see also* BROADCAST CODES). Such conventions do change over time (*see* CODIFICATION), and textual *transgressions are increasingly used with *savvy consumers: *see also* DOMINANT CODE; FILM GRAMMAR; GENRE; PICTORIAL CODES; TEXTUAL CODES; TEXTUAL SCHEMATA. 3. (*semiotics) Usually a synonym for a *code.

conventionalism 1. A pejorative term for slavish adherence to *conventions. 2. For *realists, a position which they associate with *epistemological *relativism and the denial of the existence of any knowable reality outside representational *conventions. They associate it with the 'severing' of *signs from 'real world' *referents (*see* BRACKETING THE REFERENT) and with the notion that reality is a construction of *language or a product of theories. They regard 'conventionalists' (or *constructionists) as reducing reality to nothing more than *signifying practices. They criticize as 'extreme conventionalism' the stance that theories (and the worlds which they construct) are incommensurable: *see* INCOMMENSURABILITY.

conventionality (*semiotics) A relationship between the *signifier and the *signified in a *sign (or in the signs within a *code) which is dependent on variable social and cultural *conventions rather than intrinsic or 'natural': for example, where the sound of a spoken word (or the shape of a written one) bears no relationship to what it represents. The conventional nature of codes means that they have to be learned (not necessarily formally). A traditional distinction between **conventional signs** (words) and **natural signs** (representational visual art) dates back to ancient Greece. Modern semiotic theory tends to emphasize that even the most *realistic representational images do involve conventions and many semioticians refer to learning to 'read' photographs, television, or film, for instance. *Compare* ARBITRARINESS.

conventional sign *See* CONVENTIONALITY.

convergence 1. Any process in which things get closer together. 2. (**technological convergence**) The merging of formerly discrete communication technologies/media (notably broadcast media, the *internet, and the telephone) and of their functions and associated genres, facilitated by *digitization. However, discrete *channels for radio, television, and mobile phone transmission still exist in the digital age despite the absence of any technical necessity for them to continue. At the consumer level, the *smartphone is a paradigmatic example of a convergence device. 3. (**media industry convergence**) The increasing integration of industries and markets in communication sectors such as broadcasting, film, photography, music, print publishing, and telecommunications, so that print, screens, discs, and websites can all be platforms for the same content-provider. Such developments have been associated with an increase in cross-media forms. There have been significant impacts on professional practices in the media (*see* BI-MEDIA JOURNALISM). Media convergence has also involved a convergence of *media ownership and control, often on a transnational level. It raises issues of *globalization and *homogenization. It has important *media policy implications, such as for *regulation: in the UK Ofcom was set up in 2003 as a combined regulatory body for telecommunications, television, and radio. 4. (**cultural**

convergence) Either the intermixing of *popular cultures around the world (*see also* GLOBALIZATION; McDONALDIZATION), or a shift, related to media convergence, in the relationship between media technologies, industries, markets, genres, and audiences (*see also* MEDIA ECOLOGY), accompanied by new ways of relating to media content, such as the use of the *internet by fans of television series and films (Jenkins). Such developments represent a convergence of media *production and *consumption characterized by significant *audience participation. **5. (ideological convergence)** (sociology) The 'convergence thesis' is that increasing similarities in industrial societies are in the process of making conflicts between capitalist and socialist *ideologies irrelevant. **6.** (psychology) A *cognitive style relating to problem-solving. **Convergent thinkers** are more analytical, deductive, and logical and prefer problems to which there is a correct solution: *compare* DIVERGENCE. **7.** In *visual perception, the turning inwards of the eyes to focus on an object using *binocular vision: *compare* DIVERGENCE.

convergence model A model of *interpersonal communication in terms of a process of seeking to arrive at a mutual understanding (in particular contrast to *sender-oriented communication). Such models are particularly associated with *network analysis approaches.

conversational analysis *See* CONVERSATION ANALYSIS.

conversational currency (cultural currency) *Social and *textual knowledge likely to be shared by many members of a culture which offers common ground for social conversations, in particular material drawn from the *mass media, such as '*iconic' images (*see also* COMMON SENSE; CULTURAL CODE; CULTURAL LITERACY; FOLK PSYCHOLOGY; IMAGINED COMMUNITY; SOCIAL UTILITY FUNCTION; TACIT KNOWLEDGE).

conversationalization A tendency for public *discourse to resemble the *discursive practices of *everyday life (Fairclough). This more conversational style is marked by a shift towards informality. It has been particularly associated with presentational and *interview styles in broadcast media but has also been identified in unmediated professional discourse.

conversational style An individual's general manner of speaking in *interpersonal communication in relation to tempo, pauses, and conversational *turn-taking, as identified by Tannen in a book of the same name. *See also* HIGH AND LOW INVOLVEMENT; HIGH CONSIDERATENESS; *compare* COMMUNICATION STYLE.

(⊕) SEE WEB LINKS

• Audio extracts from Tannen's *Conversational Style*

conversation analysis (CA, conversational analysis) (sociology) A technique associated with *ethnomethodology and *sociolinguistics, involving recording interpersonal speech (and the accompanying *nonverbal behaviour) in various everyday *contexts and identifying patterns in its organization: e.g. the rules of conversation *turn-taking. The *subject-matter is not the primary focus of such investigations: the primary intention is to gain insights into *roles, *social relationships, and *power relations. Harvey Sacks (1935–75), an American sociologist, pioneered this methodology in the 1970s, in close collaboration with Emmanuel Shegloff (b.1937). *See also* CONVERSATIONAL STYLE; *compare* CRITICAL DISCOURSE ANALYSIS; DISCOURSE ANALYSIS; INTERCHANGE; PHENOMENOLOGY; SYMBOLIC INTERACTIONISM.

conversation turn-taking *See* TURN-TAKING.

cool colours *See* COLOUR TEMPERATURE.

cool media *See* HOT AND COOL MEDIA.

cooperation 1. A mode of *interpersonal relations in which *co-present individuals are motivated to engage together in the same task, in which interpersonal *interaction and a shared goal is required. *Compare* COACTION; COMPETITION. 2. A primary *value in *collectivistic cultures.

co-option *See* INCORPORATION.

co-presence 1. Most broadly, any close occurrence of different things: *see also* CLUTTER; COLLOCATION; CONTIGUITY; JUXTAPOSITION. 2. The simultaneous presence of individuals in the same physical location, not necessarily engaged in *face-to-face interaction with each other: *see also* COACTION; COMPETITION; COOPERATION. 3. The engagement of individuals in *synchronous *interpersonal communication, not necessarily in the same physical location (e.g. using *mobile phones) (**co-present interaction**). 4. In any form of *mediated communication, the *phenomenological sense of 'being there' with another person in place and/or time: *see also* PRESENCE. 5. In *presence studies, how an individual's sense of 'being there' in a virtual environment is affected by the *presence of others who are also inside the *simulation in the form of *avatars.

copy 1. (*advertising) Written material produced by a *copywriter. 2. In print journalism, written material provided by a journalist for a *newspaper or magazine. 3. A 'copy without an original' (Baudrillard): *see* SIMULACRUM.

copycat behaviour An action (usually deviant) by a person or persons that resembles an incident reported in the *mass media or seen in television drama or a film. **Copycat crimes** are often attributed to the influence of the media (as *behavioural effects), though usually as *third-person effects or as a defence argument in court. *See also* CONTAGION EFFECT; VIOLENCE DEBATE.

copy editor *See* EDITOR.

copyright The legal ownership of the content and arrangement of a literary or artistic work (including computer *software) in any medium, including the right to control its reproduction, normally at least initially that of its originator(s), for whom it is a form of *intellectual property. Copyright or the right to reproduce copies may subsequently be assigned by creators to others. Ideas as such are not subject to copyright.

copy testing (*advertising) Research into the effectiveness of an advertisement before it is released. *See also* ADVERTISING EFFECTIVENESS.

copywriter (*advertising) The person who is primarily responsible for producing the verbal content of ads and ad campaigns in any *medium—including catchphrases, slogans, *straplines, jingle lyrics, and the wording of all *copy.

correlation The degree to which two or more *variables show a tendency to vary together. A **positive correlation** would be where one variable increases, the other also increases. A **negative correlation** would be where one variable increases and the other decreases. Where there is no correlation, there is no reciprocal relationship in either direction. Correlation by itself does not establish *causation; either variable could be a cause and other *intervening variables may be involved.

correlation function *See* CONSENSUS FUNCTION.

correspondence theory of truth (philosophy) The principle that truth can be established by comparing *propositions with an independent and external reality.*Realism depends on this principle. For *constructionists, reality is a construction of *discourse, so all we can compare is one discourse with another. Realists insist that things exist in the external world independently of our modes of apprehending them. *See also* FACT.

counterbricolage The practice of incorporating aspects of consumer *bricolage into commercial product design (e.g. pre-ripped jeans). *Compare* BRICOLAGE.

countercultures *See* SUBCULTURE.

coverage 1. (**News coverage, media coverage**) In news journalism, the relative priority, time, or space given to a particular *event or issue. 2. (**Camera coverage**) In filming, the different cameras used in filming a scene and/or the amount of *footage available for *editing. 3. In broadcasting and telecommunications technology, the geographic area that can receive a *signal. 4. In *marketing, the percentage of a particular *target audience that a given media outlet can reach: *see also* REACH.

cover shot *See* ESTABLISHING SHOT.

crash zoom A sudden, rapid *zoom-in on a subject. A *marked camera technique that has become a cliché in horror films. *Compare* WHIP PAN.

creative brief (*advertising) The instructions given by an account planner to a creative team (*see* CREATIVES) for the work required on an ad. It includes the background to the campaign, purpose of the ad, and a profile of the *target audience. It usually includes a schedule.

creative industries Commercial and industrial *production sectors involved in generating new cultural contributions through creativity, skill, and talent. Definitions variously include: art, music, film, performance arts, and games; architecture, design, designer fashion, and craftwork; books, publishing, and software; television and radio; *advertising and *public relations. Often a synonym for *cultural industries. In the UK, the concept of 'creative industries' arose in the late 1990s. Critics have seen it as a government-led commercialization of culture at the expense of quality. *Compare* CULTURAL INDUSTRIES; KNOWLEDGE INDUSTRIES.

creatives In an *advertising agency, the staff who formulate the ideas, and the look and feel of advertisements and campaigns, including *art directors, *copywriters, and the creative directors to whom such staff are responsible in the *production of particular ads and campaigns.

creativity (linguistics) *See* PRODUCTIVITY.

credibility *See* SOURCE FACTORS.

creolization *See* HYBRIDIZATION.

crisis The ultimate **turning point** in a *narrative structure when *resolution is imminent. Usually synonymous with the emotional *climax. *See also* CLASSICAL NARRATIVE STRUCTURE.

critical attitude (scientific attitude) In the *phenomenological sociology of Schutz, the detached and objectifying frame of mind of a disinterested observer in which phenomena are subject to critical attention rather than taken for granted as in the *natural attitude.

critical discourse analysis (CDA) A range of approaches to the analysis of texts and talk in relation to the social *contexts which give rise to them. More specifically, an approach that views language as a social practice and that seeks to identify the reproduction of *power relations and *ideological processes in *discourse (Fairclough). *Compare* CONVERSATION ANALYSIS; CRITICAL THEORY; DISCOURSE ANALYSIS; IDEOLOGICAL ANALYSIS.

(⊕) SEE WEB LINKS

• *Critical discourse analysis*: Brett Dellinger.

critical framings *See* FRAMING.

critical realism (philosophy) A stance that is distinguished from naïve or *common sense *realism in that it involves an acceptance of both the independent, objective existence of the world and of the contention that it can be known only indirectly through a *medium or vehicle of *perception.

critical theory 1. Theories associated with the neo-Marxist *Frankfurt school which involve the *ideological analysis of society and *culture. Influenced by *Marxist theory and Freudian *psychoanalytic theory. 2. Any theory which takes a critical view of society and adopts an *ideological focus, typically associated with an emphasis on the analytical importance of sociohistorical *context, an emancipatory agenda, and *reflexivity. 3. Loosely, literary or aesthetic *theory in general.

cropping 1. In photography, *photojournalism, graphics, and picture *editing, trimming the edges of a photographic image, typically to focus on a point of interest, to improve the composition, or to fit an available space. Also, in *camerawork, using tighter *framing. Both processes involve *decontextualization. 2. In video *post-production, reducing the size of the film image, typically to change the *aspect ratio.

cross-cultural communication *See* INTERCULTURAL COMMUNICATION.

cross-cutting (parallel cutting, parallel editing) In filming, *cutting between two separate scenes as both are unfolding in narrative time so as to suggest a relationship between them.

cross dissolve (cross-fade, dissolve, lap dissolve, mix) 1. In film and video *post-production, a *transition between two shots in which the first gradually fades out as the second is fading in, so that they overlap. This typically signifies the passage of time. Compared to a *cut, the relative infrequency of its use makes it a *marked transition, and it can generate *connotations of *femininity: *see* GENDERED EDITING. 2. (cross-fade) In audio *post-production, the *mixing of two sound sources together by increasing the volume of the incoming source before the mix and reducing the volume of the outgoing source after the mix.

cross-fade *See* CROSS DISSOLVE.

crossing the line (axis of action, reverse cut) In film and video *editing, a convention that a shot of a subject from one side should not be followed immediately by a shot of the same subject from the opposite side (a 180-degree shift). The traditional argument has been that most viewers would find this disorientating since it produces a mirroring effect that could threaten narrative *comprehension. For instance, filming a moving vehicle in this way might be misread as an abrupt reversal of its direction of travel or even as a head-on crash with itself. However, there are many examples of celebrated film-makers who do break this rule and, arguably, modern audiences have grown more tolerant of such transgressions because of their *knowledge of film *editing practices. *See also* 180-DEGREE RULE.

(())) SEE WEB LINKS
• Crossing the line

cross-media ownership The ownership by one organization (or by a *media mogul) of interests in more than one mass medium, especially where this includes both print media (*newspapers and/or magazines) and broadcasting companies (radio and/or television). In some countries concerns about *monopolies (especially issues of media power, *information, *access, and quality) have led to media *regulation restricting such practices. *See also* VERTICAL INTEGRATION.

CU *See* CLOSE-UP.

cue 1. In film and broadcasting, any agreed *signal indicating the start of speech and action in a studio, on a set, or on location. 2. In the psychology of *perception, visual features that facilitate *inferences about associated qualities: e.g. *depth cues. 3. (nonverbal cues) In *interpersonal communication, largely unconscious behavioural *signals that assist in maintaining interactional flows, such as *regulators in conversational *turn-taking: *see also* NONVERBAL MODIFIERS. 4. (linguistic cues) Any linguistic factors that assist readers and listeners in *comprehension and prediction, notably the contexts provided by *semantics and by predictable patterns of *syntax, *phonetics, and logographics (word shapes). 5. In classical *conditioning, a feature of a stimulus to which a behavioural response can be conditioned. **6.** (*marketing) Weak stimuli, called 'peripheral cues' in the *Elaboration Likelihood Model: *see* PERIPHERAL ROUTE.

cuelessness A relative shortage or absence of social *cues in particular forms of *interpersonal communication (e.g. sound only) compared with other forms having a greater aggregate of usable social cues (e.g. *face-to-face interaction). Such cues include physical presence and visual contact. Rutter and his colleagues found that the more of these cues that communicative participants lack, the greater the sense of *psychological distance—the feeling that the other person is 'not there'. The lack of *information had *phenomenological consequences. Cuelessness can also facilitate *anonymity. *See also* MEDIUM THEORY; SOCIAL PRESENCE.

cultivation theory (**cultivation hypothesis, cultivation analysis**) Gerbner's hypothesis that heavy television viewing tends to cultivate *attitudes towards the social world that are based on the world represented onscreen. The *mass media act as a *socializing agent, cultivating *values which are already present in a culture. Gerbner argued that the over-representation of violence on television constitutes a symbolic message about law and order (*see* SYMBOLIC VIOLENCE). For instance, the action-adventure genre acts to reinforce a faith in law and order, the *status quo, and social justice (baddies usually get their just deserts). Cultivation researchers have argued that television has long-term *attitudinal effects which are small, gradual, indirect, but cumulative and significant: viewers come to believe the television version of reality the more they watch it, most notably over-estimating the amount of violence in *everyday life. The difference in the pattern of responses between light and *heavy viewers is referred to as the **cultivation differential,** reflecting the extent to which an attitude seems to be shaped by watching television. However, critics note that *correlation is not proof of a causal relationship (*see* CAUSATION). *See also* EFFECTS; MEAN WORLD SYNDROME; VIOLENCE DEBATE.

((⊕)) SEE WEB LINKS

• Cultivation theory

cult media **1.** *Mass media forms such as music, television, and radio programmes, and above all films, that underperformed or were commercial failures at the time of their release but have subsequently developed a **cult audience,** a devoted following of fans who often define aspects of their *personal identity in relation to this genre, and who are likened to religious devotees because of the strength of their enthusiasm. **2.** Media forms targeted at niche audiences: the films of Tarantino, for example. *See* FANDOM.

cultural capital In sociology and cultural theory, the education, *knowledge, know-how, and connections available to any individual or group that give them a 'head start', confer *status, and can assist in the pursuit of *power (Bourdieu). Cultural capital is itself stratified: *popular culture is disfavoured by dominant groups, whose members cultivate *taste and discernment. There is no necessary *correlation with *economic capital: the *nouveau riche*, for instance, have high economic capital and low cultural capital. However, cultural and economic capital tend to reinforce each other and the dominant bourgeoisie has both. The convertability of one into the other reproduces *class differences. The bourgeoisie maintains its position largely through the transmission of cultural capital. *Socialization through the family and the educational system inculcates dominant *values. *See also* HABITUS; SYMBOLIC CAPITAL.

cultural code 1. Broadly, a set of standardized or normative *conventions, *expectations, or *signifying practices in a particular domain that would be familiar to members of a specific *culture or *subculture. 2. **(referential code, the voice of science)** References in a realist *narrative to cultural bodies of *knowledge. One of five *narrative codes identified by Barthes.

cultural currency *See* CONVERSATIONAL CURRENCY.

cultural determinism *Compare* SOCIAL DETERMINISM. 1. The stance that common patterns of behaviour, *attitudes, and *values which persist for generations are the result of cultural factors rather than biological or other factors (nurture vs nature). 2. The determination of *subjectivity by *ideology: a pejorative reference to Althusser's stance, in *Marxist theory, that 'individuals are always-already subjects' (*see* ALWAYS-ALREADY GIVEN; *compare* ECONOMISM).

cultural forms or formations *See* FORMATION.

cultural identity The definition of groups or individuals (by themselves or others) in terms of cultural or *subcultural categories (including *ethnicity, nationality, language, religion, and *gender). In *stereotyping, this is framed in terms of *difference or *otherness. *See also* ETHNIC IDENTITY; GENDER IDENTITY; IDENTITY; LIFESTYLE; NATIONAL IDENTITY.

cultural imperialism The influences of an economically dominant *culture on others, typically spread through trade, the *mass media, and the *internet. Often applied pejoratively to the global diffusion of American brands, *popular culture, *values, customs, and practices, allegedly at the expense of other cultures. Critics of this view argue that audiences around the world do not passively absorb American cultural exports, and are indeed often hostile to these, or interpret them within their own cultural frameworks, as Katz and Liebes demonstrated in the case of the television series *Dallas* (1978–91). Cultural *interaction is not adequately explained in terms of the absorption of local cultures by a globally dominant culture: the meeting of cultures often generates new cultural forms. *See also* ETHNOCENTRISM; EUROCENTRISM; GLOBALIZATION; MEDIA IMPERIALISM.

cultural industries *Compare* CULTURE INDUSTRY. 1. Industrial and commercial organizations producing and reproducing cultural goods and services. In the UK, 'cultural industries policies' were first developed by the left-wing Greater London Council in the late 1970s. 2. Often a synonym for *creative industries, though sometimes including *knowledge industries.

culturalism An approach to the study of *culture (associated in particular with Hoggart and Williams) with a particular emphasis on *popular culture and on the way of life of a particular community as reflected in its cultural practices and the cultural texts that it produces and consumes. This perspective tends to stress active

human *agency rather than passive *consumption (Stuart Hall). *See also* CULTURAL
MATERIALISM; CULTURAL STUDIES.

cultural literacy 1. A culturally conservative conception of what everyone
within a culture ought to know (particularly about that culture), typically including a
*knowledge of canonical works of *high culture (*see* CANON) and historical *events
associated with *national identity (Hirsch). 2. **(cultural knowledge)** *Knowledge
that is widely shared and typically assumed to be universally known within a
*culture, and upon which a great deal of communication depends. This includes
*social schemata, or knowledge of *social codes, and the recognition of '*iconic'
images. *See also* CONVERSATIONAL CURRENCY; FOLK PSYCHOLOGY; IMAGINED
COMMUNITY; SOCIAL KNOWLEDGE.

cultural materialism 1. (anthropology) A concept associated with Marvin
Harris (1927–2001), in which culture is seen as an adaptation to determinative
material conditions (primarily environmental and geographic). 2. In cultural theory,
a term used in the 1980s by Williams for an approach in which culture (including
*popular culture) is interpreted in terms of material practices and a constitutive
social process which generates different ways of life. He sought to distinguish
this approach from the *determinism of classical *Marxist theory that cultural
phenomena are secondary to, and merely the effects of, economic factors (*see* BASE
AND SUPERSTRUCTURE). Culture is not seen as autonomous from the material world
but as part of it. Cultural phenomena are seen as inseparable from the *contexts of
their *production and use. The arts, *popular culture, and the *mass media are not
merely forms of social and *cultural reproduction but also a means of *cultural
production. Dominant cultural forms and *institutions are contested. *See also*
CULTURISM; DOMINANT FORMS; EMERGENT FORMS; RESIDUAL FORMS; *compare*
DIALECTICAL MATERIALISM; MATERIALISM. 3. **(new historicism)** An approach in
literary theory, drawing on Foucault as well as Williams, which seeks to elucidate
the *ideological processes by which dominant groups seek to maintain their
*hegemony through the *appropriation of particular works, and on their subversion
by *oppositional readings. Such studies are based on close *textual analysis in the
light of the historical *context and of *intertextuality: *see also* HISTORICISM.

cultural politics In *cultural studies, the issue, and study, of relationships
between *culture, *subjectivity, *ideology, and *power: including issues of *race,
*class, and *gender. A key concern has been with marginalized *subcultures.
See also IDENTITY POLITICS.

cultural populism In *media sociology, a pejorative term for approaches to
*cultural studies (the primary target being Fiske) in which an *active audience was
seen as using the media for their own purposes and in which the pleasurable
*consumption of *popular culture was presented as having resistive and
subversive political potential, which critics such as Jim McGuigan, a British
sociologist and cultural theorist, regard as wholly illusory and *ideologically naïve.
It is criticized for overplaying human *agency and underplaying social, political,
and economic structural factors.

cultural production *Compare* CULTURAL REPRODUCTION. 1. The social processes involved in the generation and circulation of cultural forms, practices, *values, and shared understandings: *see also* CONSENSUS. 2. The work of the *culture industry.

cultural relativism (cultural relativity) The view that each *culture has its own worldview and that none of these can be regarded as more or less privileged or *authentic in its *representation of reality than another (this is the opposite of *ethnocentrism). Cultural worldviews are historically-situated social constructions (*see also* CONSTRUCTIONISM). Cultural relativists may also to be *linguistic relativists, arguing that dominant cultural worldviews are reflected in *ontologies which are built into the *language of that culture. Cultural relativism is a fundamental assumption involved in the *Sapir-Whorf hypothesis. Anthropologists and others who study *signifying practices within a culture can be seen as cultural relativists insofar as they seek to understand each culture in its own terms. However, as with *epistemological relativism (with which it is closely associated), the label is often used as a criticism, being equated with extreme *idealism or nihilism. *See also* INCOMMENSURABILITY.

cultural reproduction The maintenance and perpetuation of dominant *values, *norms, cultural forms, and *power relations across generations, that is accomplished though *socialization (particularly education) and the processes of *naturalization in *representation and *discourse. The concept was first developed by Bourdieu, who emphasized the structural reproduction of disadvantages and inequalities. *See also* CONSCIOUSNESS INDUSTRIES; CULTURAL CAPITAL; *compare* CULTURAL PRODUCTION.

cultural resistance Activist opposition to the ways in which dominant forces in capitalist society are seen as shaping people's *behaviour and ways of thinking. *See also* CULTURE JAMMING.

cultural studies The critical analysis of the texts and practices of *everyday life in contemporary society: an interdisciplinary enterprise involving both the humanities and the social sciences. Its territory (in the current context significantly overlapping with that of *media studies, *film studies, and *communication studies) includes: *mass culture (or *popular culture), *consumer culture, the *culture industry, and *cultural production and reproduction. It began as a product of the British New Left, influenced in particular by Williams (*see* CULTURALISM; CULTURAL MATERIALISM) and neo-Marxist sociologists such as Stuart Hall (*see also* ENCODING/DECODING MODEL), Bourdieu, and Foucault, and also by *feminism, *structuralism, *poststructuralism, *semiotics, *postcolonialism, *queer theory, and initially (to a lesser extent) *psychoanalytic theory. It can be seen partly as a reaction against *Leavisite cultural *elitism and the *Frankfurt school's bleak stance on *mass culture. Its emergence as a discipline is marked by the establishment of the Centre for Contemporary Cultural Studies (CCCS, or the **Birmingham school)** at the University of Birmingham in the UK in 1964 (lasting until the 1990s). Primary concerns of cultural studies include: *ideological processes, social and historical *context, *subcultures (notably youth subcultures), *representation, *identity, and *cultural politics (particularly in relation to '*race' and *gender). Cultural studies theorists see culture as a *site of struggle. Critics in the established disciplines have attacked it for eclecticism, lack of focus, or *cultural populism but it has nevertheless gained international recognition as a discipline, and it has particularly highlighted the value of the close and reflexive study of cultural forms in the specific contexts of their *production, use, and *interpretation.

cultural turn A shift in the *discourse of sociology in the 1990s reflecting a recognition of the *relative autonomy of culture from structural determination (*see* BASE AND SUPERSTRUCTURE). *See also* CULTURALISM.

culture 1. In everyday usage (and often academically in the humanities), the arts and artistic practices, in particular the creative and expressive art of *high culture rather than *popular culture or *mass culture. Associated with common usages such as 'a cultured individual' or 'lacking culture'. The exercise of 'good *taste' and discernment is a feature of the *cultural capital of the ruling *class, for whom culture is opposed to society (as *mass society). From the perspective of *cultural studies this is an *elitist conception: *see also* CANON. 2. **(cultural heritage)** A system of shared *values, and creative expressions of them, transmitted between individuals and generations through *language as well as material *artefacts; often harnessed to conservative notions of *national identity: *see also* CULTURAL LITERACY; CULTURAL REPRODUCTION. 3. In the social sciences, the entire 'way of life' of a society (Williams), including: *language, ideas, *beliefs, *values, *norms, *knowledge, customs, practices, rituals, patterns of behaviour, *dress codes, political organization, and economic activity. Its *conventions and *codes are learned through *socialization and widely shared within the culture, often being assumed by members of that culture to be universal. *Semiotics stresses *codes as the basis of culture: without shared codes there can be no communication and no culture. 4. A sociohistorical *contextualization of cultural or subcultural activities during some particular period or epoch: e.g. 'the culture of Renaissance Florence'. *See also* CONTEXT. 5. In some sociological *discourse, the values, ideas, *symbols, practices, and *artefacts of a society, as distinct from *social structure. 6. **(material culture)** The *artefacts and materials produced by a culture (fundamental for archaeology). Not to be confused with *cultural materialism. 7. In classical *Marxist theory, the social superstructure determined by the economic base (*see* BASE AND SUPERSTRUCTURE), a notion challenged within *cultural studies, e.g. by *cultural materialism, in which culture is seen as capable of influencing social change and not merely as a reflection of the existing social order. 8. That which is the product of human civilization and intelligence. A concept defined in a *binary opposition to nature. From Lévi-Strauss's *structuralist perspective, this *opposition is a fundamental organizing concept in human thought. For him, culture itself is a definitive and universal human framework underlying surface differences between societies. 9. According to the *Sapir-Whorf hypothesis, a way of experiencing the world, reflected in a shared *language. 10. An abstraction that tends to be treated as a homogeneous thing—as in it being 'a whole way of life' (*see also* REIFICATION), whereas there are diverse *subcultures in which differences are inflected by *class, age, *gender, *ethnicity, religion, and so on. A subjective construction perceived as an objective, external *fact (*see* SOCIAL CONSTRUCTIONISM) whereas it is a '*site of struggle' full of *contradictions. A product of *representation and a discursive resource for the *production of *identity through *difference and *otherness (Foucault, Said): *see also* CRITICAL DISCOURSE ANALYSIS. **11.** In prejudiced *representations such as *stereotypes, a concept that is frequently essentialized racially, whereas culture has no necessary connection with biology or genetics. **12.** A field of academic study for *cultural studies, and, because of its vast scope, for all of the disciplines in the humanities and social sciences, each of which has its own definitions.

culture industry **1.** For Adorno and the *critical theorists of the *Frankfurt school, the *mass-media *entertainment industry and commercialized *popular culture, which they saw as primarily concerned with producing not only symbolic goods but also needs and consumers, serving the *ideological function of diversion (*see also* DIVERSION FUNCTION), and thus depoliticizing the working class. Note the provocative *collocation of these traditionally antithetical terms, as in art vs commerce, *aesthetics vs *entertainment, or even rock vs pop. *See also* COMMODIFICATION; COMMODITY FETISHISM; CONSCIOUSNESS INDUSTRIES; MASS CULTURE; *compare* CONSUMER SOCIETY; CULTURAL INDUSTRIES. **2.** For British and American cultural theorists, the *press and broadcasting media framed as regulators of *information flow in relation to political issues of *media ownership and control. *See also* CROSS-MEDIA OWNERSHIP; MARKET MODEL; MEDIA CONTROLS; POLITICAL ECONOMY; PUBLIC SERVICE BROADCASTING.

culture jamming A grass-roots campaigning movement that attacks consumerist culture through the subversive use of its own mass-marketing tools and techniques, or through creative acts of civil disobedience. *See also* SUBVERTISING.

cumulative audience The number of radio listeners or television viewers (or households) tuned in during a particular time period.

cumulative effects *See* LONG-TERM EFFECTS.

cuneiform *See* WRITING SYSTEMS.

current affairs **1.** A journalistic radio and television programme *genre featuring detailed analysis and discussion of current news stories. In the UK this is normally distinguished from news reporting, special events coverage, and consumer affairs. **2.** In a broader sense, a branch of journalism encompassing issues-based investigative journalism and *documentaries where *objectivity as such has not always been a priority.

cursive **1.** Handwriting with connected letters. **2.** (*typography) Type that resembles flowing handwriting.

curvilinear perspective The rendering of perspectival depth as curving, as in a fish-eye lens, rather than in terms of the convergence of straight lines. This approximates the curved retina of the eye and also what you see if you look directly at each part of a long wall from the same position, and it is in this sense less distorting than the familiar conventions of *linear perspective. *See also* PERSPECTIVE.

cut 1. A form of *transition used in film *editing consisting of an immediate change from one *shot to another, traditionally accomplished by physically cutting the film and splicing the shots together. This is the most common form of transition (in *semiotic terms 'unmarked'), and it is virtually unnoticeable to the viewer when the juxtaposed shots follow the conventions of *continuity editing. *See also* CROSS-CUTTING; CROSS DISSOLVE; CROSSING THE LINE; FADE-IN; FADE-OUT; INTERCUTTING; JUMP CUT; MATCH CUT; MOTIVATED CUT; WIPE. 2. The spoken instruction for the camera and sound personnel to cease recording. 3. *n.* (film and video) A synonym for an *edit because the film is edited by being physically cut, **cutting** being a synonym for the *editing process. 4. An 'assembly': an ordered presentation of several sequences of shots joined together into a form that represents either an editor's draft of all or part of a film or TV programme (as in *rough cut), or what is in the director's or editor's opinion a finished version of the film or programme (*final cut): *see also* DIRECTOR'S CUT.

cutaway 1. In film and video *editing, an unmotivated *shot inserted into a sequence of a different but usually related subject in order to avoid a *jump cut. The cutaway is a necessary device in *continuity editing. Its expediency makes it vital: the advice of an editor to a junior cameraperson is always to 'get loads of cutaways'. While a cutaway can add *context and 'colour' to a scene, its unmotivated nature results in some rather odd *conventions: for example, shots of the fumbling hands of interviewees that are a staple in television news reports. *See also* GENERAL VIEWS. 2. A *motivated shot from another time or place inserted into a temporal sequence, which breaks continuity but creates a *juxtaposition intended to alert audiences to the significance of the current scene or action, or points to an alternative meaning: for example in *2001: A Space Odyssey* (1968) there is a brief cutaway to a shot of the monolith as the human-ape plays with the bone, implying its influence in the discovery of tools. *See also* FLASHBACK; FLASHFORWARD.

cutting rate The frequency of *transitions (typically *cuts) in film *editing. Faster cutting entails an increase in the number of *shots and a decrease in *shot duration. It can connote 'active'. Cutting rates have steadily increased in films and television programmes over the decades; this is often attributed to the influence of commercials and music videos (*see also* MTV).

cutting rhythm (film-making) A rhythmic pattern in the duration of *shots used to influence emotional reactions to a *scene. For instance, shot duration may be progressively shortened to increase tension. *See also* SHOT DURATION.

cybercafé (internet café) A café where people pay to use the *internet.

cyberculture Umbrella term for the various *subcultures to which the use of *computer networks has given rise and whose *interaction with each other is computer-mediated (or primarily so). Also an emergent term for a field of academic study. *See also* COMPUTER-MEDIATED COMMUNICATION; VIRTUAL COMMUNITY.

cyberfeminism A movement that began in the 1990s utilizing *cyberculture and *feminist ideas to re-theorize *gender, the *body, and *identities in relation to *technology and *power. *See also* CYBORG.

cybernetics The interdisciplinary study of the structure and flow of *information in self-regulating communication systems (technical, social, or biological): e.g. issues of *feedback and *control within *organizational communication. It was developed by the American mathematician Norbert Weiner (1894–1964), becoming popular in the 1950s and 1960s, and is closely related to *systems theory and *functionalism.

cyberpunk A science fiction *genre focusing on a blurring of distinctions between humans and machines in bleak dystopias with lawless *subcultures. The term was first applied to William Gibson's novel *Neuromancer* (1984).

cyberspace A term introduced by the novelist William Gibson in 1984 to describe an abstract *virtual space created in part by networks of interconnecting computers and in part by the human imagination. Although conceptually vague and idealized, spatial *metaphors have been a popular way to frame the communication afforded by the *internet, although they have been criticized for importing real world *ideological assumptions, such as notions of virtual property and virtual trespass. *See also* CYBERCULTURE; *compare* INFORMATION SUPERHIGHWAY; VIRTUAL REALITY.

cybertext *See* HYPERTEXT FICTION.

cyborg A hybrid being: half human, half machine (a contraction of 'cybernetic organism'). The term was first coined in 1960 by the Austrian-American space scientist Manfred Clynes (b.1925), though such creatures had featured in science-fiction since the 1920s and they have long been with us in *everyday life in the form of mechanical elements (such as prosthetic limbs) incorporated into the human body. However, they caught the public imagination, e.g. in the TV series, *Six Million Dollar Man* (1974–78). The concept was taken up by Haraway in 1985, to explore the blurring of the boundaries between the organic and the technological as a radical challenge to biological *essentialism (*see also* CYBERFEMINISM).

cyclic model of perception *See* PERCEPTUAL CYCLE.

DAB *See* DIGITAL AUDIO BROADCASTING.

DAC *See* DECODER.

daguerrotype A forerunner of the photograph in which an image was created on a light-sensitive metal plate coated with silver iodide. It was developed by the French artist and chemist Louis Daguerre (1787–1851).

dark internet Those areas of the *internet not accessible to *search engines: e.g. obsolete databases or ephemeral content such as chat. In contrast, the **dark net** or **deep web** consists of areas of the internet which are *deliberately* hidden from conventional search tools through encryption technologies.

data (*pl.*; *sing.* **datum**, though in general usage 'the data is . . .' has become widespread) **1.** Loosely, *facts, *information, or statistics. **2.** (research) Any material recorded from empirical research (*see* DATA GATHERING) from which *inferences may be made, using some form of *data analysis, in order to provide *information. **3.** (philosophy) *Facts or *propositions from which inferences can be made. **4.** Something immediately presented to the mind. Sense data or *sensory data are directly grasped by the senses. **5.** (computing) Numbers, letters, or other symbols upon which a computer can perform operations.

data analysis Searching for (normally predicted) patterns or relationships (e.g. *correlation) in *data, and making pertinent *inferences from this, using recognized methods and/or tools.

database **1.** A computer-based collection of logically related records or files organized in such a way that it can easily be accessed and maintained. **2.** A master *metaphor for understanding *new media structures as collections of individual items (every one possessing the same significance as every other), on which users can perform various operations.

data-driven processing *See* BOTTOM-UP PROCESSING.

data gathering In empirical research, the process of collecting *data relevant to the focus of a particular study, according to an explicit protocol, prior to *data analysis.

data mining Automated techniques for revealing meaningful patterns or relationships in large sets of raw *data. Often used by businesses, e.g. to analyse the shopping habits of customers online. The covert use of this technique raises issues of privacy and *surveillance.

data protection The issue of the safeguarding of confidential personal *information against unauthorized access or misuse. The use of personal *data is subject to *regulation (e.g. in the UK, the Data Protection Act, 1998).

dataveillance A portmanteau word (*data* + *surveillance*). Monitoring or profiling a person through their personal *data records, rather than by listening to or viewing their activities. The term was introduced by Roger Clarke (b.1949), a British-Australian computer scientist.

dcable *See* DIGITAL TRANSMISSION.

dead metaphor A *metaphor that has become so familiar that it is no longer recognized as being one.

dead white males *See* CANON.

decay 1. (message recall) *See* MESSAGE DECAY. 2. (sound modulation) The variable in the 'attack–decay–sustain–release' envelope that regulates how rapidly the sound falls to the sustain level after the initial peak.

decentred self (decentred subject) The concept that there is no single 'self'—there are only multiple selves, existing fleetingly moment by moment. A notion influenced by *psychoanalytic theory, *structuralism, and *poststructuralism. From the anti-humanist and *structuralist perspective of Althusser, for instance, the sense of self was an effect of *interpellation. *See also* PERFORMATIVITY.

decisive moment The influential *modernist ideal of photographing the most telling instant in a significant *event, at the same time giving 'proper expression' to the 'precise organization of forms': i.e. with attention to artistic composition. The term is that of the French photographer Henri Cartier-Bresson (1908–2004). Commonly interpreted by *photojournalists simply as the capture of a dramatic *climax.

decoder In *semiotic models of communication, the person who *comprehends and *interprets texts/messages with reference to appropriate *textual and social codes. Relating the message to *codes requires the decoder to actively construct *meaning rather than to simply 'extract' it from the text (contrast *literalism). The codes employed by the decoder may depend at least in part on their socioeconomic identity—as in Morley's study of the *Nationwide* audience, a UK television news programme. *See also* ADDRESSEE; RECEIVER; *compare* ENCODER. 2. **(encoder)** A technical device used to convert a coded *signal into another type of coded signal, such as an **analogue-to-digital converter** (ADC) or **digital-to-analogue converter** (DAC).

decoding ability *See also* COMMUNICATION COMPETENCE; RECEIVER SKILLS. 1. Sometimes a synonym for competence in *reading. 2. A *receiver's competence in establishing a *preferred meaning for a *message by applying *social and *textual codes that are appropriate to the *context. 3. Competence in identifying behavioural *cues (primarily nonverbal) in *interpersonal relations, especially in relation to emotional expression and deception. The majority of studies have shown that women tend to be better than men at decoding both emotional cues and deception.

deconstruction A *poststructuralist strategy for critical *textual analysis which was developed by Derrida. Practitioners seek to dismantle the rhetorical structures within a text to demonstrate how key concepts within it depend on their unstated oppositional relation to *absent signifiers (this involved building on the *structuralist method of *paradigmatic analysis). Texts do not 'mean what they say'. *Contradictions can be identified within texts in such backgrounded features as footnotes, recurrent concepts or *tropes, casual *allusions, paradoxical phrases, discontinuities, and omissions. Searching for inexplicit *oppositions can reveal what is being excluded. That which has been repressed can be used as a key to an *oppositional reading of the text. Poststructuralists insist that no hierarchy of meanings can ever be established and no solid underlying structural foundation can ever be located. Derrida aimed to undermine what he called the *metaphysics of presence in Western culture—the bias towards what we fondly assume to be 'unmediated' *perception and *interaction. This bias involves *phonocentrism (including that of Saussure) and the myth of the *transcendent signified. Other deconstructionists have also exposed culturally-embedded conceptual oppositions in which the initial term is privileged, leaving 'term B' negatively *marked. Radical deconstruction is not simply a reversal of the *valorization in an opposition but a demonstration of the instability of the opposition (since challenging the valorization alone may be taken to imply that one nevertheless accepts an *ontological division along the lines of the opposition in question). Indeed, the most radical deconstruction challenges both the framework of the relevant opposition and binary frameworks in general. Deconstructionists acknowledge that their own texts are open to further deconstruction: there is no definitive reading; all texts contain *contradictions, gaps, and disjunctions—they undermine themselves. More broadly, deconstructive cultural criticism involves demonstrating how *signifying practices *construct*, rather than simply *represent* social reality, and how *ideology works to make such practices seem *transparent.

decontextualization 1. A pejorative term for divorcing something from its original *context. Most commonly referring to *texts, *utterances, or artworks. As an academic practice, this is criticized as suppressing a key determinant of *preferred meanings. *See* CONTEXTUALISM; *compare* CONTEXTUALIZATION; RECONTEXTUALIZATION. 2. A *necessary condition for the development and application of abstract concepts (Vygotsky).

deduction (deductive reasoning) 1. A process of reasoning that moves from the general to the particular (the opposite of *induction). 2. A form of logic in which, if the premises are true, then its conclusion is true.

deep focus A photographic technique using a large *depth of field; everything from *foreground to *background is in sharp focus. It is the opposite of **shallow focus**, where only one plane of the image is in focus.

deep structure 1. **(deep grammar)** In *linguistics, following Chomsky, a fundamental abstract level of grammatical organization underlying the *surface structure of sentences, which are generated by applying transformational rules to such structures: *see also* TRANSFORMATION. 2. **(macrostructure)** By analogy, in *structuralist theory, fundamental patterns underlying the 'surface features' of other *sign systems, notably: for Lévi-Strauss in myth, kinship rules, and totemism; for Lacan in the unconscious; for Barthes and Greimas in the 'grammar' of *narrative.

defamation (law) A public statement about individuals, products, groups, or organizations which is untrue and may cause them harm. Termed **libel** if in written form and **slander** if spoken.

defamiliarization [Russian *ostranenie*, 'estrangement'] **1.** Shklovsky's *formalist framing of the key function of art—we need to 'make the familiar strange'—to look afresh at things and *events which are so familiar that we no longer truly see them. The formalists favoured texts which drew attention to their *constructedness and to the processes involved in their construction. As a literary technique, Shklovsky advocated the (*surrealistic) practice of placing things in *contexts in which they would not normally be found. *See also* FOREGROUNDING; RECONTEXTUALIZATION; *compare* ALIENATION EFFECT; DENATURALIZATION. **2.** A feature of many postmodern texts in the parodic use of *intertextual references to highlight the normally *transparent representational *conventions of 'realistic' *textual codes.

defence mechanisms (ego defence mechanisms) Patterns of behaviour, thought, or feeling that enable individuals to avoid the anxiety induced by conscious awareness of psychological conflicts. These mechanisms include: *denial, *displacement, *distortion, *externalization, *rationalization, *repression, and *symbolization.

defensive attribution *See* SELF-SERVING BIAS.

deferred action (nachträglichkeit) In *psychoanalytic theory, an individual's revision of memories or reinterpretation of their past.

deficit theory *See* ELABORATED CODE; RESTRICTED CODE.

definition of the situation *See* THOMAS THEOREM.

deixis **1.** [Greek 'pointing'] Sometimes termed **indexicality**. In *linguistics, the reference of an *utterance to the spatial, temporal, or locational *context within which it takes place, or to the speaker or hearer, making the *meaning of the utterance relative to that situation and those participants. This can include references within a written *text to the context established by that text. Any grammatical part of an utterance that is dependent on such reference, is **deictic** (*adj.*), such as: *I/you, us/them, here/there, this/that, now/then* (*adv.* **deictically**). **2. (deictics)** More broadly, any communicative act making reference to the context of *production: e.g. a *gesture or *symbol: *see also* INDEXICAL.

deletion **1.** One of the four logical ways in which *perception, *memory, or *description/depiction can transform an experience that is ostensibly merely reproduced. Deletion involves omitting one or more elements which were part of the original source material. For example, in reporting our behaviour on a given occasion we may consciously or unconsciously omit features which are not consonant with our self-image. *See also* ADDITION; SUBSTITUTION;

TRANSFORMATION; TRANSPOSITION. 2. In *rhetoric, *detractio*, one of Quintilian's four types of rhetorical *figures of speech involving deviation (*mutatio*): in this case, the omission of elements, e.g. of conjunctions (**asyndeton**).

demarginalization An individual's sense of the legitimation of a dimension of *identity formerly felt to be socially marginalized, as among some participants in supportive online communities of like-minded people. *Compare* MARGINALIZATION.

demassification 1. A process in which a relatively homogeneous social collectivity (or one conceptualized as such) is broken down into (or reconceptualized in terms of) smaller, more diverse elements. 2. The decline of *mass culture and *mass society (also associated with *audience fragmentation) as consumers have gained more choice of media content since the advent of satellite broadcasting and the web: *see also* MASS CONSUMPTION; NARROWCASTING; TARGET AUDIENCE. 3. (*advertising) A basic format, *appeal, or *discourse since the mid 1980s, cast in terms of self-distinction and uniqueness in a massified world (*see also* ADVERTISING FORMATS). Its themes include *authenticity, creativity, *play, *reflexivity, and diversity. Products are offered as a way of standing out from the crowd or as props for self-construction.

demassified media (narrowcast media) Communications media that reach small, fragmented, or *niche audiences (**demassified audiences**), as opposed to *mass communication via the *mass media. A development predicted by Toffler in 1980. For example, *blogs and *internet radio. The term is also applied to fringe elements of the mass media when these have demassified audiences: e.g. small FM radio stations and specialized magazines. *See also* AUDIENCE FRAGMENTATION; MASS MEDIA; NARROWCASTING.

demographic variables 1. Factors relating to the structure of human populations which particular kinds of research regard as relevant in *sampling or *data analysis. Depending on the purpose of the research, these include sex, age, household income, education level, occupation, socioeconomic group, household size, religion, *ethnicity, and nationality. Demographic variables may be dependent or independent: *see* DEPENDENT AND INDEPENDENT VARIABLES. 2. In strategic communication (such as *advertising), this refers to the characteristics of *target audiences, which form the basis for **demographic segmentation**: the division of consumers into different groups based on relevant demographic variables; *compare* PSYCHOGRAPHICS.

demography (demographics, demographic analysis) The statistical study of human populations, including size, structure, and changes.

demonization A sustained attack on an individual, a minority group, a political party, or a government in the popular press. *See also* FOLK DEVILS; MORAL PANIC.

denaturalization 1. A goal in some *semiotic analysis: revealing the socially coded basis of phenomena which are taken for granted as 'natural'. Such analysis seeks to denaturalize *signs and *codes in order to make more explicit the underlying rules for *encoding and decoding them, often also with the intention of revealing the usually invisible operation of *ideological forces. *See also* ALIGNMENT;

MARKEDNESS; *compare* NATURALIZATION. 2. Sometimes a synonym for *defamiliarization.

denial (disavowal) In *psychoanalytic theory, a *defence mechanism in which the individual shuts out unacceptable thoughts, feelings, desires, or *events.

denotation (denotative meaning) 1. The definitional, *literal, 'obvious', *common sense, or **dictionary meaning** of a word, or what an image depicts; in both cases, what is **denoted**. However, many theorists argue that there is no denotation without *connotation; no *description without *evaluation. 2. What Barthes called the first *order of signification.

( ) SEE WEB LINKS

• Denotation, connotation, and myth

dénouement [French 'unravelling'] In a narrative or drama, the final resolution of the conflicts, mysteries, or misunderstandings in the plot; the tying up of loose ends, typically in a final scene or chapter, providing narrative, structural, and, many argue, *ideological *closure. In contemporary works of high art, endings may be ambiguous and resolve nothing. *See also* CLASSICAL NARRATIVE STRUCTURE.

dependency theory 1. (sociology) A theory influential in the 1970s that the continuing poverty, social deprivation, and political instability in many poor countries was a result of their economic dependence on capitalist countries. Some argued that this was reinforced by the *ideological role of television. The adequacy of dependency theory was challenged by rapid industrialization and economic growth in some so-called Third World countries. 2. **(media system dependency theory)** A structural approach to the *mass media that presents it as an *information system with two-way **dependency relationships** between its various parts that relate to goals versus resources (DeFleur and Ball-Rokeach). On the macro level, the parts include: the 'media system', consisting of different *media industries (such as television, radio, *newspapers, and magazines) and cross-media organizations (such as news agencies, advertisers, and unions); and other social systems, such as the political system. Media-political relations are argued to be **structural dependency relations** based on fairly symmetrical patterns of interdependence, involving four interacting elements: the social system, the media system, audiences, and (potential) effects (*see* EFFECTS). At the micro level, this theory posits that individuals have come to depend on *knowledge derived from the *mass media. Here, dependency relationships exist between individuals (or groups) and the media (based on *media functions, both *personal and *social). It is argued that the degree of audience dependency (and hence potential effects) depends on the degree of social stability and the extent to which audiences are functionally dependent on the mass media, particularly as an information source. 3. **(psychological media dependency)** The popular view that individuals, groups, or society as a whole have become dependent upon the media, or some medium in particular.

dependent and independent variables *See also* VARIABLE. 1. In experimental studies, a dependent variable is an outcome factor on which an independent ('experimental' or 'controlled') variable is hypothesized and observed to have a particular measurable *effect (*see also* EXPERIMENT; HYPOTHESIS). For example, a researcher in the *effects tradition might manipulate viewers' exposure to certain types of programme content (the independent variable) in order to investigate a hypothesized impact on *attitudes or behaviour (the dependent variable). 2. In theoretical frameworks, an independent variable is a phenomenon that is seen as influencing the behaviour of some other (dependent) factor. For instance, *technological determinism presents technology as an independent variable leading to changes in social patterns (the dependent variable). Such relationships cannot necessarily be simply equated with cause and effect, and the direction of causality cannot be assumed. Note that a factor such as social *class might be treated as a dependent variable in one *context and as an independent variable in another: *see also* CAUSATION; INTERVENING VARIABLE. 3. In the rhetoric of *behaviourism, a dependent variable is any response attributed to the effects of a stimulus (the independent variable). 4. In statistics, a dependent variable is a measurable factor identified as predictably influenced by one or more independent variables: *see also* DATA ANALYSIS.

depth cues Any indications of relative distance that may contribute to *depth perception either in a three-dimensional environment (the real world or a *virtual world) or in a two-dimensional medium (e.g. *pictorial depth cues in a painting, where *binocular vision is of no assistance).

depth of field (photography) The distance in front of the camera over which the image appears clear and in sharp focus. A limited depth of field is shallow or selective focus, which may be used to emphasize a particular object. Greater depth of field can be achieved using a wide-angle lens. Large depth of field creates *deep focus. *See also* SELECTIVE FOCUS.

depth perception The *visual perception of the world in three dimensions. This is dependent on both *binocular vision and *monocular *depth cues, but it can also involve auditory and tactile cues (*see also* AUDITORY PERSPECTIVE). For pictorial *perception *see* PICTORIAL DEPTH CUES.

deradicalization *See* INCORPORATION.

deregulation Government action to reduce bureaucratic controls over an industry, typically in order to allow market forces to stimulate commercial *competition and/or to reduce public provision (*see also* MARKET MODEL). In the late 1970s and 1980s, the deregulation of media ownership was a key feature of the policies of Prime Minister Margaret Thatcher in the UK and President Ronald Reagan in the USA (*see also* MEDIA OWNERSHIP). Since the 1980s, deregulation of the *mass media has been stimulated both by technological changes which have reduced the relevance of national boundaries (*see also* CONVERGENCE; GLOBALIZATION), and by a general shift in both North America and Europe from a reliance on state intervention to a greater reliance on market forces. Critics argue that mass media deregulation leads to the neglect or closure of important but unprofitable public services and to the creation of large media corporations through mergers and acquisitions, which undermine consumer choice (*see also* CROSS-MEDIA OWNERSHIP). It has been claimed to result in more populist and less challenging media output (*see also* DUMBING DOWN). However, it has also led to opportunities for independent media producers. In practice, deregulation typically involves substituting different regulatory controls and frameworks rather than eliminating them. With respect to *censorship, pressure groups have largely focused on increasing *regulation rather than deregulation. Both Thatcher and Reagan, while committed to deregulating media ownership, were simultaneously committed to increasing moral regulation of the media (*see also* VIDEO NASTIES). *See also* MARKET MODEL; MEDIA CONTROLS; MEDIA POLICY; PRIVATIZATION OF INFORMATION; PUBLIC SERVICE BROADCASTING; REGULATION.

description 1. In modern *rhetoric, *discourse that is intended to enable audiences to picture in their minds what something is like. One of the four rhetorical modes of discourse identified by Brooks and Warren as fulfilling basic human *communicative purposes (*compare* ARGUMENT; EXPOSITION; NARRATION). It is a *referential function of language (though it may be subjective or objective) and analogous to depiction in *figurative art and *representation in photographic media. 2. The *representation of *spatial relations rather than temporality, as distinguished from *narration.

desensitization The stance, within the media *effects tradition, that heavy viewing of onscreen violence over time conditions viewers gradually to accept violence as normal, dulling their sensitivity to aggressive behaviour in *everyday life. The origin of such theories is in the tradition of behavioural *conditioning. *See also* VIOLENCE DEBATE; *compare* SENSITIZATION.

design features (*linguistics) A set of key properties of human *language that collectively distinguish it from systems of communication used by other species (Hockett). These include: a vocal/auditory channel (*see* AURAL/ORAL CHANNEL), duality of patterning (double *articulation), *productivity, *arbitrariness, *displacement, *reflexiveness, and *traditional transmission.

(((●))) SEE WEB LINKS

• Design features of human language

desktop metaphor *See* GRAPHICAL USER INTERFACE.

desktop publishing (DTP) The use of personal computers and page layout software to create documents in a finished form ready for printed reproduction ('camera-ready'). In the 1980s, the 'desktop publishing revolution' weakened the power of traditional typesetting and printing industries.

destination 1. In *Shannon and Weaver's model of communication (1949), the last stop for a *message. For example, in *speech communication, Weaver tells us that the destination would be the brain (or mind) of the person to whom it was sent. 2. For McGuire (*see also* YALE MODEL), the desired *effect, outcome, or response in an act of persuasive communication: for example, to encourage people to give up smoking, to get people to buy a product, or to generate awareness of a *brand. The desired effect might be a change in *attitudes or a change in behaviour. He also referred to this goal as the 'target'—a term nowadays more usually taken to mean the *target audience. **Destination factors** include temporal *variables: short-term or long-term *effects (raising issues such as *message decay).

determinism 1. Theories about the causes of a phenomenon which emphasize one principal (**determining**) factor (*see also* CAUSATION). More extreme versions are called **hard** (or **strong**) **determinism** and more moderate versions are called **soft** (or **weak**) **determinism**. In soft determinism, the specified factor is a *necessary condition—an enabling factor; in hard determinism, it is a *sufficient condition. The term is typically pejorative. 2. For determinism in relation to the issue of establishing *meaning in acts of communication, *see* AUDIENCE DETERMINISM; AUTHORIAL DETERMINISM; INDETERMINACY; TEXTUAL DETERMINISM. 3. In relation to the relative power of the *medium or *technology, and of society, *see* LINGUISTIC DETERMINISM; MEDIA DETERMINISM; SOCIAL DETERMINISM; TECHNOLOGICAL DETERMINISM. 4. In relation to nature versus nurture, *see* BIOLOGICAL DETERMINISM; SOCIAL DETERMINISM. 5. In relation to structures and processes versus human *agency, *see* ECONOMISM (in *Marxism); HISTORICAL DETERMINISM; STRUCTURAL DETERMINISM (in *structuralism). 6. (philosophy) The doctrine that every *event has a preceding cause, from which the event inevitably follows—a notion that in its extreme form does not allow for human free will.

development journalism The active involvement of journalists in critical coverage and awareness raising with regard to issues of socio-economic development (primarily in the southern hemisphere) from the perspective of those most affected.

deviation *See* NORM.

devil terms *See* GOD TERMS.

diachronic analysis The study of change in a phenomenon (such as a *code) over time (in contrast to *synchronic analysis). Saussure saw the development of *language in terms of a series of synchronic states. Critics argue that *structuralism fails to account for how change occurs. *See also* CODIFICATION; DOMINANT CODE; EMERGENT CODE; LANGUE AND PAROLE; RESIDUAL CODE; TRANSFORMATION.

diagonal integration Strategic acquisitions, alliances, and information partnerships between companies in order to improve access to consumers and to achieve *economies of scale and scope. Characterized by tightly-related, consumer-oriented services. *See also* DIVERSIFICATION; MEDIA OWNERSHIP; *compare* HORIZONTAL INTEGRATION; VERTICAL INTEGRATION.

diagonality The slanted directions running from corner to corner of a rectangle or other figure. In art and photography diagonals are widely argued to create a more dynamic composition. Within a *culture which is the viewer's own, *reading direction tends to determine whether a diagonal line is interpreted as 'going up' or 'going down'. For example, for those in Anglophone cultures, a line going from bottom left to top right would be rising but in Arab cultures it would be falling. *See also* CANTED SHOT; DUTCH ANGLE; ROLL.

dialect A distinct variety of a *language, with its own variations of *grammar and vocabulary, usually associated with a particular region within a country. Normally also associated with different accents, though linguists distinguish accent from dialect. *Compare* GENDERLECT; IDIOLECT; SOCIOLECT.

dialectical montage (Soviet montage, thematic montage) (*film theory) Eisenstein's term for an effect in *montage in which the *juxtaposition of two *shots (the *Kuleshov effect), when these reflect some kind of *conflict, has the potential to make an abstract concept tangible. For example, in *Battleship Potemkin* (1925), the poor treatment of the sailors is indicated intercut with shots of them filing into a mess hall with shots of maggots in the food that is being prepared for them. While a concept cannot be directly represented in an image, tensions and discord between juxtaposed images could stimulate an audience to grasp a conceptual connection by *inference. This technique could be used to generate new political insights in audiences. *Compare* ASSOCIATIVE EDITING; CONTINUITY EDITING.

dialogism (dialogics) 1. In literary works, Bakhtin's term for a style of *discourse in which characters express a variety of (potentially contradictory) points of view rather than being mouthpieces for the author: a dialogic or polyphonic style rather than a **monologic** one. 2. More broadly, the basis in dialogue of all communication.

dictionary meaning *See* DENOTATION; INTRINSIC MEANING; LITERAL MEANING; SENSE.

diegesis 1. A narrative world. 2. (*film theory) The spatio-temporal world depicted in the film. Anything within that world (such as dialogue or a *shot of a roadsign used to establish a location) is termed **diegetic** whereas anything outside it (such as a *voiceover or a superimposed caption) is **extradiegetic**. This distinction is especially associated with **diegetic sound**: for example, when a record-player is shown to be the source of onscreen music. A **diegetic audience** is an audience within the depicted world. 3. (*narratology) The relation of story *events by *telling*, as opposed to *showing* (*mimesis).

différance Derrida's term for the concept that every *signified is also a *signifier: there is no escape from the *sign system. The *meaning of signs involves endless substitutions of signifiers; there is always *slippage of meaning. His coinage alludes simultaneously to 'difference' and 'deferral', and in French the distinction from the word for 'difference' is apparent only in writing. Whereas Saussure referred to meaning being differential (based on differences between *signs), Derrida's term is intended to remind us that signs also *defer* the presence of what they signify. Meaning depends upon absence rather than *presence. *See also* ABSENT PRESENCE; DECONSTRUCTION; FREEPLAY; TRANSCENDENT SIGNIFIED; UNLIMITED SEMIOSIS.

difference 1. Being unlike something else, or unlike other people, in some way. The marking of difference constitutes *identity—especially in relation to *gender, *ethnicity, *class, and age. In some contexts, an emphasis on the differences between one group and another may be criticized for overlooking what they have in common and for perpetuating *essentialist *stereotypes. In *identity politics, on the other hand, some may celebrate a shared difference through *strategic essentialism. *See also* OTHERNESS; *compare* ALTERITY. **2. (relational meaning)** For Saussure (**différence**), a sign signifies in relation to how it is distinguished from others (*see also* RELATIONAL MODEL). This notion is reflected in *brand positioning, but it can also be applied to human identity—our sense of who we *are* depends partly on what we are *not*: *compare* DIFFÉRANCE. **3.** A comparative judgement as to whether the differences between two groups are greater than the differences within them or a typological judgement of whether differences between observed instances of some phenomenon are those of degree or of kind.

difference model (difference paradigm) An approach to communication and *gender which polarizes the *communication styles of men and women in terms of a focus by men on status and independence, reflected in an *instrumental and individualistic style, and by women on intimacy and connection, reflected in an *expressive and social/relational style. Although some theorists attribute such behaviour to subcultural factors (e.g. different treatment in the formative years of childhood and adolescence), this kind of stance often involves *gender essentialism, and fails to allow for the constitutive role of *power relations in gender differentiation (*see* DOMINANCE MODEL).

differential focus *See* SELECTIVE FOCUS.

diffusion 1. The spread of something, particularly ideas and innovations: for example, through a social system, throughout an organization, or across the globe. In this process, communication plays a key role: *see also* GLOBALIZATION; MEDIA FLOWS. **2. (cultural diffusion)** In anthropology and sociology, diffusion most commonly refers to the transmission across space from one culture to another of elements of material or non-material culture: e.g. ideas, beliefs, or practices. *See also* CULTURAL IMPERIALISM; HOMOGENIZATION; MCDONALDIZATION. **3.** The **diffusion of innovation** concerns the social and/or psychological processes involved in the diffusion and adoption of technical innovations, fashions, and so on. In *marketing, this applies to a particular market or industry: *see also* DIFFUSION RATE. **4.** The degree of *access to information, media, or technologies within a social system: as with the **diffusion of information** (including **news diffusion**) and of *communication technologies (*see also* INFORMATION FLOW; INFORMATIZATION). Whether a medium is defined as a mass medium, for instance, may depend on some threshold percentage of a population having *access to it: *see also* DIGITAL DIVIDE.

diffusion rate In the *diffusion of innovation, the rate at which new ideas, practices, or products are adopted throughout a population. According to Everett Rogers (1931–2004), an American sociologist, the rate of adoption tends to follow an S-shaped curve, in which the x-axis represents time and the y-axis represents the cumulative percentage of the population. The variance lies in the relative steepness of the slope.

digicut 1. A portmanteau word (*digital* + *cut*). Typically, the final assembly of a finished *offline *edit. 2. The physical video cassette or exported digital video film that contains the final offline cut: *see also* FINAL CUT.

digital 1. *Signs and *codes involving discrete units such as words and numerals that progress in step changes without traversing intermediate positions, in contrast to *analogue signs and codes which are continuous and theoretically infinitely divisible. Note, however, that digital technology can transform analogical signs into high *resolution digital reproductions where the step changes are so minute that they may be perceptually indistinguishable from the 'originals', and also that texts generated in a digital medium can be 'copies without originals', e.g. a word-processed text. *Compare* ANALOGUE. 2. Any *information that has been digitized. 'Digital' does not signify that physical phenomena have been transformed into binary information, merely that binary numbers have been assigned to represent analogue encodings of physical phenomena. For example, the light rays that hit the **charge-coupled device** (CCD) in a digital camera are converted into electricity in exactly the same way as in an electronic analogue camera. It is only when the electrical signal is digitized by being assigned a set of binary values that the photograph becomes digital. Consequently *digital photography is still *indexical. However, the ease with which photographs can be manipulated once they are in the digital domain means that their indexical qualities cannot be guaranteed. *See also* DIGITAL TRANSMISSION; PHOTOSHOPPING.

digital audio broadcasting (DAB) A form of broadcast digital radio, as opposed to digital radio on the *internet. In the UK and Europe DAB is encoded according to the Eureka 147 Digital Audio Broadcasting standard. The US has adopted the HD Radio standard which allows digital radio signals to 'piggyback' on top of AM or FM analogue transmission.

digital bit stream *See* DIGITAL TRANSMISSION.

digital broadcasting *See* DIGITAL TRANSMISSION.

digital cable *See* DIGITAL TRANSMISSION.

digital divide A disparity between those who have easy *access to computers and the *internet and those who do not. Patterns of unequal access are often related to global inequalities and to individual factors such as income, age, and/or *gender issues. Often treated as a synonym for the *knowledge gap between the *information rich and poor.

digital editing *See* NONLINEAR EDITING.

digital journalism (electronic journalism) The practice of journalism in digital environments. This can include online *newspapers, magazines, and other journalistic websites run by existing broadcasting organizations, print newspapers, and magazines, as well as independent *blogs, student radio stations, and so on.

digital media An umbrella term often treated as synonymous with *new media or *computer-mediated communication. A distinction can be made between media which are based on encoded physical qualities such as light or sound waves through the re-encoding of analogue information (e.g. with digital cameras or digital sound equipment), and media which are based on the re-encoding of previously encoded cultural forms such as such as *writing, mathematics, *linear perspective, or the Cartesian coordinate system that is used to represent physical space in *virtual reality applications.

digital photography A form of imaging produced by a digital camera. Instead of the light from the lens being stored on light-sensitive film, sensors convert it into electrical charges and an analogue-to-digital converter turns this into data that is compressed and stored in the camera on a memory card as image files.

digital recording The conversion of analogue video and/or sound *signals to digital *data through a process of *digitization and the storage of this in the form of a discontinuous *signal consisting of a series of voltages on magnetic tape, hard drives, or optical drives.

digital television A television with a built-in digital-to-analogue converter to change digital signals into analogue picture information. A **set-top box** performs this function for analogue televisions.

digital-to-analogue converter *See* DECODER.

digital transmission A method of sending television, radio, and *mobile phone data over long distances by using digital encoding to modulate a continuous beam of charged *electromagnetic particles (typically radio waves, but also microwaves, electricity through wires, and visible light via fibre-optic cables). Digital signals consist of binary information which is *symbolic and therefore *arbitrarily related to its source; however, in the case of picture and sound information it is *analogue signals that are being digitized so the *indexicality of the information is preserved. Digital signals encode information in discrete bursts, unlike continuous *analogue signals, and their modulations are expressed in abrupt changes (steps) rather than smoothe transitions (slopes). The main advantages of digital over analogue signals are that they can be compressed and that *noise can be identified and removed. Digital transmission systems use a variety of methods: **pulseband systems,** such as those used for broadcast digital television, use digitized analogue waveforms while **baseband systems,** such as those used on the *internet, send information in discrete bundles or 'packets'. Digital television transmission allows for **multiplexing,** whereby multiple channels are bundled together and sent simultaneously in a single stream of data. *See also* MPEG2; TRANSMITTER.

(●) SEE WEB LINKS

• Digital broadcasting

digital video effects (DVE) A dedicated piece of equipment in an *online edit suite that creates *real-time digital transition and picture manipulation effects such as picture-in-picture boxes and page-turns.

digitization 1. The conversion of *data from *analogue to *digital form. 2. The computerization of *information. 3. The *diffusion of such technologies and techniques: *see also* CONVERGENCE.

direct address Communication that is explicitly indicated as being targeted at a current listener, reader, or viewer as an individual. In *face-to-face interaction, this is when you are being spoken to or gestured at: signified by *eye contact, the use of the word 'you', your name, or a pointing finger (*see also* DEIXIS). In the case of television and photography, an example would be someone talking while looking into the camera lens, as if they were communicating directly with the current viewer. This *mode of address is common for presenters in certain *television genres: notably newscasters, weather forecasters, and chat-show hosts. It is only occasionally used in *narratives, where such communication is extradiegetic (*see* DIEGESIS); in such contexts this is typically a humorous device or an *alienation effect. *See also* INTERPELLATION; PIECE-TO-CAMERA.

direct effects In simplistic causal models, patterns of variation in the phenomenon under investigation which are attributed solely to the influence of one factor, without any *mediation by *intervening variables (*see also* DEPENDENT AND INDEPENDENT VARIABLES). An example would be if an increase in violent behaviour on the streets were to be attributed solely to the influence of an increase in depictions of violence in the *mass media, with no allowance made for any other factors (such as differences between viewers or different kinds of violence). This kind of *reductionism is a feature of hard *determinism, as in the *hypodermic model. *See also* CAUSATION; EFFECTS; *compare* INDIRECT EFFECTS.

direction of relationship *See* CAUSATION.

direct marketing Sending promotional communications by mail, *email, *mobile phone, or similar means, to specific consumers in a *target market.

director 1. (film) The person who controls the creative realization of the script, working closely with the actors and the technical crew (especially the cinematographer and the editor). Alongside the *producer (to whom the director is responsible), the director is often termed a *film-maker: *see also* AUTEUR THEORY. 2. (television and radio) The creative coordinator who is responsible for realizing the scripted concept: *compare* PRODUCER.

director's cut 1. In *post-production, the *final cut of a film, TV programme, or pop video, which is approved by its *director but which may be subsequently re-edited: for example as a response to studio pressure from poor test screenings. A director's contract normally stipulates that final cutting rights belong to the studio. 2. A *marketing device for films whereby a director's approved cut is re-issued as the definitive version of a film. The director's cut of *Blade Runner* (1982) is an example. On some occasions, the commercial imperatives of this practice outweigh its artistic merits.

direct perception A theory of *perception, developed by James Gibson, in which the invariants in moving patterns of light provide sufficient indication of spatial arrangements and surfaces without the intervention of *inference or *memory. *See also* BOTTOM-UP PROCESSING; *compare* TOP-DOWN PROCESSING.

disavowal *See* DENIAL.

disclosure 1. **(self-disclosure)** The communication of personal *information about oneself (especially intimate feelings and experiences) that others are unlikely to know from other sources. Usually, but not necessarily conscious and voluntary. This often signifies a sense of *affiliation with or attraction to the other party, while reciprocal disclosures contribute to deepening relationships based on trust and intimacy, often referred to in terms of the metaphor of peeling an onion (*see also* JOHARI WINDOW; RECIPROCITY). In *asymmetrical relationships subordinates tend to engage in more self-disclosure to superiors than vice versa, allowing *information to flow towards those with greater *status or power. Self-disclosure can occur where the social cost or accountability is low (the 'strangers on the train' phenomenon). The relative *anonymity of purely textual forms of *computer-mediated communication (notably non-visibility and pseudonyms) tends to be associated with de-individuation or increased private self-awareness, which can lead to reduced inhibition and greater self-disclosure. Online *discussion groups with higher proportions of women tend to exhibit more self-disclosure than others. The term was coined by Sidney Jourard (1926–74), a Canadian psychologist. 2. **(narrative disclosure)** In *genres which depend on maintaining suspense, the process whereby an author strategically withholds information from the audience, only gradually revealing what they need to know.

discourse 1. In some contexts, speech, talk, or conversation. 2. A unit of linguistic analysis larger than the sentence: *see also* COHESION. 3. Written or spoken communication, formerly more narrowly framed as a formal *exposition. 4. More broadly, all forms of human *interpersonal communication: *see also* MULTIMODALITY. 5. A language variety, *register, *genre (e.g. poetic discourse), or usage within a particular domain (as in *advertising discourse). 6. Communication within the social *context of its use (*see* CRITICAL DISCOURSE ANALYSIS). Not synonymous with *language since it focuses on *parole* (language in use) as distinct from *langue* (the language system); *see* LANGUAGE AND PAROLE. An intersubjective practice with its own rules and *conventions. Furthermore, for *constructionists, a constitutive practice that constructs social realities. 7. For contemporary theorists influenced by Foucault, a system of *representation consisting of a set of representational *codes (including a distinctive *interpretive repertoire of concepts, *tropes, and *myths) for constructing and maintaining particular forms of reality within the *ontological domain (or *topic) defined as relevant to its concerns (such as science, law, government, medicine, journalism, and morality). Representational codes thus reflect relational principles underlying the symbolic order of the 'discursive field'. According to Foucault, whose primary concern was the analysis of *discursive formations in specific historical and sociocultural contexts, each formation maintains its own 'regime of truth'. He adopted a stance of *linguistic determinism, arguing that the dominant tropes within the discourse of a particular historical period determine what can be known—constituting the basic *épistème of the age. A range of discursive positions is available at any given time, reflecting many determinants (economic, political, sexual, etc.). Foucault focused on *power relations, noting that within such contexts, the discourses and *signifiers of some *interpretive communities (e.g. 'law', 'money', 'power') are privileged and dominant while others are marginalized. He declared that 'It is in discourse that power and *knowledge are joined together.' 8. In *narratology, the *narration rather than the narrated.

discourse analysis 1. Most broadly, the study of *language in use, and of its *functions and patterns of use in particular *contexts, in contrast to *structuralist approaches: *see also* LANGUE AND PAROLE. 2. *Text linguistics: the linguistic analysis and *description of the defining properties of written and spoken communications that serve different functions. 3. Other descriptive approaches to *discursive practices, as in applied *linguistics: *pragmatics and *sociolinguistics. In social psychology, this includes the functional analysis of the variability of spoken and written communication in relation to the goals of communicators in particular *contexts. 4. In the philosophy of language, *speech act theory in the tradition of Searle and Austin. 5. The sociological analysis of conversation arising from *ethnomethodology: *see* CONVERSATION ANALYSIS. 6. 'Critical' approaches arising from functional linguistics inflected by social theory. Linguistic analysis of discourses focusing on an *ideological critique of their role in reproducing *power relations: *see* CRITICAL DISCOURSE ANALYSIS. 7. **Colonial discourse analysis**: *see* POSTCOLONIALISM.

(⊕) SEE WEB LINKS

• *Discourse Analysis Online*

discourse community *See* INTERPRETIVE COMMUNITY.

discourse genres *See* GENRES; REGISTER.

discursive formation (discourse formation) For Foucault, 'the general enunciative principle that governs a group of verbal performances'. The term is also used to refer to the particular *discourse governed by this principle, in which different examples share the same patterns of concerns, perspectives, concepts, or *themes. For instance, the discourses of medicine or economics. Said analysed *orientalism as a discursive formation. Their relationship with non-discursive formations (*institutions, political events, and economic processes) is one of *relative autonomy. *See also* EPISTEME.

discursive practices Foucault's term for communicative practices based on rules that define and construct their *referents. *See also* CONSTITUTIVE MODELS; *compare* SIGNIFYING PRACTICE.

discursive turn *See* RHETORICAL TURN.

discussion lists *See* ELECTRONIC MAILING LISTS.

disembedding In sociology, a process associated with *modernization in which *social relations have become increasingly spread across time and space, associated with a decline in traditional *social ties (Giddens). *See also* DISTANCIATION; WEAK TIES; *compare* RE-EMBEDDING.

disinformation (black propaganda) A form of *propaganda involving the dissemination of false *information with the deliberate intent to deceive or mislead. It is *misinformation that the term has Russian roots: *dezinformatsia* (misinformation) is derived from French (*dés* + *information*).

disinhibition *See* DISCLOSURE.

disinhibition theory A *hypothesis formerly advanced by Berkowitz that people are naturally aggressive, but that they normally repress this aggression; heavy viewing of violence on television weakens their inhibitions and leads them to feel that aggression is acceptable. *See also* VIOLENCE DEBATE.

Disneyfication A pejorative term for the metaphorical resemblance of some cultural phenomenon to a theme park. The connotations typically include cultural *homogenization, *McDonaldization, sanitization, 'family values', *dumbing down, and artificiality. *See also* HYPERREALITY.

displacement 1. Most broadly, any shift of position. 2. (psychology) Any form of behaviour **(displacement activity)** acting as a substitute for another which is blocked or thwarted. 3. In *psychoanalytic theory, a *defence mechanism in which unconscious desires are transformed into an associated *symbol (a concept introduced by Freud for the *interpretation of dreams). Lacan makes an analogy with *metonymy. *See also* DREAM-WORK; *compare* CONDENSATION. 4. (*linguistics) The power of words to refer to things in their absence (displaced in time and space). Displacement was identified by Hockett as a key *design feature of human *language: in this case a feature shared with bee dancing, the 'language' of bees (Hockett). It enables signs to be more than simply *indexical and facilitates reflective thought and communication using *texts which can be detached from their authors. *See also* ABSENT PRESENCE.

displacement activities Small, apparently unmotivated body movements (e.g. *self-touch movements such as scratching one's head) which are inferred to reflect frustration or inner conflict.

display rules *See* AFFECT DISPLAYS.

display text In text design, titles, headlines, headings, subheadings and so on— as distinct from the *body text. It is usually visually distinguished by the use of *display types.

display type (display faces) *Typeface(s) used for *display text, which in a particular document may differ from the font used for the main *body text. A *font size larger than that of the *body type is normally used, with relative sizes of the same display type being proportional to levels of organization (and importance) within the text. The type used for display is more prominent, and the more striking typefaces are especially associated with advertisements.

dissensus 1. Lack of *consensus; difference of opinion. 2. An agreement to disagree. 3. A minority opinion in response to a consensus position. 4. Specific areas of disagreement.

dissolve See CROSS DISSOLVE.

dissonance reduction See COGNITIVE DISSONANCE.

dissonance theory See COGNITIVE DISSONANCE.

distance 1. In nonverbal communication: *see* PROXEMICS. 2. **(camera distance)** See CLOSE-UP; MID-SHOT; LONG-SHOT. 3. (aesthetics) See AESTHETIC DISTANCE; DISTANCIATION. 4. (psychological) See PSYCHOLOGICAL DISTANCE.

distance communication 1. Any *interpersonal communication in which the physical gap between the participants is beyond the physiological limits of unaided human *perception. 2. *Asynchronous communication using portable media that are physically transported. Innis argued that the use of papyrus in Ancient Egypt made long-distance communication, and thereby empire expansion, much easier. 3. *Synchronous communication that does not require physical transportation: the first of these being the telegraph and the telephone (notably both prefixed with the Greek for 'far').

distanciation 1. A synonym for *aesthetic distance. 2. A synonym for the Brechtian *alienation effect. 3. (sociology) A concept with both spatial and emotional dimensions, in which for individuals in modern society there is increasingly less connection between *psychological distance or closeness and physical distance or *proximity in regular *social relations. This is in part related to the *affordances of modern media of *interpersonal communication, which can help to sustain what might otherwise be *weak ties. It is also a feature of *disembedding.

distancing See AESTHETIC DISTANCE.

distortion 1. Misrepresentation or inaccuracy in the ostensibly objective reporting or *representation of something: *see also* BIAS; OBJECTIVITY. 2. In relation to *perception and *memory, unconscious modifications to the source material: *see also* ADDITION; ASSIMILATION; DELETION; LEVELLING AND SHARPENING; SUBSTITUTION; TRANSPOSITION. 3. In *psychoanalytic theory, a *defence mechanism that disguises dream content: *see also* CONDENSATION; DISPLACEMENT. 4. In relation to lenses (both in physiology and optical devices), any contortion of the image due to characteristics of the lens. 5. In photography, design, and audio and video recording or broadcasting, either a malfunction or unwanted *artefact of the technical process *or* the deliberate use of such artefacts to transform images or sounds for *aesthetic effect (e.g. using a wide-angle lens or an overdriven guitar sound).

distribution 1. (*marketing) The delivery of goods to consumers. 2. The *circulation of a publication. 3. Frequency of publication. 4. The act or process of disseminating something (e.g. information). 5. The means by which it is disseminated (e.g. via a **distribution network**). 6. The extent of its *diffusion at some point in time within some population.

divergence 1. (psychology) A *cognitive style relating to problem-solving. **Divergent thinkers** tend to generate more ideas and prefer open-ended problems.

See also TOLERANCE OF AMBIGUITY; *compare* CONVERGENCE. 2. In *visual perception, the turning outwards of the eyes as the distance between the perceiver and the point of focus increases: *compare* CONVERGENCE.

diversification Strategic acquisitions and investment in new activities, usually on an 'arm's length' basis by companies seeking to minimize financial risks by spreading them across different market sectors (e.g. Virgin operating both a train and airline service). *Compare* DIAGONAL INTEGRATION; HORIZONTAL INTEGRATION; MEDIA OWNERSHIP; VERTICAL INTEGRATION.

diversion function In relation to general types of use by individuals of the *mass media, a single medium, a media *genre, or specific media *content, usage for purposes such as stimulation (escape from boredom, routine, or problems), relaxation, or emotional release. This is what Schramm calls the *entertainment function. Diversion is seen as a basic human need. For *Frankfurt school theorists this is an *ideological function serving to depoliticize the working class. *See also* CATHARSIS; ESCAPISM; IDENTIFICATION; MEDIA FUNCTIONS; USES AND GRATIFICATIONS.

division of labour *See* GENDER.

docudrama A portmanteau word (*documentary* + *drama*). A *hybrid genre in which actual *events are dramatized for film, television, or radio. Sometimes also called **docufiction**. *Compare* DOCUMENTARY; DOCUSOAP; DRAMADOC; FACTION.

documentary A *genre closely associated with film and television, but also found in radio, theatre, and photography, dealing with a particular theme, and seeking to represent actual people, places, and *events in a manner intended to leave viewers or listeners feeling that they have gained some insight into the *subject matter. Although often categorized as a serious, *factual, or non-fiction genre, this tends to neglect the extent to which particular examples can represent many blends of *communicative functions: *description*: seeking to record or represent events as accurately as possible without overt commentary; *exposition*: seeking to explain, contextualize, and interpret events or issues in an unbiased, impartial, objective, and evidential manner; *persuasion*: seeking to present a provocative case for a particular perspective; *education*: seeking to teach us something; and *entertainment*: seeking to amuse us, or encourage us to indulge in *voyeuristic pleasures. *Compare* CINÉMA VÉRITÉ; DOCUDRAMA; DOCUSOAP; FACTION; FLY-ON-THE-WALL; MOCKUMENTARY; REALITY TV.

documentary style The use of techniques particularly associated with the television *documentary genre (such as real-world locations, apparently unrehearsed dialogue, and hand-held *camerawork) in commercials, fictional films, and television *series, in order to connote *authenticity.

docusoap A portmanteau word (*documentary* + *soap opera*). A *hybrid genre on television or radio in a *serial format which follows the experiences of real people over a period of time. *Compare* DOCUDRAMA; DOCUMENTARY; DRAMADOC; FACTION; FLY-ON-THE-WALL; REALITY TV.

dolly shot *See* TRACKING SHOT.

domestic communication technologies 1. Those *information and communication technologies found in the home. 2. The domestic environment as a communication *context, with its own *media ecology, *power relations, domestic politics, *communicative purposes, practices, and styles: *see also* COMMUNICATION STYLE.

dominance 1. *Status, *power, and/or degree of influence over others, relative to deference or **submissiveness**—in communication, a key interpersonal relation between interactive partners communicated by *nonverbal behaviour: strong/weak, superior/subordinate, active/passive: *see also* POWER RELATIONS. 2. (*Marxist theory) Relative power in a social *formation. Althusser famously referred to 'a complex unity, structured in dominance': *see* DOMINANCE MODEL; HEGEMONY. 3. In *cultural materialism, the relative status of cultural forms: *see* DOMINANT FORMS; EMERGENT FORMS; RESIDUAL FORMS. 4. In *Jakobson's model of communication, the relative status of the *linguistic functions operating within a hierarchy in an *utterance, determined by the social *context of use, leading the key function to influence the general character of the *message.

dominance model (**dominance paradigm**) 1. A stance in which a small elite of powerful interests is seen as controlling the *mass media. The *hidden agenda in political and economic coverage is largely that of primary definers—notably authoritative and official sources (*see* PRIMARY AND SECONDARY DEFINERS). This is a feature of *Marxist theory, in which the mass media are seen as reproducing the *ideology and *values of the dominant groups in society and alternative voices are filtered out. A relatively passive *mass audience is seen as conditioned to accept the dominant worldview. The media thus reinforce the *status quo. *See also* AGENDA SETTING; DOMINANT IDEOLOGY; MANIPULATIVE MODEL; MANUFACTURE OF CONSENT; MEDIA HEGEMONY; *compare* PLURALIST MODEL. 2. An approach to communication and *gender in which *power relations are seen as reflected and reproduced in everyday social *interaction, *conversational style, and *nonverbal behaviour. For instance, men are often reported to be more likely than women to adopt an *instrumental communication style, to interrupt more, to have larger *personal space, and feel far freer to look at and touch women than vice versa. Less patriarchal contexts would reveal such behaviour to be about *power rather than sexual difference: *compare* DIFFERENCE MODEL.

dominant code 1. (**hegemonic code**) The standard textual *conventions framing *texts within a particular *genre and/or the defining assumptions of a prevailing *ideology framing a particular text (*see* DOMINANT IDEOLOGY). A concept associated with Stuart Hall's notion of the *hegemonic reading of *mass media texts. *See also* IDEOLOGICAL CODES; *compare* NEGOTIATED READING; OPPOSITIONAL READING. 2. A synonym for Williams's concept of a *dominant form. Adopted as a concept in *marketing trend-spotting referring to the prevailing *values, styles, and fashions of the present day, which are particularly hard to identify as *codes because their familiarity often renders them *transparent: *see also* EMERGENT CODE; RESIDUAL CODE.

dominant forms (**dominant formations**) Williams's term for one of three categories of cultural forms or *codes that coexist within a society at any particular moment in history, the dominant form reflecting currently prevailing cultural *institutions, traditions, *styles, movements, social forces, *values, practices, and *identities. The dominant *culture and its institutions seek to incorporate aspects of rival forms in order to maintain their *hegemony. Williams advanced the concept of coexisting forms in order to avoid stark periodicity of historical 'epochs' and to emphasize the simultaneous presence in society of dynamic and contradictory cultural processes. *See also* CULTURAL MATERIALISM; EMERGENT FORMS; RESIDUAL FORMS.

dominant ideology 1. The ideas, *attitudes, *values, beliefs, and *culture of the ruling *class in a society; usually also the function of these in validating the *status quo. The nature and coherence of capitalist *ideology is disputed, but it is usually held to include the belief in private property and economic growth. 2. **Dominant ideology thesis**. In *Marxist theory, the argument that the dominant classes in society exercise considerable control over the circulation of ideas (*see also* MANIPULATIVE MODEL) and that the working class tends to accept its subordination because the prevailing *ideology functions to naturalize and legitimize the social inequalities of the *status quo, for instance by promoting the value of hard work (*see also* COMMON SENSE; LEGITIMATION; NATURALIZATION; SYMBOLIC VIOLENCE). This is argued to generate a '*false consciousness' among the masses. In capitalist societies this *ideology thus functions to sustain social order and *cohesion. Critics question the *ideological power of the dominant classes and the degree of acceptance of such ideas by subordinate groups. They also argue that the thesis underestimates the role of factors such as economic constraints, legal and political coercion, and institutional *socialization in maintaining social order. Such factors may be so powerful that the dominant classes can afford a degree of *pluralism and tolerance of political, social, and cultural deviance. Critics also note that the thesis overestimates the extent and importance of social *integration and *cohesion in modern societies and fails to account for persistent *conflict: *see also* MEDIA HEGEMONY.

dominant reading *See* HEGEMONIC READING.

dot-com An *internet-based company, based on the internet addresses of commercial websites, which often end in '.com'.

dots per inch *See* DPI.

double coding 1. Any *sign or *text which is open to two different *interpretations depending on the *frame of reference which is used to interpret it, as in 'I used to miss him . . . but my aim has improved'. *Irony has sometimes been referred to as a form of 'double coding'. In irony, double coding is open to both a *literal and an ironic interpretation: the former can be seen as depending on a *broadcast code and the latter as depending on a *narrowcast code. Thus interpretations would diverge. However, referring to irony as double coding obscures the role of *context as well as code: determining that the *preferred reading is ironic can be seen as requiring a greater sensitivity to context, rather than requiring access to another code. In this sense, one might argue that all signs are double coded, requiring reference both to codes and to contexts: *see also* JAKOBSON'S MODEL. 2. For the American architectural theorist Charles Jencks (b.1939), a defining characteristic of *postmodern architecture, art, and literary works in which modern techniques are combined with 'quotations' of traditional or historical styles.

double hermeneutic *See* HERMENEUTIC CIRCLE.

downmarket (downscale) Relating to consumer goods in the cheaper sector of the market, targeted at those with lower-than-average incomes. *Compare* UPMARKET.

downward communication (top-down communication) *Message sending, and *information flow, within organizational hierarchies from superiors to subordinates, often taking highly directive forms such as instructions and orders. Such communication reinforces the hierarchical nature of organizations. It is characteristic of an organizational structure termed 'mechanistic', in which *roles are clearly defined. *See also* ORGANIZATIONAL COMMUNICATION; SYSTEMS THEORY; *compare* LATERAL COMMUNICATION; ONE-WAY COMMUNICATION; UPWARD COMMUNICATION.

doxa *See* COMMON SENSE.

dpi (dots per inch) A unit of measurement representing the *resolution of the output of computer printers or the input of image scanners in terms of the number of points per linear inch: the larger the number, the greater the detail. The term is sometimes misapplied to screen resolution, where the term is *pixels per inch (ppi).

drama 1. Often used as a synonym for a *play. However, according to some literary definitions, only dramas intended for *performance before an audience (usually in a theatre) are plays. 2. A major *genre in literature, performance, film, television, and radio. Nowadays, drama is seen more often on the screen than on the stage, and both television and radio feature drama *serials as well as one-off plays. The major dramatic genres, as defined by Aristotle, are *comedy and *tragedy, but such terms hardly encompass the range of forms that drama has subsequently taken (for instance *docudrama, *dramadoc). 3. For Plato and Aristotle, drama was about *mimesis, the imitation or *representation of reality, and involved *showing* rather than *telling* (the latter being the task of *narrative).

dramadoc A portmanteau word (*drama* + *documentary*). A *hybrid genre on television or radio which aims to be a faithful *representation of actual *events drawing on documentary evidence but using actors. *Compare* DOCUDRAMA; DOCUMENTARY; FACTION.

dramatic irony A dramatic effect in which the audience for a drama (in any medium) or the reader of a novel has *information that characters lack that enables the audience or reader to understand the implications of a situation or of what is being said while the characters do not. The film *Valkyrie* (2008) is no less a suspense thriller because the audience knows that the plot to assassinate Hitler failed, and dramatic irony is a device intended to elicit *empathy for the doomed *protagonist.

dramatic licence *See* ARTISTIC LICENCE.

dramatics *See* DRAMATURGY.

dramatization 1. A version of a *narrative that has been adapted into the form of a *drama. 2. The act of converting a narrative in some other form (e.g. a novel or a short story) into a drama for stage, screen, or radio.

dramaturgy 1. **(dramatics)** The principles and practice of dramatic composition and theatrical artistry (a **dramaturge** or **dramaturgist** is a playwright). 2. The study of everyday social *interaction by analogy with theatrical performance. As Shakespeare wrote, 'All the world's a stage, And all the men and women merely players,' and this idea goes back to ancient Greece. *See also* PERFORMANCE; ROLE; SCENARIO; SCENE; SCRIPT. 3. **(dramaturgical perspective, dramaturgical theory, dramaturgic approach)** Goffman's sociological approach in which everyday social *interaction is seen as following familiar, relatively predictable *scripts. He makes extensive use of *metaphors of the stage, actors, *roles, props, and audiences, viewing social *interaction as a *performance in which social actors stage-manage their own behaviour. His primary focus is on expressive rather than purely functional aspects of performances. His approach arose from *symbolic interactionism. *See also* BACK STAGE; EVERYDAY LIFE; IMPRESSION FORMATION; IMPRESSION MANAGEMENT; MOTIVATION; PUBLIC AND PRIVATE SPHERES; ROLE DISTANCE; ROLE PLAYING; ROLE TAKING; SCENE; SELF-PRESENTATION. 4. **(dramatism)** Kenneth Burke's rhetorical approach to *language as a mode of action in the world rather than a means of conveying *information. In his **grammar of motives** he isolates five components (the **dramatistic pentad**): act (what is done), scene (the context), agent (who performs the act), agency (the means employed), and purpose (the goal of the act). This forms the basis for the *structural analysis of any kind of *text.

dream-work In *psychoanalytic theory, Freud's term for the processes through which the raw materials of dreams (fragments of recent *events and memories) are transformed into *manifest content, disguising the *latent meaning from the sleeper so that they may continue to sleep undisturbed. The primary processes involved are *condensation and *displacement.

dress code 1. Explicit rules for how people may and may not dress in a specific *context, specified by those with ownership and/or control of that location. Usually associated with 'formal dress', but including any such *code, including that for nudist beaches. 2. The unwritten cultural *codes of dress and general *appearance that reflect *norms in particular contexts. Natives of a *culture learn these through *socialization while strangers to that *culture may infer them from the behaviour of the majority of people within it.

drip 1. **(drip effect, drip-drip effect)** In theories of media *effects, the notion that the *mass media contribute towards gradual changes in the long term, either in individual *attitudes or behaviour (e.g. among *heavy viewers of television: *see*

CULTIVATION THEORY), or in the form of social changes (alongside other social forces). **2. (drip campaign)** In *advertising, a campaign in which media expenditure is stretched over a relatively long period, in contrast to *burst campaigns. This strategy is often used for 'reminder campaigns' or when the goal is to achieve longer-term *attitudinal effects.

dropout 1. An *artefact found in *analogue recording where a speck of dust gets between the tape and the recording head. This results, in audio, in a pop or crackle sound, and in video in a break in the recording which manifests as a horizontal black line visible on the screen: *compare* CONCEALMENT ERROR. 2. (*colloquial*) A person who declines to conform with the behavioural *norms of society.

Droste effect *See* MISE-EN-ABÎME.

DSAT *See* DIGITAL TRANSMISSION.

DTP *See* DESKTOP PUBLISHING.

DTT *See* DIGITAL TRANSMISSION.

dual audience In *marketing, a *target audience with two distinct subgroups requiring different strategies. For instance, children and parents, males and females, heterosexual and gay, local and international. Sometimes one of the two groups is the larger or *primary audience but the dual audience concept ensures that the *secondary audience is not neglected. *See also* TARGET AUDIENCE.

dual coding theory The hypothesis in cognitive psychology that human *memory employs two coding systems: one based on visual *imagery and the other on verbal coding.

dualism 1. Any *theory or belief based on the fundamental difference between two concepts, or categories, e.g. a religious belief in good and evil as absolutes rather than as relative: *compare* BINARISM. 2. Mind-body dualism: *see* CARTESIAN DUALISM. 3. In sociology, dichotomies such as nature versus nurture or *agency versus *structure. These are typically seen as being involved in a dialectical interaction. 4. Linguistic dualism: *see* CLOAK THEORY.

duality of patterning *See* ARTICULATION.

dub 1. In video or sound recording, an *analogue (machine to machine) copy of an analogue or *digital source. A **digital dub** is a digital copy of either an analogue source, or a digital source that is being copied to a different format: for example, an *NTSC programme that is being converted to *PAL. 2. A synonym for sound *mixing in television and film *post-production. 3. **(dubbing)** The process of using actors to re-record the dialogue *track of a film, television programme, or commercial in another language for foreign *distribution: *compare* ADR. 4. A *genre of reggae music that remixes existing recordings, typically removing the vocals and emphasizing the drums and bass.

dumbing down A pejorative term for a perceived cultural trend in which important concepts or issues are glossed-over, condensed, over-simplified, or trivialized to make them more popular or accessible to a larger (and more lucrative) audience. In relation to the *mass media, the argument is that media output is increasingly focused on *popular culture *entertainment values at the expense of more demanding *high culture content (*see also* FICTION VALUES). The phrase seems to have originated in Hollywood in the 1930s.

duopoly 1. A market in which there are only two companies. 2. The dual dominance of the BBC and ITV over UK television in the period between 1957 and 1982. Although ostensibly in *competition with each other, both corporations operated what became known as a 'cosy duopoly'. Both broadcasters were obligated to fulfil public service obligations, but such *regulation meant that they had protected and very lucrative income streams since the BBC was government-funded, leaving ITV with a commercial *monopoly. The advantage of the duopoly was that it allowed for experimental and challenging programming. The disadvantage was a lack of *pluralism (especially in programmes catering for minority audiences) and the two companies presented a closed shop to independent programme-makers.

Dutch angle shot (canted shot, oblique angle) An oblique or 'crooked' shot in which the camera is angled clockwise or anticlockwise (*see also* CANTED SHOT). Some reserve the term *Dutch angle* for *shots which in addition involve a vertical *tilt. Typically used to signify a subjective view, or to generate *connotations of disorientation or dramatic tension (*see also* DIAGONALITY). In *semiotic terms, a *marked shot.

DVD (digital video disc, digital versatile disc) An optical disc storage medium mainly used for films.

DVE *See* DIGITAL VIDEO EFFECTS.

dwindling size perspective (dwindling scale perspective, relative size) A *depth perception cue in both three-dimensional (as in real and *virtual worlds) and two-dimensional contexts (as in photographs, paintings, and films) in which objects assumed to be of comparable size but which appear smaller are assumed to be further away than others that appear larger. *See also* PERSPECTIVE; PICTORIAL DEPTH CUES; SIZE CONSTANCY; TEXTURE GRADIENT.

dyad In the study of *interpersonal communication, a basic unit of two communication partners. Communication within such a unit is termed **dyadic communication**. A communication unit with three participants is a **triad**. *See also* COMMUNICATION NETWORK.

dynamic range The difference between the quietest and loudest sounds in an audio recording.

e-book (electronic book) A digitized version of a printed book which can be read on a computer or a hand-held electronic device, or a book-length text designed to be read on a screen.

economic capital Economic resources (monetary and property assets). For the wealthy bourgeois this is 'the dominant principle of domination', transferable from generation to generation and thus effective in reproducing social *power relations over time. Sections of the dominant *class with relatively less economic capital and greater *cultural capital (e.g. professionals, academics, and artists) endeavour to establish the latter as a rival principle of domination. However, economic capital can also be converted into cultural capital at a better exchange rate than vice versa. *Compare* SOCIAL CAPITAL.

economic determinism, economic reductionism *See* ECONOMISM.

economies of scale The reduction of costs in the long term through increasing mass *production: for example, as a consequence of *diagonal integration, *horizontal integration, or *vertical integration.

economies of scope The reduction of costs in the long term when the scope of a company's activities increases: for example, as a consequence of *diagonal integration. This is possible where a product can be sold in different markets or in different forms for different media.

economism **1. (economic determinism)** Theories, such as *Marxism, in which political and historical developments, *social relations, *culture, ideas, and social consciousness are seen as determined by the underlying economic system based in the relations of *production. In an extreme version, the social consciousness of individuals is determined by their position in the economic structure, a stance which would deny free will and the role of human ideas and *agency in social change. In a more moderate version, the relations of production are merely a constraining factor. *See also* BASE AND SUPERSTRUCTURE; DETERMINISM.
2. (economic reductionism) A pejorative term for the reduction of social phenomena to economic factors. Extreme economic determinism is a prime example of such reduction, and economism is often used as a synonym for economic determinism. *See also* REDUCTIONISM.

ECU *See* BIG CLOSE-UP.

edge numbers A series of numbers printed along the edge of movie film formats that identifies sequences of *frames, performing a similar function to *timecode.

edit 1. *v. See* EDITING. 2. *n.* A specific change made to an audio- or audiovisual recording. 3. *n.* An edited version of an audio- or audiovisual recording.

edit decision list (EDL) In video *post-production, a list of instructions for re-assembling a video sequence that has been created in an offline *edit. In video an EDL consists of *timecodes; in film it consists of *edge numbers.

editing 1. Making revisions to any *text. 2. Preparing written material for publication by making corrections, stylistic amendments, making it shorter, and so on. 3. Selecting, arranging, and assembling elements of audio- or audio-visual material for recording or broadcasting. For film and video editing, *see* ASSEMBLE EDITING; ASSOCIATIVE EDITING; CONTINUITY EDITING; CROSS-CUTTING; CUT; CUTTING RATE; INSERT EDITING; LINEAR EDITING; MONTAGE; NONLINEAR EDITING; OFFLINE EDITING; ONLINE EDITING; POST-PRODUCTION; TRANSITION. 4. The job done by an *editor.

editor 1. (book publishing) A role involving the commissioning of new books and the coordination of their creation and *production. A **copy editor** checks manuscripts for errors and consistency ready for *printing. 2. In the compilation of edited books and the *production of journals, the role of coordinating the work of contributors. 3. (periodical publishing) A role involving the overall control of *content, format, and publication. 4. (film) A role involving logging, cutting, and assembling film *rushes into a presentable form (although today it is invariably done using a *nonlinear editing system). An editor usually makes decisions in close association with the *director, or sometimes the *producer. 5. In video and audio *post-production, a role that is very similar to a film editor, but using videotape or audio recordings instead of film.

editorial *Compare* ADVERTORIAL. 1. Material in *newspapers or magazines reflecting the opinions of the *editor or editorial team, generally appearing in an editorial column or on an editorial page. 2. Collectively, the non-*advertising elements of a magazine: its various subject areas (such as food and sports).

editorializing In journalism and *factual genres such as *documentary, any overt personal comments expressing an opinion or reflecting an *attitude. Typically a pejorative reference to commentary which is seen as breaching an expectation of objective reporting.

EDL *See* EDIT DECISION LIST.

educational function (instructional function) One of four basic kinds of uses of social communication listed by Schramm from the perspective of the individual, in which the normative objectives are for the *sender to teach and for the *receiver to learn. He distinguishes this from a purely *informational function. From the perspective of society, Schramm argues that this function is analogous to the function of *socialization. *See also* MEDIA FUNCTIONS; PERSONAL FUNCTIONS.

edutainment A portmanteau term (*education* + *entertainment*). A *hybrid genre such as in educational games or *videogames with an educational dimension, where forms of *entertainment are related to educational goals. Sometimes used pejoratively in the context of *dumbing down. *Compare* INFOTAINMENT.

effective frequency In *advertising, the level of *exposure of a *target audience to a medium carrying the advertiser's message during a given period that is regarded as meeting a specified objective in relation to *brand awareness, *ad retention, or consumer action. This relates to the number of times the average person within the target audience has an opportunity to be exposed to the advertising within that period.

effective reach In *advertising, the number of different individuals (or homes) with the opportunity to be exposed to the *medium carrying particular advertisements (rather than those directly exposed to the advertising itself). It is assessed in relation to a specified objective for *brand awareness, *ad retention, or consumer action. *See also* REACH.

effects 1. Any *events that predictably follow another event (or combination of events). Specific effects may be attributed to a determining cause (*see also* SUFFICIENT CONDITION) or to contributory influences (*see also* CAUSATION; DETERMINISM; NECESSARY CONDITION). 2. The outcomes of an act of communication, as in Lasswell's famous formulation in 1948 that such acts can be described in terms of 'who says what, in which channel, to whom, with what effect?' Such effects may be planned or unplanned, short-term or long-term. The study of 'the impact upon audiences' is **effect analysis**: *see* EFFECTS TRADITION. 3. In the discourse of the *effects tradition, any human behaviour or social phenomenon ascribed to the influence of the media (or *advertising). *See also* ATTITUDINAL EFFECTS; BEHAVIOURAL EFFECTS; COGNITIVE EFFECTS; HIERARCHY OF EFFECTS; INDIRECT EFFECTS; LIMITED EFFECTS THEORY; PRIMARY AND SECONDARY EFFECTS; SOCIAL EFFECTS; THIRD-PERSON EFFECTS. 4. In experimental research, consistent patterns of influence of one or more factors on another (*see* DEPENDENT AND INDEPENDENT VARIABLES). The identification of causal effects is the primary focus of *experiments.

effects, special *See* SOUND EFFECTS; SPECIAL EFFECTS.

effects tradition (effects model) A *paradigm in academic media research which focused on what was initially assumed to be the potentially major influence of the *mass media on their *audiences (*see also* HYPODERMIC MODEL). Heavily influenced by *behaviourism, it was dominant from the 1920s until the 1950s in the USA, a particular concern being with anti-social *behavioural effects (*see also* VIOLENCE DEBATE). Later research came to see any such influences as being minimal, *limited, *indirect (*see also* TWO-STEP FLOW), and subject to *selective perception. By the early 1960s attention was turning from what media did to people to what people did with media (*see* USES AND GRATIFICATIONS). Effects rhetoric continues to flourish in the ironic setting of the *tabloid press (*see also* MANIPULATIVE MODEL; MORAL PANIC). There is little doubt that both the *mass media and the mass use of technologies of interpersonal communication are inextricably linked to social change, but framing this in terms of effects neglects the

rich complexity of human *social relationships to technologies. *Compare* ACTIVE
AUDIENCE THEORY.

(⊕) SEE WEB LINKS

• Ten things wrong with the 'effects model'

ego appeals (self-esteem appeals) In *advertising, and in any persuasive
communication, a psychological and rhetorical strategy which emphasizes the
benefit of some product or course of action in terms of your *self-esteem, pride,
or vanity. It may flatter your intelligence, play on your desire for *status, challenge
you to demonstrate your strength of character, *masculinity or *femininity, and/or
encourage self-indulgence. A characteristic feature is the use of *direct address.
An example of such an appeal is L'Oréal's slogan: 'because you're worth it!'
See also ADVERTISING APPEALS.

ego involvement *See* RECEIVER FACTORS.

80/20 rule *See* POWER LAW DISTRIBUTION.

elaborated code 1. Within linguistic **deficit theory**, Bernstein's term for the
relatively formal, abstract, flexible, and extended linguistic patterns argued to be
largely limited to the language use of the middle- and upper-classes, and the
dominant mode employed in the schooling system (*see also* LOW-CONTEXT). Deficit
theory, which sees the language of the working class as limited to a more *restricted
code, has been widely contested by linguists. 2. In cultural theory, an *aesthetic
code which Fiske suggests is employed in *high culture works of art aimed at a
limited audience, which has to learn the codes needed to interpret such texts:
see NARROWCAST CODES.

elaboration (cognitive elaboration) The extent to which an individual
processes *information (or the relative amount of cognitive effort involved). This
involves restructuring *information, *arguments (or any external stimulus), and
making *inferences by relating such input to existing *knowledge or beliefs. The
likelihood of elaboration or critical thinking depends particularly on perceived
relevance. New information that is elaborated is more easily recalled than
information that is not elaborated. *See also* HIGH AND LOW INVOLVEMENT.

elaboration likelihood model (ELM) A model of *persuasion and *attitude
change in which there are two routes to persuasion: a *central route (relying on
*argument) and a *peripheral route (relying on less central factors). The model was
developed by Petty and Cacioppo. The choice of a persuasive strategy depends on
the likelihood of *receivers engaging in cognitive effort or *elaboration. The
central route is more likely to lead to longer-term attitude change, but only if
elaboration occurs.

electromagnetic spectrum A division of electromagnetic radiation into
categories distinguished by *wavelengths. The electromagnetic spectrum represents
a conventional division in a range from large to small: *radio waves, microwaves,
infrared light, visible light, ultraviolet light, X-rays, and gamma rays. Radio waves
and microwaves are used as transmission media for communications signals. A very

small percentage of the wavelengths of the electromagnetic spectrum can be seen by the human eye—the frequencies between 400 and 789 terahertz (THz) known collectively as 'visible light'. In humans, different wavelengths of visible light are perceived as different *colours. Longer wavelengths in the 400 to 600 THz range are perceived as reds and oranges while shorter wavelengths in the 600 to 789 range are perceived as blues and violets. Some insects and birds can 'see' in infrared or ultraviolet. Rock declared that 'If we had the sensory apparatus of some other of the Earth's organisms, "reality" would seem quite different.' *See also* SPECTRUM SCARCITY.

electronic book *See* E-BOOK.

electronic journalism *See* DIGITAL JOURNALISM.

electronic mail *See* EMAIL.

electronic mailing lists Any *email lists used to circulate emails to multiple recipients who have subscribed to them. Such lists include: **announcement lists** or newsletters, which are primarily for *one-way communication, and **discussion lists**, which are usually *topic-oriented and monitored by a *moderator. Past messages may be made available in online *archives.

electronic newsgathering (ENG) In television broadcasting, on-the-spot news coverage in which reports are shot and edited on location using digital equipment operated by the journalist and/or a cameraperson, and transmitted over the *internet, via satellite, or by line-of-sight microwave relays.

electronic press kit *See* VIDEO NEWS RELEASE.

electronic publishing (ePublishing) The publication of *e-books, e-journals, *e-zines, and articles in digital form online or on disc.

electronic recording (electromagnetic recording) The preservation of *information by a process of electromagnetism whereby a *signal consisting of a series of modulating voltages is fed through an electromagnet (the record head) which selectively magnetizes the ferromagnetic particles coating the surfaces of the recording medium: either audio or video tape, or a computer hard drive. These particles reproduce the same voltages when another electromagnet (the playback head) is passed over them, thereby reconstituting the signal. *See also* ANALOGUE; COMPRESSION; DIGITAL; GENERATION LOSS.

elevation 1. **(height in field)** A *pictorial depth cue whereby similar shapes of the same height which are lower in the *frame tend to appear closer to the viewer than those higher in the frame. 2. A principle identified by Goffman in visual *representation, notably in advertisements, whereby in Western society, higher physical place seems to signify higher social *status, as in magazine advertisements over several decades which he reviewed in 1976, where he found that men tended to be positioned *symbolically higher than women, signifying the subordination of women to men.

elite interpreter A pejorative term for scholars who uncritically offer their own *interpretations of a phenomenon (e.g. a *sign, *text, *code, or practice) as if it were the most reasonable interpretation—perhaps because they see themselves as particularly skilful and well-informed interpreters.

elitism 1. In relation to *culture, a typically pejorative term for the assumption that *high culture is inherently superior to *popular culture or *mass culture. Its conservative form is associated with the creation and maintenance of a *canon of 'great works' and its radical elements with the avant-garde. In either case, it champions what it defines as artistic, intellectual, and creative excellence, and the aesthetic value of 'discrimination' with which it associates itself. 2. In political theory, a political system based on rule by a minority, or a belief in such systems (**elite theory**).

ellipsis (*pl.* **ellipses**) 1. (**syntactic ellipsis**) In *grammar and *rhetoric, the deliberate omission of part of a grammatically complete sentence (or three dots indicating such an omission in writing). It is an important device in grammatical *cohesion. It permeates everyday speech, where *redundancy usually enables the listener to fill in the gaps by *inference and reference to *context, but in writing it can produce a *telegraphic style (as in newspaper headlines), and it is avoided in legal *contracts to avoid *ambiguity: *see also* ANAPHORA. 2. In philosophy, a fallacious *argument from a premise directly to a conclusion. 3. Loosely, in any form of *representation, an omission: *see also* DELETION. 4. In *narratology, an implicit or explicit gap in the temporal *representation of sequential *events; in film, usually signified by a *cut (or other *transition).

ELM *See* ELABORATION LIKELIHOOD MODEL.

email (electronic mail) 1. A software application which allows users to communicate through typed messages, sent from computer to computer over the *internet. The first email system appeared in 1965, linking users of the same mainframe computer. 2. A form of electronic mail which could be sent to different computers over ARPAnet, devised in 1971 by the computer programmer Ray Tomlinson (b.1941). Notable for its use of the '@' symbol separating a sender's name and their location. 3. A form of *interpersonal, *group, and *mass communication characterized by being text-based, instantaneous, and *asynchronous. Unlike postal mail, there is normally no delay between sending and receiving, and unlike a *telephone call, the sender and receiver do not have to be temporally *co-present. *See also* ELECTRONIC MAILING LISTS; *compare* POST; SNAIL MAIL.

embargo A formal request not to publish or broadcast particular information before a specified date. Embargoes are used by governments and corporations to control the timing of news and for marketing purposes where media products are made available to reviewers in advance of their release, but with penalties attached for breaking the embargo.

embedded reporters Journalists assigned to specific military units during armed conflicts. The term arose from a strategy devised by the Pentagon in 2002 which reflected changing conditions in war reporting, including: the impact of new technologies, increased risks to reporters, and more sophisticated media manipulation by government. Research has found that embedding does not affect the overall impartiality of reports, although some studies detect a more pro-military tone. While there is no lack of *information, critics have argued that the perspective of reporters is severely narrowed, foregrounding the *spectacle of war and overlooking wider *contexts.

(((()))) SEE WEB LINKS

• Embedded reporters

emblems 1. Visual images of objects or patterns representing abstract concepts or specific organizations and taking the form of distinctive badges or *logos. Today's emblems are found in corporate logos, for example the Mercedes three-pointed star and the Nike 'swoosh'. 2. Broadly, in *nonverbal communication, *gestures, usually in the form of hand-movements, defined functionally as having a direct verbal translation and as intentional *signals. One of five types of nonverbal acts according to Ekman and Friesen (the others being *adaptors, *affect displays, *illustrators, and *regulators). In the USA in 1975, emblems performed and interpreted in a similar way by 100% of encoders and decoders and regarded by them as 'natural' signified the following: sit down beside me; be silent; come here; I can't hear you; wait; screw you (finger); OK; no, or I disagree (head); I don't know; yes, or I agree, or I like it; woman or nice figure; you (finger point); me (own chest). 3. **(symbolic gestures)** In more restricted usage, gestures defined in relation to *form rather than *function, being distinguished (by some) from *illustrators as not resembling their *referents: as *symbolic rather than *iconic forms.

emergence A process where complex forms are generated at first by the ordering of simple objects into patterns which then reach a higher level where they start to order the original patterns of objects, producing nested patterns. This jumping across levels and successive ordering continues until forms are created which consist of multiple iterations of the same basic pattern reproduced at many different scales: for example, fern leaves. Like the theory of evolution, emergence explains how complexity can arise through simple *bottom-up processes. A variation of it is applied in the design and business models of *new media forms such as Wikipedia, Linkedin, and Second Life as a strategy for allowing *user-generated content to organize itself.

emergent code A synonym for Williams's concept of an *emergent form. Adopted as a concept in *marketing trend-spotting referring to as yet loosely-defined *values, *styles, and fashions, some of which may be perceived as subversive, which compete to be among those which may eventually become dominant. *See also* DOMINANT CODE; RESIDUAL CODE.

emergent forms (emergent formations) Williams's term for one of three categories of cultural forms or *codes that coexist within a society at any particular moment in history, the emergent form reflecting new subcultural *institutions, traditions, *styles, movements, social forces, *values, practices, and *identities (though it can be difficult to distinguish what is genuinely emergent from what is merely novel). Emergent subcultures express *structures of feeling that may be neglected, ignored, marginalized, denied, opposed, repressed, or not even recognized by the dominant culture, which nevertheless selectively incorporates aspects of these *subcultures in order to maintain its *hegemony. He also refers to **pre-emergent** forms that have not yet fully taken shape. *See also* CULTURAL MATERIALISM; DOMINANT FORMS; RESIDUAL FORMS.

emic and etic *adj.* 1. (*linguistics) Terms derived from *phonemic* and *phonetic* referring to different approaches to the study of linguistic data (*see also* PHONEME). An **emic** approach is based on the linguist's framework of functional relationships; an **etic** approach is based on the objective *description of the physical patterns of language. 2. (anthropology and sociology) **Emic** approaches are those based on the description of the *frames of reference of insiders within a culture; **etic** approaches are those based on the observer's application of broader theoretical models (an outsider's view). Emic concepts are not always easy to translate into etic constructs.

emoticon (smiley) A portmanteau word (*emotion* + *icon*). A kind of image originally based purely on *ASCII characters representing a simplified face turned on its side and with an expression such as smiling or frowning. Originally used in *email messages, which as a medium of relative *cuelessness sometimes leads to the misinterpretation of the sender's mood. In informal messages, a smiley emoticon, for instance, helps to indicate that the writer is in a good mood. Textual emoticons are also used in *SMS text messages on *mobile phones. The term has additionally come to be applied to the corresponding visual images automatically generated by the use of standard textual emoticons in online environments such as *instant messaging systems and online *chatrooms.

emotion An imprecise term for any affective psychological state, including happiness, sadness, anger, disgust, surprise, and fear (*see also* AFFECT). Some theorists suggest that emotions can be interpreted in terms of *evaluation. The reason that everyday language lists hundreds of emotions may be that any given emotional state may be experienced as if it were a different emotion depending on the situational *context giving rise to it. The conventional distinction between emotion and reason depends on *Cartesian dualism—emotion and reason are often intermingled in human experience. The Freudian metaphor of emotion as a safety valve for the individual has little currency outside *individualistic cultures. Some sociologists have argued that emotions may at least in part be socially constructed. Goffman argues that they function as ritual 'moves' in *interaction (*see also* INTERACTION RITUAL; RITUAL INTERACTION).

emotional appeals In persuasive communication such as *advertising and political communication, rhetorical strategies intended to evoke feelings in the audience. This can include the use of humour or nostalgia, the evocation of personal pride, love for one's family and children, patriotism, and even sexual *arousal. Such 'positive' emotional appeals are deployed in order to develop bonding between the audience and a brand, individual, or political party. However, emotional appeals may be negative as well as positive: they include *fear appeals and *guilt appeals. Shock tactics are often employed in health and safety campaigns.

Emotional appeals in audio-visual media are based primarily on *visual imagery, *connotation, and music rather than *information or *argument (*see also* PERIPHERAL ROUTE). Advertisers' choices between emotional and *rational appeals is influenced by whether the product or service is seen as being likely to entail high or low affective or cognitive involvement (*see also* ELABORATION LIKELIHOOD MODEL). Bread, for instance, may be seen as involving high affective involvement but low cognitive involvement, and advertisers may choose to employ emotional appeals (such as the appeal to nostalgia in Hovis ads). *See also* AFFECTIVE COMMUNICATION; HIGH AND LOW INVOLVEMENT; PERSONALIZED FORMAT; SOFT SELL.

emotional expressions *See* AFFECT DISPLAYS.

emotional realism A representational quality in a *narrative that is felt to be 'true-to-life' by audiences in terms of the enactment of recognizable subjective experiences. The cultural theorist Ien Ang (b.1954) suggests that for some viewers, watching a *soap opera involves this kind of psychological *realism, perhaps in part because long-running serials give viewers a chance to develop a form of parasocial relationship with the characters (*see* PARASOCIAL INTERACTION), of whom we are often offered *close-up shots focusing on their *facial expressions. For Ang, emotional realism depends on *connotation more than *denotation. Even if at the level of content the treatment is unrealistic, what is recognized as real is **truth to feeling**. For many viewers of the glamorous, melodramatic, and (many would say) unrealistic US soap opera *Dallas* (1978–91), this was a tragic *structure of feeling, evoking the idea that happiness is precarious. *See also* CLASSIC REALIST TEXT; REALISM; SOCIAL REALISM.

emotive function *See* EXPRESSIVE FUNCTION.

emotive language *See* EXPRESSIVE COMMUNICATION.

empathy (*adj.* **empathic**) 1. The capacity to understand another person's feelings or to experience something from their point of view in a particular situation. 2. A mode of psychological involvement (sometimes termed a form of *identification) with a particular person, creature, or even an inanimate object (such as a doll)—either directly observed in the world, or represented in any medium (such as in a novel or a film). It is characterized by the observer, reader, or listener having some physical sensations almost as if they were experiencing the world for a short while as the entity with which they are empathizing. When thoroughly absorbed in contemplating such phenomena, we may even engage in mimicry, such as when our muscles involuntarily respond to watching a dancer or a soaring bird, or when we hold our breath along with a hiding victim in a film thriller. The term was introduced into English by the psychologist Edward B. Titchener (1867–1927) as a translation of the German word *Einfühlung* ('feeling-into'). Brecht's use of the *alienation effect is intended to inhibit both empathy and *sympathy on the part of the audience towards the *protagonists in order to encourage a critical attitude towards the represented social realities.

empty signifier (**floating signifier**) (*semiotics) Variously defined as a *signifier with a vague, highly variable, unspecifiable, or non-existent *signified.

Such signifiers mean different things to different people: they may stand for many or even any signifieds; they may mean whatever their interpreters want them to mean. Those who posit the existence of such signifiers argue that there is a radical disconnection between signifier and signified (*see also* POSTSTRUCTURALISM). For a Saussurean semiotician no signifier can exist without a corresponding signified—to qualify as a *sign something must be signified.

encoder 1. In communication theory, the producer of *texts or *messages, both in *interpersonal and *mass communication—a term that alludes to the role of *codes and which is therefore frequently associated with *semiotic discourse: *compare* ADDRESSER; SENDER. 2. A technical device such as an **analogue-to-digital converter** or a **digital-to-analogue converter**. *See* DECODER.

encoder skills *See* SENDER SKILLS.

encoding (opposite of **decoding**) 1. In *interpersonal and *mass communication, the process of producing *messages by adapting to the *affordances of the *medium, together with any relevant *genres and *discourse *conventions (such as *register), drawing upon appropriate *textual and *social codes likely to be shared by the intended *decoders, bearing in mind appropriate *communicative relationships, and in *face-to-face interaction framing communication within the specific *context in which it takes place. Thus, not only are messages encoded, but also the *values, beliefs, and assumptions of the encoders. 2. In some *semiotic discourse, the perceptual process of making sense of reality: *see also* PERCEPTUAL CODES. 3. The process of converting *information systematically into another form using a *code (*see* ANALOGUE; DIGITAL). 4. In cognitive psychology, the transformation of an external stimulus into an internal *representation. Four stages have been postulated: preattentive analysis (combining features into recognizable objects), focal *attention (conscious representation), *comprehension, and *elaboration. *See also* MENTAL REPRESENTATION.

encoding/decoding model 1. **(semiotic model)** Any *model representing communication as a process of *encoding and decoding *messages. In *information theory, the coding involved is a technical process, but semioticians underline the importance of the *production and *interpretation of *messages/*texts within relevant *textual and *social codes. The centrality of *codes to communication is a distinctive semiotic contribution which emphasizes the social nature of communication and the importance of *conventions (though *context is seen as equally important in *Jakobson's model). Such codes are expected to be largely shared by the participants. 2. Stuart Hall's model of *mass communication, also called the *circuit of communication (1980). In the context of the *production and reception of television news and current affairs programmes, Hall argued that *events had to be encoded into *televisual stories reflecting an *intended meaning. The apparent naturalness of television *codes disguises their *ideological potential. However *transparent such codes may seem to be, they are rich in *connotations and require decoding (*interpretation). In order to make sense of what we are seeing and hearing, we unconsciously draw on *common sense (i.e. what we have in common with those employing such codes) to establish the *preferred meaning. Insofar as we accept such *framings, we adopt a **hegemonic reading**. However, Hall rejected *textual determinism, noting that decodings do not follow inevitably from encodings. He outlined two less compliant stances: *negotiated reading and *oppositional reading, which could be argued to be a form of re-coding. They are linked to such reception factors as *class, *gender, *ethnicity, *interpretive repertoires, and *context.

((⊕)) SEE WEB LINKS

• Encoding/decoding

enculturation *See* SOCIALIZATION.

endorsement 1. In *advertising, the use of personalities lending their support to the product or service, either by explicitly indicating that they approve of it, and/or implicitly by their mere presence. This persuasive strategy may operate through increasing *source credibility or through *meaning transfer. Endorsers include not only celebrities (**celebrity endorsement**) and experts but also typical users from the *target audience with whom the consumer may be expected to identify, and anonymous models who are likely to be perceived as being aspirational. *See also* IDENTIFICATION. 2. A 'seal of approval' for a product or service from some relevant third-party organization.

ENG *See* ELECTRONIC NEWSGATHERING.

engineering of consent *See* MANUFACTURE OF CONSENT.

enigma code *See* HERMENEUTIC CODE.

Enlightenment (Age of Enlightenment, Age of Reason) A period of ferment in European intellectual history often seen as beginning at some point in the second half of the 17th century and extending through the 18th century to the period of the French Revolution (1789–99). It is widely regarded as the foundation of modern Western intellectual culture, most clearly marked by the radical questioning of traditional modes of thought and authority, the growth of secularism, the rejection of religious dogma and superstition, a belief in social progress through the pursuit of reason and science, and an emphasis on individual freedom of expression. Habermas sees the Enlightenment as witnessing the rise of the (bourgeois) public sphere (*see* PUBLIC AND PRIVATE SPHERES). Freedom of opinion was, of course, for intellectuals (in such places as the coffeehouses and the Republic of Letters) rather than for 'the populace'. Nevertheless, the French and American revolutions and the abolition of slavery had their philosophical roots in Enlightenment principles of equality and natural rights. This was the era of the compilation of the first modern encyclopaedias, demonstrating the thirst for *knowledge and understanding based on the triumph of rational thought. **Post-Enlightenment** thinking by *poststructuralists and *postmodernists since the Second World War has reflected intellectual disquiet in particular over the legacy of overconfidence in reason, progress, and universal truths (e.g. Foucault, Lyotard). *Marxist theorists (Adorno, Horkheimer) have argued that Enlightenment reason has been reduced to *instrumental reason and rationalization in *mass society (*see also* FRANKFURT

SCHOOL; RATIONALIZATION). *Postcolonialism critiques its *Eurocentrism. *See also* POSTMODERNITY.

énonciation (enunciation) Broadly, where an **énoncé** is an *utterance, énonciation is the act of uttering it. Saussure chose to ignore the circumstances of enunciation (*see* LANGUE AND PAROLE) but in *structuralist linguistic theory, enunciation refers specifically to the aspect of an utterance which addresses and positions its *receivers (*see* POSITIONING). In *realist texts the act of enunciation is backgrounded: for instance, Metz argued that *realist cinematic *modes of address mask their own enunciation, implying no *addresser or addressee.

entertainment function A function of both *interpersonal and *mass communication in which the *sender seeks to please and the *receiver is expected to enjoy. For Schramm, entertainment is one of the key functions of communication from the point of view of the individual (others call this a **diversion function**), and also viewed socially (*see also* SOCIAL FUNCTIONS). In relation to *mass communication, entertainment can be seen as a function of media use (*see also* MEDIA FUNCTIONS): it is widely listed as one of the *uses and gratifications of media use for users. One of the objectives of the *mass media is to entertain, while the related objectives of the individual include enjoyment, relaxation (*see also* CATHARSIS), and escape. Unlike other functions, Schramm notes, entertainment requires a certain 'willing *suspension of disbelief'. For the *Frankfurt school, this was akin to political passivity, and Adorno argued that the real function of *mass-media entertainment was to subdue the working-class. From another perspective, the entertainment function can be seen to be analogous to the aesthetic function (*see* AESTHETIC CODES) featured in other framings of *communicative functions, an analogy which flouts the distinction between *high culture and *popular culture.

environmental determinism *See* SOCIAL DETERMINISM.

environmental uses (Lull) *See* STRUCTURAL USES.

episode 1. One of the instalments of a broadcast *serial. 2. One of a series of related *events. 3. **(social episode)** In social psychology and sociology, a basic temporal unit of social *interaction taking the form of a number of recurrent and familiar situational activities with relatively predictable patterns about which members of a *culture share various *conventions and which can be seen as the building blocks of social life. *See also* CONTEXT OF SITUATION; INTERCHANGE; SCRIPTS.

episodic *adj.* 1. Occurring or presented in *episodes. 2. The structure of a *narrative that is composed of a series of incidents: for example, the film *Citizen Kane* (1941). 3. A pejorative term for a *plot that has relatively little continuity or dramatic logic, so that *events seem unrelated even at the end. 4. Occurring at irregular intervals.

épistème Foucault's term for the total set of relations within a particular historical period uniting the *discursive practices which generate its *epistemologies. *See also* DISCOURSE; DISCURSIVE FORMATION; *compare* PARADIGM.

epistemic community (epistemological community) *Compare* IMAGINED COMMUNITY; INTERPRETIVE COMMUNITY; VIRTUAL COMMUNITY. **1.** A group of people with shared *knowledge, expertise, beliefs, or ways of looking at the world: for example, 'the scientific community', a group of professional specialists, or a school of thought. Those who share a disciplinary *paradigm in the Kuhnian sense or are subject to the same Foucauldian *épistème, though note that neither Kuhn nor Foucault use the term *epistemic community*. *Compare* INTERPRETIVE COMMUNITY. **2.** In political contexts, technical specialists who influence policy-making by decision-makers; here, epistemic communities are sometimes distinguished from **interest groups** (in the sense of issue-oriented groups with an agenda, such as environmentalists). **3. Communities of interest**: loosely, any group with shared interests or identities. The *internet has created a global infrastructure particularly well suited to the development and maintenance of specialized communities of interest, including stigmatized groups constituted by *difference: *see* DEMARGINALIZATION.

epistemological community *See* EPISTEMIC COMMUNITY.

epistemology (*adj.* **epistemological**) A branch of philosophy concerned with the theory of *knowledge. The term refers to how the world can be known and what can be known about it. *Realism, *idealism, and *constructionism are all epistemological stances regarding what is 'real'. Epistemologies embody *ontological assumptions (*see* ONTOLOGY). Kuhn referred to scientific communities which were characterized by shared *texts, *interpretations, and beliefs: these are sometimes referred to as *epistemic communities (*see also* PARADIGM).

EPK (electronic press kit) *See* VIDEO NEWS RELEASE.

ePublishing *See* ELECTRONIC PUBLISHING.

ergodic *adj.* [Greek *ergon* 'work', *hodos* 'path'] The conscious effort the reader/player exerts to navigate, influence, or produce *events that would simply be told or shown in the context of a story or play. A means of distinguishing *hypertext fictions or *videogames from traditional *narratives by focusing the analysis on the activity that produces the narrative rather than regarding its existence prior to *interpretation as a self-evident *fact (Aarseth).

escapism A typically pejorative term for behaviour perceived as a retreat from the problems, routines, and tensions of everyday reality by seeking distraction or relaxation in entertainment or fantasy (*see also* CATHARSIS). The term was first recorded in 1933. Schramm lists **escape** as one manifestation of the *entertainment function of (mass) communication (*see also* DIVERSION FUNCTION). For the *Frankfurt school, the entertainment function of the mass media was reducible to escapism: Adorno argued that it diverted the working class from thinking about their oppression.

essentialism **1.** (philosophy) The view that certain key concepts (or, in *semiotics, *signifieds) are distinct, autonomous entities which have an objective existence and essential properties and which are definable in terms of some kind of absolute, universal, and transhistorical 'essence'. These concepts (such as reality, truth, *meaning, *facts, mind, consciousness, nature, beauty, justice, freedom) are granted an *ontological status in which they exist 'prior to' *language (*see* FOUNDATIONALISM). Essentialism is a form of *idealism. **2.** A belief about human nature. In relation to people, the term refers to the stance that human beings have an inherent, unchanging, and distinctive nature which can be 'discovered'. To say this of women or men is *biological or *gender essentialism. **3.** Beliefs about the individual. The stance known as humanism (which is deeply embedded in Western culture) is essentialist, based on the assumption that the individual has an 'inner self' (a secular version of a 'soul' consisting of 'personality', *attitudes, and opinions) which is stable, coherent, consistent, unified, and autonomous and which determines our behaviour. Bourgeois *ideology is essentialist in characterizing society in terms of 'free' individuals whose pre-given essences include 'talent', 'efficiency', 'laziness', or 'profligacy'. **4. Anti-essentialists** such as *relativists and *structuralist and *poststructuralist semioticians deny that things have essential properties which are independent of our ways of defining and classifying them—they emphasize the contingency of concepts (in particular the sociocultural and historical *contexts). For *constructionists many *signifieds which *common sense regards as having essential properties are socially constructed. 'Nature vs nurture' debates reflect essentialist vs constructionist positions. *Materialism is an anti-essentialist position which counters essentialist abstraction and *reification with a focus on the material conditions of lived existence.

establishing shot (orientation shot, cover shot, opening shot) In film or video *editing, the opening *shot (or shots) of a *sequence (notably, at the start of a *scene), which establishes the time, location, and sometimes also the mood. Such shots are usually *long-shots, *tracks, *pans, or *zooms that indicate a wider *context, although a *close-up can also be used: for example, a café sign. In science fiction and fantasy *genres, whole sequences can be regarded as establishing shots since they serve an expository function of introducing an unfamiliar storyworld to the viewer. But other genres also use sequences for this purpose: for example, the exterior of a building is typically followed by a shot inside that building. **Re-establishing shots** are sometimes used later in the sequence as reminders. *See also* GENERAL VIEWS.

estrangement *See* DEFAMILIARIZATION.

ethics *See* MEDIA ETHICS.

ethnic **1.** In anthropology, a term used since the mid 19th century to refer to social grouping based on both physical and cultural characteristics. **2.** From the 1930s, a euphemism for racial difference. **3.** Having shared national, linguistic, or cultural traditions. **4.** Identified by birth, descent, or kinship rather than current nationality. **5.** An *ethnocentric reference to *otherness, as in colloquial usage by those within a dominant *culture, in which it serves to label those whose ways seem foreign or whose skin-colour is different from their own.

ethnic identity A distinctive *identity felt, shared, or claimed by individuals or a group, or ascribed to them, based on shared characteristics associated with a definition in terms of *ethnicity and forming the basis for their *subcultural and/or political differentiation from other groups in a society. A *salient aspect of identity for individuals from ethnic minorities.

ethnicity 1. A *cultural identity (usually that of a *subcultural minority) defined in terms of shared traits, variously including *race, ancestry, country of origin, skin colour, religion, *language, traditional culture, and shared customs. Sometimes associated with particular regions of a country. Often a basis for nationalism or the oppression of minorities. 2. In general usage, a euphemism for racial difference, though social scientists note that ethnicity has no necessary relation to *race. 3. For Stuart Hall, a 'project' in which we are all positioned in relation to history, *language, and *culture, in the process of the construction of our *subjectivity and *identity.

ethnic stereotypes *Representations of a group identified by an *ethnic label (such as Jews) which reproduce the most frequently represented traits associated with such groups. *Selective perception or *salience tends to reinforce such stereotypes by drawing attention to examples confirming it and blinding the observer to individual differences. So too does the *imagery of *mass-media *entertainment genres. In popular usage, *ethnicity is a euphemism for *race, and such stereotypes are often *racial stereotypes (*see also* RACISM; STEREOTYPING).

ethnocentrism *Compare* EUROCENTRISM; RACISM; STEREOTYPING. 1. A form of *observer bias in relation to other ethnic groups, *cultures, societies, or nations which (typically unconsciously) reflects embedded assumptions and criteria derived from the observer's own culture (*see also* COMMON SENSE). This may imply negative *value judgements or the inferiority of that culture: for example, a Western tendency to assume that *consumer culture and Western conceptions of democracy represent some kind of ideal for the rest of the world. Anthropologists and sociologists seek to avoid ethnocentrism, but overzealous avoidance of ethnocentrism can be criticized as *cultural relativism. *See also* EUROCENTRISM. 2. Prejudice or mistrust within a cultural group regarding outsiders. An insular tendency to look inwards towards the *norms of the group and to cast issues in terms of 'us vs them'. This functions to bolster the *identity and solidarity of the group. *See also* GROUP IDENTIFICATION; IN-GROUP. 3. A personality trait associated with authoritarianism, dogmatism, and political and economic conservatism, in which hostility towards one 'out-group' tends to be projected onto other groups. It is analogous to egocentrism.

ethnography 1. Academic fieldwork involving direct, detailed, and relatively long-term observation of social life and *culture in a particular social system. A key *qualitative research method in anthropology (with which it is almost synonymous) and sociology. It seeks to study cultures 'from within' using *participant observation. In addition to direct observation, ethnographic studies derive information from informants by using *interviews, group discussion, diaries, written documents, pictures, and other sources. It often involves the use of audio- and/or video-recording, which are then transcribed. 2. The written *description and analysis produced by such fieldwork and observation. This seeks to provide an account of activities and *meanings from the perspectives of members of the culture being studied and includes verbatim quotations from informants (*see also* EMIC AND ETIC). In order to avoid forms of *observer bias such as *ethnocentrism, such texts should show evidence of *reflexivity on the part of the researcher.

ethnomethodology In sociology, the study, initiated by the American sociologist Harold Garfinkel (b.1917), of the implicit *common-sense *knowledge and reasoning employed in the mundane routines or *interaction rituals of *everyday life that people tend to take for granted (*see also* NATURAL ATTITUDE). This forms a basis for exploring how social reality is constructed and maintained by individuals in social *interaction (though it ignores the issue of what kinds of realities are produced). Since common-sense knowledge is largely *tacit knowledge, this approach employs techniques designed to elicit it. One of these consists of the use of **breaching experiments,** in which researchers deliberately breach a conventional *expectation in an everyday routine, the most famous example being when Garfinkel instructed his students to go home and behave as if they were lodgers. Another strategy was to get informants to ask the advice of a 'psychotherapist' to which the answers were restricted to 'yes' or 'no'. They were required to interpret these answers before asking for further advice. The best-known ethnomethodological technique, however, is *conversation analysis. These methods are used in order to reveal the shared understandings on which social life depends. Two key concepts are that meaning is *indexical (dependent on *context), and that conversations constitute the situations to which they relate (*see also* REFLEXIVITY). *See also* INTERPRETIVISM; MICROSOCIOLOGY; QUALITATIVE RESEARCH; RECIPROCITY; RITUAL INTERACTION; SOCIAL NORMS; *compare* DISCOURSE ANALYSIS; PHENOMENOLOGY; SYMBOLIC INTERACTIONISM.

etic *See* EMIC AND ETIC.

etymological fallacy The view that the linguistic roots of a word determine its correct *meaning. Linguists argue that the meaning of a word has to be established from its current usage.

Eurocentrism A *bias in which European cultural perspectives are privileged (often unconsciously, as if it were *common sense) over others. *Postcolonialism has exposed many of the ways in which such biases are manifested. *See also* ETHNOCENTRISM.

evaluation 1. The (value) judgement of whether something is good or bad, or of how good or bad it is. This was the basis of *Leavisite academic criticism of literary *texts, and the elevation of certain texts to the *canon. Such approaches have largely been rejected on the basis of their *subjectivity and *ideological bias. 2. The attachment of *emotion or a point of view to *meaning. *Description is rarely, if ever, free of evaluation or *subjectivity (nor *denotation of *connotation); *see also* LOADED LANGUAGE. *Ideological analysis of *discourse is alert to such usage. It is arguable whether even *perception is at any stage free of evaluative *interpretation: *see also* VALUE. 3. A feeling of *liking (**positive evaluation**) or disliking (**negative evaluation**). In *communication, this is one of the main kinds of interpersonal *attitudes that may be reflected in or inferred from *nonverbal behaviour (*see also* AFFILIATION). Goffman notes that mutual evaluation is noticeable in the smallest details of *face-to-face interaction. In *mass media research, evaluation might refer to a viewer or listener's evaluation of a fictional character (as in Livingstone's research into viewers of the UK television soap opera *Coronation Street* (1960–) or to the positive evaluation associated with the attractiveness or likeability of the *source in *advertising *endorsement. In Osgood's *semantic differential, this is one of the three dimensions hypothesized to be universal in the *connotational dimensions of verbal meaning. **4.** The judgement of *modality in relation to the *content of a text: e.g. assessment of whether a *representation or *genre is *factual or *fictional, or whether some depicted phenomenon is possible or plausible, *live or recorded, staged or not. *See also* PERCEIVED REALITY. **5.** The formal assessment of the worth or *value of some project or service, and/or the extent to which it has met specified goals, often in response to a policy of accountability. **6. Summative evaluation**: retrospective testing of the effectiveness of some product or procedure. **7. Formative evaluation**: a trial of some product or procedure to establish whether and how it could be improved. **8.** Normative evaluation: a comparative method of assessing the quantitative results of the formative or summative evaluation of a product or procedure with reference to the results for comparable products or procedures. **9. Criteria-referenced evaluation:** a method of assessing the quantitative results of the formative or summative evaluation of a product or procedure with reference to specific benchmarks reflecting *expectations for performance.

event **1.** Any phenomenon experienced within some framework as an incident of change which has a beginning (and usually an end). From a *constructionist perspective, any 'event' is a social construction—bounded 'events' have no objective existence. Furthermore, the frameworks within which events are defined as such are frequently implicit, masking the *subjectivity of such definitions. **2.** (*narratology) An action or happening reflecting a change of state in *narrative *discourse: *compare* EPISODE. **3.** (news journalism) An occurrence judged to have *newsworthiness as part of a 'story' (Galtung and Ruge). For the viewer of television news, such events are contextually framed by the flow of the news programme. *See also* J-CURVE. **4.** A major happening featured in the *mass media (*see* MEDIA EVENTS; PSEUDO-EVENT). **5.** For Lyotard, a major cultural turning-point that transforms people's perspectives, examples being the revelations about Auschwitz and the Paris riots of 1968. **6.** (philosophy) Any occurrence, change, happening, or *episode, regardless of its importance. There is disagreement about whether events can be described in different ways and remain the same events, or whether they are more like *facts which are dependent on the concepts framing them. One event may have the *effect of causing another.

everyday life *See also* LIVED EXPERIENCE. **1.** Daily activities in the social world, and the field of enquiry for which this forms a focus. **2.** The realm of social life, the traditional focus of anthropology and *ethnography, applied to everyday actions and *social relations in our own familiar *cultures as well as others. **3. (lifeworld)** The mundane world with which we are familiar and which we ordinarily take for granted as our paramount reality: the key focus for *phenomenological sociology, as for Schutz, Peter Berger, and Luckmann: *see also* NATURAL ATTITUDE.

4. (*ethnomethodology) The world of mundane routines in which individuals interact and unconsciously participate in the construction and maintenance of intersubjective reality: *see* INTERSUBJECTIVITY. **5.** In *symbolic interactionism, the world of *face-to-face interaction, the workings of which form the focus of this approach: *see also* DRAMATURGY. **6.** For the French sociologist Henri Lefebvre (1901–91) and for de Certeau, the focus for the creative 'tactics' or 'ways of operating' in the generic daily activities of 'very ordinary culture' such as talking, working, eating, and drinking. **7.** The focus for *critical theories which seek to explain how social practices are constrained by and/or resist powerful *social structures and *institutions: *see* IDEOLOGY.

exchange theory (social exchange theory, SET) **1.** Most broadly, the argument that most social *interaction is based on the *expectation that actions directed towards others will receive a commensurate response and create reciprocal relationships (*see also* RECIPROCITY). 'All contacts among men rest on the schema of giving and returning the equivalence' (Simmel). Without this, *social relationships are destabilized. Communication can be seen as such an exchange system. **2.** In rational choice theory, an individualistic and transactional model of social *interaction (primarily for *dyads) as the exchange of social or symbolic resources with others based on the rational calculation of costs and the maximization of rewards (an aspect of **rational choice theory**). This concept is most associated with the American sociologist G. C. Homans (1910–89) and the Austrian-American sociologist P. Blau (1918–2002). **3.** A European collectivistic model of the *interaction between individuals and larger social collectivities based on shared *values, *cooperation, trust, and loyalty rather than on self-interest. The French sociologist Marcel Mauss (1872–1950) sees **gift exchange** as the basis of social solidarity (*see also* RECIPROCITY). Lévi-Strauss sees the exchange of women as marriage partners as the origin of kinship systems; in his *structuralist perspective, the exchange of women is controversially presented as a form of communication.

exchange value *See* COMMODIFICATION; COMMODITY.

exclusion *See* MARGINALIZATION.

executive producer In film and broadcasting, the role of procuring and disseminating *production funds. Occasionally, a 'vanity title' given to a star performer, or prominent financier.

exegesis (*adj.* **exegetic** or **exegetical**) Critical *interpretation or explanation of a *text, traditionally associated with religious scriptures, but now used with reference to close readings and analyses of any text.

exhibitionism *See* VOYEURISM.

exnomination Barthes' term for the phenomenon whereby the bourgeoisie hides its name (and identity) by not referring to itself as such in order to naturalize bourgeois *ideology and maintain its *hegemony, representing itself, for instance, as the nation (*see* NATURALIZATION). Similarly, as Dyer has shown, whiteness has been exnominated or made invisible in Western culture so that it becomes simply the *norm (*see also* RACISM). Dominant groups still frequently present themselves as beyond naming in relation to aspects of *identity: in many contexts, white, male, and heterosexual 'go without saying'. The *markedness of '*small talk' as that of women reflects the exnomination (unmarkedness) of men's talk.

exoticism A romanticization, *fetishization, and/or *commodification of *ethnic, racial, or cultural *otherness, as in orientalism, or primitivizing *representations of the 'noble savage'. *Ethnocentric *stereotyping (as in *Eurocentric views of non-European *cultures), in which the *other is marked by *difference (*see* MARKEDNESS). In *post-colonial theory, this is identified as a form of *objectification, *marginalization, domination, oppression, and exploitation.

expectations 1. **(expectancy effect)** A *top-down factor in *perception generated by particular *contexts and/or *purposes that contributes to the relative *salience of *data: *see also* CONTEXTUAL EXPECTATIONS; PERCEPTUAL SET. 2. **Social expectations theory**: shared cultural expectations about *norms, sanctions, *roles, and rankings for routine social *interactions in various *contexts. DeFleur argues that *mass-media *socialization has a function in the development of such expectations, and in this way has an indirect and long-term influence on behaviour. 3. In *communicative relationships, *see* CONTRACT. 4. In *reception theory, *see* HORIZON OF EXPECTATIONS.

( ) SEE WEB LINKS

• Contexts and expectations

experiment A scientific research method for testing a *hypothesis about cause-and-effect relationships between variables (*see also* CAUSATION; DEPENDENT AND INDEPENDENT VARIABLES). The basic form compares two groups which are as similar as possible both demographically (*see* DEMOGRAPHIC VARIABLES) and in relation to any factors likely to have any bearing on the study. The **experimental group** is exposed to a condition that is hypothesized to have some causal effect (such as watching a violent film-clip). The **control group** is not, so that they act as a baseline with which to compare the results from the experimental group. The attitudes and/or behaviour of the two groups are subsequently assessed. If the results differ between the groups, then it may be concluded that the difference is caused by the varying conditions, but the **external validity** of this conclusion is dependent on a number of factors such as the size of the groups, the length of time they are studied, and the attention paid to *context. The **internal validity** of an experiment is the extent to which causal conclusions may be biased by the research method, the *context, or the sample (*see* SAMPLING). Experimental studies are designed to be repeatable for purposes of verification.

explicit meaning The *literal or *denotative meaning of a *text or *utterance. Most theorists would question whether such *meaning can ever be wholly explicit, arguing that to interpret a *message requires the user to 'go beyond the information given' (Bruner), drawing on *social and *textual knowledge, and bearing in mind the *context. *See also* ELABORATED CODE; LOW-CONTEXT; *compare* IMPLICIT MEANING.

exposition [Latin *exposition* 'setting forth'] 1. In modern *rhetoric, *discourse which is intended to inform an audience about something or to explain it to them (*see also* INFORMATIONAL COMMUNICATION; INFORMATION FUNCTION). One of the four rhetorical modes of discourse identified by Brooks and Warren as fulfilling basic human *communicative purposes (*see also* ARGUMENT; DESCRIPTION; NARRATION). 2. The first phase in *classical narrative structure, presenting circumstances preceding the action of the *narrative. 3. In *drama, a kind of writing where characters talk about the plot: for example, in crime dramas this may take the form of a police briefing where officers are told about the case they have to solve. This kind of writing is sometimes necessary but is often undramatic: screenwriters, for example, are advised to avoid lengthy or explicit exposition.

exposure 1. In conventional photography, the chemical reaction caused by allowing light rays to reach the photosensitive film for a fraction of a second. The amount of light reaching the film is determined by the camera's shutter speed and lens *aperture. **Overexposure** or **underexposure** results in images that are either too light or too dark. **Double exposure** involves the superimposition of two images whereby a photograph is taken and the film is wound back before a second picture is taken. 2. The amount of light energy reaching a photographic film as determined by the shutter speed and lens aperture. 3. An individual's auditory and/or visual contact with a specific *medium or *message, or a measurement of the amount of such contact. In relation to *advertising, *see also* EFFECTIVE FREQUENCY; EFFECTIVE REACH. 4. (research) Being subjected to an experimental condition or treatment. 5. Of the body: *see* EXHIBITIONISM. 6. (**media exposure**) (*public relations) The amount of media coverage a client (such as a performer or a politician) is getting, and whether this is sufficient, insufficient (**under-exposure**), or in danger of cheapening them as a *brand (**over-exposure**).

expression 1. Loosely, *communication, as in 'the expression of opinions'. 2. Any word or phrase that is a unit of *meaning. 'Mind your Ps and Qs' is an English expression. 3. *How* something is communicated as distinct from *what* is communicated; often referred to as *form rather than *content. Hjelmslev, referring specifically to language, argued that expression (similarly distinguished from *content) consisted of both *form (*language, formal syntactic *structure, and *style) and material substance (*phonemes or *graphemes).

expressive behaviour Any action or *interaction consciously or unconsciously communicating *emotions, desires, intents, and/or personality. *See also* AFFECTIVE COMMUNICATION; EXPRESSIVE COMMUNICATION; FACIAL EXPRESSION; NONVERBAL COMMUNICATION; SELF-TOUCH.

expressive communication Any communication in which the primary *function is to express or arouse *emotion (respectively *sender-oriented or *receiver-oriented modes), or in which the mode of expression (e.g. textual form) is characterized more by *connotation than *denotation, unlike referential communication (*see* INFORMATIONAL COMMUNICATION; REFERENTIALITY). These three meanings (as related to the *sender, to the *receiver, and to *textual features) are rarely separable. **Expressive, emotive,** or **affective language** ranges from swearing to love poetry. *Gender stereotypes often frame expressive (as opposed to *instrumental) communication as a feminine style (*compare* RELATIONAL

COMMUNICATION). Theories influenced by the primacy of language in *structuralism often problematize the *sender-oriented notion of expression by arguing that rather than expressing ourselves *in* *language, human beings are expressed *by* language. *Compare* AFFECTIVE COMMUNICATION.

expressive function (emotive function) In *Jakobson's model of linguistic communication, a key *linguistic or *communicative function oriented towards the *addresser and serving to express feelings or *attitudes. *See also* SENDER-ORIENTED COMMUNICATION.

expressive meaning *See* AFFECTIVE MEANING.

expressive model *See* RITUAL MODEL.

EXT (exterior, exterior shot) In *screenplays, an outdoor scene. *Compare* INT.

externalization 1. The *representation in the external world of something from the inner mental world of the individual. Freud's advice to a colleague for exploring ideas was to 'write it, write it, put it down in black and white . . . get it out, produce it, make something of it—outside you, that is; give it existence independently of you.' 2. (*psychoanalytic theory) A *defence mechanism in which inner impulses are unconsciously attributed to something, or more often someone, in the external world. Also termed **projection**. 3. (social psychology) An individual's attribution of the cause of their behaviour to external factors over which they have little control.

external validity *See* EXPERIMENT.

extracinematic code *See* MISE-EN-SCÈNE.

extradiegetic *See* DIEGESIS.

extralinguistic Outside *language, e.g. the extralinguistic reference of a word would be what it referred to in the world outside the language system itself. *Compare* BRACKETING THE REFERENT.

extraversion (extroversion) A personality factor related to a hypothetical spectrum from extraversion to *introversion, introduced by Jung. Extraversion is characterized by behavioural traits such as sociability and assertiveness.

extreme close-up (XCU) *See* BIG CLOSE-UP.

extreme long-shot (ELS, XLS) An extremely wide angle *shot at long-range and/or using a short focal-length lens, showing a broad, vast, panoramic view. Often used as an *establishing shot. *See also* LONG-SHOT.

eyebrow flash A barely-detectable raising and lowering of the eyebrows that can variously signify friendly recognition, approval, agreement, confirmation-seeking, thanks, or flirtation. In conversation it can mark the start of a turn (*see also* TURN-TAKING) or indicate emphasis.

eye contact (mutual gaze) The phenomenon of two individuals looking towards each other's eyes. Eye contact is important in regulating *interaction, especially in conversational *turn-taking. To start a conversation you first establish eye contact and then speak, breaking eye contact. To transfer the floor near the end of an *utterance a speaker looks away briefly, then returns the *gaze. People generally gaze much more when listening than when speaking. Women have been found to engage in more eye contact than men, especially with each other, and to hold mutual gaze longer. Heterosexual males show a striking avoidance of eye contact with other males. Although most people like some friendly eye contact, prolonged eye contact is uncomfortable. Minimal eye contact can lead to *inferences of nervousness, evasiveness, or defensiveness.

eyeline match A technique associated with *continuity editing consisting of two shots. In the first, a performer looks offscreen in a particular direction; in the second, the person or object they are looking at is shown framed in such a way that it matches the trajectory of their gaze.

eye movements Voluntary and involuntary movements of the eyes, including *convergence, *divergence, *fixation, and the *saccade. In studying eye movements in the 1950s and 1960s, Yarbus found that in looking at images we tend to look most at areas with high contrast, fine detail, and signs of life, and with faces we give special attention to relationships between key features. However, scanning patterns depend above all on our current *purposes and interests. He found that asking different questions about an image produced very different scanning patterns and points of *fixation.

eye tracking The recording of the moving path of the focus of the gaze of an individual over an image or a three-dimensional scene, or alternatively the recording of the motion of the eye. The most influential studies employing this method were by Yarbus. Subsequent applications in relation to media use have included the tracking of *eye movements over printed advertisements, producing *data that can be employed in *communication design.

e-zine An online magazine.

fabula [Latin 'story'] In Russian formalist theory (*see also* FORMALISM), the underlying **story** as a chronology of *events, as distinct from the surface level **plot** or narrative structure—the latter being **syuzhet** (Shklovsky). In simple *narratives the two normally coincide.

face-ism (body-ism) A tendency for mass-media images (notably photographs in newspapers and magazines) to emphasize the faces of men and the bodies of women, thus reinforcing a *gender stereotype aligning males with the mind and females with the body, as well as objectifying women as objects of the *male gaze (*see* OBJECTIFICATION).

face-saving The protection of one's own public image, reputation, or dignity, or that of someone whose image may be affected by your words or deeds. The avoidance of 'loss of face'. *See also* FACE-WORK.

face-to-face interaction *Synchronous social *interaction between individuals *co-present in the same physical location, normally through speech and *nonverbal communication. It is a particular concern in social psychology and *sociolinguistics, and a primary focus for the sociologist Goffman (*see also* FACE-WORK; INTERCHANGE). In sociological terms, such a concern reflects a microsocial level of analysis (*see* MICROSOCIOLOGY). Face-to-face speech communication is traditionally phenomenally privileged (as in Plato) as the most meaningful mode of human communication (*see* PHONOCENTRISM). In *presence studies it typically represents the 'gold standard' to which other forms of mediated interaction aspire.

face-work Goffman's term for what he regards as a basic condition and structural feature of social *interaction (especially in *face-to-face interaction) which involves all participants conducting themselves in accordance with a *social code involving a set of unwritten ground rules and standardized practices. These function to maintain the positive public image of all of those involved in any given encounter and to counteract incidents (such as gaffes or faux pas) which might threaten this and cause the kind of embarrassment that leaves a participant wanting to 'fall through the floor' (*see also* FACE-SAVING). In some contexts, for instance, people will act as if they are wholly deaf to someone's stomach rumbling loudly (especially if it is their own). Particular social skill in this regard is referred to as tact, savoire faire, or diplomacy. Gaucheness is a lack of such skill: as in the adolescent ploy that the mis-speaker was 'only joking'. Goffman uses the term 'ritual' to refer to these practices because he argues that these are symbolic displays of respect (*see also* INTERACTION RITUALS; RITUAL INTERACTION). The specific practices employed are culturally and subculturally variable but the basic phenomenon seems to be universal.

facial expression A configuration or movement of the facial muscles, reflecting some form of *arousal or mental state, either deliberately or unwittingly. A primary nonverbal *cue for inferring *emotion in others and for detecting deception, though some facial expressions indicate cognitive reactions (*see* EYEBROW FLASH). Six **primary emotions** reflected almost universally in the same ways in facial expression have been identified as: happiness, sadness, anger, disgust, surprise, and fear (Ekman and Wallace Friesen). However, there are also different cultural *conventions concerning facial displays. Furthermore, facial expression cannot be separated from *context: for instance, a frown may variously signify dislike, disapproval, puzzlement, weariness, or boredom. It is sometimes referred to as a form of *gesture. The study of facial expression is an aspect of *kinesics. *See also* AFFECT BLENDS; AFFECT DISPLAYS.

fact 1. In common usage, any statement which is true. This, of course, raises issues such as how its truth is established. 2. (social science) A *proposition that has been repeatedly confirmed and that is provisionally considered true until proven false. 3. In the *discourse of news journalism, an item of *information reported in the spirit of *objectivity without interpretive commentary, based on direct observation or on the testimony of more than one reputable source, and meaningfully related to other facts. 4. (philosophy) Statements which are objectively true and do not involve *value judgements—a disputed distinction between fact and *value: *see also* EVALUATION. 5. In the *correspondence theory of truth, things in the world that exist independently of thought and *language and that correspond to statements, making them true. 6. From a critical perspective, a *proposition forming part of a *theory. As the German polymath Johann Wolfgang von Goethe (1749–1832) put it, 'every fact is already theory.' Such frameworks are amenable to *ideological analysis. 7. (sociology) According to the *Thomas theorem, an observation of social reality experienced as real but which is always dependent on the interpreter's definition of the situation (*see also* FRAME OF REFERENCE; FRAMING). 8. **(social fact)** Any of the cultural or structural features of social systems that we experience as external to us and which constrain the behaviour of those within these systems (Durkheim).

faction A portmanteau term (*fact* + *fiction*). Typically pejorative, it refers to a form of *narrative based on real *events but employing *dramatic licence (for instance through the use of imagined conversations). *See also* DOCUDRAMA.

factoid 1. An unverified assertion that is presented as a *fact in the popular press. A term first used in 1973 by the American novelist Norman Mailer (1923–2007). 2. An unverified assertion that has been repeated so often that it is widely assumed to be true. 3. A trivial snippet of *information.

factual 1. As opposed to fictional, relating to the real world (*see also* FICTION); as in *factual genres. 2. As opposed to evaluative or interpretive, relating to what is objectively true: *see also* EVALUATION; INTERPRETATION; OBJECTIVITY. 3. As opposed to theoretical, what can be empirically observed: *compare* THEORY. **4.** As opposed to logical, what is contingent: *see* CONTINGENCY.

factual genres **1.** In writing, this includes certain rhetorical modes of *discourse (*exposition, *description, and *argument), and particular forms such as reports, interviews, surveys, biographies, dictionaries, encyclopaedias, academic monographs, and textbooks. The organization of public libraries suggests that the distinction between *fiction and non-fiction is one of the most fundamental contemporary written *genre distinctions—a categorization which highlights the importance of *modality judgements. However, even such an apparently basic distinction is revealed to be far from straightforward as soon as one tries to apply it to the books on one's own shelves. **2.** In television, factual genres include news reports, current affairs programmes, *documentaries, public 'events' coverage, sports and leisure programmes, consumer programmes, and specialist programmes (history, religion, and so on). Even within genres acknowledged as factual (such as news reports and documentaries) 'stories' are told—the purposes of factual genres in the *mass media include entertaining as well as informing. Genre labels in the television industry are highly fluid (*see also* TELEVISION GENRES). In the UK at present the term **popular factual television** commonly includes such forms as celebrity profiles and entertaining *documentaries. Sometimes the term **factual entertainment** is employed in relation to *hybrid genres such as *docudrama (a form of *faction). *Reality TV is variously classed as popular factual television and sometimes as factual entertainment. *See also* FICTION VALUES; HYBRID GENRE; STORY MODEL; TABLOIDIZATION.

fade-in (fade-up) **1.** In video *post-production, a slow *transition from black to the full, delineated image. **2.** In sound recording, a slow transition from silence to sound.

fade-out (fade-down) **1.** In video *post-production, a slow *transition from a fully delineated image to black. **2.** In sound recording, a slow transition from sound to silence.

falling action *See* FREYTAG'S PYRAMID.

false consciousness (*Marxist theory) Class consciousness or *ideology which does not match the political and economic realities or interests of those exhibiting it, but which is the product of the social structure. The term derives from Engels rather than Marx. The orthodox Marxist concept of 'false consciousness' implies that ideology is like a curtain masking reality, but for Althusser, it is the unavoidable fabric of reality: 'ideology represents the imaginary relationship of individuals to their real conditions of existence' (*see* IDEOLOGICAL STATE APPARATUS). *See also* COMMODITY FETISHISM; DOMINANT IDEOLOGY.

falsified metacommunication *Compare* METACOMMUNICATION. **1.** In *communication based on the pathological exploitation of unequal *power relations, the reframing of oppression as benevolent and protective (Bateson). **2.** For the American sociologists Robert Goldman and Stephen Papson, a reflexive strategy employed in any advertisement targeted at *savvy consumers which involves calling attention to assumptions that are normally implicit in communication (e.g. drawing attention to its status as an advertisement, or to its *constructedness) and thus giving the disarming appearance of being honest in demystifying the process; *see also* REFLEXIVITY. This can be seen as a form of misdirection. In such a strategy the focus is not on the product, *brand, or service itself but on the *audience, or rather the audience's relationship to the advertiser and to the communicative *code employed. We are aligned with the advertiser, the idea being that we are won over by this refreshing honesty, and flattered by this invitation into the advertiser's confidence and by this tribute to our own sophistication, so that we are inclined to favour the brand.

familiar size In *depth perception, an interpretive cue in three-dimensional environments and a *pictorial depth cue whereby our *social knowledge of the usual scale of particular objects helps us to judge their relative distance from each other. Our routine estimates of size in everyday life are guided by familiarity, where this is a more reliable guide to relative distance than it is in pictures.

fandom 1. An *interpretive community consisting of dedicated followers of any cultural phenomenon, such as a television *series or *serial or a particular *film genre or film star. 2. An interconnected *social network of such *subcultural communities. 3. A form of consumer activity in which ardent enthusiasts, referred to by Jenkins as 'textual poachers', subversively appropriate their favourite *mass-media texts for their own *purposes, sometimes actively rewriting them. *See also* TEXTUAL POACHING; *compare* PARTICIPATORY CULTURE. 4. The process of becoming a fan. 5. Any or all of these as a field of academic study.

fantasy 1. A process or product of the imagination. 2. Any *representation defined by its contrast to the reality of the known world, and which critics may dismiss as *escapism. 3. A *genre of *fiction or storytelling in any *medium encompassing many other genres (fairy tale, ghost story, *melodrama, *romance, science fiction, utopian fiction), particularly associated with magic and the supernatural. 4. **(phantasy)** In Freudian *psychoanalytic theory, the psychic content of dreams representing repressed desires. Fantasies are seen as central to our sense of *identity; the *subject usually plays the leading role.

fanzine A portmanteau term (*fan* + *magazine*). A magazine for enthusiastic followers of a particular sports team, star, television series/serial, or *mass-media genre, produced by fans themselves, often on a non-profit-making basis. A term originally used in 1949 in the USA in relation to science fiction magazines. They can be seen as a form of *alternative press.

fear appeals A psychological and rhetorical strategy in persuasive communication such as *advertising that seeks to evoke a response of fear or anxiety in the audience by showing them an undesirable outcome that they can avoid by heeding the warning. This strategy is intended to increase the effectiveness of the message and it is commonly used in health and safety campaigns, such as those warning motorists not to drink and drive. *See also* ADVERTISING APPEALS; EMOTIONAL APPEALS; NEGATIVE APPEALS.

feature film *See* FILM; NARRATIVE FILM.

feed 1. (engineering) A generic term for an audio or video *signal (analogue or digital) which has to be routed (or fed) to an edit suite or sound studio, usually from some other location. 2. A generic term for number of inputs to a vision or audio *mixer, designated as active when they are connected to a source. 3. **Satellite feed**: material sent via satellite to a *news agency or television company either in an edited form or as *rushes. 4. (journalism) *See* NEWS FEED. 5. On the web, *see* RSS.

feedback 1. **(servomechanism)** In *cybernetics, the modification of any process or system by its *effects (as with a thermostat). 2. In communication generally, any reaction on the part of the *receiver to a *sender's *message. The term is usually restricted to reactions that reach the sender, enabling them to monitor the effectiveness of the communication and to adapt as necessary. Without feedback from the audience in the form of laughter, the comedian isn't funny. In linear *communication models, this is indicated as a **feedback loop** with a directional arrow back from the receiver to the sender. However, a feedback loop does not transform a *transmission model from being *sender-oriented into an *interaction model. 3. In face-to-face interpersonal speech communication, this includes both reactions that are vocalized and those that are nonverbal (for the latter, *see* BACK-CHANNEL). 4. In mediated interpersonal communication, feedback is comparatively attenuated depending on the *affordances of the medium employed: *see also* CUELESSNESS. 5. In mass communication, potential feedback is typically minimal, indirect, and usually significantly delayed. *Audience research can provide formal feedback. However, for some kinds of broadcast shows a studio audience is seen as providing essential immediate feedback. Such a forum is also sometimes used for formal 'feedback' programmes. In responding to media output, individual viewers, listeners, and readers are largely limited to *emails, phone calls, and letters. *Mass communication is, of course, essentially one-way. 6. The *information gained from formative *evaluation. 7. Speakers' immediate awareness of their own vocal *production of sound. 8. **Acoustic feedback** (**howl round**): an unpleasant high-pitched noise that occurs when a microphone is placed too close to a speaker so that its sound is picked up by the speaker and in turn by the microphone and exponentially amplified in a process called **loop gain**. 9. **Video feedback**: the effect created when the output of a video *signal is fed into its input: for example, when a camera films a television shooting pictures from that camera. The tunnelling effect produced is an example of *mise-en-abîme (also recursion).

feedforward Information about *receivers that is available to the *sender prior to communicating with them and that can be used to improve the effectiveness of the communication. Knowing the *target audience is important in all forms of communication, and fundamental in such contexts as *advertising, where it determines even the choice of *medium.

female gaze 1. A term coined by *feminists in response to the claims made by Mulvey that the *conventions established in classical Hollywood films required all spectators, regardless of their sex, to identify with the male *protagonist and to adopt the controlling *male gaze around which such films were held to be structured. 'The female gaze' thus marked out neglected territory. For many, the term alludes to the right of women to adopt the active and objectifying gaze that has traditionally and stereotypically been associated with males, undermining the dominant cultural *alignment of *masculinity with activity and *femininity with passivity. Despite the label, this need not involve replacing one form of *gender essentialism with another: the objects of the gaze need not be confined to males. 2. The ways in which women and girls look at other females, at males, and at things in the world. This concerns the kinds of looking involved, and how these may be related to *identification, *objectification, *subjectivity, and the *performance and construction of *gender. *See also* GAZE. 3. The gendered *attention anticipated in visual and audiovisual texts addressed to female viewers.

femininity *See also* GENDER; GENDER STEREOTYPES; *compare* MASCULINITY.
1. For *constructionists, a culturally-constructed and historically-variable set of gendered *subject positions conventionally associated with females (*see also* CONSTRUCTIONISM; POSITIONING). Marxist-feminist accounts emphasize the sexual division of labour (in which women are cast as natural carers) as the prime determinant of the social construction of femininity. The concept is nevertheless an *ideological *site of struggle (*see also* IDEOLOGY). *Masculinity as an unmarked category is dependent on notions of femininity constructed in terms of *difference: *see* MARKEDNESS. 2. From the *reductionist viewpoint of *gender essentialism, biologically-determined **femaleness**: anatomical, genetic, and hormonal. Women are consequently seen as naturally well-equipped for certain subordinate social roles and not for others. Such roles are associated primarily with the private sphere of domesticity (*see also* PUBLIC AND PRIVATE SPHERES). From this perspective femininity is conceived of as a core feature of *identity. 3. Any cultural forms, aspects of *appearance, *values, personality traits, or patterns of behaviour conventionally associated with women. Certain personality traits are stereotypically regarded as distinctively feminine: these typically include emotionality, passivity, dependence, and warmth. *Communication styles associated with stereotypical femininity are *expressive, social/relational, and/or *person-oriented.

feminism *Compare* MASCULINISM. 1. An *ideology and a social movement based on the need to end the subordination of women to men in contemporary society. Beyond this shared perspective, there are multiple **feminisms** organized around a polarization between those stressing the basic *sameness* of men and women (androgyny) and those emphasizing *difference* (whether biological, cultural, or social)—the latter sometimes adopting *essentialist stances and/or separatist strategies. It is conventionally divided into three historical 'waves': the *first wave* from the *Enlightenment thinking of the late 18th century, based on advancing women's rights; the *second wave* of the anti-sexist women's liberation movement from the late 1960s; and *third wave* feminism from the 1990s, an era of theorization which has witnessed increasing *fragmentation. 2. **Socialist** and **Marxist feminism**: the stance that sexual inequality is the result of the socioeconomic relations of capitalism. Social *class is the key factor in women's subordination and social distinctions between men and women must be addressed. 3. **Radical feminism**: the view that sexual inequality is the result of patriarchy, and men are the main enemy, dominating the major social *institutions. Capitalism, militarism, authoritarianism, and *competition are the core values of patriarchy through which men maintain their *hegemony. It calls for a radical reordering of *gender roles. 4. **Cultural feminism**: an overtly *essentialist stance celebrating traditional feminine values, such as emotionality, intuition, *cooperation, caring, and nonviolence, and emphasizing the differences between women and men—domination and aggression being seen as inherent male tendencies. Cultural feminism was an offshoot of radical feminism. 5. **Liberal feminism**: the stance that sexual inequality is primarily the result of *socialization and barriers to equality and that it can be addressed through political and legal reform. 6. **Psychoanalytic feminism**: the view that *gender is a product of psycho-social development. 7. **Lesbian feminism**: a separatist critique of institutionalized heterosexuality, with a slogan in the 1970s that 'feminism is the theory; lesbianism is the practice.' 8. **Black** and **postcolonial feminism**: a 'womanist' critique of feminism as reflecting the concerns of white, predominantly middle-class women in advanced capitalist countries, and as implicitly *racist. *See also* ETHNOCENTRISM; EUROCENTRISM. 9. **Ecofeminism**: the view that the oppression of women by men is inextricable from the masculine exploitation of nature and the third world. 10. **Postmodern** and **poststructuralist feminism**: the stance that since 'the master's tools will never dismantle the master's house', concepts of *gender and of 'woman' require *denaturalization and radical *deconstruction—including the binaries of sameness and *difference. *See also* POST-FEMINISM; *compare* QUEER THEORY.

feminization *Compare* GENDERING; MASCULINIZATION. 1. (sociology) A process in which certain social *roles or occupations become associated primarily with women. This has historically led to such roles having a lower status (e.g. school-teaching and nursing). 2. (cultural theory) The concept that a decline in male power in the 20th century was reflected in tendencies within the culture of *modernism such as an increasing focus on personal *values and the private sphere: *see also* PUBLIC AND PRIVATE SPHERES. 3. The thesis that American mass culture in the 19th century reinforced traditional *gender stereotypes about women.

fetishism 1. Originally in anthropology, the attribution of mysterious or supernatural qualities to material objects which then become the object of idolatry: *see also* COMMODITY FETISHISM. 2. (psychology) A pathological sexual fixation on an object or seemingly inconsequential part of the body on which the **fetishist** depends for sexual *arousal and gratification. 3. In Freudian *psychoanalytic theory, the substitution of an object for the penis as a defence against the castration anxiety argued to be generated by a boy's discovery that his mother lacks a penis. 4. In Mulvey's *psychoanalytic theory of the *male gaze in film spectatorship, **fetishistic looking** is theorized as one response to male castration anxiety, in which the physical beauty of a woman represented onscreen, or some aspect of her *appearance, becomes an erotic focus that makes this kind of looking gratifying; she suggested that this led to the cult of the female movie star. *See also* OBJECTIFICATION; VOYEURISM; *compare* SCOPOPHILIA. 5. In *postcolonial theory, *racism is seen as involving the **fetishization** of *difference.

fiction 1. A generic term for a *narrative in any *medium that tells a story which is not primarily an account of real *events and/or people but of imaginary events and/or characters. Historical narratives based on real people or events but with an invented plot are sometimes referred to as *faction. 2. **(narrative fiction)** A broad category of literary work, usually regarded as excluding (at least non-narrative) poetry and drama and including novels, novellas (short novels), fables, and short stories. 3. A falsified (**fictitious**) statement or an unjustified belief. 4. A *modality *ontologically distinguished from *fact, truth, or reality, or generically from non-fiction.

fictionalization 1. The transformation of actual happenings into *fictional form; to represent real people or *events in the manner of fiction and as if they were fictional: as in **fictionalizing** a biography. *See also* DRAMATIZATION. 2. A pejorative term for an overindulgence in *dramatic licence. 3. A *narrative based partly or wholly on *fact but written as if it were *fiction. Films and broadcast dramas of this kind often bear the label 'based on a true story'. *See also* DOCUDRAMA; FACTION.

fiction film *See* NARRATIVE FILM.

fiction values A euphemism for the *entertainment function of television. In relation to television programmes in the UK, an allusion to a tendency for *factual genres to seek to be entertaining, inverting the old Reithian priorities (*see* REITHIANISM). This is part of the rhetoric of the debate about the 'falling standards' of programmes attributed to a populist approach to retaining and increasing *audience share. The implied contrast is with *news values. In factual genres on television the boundaries between *fact and *fiction have become blurred. *See also* STORY MODEL; TABLOIDIZATION.

field 1. A bounded area. 2. **(field of study)** A particular academic area of investigation, traditionally within a single academic discipline (such as sociology or *linguistics), but often in contemporary research, crossing traditional disciplinary boundaries. For instance, the *internet is a field of study for researchers from many disciplines in the humanities, the social sciences, and the sciences. 3. For Bourdieu, a network of individuals and *institutions which forms the context for individual endeavour in a particular domain (cultural, philosophical, political, or scientific) and which competes for dominance with other fields (e.g. the literary field and the educational field). 4. The everyday setting of ethnographic research: *see* ETHNOGRAPHY. 5. (video engineering) One of two subdivisions of a video *frame: one field contains all the odd TV lines; the other all the even ones. Each field decodes as a still image of video, but in interlaced video standards (which include *PAL and *NTSC) the images captured in each field are slightly different. Since the playback head cycles between these, a still frame of interlaced video is not a static image like a frame of film. *See also* INTERLACE FRAME. 6. **(data field)** In a *database, a single category of *data (typically displayed as a column), with a **field heading** such as 'surname' or 'age'. Such fields apply to all of the records listed, so that for each individual, the surname and age fields would contain the corresponding data for that person. Surname would be an *alphanumeric field so that the records could be sorted into alphabetical order. Age would be a **numeric field** so that the records could be sorted into ascending or descending order by age. 7. **(visual field)** In the psychology of *perception, the area that can be seen from a particular location at a particular moment. For James Gibson, the *ambient optical array on the retina. 8. **(attentional field)** (cognitive psychology) All objects, thoughts, and concepts presently within consciousness: *see also* ATTENTION. 9. **(field theory)** (social psychology) An approach which views behaviour holistically in terms of the individual's overall psychological environment (**field** or **life-space**)—in which individuals, their *significant others, and their needs, goals, and perceptual framings are seen as dynamically interacting. The concept derives from Kurt Lewin (1890–1947), a German-American psychologist.

field dependence and independence A continuum mapping a *cognitive style which refers to the relative ease of difficulty with which an individual is able to disembed a figure from its ground or *context (notably in *visual perception); *see also* FIGURE AND GROUND. Those who find this relatively easy are termed more **field independent**; those who find it relatively difficult are more **field dependent**. Men tend to be more field independent than women. This psychological dimension was identified by the American psychologist Herman A. Witkin (1916–79).

field of view (field of vision) In *visual perception and in photography, the angular extent of the observable world that is visible from a particular point in a single direction. Unaided human sight spans nearly 180 degrees, 140 degrees being covered by *binocular vision, though only a small area is in sharp focus at any moment (*see* FOVEAL VISION).

fifth estate A colloquial term for *broadcasting, as distinct from the *fourth estate (print media).

figurative art (representational art) Visual works of art which recognizably represent aspects of the real world (even if in distorted form), as opposed to 'abstract art'. See also MIMESIS; REPRESENTATION.

figurative language (metaphorical language) *See also* RHETORIC; *compare* IMAGERY. 1. Language that employs *figures of speech, especially *metaphor. 2. As opposed to *literal language, language that is not intended to be taken literally: *see* METAPHORIC MEANING. 3. Language that is more connotative than denotative: *see also* CONNOTATION; DENOTATION. 4. Language that is more expressive and/or *poetic than *referential in its *linguistic function. This can include all **literary language** (not just 'poetic language'); however, references to it as literary language or **literary imagery** ignore the fact that such language is ubiquitous in everyday speech. It is also particularly associated with the language of *advertising. *See also* EXPRESSIVE FUNCTION; POETIC FUNCTION; *compare* REFERENTIAL FUNCTION. 5. Any use of language that is stylistically or semantically *marked, deviating from conventional usage or meaning. 6. Language that is perceived as decorative, ornamental, or colourful rather than plain and instrumental; this may lead to connotations of *femininity. *See also* CLOAK THEORY. 7. For the scientists of the Royal Society in 17th-century England, the kind of language that distorts reality and truth, and which they consequently sought to eliminate in scientific *discourse. 8. Language that has been argued to shape thought (*see* LINGUISTIC DETERMINISM) or *express us* (Barthes) rather than merely expressing preformed thoughts: *see also* MOULD THEORY. 9. For *critical discourse analysts, language that sheds light on the *framing of reality within discourse: *see also* CRITICAL DISCOURSE ANALYSIS. 10. For deconstructionists, the root of all *language, which cannot be eliminated in supposedly literal forms (*see also* DECONSTRUCTION).

figurative meaning *See* METAPHORIC MEANING.

figure and ground In the psychology of *perception, the organization of a perceptual *field into a **figure** (the subject) with a *form or *structure that stands out against and in front of a relatively undifferentiated **ground** (its background). In deliberately designed ambiguous images (such as the famous vase-and-faces image), what is figure (or *signal) and what is ground (or *noise) is capable of reversal, and what is initially perceived as figure depends on the observer's current interests and *purposes and the immediate *context within which the image is framed (*see* PERCEPTUAL SET). We owe the concept of 'figure' and 'ground' in perception to the gestalt psychologists: notably Wertheimer, Köhler, and Koffka. *See also* FIELD DEPENDENCE AND INDEPENDENCE; FOREGROUNDING; GESTALT LAWS; SALIENCE.

figure of speech Any form of *expression in which *language is manipulated for rhetorical effect. Around AD 95, Quintilian defined the figure of speech as 'a departure from the simple and straightforward method of expression.' He listed four types of rhetorical deviation (*mutatio*): *adjectio* or *addition, *detractio* or omission (*see* DELETION), *transmutatio* or rearrangement (*see* TRANSPOSITION), and *immutatio* or *substitution. In classical *rhetoric, figures of speech were traditionally divided into schemes and *tropes. **Schemes** are patterns of expression. They include: alliteration, *anaphora, antithesis, asyndeton (*see* DELETION), and *climax. Tropes radically transform the meaning of words. These include: allegory, conceit, *hyperbole, *irony, *metaphor, *metonymy, *onomatopoeia, oxymoron, paradox, personification, pun, rhetorical question, *simile, and *synecdoche. However, nowadays in many contexts the term trope is synonymous with figure of speech.

((⊕)) SEE WEB LINKS

• Rhetorical tropes

file In computing, a collection of *data stored on a computer which decodes as a text, graphic, song, photograph, or movie. File information is stored along with identifiers, or instructions for opening and use.

file sharing In computing, the activity of exchanging *data over a *peer-to-peer network.

filled pauses Meaningless *vocalizations (such as 'um' and 'er') that signify a break in a speaker's fluency. These need not be signs of nervousness or lack of skill but may reflect pauses for thought. They also have *back-channel functions, such as in *turn-taking.

film *Compare* CINEMA. 1. The medium for both still *photography and motion pictures. A thin, transparent strip of flexible plastic (originally cellulose) coated in an emulsion of light-sensitive particles called silver halides with small sprocket holes down one or both sides (depending on its size or 'gauge'). When a photograph is taken, a segment of the film strip (or frame) is exposed to light causing a chemical reaction which forms a *latent image (*see* EXPOSURE). In still cameras exposed film typically consists of a series of *photographs of different subjects, whereas in movie cameras 24 photographs of the same subject are taken automatically every second (*see* SHOT). The latent images from the camera are fixed and developed in a darkroom producing a negative from which either positive copies or prints are made. Film takes time to develop and must be physically copied to be disseminated through distribution networks. These processes are complex, time-consuming, and costly, which accounts for their professionalization (*see* ASYNCHRONOUS COMMUNICATION). 2. A mechanical technology that produces (and reproduces) images on film using a number of photographic processes and devices including cameras, darkrooms, printers, and projectors. 3. **(movie, motion picture)** A mass medium particularly dominant in the early to mid 20th century, consisting of a visual presentation of (apparently) moving pictures (*see* APPARENT MOTION), since the 1930s synchronized with sound. This is intended to be experienced in a *cinema by being projected onto a screen and viewed by a paying audience. Today, **feature films** usually take the form of audiovisual stories and are usually between 70 and 240 minutes in length but can take other forms, such as a newsreel. 4. A *metonym for the entire subject area of moving pictures, including the film industry, *production, *marketing, *distribution, exhibition, viewing, reception, and study. 5. *v.* To photograph something with a movie camera.

SEE WEB LINKS

• The Internet Movie Database (IMDb)

film audience (cinema audience) *See also* AUDIENCES. 1. A group of *viewers of a film: either in a *cinema, or at home watching on *DVD and other *formats (though often used synonymously with film *spectators). 2. In *film studies, a group of people watching a film, either conceived of as an idealized discursive construct, about which theoretical assumptions are made (*see also* IMPLIED READER; SUBJECT), or specific individuals or groups defined as the focus of investigation using *quantitative and/or *qualitative methods (*see* AUDIENCE RESEARCH). Traditionally, film scholars have paid little attention to audiences, instead focusing on the film as a *text and conceiving the audience as an undifferentiated and sometimes passive 'mass' vulnerable to the *ideological effects of film (*see* HYPODERMIC MODEL). More recently approaches have sought to differentiate and contextualize film audiences as active creators of meaning: *see* ACTIVE AUDIENCE THEORY; USES AND GRATIFICATIONS. 3. For film practitioners, the group representing the *target market for a film. Film audiences have changed over time: for example, with the arrival of television. Since the 1950s, the average age of film audiences has grown steadily younger. Today young people aged 15–24 are the most likely to be regular cinemagoers. Men are generally regarded as more avid cinemagoers than women. Films reflect these changing audience *demographics. However, Hollywood in particular has been criticized for not understanding its audience, resulting in expensive flops and surprise hits. Although film-makers try to reach a *mass audience, some *genres are targeted more specifically at certain demographics, e.g. action genres at men and romantic comedies at women. Certain films that flop on their initial release attract a dedicated audience over time: *see* FANDOM.

film criticism *See* FILM THEORY.

film genres The ways in which the film industry, critics, academics, and audiences classify film, forming structures that shape the *production and *marketing of particular films and manage the *expectations of both critics and *audiences towards them. The classic film genres are westerns, comedies, musicals, and war films, with thrillers, crime or detective films, *film noir, horror, and science fiction also prominent. The major film genres have distinctive *textual features including *subject matter and *themes, *setting, *narrative form, characterization, *iconography, and filmic techniques. Some tend to be defined primarily by their *subject matter* (e.g. detective films), some by their *setting* (e.g. the western), and others by their *narrative form* (e.g. the musical). In addition to textual features, different genres also involve different functions, pleasures, *audiences, modes of involvement, styles of interpretation, and *text-reader relationships. Many are *hybrid genres: for example, romantic comedy or action adventure, problematizing the notion that *genres can have clear and distinct borders.

(((∰))) SEE WEB LINKS
• Film genres and themes (BFI)

film grammar Conventions governing the techniques of film and how they are used to tell a story. Film techniques include *cinematography, *mise-en-scène, and *editing (*see* CLOSE-UP; CONTINUITY EDITING; LONG-SHOT; MID-SHOT) and the way in which these conventions are used by practitioners of the medium to signify certain *meanings (*see* CUTAWAY; ESTABLISHING SHOT; POINT-OF-VIEW SHOT; SHOT/REVERSE-SHOT). 'Grammatical rules' can also be broken: for example, through *jump cuts or by *crossing the line. Semioticians have disputed its comparability to *grammar in the strict linguistic sense.

(((∰))) SEE WEB LINKS
• The grammar of television and film

filmic *adj.* **(cinematic)** That which pertains to film in the sense of any *style or *content that is associated with film, when incorporated into other media (*compare* TELEVISUALISM).

film mode The approximation of the *progressive scanning movement of film on video achieved by duplicating either *field 1 or field 2 of the video *frame. In the early days of *nonlinear editing, the *software would only *digitize a single field of video to save disc space. This produced a film-like movement favoured by some *producers and *directors. The disadvantage of film mode is that duplicating a video field effectively halves the vertical picture *resolution.

film noir A *genre of crime films popular in the 1940s and 1950s, characterized by the use of expressionist, *chiaroscuro black-and-white *cinematography, complex mystery plots, and stock characters such as the cynical detective and femme fatale. Film noir deals with morally *ambiguous themes, in contrast to the dominant convention in Hollywood. Notable films include *Out of the Past* (1947) and *The Big*

Sleep (1946). Certain modern films shot in colour have borrowed its stylistic and thematic conventions, notably *Chinatown* (1974) and *Blade Runner* (1982).

film script *See* SCREENPLAY.

film studies An academic discipline taking film as its subject and investigating issues such as the processes of film-making, the film *text, *film genres, and *audiences and reception. These may be studied historically or thematically, within or across cultures. Film studies can be divided into *practice*-based and *theory*-based approaches. The former concentrates on vocational training and hands-on practice in the techniques of film-making; the latter is regarded as a discipline within the humanities.

((())) SEE WEB LINKS

• *Through Navaho Eyes: Film Communication and Anthropology*: Sol Worth

film theory The aesthetic, historical, and/or ideological analysis of film, or the academic study of the nature of the cinematic experience, as distinguished from **film criticism**, which is typically concerned with the evaluative interpretation of films. The history of film theory can be loosely divided into three phases. The first (1910s–30s) was *formalist* and attempted to elevate the status of film as an art form as opposed to a mere document of reality. Notable theorists include the German Rudolph Arnheim (1904–2007), and Eisenstein. The second phase (1930s–60s) is characterized as *realist*, embracing the photographic aspect of film as an art form that most closely reflected nature. Theorists associated with this stance included the German author Siegfried Kracauer (1899–1966), and the French film theorist André Bazin (1918–58) who was also the co-founder of the influential journal *Cahiers du Cinema*. The third phase (1960s–90s) was a period of eclecticism that can be separated into three interweaving strands: *political* theory influenced by Marx and Althusser that attempted to identify the *ideological strategies of film in the maintenance of bourgeois values (Baudry, MacCabe); *formalist* theory influenced by the *semiotics of Saussure, associated with Metz and the British film theorist and screenwriter Peter Wollen (b.1938); *psychoanalytic* theory drawing on Freud and Lacan (Mulvey and the UK journal *Screen*). This period is associated with *grand theory. Since the 1990s the influence of *postmodernism and a reaction against the excesses of grand theory has seen a return to more modest interpretive approaches associated with Bordwell and the American philosopher Noël Carroll (b.1947). *See also* AUTEUR THEORY; COGNITIVE FILM THEORY; CONSTRUCTIVISM; NEOFORMALIST FILM THEORY.

final cut (final assembly) In *post-production, the finished film print or television programme that is no longer a work in progress. The completion of the offline stage by the *editor and *director which has been approved by the production executives and which guides the rest of the *post-production process. *Compare* ROUGH CUT.

first-person point of view *Compare* SECOND-PERSON POINT OF VIEW; THIRD-PERSON POINT OF VIEW. **1. (first-person** or **subjective narration)** In literary *narratives (novels, novellas, and short stories), subjective *narration by a character in the plot—normally, but not always, a major participant. The *narrator refers to himself or herself as 'I' and relates *events as they occur, from *memory and/or from hearsay, making judgements on these and on other characters (*compare* OBJECTIVE NARRATION). Readers thus experience narrative events from that character's *point of view. This does not guarantee that they will interpret events in the same way as the character or that they will empathize with them: they are at liberty to find them naïve, self-deceptive, or simply dislikable. A novel sometimes employs more than one narrative *point of view, though frequent shifts are rare. *See also* PERSONA. **2. (subjective point of view)** In film *narratives, a narrative *point of view in which the audience either views the action as if through the eyes of a particular character or hears the character commenting on the depicted events as a *voiceover. Although the dominant point of view in cinema is usually neutral (*see* FOURTH WALL), brief *point-of-view shots are not unusual. However, a sustained first-person perspective in cinema is rare and thus highly *marked. *Lady in the Lake* (1947) is a rare example in which we see the action directly and entirely from the *protagonist's point of view and in which all the *shots are subjective *point-of-view shots (we only glimpse the character's face in reflections). This is the dominant view in first-person shooter *videogames and *virtual reality. *See also* SUBJECTIVE CAMERAWORK.

fixation **1. (fixation pause)** In *visual perception, a brief moment at which the eye is at rest between *saccades. Processing of the retinal image takes place in these pauses. We never see 'the whole picture': only the areas where the eyes rest are consciously registered and only these can be recalled. *See also* EYE MOVEMENTS. **2. (affective fixation)** In *psychoanalytic theory, the persistence of an excessive or irrational affective attachment to an object or person from an earlier stage of psychosexual development. **3.** An obsessive interest.

flaming **1.** The act of posting angry or insulting messages (flames) to an internet *newsgroup or other online forum. A **flame war** is an exchange of such messages. **2.** Slang, derogatory term applied to a man acting in an exaggeratedly effeminate manner.

flâneur [French *flâner* 'to stroll'] **1.** For the French poet Charles Baudelaire (1821–67), an idle stroller who is in their element as one of the crowd; a dashing young gentleman whose wealth and education allows him to explore the new urban arcades of 19th-century Paris. A passionate observer who is at the centre of his world and yet remains inconspicuous. **2.** For Benjamin, not so much a hero but a tourist in commodity culture, who roams the city, becoming affected by its architecture and nurturing an enduring passion for things seen only in passing. **3.** The street photographer, attracted to 'dark seamy corners' (Sontag). **4.** Either the cinema *spectator who enjoys the voyeuristic pleasures of seeing everything while remaining hidden or one who resists being sutured into the film. *See also* SUTURE; VOYEURISM. **5.** The TV channel-hopper or *surfer; a detached indifferent observer. **6. (cyber, digital,** or **virtual flâneur)** A *surfer of the *internet, exploring *cyberspace in search of virtual pleasures. The *anonymity of the flâneur is especially embodied in the figure of the *lurker.

flashback 1. **(analepsis)** (film) A *shot or *sequence of a past *event, or past events, inserted into a *narrative, disrupting its chronology. Flashbacks are often used to deepen the *significance of events taking place in the present, or to illuminate a back-story: for example, the sequence showing Rick and Ilsa's time in Paris in the film *Casablanca* (1942). *Transition effects are sometimes used to signal a flashback: the ripple dissolve became a cliché in Hollywood films of the 1930s and 1940s. 2. (psychology) A term borrowed from film and originally used to name a residual drug hallucination, although today more commonly applied to the re-experiencing of a past traumatic event which is a symptom of post-traumatic stress disorder.

flashbulb memory A very vivid, detailed, and persistent subjective and episodic *memory of an emotionally-charged *event in one's life. This usually includes the memory of where one was and what one was doing when the event occurred. Its vividness is no guarantee of its accuracy.

flashforward (prolepsis) In film, a glimpse of a future *event inserted into a *narrative, disrupting its chronology. Flashforwards are less common than *flashbacks because they kill suspense, but foreknowledge can sometimes deepen the significance of a scene, either through *dramatic irony, or by communicating fatalism: for example, in *Barry Lyndon* (1976). They can also be unsettling, as in the work of the British film director Nicholas Roeg (b.1928), where they often signify clairvoyance: for example, in *Insignificance* (1985) where a character based on Marilyn Monroe has a vision of her future miscarriage when she enters a hotel bathroom.

flash mob People who make use of *social media and mobile communication technologies to arrange a meeting at a specified location in order to perform some collective action. *Compare* SMART MOB.

flicker fusion The phenomenon where the strobing of a light source flashing on and off appears to disappear when the frequency of its flashes exceeds 48 times a second. Flicker fusion is a symptom of a limitation of human vision that fails to detect rapid movement of any kind. It is exploited in fluorescent lighting and in the cinema serves to mask the rapid blackouts between projected frames. Discredited *persistence of vision theories link it to *apparent motion.

flipped image 1. **(reverted image, flopped image)** An image that has been laterally reversed, so that the right-hand side is now on the left. Photographers sometimes flip images, subjectively judging the flipped version to be more effective. This seems to be based partly on the assumption of left to right reading: either because (as, for instance, in athletics photographs) speed is thought to be phenomenally greater when the direction of action matches this *reading direction, or because of the notion that we are more like to identify with the near-side, which in this reading direction would be the left (many us/them images follow this pattern). Certainly, a vertically split before-and-after image (as in an advertisement) would only make sense in left-right reading cultures if the 'before' state appeared on the left. Where images appear in sequence, the issues of *match cuts in film *editing come into play. However, as Yarbus demonstrated, where viewing is driven by particular purposes, the actual scanning pattern for single images is more likely to be subservient to these than to reading direction: *see* EYE MOVEMENTS. *See also* GLANCE CURVE. 2. In television *post-production, an image rotated around the horizontal axis as opposed to a *flopped* image which is rotated around the vertical axis. 3. In computer graphics, an image mirrored vertically.

flipping In relation to television viewing, *see* GRAZING.

floating signifier *See* EMPTY SIGNIFIER.

flopped image *See* FLIPPED IMAGE.

flow *See* ACOUSTIC FLOW; AUDIENCE FLOW; IMMERSIVE FLOW; INFORMATION FLOW; INTERACTIONAL SYNCHRONY; MEDIA FLOWS; NARRATIVE FLOW; SPACE OF FLOWS; TELEVISION FLOW; TWO-STEP FLOW.

fly-on-the-wall 1. A style of non-interventionist *documentary film-making that typically films its subject for a sustained period of several months, generating thousands of hours of *footage which is then edited to tell a story without overt commentary, interviews, or the onscreen presence of a *narrator. 2. A *documentary or *drama that appears to be filmed in a naturalistic style.

FM *See* FREQUENCY MODULATION.

FM radio *Analogue radio stations that broadcast using *frequency modulation typically between 87 and 108 MHz. FM radio can be broadcast in stereo and has clearer sound quality than *AM but lacks its range. In the US, it is particularly associated with college radio stations.

focal length In *optics, the distance from the middle of the lens to its focal point. Light rays run in parallel to one another, while lenses distort light rays: a convex lens (the type that is thicker in the centre than at the edges) brings them closer together and a concave lens (the type that is thinner in the centre) forces them apart. Cameras use convex lenses to bring the light rays together to a point where they converge and the image is in focus: this is where the film or light sensitive diode goes. The more convex (or thicker) the lens, the more severely the light rays are bent and the shorter the focal length (conversely, the thinner the lens the longer the focal length). Different focal lengths create different kinds of image effects. Lenses with very short focal lengths (or wide angle lenses) allow more of the picture to be seen and emphasize *foreground elements, whereas lenses with very long focal lengths (or telephoto lenses) allow less of the picture to be seen and emphasize *background elements which appear to be magnified. These different effects are dramatically illustrated by a technique used in feature films called a **Hitchcock zoom,** where the camera *tracks out at the same time as it *zooms in (or vice versa), an effect used in the film *Vertigo* (1958).

focused viewing *See* HIGH AND LOW INVOLVEMENT.

focus group A *qualitative research method in which a group of individuals engages in an organized discussion of a predetermined topic in the presence of a *moderator. Pioneered in the 1940s and 1950s by Merton, who called it a 'focused group interview', it is often used to gauge views or reactions likely to be encountered in the general population. In *market research, participants are selected as representatives of a *target audience. The validity of focus groups has been questioned, primarily since individuals can be unduly influenced by *group dynamics.

Foley In film and television, the recreation of ambient sound effects in *post-production for foreign language versions of films where dialogue is replaced, or in situations when no *natural sound has been recorded. Named after the American sound technician Jack Foley (1891–1967). *See also* M&E; ADR.

folk devils Stereotypical *representations that demonize certain rule-breaking minorities (*see* DEMONIZATION), which are circulated in the *mass media as examples of deviance, so that these groups function as scapegoats (Cohen). Examples in the UK have included drug users and black youth. Campaigns against them can become *moral panics. *See also* AMPLIFICATION OF DEVIANCE.

folk psychology *Common-sense assumptions, principles, and beliefs within a *culture on which people draw and to which they refer in seeking to account for aspects of behaviour encountered in *everyday life or represented in *texts. Livingstone notes how viewers of television *soap operas differed in the particular principles of such 'culturally consensual knowledge' which they invoked or in how they applied them in their *interpretation and *evaluation of the behaviour of characters (these related to issues such as maternal feelings, the nature of relationships, and ways of helping or influencing others). *See also* COMMON SENSE; CONVERSATIONAL CURRENCY; CULTURAL CODE; CULTURAL LITERACY; TACIT KNOWLEDGE.

following pan A horizontal *camera movement filmed from a fixed position that keeps subjects constantly in *frame as they move across the screen.

font 1. Traditionally, a complete set of characters for one size (e.g. 10 point) and style (e.g. italic) of a particular *typeface design (e.g. Garamond). 2. In digital contexts, the whole character set for a particular typeface regardless of size, since any size can be rendered from a single font file.

font family 1. **(type family)** (*typography) The complete set of characters in a single *typeface design (e.g. Palatino) in all its sizes (e.g. 10 point, 12 point) and styles (e.g. italic, bold). 2. In *HTML and stylesheets, **generic font families** are general categories of fonts: these include *serif, *sans-serif, and *cursive.

footage 1. In motion pictures, a measure of film taken in feet. There are 16 *frames to every foot of 35-mm film and the film travels through the projector at a rate of 1.5 feet per second. 2. A generic term for an amount of uncut film, or video *rushes: *see also* ARCHIVE.

Fordism *Compare* POST-FORDISM. 1. The highly automated assembly-line mass *production of standardized products for a *mass market, based in large factories—reducing production costs and prices. The founder of the Ford Motor Company, Henry Ford (1863–1947) introduced moving assembly belts into his automobile production plants in 1913. This model of mass production subsequently flourished in industrial societies, beginning to decline only in the 1960s. **2.** An associated method of organizing production and improving efficiency based on 'scientific management' or **Taylorism**: this involved centralized control, a high degree of job specialization, and the use of semi-skilled labour for highly repetitive tasks. **3.** Gramsci's term, coined in the 1930s, for this form of production and of regulation of workers that he saw as characteristic of advanced capitalism, and which offered high wages in return for compliance with mechanical discipline, separating this group of workers from the rest of the working class. **4.** (cinema) The coordinated *production process, specialized tasks, and standardized output that characterized the Hollywood *studio system from the 1920s until the late 1940s.

foreground **1.** In visual images which involve the *representation of spatial depth (originally paintings, but subsequently also photographs), the depicted area that appears to be closest to the viewer. One of the three *zones of recession lying behind the *picture plane in the visual representation of depth. *See also* PICTORIAL DEPTH CUES; *compare* BACKGROUND; MIDDLE DISTANCE. **2.** That which is *salient: *see* FOREGROUNDING.

foregrounding [loose rendering of Czech *aktualisace* 'actualization'] **1.** For the Prague school linguists this referred to a stylistic feature characterizing poetic language (and literary language in general), in which verbal devices (e.g. rhetorical *figures of speech) draw particular attention to themselves. Jan Mukařovský (1891–1975), a Czech literary theorist, declared: 'It is not used in the services of communication, but in order to place in the foreground the act of expression'. In other words, in this form of language use, 'it ain't what you say, but the way that you say it' that counts. In *Jakobson's model, this is the *poetic function (being used 'for its own sake')—in particular contrast to the *referential function. In semiotic discourse, foregrounding of this kind involves *signifiers attracting attention to themselves rather than simulating *transparency in representing their *signifieds. Drawing attention to the *medium can function as a form of *defamiliarization. **2.** (*stylistics) Attracting attention to a particular feature of a *discourse or *representation by deviating from conventional *norms or *expectations: *see also* MARKEDNESS. **3.** More loosely, making some aspect of a *discourse or *representation the primary focus of attention (*see also* SALIENCE). This relates more closely to the gestalt psychologists' distinction between *figure and ground (which influenced the Russian formalists). Note that in this usage, commentators may refer to *content being foregrounded, while *form or *style retreats to *transparency, as in the *codes of aesthetic *realism. For instance, in *classical Hollywood movies, the storyline is foregrounded while stylistic features are **backgrounded** through such practices as 'invisible' *continuity editing. Such practices serve to *naturalize the codes employed (the *opposite* of defamiliarization).

forgetting rate The rate at which we lose from *memory *information that we have just learned. As the German psychologist Hermann Ebbinghaus (1850–1909) showed in 1885, without reinforcement, our memory of newly learned information rapidly declines, but after that it gradually levels off (the **forgetting curve**).

Repetitions, as in *advertising, assist retention, but *wearout becomes a factor: repetition with variation is one solution adopted. The forgetting rate is influenced by factors such as how meaningful the material is (*see* FLASHBULB MEMORY). *See also* AD RETENTION; MESSAGE DECAY.

form 1. The shape, outline, or overall structure of an object or figure. 2. (as in 'form and content') The *structure, and sometimes also the *style, of an *utterance, *text, or artwork in any *medium as distinct from its *content, *subject, or *literal meaning. These are sometimes referred to as its **formal features**. Aesthetic texts tend to *foreground form (in contrast to *informational texts); *see also* FOREGROUNDING. Form and content can only be separated for analytic purposes. Although linguistic 'dualists' argue that the same content can be expressed in different forms (*see also* CLOAK THEORY), 'monists' argue that changing the form changes the meaning (*see* MOULD THEORY). Despite the *conduit metaphor, form is not a 'container' of meaning and can itself be meaningful. For instance, in visual *representation (even in *typography), curvy shapes have *connotations of *femininity. 'Abstract' art may not refer directly to the world, but connotation ensures that it is never 'pure form'. In this sense, form can be seen as a kind of content (*see also* FORMALISM). 3. The general categories to which a particular text or artwork can be assigned: how it can be related to existing types, *genres, or *formats. Genres are associated not only with certain formal and stylistic features, but also with particular kinds of *content (*see also* ICONOGRAPHY). Insofar as content is adapted to pre-existing forms, form can be seen as preceding content (a structuralist notion), but the process of adaptation may sometimes contribute to the development of *hybrid genres. 4. A particular configuration in relation to its *function (*see also* FUNCTIONALISM). The principle that 'form follows function' implies that the means employed should be well-adapted to some generic *function. Functional frameworks have been applied not only to the design of tools and techniques but also to forms which have evolved rather than been designed: such as *conventions, *genres, and *language (*see also* COMMUNICATIVE FUNCTIONS; DESIGN FEATURES; LINGUISTIC FUNCTIONS). In either case, functions are ultimately subordinate to the actual *purposes of real users in specific *contexts: *see also* COMMUNICATIVE PURPOSES. 5. (philosophy) The ideal and abstract character or essence of a thing as distinct from any specific material manifestation (Plato), or what places a thing in a species or kind (Aristotle). 6. (in relation to **substance**) In Hjelmslev's framework, the **form of expression** (language, formal syntactic structure, technique, and *style) and/or the **form of content** (semantic and thematic structure) as distinct from the substance of expression (physical, material form) and/or the substance of content (subject matter or genre). In other words, it refers to the relative abstractions of *structure and *style rather than to the concrete specificities of material form and content. 7. In *gestalt perceptual theory, a pattern perceived as a whole 'greater than the sum of its parts'. 8. **(cultural forms)** *Codes, *conventions, and practices associated with a particular *culture or *subculture: *see also* DOMINANT FORMS; EMERGENT FORMS; RESIDUAL FORMS. 9. A structured document, either on paper or onscreen (e.g. online), requiring the provision of specific items of *information. Such forms are employed in *survey-based research: for instance, in *market research.

formal analysis A mode of analysis focusing primarily on the identification and *description of the *formal features (*see also* FORM) of a *text or artwork and on their relations—rather than on its explicit *content, or without reference to its specific cultural or historical *context (*see also* DECONTEXTUALIZATION). It can involve treating examples as typical of a particular period, movement, and/or *style— tending to underplay differences within such codified 'isms'. Even where a particular theoretical approach leads form to be analytically separated from content (a problematic strategy often associated with *formalism and *structuralism), this form of analysis can (but does not always) include the exploration of stylistic *connotations (including the expressivity of material form, such as brushwork in painting) and the *ideological analysis of forms (*see also* CLOSED FORMS; OPEN FORMS). Formal analysis can only be a partial analysis, since it backgrounds content, context, and *audience factors, and as such it may form part of a larger analytical project. Purely formalist approaches may seek to be objective, but they can also be criticized as privileging the *elite interpreter, and their relative abstraction leads to them sometimes being perceived as 'arid'. *See also* TEXTUAL ANALYSIS.

formal features 1. Structural and/or stylistic aspects of an *utterance, *text, or artwork in any *medium. *See also* FORM; STRUCTURE; STYLE; TEXTUAL ANALYSIS; TEXTUAL FEATURES. 2. The structural and stylistic *conventions of a *genre: *see also* ICONOGRAPHY. 3. The *affordances and technical *conventions of a particular medium; in relation to *language; *see* DESIGN FEATURES.

formal function *See* POETIC FUNCTION.

formalism 1. Aesthetic approaches emphasizing *form over *content, in which form is an end in itself. Sometimes used pejoratively (especially by *realists) to refer to what they regard as an *idealist reduction of referential content and of material substance and practices to abstract systems. *See* FORMAL ANALYSIS. 2. **Russian formalism** was an anti-realist aesthetic doctrine whose proponents included Shklovsky and Jakobson. Formalism represented a linguistic focus on literary uses of language. As the name suggests, the primary focus was on *form, *structure, technique, or *medium rather than on *content. The formalists saw literary language as language 'made strange' (*see* DEFAMILIARIZATION) and their model was poetry rather than prose. They were particularly interested in literary 'devices' such as rhyme, rhythm, metre, *imagery, *syntax, and *narrative techniques—favouring writing which 'laid bare' its devices (*see* FOREGROUNDING). Formalism evolved into *structuralism in the late 1920s and 1930s. 3. A term applied to the films of Eisenstein, Kuleshov (*see* KULESHOV EFFECT), and Dziga Vertov (1896–1954) in Russia in the 1920s. Their use of *montage foregrounds the *formal features of the medium, and they tended to background narrative. In 1934 the government put an end to this movement by requiring all art to be based on socialist realism. 4. In literary theory, this sometimes refers to the **New Criticism**—a school of literary criticism that flourished in Britain and the USA from the 1930s to the 1950s. The formalists sought to develop an approach that was 'objective' rather than 'impressionistic'. The 'meaning of a text' was immanent—it lay within it: the text itself told you everything you needed to know, and so they focused on *textual analysis in the form of 'close reading'. They did not relate meaning to what they saw as extrinsic factors such as *authorial intentions (*see* INTENTIONAL FALLACY) and socio-historical *context. Although not directly related to Russian formalism, this school of thought shared the emphasis on poetic language as a special kind of language. **5.** Another term for **formal sociology,** originating with Simmel, which focuses on generic social 'forms', patterns, and processes that are found throughout social life (e.g. *identities, *roles, *conflict, and *competition) as distinct from specific 'content' (politics, the *mass media, and so on). **6.** *See* NEOFORMALIST FILM THEORY.

formality **1.** In *sociolinguistics and *stylistics, variations of linguistic *style or tone in relation to *conventions regarding appropriateness to the social *context of use: in particular in relation to the situation, *setting (public or private), communicative *genre, audience size, and *communicative relationships (including degree of acquaintance). Martin Joos (1907–78), an American linguist, identified five degrees of formality in *language: intimate, casual, consultative, formal, and frozen. These are sometimes referred to as *registers. *Compare* ELABORATED CODE; RESTRICTED CODE. **2.** In *communication theory, an aspect of *modes of address: relative formality or social distance being one of the ways in which these differ. Using Edward T. Hall's terms for 'zones' in *proxemics, a distinction can be made between *intimate, *personal, *social and *public (or *impersonal) modes of address. In *camerawork this is reflected in *shot sizes—*close-ups signifying intimate or personal modes, *medium shots a social mode, and *long shots an impersonal mode. **3.** A dimension of *connotation in relation to communicative choices, where some forms may be subjectively evaluated as relatively formal or casual: as in choosing Times or Lucida Handwriting (*fonts), word-processing or handwriting, post or *email. Such choices may be interpreted as implying either a formal or a casual *communicative relationship which may be evaluated in terms of appropriateness.

format **1.** *n.* In *mass media *production, a distinctive structural and stylistic design template, notably for a particular programme or magazine. **2.** *n.* In radio or television, a plan of a series which defines the *content as well as the look and feel of the programmes. In recent years, the process of formatting has been refined to such an extent that the formula of a successful series is offered as a 'kit of parts' (including running order, set design, and music cues) to broadcasters around the world. A notable example of this trend is *Who Wants to Be a Millionaire?*, first broadcast in the UK in 1998: *see also* FRANCHISE. **3.** *n.* In relation to *advertising, *see* ADVERTISING FORMAT. **4.** *n.* For newspaper formats, *see* NEWSPAPERS. **5.** *n.* (television engineering) The technical specifications which distinguish one kind of recording process from another. This includes different television systems like *PAL and *NTSC and different products used within those systems: Digi Beta, VHS, etc. In tape-based systems, the 'footprint,' or the way in which the electromagnetic information is laid down onto videotape. **6.** *v.* To prepare a videotape for *insert editing: *see* STRIPING. **7.** *v.* (computing) To prepare a hard-drive or disc for use by specifying the structure for data storage and retrieval.

formation **1.** For Foucault's usage, *see* DISCURSIVE FORMATION. **2.** **Social formation**: in *Marxist theory, a particular *social structure such as that of feudal or bourgeois society. Althusser saw *Marxism as charting the history of social formations, which are determined 'in the last instance' by the economic base: *see* BASE AND SUPERSTRUCTURE. 3. **Cultural formation** (Williams): any cultural group, artistic movement, or tendency with a shared aesthetic and political *ideology and *class position, such as the Bloomsbury group in England in the 1920s and 1930s. *See also* DOMINANT FORMS; EMERGENT FORMS; RESIDUAL FORMS.

form constancy *See* SHAPE CONSTANCY.

forward integration *See* VERTICAL INTEGRATION.

foundationalism (priorism) Theories granting *ontological priority to certain 'foundational' entities which are regarded as givens or first principles. Various theorists assign causal priority to God, material reality, *perception, human nature, *language, society, *ideology, *technology, and so on, raising the problem of how we are to explain these entities and their origins. *Common sense suggests that reality exists prior to and outside *signification. In a *naïve realist form, materialism posits a materiality prior to signification and attributes to it causal primacy. *Essentialism grants an *ontological status prior to and independent of language to some 'essence'. Althusser declared that ideology was *always-already given. *Structuralism involved an attack on foundationalism, emphasizing that 'reality' is a construct and that there is no way in which we can stand outside language. However, both structuralists and poststructuralists thus give priority and determining power to language—which pre-exists all individuals. This is sometimes expressed as the *primacy of the signifier. *Social determinists reject the causal priority given to language by *linguistic determinists and to technology by *technological determinists. Derrida dismissed as 'metaphysical' any conceptual hierarchy which is founded on a sacrosanct first principle and his deconstructive strategy was directed against such priorism. Some theorists would argue that while we may become more conscious of foundationalism it may nevertheless be as inescapable as 'which came first—the chicken or the egg?'

four Ps (*marketing) A traditional formulation of the priorities in the *marketing mix and product *positioning, namely: product (quality and features), price (and *value), place (*distribution, delivery etc.), and promotion (marketing/*advertising).

fourth estate *See also* PUBLIC AND PRIVATE SPHERES; *compare* FIFTH ESTATE. 1. *Newspapers in particular, and the news media in general, regarded as a legitimate political force performing a *watchdog function. A vague metaphor that draws upon the medieval concept of the three estates of the realm: the spiritual authority of the church, the secular authority of nobles, and the mass authority of the 'commons' (or the people, later the bourgeoisie). The concept is attributed to the Irish statesman Edmund Burke (1729–97). 2. For Marx, the urban proletariat.

fourth wall A theatrical convention of an imaginary barrier that separates the performers on stage from the audience. It also applies to film and television where actors rarely look directly into the camera (*see* MODE OF ADDRESS). The fourth wall is broken by a performer directly addressing the audience (*see* DIRECT ADDRESS). *See also* ILLUSIONISM.

foveal vision The small area of vision (about 2 degrees of visual angle) within which human beings have sharp focus. *Compare* PERIPHERAL VISION.

fps *See* FRAME RATE.

fragmentation 1. **(social fragmentation)** Of Western, *postmodern societies: *see* INDIVIDUALIZATION; *compare* HOMOGENIZATION. 2. Of audiences and markets: *see* AUDIENCE FRAGMENTATION. 3. **Body fragmentation**: the way in which the human body is represented in contexts such as advertisements in a fragmentary way and thus objectified (*see* OBJECTIFICATION)—particularly associated with a long history of the fragmented *representation of women's bodies in advertisements, though increasingly with male bodies also. *See also* FACE-ISM. 4. Of the *subject: *see* DECENTRED SELF. 5. **Disconnectedness**: a characteristic stylistic and structural feature in both *modernist and *postmodernist artworks and poststructuralist *theory.

frame *See also* FRAMING. 1. A physical structure within which a painting, drawing, or photograph is formally displayed: *see also* LANDSCAPE FORMAT; PORTRAIT FORMAT. 2. A printed border around material on a page. 3. A single image belonging to a sequence of images: for example, a single frame of a film, video, or digital movie, or a single picture in a comic. 4. **(film frame)** A single image on a filmstrip. 5. **(video frame)** A single interlaced image of video consisting of two *fields: *see also* INTERLACE FRAME. 6. A synonym for a *frame of reference. 7. For Goffman, a 'definition of a situation' within which we make sense of social *events. *See also* THOMAS THEOREM; *compare* SOCIAL SCHEMATA. 8. Any format or criterial template which filters the reporting of current *events in the *mass media: *see* NEWS FRAMES. 9. On the web, a subdivision of the viewing window within which separate material may be displayed: for instance, a frame running down the left-hand side may contain a static menu of options. Each choice may load different textual and graphical material into the main frame on the page. Material within such frames can be independently scrolled: *see* SCROLLING. 10. In page layout software, a moveable element on the screen into which text or images may be inserted. 11. In *discourse analysis, a transition marker between topics or sections of a discourse (such as 'now', or 'OK'). 12. In artificial intelligence, a concept analogous to a *schema. 13. In literary theory, a **frame narrative** is a story within which other stories are told (as in Chaucer's *Canterbury Tales*).

frame of reference 1. In *perception, human factors which influence the way in which a figure, object, *event, or situation is perceived; the perceptual *context which influences the selectivity of perception (*see* SALIENCE; SELECTIVE PERCEPTION). The frame of reference may lead to the transformation of the object of perception by *addition, *deletion, *substitution, and/or *transposition as well as by *foregrounding or backgrounding. 2. More generally, any analogous process of *framing, as when *genres are referred to as frames of reference.

frame rate 1. In any motion picture technology the number of images exposed to the viewer in a given time period: a sufficiently high frame rate produces the illusion of moving pictures. 2. In film, the number of individual images or frames passing through a camera or projector, measured in **frames per second (fps)**. The standard frame rate for film is 24 fps, although slow and fast motion effects can be achieved by varying the frame rate in the camera.

framing *See also* FRAME. 1. Putting a border (or *frame) around an image (or text) to mark its boundaries and to establish some degree of conceptual autonomy from its current *context. The *metaphor of framing in other contexts derives from its use in visual art. In the proscenium arch format of the traditional stage performance, '**breaking frame**' refers to theatrical devices in which the performer uses *direct address to the audience (*see also* FOURTH WALL). Bateson notes the importance of a *metamessage in interpreting a communicative act: a recognizable cue is needed for a nudge not to be misinterpreted as a sign of aggression. **Contextual** cues are needed to signal the use of *irony. 2. Representing a *figurative image as if it were a *slice of life, by allowing its edges to cut across figures appearing only partly within it—as in some paintings by Edgar Degas (1834–1917), which in this respect resemble the art of the photographic snapshot. 3. Making explicit the ground rules of an encounter or the boundaries of an academic investigation: *compare* BRACKETING THE REFERENT. 4. In perspectives influenced by the *Sapir-Whorf hypothesis, the way in which *language filters our *perception of reality. More specifically, psychological research has established that verbal labels can influence the accuracy of our *perception and/or recall of the phenomena to which they are applied. 5. Relating experiences to a *frame of reference. 6. For Goffman, the way in which we define situations in terms of regularized encounters or social *episodes in order to make sense of the social world. 7. The way in which individuals and the *mass media turn the flow of *everyday life into narrative *events: *see also* NEWS FRAMES. 8. The way in which mental templates or *schemata help us to make sense of (or contextualize) new experiences with reference to the *expectations established by previous experiences. *See also* PERCEPTUAL SET; PRIMING; SCHEMA THEORY; SELECTIVE EXPOSURE; SELECTIVE RECALL; SELECTIVE RETENTION; STEREOTYPING. 9. The *modality status given to situations, *events, or forms of *representation, as in the *Thomas theorem. 10. The ways in which *representations function to recontextualize (and thus change the meaning of) that which they represent: *see* RECONTEXTUALIZATION. 11. The role of particular techniques and devices employed in *representations as a means of constraining *interpretation: *see also* PREFERRED READING. 12. The ways in which representational *conventions naturalize the process of *representation within a particular *discourse or *code: *see also* NATURALIZATION. 13. In photography, composing an image either when taking a photograph, or subsequently, by *cropping it. Such framing unavoidably cuts the image off from its *context, and the selection of what to depict and what to exclude leaves viewers to infer the basis of this selectivity. 14. The different *frames of reference applied by audiences to the same *text. Katz and Liebes, for instance, distinguish between **referential framings,** in which viewers relate a *soap opera to their own lives, and **critical framings,** in which they comment on how it is constructed and performed.

franchise 1. A licence to reproduce an idea, design or trademark for a fee: for example, the quiz show *Who Wants to Be a Millionaire?* which was originally produced for British television in 1988 but became an international success.

2. Loosely a series of media products, especially if they are authored by different people, as with the James Bond books and films. 3. A media product, the success or predicted success of which motivates the production of other media products, such as novelizations, films, videogames, and toys. Certain *genres, such as science fiction or fantasy, are more conducive to becoming franchises than others, such as musicals or biopics.

Frankfurt school Neo-Marxist social theorists associated with the Frankfurt Institute for Social Research (1922–69), which developed what they called a '*critical theory of society' (in which 'critical theory' was a coded reference to *Marxism). Leading figures associated with this school included Adorno, the German social psychologist Erich Fromm (1900–80), Horkheimer, and Marcuse. Benjamin was on the fringe, and Habermas is of the second generation. They represented a broad range of disciplines within social science, sharing an antagonism to *positivism and the notion that any research could be *value-free. They felt that the *Enlightenment ideal of reason had been reduced to a dehumanizing and oppressive *instrumental rationality concerned only with efficiency and control (*see also* RATIONALIZATION). This was hardly surprising against the backdrop of the rise of the Nazis: they emigrated to the USA in the 1930s, returning only in 1950. They strongly opposed Marxist *economism: unlike classical Marxist theorists, they did not see *culture as a mere reflection of the economic base (*see* BASE AND SUPERSTRUCTURE). Culture was indeed seen as involved in the reproduction of the *status quo. Adorno and Horkheimer are associated with the pessimistic view that the working class is manipulated and depoliticized by what they referred to as the *culture industries (primarily the *mass media), which functioned to sustain the interests of the dominant class. They stressed the need for a critical approach to art and *aesthetics, and they admired *modernist art, which they saw as resistant to *commodification. They incorporated Freudian *psychoanalytical theory into *Marxist theory, allowing for the role of the individual. Horkheimer and Adorno argued that *audiences were not duped but could not resist the attractions of *consumerism. Adorno developed his 'negative dialectics' as an ideological critique of the *contradictions in *social relations in capitalist societies. Engaging in such a critique offered the possibility of breaking the cycle of *cultural reproduction. The ideas of the Frankfurt school diverged over time, especially after some of them remained in the USA while others returned to Germany. *See also* IDEOLOGICAL ANALYSIS.

freedom of information The right for citizens to have *access to records of the deliberations and decisions of governments, public authorities, or anyone who works for these in an official capacity. This applies to all matters except those which affect state security or infringe upon the right of individuals to privacy. In the UK this is interpreted as the right for people to have access to *information if it is in the 'public interest'.

((⊕)) SEE WEB LINKS

• Freedom of information in the UK

freedom of the press The right of free expression extended to media publications. This is designed to uphold the independence and diversity of opinions

and voices (*pluralism) of the media. *See also* FREE PRESS; JOURNALISTIC
AUTONOMY.

freeplay [French *jeu*] A reference by Derrida (originally in the 1960s) to *signifiers
not being fixed to their *signifieds but pointing beyond themselves to other
signifiers in an 'indefinite referral of signifier to signified'. Signs thus always refer to
other signs, and there is no final sign referring only to itself—no *transcendent
signified. *Meaning is endlessly deferred (*see* DIFFERENCE). Denying that there were
any ultimate determinable meanings (*see also* INDETERMINACY), Derrida
championed the *deconstruction of Western *semiotic systems. *See also* SLIPPAGE
OF MEANING; *compare* UNLIMITED SEMIOSIS.

free press Publications which are not controlled by government or restricted
by *censorship laws, where writers can voice their opinions without fear of
retribution. The right to a free press was enshrined in the first amendment to the
US constitution and in article 19 of the Universal Declaration of Human Rights.
See also FREEDOM OF THE PRESS.

(((⊕))) SEE WEB LINKS
• The Universal Declaration of Human Rights

free speech (freedom of speech) The right of any person to express their ideas
or views without the threat of official censure. Societies that enshrine free speech in
law also recognize limits when it conflicts with other human rights. *See also*
POLITICAL CORRECTNESS.

freeze frame In moving images, a still image that is created by multiple
repetitions of the same picture.

frequency and reach *See* EFFECTIVE FREQUENCY; EFFECTIVE REACH; REACH.

frequency modulation (FM) A method of *encoding *information into the
wave of a carrier signal by increasing and decreasing its length but not altering its
height. *Wavelengths can be astronomically large so **frequency** (or the number of
times they pulse in a second) is the preferred measurement. *See also* FM RADIO.

Freudianism A usually pejorative reference to Freudian *psychoanalytic theory,
often caricatured as seeking to reveal *sex as the basis of all human *motivation.

Freudian slip *See* PARAPRAXIS.

Freytag's pyramid A sequence of five structural phases in a drama:
introduction, rising action, climax, falling action, and **catastrophe.** *Compare*
CLASSICAL NARRATIVE STRUCTURE.

frontality 1. The *representation of figures or objects so that they face directly
toward the viewer and tend towards bilateral symmetry (a 'front view' or 'head-on'
view). 2. Broadly, the depiction of figures, objects, or scenes in any visual medium
at a non-oblique angle to the viewer (facing towards them or at right-angles to
them). 3. The depiction of figures, objects, or scenes oriented parallel to the *picture
plane in one-point or parallel *perspective: *see also* LINEAR PERSPECTIVE. 4. A
pictorial *convention (characteristic of ancient Egyptian art and sometimes called

'frontal-profile') in which the human figure was represented with the head in profile, the eye and shoulders in front view, and the lower body in profile.

front end 1. In software design, the part of an application that is seen and used by consumers. 2. In *videogaming, the opening screen of a game that typically displays configurable options to the user.

front region (front stage) *See* BACK STAGE.

full-duplex A transmission system that is active in both directions at the same time. A *mobile phone is a full-duplex device. *See also* HALF-DUPLEX; SIMPLEX.

full height anamorphic (FHA) In television, a 16:9 picture that is filmed by being electronically squeezed along the horizontal axis into a 12:9 (4 x 3) frame and expanded using an *aspect-ratio converter. This method utilizes the full height of the image and thus all the available TV lines (unlike *letterboxing) and it is how video *footage has been transmitted for showing on standard definition *widescreen televisions since the 1990s.

full-service agency An *advertising agency with its own departments for creative work, *market research, and *media planning and buying. Many of the major agencies have 'unbundled' some of their services, focusing on account handling (*see* ACCOUNT HANDLER). Smaller **advertising boutiques** are variously media independents (specialist media agencies handling *media buying and planning), creative specialists (*see* CREATIVES), and *production specialists (video and broadcast production companies).

function 1. A generic application for which some tool or *medium is primarily designed, or which is attributed to it within a *functionalist framework, as distinct from the specific *purposes of users on particular occasions. 2. The role of something in satisfying particular *needs. In the case of human beings these may be either biological or social. Where this notion is applied to society itself, critics note that social systems cannot be assumed to be analogous to human organisms. 3. Requirements regarded as essential (prerequisites or *necessary conditions) for the maintenance and continuation of some system. Examples from a *functionalist perspective on society (where these are sometimes called **functional imperatives**), include reproduction and *socialization. Not all functions so formulated can be easily established. 4. The consequence of some action for the maintenance of the social system as a whole. These may be intended or unintended. Critics have suggested that such explanations are teleological in accounting for functions in terms of their effects on the system of which they are a part. 5. (*syntax) The relation between a linguistic form and other parts of the unit in which it occurs (e.g. *subject or *object). 6. (*phonetics) The contrastive basis for differentiating *phonemes. 7. A generic kind of *utterance within an *interchange: e.g. question, answer, or statement. 8. For relationships between linguistic form and social or interpersonal *settings or situations, *see* LINGUISTIC FUNCTIONS. 9. For usage related to *roles in *interpersonal communication, *see* COMMUNICATIVE FUNCTIONS. 10. For uses of the media, *see* MEDIA FUNCTIONS; PERSONAL FUNCTIONS; SOCIAL FUNCTIONS. 11. (mathematics) A dependency relation. For example, the items in a typology are a function of the *theory within which they are framed. 12. In Propp's *narratology, a standardized element in the plot of a *narrative, defined in terms of its role within it. 13. For Barthes, the smallest narrative unit.

functionalism 1. An instrumental and utilitarian design principle that *form should be dictated (at least primarily) by practical function rather than by any other factors—notably *aesthetic considerations. It is reflected in such phrases as 'form follows function' (originally employed in relation to architecture) and 'fitness for purpose' (which has recently enjoyed a revival in political *rhetoric). 2. Any approach focusing on the function or role of parts within a whole system. 3. **(structural functionalism)** An umbrella term for various theories explaining social and cultural practices and *institutions in terms of their functional roles within sociocultural systems (*see also* MEDIA FUNCTIONS). Society is seen as a system greater than the sum of those who comprise it. It is based on a common system of *norms or a *consensus about *values and goals, and these are seen as the basis of social order and social *integration. Deviance is a malfunction. It was established by the British sociologist Herbert Spencer (1820–1903) and Durkheim, the latter arguing that sociology involved both causal and functional explanations. Functionalism was later adopted by the anthropologists Malinowski and Radcliffe-Brown and the sociologists Parsons and Merton. It has been criticized (not always accurately) for neglecting human *agency, social *interaction, *competition, *conflict, and social change, and as being inherently conservative and *ahistorical. Others note that such theories tend to neglect the role of dominant groups in shaping societies in their own interests rather than in the interest of society as a whole. However, functionalist concepts are still widely invoked in contemporary sociology, and as Durkheim suggested, functional and causal approaches need not be incompatible.
4. (*linguistics) Functionalism is the view that the structure of *language is determined by the *functions that it serves. Consequently, functionalist linguists focus on the function of linguistic forms. This perspective is closely linked with *structuralism. Structuralist phonemic analysis focuses on the basic functional differences between *phonemes. Linguists within this tradition include: the Russian formalists (including Propp, Voloshinov, and Bakhtin); the Prague school (including Jakobson); Hjelmslev, the Frenchman André Martinet (1908–99), Sapir, Whorf, Halliday, and the Dutchman Teun A. van Dijk (b.1943). *See also* FORMALISM; LINGUISTIC FUNCTIONS. 5. (psychology) A perspective emphasizing mental experience and behaviour in relation to its functional value to the organism in adapting to the environment rather than in relation to its *content. This approach was superseded by *behaviourism in the 1930s. 6. (philosophy) An approach viewing mental states as functional states, as in artificial intelligence.

functions *See* COMMUNICATIVE FUNCTIONS; LINGUISTIC FUNCTIONS; MEDIA FUNCTIONS.

function words *See* GRAMMATICAL WORDS.

future shock Individual anxieties in Western societies about the increasing pace of social and technological change. Toffler coined the term in 1965, popularizing it in the title of a bestseller in 1970. *See also* INFORMATION OVERLOAD.

game In many languages a term synonymous with *play, but distinguished in English as specifying a certain activity associated with play (as opposed to a general activity performed playfully) which is contextualized and structured according to certain rules and social *conventions (and typically, goals and winners). *See also* COMMUNICATION GAME; LANGUAGE GAMES; VIDEOGAME.

gamer A person who regularly plays *videogames. Gamers can be **casual** or **hardcore** depending upon the degree of commitment they exhibit.

game studies *See* VIDEOGAME STUDIES.

gatekeepers Key personnel who regulate *access to *information, goods, services, or those in power. For example, in news journalism, the job description of editors includes strategic decision-making on matters such as *newsworthiness and *taste. It also includes owners, executives, producers, and managers throughout the *media industries. Gatekeeper studies have explored various factors influencing decision-making by gatekeepers, including the largely unconscious role of dominant *value systems. It has been argued that those in positions of power and influence selectively recruit others like themselves, consequently excluding other values. However, such power is not uncontested within the media industries. *See also* TWO-STEP FLOW.

gatekeeping A concept in sociology and social psychology based on functions regulating *access to *information, resources, and those in power within hierarchical social structures and organizations. It can refer either to the limitation and control of access to goods and services or to filtered *downward communication. Some theorists have criticized the emphasis on such top-down processes, arguing that this fails to account for processes of negotiation. Suggestions that the *internet is less susceptible to this function seem somewhat utopian; indeed, information *portals are valued for their filtering function. *See also* INFORMATION FLOW.

gaze *See also* SPECTATOR; VIEWING. **1.** *v.* To look steadily and intently at someone or something. **2.** *n.* A steady and intent look. **3.** (social psychology) Looking at other people in the general direction of their eyes: a key form of *nonverbal communication. Increased gazing can signify *liking, attraction, or *dominance (though greater looking while listening can signify submissiveness or lower *status). It is closely involved in the regulation of conversational *turn-taking in *face-to-face interaction. The study of **gaze behaviour** is an aspect of *kinesics. *See also* EYE CONTACT; GAZE AVERSION. **4.** In

gender

Western society, the way in which (heterosexual) males have traditionally felt free to survey females visually; women have frequently been represented as the passive objects of this objectifying and 'active' gaze. This is both a *symbolic reflection of dominant *power relations in patriarchal societies, and at the same time a *performance and mode of maintenance of such relations. Only since the mid 1980s have men themselves also begun to be publicly depicted as objects of the gaze, notably in *advertising. The study of the gaze in *visual culture is termed **gaze theory**. *See also* CODES OF LOOKING; OBJECTIFICATION. **5.** For Freud, a look which is an uneasy mixture of partial *identification with desire. **6.** [French *le regard*, rendered as 'the gaze'] In Lacan, the look of the infant that is reflected back by the mirror as a coherent but illusory image of the self (*see also* IMAGINARY). Lacan later counter-intuitively presents the gaze as a property of the object of *perception which 'captures' our attention: rather than us freely choosing to look, the object pictures us. **7. (the look)** (*film theory) A form of viewing associated by Mulvey with a *male gaze which was dominant in *classical Hollywood cinema: *see also* FEMALE GAZE; MALE GAZE. **8.** [French *le regard*, often rendered as 'the look'] For Sartre, a look of which one is the *object, which limits one's freedom and may lead to shame. **9.** For Foucault, the process of being objectified and subordinated when we are surveyed by those with power: *see also* PANOPTICISM. **10.** (screen theory) A type of look associated with film, rather than the *glance associated with television: *see also* SPECTATOR.

(((🌐))) SEE WEB LINKS

• Notes on 'the gaze'

gaze aversion (gaze avoidance) Discontinuation or deliberate avoidance of *eye contact: for instance, because looking longer would be staring, because of feeling dominated, because we are ignoring someone, or because we are embarrassed, uncomfortable, or depressed. Adults avert gaze by glancing to one side or the other. Gaze aversion after brief eye contact is part of a pattern of behaviour known as **civil inattention**. An **averted gaze** thus signals disengagement.

gender **1.** The origin of the term is in *grammar, where it refers to a class in some languages in which nouns and pronouns are located, marked by inflections distinguishing them as masculine, feminine, or neuter. **2.** In common usage, sometimes driven by a misguided sense of *political correctness or a prudish avoidance of the term *sex*, the state of being male or female. **3.** (social science) The sociocultural construction of male and female *identity as the primary social category, with differentiated cultural *norms for (stereotypical) masculine and feminine traits, *roles, *values, *discourse practices, and forms of behaviour (*see also* FEMININITY; MASCULINITY). *Socialization naturalizes such differences, so that natives of a *culture may treat as natural an identity between male and masculine, female and feminine, and may be unaware of the extent to which gender differences may involve conventions to which they have become thoroughly accustomed (*see also* GENDER DIFFERENCES; GENDER ESSENTIALISM; NATURALIZATION). For social scientists, gender is culturally and historically variable and cannot be equated with biological sex. From this perspective, gender does not explain differences: gender results from the creation of differences. Furthermore, genders are not homogeneous categories: 'masculinities' and 'femininities' are inflected by factors such as *class, age, and *ethnicity. **4.** A mode of human differentiation based on a hierarchical *binary opposition, in which, as the French philosopher Simone de Beauvoir (1908–86) was the first to note, woman is marked as 'other' (*see also* DIFFERENCE; MARKEDNESS; OTHERNESS). This opposition reinforces both patriarchy and *heteronormativity. Bem has demonstrated that traditionally masculine and feminine qualities are exhibited in varying degrees by both sexes. **5.** In *feminist theory, an *ideological mechanism for the subordination of women which feminists seek to critique, denaturalize, or deconstruct (*see also* DECONSTRUCTION; DENATURALIZATION; FEMINISM). Although *gender essentialists insist that certain basic values, skills, 'ways of seeing', and so on, variously attributed to nature and/or culture, distinguish males from females, from the 1970s onwards many have argued that gender is a locus of *power relations, so that what may appear to be differences related to sex can be seen primarily as differences related to inequalities of power in patriarchal societies. **6.** In structuralist sociology (*see* FUNCTIONALISM), sexually-differentiated roles seen as generated by social structures: particularly the **division of labour** in traditional families, which reproduces the *alignment of male-earner-instrumental and female-carer-expressive (*see also* COMMUNICATION STYLE; EXPRESSIVE COMMUNICATION; INSTRUMENTAL COMMUNICATION). **7.** In Freudian *psychoanalytic theory, sex-based roles that are assigned through the Oedipus complex, in which *identification with the same-sex parent leads to the incorporation of this role into the self as part of the superego, and to the alignment of *masculinity with activity and *femininity with passivity: *see also* MALE GAZE. **8.** In *symbolic interactionism and in *queer theory, a sociocultural *identity which one performs in order to 'pass' as male or female, gay or straight. Gender is thus a practice and a process, not a given: *see also* PERFORMANCE; PERFORMATIVITY.

gender bias **1.** In sociology and gender studies, prejudice associated with sex roles in society (*see* GENDER ROLES) and gender terms in language (*see* MALE NORM). Such a *bias is often expressed in casual *stereotyping. *Communication styles associated with women are often evaluated negatively: women's conversation is '*small talk'. **2.** Unconscious reliance on one's own gendered practices in communicating with, or creating *representations for, a general audience (or tools for general use), particularly the *male norm in patriarchal cultures, since the specificity of the worldview of those with *power is normally unmarked and invisible even to themselves: *see also* MARKEDNESS. **3.** *Sexism. **4.** *Heteronormativity. **5.** The habitual under- or over-representation of one sex or sexual identity in *mass media depictions—or the more frequent depiction of one *sex or *sexual identity in subordinate *roles. *Content analysis has been widely employed to identify such gender biases in mass media *texts. *See also* GENDER STEREOTYPES; SYMBOLIC ERASURE. **6.** *Institutional bias that produces *gender role inequalities. The under- or over-population of certain jobs by one sex (*see also* FEMINIZATION; MASCULINIZATION), not necessarily as a result of overt discrimination. Where such jobs are within the *mass media, this is likely to be an influence on gender depictions.

gender differences (sex differences) 1. Often used synonymously with
*gender. 2. Differences in *attitudes, *values, or behaviour attributable to social
constructions of gender rather than to biological differences but which are
naturalized within *cultures through *socialization (*see also* GENDER ROLES;
NATURALIZATION). Some theorists argue that the differences between cultures in
their construction of gender suggest that gender differences constitute relatively
arbitrary *codes. 3. Differences attributable to the ways parents and others treat
children according to their *sex, within cultural *norms. 4. Differences reproduced
by the influence of *gender stereotypes on children at an impressionable stage.
5. **(gender inequalities)** *Gender role inequalities caused by institutional *gender
bias. 6. Differences attributed to biological factors, such as chromosomal and
hormonal differences and (controversially) differences in brain structure and
function. 7. Psychological differences between the sexes. Eleanor Maccoby and
Carol Jacklin's *The Psychology of Sex Differences* in 1974, identified a tendency
for males to perform better than females on mathematical and visual-spatial tasks
(*see also* FIELD DEPENDENCE AND INDEPENDENCE; SPATIAL PERCEPTION), for females
to perform better than males on verbal tasks, and for males to be more aggressive
than females. On most tasks, there were no consistent differences. Subsequent
studies have tended to indicate fewer differences in these domains, but have noted
that females tend to conform more in groups, to be more easily persuaded, and to
be better at decoding *nonverbal behaviour than males (*see also* DECODING
ABILITY). Differences have also been noted in *communication styles (*see also*
EXPRESSIVE COMMUNICATION; INSTRUMENTAL COMMUNICATION). However,
differences between members of the same sex often outweigh differences between
the sexes. 8. A posited tendency for females to be markedly less resistant to
*identification with characters of the other sex in *narratives than are males: *see also*
GENDERED IDENTIFICATIONS; MALE GAZE. 9. In traditional Freudian *psychoanalytic
theory, differences produced in childhood by the passage through the Oedipus
complex: *see also* IDENTIFICATION THEORY. 10. In *Marxist theory, inequalities
between the sexes produced by the *power relations in capitalist society.

gendered camerawork A tendency to use some photographic techniques
more or less often depending on whether the *target audience is male or female.
For instance, *close-ups can have feminine *connotations partly because of their
frequency in 'feminine' screen *genres, where they are used to *foreground *facial
expressions of *emotion.

gendered editing A tendency to use some film *editing techniques more or
less often depending on whether the *target audience is male or female. For
instance, a more rapid *cutting rate has masculine *connotations because of its
association with the stereotypically masculine action *film genre. Similarly, *cross
dissolves can have feminine connotations (they are far more common in
commercials for girls than in those for boys).

(((🌐))) SEE WEB LINKS

• Gender-differentiated production features in toy commercials

gendered genres *See also* GENRE. 1. *Formats in any *medium for which the
primary *target audience is one sex rather than the other. In relation to *television

genres, *soap operas are often characterized as a feminine genre, although it is notable that the actual audience split by sex for British soap operas is usually about 60:40 female to male. Members of a *secondary audience may sometimes notice themselves being targeted, as when soap operas incorporate elements of crime drama, or when crime drama switches to a focus on relationships. 2. *Narrative forms which, in relation to their relative *closure, can be perceived as having masculine or feminine associations (*see* CLOSED FORMS; OPEN FORMS). This need not reflect a naïve *essentialism, since cultural forms can acquire (as well as lose) cultural *connotations over time: *see* GENDERING.

gendered identifications 1. In relation to *text-reader relations, the notion in theories of *identification, that *audiences tend to identify with those who are most like themselves (albeit in an idealized form), and that this normally includes those of the same sex. Some (e.g. Horton, Wohl, and the British psychologist Grant Noble) have argued that females are much more likely than (heterosexual) males to identify with an opposite-sex character. Film theorists such as Mulvey (*see* MALE GAZE) have endorsed this stance, arguing that 'for women (from childhood onwards) trans-sex identification is a habit that very easily becomes second Nature'. Others, such as Eleanor Maccoby and William Cody Wilson, have argued that if strong female roles were to be given equal *representation, this divergence would disappear. *See also* FEMALE GAZE. 2. In relation to interpersonal *interaction, *see* IDENTIFICATION THEORY.

((())) SEE WEB LINKS
• Gendered readings of *Big Brother 2*

gender inequalities *See* GENDER DIFFERENCES.

gendered technologies The association of a *technology primarily with one sex. For example, the domestic (landline) *telephone was culturally feminized by its fixed location in the private sphere (*see* PUBLIC AND PRIVATE SPHERES), which meant that men associated the domestic phone with feminine '*small talk', and they were much more likely to dislike using it than women were. This led to a famous *advertising campaign in the UK in the 1990s, fronted by the 'man's man' Bob Hoskins, who reassured men that 'it's good to talk'. The *mobile phone is free of domestic *connotations and thus defeminized. *See also* BROWN GOODS; FEMINIZATION; MASCULINIZATION; WHITE GOODS.

gender essentialism 1. The belief that males and females are born with distinctively different natures, determined biologically rather than culturally. This involves an equation of *gender and *sex. The term is often used pejoratively by constructionists (*see* CONSTRUCTIONISM), but *strategic essentialism is a common activist strategy, and *biological essentialism surfaces in the insistence of some *feminists that the physical facts of sexual difference do have entailments. *See also* DIFFERENCE MODEL; ESSENTIALISM. 2. The belief that gay people are born gay (a form of *biological determinism) and/or that there is a distinctive 'gay sensibility'. 3. The attribution of a homogeneous identity to a labelled group (such as women or gay males), ignoring differences within it. This can be either a naïve essentialism (for instance, labelling people in widely-different *cultures and historical periods simply as 'gay'), or a politically-motivated *strategic essentialism.

gender identity 1. The role in one's subjective sense of self of one's own personal negotiation with *masculinity and *femininity as framed within our own *culture. Sometimes distinguished from the public expression of this in *gender roles. 2. The psychological *internalization of traits framed as masculine or feminine. 3. A *context-sensitive performance of *roles in social *interaction that relates either normatively or subversively to prevalent *expectations about one's *sexual identity, particularly as reflected in public behaviour and *appearance.

gendering The sociohistorical process in which particular cultural forms come to be associated more with one sex than the other within a culture, generating *gender *connotations and playing a significant part in the construction of gender. Such forms include *discourses, *genres, shapes, *colours, media, tools, and *technologies. In the contemporary world, pink is so *marked as feminine that this can feel a natural association, yet it was not always so. In June 1918, this observation appeared in a Chicago-based trade magazine called *The Infants' Department*: 'Pink or blue? Which is intended for boys and which for girls?... There has been a great diversity of opinion on this subject, but the generally accepted rule is pink for the boy and blue for the girl. The reason is that pink being a more decided and stronger color, is more suitable for the boy; while blue, which is more delicate and dainty is prettier for the girl.' Nor is this an isolated source for the same sentiments in the early decades of the 20th century. This is a powerful example of how the gendering of cultural forms can change over time. *See also* BROWN GOODS; FEMINIZATION; GENDERED TECHNOLOGIES; MASCULINIZATION; WHITE GOODS.

genderlect In *sociolinguistics, a speech variety or *communication style particularly associated with one sex (a kind of *dialect). Such styles are shaped by cultural factors: Robin Lakoff, an American linguist (b.1942) argues that they are a result of differences in male and female social *roles. Speech differences are a key feature in *gender stereotypes: as in the man of few words and the garrulous woman. The most widespread distinction with some basis in current social reality is between feminine expressivity and masculine instrumentality (*see* EXPRESSIVE COMMUNICATION; INSTRUMENTAL COMMUNICATION). In everyday *face-to-face interaction, compared to men, women tend to be more relational than task-oriented (*see* RELATIONAL COMMUNICATION; TASK-ORIENTED COMMUNICATION). Tannen identifies different *values in conversational *language: 'status and independence' in male language and 'connection and intimacy' in women's language. According to some theorists (such as Robin Lakoff), women's use of language tends to involve more verbal 'fillers', *hedges, *qualifiers, and politeness markers; being less definitive ('perhaps . . . '); using more justifiers ('because . . . '); asking more questions; agreeing more with conversational partners; not interrupting and not monopolizing topic choice. However, ultimately such differences are about relative *power in societies rather than about innate differences between the sexes. *Compare* DIALECT; IDIOLECT; SOCIOLECT.

gender roles (sex roles) 1. Socially assigned *roles traditionally associated with each *sex within a *culture (such as mother or provider). 2. Loosely-connected sets of traditional cultural *norms and social *expectations for psychological traits, *attitudes, *perceptions, behaviour, affective reactions, and *appearance regarded as appropriate in particular *contexts for each sex, widely regarded within that culture as universal but in fact culturally variable (or differently valued). These roles are learned through *socialization, including through the *mass media (*see* GENDER STEREOTYPES). Individuals feel expected to reproduce them by virtue of their being male or female: *see also* GENDER DIFFERENCES. 3. Sometimes applied to the public expression of *gender identity, where the latter is distinguished as a private and personal experience.

gender stereotypes (sex role stereotypes) *See also* STEREOTYPING. 1. Personal beliefs about *gender differences in traits and behaviour, largely attributable to *socialization. 2. Standardized *representations of men and women within a culture, particularly in the *mass media, which polarize differences between the sexes, notably in their physical *appearance, traits, behaviours, and occupations. The stereotypes are so widely known that on the basis of identifying any one element in a gender stereotype (such as physical appearance), people regularly make *inferences about other elements associated with it. Hence the widespread use of such stereotypes as a convenient shorthand in the various fiction *genres in the mass media. Such representations are widely regarded as a key factor in *gender role socialization, functioning as a conservative influence on *cultural reproduction. They have often been studied using *content analysis and *semiotic approaches. 3. A cultural system of *binary oppositions of concepts with gendered *connotations such as, in traditional Western cultures: active/passive, mind/body, reason/emotion, objective/subjective, public/private, culture/nature. In each case the first term in the pair is gendered as masculine. Similarly, the *connotations of *formal features such as straight vs curvy, plain vs fancy or colourful, literal or denotational vs metaphorical or connotative, hard vs soft, coarse vs fine, and heavy vs light. 4. In *communication styles, the gendering of *instrumental and *task-oriented communication as masculine and of *expressive and *relational communication as feminine.

(((●))) SEE WEB LINKS

• GLAAD's advertising media program

generalized other A general *model of the *status, behaviour, and *attitudes associated with particular social *roles which is internalized by the individual as part of *socialization and forms the basis of *expectations in social *interaction and the individual's own *performance of roles. For Mead being able to take the role of others emerged in the 'game-stage' of childhood and was the third and final stage in the development of the self. This concept had a key influence on *symbolic interactionism. *Compare* SIGNIFICANT OTHERS.

general semantics A philosophical movement, initiated in the 1930s by the Polish-American philosopher Alfred Korzybski (1879–1950), seeking to develop public awareness of the conventional basis of the relationships between words and things in order to improve clarity of thought and communication. This bears comparison with the Saussurean emphasis on the conventional nature of the relationship between the *signifier and the *signified in linguistic *signs. *See also* SEMANTICS.

general views (GVs) In the logging notation of film and video rushes, a shorthand term for *shots that establish a specific location, subject, or activity. Normally GVs are additional shots that are not the main focus of the filming but can be used by editors as *establishing shots or *cutaways.

generation loss In *analogue recordings, a progressive loss of quality that occurs every time a tape, film, or vinyl disc is copied. The problem of generation loss has been reduced but not eradicated in *digital media. *See also* COMPRESSION; CONCEALMENT ERROR.

generation X (Gen X) The *age cohort born between 1964 and 1984, characterized by their pessimism and cynicism. For the Canadian novelist Douglas Copeland (b.1961), they are stereotypically the children of divorced parents who are distrustful of authority and who define themselves in relation to their *lifestyle choices, behaving as *savvy consumers. *Compare* BABY BOOMERS; GENERATION Y.

generation Y One of the names given to the *age cohort born after 1984 and before 2000, characterized by their optimism and technical confidence (especially with computers and the *internet). 'Y' alludes to their questioning 'Why?'. The children of *baby boomers, they tend to be affluent, although they often have issues with obesity and underage drinking. *Compare* GENERATION X.

generic representation A generalized *representation of a category, such as Man or Woman, sometimes employing an individual example to stand synecdochally for such a category and sometimes a more abstract *idealization. *See also* METONYMIC FALLACY; SYNECDOCHE.

genetic determinism *See* BIOLOGICAL DETERMINISM.

genetic epistemology *See* CONSTRUCTIVISM.

genre 1. In literary, film, and aesthetic theory, a type of *text recognized by particular *conventions of *form and content which are shared by other texts of that type (e.g. westerns, thrillers, historical romances). Audience *expectations about a text are 'managed' by genre conventions and genre features in the *production and the *marketing of many media products from indie music to blockbuster films. However, genre is not an unproblematic basis for taxonomy because individual texts within a genre rarely if ever have all of its characteristic features, and texts often exhibit the conventions of more than one genre. Genres also evolve over time, generating hybrid forms that in turn may spawn new genres (*see* HYBRID GENRE). They cannot be adequately defined purely in terms of *textual features, partly because they also involve varying relationships between producers and *audiences (*see* TEXT-READER RELATIONS). Traditionally, literary and film critics in particular have regarded 'generic' texts (by which they mean 'formulaic' popular texts) as inferior to texts that are **genre transgressive** works of art (*see* TRANSGRESSION). However, Derrida argued in 1981 that 'there is no genreless text'. *See also* FILM

GENRES; GENDERED GENRES; LITERARY GENRES; RADIO GENRES; TELEVISION GENRES; VIDEOGAME GENRES. 2. **(discourse genres)** In *linguistics and *discourse analysis, any variety of speech **(speech genres)** or writing **(written genres)** that is widely recognized, such as a conversation, a joke, or a menu. Genres such as conversation can have subgenres, such as telephone conversation. Each form has its own formal stylistic properties, social *functions, and associated *contexts. Sometimes used synonymously with *register. *See also* COMMUNICATIVE PURPOSES.

(⊕) SEE WEB LINKS
• Introduction to genre theory

genre fiction *See* LITERARY GENRES.

geographical identity (geographic identity) *See also* IDENTITY. 1. An individual or group's sense of attachment to the country, region, city, or village in which they live. 2. The key characteristics with which a particular country, region, city, or village is associated.

geographic segmentation (geographics) (*marketing) The division of markets into different geographical areas (global regions, countries, local regions, cities) based on significant commonalities of needs, wants, and purchasing habits within such areas and differences from others, primarily in the interests of effective *targeting. *See also* SEGMENTATION.

gestalt (Gestalt, *pl.* Gestalten) 1. In the psychology of *perception, a unified structure, shape, or *form that is greater (i.e. more meaningful) than the sum of its parts, and which takes perceptual precedence over these. Perception always involves the separation of a meaningful figure from its ground (*see* FIGURE AND GROUND; GESTALT LAWS). **Gestalt theory** is a school of thought in psychology: the key figures were Wertheimer, Köhler, and Koffka. It contrasts strongly with the stimulus-response model of *behaviourism. 2. In Iser's *reception theory, interpretive *frames formed by readers as they read a *text.

gestalt laws (Gestalt principles of perceptual organization) (psychology) Unconscious and apparently universal principles of *perception that favour particular forms of *perceptual organization. *See also* COMMON FATE; FIGURE AND GROUND; GOOD CONTINUATION; GROUND; PRÄGNANZ; PROXIMITY; SIMILARITY; SMALLNESS; SURROUNDEDNESS; SYMMETRY.

(⊕) SEE WEB LINKS
• Laws of organization in perceptual forms

gestural language *See* SIGN LANGUAGE.

gesture A meaningful body movement, usually of the hand or head, though the term can include *facial expression and expressive movements of the whole body. The main kinds of gestures are manual ones, primarily: *emblems, *illustrators, *batons, and *self-touch. They are culturally highly variable, although a few are universal (*see* EMBLEMS). Sapir referred to gesture as 'an elaborate code that is written nowhere, known by none, and understood by all.' The study of gesture is an aspect of *kinesics.

GIGO (garbage in, garbage out) A maxim of computing which states that if invalid *data is input to a computer the output will always be invalid.

given and new (given information, new information) In *discourse analysis and *text linguistics, with reference to the *information structure of *utterances and *texts, **given** refers to *information that has already been provided in the preceding linguistic *context; **new** refers to fresh information. **Given** and **new** are sometimes called *topic and comment. *Compare* THEME.

givenness *See* ALWAYS-ALREADY GIVEN.

given off meaning *See* UNINTENTIONAL COMMUNICATION.

glance A term sometimes used to refer to the kind of casual viewing associated with watching television, as distinct from the *gaze—the term usually applied to watching films in the cinema. Such a distinction relates partly to the generally more casual social *setting of domestic viewing compared to cinema-going, but arguably sometimes also to an elitist conception of television as an inherently less demanding medium of *popular culture and to film as a potentially more serious form of art.

glance curve In relation to the *perception of visual art, the German psychologist Mercedes Gaffron (1908–93) argued in 1950 that Western viewers unconsciously followed a basic perceptual path in looking at two-dimensional perspectival *representations—a left-to-right movement—running upwards from the lower left *foreground, across to the right, into three-dimensional depicted space. We become aware of this phenomenon only when an image is laterally flipped. It is not clear how this is related to physical *eye movements. Wölfflin had already argued that there was a general tendency for the (Western) viewer to follow a visual path from the lower left of the picture, first going up, then going down (perhaps a tendency in Western art to assume such a path), but he had focused on the *picture plane rather than relating it to pictorial depth. *See also* READING DIRECTION.

Glasgow media group (Glasgow University Media Group, GUMG) An influential group of media researchers formed in 1974 which has investigated the role of television news journalism in relation to *agenda setting, making notable use of *content analysis. They are best-known for arguing that an implicit journalistic *ideology tends to uphold the *status quo and that *events are not adequately contextualized.

(🌐) SEE WEB LINKS

• Glasgow University Media Group

globalization *Compare* McDONALDIZATION. 1. A planet-wide systematic interrelationship of all *social ties so that no given relationship or set of relationships can remain isolated or bounded and consequently geographical boundaries become unsustainable. In the social sciences this is marked by a shift away from the nation-state to the transnational (the new world order, global capitalism, environmentalism) as the analytical theme. **2.** The phenomenon of a shrinking world and an increasing awareness among individuals of being global citizens (*see* DISTANCIATION; GLOBAL VILLAGE; TIME-SPACE COMPRESSION) where transportation and *communication technologies have augmented immediate experience of localities, supplanting them with actual or mediated impressions of the globe: a trend that is not always embraced by individuals or cultures. *See* GLOCALIZATION; LOCALIZATION. **3.** A process contemporary with *modernization proceeding since the 16th century (although much accelerated in recent times) involving economic systematization, international relations between states, and an emerging global consciousness. Robertson contends that this does not imply that the world is more harmoniously integrated but merely that it is more systematically unified: *see* HOMOGENIZATION; HYBRIDIZATION. **4.** For Giddens, a multicausal process aligned with *modernity, the progress of which appears to be inexorable but the outcome of which is uncertain because it operates within four relatively autonomous arenas: capitalism, *surveillance, military order, and industrialism, which are insulated from one another.

(⊕) SEE WEB LINKS

• Globalization

global media Media bought up through mergers and acquisitions and owned by a handful of transnational corporations such as News International and Google. The American political economists Herman and Robert McChesney argue that the presence of global media is a cause for concern because their power challenges governments. It also has an adverse effect on media diversity because although there appear to be lots of outlets, they are owned by only a few companies. *See* VERTICAL INTEGRATION.

Global Positioning System (GPS) A technology that works out a person's latitude and longitude based on triangulating their position using satellites and sends the data to a dedicated GPS unit or a portable device such as a *mobile phone.

global village A term popularized by McLuhan, long before the *World Wide Web, for a world that has been phenomenally shrunk by *communication technologies and transport systems so that news and *information spreads rapidly across the planet and those with direct *access to such technologies feel more interconnected, as if they were members of the same community. *See also* McLUHANISM.

glocalization A portmanteau term (*globalization* + *localization*). *See also* RE-EMBEDDING. **1.** A term that emphasizes that these two concepts do not exist in polar *opposition, but rather that they operate in mutual interdependence in a globalized world. Typified by the slogan, 'Think globally, act locally'. People understand the significance of *globalization when it impacts on their local environment, which leads to the perception that global phenomena are local (e.g. through media *representations of far-off places) and local phenomena are global (the imported food in our supermarkets). The term was introduced by

Robertson in 1992. 2. (*advertising) The tailoring of global techniques and resources to appeal to increasingly differentiated markets.

god terms (god words) Words reflecting core sociohistorical *values in a *culture or *subculture in a particular period, which are consequently prominent in cultural *rhetoric. For instance, in the USA, such terms include *freedom*, *motherhood*, and *justice*. These are positively-evaluated, potent, but vague concepts. **Devil terms** are negatively-evaluated, but similarly potent and vague (for example, *un-American*). The concept derives from Richard M. Weaver (1910–63), an American rhetorician.

golden mean (golden section, golden ratio) A supposedly ideal visual proportion in composition and design in painting, architecture, sculpture, and photography. It is based on the ratio between two unequal parts of a whole where the proportion of the smaller part to the larger one is equal to that of the larger part to the whole. For instance, a straight line or a rectangle can be divided in this way: hence its use in pictorial composition. It is mathematically expressed as *phi*: 1 plus the square root of 5, divided by 2 (roughly equivalent to 1.618:1). The concept can also be applied to the *aspect ratio of the *frame.

gonzo journalism [*slang* 'crazy', 'off the wall'] A style of reporting that places the reporter and their quest for *information at the centre of the story. A kind of journalistic equivalent to *participant observation, which often includes verbatim transcriptions of telephone conversations, telegrams, and *interviews. Hunter S. Thompson (1937–2005), an American journalist, claims that he originated the style when, in the rush to meet a deadline, he simply pulled pages out of his notebook and sent them to the publisher in desperation.

good continuation In the *gestalt laws of *perception, the principle whereby in visual patterns, smooth continuity is preferred to abrupt change. A roughly-drawn X-shape, for instance, is more likely to be seen as two diagonal lines than as a V-shape on top of an inverted V-shape, because in the former each line would represent a smooth continuity of an established direction.

Google journalism Reportage based largely on *internet searches. Normally a pejorative term.

governmentality *See* POWER.

GPS *See* GLOBAL POSITIONING SYSTEM.

grader *See* COLOURIST.

grading The process of colour-correcting video or film *footage. Grading can also be used to create a distinct look for a film or television programme: e.g. *Traffic* (2000). *See also* COLOURIST; TELECINE; *compare* COLOUR TIMING.

grammar 1. The branch of *linguistics concerned with the *structure of *language. 2. *Syntax (the structure or clauses and sentences) and *morphology (word structure). 3. In generative grammar, the linguistic *knowledge internalized by a native speaker. 4. **(narrative grammar)** In *narratives, abstract structural forms in which, for instance, the *subject is the actor (**actant**) and the *object is the 'receiver' of an action: *compare* STORY GRAMMAR. **5.** Even more broadly, patterned structural relationships in any *medium, and/or the user's *knowledge of this. Some theorists (most formally in structuralist *semiotics) refer to the 'grammar' of media other than language, in particular in relation to visual media, while others have challenged this application of a linguistic model to media which move beyond the verbal. *See also* FILM GRAMMAR; VISUAL GRAMMAR.

grammar of motives *See* DRAMATURGY.

grammatical words (function words) (*linguistics) Words for which the primary *function is to indicate grammatical relationships, as distinct from **lexical words**, the primary function of which is *referential (**content words**). Grammatical words include articles, pronouns, and conjunctions. Lexical words include nouns, verbs, and adjectives.

grammatology **1.** The study of *writing, particularly its historical origins and development. **2.** Derrida's *deconstructionist critique of the *phonocentrism of Plato, Rousseau, and Saussure.

grand narratives (metanarratives, master narratives) [French *grands récits* 'big stories'] Lyotard's term for the totalizing *narratives or metadiscourses of *modernity which have provided *ideologies with a legitimating philosophy of history. For example, the grand narratives of the *Enlightenment, democracy, and *Marxism. Hayden White (b.1928), an American historian, suggests that there are four Western master narratives: Greek fatalism, Christian redemptionism, bourgeois progressivism, and Marxist utopianism. Lyotard argues that such authoritarian universalizing narratives are no longer viable in *postmodernity, which heralds the emergence of 'little narratives' (or **micronarratives**, *petits récits*): localized representations of restricted domains, none of which has a claim to universal truth status. Critics suggest that this could be seen as just another grand narrative, and some have seen it as *Eurocentric.

grand theory Any theorizing involving a general explanation of society or human experience rather than the study of particular societies or experiences. Often used pejoratively within empiricist perspectives.

grapheme Any individual character in written *language; in alphabetic languages, a letter or other *alphanumeric character. The smallest unit in written language. *Compare* PHONEME; *see also* WRITING SYSTEMS.

graphical user interface (GUI) In computer design, the way in which the operating systems of computers represent *data by employing two main *pictorial metaphors. Firstly, the **desktop metaphor** of the office with files and folders representing *information and programs, the hard drive represented as a file store, a desktop area, and even a waste paper basket for unwanted files. Secondly, the **window** where programs open within a rectangular frame and can be displayed and run. Research began on GUIs in the 1960s as a user-friendly alternative to the command line structure used by computer programmers. *See also* HUMAN-COMPUTER INTERACTION.

graphic communication *See* PICTORIAL COMMUNICATION.

graphocentrism *See* SCRIPTISM.

grazing (channel surfing, flipping) Using a remote control device to switch frequently from one television programme to another, sampling what is currently being broadcast without settling for long on any single programme. *See also* CHANNEL HOPPING; ZAPPING.

great divide theories *Theories in the comparative analysis of modes of communication which assume or refer to a *binary divide or dichotomy between different kinds of society or human experience: primitive vs civilized, simple vs advanced, pre-logical vs logical, pre-rational vs rational, pre-analytic vs analytic, mythopoeic vs logico-empirical, traditional vs modern, concrete vs scientific, oral vs visual, or pre-literate vs literate. Such pairings are often also regarded as virtually interchangeable with each other: so that modernity equals advanced equals civilization equals *literacy equals rationality and so on (*see* ALIGNMENT). They can also be *Eurocentric. The French anthropologist Lucien Levy-Bruhl (1857–1939) created a storm of protest early in the 20th century by labelling as 'pre-logical' the thinking of people in hunter-gatherer societies. Such theories tend to suggest radical, deep, and basic differences between modes of thinking in non-literate and literate societies. They are often associated with attempts to develop *grand theories of social organization and development. Like any form of simplification they can be interpretively illuminating. However, the sharp division of historical continuity into periods 'before' and 'after' a technological innovation such as writing assumes the *determinist notion of the primacy of 'revolutions' in *communication technology, and differences tend to be exaggerated. The interpretive alternatives to great divide theories are sometimes called **continuity theories**: these stress a continuum rather than a radical discontinuity between oral and literate modes, and an ongoing dynamic *interaction between various media.

(⊕) SEE WEB LINKS
• Biases of the ear and eye

Greek visualism *See* OCULARCENTRISM.

green consumerism *See* CONSUMER CULTURE.

green screen In film and television, a uniformly-lit plain background that is used to create a *travelling matte for special-effects shots using a process called **colour separation overlay**. Green and blue are the preferred colours because they are not found in human skin or hair tones (*see also* CHROMA KEY). The live action component of films such as *Avatar* (2009) and *300* (2006) are almost entirely photographed with actors performing in front of green screens.

griefer A person or group of people typically performing as a single *avatar in an online environment (or a participant in an online forum), who participates in the activity of **griefing**: deliberate attempts to disrupt activities or cause distress to others. Griefers often use malicious software: for example, by initiating automated programs that replicate themselves, which can overload servers and cause whole *virtual worlds to crash. The antics of a griefer can range from mildly annoying to sociopathic. *Compare* FLAMING; TROLL.

( ) SEE WEB LINKS

• Julian Dibbell on griefers

gross rating points *See* RATINGS; REACH.

ground 1. For usage in literary theory, *see* METAPHOR. 2. For usage in relation to *perception, *see* FIGURE AND GROUND.

group communication (small group communication) The process by which verbal and nonverbal *messages are exchanged between a limited number of people, usually from 3 to about 20, the upper limit being determined by the extent to which each member can interact with every other member with the potential for mutual influence. Traditionally, this refers to *interpersonal communication between group members in *face-to-face interaction. Sociologists (such as Goffman) tend to be concerned with how small groups maintain a shared definition of reality. The group is the smallest social system in which a *communication network can exist: a *dyad has only one link whereas a minimal group (a **triad**) has three (*see also* SOCIAL NETWORKS).

group dynamics 1. The structure and interactional processes that take place within small groups in *face-to-face interaction: *see also* COMMUNICATION NETWORK. 2. The study of small groups and the *interaction processes within them, such as *power relations, leadership, decision-making, productivity, *cohesion, *conformity, *cooperation, and *conflict.

group identification (social identification) In social psychology, an individual's sense of belonging to a particular social, cultural, or subcultural group. *Social identity theory focuses on the contribution of group membership to the self-concept. The American sociologist Robert E. Park (1864–1944) proposed that a universal preference for the familiar and for those who are perceived as being like oneself underlies group identification. *In-group identification is associated with *ethnocentrism. *See also* PRIMARY AND SECONDARY GROUPS; REFERENCE GROUP.

GRP (gross rating points) *See* RATINGS; REACH.

GUI *See* GRAPHICAL USER INTERFACE.

guilt appeals A psychological and rhetorical strategy in persuasive communication such as *advertising, classified as both emotional and negative, which seeks to arouse in the individual feelings of guilt which the desired response would be perceived as likely to assuage. Guilt appeals are ubiquitous in charitable appeals. *See also* ADVERTISING APPEALS; EMOTIONAL APPEALS; FEAR APPEALS; NEGATIVE APPEALS; SOCIAL ACCEPTANCE APPEALS.

GUMG *See* GLASGOW MEDIA GROUP.

GVs *See* GENERAL VIEWS.

habitus A set of *norms and *expectations unconsciously acquired by individuals through experience and *socialization as embodied dispositions, 'internalized as second nature' (Bourdieu), predisposing us to act improvisationally in certain ways within the constraints of particular social fields. The concept of the habitus was proposed by Bourdieu as an integral part of behaviour reflected in a 'way of being': including ways of seeing, moving, talking, and so on. It functions to mediate between individual *subjectivity and the social structures of relations.

hacker 1. Negatively, a person skilled in computer programming who uses their abilities to gain unauthorized access to the data in other people's computers, illicitly copying or wantonly destroying *data and disrupting *computer networks through viruses. **Hacking** is the activity of the hacker. 2. A computer programmer dedicated to finding optimum solutions to programming problems through hands-on experimentation and the sharing of *knowledge among *peer groups. Hence, **hack** *n.*: an ingenious and elegant technical solution to a problem.

((⊕)) SEE WEB LINKS

• *Hackers*: Steven Levy

hailing *See* INTERPELLATION.

half-duplex A two-directional transmission system that is only active in one direction at a time. Walkie-talkies use this system: the user presses a 'talk' button to speak to the other party. *Compare* FULL-DUPLEX; SIMPLEX.

halo effect In *impression formation, a tendency to allow a positively-evaluated attribute (such as physical attractiveness) to positively bias one's assessment of other traits. *See also* PERSON PERCEPTION.

haptics Touching and its study. Argyle suggests that touch is a powerful social *signal because it is associated with both *sex and aggression. Touching may be self-focused or other-focused. Self-focused touch is not normally intentionally communicative and *self-touch *adaptors may reflect the person's current state of mind (e.g. anxiety) or may be merely a habit. However, touch is also part of the *performance of *identity, not least of *gender. Desmond Morris notes that self-touching of hair shows a three-to-one bias in favour of women, while temple-supporting shows a two-to-one bias in favour of men. As for other-focused touch, for Henley, one of its functions is to maintain the social hierarchy. She asks us to consider who would be more likely to touch the other: teacher/student, police officer/accused person, doctor/patient, minister/parishioner, adviser/advisee, foreman/worker, businessman/secretary? Social psychologists in the

USA have argued that the fear of being seen as homosexual accounts for the common finding that women engage in more same-sex touch than do men. Social codes of touch are culturally variable: *see* HIGH-CONTACT CULTURES; LOW-CONTACT CULTURES.

hard news Up-to-date *factual reporting of consequential newsworthy *events (usually on a national or international level) (*see also* NEWSWORTHINESS). Note the stereotypical *connotation of *masculinity. *See also* STORY MODEL; *compare* SOFT NEWS.

hard sell In *advertising, heavy promotion using a direct and overt sales message, typically employing *logical appeals and focusing on *information stressing the tangible benefits of the product or service and aiming to stimulate immediate purchases. *Compare* SOFT SELL.

HA shot *See* HIGH-ANGLE SHOT.

hash tag An economical and searchable means of specifying the subject of a message on Twitter, created by prefixing a word or short hyphenated phrase with a hash symbol (#). Multiple messages labelled with identical hash tags generate **trending topics** which can be automatically collected and ranked according to their popularity.

hate speech *See* POLITICAL CORRECTNESS.

hate stare Intense, directed, and sustained *eye contact, asserting *dominance and experienced as threatening and intimidating: frequently associated with inter-racial bigotry and once commonly directed against African Americans by white Americans in the southern states of the USA.

Hawthorne effect (research) An 'experimenter effect' in which the behaviour of subjects changes simply because they are aware of being the subject of research.

Hays Code (Motion Picture Production Code) A set of *censorship guidelines for the United States motion picture industry in force from 1930 to 1968, introduced by Will Hays (1879–1954), President of the Motion Picture Producers and Distributors of America (MPPDA). One of its general principles was that 'No picture shall be produced that will lower the moral standards of those who see it'. Restrictions included a prohibition on any reference to 'sex perversion' (such as homosexuality). Replaced by the age-based rating system that is still in use (*see* CERTIFICATION).

HCI *See* HUMAN-COMPUTER INTERACTION.

HDTV *See* HIGH DEFINITION TELEVISION.

header *See* MASTHEAD.

headline 1. The title of a story in a *newspaper or magazine (a convention carried over to television news programmes and webpages) displayed in larger and bolder type so as to attract *attention: *see also* BYLINE. 2. The title of the main story that appears in *newspapers on page one *above the fold.

head nod A brief and slight lowering and raising of the head. Head nods function as *regulators to assist *turn-taking: a nod can signify that someone should keep talking; rapid nodding can indicate that the nodder wants to speak. For head nods in televised interviews, *see* NODDIES.

headroom 1. In audio engineering, the amount an audio *signal can exceed a designated maximum level without clipping or distorting. 2. In film and video camerawork, the space above the subject's head in the *frame: too much space makes the subject appear less important.

heavy viewers In Gerbner's *cultivation theory, people who watch television more than four hours a day. These are the television viewers who Gerbner found to be most likely to be subject to *attitudinal effects based on the ways in which the world is framed by television programmes, especially regarding topics of which the viewer has little first-hand experience. Light viewers may have more sources of *information than heavy viewers. Heavy viewers are also seen as more likely to be affected by *mainstreaming.

hedging The employment of linguistic devices by speakers or writers in order to evade responsibility for making a statement which might be disproven. For example, 'It might be suggested that . . . ' or 'It could conceivably be the case that . . . '. A habit of politicians and academics in particular. *See also* QUALIFIERS.

hegemonic code *See* DOMINANT CODE.

hegemonic masculinity The mythology of *gender dominant within cultural *representations of males, reflecting normative behavioural ideals for males in a culture in a particular period (regardless of the actual prevalence of such behaviour in that society). Such representations promote stereotypical masculine heterosexual *values (*see also* MASCULINITY). Also, those men who exemplify, perform, and perpetuate the mythology of dominant masculinity, who are implicated in the subordination of women and of men who represent marginalized masculinities (such as gay men). In contemporary Western cultures, masculinity is typically associated with personality traits such as independence and competitiveness, role behaviours such as being the primary provider and initiative-taking, and physical characteristics such as muscularity and a deep voice. However, the form of masculinity occupying the hegemonic position in a culture at any particular time is always contestable.

hegemonic reading (dominant reading) Within Stuart Hall's *encoding/decoding model, the *interpretation of a *mass-media text by a *decoder who fully shares its *ideological code and accepts and reproduces the *preferred reading—a reading which may not have been the result of any conscious intention on the part of those who produced it. In such a stance the *dominant code seems natural and *transparent. *Compare* NEGOTIATED READING; OPPOSITIONAL READING.

hegemony [Greek *hēgemōn* 'leader'] 1. In sociology, history, political science, and international relations, *dominance or control, especially that of one state or social group. 2. **(bourgeois hegemony)** In classical *Marxism, the political and economic *dominance of the bourgeoisie exercised through the legislative and coercive power of the state. 3. **(cultural or ideological hegemony)** For Gramsci, the cultural and ideological *dominance of the ruling *class, which exercises control by using its influence in the major *institutions (such as education and the *mass media) to engineer consent through projecting its own *ideology as *common sense while excluding, or absorbing and transforming, alternatives (*see also* MANUFACTURE OF CONSENT; MEDIA HEGEMONY). The *status quo is thus accepted as in their own best interests by those who are subordinated by it. Marxist intellectuals may nevertheless engage in a 'counter-hegemonic project'. The struggle for ideological hegemony is a primary factor in radical change.

height in field *See* ELEVATION.

hemispheric lateralization (hemispheric localization, hemispheric specialization, laterality, cerebral dominance) The *hypothesis that the left and right hemispheres of the human cerebral cortex differ in their psychological functions. For most people (most right-handed people and some left-handers) the left hemisphere is dominant for *language functions and the right hemisphere is dominant for visual-spatial tasks and *nonverbal communication. The right hemisphere processes the *left* visual *field and tends to produce an *attentional bias to the left (though *reading direction also plays a part in this). Males tend to have more lateralized, less coordinated, brain functions than females, leading some to suggest that this may help to account for greater nonverbal sensitivity among females.

hermeneutic circle 1. In philosophy, the problem of the circularity of understanding: where understanding **A** presupposes understanding **B**, which in turn presupposes understanding **A**. 2. In *hermeneutics a dialogical relation between the part and the whole in texts: we have to refer to the whole to understand the parts and the parts to understand the whole (e.g. in understanding sentences and the words within them). This concept was introduced by Schleiermacher although the term was coined by Dilthey. In hermeneutics, it is seen as the path to greater understanding rather than a problem: unlike a 'circular definition', it is not meant to suggest 'going round in circles', since, as noted by the Greek philosopher Heraclitus (*fl.* 500 BC), 'No man ever steps in the same river twice, for it's not the same river and he's not the same man.' Some commentators therefore refer to the process as more like a spiral. It has been applied to the relations between *texts and *genres, between text and *context, and between *theory and *data. Giddens refers to a **double hermeneutic** in which social scientists seek to engage with both *emic and etic perspectives on social reality. 3. The *poststructuralist, anti-hermeneutic notion that since all *signs refer to other signs, no ultimate meanings can be established.

hermeneutic code (enigma code, the voice of truth) Barthes' concept of a *narrative formula consisting of three stages: the enigma, the delay, and the resolution. *See also* CLASSICAL NARRATIVE STRUCTURE; DISCLOSURE; NARRATIVE CODES.

hermeneutics *See also* INTERPRETIVISM. 1. The art or technique of *interpretation, especially of *texts. 2. Most broadly, the interpretation of human behaviour and the social world. 3. Originally, in theology, Biblical *exegesis to establish a correct interpretation of holy scripture. For Schleiermacher, hermeneutics involved the application of historical *contextualism to the study of texts, in order 'to understand the author better than he understood himself' (Dilthey). Such approaches led to the cynical jibe that hermeneutics is the art of finding what is not there. 4. Traditionally in jurisprudence, interpreting juridical texts in order to establish an authoritative statement of law. 5. In philosophy and literary theory, the theory of interpretation. For Dilthey, hermeneutics represented *verstehen*, the subjective *understanding* needed to deal with historical, social, and cultural *knowledge, as distinct from the explanation required in objective, scientific method. It thus distinguished the human sciences from the natural sciences. For the German philosopher Hans-Georg Gadamer (1900–2002), interpretation is always situational and subjective: there can be no objective interpretation of the *meaning of a text. This conception has a considerable influence on *reception theory. The French philosopher Paul Ricoeur (1913–2005) argues that 'Every reading takes place in a culture which imposes its own framework of interpretation.' Such stances are rejected as *relativism by Hirsch, who regards only the 'verbal meaning' of the text as within the provenance of hermeneutics. 6. (psychology) The *interpretation of behaviour, speech, and writing in terms of *meaning and intention. 7. In recent theory, a focus on the way in which *interpretation constructs its *object. 8. (*semiotics) A relatively open, loose, and often unconscious system of implicit interpretive practices, in contrast to the more formal and explicit character of a semiotic *code (Guiraud).

hero or heroine 1. In common usage, a man or woman admired for some positively-evaluated trait or for their achievements. 2. In literary and *film theory, the main male or female character in a narrative, regardless of whether their qualities are admirable. When not distinguished by admirable qualities, the term *anti-hero may be applied. Usually a hero or heroine is the *protagonist, but not always: as in the film *Dances with Wolves* (1990), where Dunbar is the hero and Stands with a Fist is the heroine, but only Dunbar is the protagonist.

heteronormativity A deeply-embedded cultural presumption that humanity and heterosexuality are synonymous. The term was coined in 1993 by the American literary critic Michael Warner (b.1958), who quoted the French feminist Monique Wittig (1935–2003): 'To live in society is to live in heterosexuality . . . Heterosexuality is *always already given within all mental categories.' Gayle Rubin (b.1949), an American anthropologist, had already coined the phrase **compulsory heterosexuality** in 1975 to refer to the taboo on homosexuality as being more basic than that on incest, while the American poet Adrienne Rich (b.1929) used the same term in 1986 to argue that heterosexuality is a social construct sustained by social sanctions. Heteronormativity permeates social life and social *institutions, from the reactions of all-male groups when an attractive woman passes to the checkbox for 'married or single'. However, the presumption of universal heterosexual desire is an inherently unstable *myth.

heterosexism Social practices reflecting tacit or overt *bias in favour of heterosexuals and prejudicial to gay men, lesbians, or bisexuals, not necessarily involving the aversion or hatred implied by *homophobia. Often based on the presumption of heterosexual *norms (*see* HETERONORMATIVITY).

heuristic function Halliday's term for a *linguistic function in which one uses *language as a means of exploring, learning, and acquiring *knowledge about one's environment, typically through the use of questions. For example, 'What happened?'

heuristics A method of reasoning or *inference that proceeds by guessing and by trial and error, rather than by deducing the answer by following a series of explicit rules.

hidden agenda 1. A covert *subtext within any act of communication. 2. A pejorative reference to a conscious but unstated plan motivating the actions of an individual, group, or organization.

hierarchy of effects (HOE model or paradigm, hierarchy of influences) 1. A model of *persuasion based on learning theory in which the *target audience is assumed to go through these stages of influence: *attention, *comprehension, and acceptance. This model was originally proposed by Hovland and colleagues in 1953 (*see also* YALE MODEL). Later versions added the stages of retention and yielding. 2. Various related models of *marketing communication consisting of stages of influence through which the consumer is hypothesized to pass in relation to a product or service based on the sequence: learning (cognitive), feeling (affective), and doing (conative or behavioural); alternative sequences have also been proposed. Such models have been criticized as theoretically weak. Contemporary psychology has abandoned the traditional distinctions between these dimensions on the grounds that they are highly interdependent.

hieroglyphic *See* WRITING SYSTEMS.

high and low involvement 1. The degree of cognitive effort or *elaboration required on the part of the *audience in relation to the *form of the *message. Some *texts demand more active *interpretation than others, even within the same *medium. For example, some television commercials are designed to be more open-ended, as when the *target audience is expected to be more highly-educated and to find such interpretation intrinsically gratifying. 2. The amount of cognitive effort required from the audience in relation to the nature of the medium. Reading printed text is generally regarded as requiring more active cognitive involvement than watching television, although clearly this is partly dependent on the *content: casually flipping through a magazine is likely to be less demanding than watching a whodunnit on TV. *See also* HOT AND COOL MEDIA. 3. A characterization of television *viewing styles in terms of the degree of *attention paid to the screen. The British marketing analysts Patrick Barwise (b.1946) and Andrew Ehrenberg (b.1926) reported in 1988 that, based on UK data, of those in a room with a TV switched on during programme transmissions, 40% were not attentively viewing, and during commercials, that figure rose to 60%. The *attention of individual viewers varies dramatically, from rapt attention to no attention at all. In 1983, Jeremy Tunstall, a British sociologist, proposed a three-tier categorization of audience involvement

with television programmes. **Primary involvement (focused viewing)** denotes watching TV attentively and critically, evidenced in the viewer's ability to effectively recall and evaluate what they have just seen. **Secondary involvement (monitoring)** denotes watching while engaged in another activity, e.g. ironing, or where something else is going on in the background. **Tertiary involvement (idling)** denotes the situation when the TV is on in the background but is not the subject of conscious attention (*see also* SIT UP OR SIT BACK; TELEVISION VIEWING STYLES).
4. (*marketing) The relative level of *cognitive* effort and problem-solving in which the consumer is expected to engage when purchasing particular types of product. This typically corresponds to how expensive mistakes could be: so purchase decisions in relation to cars or computers are expected to involve more cognitive involvement than for soap or bread. *See also* ELABORATION LIKELIHOOD MODEL.
5. (*marketing) The relative level of *affective* involvement anticipated on the part of consumers in relation to the purchase of particular types of product: *see also* AFFECT; EMOTIONAL APPEALS. 6. (*linguistics) The *conversational style of an individual speaker in *interpersonal communication whose speech, reflecting their enthusiasm and interest, is characterized by such features as rapidity, relatively short pauses, abrupt topic shifting, faster *turn-taking, and a tendency to speak without necessarily waiting for others to finish their turns. Tannen used the term to describe a style she observed among New Yorkers. She noted that a high-involvement style of speaking is evaluated positively by other users of this style but is seen as dominating by those who do not. The comparison here is with a style she referred to as *high considerateness.

high-angle shot (HA shot) A photographic composition in which the viewing position is above the subject, giving the impression that the camera is looking down. In film and video logging conventions, a high-angle shot tends to imply a static shot. So, for example, a shot from the top of a building would be high-angle, although a shot from a helicopter would be an **aerial shot**. A **crane shot** is typically a high-angle shot that sweeps over the action. In *semiotic terms, such unusual shots are *marked compared with level shots, drawing attention to themselves. *See also* TILT.

high concept Media *productions which are easy to market because they feature established stars, have cross-media potential and have a straightforward premise which is easily communicated and comprehended, often by being reducible to a single sentence. The high concept approach originated in American television but is particularly associated with film; it has defined mainstream Hollywood cinema since the 1980s.

high considerateness (*linguistics) The *conversational style of an individual speaker in *interpersonal communication whose speech is characterized by a relatively slower pace and longer pauses than in a *high involvement* style (Tannen). *See* HIGH AND LOW INVOLVEMENT.

high-contact cultures *Cultures in which, compared to those in most cultures, people tend to touch each other more often, maintain closer *interpersonal distance, make more *eye contact, and speak louder. For example, Latin America and the Mediterranean. *See also* INTERCULTURAL COMMUNICATION; *compare* LOW-CONTACT CULTURES.

high-context *See also* INTERCULTURAL COMMUNICATION. 1. **(high-context communication)** A *communication style in which much of the *meaning is implicit (*see* IMPLICIT MEANING) and context-dependent (*see* CONTEXTUAL MEANING) rather than explicit in the *message (Edward T. Hall). To interpret the message the *receiver must invoke the *context. This is a *process-oriented style. All communication involves some degree of context-dependence, but there is considerable variation between cultures. *Compare* LOW-CONTEXT. 2. **(high-context cultures)** *Collectivistic cultures (such as in China) particularly associated with a high-context communication style. By comparison with *low-context cultures, people are more tolerant of silences in conversation, use silence more strategically, and are more alert to nonverbal *cues. People in high-context cultures often adopt a *role-oriented style.

high culture 'Authentic' works of art and individual creativity and the aesthetic pleasures associated with their appreciation which require the demonstration of *taste, discrimination, and sophistication derived from and contributing to the *cultural capital of an elite as distinct from the 'mere *entertainment' values associated with *popular (mass) culture, commercial *commodification and uncritical *consumption. A polarizing term, originating in the mid 19th century, explicitly linked to *class distinctions. However, Adorno and Horkheimer from the *Frankfurt school offer a Marxist perspective in which high culture is a context within which *dominant ideologies can be challenged.

high definition television (HDTV) Television with more TV lines and therefore a higher *resolution than standard definition systems. The system took off in the late 1990s with the rise of *digital transmission, LCD and plasma technology replacing bulky, heavy cathode-ray equipment. Today, a high definition television image is defined as 1080 TV lines as opposed to 625 for *PAL and 525 for *NTSC. However, in the 1980s an analogue system was marketed with a resolution of 1120 TV lines. In 1940, the British inventor John Logie Baird (1888–1946) demonstrated a 600-line colour television system.

((⊕)) SEE WEB LINKS

• The world's first high definition colour television

high modernity *See* POSTMODERNITY.

historical determinism 1. A belief that historical processes have a certain inevitability, based on some fundamental factor. Its application ranges from a pessimistic fatalism which denies human free will (which 'soft *determinism' permits) to the far looser optimistic *Enlightenment notion of progress as inevitable. Benjamin refers to this evolutionist faith in the irresistible progress of humankind as *historicism (contrasting it with **historical materialism**). Some, such as the Austrian-British philosopher Karl Popper (1902–94), point to historical determinism in classical *Marxism; others (e.g. Althusser) reject this. 2. **(historical relativism)** The view that our ideas are determined by our historical situation.

historical relativism (historical particularism) The stance adopted by the German-American anthropologist Franz Boas (1858–1942), and others, that a historical era can only be understood on its own terms (*see also* HISTORICISM). In its extreme form, a rejection of the validity of historical (or cross-cultural) comparisons and evolutionary schemata.

historicism 1. A pejorative synonym for *historical determinism or *historical relativism. 2. **(historism)** The stance that *events and/or ideas need to be interpreted within their historical *context **(historical contingency),** or that human phenomena should be seen in terms of their historical development. Such standpoints are often framed in opposition to *universalism, *essentialism, and *formalism. However, over-emphasis on historical variability and the uniqueness of circumstances is criticized as relativistic. 3. The *hermeneutic approach in which it is argued that historical *interpretation requires us to adopt the *values and assumptions of the time, seeing the phenomenon in its own terms and not ours. 'Always historicize,' declared Jameson in 1981. Critics have either branded this approach as *cultural relativism or have emphasized that interpreters cannot escape their own historical situatedness. 4. **(new historicism)** A form of *textual (and contextual) analysis originating in the USA in the 1980s which has been seen as allied with *cultural materialism in the UK. Rejecting traditional literary and cultural history and *grand narratives, this approach emphasizes *contradictions and discontinuities within historical cultural forms, marginalized minorities, and the importance of the cultural and social context. 5. In architecture and design, styles drawing inspiration from the past. The term is often used pejoratively, particularly within *modernist discourse.

historicity The historical dimension of human phenomena, or the distinctive sociohistorical circumstances of a specific *event or series of events. Theories ignoring this dimension are *ahistorical.

historic turn A change in emphasis in the discourse of the humanities and social sciences reflecting a recognition (beyond the academic bounds of history itself) of the importance of historical *context and historical processes. This has included the new *historicism in literary theory, ethnohistory, and historical sociology. One of several turning points identified in the evolution of these disciplinary discourses; it is seen as having followed the *rhetorical turn.

Hitchcock zoom *See* FOCAL LENGTH.

HOE model or paradigm *See* HIERARCHY OF EFFECTS.

homogenization (homogeneity) [Greek, *homos* 'same', *genos* 'kind'] The combining of different elements into a uniform whole; the fear that the global *diffusion of Western (particularly American) cultural goods and *values will result in an erosion of cultural diversity. *See also* CULTURAL IMPERIALISM; MCDONALDIZATION; *compare* FRAGMENTATION; HYBRIDIZATION.

homonymy *See* POLYSEMY.

homophobia Negative *attitudes towards homosexual people and homosexuality which may be manifested in discrimination, hostile behaviour, or hate crimes. The term was adopted in 1972 by George Weinberg (b.1935), an American psychologist. The use of 'phobia' has been criticized as implying a pathological and irrational fear rather than a form of prejudice analogous to *racism. The term is sometimes reserved for more extreme forms reflecting hatred and revulsion, the term *heterosexism being favoured in other cases. Homophobic attitudes have been associated with conservative *ideologies and authoritarian personalities. Extreme homophobia is often attributed to unconscious homosexual desires but it can also be due to ignorance or function as a means of gaining approval from a *reference group. **Institutional homophobia** is reflected in laws, policies, practices, and the history of *invisibility of gay people in the *mass media. One theory is that the social function of homophobia is to enforce rigid *gender distinctions (*see also* HETERONORMATIVITY). **Internalized homophobia** refers to gay and lesbian people themselves adopting negative attitudes about homosexuality from *socialization into a homophobic culture, leading to denial or self-hatred because they feel that they cannot live up to dominant cultural gender *expectations.

hook In journalism and broadcasting, an element at the outset of an item that seeks to grab audience *attention.

horizon of expectations The shared 'mental set' or framework within which those of a particular generation in a culture understand, interpret, and evaluate a *text or an artwork. This includes *textual knowledge of *conventions and *expectations (e.g. regarding *genre and *style), and *social knowledge (e.g. of moral codes). It is a concept of reading (and the *meanings this produces) as historically variable. The term is central in Jauss's *reception theory.

horizontal communication *See* LATERAL COMMUNICATION.

horizontal integration (lateral integration) Strategic acquisitions and collusions between companies in the same sector and at the same level in order to operate as a single entity with a supply-oriented focus. The motives are to reduce the *competition, to achieve *economies of scale, and to concentrate ownership and power. *See also* MEDIA OWNERSHIP; *compare* DIAGONAL INTEGRATION; VERTICAL INTEGRATION.

horizontal–vertical illusion Bisecting a horizontal line with a vertical line of equal length (producing an inverted T-shape) tends to generate an optical misperception in which the vertical line seems longer. This has been argued to be caused by a tendency for those used to large open spaces and/or the *pictorial depth cues associated with *linear perspective to see such lines as retreating into depth, and thus longer than they appear in two-dimensional *representations. The illusion was first reported in 1858 by the German psychologist Wilhelm Maximilian Wundt (1832–1920).

hot and cool media A distinction made by McLuhan between media such as print, photographs, radio, and movies (**hot media**) and media such as speech, cartoons, the telephone, and television (**cool media**). Hot media are 'high definition' because they are rich in sensory data. Cool media are 'low definition' because they provide less sensory data and consequently demand more *participation* or 'completion' by the audience (a useful mnemonic is to imagine that hot media are too hot to touch). Note that McLuhan was not referring to the issue of the relative cognitive effort involved in the use of different media. Arguably, in McLuhan's terms, television has grown hotter since the 1960s as its technical picture quality has improved, so these terms are relative. Critics of McLuhan's concept have argued that it reifies the medium, underestimating differences within the same medium; the degree of audience engagement does not depend primarily on the *medium itself (although its *affordances may play a part), but on its *content and the ways in which the medium is used on specific occasions within specific *contexts. *See also* McLuhanism; *compare* high and low involvement.

howl round *See* feedback.

HTML (Hypertext Markup Language) A way of formatting a *text document so that it can be displayed on a *web browser. HTML uses elements of code called *tags to specify stylistic parameters, to embed other digital content like image, sound, and movie files, and to define *hyperlinks.

hue 1. Loosely, a synonym for *colour, as in 'red, green, and blue hues'. 2. The subjective psychological experience of a distinct colour. One of the three major psychological dimensions of *colour, the others being *brightness and *saturation (*see also* colour constancy). The visual sensation relates to the physical dimension of the *wavelength of light (and its amplitude or intensity) as reflected by objects or surfaces.

human-computer interaction (HCI) The study of people using computers: a mixture of engineering, design, and behavioural science. HCI can be separated into four dimensions: the 'task dimension', dealing with goals and *purposes of the engineers, designers, and the users of computers; the 'dialogue dimension', concerning how the computer and user are intended to interact; the 'structural dimension', dealing with specifics of the layout and the grouping of tasks; and the 'usability dimension', dealing with the ways in which users and computer actually interact. The **human-computer interface** is both the hardware and software of the computer and includes elements such as the keyboard, mouse, screen, *graphical user interface, windows, drop-down menus, and other means of accessing *information. *See also* computer-mediated communication; front end; Turing test.

human interest story In journalism, an item in which the primary appeal is its focus on individuals and the details of their personal experiences, rather than its *news value. Such stories typically involve an *emotional appeal, and may seek empathic audience *identification with those who are sympathetically represented. Where such stories feature at the end of news programmes they typically function to lighten the mood, or, as Charlotte Brunsdon and Morley argued in 1978, to *ideologically unify the audience.

hybrid genre [Latin *hybrida* 'mongrel'] In *genre theory, the combination of two or more genres. *Back to the Future 3* (1990) combines elements of science fiction and western films. Such combinations can also cut across categories such as *fact and *fiction. *Docusoaps, which combine *documentary and *soap opera, have been criticized for trivializing documentary by associating it with soaps. *See also* ADVERTORIAL; DOCUDRAMA; DRAMADOC; EDUTAINMENT; FACTION; FILM GENRES; INFOMERCIALS; INFOTAINMENT; TELEVISION GENRES.

hybridization (hybridity) 1. The combinability of different *forms.
2. (*linguistics) The phenomenon whereby particular words are composed of elements from different languages: for example, the word *television* is a **hybrid word**, *telē* coming from Greek and *visio* from Latin. 3. (*postcolonial theory) What Bhabha refers to as the 'in-between spaces' where cultural differences meet and conflict, unsettling established oppositions: a 'third space' which offers an escape from singular, ostensibly stable, *essentialist identities constructed around *class, *race, or *gender. This is distinct from the older concept of **creolization,** which, it has been argued, combined different *identities into new forms of essentialism. In late *modernity, *globalization is seen as stimulating hybridity: different elements combine in ways which preserve some of the original diversity, albeit in different forms. *Compare* HOMOGENIZATION. 4. More broadly in postmodern cultural theory, the stance of the French anthropologist Bruno Latour (b.1947) that all cultural forms are infinitely combinable, that any boundary can be breached, and that any argument defending an absolute separation between spirituality and science, nature and culture, reality and reality-construction, has the status of a modern reworking of an ancient taboo. He suggests that a radical anthropology is needed to study modern culture that would draw upon the myths, ethnosciences, genealogies, political forms, techniques, religions, etc., cutting across the *binary distinctions separating these.

hyperbole (*rhetoric) A *figure of speech involving emphatic exaggeration or overstatement, sometimes based on *irony and/or for comic effect. Sensational reporting often employs hyperbole (informally called **hype**). The opposite figure is understatement.

hyperlink *See* LINK.

hypermedia 1. *Digital media which employ *links. 2. Computer applications connecting multiple media texts, representing several viewpoints simultaneously (*see also* POLYVOCALITY). Bolter and Richard Grusin, American new media theorists, argue that with hypermedia we can take pleasure in the act of *mediation: *see also* REMEDIATION; *compare* IMMEDIACY.

hyper-realism *See* SUPER REALISM.

hyperreality (*adj.* **hyperreal**) 1. In a mediated context, an artificially created copy that is perceived as somehow more real than the real thing, or too real to be real: modelled on reality but with an exaggerated intensity, such as computer-generated films with unnaturally bright and vibrant *colours. In visual art, often a synonym for *photorealism. 2. For Eco, the celebration of the fake in *popular culture: for example, theme parks such as Disneyland feature automata, which are combinations of robotics and waxworks models, fashioned to look like famous characters from history. **3.** For Baudrillard, that which has gone beyond the real, supplanting or erasing it: *see also* SIMULACRUM.

hypertext **1.** A method, devised by Berners-Lee as part of his *World Wide Web software, of embedding omni-directional *links within a given digital *text (encoded in the form of an *HTML document and displayed on a *web browser) which connect to other HTML texts without the need for extra navigation. For example, a selected word of a text document, or an area of an image document, is defined as a *hyperlink which, when clicked on, loads the document at that address into the browser window. Hypertext is designed to be media independent (a text can link to a sound file, an image, or even a location in a *virtual world), which makes it a *metonym for the versatility of *digital media generally. **2.** A visionary concept of Ted Nelson (an American new media theorist, b.1937) for a *human-computer interface in which computers present a given text from multiple viewpoints, making it a malleable object that can be 'played with' in order to deepen a person's understanding. For example, a hypertext version of Hamlet's 'To be, or not to be' soliloquy might consist of a standard-edition printed text, a facsimile of the earliest known version, a video recording of a performance, critical notes, and articles, etc.—all of which could be expanded from or collapsed back into the original text by clicking on a series of bi-directional links. **3.** For Genette, literary works which derive from, relate, or allude to an earlier work: *see also* INTERTEXTUALITY. **4.** Any text structured in a way that is nonlinear or nonsequential, having no clear beginning, middle, and end, or in which the reader has control over the sequence. Where such texts link to others through *hyperlinks, the boundaries of the text may be blurred or the text may be perceived as unbounded.

(⊕) SEE WEB LINKS
• Project Xanadu

hypertext fiction An experimental story form which uses some variant of *HTML to create a branching structure, offering the reader choices at each stage of the *narrative so that a different story is produced by each reading (albeit one limited to the branches built into the narrative). Certain characteristics have been attributed to hypertext fiction: that it is nonlinear, indeterminate, and interactive. All of these are problematic, however, because they can arguably apply to traditional fiction at the level of the reading. In response, Aarseth defines **cybertext** as a mechanism for producing a variety of expressions at the level of the text rather than an ambiguous text open to a number of different readings. *See also* INTERACTIVE FICTION.

Hypertext Markup Language *See* HTML.

hypodermic model (hypodermic needle model, hypodermic syringe model, magic bullet theory) **1.** Not so much a *model or a *theory as a *metaphor for a popular assumption that communication involves the transfer of ideas, thoughts, feelings, *facts, *information, *knowledge, or *meanings from *sender to *receiver (a one-way linear process)—a notion long ago discredited in academic contexts (*see also* TRANSMISSION MODELS). It is reflected in everyday speech in the *conduit metaphor. 2. A feature of the *behaviourist 'stimulus-response' rhetoric reflected in academic discourse up until the early 1950s, in which the *mass media were argued to have direct effects on their audiences, particularly *behavioural effects. This concept was gradually abandoned in academic theory and research in favour of a conception of the *audience as highly active and selective rather than a passive and defenceless sitting target (*see also* ACTIVE AUDIENCE THEORY; BEHAVIOURISM; EFFECTS TRADITION). Ironically, the notion persists in the rhetoric frequently employed by the popular press, particularly in relation to violent crimes attributed to media influence (*see also* VIOLENCE DEBATE).

hypotext *See* HYPERTEXT.

hypothesis A provisional explanation of a phenomenon, formally framed as a *proposition. It may be debated by rational *argument and/or tested empirically. **Hypothesis testing** requires a precise and testable statement of such a claim or prediction, and the collection of appropriate *data against which it can be tested. More loosely, the British psychologist Gregory sees *perception as a process of hypothesis-testing. Gombrich offers this example: 'Take a man in the dark trying to gain information about the unseen environment. He will not grope and thrash about at random, but will use every finding to form a hypothesis about the meaning of his encounters, a hypothesis which subsequent gropings will serve to confirm or refute.'

hypothesis-led processing *See* TOP-DOWN PROCESSING.

IC *See* INTRAPERSONAL COMMUNICATION.

iconic 1. *adj.* (*semiotics) A mode of relationship in a *sign between a *sign vehicle and its *referent in which the former is perceived as resembling or imitating the latter (recognizably looking, sounding, feeling, tasting, or smelling like it)—being similar in possessing some of its qualities (e.g. a portrait, a diagram, onomatopoeia, *metaphor, 'realistic' sounds in music, sound effects in radio drama). Note that in semiotics, **iconicity** is not confined to visual resemblance. The iconic mode, the *indexical mode, and the *symbolic mode are concepts in the *Peircean model of the sign, where they represent relationships between the *representamen and the *object. Where the relation is solely iconic, the sign may be referred to as an **icon**; however, most signs involve more than one mode. *Photographs are sometimes misleadingly labelled as iconic in the semiotic sense. Although this may be legitimate where what is being stressed is the use of photographic *conventions, the primary characteristic of the *medium is that it is *indexical, since it is hardly an accident that photographs 'resemble' what they depict. 2. In popular usage, anything expected to be instantly recognized as famous (a popular **icon**) by any fully-fledged member of a particular *culture or *subculture. Any famous visual image can thus be iconic (*see also* CONVERSATIONAL CURRENCY). In this non-semiotic sense, an **iconic photograph** is one which is famous in its own right, especially if it is a memorable depiction of a famous person or *event. Note that events themselves are not iconic: only famous *representations of them. However, major celebrities or stars (not just famous representations of them) are often described as (cultural) icons, where there is an added connotation of widespread admiration. 3. (*signage) Relating to pictorial signs signifying familiar concepts (not necessarily based on resemblance). In this sense, **iconic communication** is the *informational use of simple pictorial signs or 'icons', notably in computing environments and public signage and usually in coordinated sets, as a kind of visual shorthand for certain basic functions or standardized messages. For instance, a simplified outline of a house on a webpage button is widely used to indicate that clicking on it will take the user to the website homepage. 4. Each of the above senses can be seen as deriving from different aspects of the ancient idea of *religious* icons: works of visual art representing sacred figures which may be venerated as holy images by devout believers.

iconic gesture *See* ILLUSTRATOR.

iconic index *See* PHOTOGRAPH.

iconic memory *See* AFTER-IMAGE; MEMORY.

iconography 1. A familiar stock of images or *motifs associated with a particular *film genre, the *connotations of which have become fixed. Iconography is primarily but not necessarily visual and includes: décor, costume, and objects, certain 'typecast' performers (especially film *stars, some of whom may have become '*icons'), familiar patterns of dialogue, characteristic music and sounds, and appropriate physical topography. 2. In art history, the study of the *subject, *content, *themes, *imagery, *symbols, and/or *meaning of works of art rather than their *style or *form. Also, a collection of related portraits.

ICT *See* INFORMATION AND COMMUNICATION TECHNOLOGY.

idealism 1. In everyday usage, the pursuit of lofty goals (typically a pejorative reference to these as unrealistic or impractical ideals, contrasted with *realism). 2. In *representation, *see* IDEALIZATION. 3. A philosophical (specifically *epistemological) stance on 'what is real?' in which it is argued that external reality is dependent on consciousness, or even that it is purely *subjective and constructed in our use of *signs (notably *language). Philosophical idealism is strongly opposed by *materialists and *realists. Left-wing critics in particular object that idealism ignores the material conditions of human existence. *Constructionists criticize the blindness of idealism to the social dimension. Divorcing texts from their social *contexts is sometimes referred to as **textual idealism**. Note that the belief that nothing exists except oneself and one's own mental states is referred to as **solipsism**. *Compare* OBJECTIVISM.

idealization The *representation of something as a perfect example or model (in contrast to **naturalism**).

ideal reader The role in which a reader of a *text is *positioned as a *subject through the use of particular *modes of address. For Eco this term is not intended to suggest a 'perfect' reader who entirely echoes any *authorial intention but a *model reader whose reading could be justified in terms of the text. Note that not every *reader takes on the reader's role which may have been envisaged by the *producer(s) of the text.

ideational function Halliday's term for a *linguistic function referring to the *content or idea expressed in an *utterance. This is presented as one of three essential metafunctions reflected in all adult language usage (*compare* INTERPERSONAL FUNCTION; TEXTUAL FUNCTION).

ideational meaning (cognitive meaning, conceptual meaning, propositional meaning) The ideas, concepts, or *propositions in a *message. As opposed to *affective meaning. Its scope includes referential meaning (*see* REFERENTIALITY).

ident (station identification) In broadcasting, the *channel branding that takes the form of short video or audio segments of high *production values, typically featuring the name or *logo of the channel. A **bug** is a caption or channel *logo that identifies which channel the viewer is watching and is usually positioned in a corner of the television screen.

identification 1. Recognizing and naming somebody or something. 2. Loosely, a fleeting feeling of *empathy with someone. 3. (audience theory) A largely unconscious psychological relationship posited to exist (or phenomenally experienced) between us as viewers, readers, or listeners and a represented character when we become absorbed in a *narrative. The *hypothesis is that we identify with one or more of sympathetically-presented characters (usually the *protagonist), seeing *events from their perspective, at least at particular moments. Theorists have suggested that there may be several related factors: *liking the character (*affiliation), seeing oneself as like the character (*similarity), wanting to be like the character (*modelling), and being able to put oneself in the character's shoes (*empathy). See also GENDERED IDENTIFICATION. 4. (*advertising) More loosely applied to an implicit invitation for *target audiences to admire and/or wish to be like an attractive *role model (see ENDORSEMENT), even without a *narrative format (as in print ads). However, the use of such models is usually framed in terms of *meaning transfer. 5. (social psychology) The close *affiliation of individuals with *significant others or *reference groups leading to the adoption of their *values. 6. (*psychoanalytic theory) See IDENTIFICATION THEORY.

identification theory 1. The traditional Freudian *psychoanalytic theory of sex-role development that argues that psychological *identification with the same-sex parent (as a resolution of the Oedipus complex) is how children learn sex-role behaviours: see GENDER ROLES. 2. In Lacanian *psychoanalytic theory, the construction of the ego in the mirror phase in which the infant's first sight of their mirror image induces the illusion of a coherent *personal identity.

identity See also CULTURAL IDENTITY; ETHNIC IDENTITY; GENDER IDENTITY; GEOGRAPHICAL IDENTITY; GROUP IDENTIFICATION; LIFESTYLE; NATIONAL IDENTITY; PERSONAL IDENTITY; RACE; SEXUAL IDENTITY; SOCIAL IDENTITY; compare DIFFERENCE. 1. The persistent sameness of a person despite changes over time. 2. One's subjective sense of oneself as an individual. 3. The widespread *common-sense notion of a core, inner, authentic, or 'true self' which individuals experience as stable, unified, coherent, and autonomous of external influences (an *essentialist stance) but which contemporary theorists have characterized as constructed, fluid, multiple, hybrid, fractured, and decentred (see also DECENTRED SELF). The core self is now seen as a mythology derived from the individualistic legacy of *Cartesian dualism. In contrast to this notion, identity is conceived to be a dialectical relationship between self and others. 4. The process in which the child differentiates itself from its parents and family and which develops through adolescence in social *interaction. This usage derives from the American psychologist and psychoanalyst Erik Erikson (1902–94). 5. **(identifications)** The socially constructed and culturally-variable categories to which individuals relate in the process of producing a sense of *personal identity: notably *gender identity, *sexual identity, *ethnic identity, and *social (*class) identity. This perspective is found in *symbolic interactionism and social *constructionism. In structuralist framings identities are constituted through the *positioning of the subject through *language (or, in

Foucault, *discourses). In contemporary societies these identifications are multiple
and fluid. 6. The relationship of individuals to their social roles, the *expectations
for which are internalized through *socialization. 7. The active construction by
individuals of a sense of self from the cultural resources available: *see also*
BRICOLAGE. 8. The *discursive practices and *performances of individuals in
relation to their *similarity to and *difference from others within their cultural
*contexts.

((⊕)) SEE WEB LINKS

• Youth identity and digital media

identity politics Political positions and activism based on an aspect of *identity
(e.g. *ethnicity, religion, sex, or sexual orientation) shared by a group which feels
that its concerns are not adequately represented. It seeks the defence of its rights as
a subordinated minority and is reflected in such forms as *feminism, gay activism,
and religious fundamentalism. Attacked by critics (*see also* QUEER THEORY) as
*essentialism, its apologists sometimes refer to it as a pragmatic strategy of *strategic
essentialism in a struggle for equal rights. The related concept of **identity work**
frames identities as the product of processes such as political struggle.

identity theft A crime in which a person's credit card or bank details are stolen
and the criminal attempts to buy goods and services by posing as that person.

ideological analysis (ideological criticism) The investigation of embedded
*values, beliefs, *biases, and assumptions within a specific *text, in some domain of
*discourse, or in social practices within a particular cultural *context, and of the
*motivations and *power relations underlying these. **Ideology critique** [German
Ideologiekritik] originated with the *Frankfurt school, and its focus on identifying
the workings of dominant ideologies and the *contradictions involved in
maintaining them has endured in cultural and *critical theory. Approaches such as
*critical discourse analysis and *semiotic and sociological theory in media and
*cultural studies stress the role of *ideology, which semiotic theory frames in terms
of the construction of individuals as *subjects through the operation of *codes.
According to the theory of textual *positioning, understanding the meaning of a text
involves taking on an appropriate ideological identity (*see* IDEAL READERS). Barthes
argues that the *orders of signification called *denotation and *connotation
combine to produce ideological *myths. Ideological forces seek to *naturalize
codes—to make dominant cultural and historical values, *attitudes, and beliefs
seem natural, self-evident, *common sense, although the operation of ideology in
signifying practices is typically made to appear *transparent. Barthes saw myth
as serving the ideological interests of the bourgeoisie. Semiotic approaches involve
ideological analysis when they seek to *denaturalize codes.

ideological bias 1. Implicit *values and assumptions embedded within *texts,
*discourse, or social practices, e.g. *loaded language. For those inclined towards
*realism, ideology involves a distortion of an objective reality. However, following
Bakhtin and Voloshinov in the 1930s, many contemporary theorists argue that there
are no ideologically neutral *sign systems: *signs function to persuade as well as to
refer. 2. Certain tendencies beyond mere functionality which are favoured by the

*affordances of a particular *technology. Neil Postman argues that every *medium involves an ideological bias, having several aspects: intellectual and emotional bias, political bias, sensory bias, social bias, and content bias (*see* BIAS).

ideological codes (*semiotics) Interpretive frameworks for making sense of *texts and the world from the shared perspective of a particular *epistemic or *interpretive community. The most obvious ideological codes are the 'isms', such as: anarchism, capitalism, conservatism, *consumerism, *feminism, individualism, liberalism, nationalism, populism, *racism, and socialism. One of three broad types of codes, the others being *social codes and *textual codes, although insofar as there is no *denotation without *connotation, all codes can be seen as ideological. *See also* DOMINANT READING; NEGOTIATED READING; OPPOSITIONAL READING.

ideological criticism *See* IDEOLOGICAL ANALYSIS.

ideological state apparatus (ISA) For Althusser, the social agencies which help to maintain the current social order, not through coercion (as with what some Marxists have called the 'repressive state apparatus' of the armed forces and the police), but by engineering consent (*see also* LEGITIMATION; MANUFACTURE OF CONSENT). Such agencies include the educational system, the family, religion, the legal system, and the *mass media. These function to reproduce the *social relations of *production, inculcating the *values of the state and *positioning the subject in such a way that their *representations are naturalized—taken to be reflections of everyday reality. *See also* CONSCIOUSNESS INDUSTRIES.

ideology [French *idéologie* 'science of ideas'] (*adj.* **ideological**) 1. A highly contested term most broadly referring to: *attitudes, ideas, ideals, beliefs, doctrines, *values, worldviews, moral views, and political philosophies acting as an interpretive *frame of reference. Usually relating to relatively coherent systems of ideas held by social groups or those in particular social *roles within a *culture, but sometimes also to the more fragmentary forms of *common sense. *See also* IDEOLOGICAL CODES. 2. A pejorative reference to ideas reflecting *bias or prejudice, or to generalizations which are not scientific or objective and cannot be empirically verified or falsified. Based on an *ontologically problematic *realist distinction between objective reality and subjective ideology distorting our *knowledge of the world. *See also* IDEOLOGICAL BIAS. 3. In *Marxist theory, ideas shaped by *class interests, or more specifically, a system of ideas (and practices) reflecting a distorted view of social reality propagated by the ruling class to mask its *class domination, justifying or legitimating its subordination of the working class as natural (e.g. as 'in the national interest'), and serving to maintain the *status quo (*see also* SYMBOLIC VIOLENCE). This leads to '*false consciousness', which distorts people's understanding of what is in their best interest. For Althusser, the ideological mechanism is that of *interpellation. For him, 'ideology represents the imaginary relationship of individuals to their real conditions of existence.' Gramsci emphasizes that this relationship is a *site of struggle. 4. In classical *Marxist theory, ideas and consciousness—part of the cultural superstructure of society determined by the techno-economic base and its associated *social relations (*see* BASE AND SUPERSTRUCTURE). In Althusserian neo-Marxism, intellectual ideas and cultural forms which enjoyed a *relative autonomy from the structural base of society and which could thus influence society. Note that, for Althusser, ideology is so ubiquitous that it is virtually synonymous with *culture. **5.** Any doctrine in which the dominant group justifies its subordination of another: for instance, those used to justify *racism, sexual discrimination, *homophobia, or religious oppression: *see also* SEXISM. **6.** For Parsons, an interpretive framework employed by social groups in order to make sense of the world from their own perspective. **7.** For Voloshinov, the inscription of social *power relations in *discourse: *see also* CRITICAL DISCOURSE ANALYSIS.

(⊕) SEE WEB LINKS

• Ideology

ideology critique *See* IDEOLOGICAL ANALYSIS.

idiolect *Compare* DIALECT; GENDERLECT; SOCIOLECT. **1.** (*sociolinguistics) The distinctive ways in which *language is used by *individuals. **2.** In broader semiotic usage, the stylistic and personal *subcodes of individuals.

idling *See* HIGH AND LOW INVOLVEMENT.

ilinx [Greek 'whirlpool'] Games that induce a sense of disorientation or vertigo: e.g. racing *videogames. This is one of four game categories introduced by Caillois. *See also* AGON; ALEA; MIMICRY.

illocutionary act In *linguistics, and more specifically *pragmatics, an interpersonal act performed by saying something in a sufficiently explicit form to be understood (in a relevant *context) to have 'conventional consequences'. The most obvious examples employ performative or illocutionary verbs (describing the *performance of an action): for example, *promise, arrest, baptize*. The definitive focus here is on a particular *communicative purpose or *function rather than on *effects; recognition of the communicative intent is crucial. Such acts are said to have **illocutionary force**: in such acts to *say* is to *do*, as in 'You're fired!'. The term was introduced into *linguistics by Austin and developed by Searle (for the latter the term is synonymous with 'speech act'). *See also* LOCUTIONARY ACT; PERFORMATIVES; PERLOCUTIONARY ACT; SPEECH ACT.

illusion *See* VISUAL ILLUSION.

illusionism **1.** Any artistic *style that is designed to background or render *transparent the techniques of an artwork's *production, and is intended to fool the audience into thinking that the artwork represents a *slice of life or a *window on the world: for example, *continuity editing in film: *compare* REFLEXIVITY. **2.** The skilful use of artistic techniques designed to deceive the viewer into thinking that a painting is of a real scene: for example, **trompe-l'œil,** which renders the colours and textures of a wall or ceiling in paint and extends its perspective lines so that from a certain angle it looks as if the painted scene is an actual part of the building.

illusory motion *See* APPARENT MOTION.

illustrator 1. A person who creates artwork to accompany text in *advertising, a periodical, or a book. 2. For Ekman, any of the communicative hand movements following the rhythm or content of speech. This includes *batons. One of five types of nonverbal acts according to Ekman and Friesen: the others being *adaptors, *affect displays, *emblems, and *regulators. 3. **(iconic gesture, mimic sign)** A *gesture illustrating speech content graphically. Distinguished by some from an *emblem as being *iconic in the *semiotic sense through a perceived resemblance to its *referent: for instance, a partially-closed hand with the extended little finger close to the mouth and the extended thumb close to the ear, usually signifying either 'I'll phone you' or 'phone me'. Illustrators are common among people who do not share the same language.

image 1. A visual *representation of something (e.g. *figurative art or a photograph). The analysis of such images is the focus of *pictorial semiotics. 2. In relation to film, a single *shot: the domain of the *mise-en-scène. 3. A mental picture of something, sometimes incorporating sensory modalities other than the purely visual: *see also* MENTAL REPRESENTATION. 4. (literary theory) A mental impression evoked by the use of words: either in *figurative language such as *metaphor and *simile, or more generally in *descriptions. 5. The general public impression of a person, organization, or *brand (*see also* BRAND IMAGE). In relation to the cinema, the term is often applied to the branding of *stars. For Boorstin (*The Image*, 1961), it refers to an inauthentic **public image** instrumentally calculated to create a distinctive and favourable impression. Boorstin argued that thinking in terms of public image had displaced ideals as well as becoming 'more real than reality' (*see also* PSEUDO-EVENT). Baudrillard goes further, arguing that images have become wholly detached from reality: *see* SIMULACRUM. 6. Loosely, a general conception or vision of something, as in having an image of the future. 7. For the British-American economist Kenneth Boulding (1910–93) in his book *The Image* (1956), an internalized model of one's *knowledge of the world, and one's associated *value system, built up from experience and governing behaviour, much of which is shared by 'people like ourselves' within a *culture or *subculture. In this framework, 'the meaning of a message is the change which it produces in the image.'

imagery 1. Descriptive *language (literal imagery) referring to concrete objects, scenes, actions, or sensory experiences, which tends to generate vivid mental impressions (not visual reproductions, and not necessarily visual). Research has shown such language to be easier to recall than the more abstract language of *argument or *exposition. *See also* VISUAL IMAGERY. 2. (literary criticism) *Figurative language, especially the use of *metaphor and *simile. The New Criticism stresses imagery in this sense as the essential element in poetry: *see also* FORMALISM. Such critics argue that it is crucial to analyse patterns of imagery in a literary work in order to understand its *meaning. Repetition of an image in a work can make it *symbolic.

imaginary 1. *adj.* In everyday usage, existing only in the imagination. 2. *n.* [French *imaginaire,* connoting 'illusion'] 'The imaginary' is Lacan's term for an internalized *representation of the visual world in which the construction of the self as *subject is initiated. Initially the infant has no centre of *identity and there are no clear boundaries between itself and the external world. Lacan argues that in the **mirror phase,** or stage, (at the age of six- to eighteen-months, before the acquisition of speech), seeing one's mirror image induces a strongly-defined illusion (**misrecognition** or *méconnaissance*) of a coherent and self-governing *personal identity. In the realm of images, we find our sense of self reflected back by another with whom we identify (who is paradoxically both self and other). The imaginary is one of Lacan's three orders of *subjectivity, the *symbolic and the *real being the others. Kristeva renamed Lacan's imaginary the *semiotic. 3. *n.* For Althusserian neo-Marxist theorists, *representations which mask the historical and material conditions of existence (e.g. the heterosexual imaginary naturalizes heterosexuality and conceals its *constructedness, making homosexuality a marked category). *See also* MARKEDNESS.

imaginary signifier A term used by Metz to refer to the cinematic *signifier—the *medium of film. 'What is characteristic of the cinema is not the imaginary that it may happen to represent, but the imaginary that it *is* from the start, the imaginary that constitutes it as a signifier.' It is argued to have a 'dual character', involving both photographically and auditorily faithful perceptual plenitude and at the same time the unreality of fiction (we know we are watching a film). Its perceptual *transparency renders it an *absent signifier. Metz relates the concept to Lacan's *imaginary—the cinematic signifier is theorized as inducing identifications related to those of the mirror phase (where the screen is the mirror), though in cinema the *identification is paradoxically argued to be with oneself as 'a condition of the possibility of the perceived'. Prior to Metz's book *The Imaginary Signifier* (1977), film theorists had ignored the role of the *spectator.

imaginative function Halliday's term for a *linguistic function in which one creates and explores a private world. For example, 'Let's pretend...'

imagined community A group sharing an abstract, symbolic, but distinctive *identity whose members cannot collectively meet or know each other but to which its members nevertheless feel they belong. In 1983, the American political scientist Benedict Anderson (b.1936) referred to a nation as 'an imagined political community', emphasizing that it is imagined rather than imaginary. In modern nations, the *mass media have been important in developing and sustaining a collective sense of *national identity and 'the people', sustained through what Barthes refers to as *myth—reflected, for instance, in '*iconic' images. *See also* CONVERSATIONAL CURRENCY; CULTURAL LITERACY; SOCIAL UTILITY FUNCTION; *compare* EPISTEMIC COMMUNITY; INTERPRETIVE COMMUNITY; VIRTUAL COMMUNITY.

IMD *See* INDIVIDUAL-MEDIA DEPENDENCY.

imitation 1. (psychology) *See* MODELLING. 2. (representation) *See* MIMESIS.

immediacy 1. Lack of an intervening or mediating agency; unmediatedness; directness. *Face-to-face interaction is often *phonocentrically framed as unmediated (*see also* PRESENCE; SOCIAL PRESENCE). However, many theorists argue that communication and reality are never unmediated: *see also* MEDIATION. 2. A phenomenal quality attributed to any *medium that seems to achieve *transparency by *backgrounding the presence of the medium and the process of *mediation:

for example, photography. Bolter and Richard Grusin, American new media theorists, argue that it is always represented as a *first-person point of view. *See also* REMEDIATION; *compare* HYPERMEDIA. **3.** (journalism) A key *news value: reporting *events 'as they happen'; often seen as a strength of *live broadcasting, it tends to operate against *contextualization. **4.** A lack of systemic delay in a particular form of *interpersonal communication, offering the potential for immediate *feedback: *see also* REAL-TIME; SYNCHRONOUS COMMUNICATION. **5.** A quality reflected in specific verbal and nonverbal behaviour (e.g. *proximity, *open postures, postural *orientation, *eye contact, affectionate touch, positive *facial expressions, warm vocal tones) from which *liking, warmth, involvement, and relational closeness may be inferred. A measure of *psychological distance.

immersive flow (flow) A state of total absorption in a task or activity (e.g. playing a *videogame) that is negatively characterized by a non-awareness of oneself, one's surroundings, and of the passing of time. The concept derives from the Hungarian-born American psychologist Mihaly Csikszentmihalyi (b.1934).

impartiality **1.** A democratic ethical principle that official judgements and reports should be based on objective and relevant criteria, without *bias or prejudice, and not take sides (as opposed to being *partial*; *see also* NEUTRALITY; POLITICAL BIAS). Impartiality involves treating everyone as an equal rather than necessarily treating them in exactly the same way since it has been argued that sometimes individuals may be objectively judged to require different treatment. *See also* OBJECTIVITY. **2.** (journalism) An umbrella term for a cluster of associated concepts in professional ethics. In broadcast journalism these are reflected in editorial policies such as the need for programmes to reflect a wide range of views and opinions, to avoid bias or an imbalance of views on controversial issues (*see also* BALANCE), and, where a single view is expressed, to avoid misrepresenting opposing views and allow a right of reply. This particular list is adapted from the BBC's editorial guidelines.

(∰) SEE WEB LINKS

• Safeguarding impartiality in the 21st century

impersonal *adj.* **1.** Not reflecting personal feelings. For example, many people would regard the relative *formality of a word-processed letter as connoting **impersonality** by comparison with an otherwise identical handwritten one. **2.** Unconcerned with the feelings of individuals. **3.** (*linguistics) A formal use of language which avoids the personal mode (and personal pronouns), as in 'Smoking is not permitted'—a passive form with the agent deleted. Such usage is common in legal documents, public notices, and other similar *registers.

implication *See* IMPLICIT MEANING.

implicature (conversational implicature) In *linguistics, and more specifically in *pragmatics, the inexplicit implications deduced from the form of an *utterance in the light of conversational *expectations (notably regarding relevance to *context). For example, 'Were you brought up in a barn?' implies that you should close the door. The term derives from Grice, who demonstrated that the utterances often mean far more than they say.

implicit communication The *connotations (intended or not) of a particular environment or of *spatial relations, such as sitting 'at the head of' a rectangular table. *See also* ELEVATION.

implicit meaning (implied meaning, implication) The import of a *message: a *meaning implied but not directly stated; connoted rather than denoted (*see also* CONNOTATION; DENOTATION). Such meanings must be inferred by the reader or listener, often by reference to the *context (*see also* INFERENCE; HIGH-CONTEXT; RESTRICTED CODE). *Compare* EXPLICIT MEANING; SIGNIFICANCE.

implied author *See* AUTHOR.

implied reader In Iser's *phenomenological theory of reader-response, a hypothetical 'role' or 'model' of someone assumed by the author to share the *knowledge necessary in order to fully understand the *text, as distinct from any actual readers. The difference between an implied reader and an actual reader is likely to be most apparent in reading works from a period when conventional *values were very different. The implied reader is embodied in the way in which text structures responses, in the form of a network of *schemata, patterns, points of view, and *indeterminacies that require and constrain *interpretation. *See also* READER-RESPONSE THEORY; RECEPTION THEORY; *compare* MODEL READER.

impression formation (person perception) *See also* DRAMATURGY; EXPECTATIONS; HALO EFFECT; PERSON PERCEPTION; PRIMACY EFFECT; PRIMING, SALIENCE; SOCIAL PERCEPTION; STEREOTYPING. 1. (social psychology) The rapid development of initial *perceptions and *evaluations of the character or personality of others. This involves both data-driven and theory-driven processes: *see* BOTTOM-UP PROCESSING; TOP-DOWN PROCESSING. 2. More broadly, how we perceive or understand other people, objects, or situations.

impression management The various ways in which people seek to influence the impressions formed by others. These may relate to a person (oneself or others), an organization, an object (such as a product), or an *event. Where this is focused on impressions of oneself this is called *self-presentation. *See also* DRAMATURGY.

impulsivity *See* REFLECTIVITY–IMPULSIVITY.

inbetween frames *See* KEYFRAME.

incommensurability A problem whereby one *theory or set of beliefs makes no sense in terms of another. This is an argument about *translatability: a stance sometimes criticized as involving *relativism, as in the *Sapir-Whorf hypothesis. Some theorists argue that competing scientific *paradigms are incommensurable.

incorporation 1. (ideological incorporation) In *Marxist theory, the disputed notion that the *dominant ideology in a capitalist society functions to incorporate the working class, thus maintaining social order and *cohesion. 2. The Marxist stance that working-class consciousness has been shaped by the *ideology of the dominant *class. The *mass media are argued to play a major part in this process, leading to the working class taking for granted the *status quo (and to working-class conservatism): a process Marcuse referred to as **deradicalization**. 3. **(co-option, recuperation)** The process in which popular countercultural forms (especially youth *subculture fashions) are commodified by the *culture industries: *see also* COMMODIFICATION; DOMINANT FORMS; EMERGENT FORMS; RESIDUAL FORMS.

independent media 1. Small media *production, *marketing, or *distribution companies not affiliated with a 'major' commercial company. This includes those which may seek public funding, such as in the 'independent film sector'. 2. Media companies defining their productions in opposition to the values of mainstream *entertainment: *see also* ALTERNATIVE MEDIA. 3. Commercial media companies which are independent of state ownership and funding: for example, in the UK, ITV (Independent Television)—a *terrestrial broadcast channel operated regionally on a *franchise basis.

independent variable *See* DEPENDENT AND INDEPENDENT VARIABLES.

indeterminacy (indeterminism) 1. (philosophy) The view that some *events have no causes or that future events are unpredictable. Such positions are encountered in quantum mechanics—the 'uncertainty principle' of the German theoretical physicist Werner Heisenberg (1901–76)—as well as some theories of human social behaviour. This stance is the opposite of *determinism. 2. In *reader-response theory, the interpretive openness of those elements of a *text which are open to more than one *interpretation and require the reader to decide on the *meaning: *see also* RECEPTION THEORY; WRITERLY. 3. **(undecidability)** In *deconstruction, the notion that the meaning of texts can never be definitely or finally established: *see also* APORIA. 4. **(indeterminacy of reference and translation)** In the philosophy of W. V. Quine (1908–2000), the notion that translation (including paraphrase and perhaps even synonymy within the same *language) is impossible without changing the meaning or truth of the original: *see also* TRANSLATABILITY.

indexical 1. *adj.* (*semiotics) A mode of relationship in a *sign between a *sign vehicle and its *referent in which the former is not purely *arbitrary or *conventional but is directly connected in some way (physically or causally) to the latter. This link can be observed or inferred: e.g. between smoke and fire, a weathercock and the direction of the wind, a thermometer and the temperature, a footprint or fingerprint and the person or creature that made it, and all symptoms of disease (quickening pulse rate, rashes, paleness, and pain). Indexical relations connect *meanings to *context. A photograph is indexical in the sense that the image is created by light. *Metonymy and *synecdoche are indexical forms. The indexical mode, the *iconic mode, and the *symbolic mode are concepts embodied in the *Peircean model of the sign, where they represent relationships between the *representamen and the *object. Where the relation is solely indexical, the sign may be referred to as an **index** (*pl.* **indices**); however, most signs involve more than one mode. **Indexicality** is the noun for the quality of being indexical. 2. For indexicality in *linguistics, *see* DEIXIS. **3.** In the study of social *interaction, the concept that meaning depends on social *context, a notion especially important in *ethnomethodology.

indirect address Behaviour by those represented within a *medium in which they are either unaware of having an *audience (as with the characters in most *narratives), or behave as if they were (as with actors in most drama). In photographic and filmic media, those within the *frame also behave as if there were no camera present (as in many *documentaries). The audience or reader is positioned in the role of a hidden voyeur (*see* VOYEURISM). This is the dominant *mode of address in narratives in any medium. It serves to suggest the unconstructedness of the narrative when the audience is willing to 'suspend disbelief' (*see* SUSPENSION OF DISBELIEF). *Compare* DIRECT ADDRESS.

indirect effects The *effects of one factor on another through one or more *intervening variables (*see also* DEPENDENT AND INDEPENDENT VARIABLES). Not to be confused with *secondary effects. *See also* CAUSATION; *compare* DIRECT EFFECTS.

indirect perception An approach to *perception associated with psychologists Gregory and Rock, in which it is conceptualized as a very active cognitive process of meaning-making (*see also* CONSTRUCTIVISM). The emphasis is on *top-down processes and on perception as primarily theory-driven: led by *schemata, *hypotheses, and *expectations which draw on our past experience and *knowledge of the world (which can be seen as constituting an internal *representation of it). These may be modified by *sensory data in particular *contexts (such *data may also trigger a change in which schemata or hypotheses are currently active, where these offer a better fit to the data). Processes of *inference allow us to go beyond the available data. Both top-down and *bottom-up processes feature in Neisser's *perceptual cycle. *Compare* DIRECT PERCEPTION.

indirect realism *See* REPRESENTATIONALISM.

indirect relationships *Impersonal, institutional relationships between people, mediated by bureaucracies, organizations, markets, corporations, and technological systems (especially *information technology). The large-scale proliferation of such relationships is seen by the American sociologist Craig Calhoun (b.1952) as a distinctive feature of modern social *integration (*see also* MODERNITY). He argues that they constitute more abstract levels of relationship beyond those termed primary and secondary (*see also* PRIMARY AND SECONDARY GROUPS). *Compare* SOCIAL NETWORKING.

individualistic cultures *Cultures that emphasize individual autonomy and competitiveness (*see* COMPETITION) rather than social *cohesion, cultural *norms, harmony, and *cooperation (the basis of what many regard as a fundamental distinction between cultures). Hofstede identifies as the most individualistic cultures the USA, Australia, Great Britain, Canada, and the Netherlands. Individualistic cultures tend also to be low *power distance cultures. *See also* INTERCULTURAL COMMUNICATION; LOW-CONTEXT; TASK-ORIENTED COMMUNICATION; *compare* COLLECTIVISTIC CULTURES.

individualization 1. The *fragmentation of traditional social groupings within modern Western societies and a movement towards what the Polish sociologist Zygmunt Bauman (b.1925) calls a 'society of individuals' characterized by a growth in the diversity of *lifestyles, a widening of options for individuals, and increasing pressures on them to take more decisions for themselves. This process has also led to the fragmentation of *mass-media audiences and of consumer markets (*see* AUDIENCE FRAGMENTATION). It is closely associated with the dominance of individualism as a cultural *value. *See* INDIVIDUALISTIC CULTURES; *see also* DEMASSIFICATION; *compare* HOMOGENIZATION. 2. **Pseudo-individualization**: the pretence of one-to-one relationships in commercial culture (as in 'just for you'). Criticized in the 1940s by Adorno: *see* FRANKFURT SCHOOL.

individual-media dependency (IMD, individual media-system dependency) The dependency relationships of individuals with the *mass media. For instance, Ball-Rokeach argues that *audiences might turn to *books or magazines for social understanding, to pop psychology books for self-understanding, and to *radio for orientation to action and *interaction. She reported that for *television the most common relationship for the individual was based on social understanding, but that all of these relations are found in relation to this *medium. She argues that these relations apply also to particular *genres and particular *texts (e.g. specific programmes, films, or magazines). *Compare* USES AND GRATIFICATIONS.

induction (inductive reasoning) A process of inferring a general principle from particular instances. The opposite of *deduction.

inference The general term for the *cognitive or logical process of going beyond the explicit evidence by making *hypotheses (or drawing conclusions) based on *information implicit in *data or premises or on what is implied or assumed within a *text or *utterance; alternatively, any conclusion drawn from such a process. *See also* DEDUCTION; INDUCTION.

inferential model *See* RELEVANCE THEORY.

infinite regression *See* MISE-EN-ABÎME.

inflection 1. The modulation of vocal *intonation or *pitch. 2. A change in the form of a word to indicate a grammatical function: e.g. adding the letter 's' to make a simple plural in English. 3. Often used in social science to refer to how one dimension of *identity (e.g. *class) is affected **(inflected)** by others (e.g. *ethnicity and *gender).

influence 1. The capacity to persuade: being able to affect people's *attitudes, *values, and/or behaviour due to *power, *status, *knowledge, contacts, and/or wealth; alternatively, the *effect or *agency. 2. In the *rhetoric of media and *technology *effects, a term associated with soft *determinism (rather than hard determinism), implying that a particular factor contributes to, or facilitates, some effect but that it is not a *sufficient cause or perhaps even a *necessary cause. *Compare* TECHNOLOGICAL DETERMINISM.

Infobahn *See* INFORMATION SUPERHIGHWAY.

infographics (information graphics) Visual *representations of *data, *information, or concepts.

infomercials A portmanteau term (*information* + *commercial*). Extended television commercials including product demonstrations, designed to stimulate direct purchases via an onscreen telephone number.

informant Someone who provides *information. In social science, this is for a researcher, usually in relatively informal research contexts such as unstructured and semi-structured *interviews and more generally in *ethnography. *Compare* RESPONDENT.

information 1. Often used loosely as a synonym for *data, *facts, or *knowledge. 2. A primary *function of communication (*see* INFORMATION FUNCTION); also, the broad classificatory basis for forms of *discourse concerned with imparting *facts or *knowledge: *see* EXPOSITION. 3. The referential or semantic *content of a *message: *see also* INFORMATIONAL COMMUNICATION; REFERENTIALITY. 4. *Data interpreted within a framework (e.g. a *schema or a *theory). In this sense, there is no information in books, computers, or the world: data only becomes information when it is interpreted. 5. New or previously unknown *knowledge or *facts. 6. *Knowledge acquired by learning or research. 7. In *information theory, that which contributes to the reduction of uncertainty; not to be confused with *meaning. *See also* REDUNDANCY. 8. In *discourse analysis and *text linguistics, the degree of unexpectedness or familiarity in the content of a message: *see* GIVEN AND NEW.

information age 1. A period commonly regarded as having begun with the rise of the *internet in the 1990s (although the phrase was coined in Japan in the mid 1960s) which is characterized by the dominance of an *information economy, an *information society, and (negatively), fallout from *information overload. 2. A rhetorical device that tries to grasp the significance of the changes brought about by digital communications by characterizing them as being on the same order of magnitude as the shift from an agrarian society to an industrial one (Toffler).

informational communication (referential communication) *Messages in which the primary *content is referential (*see also* CONTENT MESSAGE; REFERENTIALITY). **Referential language** functions primarily to record or communicate *information. For example, the language of science (in particular contrast to poetic language). It is intended to denote (*see* DENOTATION) rather than connote (*see* CONNOTATION), unlike *expressive communication. *Gender stereotypes often frame informational communication as a *masculine style. *See also* EXPOSITION; *compare* EXPRESSIVE COMMUNICATION; INSTRUMENTAL COMMUNICATION; RELATIONAL COMMUNICATION.

informational function *See* INFORMATION FUNCTION.

information and communication technology (ICT) An umbrella term for all of the various media employed in communicating information: for example, in an educational context ICT may include computers, the *internet, television broadcasts, and even printed or handwritten notes.

information architecture In computer science and web design, the systematic structural organization of *database *information to support ease of use. *Compare* INFORMATION DESIGN.

information culture 1. A hypothetical *culture in which the main role of its *institutions and laws is to support the *production, exchange, and dissemination of *information and where the majority of its art and *artefacts exist as information. *Virtual worlds like Second Life are arguably information cultures, although the extent to which any post-industrial Western culture qualifies is less certain. 2. In business, the corporate ethos of a company, the product of which is *information, including the structures and behaviours associated with *knowledge acquisition, communication, and dissemination among staff and customers.

information design The organization and presentation of *information in order to make it easier to navigate and understand, particularly through graphical means (*see* INFOGRAPHICS). *See also* CHUNKING; COMMUNICATION DESIGN; SIGNPOSTING; *compare* INFORMATION ARCHITECTURE.

information economy An economy in which the majority of the wealth is produced through the buying and selling of *information: both as a *commodity and as a service. In 1967, the economist Marc Porat (b.1947) distinguished between the domains of 'matter and energy' and information, dividing *information* into a primary sector consisting of companies that produce information goods and services and a secondary sector consisting of information services used by public *institutions and private companies. On this basis, he estimated that 53% of all labour income in the US could be attributed to information work. *Compare* KNOWLEDGE ECONOMY.

information flow The movement, control, and direction of *data or *messages within systems. *See* ASYMMETRICAL RELATIONSHIPS; CYBERNETICS; DEPENDENCY THEORY; DIFFUSION; DISCLOSURE; DOWNWARD COMMUNICATION; GATEKEEPERS; GATEKEEPING; INFORMATIZATION; MARKET MODEL; MEDIA-CENTRICITY; PLURALISM; TWO-STEP FLOW; UPWARD COMMUNICATION; WEAK TIES; *compare* INFORMATION GAP.

information function The use of communication for imparting *facts or *knowledge. It presupposes a normative relationship in which the sender's purpose is to inform and the *receiver's purpose is to understand. In communication where the primary function is informational, *content tends be *foregrounded (rather than *form or *style). It is a major purpose for individuals in both *interpersonal communication and in their use of the *mass media, although in that context it is often referred to by sociologists as the *surveillance function (*see also* COMMUNICATIVE FUNCTIONS; PERSONAL FUNCTIONS; USES AND GRATIFICATIONS). The circulation of *information and news is also one of the major roles of the *mass media from the functional perspective of society, again often termed the surveillance function (*see also* MEDIA FUNCTIONS). Communication is often reductively defined as the transmission of *information (*see also* TRANSMISSION MODELS). *See also* EXPOSITION; INFORMATIONAL COMMUNICATION; REFERENTIAL FUNCTION.

information gap 1. An asymmetry of *information where one party has *access to more than another: *see also* ASYMMETRICAL RELATIONSHIPS; DISCLOSURE; INFORMATION FLOW; JOHARI WINDOW; OMNISCIENT POINT OF VIEW. 2. Social division based on inequality of *access to *information: *see also* INFORMATION RICH AND POOR; KNOWLEDGE GAP; *compare* FREEDOM OF INFORMATION; INFORMATION FLOW; INFORMATION LITERACY; PUBLIC DOMAIN.

information graphics *See* INFOGRAPHICS.

information literacy A person's competence measured by their ability to identify, access, evaluate, and organize *information in order to complete a task or solve a problem.

information model *See* STORY MODEL.

information overload A term coined by Toffler referring to a subjective experience of individuals in the modern world in which they feel overwhelmed by more *data than they feel able to handle. *See also* FUTURE SHOCK; *compare* NARCOTIZATION.

information processing 1. (computing) Performing operations on input *data in a sequence of functional steps, transforming it into different output data in accordance with a specific goal. 2. (cognitive psychology) A model of human *cognition based on the *metaphor of the computer (*see also* COGNITION). This conceptualizes *sensory data as input (*see also* BOTTOM-UP PROCESSING), and thinking as performing operations on this, generating output which guides the selection and execution of goal-directed actions (*see also* TOP-DOWN PROCESSING). *Constructivist critics argue that this reductively ignores the centrality of *meaning rather than *information in human cognition, the inseparability of cognition and *affect, and the importance of social *interaction and bodily experience.

information retrieval The process of accessing *information in documents or *databases. A term associated with the American computer scientist Calvin Mooers (1919–94).

information rich and poor The division of the general public into two groups depending upon the way in which they use and relate to *information. The information rich tend to be of a higher socioeconomic status, are better educated, have better *access to technology and are more technologically savvy than the information poor. *See also* DIGITAL DIVIDE; KNOWLEDGE GAP.

information science The systematic study of *information in all its forms, including its collection, storage, retrieval, classification, manipulation, dissemination, and *evaluation.

information society 1. A reconstitution of the social world due to the *diffusion of specific technologies (including cable and satellite television, computers, and the *internet). Toffler suggests the world has been shaped by three waves of technological innovation: the agricultural revolution, the industrial revolution, and the information revolution. The term started to appear from the 1960s in Japan to account for the transformations that began after the Second World War. However, as Giddens points out, all nation states can already be considered as information societies because of their reliance on information for communication and control: *see* IMAGINED COMMUNITY. 2. The occupational shift from manual to office work in advanced industrial societies (Bell).

information structure *See* GIVEN AND NEW.

information superhighway [German *Infobahn*] An outmoded *metaphor for the *internet which, while emphasizing its vast capacity as a delivery system for *information, conceptualized it inaccurately in terms of a linear broadcast model rather than as a distributed network. The term was attributed to the American politician Al Gore (b.1948) in the 1990s, although the Korean-American artist Nam June Paik (1932–2006) named a hypothetical thousand-channel television system the 'electronic superhighway' in 1974. *See also* TRANSMISSION MODELS.

information technology (IT) Commonly a synonym for computers and computer networks but more broadly designating any technology that is used to generate, store, process, and/or distribute *information electronically, including television and the telephone.

information theory A mathematically-based approach to *information that ignores *semantics (its *meaning) and quantifies it in terms of units or *bits. This method allows information exchanges between a *sender and a *receiver to be expressed as a series of equations and is of particular use to engineers attempting to maximize the potential output of a transmission system. *See also* FEEDBACK; NOISE; REDUNDANCY; SHANNON AND WEAVER'S MODEL.

information transmission *See* TRANSMISSION MODELS.

informative function (representational function) Halliday's term for a *linguistic function in which one uses language to make statements, to communicate *information, or to represent one's understanding of *facts and *knowledge. For example, 'I want to tell you about . . .' *Compare* INFORMATION FUNCTION; REFERENTIAL FUNCTION.

informatization *See also* INFORMATION ECONOMY; INFORMATION SOCIETY; KNOWLEDGE ECONOMY; KNOWLEDGE INDUSTRIES; POST-INDUSTRIALISM. 1. Broadly, an increasing flow or *diffusion of *information throughout a social system. 2. The *diffusion of *information and communication technologies. 3. The policy of using *information technologies to promote socioeconomic development.

informed consent A formal process in which the purposes and consequences of research are explained to *subjects, who must sign a *consent form before any research is carried out.

infotainment A portmanteau term (*information + entertainment*). The presentation of *factual *information in an entertaining manner, normally in broadcast media and especially on television (*docudrama can be seen as an example). Sometimes regarded as a *hybrid genre. Often used pejoratively in the *rhetoric of *dumbing down, especially where coverage of political issues takes the form of more popular formats (*see also* FICTION VALUES; SENSATIONALISM; STORY MODEL; TABLOIDIZATION). *Compare* EDUTAINMENT.

in-group A group to which individuals see themselves as belonging, an **out-group** being a group to which they do not. *See also* GROUP IDENTIFICATION; *compare* REFERENCE GROUP.

inherited audience Term used in research within the broadcast media for an *audience that carries over from a previous programme.

inner speech The silent mental use of words in formulating ideas, including rehearsal for external expression. Vygotsky saw this as an essential part of thinking. The notion of thinking as internal conversation also reflects the perspective of *symbolic interactionism. *Compare* INTRAPERSONAL COMMUNICATION.

innocent eye A term used by Gombrich and the American philosopher Nelson Goodman (1906–98) to refer to a common assumption that images do not need to be read, whereas Gombrich stressed 'the *beholder's share': 'reading an image, like the reception of any other message, is dependent on prior knowledge of possibilities; we can only recognize what we know.' He added that 'the innocent eye is a myth' and Goodman commented that 'The innocent eye is blind and the virgin mind empty.' The viewer is cognitively active, not passive. *See also* ACTIVE AUDIENCE THEORY.

(⊕) SEE WEB LINKS

• Gombrich archive

inoculation theory The notion, developed by McGuire and subsequently repeatedly demonstrated in research, that to promote resistance to *persuasion by opposing viewpoints (for instance, in political or health campaigns), the persuasive message should include small 'doses' of a counterargument, followed by a refutation.

insert editing 1. **(splice in)** (*nonlinear editing) An option that allows for a new element (consisting of either video or audio) to be added to a sequence on a *timeline while preserving the material that is already there by shunting it forward by the length of the *shot. Distinguished from **overwrite editing,** an option where a new element replaces existing material on a *timeline. 2. (*linear editing) A technique of editing onto a pre-formatted (or striped) videotape which allows for individual shots to be dropped in at any point without creating a picture disturbance (*see also* STRIPING). (Confusingly, in a linear context, an insert edit is the equivalent of an overwrite edit in nonlinear editing, because it replaces existing material on the tape).

inserts In television and radio, pre-recorded elements that have been prepared to supplement an otherwise live broadcast.

instant messaging A form of *synchronous text-based communication between two or more individuals over the *internet.

institutional bias (institutionalized discrimination, systemic bias) A tendency for the procedures and practices of particular *institutions to operate in ways which result in certain social groups being advantaged or favoured and others being disadvantaged or devalued. This need not be the result of any conscious prejudice or discrimination but rather of the majority simply following existing rules or *norms. Institutional *racism and institutional *sexism are the most common examples. *See also* BIAS.

institutionalization The development of patterns of social behaviour into enduring and pervasive forms: the process in which *institutions emerge. Peter Berger and Luckmann argue that institutionalization occurs when the first generation to say 'let's try it this way' passes down a practice to following generations who see this as 'the way it's done' (*see also* CONTRUCTIONISM).

institutions 1. In most everyday usage, organizations (such as schools, banks, hospitals, prisons, and broadcasting corporations). 2. **(social institutions)** (social sciences) A term frequently used loosely to refer to established ways of behaving or, more formally to major social systems or structures which organize the primary social practices, *roles, and relationships within a *culture. Broadly, there are four main types of social institution: political, economic, cultural, and kinship institutions. Most frequently cited as social institutions are the family, the state, and the law, but social *constructionists often refer to *language as the foremost social institution. In *functionalist approaches, social institutions have been seen as *social structures serving to maintain society through meeting social 'needs' in their organization of essential activities. For instance, for Malinowski they meet basic and universal individual human biological and psychological needs. In contemporary sociology, functionalist approaches have been overtaken by a more fluid notion of institutions reflecting less clearcut distinctions between institutional structures and functions and less *consensus over *values. Social institutions offer the psychological value of predictability and stability but they can also be experienced as autonomous forces constraining our options. Although they transcend the lives of individuals, institutions and patterns of behaviour are always in the process of formation, transformation, and decline. 3. A central theme in *media studies deriving from sociological and *political economy approaches. The primary focus is on *mass-media institutions rather than *textual analysis or *audience research, although Stuart Hall and others have emphasized the interconnectedness of *production and *regulation with the other elements in the *circuit of culture. Key themes include *power relations, *globalization, concentration of ownership (*see* MEDIA OWNERSHIP), *regulation, and occupational practices and values within *media culture. It includes, on the macro-level, the study of media organizations such as *production and *distribution companies and the relationships between them, and on the micro-level, of groups of media workers such as unions and news teams. Media institutions are seen as shaped by economic and political factors in particular. In the broadcast media, commercial factors are seen as influencing not only commercial broadcasting but also *public service broadcasting. The polar opposites in debates about media power are the *market model and the *manipulative model. While *pluralist approaches frame the role of the mass media in terms of a liberal *ideology of freedom, Marxist approaches foreground the power of media institutions to determine what appears in the marketplace, where media products are treated as *commodities rather than a public good. In relation to film, the primary focus of institutional analysis has been on the *studio system of *classical Hollywood cinema, foregrounding the socio-historical *context, and demonstrating the pervasive influence of the institutional drive for the maximization of profit. Bordwell has argued that the *form and *content of classical Hollywood films was primarily determined by the institutional context of their *production.

instructional function *See* EDUCATIONAL FUNCTION.

instrumental communication (outcome-oriented) Communication in which the primary goal is to 'transmit' an *intended meaning (*informational and/or persuasive) accurately and effectively, and in which communication is merely a means to an end. The primary focus is on explicit *content (and/or *effects) rather than on *form or stylistic features. It is a communicative style that *foregrounds clarity of *denotation and backgrounds *ambiguity, *connotation, and *aesthetic and *expressive functions. *Gender stereotypes often frame instrumental communication as a *masculine style. *Compare* EXPRESSIVE COMMUNICATION; INFORMATIONAL COMMUNICATION; RELATIONAL COMMUNICATION.

instrumental function Halliday's term for a *linguistic function in which one uses *language to satisfy basic material needs, to manipulate the environment, and to accomplish things. For example, 'I want...'

instrumentalism 1. Goal-oriented, *instrumental, or *task-oriented communication or behaviour or pragmatic or *instrumental values, often contrasted with *expressive or *relational communication or behaviour and aesthetic or social *values. 2. (philosophy) A pragmatic approach in which theories are evaluated in terms of their usefulness as a means of achieving a particular *purpose.

instrumental rationality A term used by *Frankfurt school critical theorists to refer to what they regarded as the reduction of the *Enlightenment ideal of reason to a dehumanizing technical rationalism in modern industrial societies. Instrumental rationality views the natural and social world in terms of how they can be exploited, and has no regard for human *values. *See also* CRITICAL THEORY; RATIONALIZATION.

instrumental values The *evaluation of things (whether concrete objects or abstractions) in terms of their utility or suitability for one's own *purposes rather than in terms of intrinsic worth or aesthetic merit.

INT (interior shot) In *screenplays, an indoor set. *Compare* EXT.

integration 1. (social integration) (sociology) Social *cohesion based on the functional interdependence of all aspects of a sociocultural system and on shared *norms and *values maintained by consent and *cooperation rather than coercion.

For *functionalists, an essential condition for the functioning of society, as also are *institutions of integration including written *language and a legal system. Sometimes a reference to the degree of such cohesion. Critics argue that such theories overemphasize the importance of shared *values and underestimate the degree of *conflict. *See also* FUNCTIONALISM. **2.** An individual's sense of belonging to a social group through sharing its norms, values, and beliefs (a concept derived from Durkheim). One of the primary *uses and gratifications or *social functions of media use: *see* SOCIAL UTILITY FUNCTION. **3.** The process by which a minority group adapts to the culture of a majority. **4.** Unified access to public facilities previously segregated on the basis of race as formerly in the USA and South Africa. **5.** (business management) A strategy in which a company acquires others within the same field in order to reduce *competition, pool resources and increase profit, market share, and/or sales. *See also* DIAGONAL INTEGRATION; HORIZONTAL INTEGRATION; VERTICAL INTEGRATION.

intellectual property The rights or entitlements that are attached to products of the intellect (as opposed to physical property) which include forms of artistic expression such as songs, books, films, and images, as well as technological inventions such as hardware and software. Laws based around the protection of intellectual property such as *copyright and the patent system are claimed to encourage creativity by rewarding creators and protecting their interests.

intended meaning *Compare* PREFERRED READING. **1.** In *interpersonal communication, how a speaker expects an *utterance to be interpreted, which may or may not correspond with how it is actually interpreted: *see also* COMMUNICATIVE PRESUMPTION; INTENTIONAL COMMUNICATION. **2.** A reader's understanding of how the author of a *text expected a particular work, or part of it, to be interpreted, which they may infer from the text and/or from external evidence. In the case of films, the 'author' is typically seen as the *director (*see* AUTEUR THEORY). In literary and filmic contexts audiences commonly privilege what they understand to be the creator's intentions. For problems with this stance *see* INTENTIONAL FALLACY.

intensity *See* LUMINANCE.

intentional communication Conscious, deliberate, and often explicit communication as opposed to unintentional communication 'given off' through *leakage in *nonverbal communication. Intentionality is important in *speech act theory. *See also* COMMUNICATIVE PRESUMPTION.

intentional fallacy An alleged interpretive fallacy, identified in literary theory by Wimsatt and Beardsley, that involves relating the *meaning of a *text to its author's intentions. Although these theorists regarded meaning as residing within the text, some other theorists not sharing this standpoint have also dismissed the author's intentions in relation to meaning (*see also* AUTHORIAL INTENTION). Privileging the author's intentions is a stance which has several flaws. In particular, it assumes that authors are always aware of their own intentions; it underestimates the debt of the author to other sources (*see* INTERTEXTUALITY); and it ignores the importance of *readers' purposes (which Wimsatt and Beardsley also dismissed as the *affective fallacy). The intentional fallacy implicitly involves a *transmission model of communication which privileges the *sender. An author's intentions are of no concern to formalist or structuralist analysts (*see also* FORMALISM; STRUCTURALISM). Although the literary theorist Hirsch insists that 'a text means what its author meant', an emphasis on the importance of the historical *context of a text's *production and of the author's biography can be associated with an approach in which authorial intentions are seen as contributing to an understanding of the *significance of the text rather than as determining its meaning. In relation to the *mass media, the concept of a *preferred reading is built on the assumption that the producers of texts seek to constrain their *interpretation even if readers decline the preferred reading. In relation to *interpersonal communication, there is similarly argued to be a *communicative presumption.

interaction 1. Reciprocal action or influence (*see* RECIPROCITY). This includes interaction between people, animals, and objects such as machines: *see also* COACTION; COMPETITION; CONFLICT; COOPERATION; HUMAN-COMPUTER INTERACTION. 2. **(social interaction, interpersonal behaviour, social behaviour)** The verbal and *nonverbal behaviour of two or more individuals (or groups) in relation to each other in a social *context, including reciprocal communication. It is widely argued to be dependent on shared, taken-for-granted *expectations. In (social) **action theory**, social interaction consists of intentional actions in *social relations which are made in anticipation of, and in response to, those of others. In *symbolic interactionism, the self is seen as the result of such interaction. In *constructionism, social interaction is seen as constructing and maintaining social reality. *See also* COACTION; COMMUNICATIVE FUNCTIONS; COMMUNICATIVE PURPOSES; COMMUNICATIVE RELATIONSHIPS; FACE-TO-FACE INTERACTION; INTERCHANGE; INTRAPERSONAL COMMUNICATION; RITUAL INTERACTION; SYMBOLIC INTERACTIONISM; *compare* PARASOCIAL INTERACTION. 3. Sometimes a synonym for *communication.

interactional function Halliday's term for a *linguistic function in which one uses *language to mediate relationships with others. For example, 'We're friends'.

interactional synchrony (interactional flow) In *interpersonal communication, the way in which conversations are unconsciously coordinated to maintain a flow and to minimize unintentional interruptions. Nonverbal cues have been argued to perform this function in *face-to-face interactions, though it seems to work fairly well even in the relative *cuelessness of telephone conversations. *See also* POSTURAL ECHO.

interactionism *See* SYMBOLIC INTERACTIONISM.

interaction model *See also* COMMUNICATION MODELS; INTERACTION-ORIENTED COMMUNICATION. 1. Generally, a conceptualization of communication as a two-way, cyclical process (including *feedback) in contrast to the *sender-oriented asymmetry and unidirectionality of linear models, Schramm's 1954 model, emphasizing the active *interpretation of meaning being the most well-known example. *See also* ENCODING/DECODING MODEL; MEANING-ORIENTED COMMUNICATION; *compare* TRANSMISSION MODELS. 2. More specifically, conceptualizations of communication as sharing, exchanging, or negotiating *meanings through *interaction in situational *contexts (*see also* RECIPROCITY; SYMBOLIC INTERACTIONISM). Various types of situations are associated with normative functions or purposes: *see* COMMUNICATIVE FUNCTIONS; COMMUNICATIVE PURPOSES. *Compare* COMMUNICATION GAME; RELATIONAL MODEL.

interaction-oriented communication (interaction-centred)
1. Communication in which the main focus is on *phatic functions, social *context, and/or *interpersonal relations. Variously contrasted with *task-oriented communication or *sender-oriented communication. *Compare* SOCIO-ORIENTED COMMUNICATION. 2. *Discourse which is heavy in contextual information: *see also* HIGH-CONTEXT. 3. The primary *communication style favoured in *collectivistic cultures.

interaction rituals Goffman's term for relatively standardized routine *interchanges or social *episodes in the *microsociology of interpersonal *social relations in which shared realities and *identities are enacted. This includes such everyday rituals as greetings, departures, flirting, and joke-telling. *See also* RITUAL INTERACTION.

interactive fiction 1. A *videogame genre also known as **adventure games** in which players are given a goal and must solve puzzles or fight opponents in order to reach it. Such games can be text-based such as *Adventure* (1976) or graphics-based such as *Myst* (1993). 2. A hypertext novel with multiple branching plots.

interactive media Media (typically online, disc-based, or broadcast) that enable users not only to access the materials on offer but also (within a limited framework) to communicate specific responses which may influence subsequent *events (e.g. triggering an alternative ending to a *narrative).

interactive movies 1. A *videogame genre, popular in the 1990s, which makes extensive use of full-motion video segments, employing a branching 'decision-tree model' whereby the user's actions determine which pre-filmed scene would introduce the next challenge for the user. 2. A pejorative term for a *videogame containing lots of non-interactive mini-movies (known as *cut scenes*) which interrupt the gameplay.

(⊕) SEE WEB LINKS

• The challenge of the interactive movie

interactive television A broad category of actual and potential television applications that opens up a channel of communication between the programme-maker and the viewer or develops the television along the lines of an *internet *browser through which viewers can order products and services and access *information. Traditionally, interacting with television was restricted to choosing which programmes to watch, writing a letter to a broadcaster, or participating in a phone-in. Digital television has enhanced but not radically extended these capabilities. Some sports services allow viewers a choice of various *camera angles filming an *event. In the 1980s, *teletext applications were introduced that allowed viewers to browse 'pages' of *information such as channel guides, weather reports, and national and local news. Digital television has extended these facilities. In the UK, many programmes supply supplementary information accessed by pressing the red button on the remote control. In the 1990s web TV products were introduced, that afforded web browsing and *email through the television, although it lacked *mass-market appeal, possibly because of the difficulty of reading text on a standard definition television screen.

interactivity 1. A dynamic and reciprocal communicative relationship between a *user and a computerized media device where each new action is contingent on a previous action. When taken to be a property of a *medium, interactivity measures the degree to which users can influence and vary *form and/or *content. This is conceptualized by the American HCI researcher Brenda Laurel (b.1950) according to the frequency, range, and significance of the choices that the medium offers to the user. Critics of this position argue that since the computer is not an active participant in the communication process, only *interpersonal communication can be truly interactive. 2. Any communication between two or more individuals that is dynamically shaped by the participants of the exchange (*see also* INTERACTION). When taken as a property of the communication process, interactivity is characterized as being active, intentional, and occurring only in conditions where the roles of *sender and receiver are fully interchangeable. Examples include a face-to-face meeting, a telephone conversation, and an SMS text message exchange. Critics of this position argue that it is overly reliant on a linear, *transmission model of communication, whereas interactive environments are virtual spaces in which a person can be both the *sender and *receiver of *information because their actions define their experience of the medium. 3. In broadcast media, a limited potential for programme *content to be dynamically shaped by *feedback from viewers/listeners in forms which include audience participation, telephone calls, emails, and text messages. *Digital television has extended the possibilities for interactive broadcasting: *see* INTERACTIVE TELEVISION.

interchange (ritual interchange) Goffman's term for a unit of social *interaction involving two or more 'moves' and two or more participants. For example: 'Excuse me' followed by 'Certainly'. He argues that a conversational interchange is not merely a dialogue but a basic unit of social interaction (*compare* EPISODE): hence, he refers to the second move as a *response* rather than a *reply*. *See also* RITUAL INTERACTION; SYMBOLIC INTERACTIONISM; *compare* ADJACENCY PAIRS.

intercultural communication (cross-cultural communication) 1. Loosely, an umbrella term for *interaction between people from different *cultural or *subcultural backgrounds intended to lead to shared understandings of *messages. 2. In discourses where cross-cultural communication refers to entire cultures (as in relation to *collectivistic cultures, *high-contact cultures, *high-context cultures, *individualistic cultures, *low-contact cultures, *low-context cultures, *power distance), intercultural communication may be restricted to *interpersonal communication between individuals from different cultures and **intracultural communication** to that between individuals with a shared cultural background. 3. A branch of *communication studies concerned with this field.

intercutting 1. (*editing) A technique of cutting back and forth between two or more discrete *narrative *sequences typically filmed in different locations or at different times which combine to produce a sense of the convergence or divergence of several story strands in a complex plot: for example, in the films of Robert Altman. Another classic example of this device is a *shot of a bomb timer counting down intercut with shots of the attempts of the *protagonists to escape. 2. In less narrative-driven content, such as pop videos, cutting back and forth between different segments: for example, between an artist's performance and a dance sequence or other *imagery.

interest groups *See* EPISTEMIC COMMUNITY.

interface 1. The means of 'communication' between a human user and a computer (or any electronic device). In computing, the interface consists of both hardware (computer, screen, keyboard, mouse), and the *software. *See also* HUMAN-COMPUTER INTERACTION. 2. Loosely, the *graphical user interface. 3. Any means by which two electronic devices 'communicate' with one another: for example, a printer cable is a means for a computer to interface with a printer.

intergroup communication *Interaction between two or more different social groups. *Compare* INTERPERSONAL COMMUNICATION; INTRAGROUP COMMUNICATION.

interlace frame A single *frame of video consisting of two *fields encoded with separate information representing two successive 'snapshots'. *Compare* PROGRESSIVE SEGMENTED FRAME.

interlace scanning (interlacing) In the majority of standard definition television systems, a process where all the odd lines of a television picture are scanned first—from the top left to the bottom right of the screen—and then the electron beam 'flies back' and scans all the even lines. Interlace scanning is a way of evening out the picture brightness and reducing flicker.

(((⬤))) **SEE WEB LINKS**
• Interlacing

intermediality A generic term for phenomena at the point of intersection between different media, or crossing their borders, or for their interconnection, typically in the context of *digital media. The term emerged in the 1990s, but usage beyond this basic concept varies greatly. *See also* CONVERGENCE; HYBRIDIZATION; MULTIMEDIA; MULTIMODALITY; *compare* DIALOGISM; INTERTEXTUALITY.

internalization 1. (social psychology) The adoption by individuals of the normative *attitudes, beliefs, *values, or *role behaviour of a group or the broader social system to which they belong: the psychological dimension of *socialization (*see also* REFERENCE GROUP). This is the basis of social control. Where *norms are imposed rather than accepted (*see* CONFORMITY), this represents compliance with coercion rather than internalization. 2. (*psychoanalytic theory) The adoption of (primarily) parental standards and values into the mental structures of the individual, leading to the development of the superego. 3. The learning of abstract rule systems (such as grammatical rules).

internal validity *See* EXPERIMENT.

internet A portmanteau word (*interconnected* + *network*). 1. A vast *network of interconnected computers that acts as a worldwide *distribution system for digital *information. The internet operates according to two principles. Firstly, it is a non-centralized or 'distributed network' so that if a computer (or node) should fail, the fidelity of the network as a whole can be preserved by routing information around it. Secondly, the information itself is broken down into 'packets' which are separately addressed, and sent and received according to specific protocols. A prototype of the internet (ARPAnet) was designed in the US in the 1960s at the height of the Cold War as a communications system sufficiently robust to survive a full-scale nuclear attack. In 1984, ARPAnet became the internet by being divided into five domains identified by a 'dot' prefix: for example, .mil for the US military or .gov for governments. In 1991, the internet was commercialized and a *dot-com domain was added which led to a huge rise in its popularity. 2. A *medium associated with a variety of *communication technologies including the *World Wide Web, *email, chat (*instant messaging, *IRC), *newsgroups, *blogs, and *streaming video. Sometimes distinguished from *mass communication as a **many-to-many** medium of communication.

internet café *See* CYBERCAFÉ.

Internet Relay Chat (IRC) An online forum in which people can 'chat' by typing text messages to one another, thereby holding a 'conversation' in *real time. IRC was created in Finland in 1988 by Jarkko Oikarinen (b.1967).

Internet Service Provider (ISP) A company that provides access to the *internet in exchange for a fee for members of the public who have the requisite personal computer and connection equipment.

interpellation (appellation, hailing) Althusser's term to describe a mechanism whereby the human *subject is 'constituted' (constructed) by pre-given structures (a *structuralist stance). By being named or 'hailed' as a member of a group, a person is led to see themselves as an *ideological *subject. For example, when a politician addresses a crowd as 'citizens', or a teacher addresses a class as 'students', the people in those situations are being asked to adopt a certain *subject position or social *role that is conducive to the maintenance of the social order. The situation would be different if they were addressed as 'comrades'. This concept is used by *Marxist theorists to explain the *ideological function of *mass-media *texts. According to this view, the subject (viewer, listener, reader) is constituted by the text, and the power of the mass media resides in their ability to 'position' the subject in such a way that their *representations are taken to be reflections of everyday reality. Such framings reflect a stance of structural or *textual determinism which has been challenged by contemporary social semioticians who tend to emphasize the 'polysemic' and 'multiaccentual' nature of texts, together with the diversity of their uses. *See also* IDEOLOGICAL STATE APPARATUS.

interpersonal behaviour *See* INTERACTION.

interpersonal communication (IPC) 1. *Interaction between individuals, typically 'one-to-one' (**dyadic communication**), although it can also include small groups (*see* GROUP COMMUNICATION). It may be either *synchronous or *asynchronous. Synchronous interpersonal communication may involve both speech and nonverbal cues (e.g. direct *face-to-face interaction, videolinks), or speech alone (e.g. *telephone); or mainly text (e.g. *internet chat systems). Asynchronous interpersonal communication tends to be primarily through text (e.g. letters, fax, *email). 2. A branch of *communication studies concerned with this field.

interpersonal distance (IPD) The relative distances between people in *face-to-face interaction, the study of which is termed *proxemics (*see also* INTERPERSONAL ZONES; PROXIMITY).

interpersonal function (**pragmatic function**) Halliday's term for a *linguistic function in which *language expresses the relations between speaker and listener. This is presented as one of three essential metafunctions reflected in all adult language usage (*compare* IDEATIONAL FUNCTION; TEXTUAL FUNCTION). *See also* COMMUNICATIVE FUNCTIONS.

interpersonal interaction *See* INTERACTION; INTERPERSONAL COMMUNICATION.

interpersonal perception *See* PERSON PERCEPTION.

interpersonal relations The relations between individuals, including friendship and romantic relationships. *See also* COACTION; COOPERATION; COMPETITION; CONFLICT; INTERACTION; INTERPERSONAL COMMUNICATION; INTRAPERSONAL COMMUNICATION; POWER RELATIONS; RECIPROCITY; SOCIAL RELATIONS.

interpersonal zones A typology of significantly different ranges of physical distance between people in *face-to-face interaction (*see also* PROXEMICS). Edward T. Hall outlines four main ranges based on 'sensory shifts' (e.g. from communication in whispers to shouting): intimate (18 inches or less), personal (1.5 to 4 feet), social (4 to 12 feet), and public (12 feet or more). The **intimate zone** is that of parents and children, lovers, spouses, and partners; the **personal zone** is that of close friends; the **social zone** is that of friends and co-workers; the public zone is that of strangers and officials. Hall notes that the intimate zone is an area which can easily feel 'invaded' and that 30 feet is the distance that is automatically set around important public figures. These zones are based on North American norms, and such zonings are culturally variable (*see* HIGH-CONTACT CULTURES; LOW-CONTACT CULTURES). They can also be related to *shot sizes in photography and film. *See also* PERSONAL SPACE; TERRITORIALITY.

interpolation (computing) A method of constructing new *data points taking a *value that lies somewhere between a range of known data points. For example, if you want to display a 600 *dpi image on a 72 *ppi screen you might construct an algorithm that simply divides the former value by the latter and tells the computer to display only 1 pixel in 8. In practice interpolating images involves a trade-off between efficiency, smoothness, and sharpness.

interposition *See* OCCLUSION.

interpretant In the *Peircean model of the *sign, not an interpreter but rather the *sense made of the sign. Its function is to connect the *representamen with its *object in the form of a mediating *representation which creates a triadic relation that Peirce argues is the basis of *semiosis. The interpretant divides into three subsidiary categories: the *immediate interpretant*, which is the grasped *meaning of the sign, the *dynamical interpretant*, which is the actual effect of the meaning of the sign, and the *final interpretant* which is a habit of thought that is either reinforced, modified, or created anew by the meaning of the sign. *Compare* OBJECT; REPRESENTAMEN.

interpretation 1. The process of explaining or clarifying the subjective or intersubjective *meaning, *significance, and/or relevance of something (e.g. *signs or *texts); also, the product of this process. Interpretation is the primary focus of *hermeneutics and *deconstruction. It is widely regarded as inseparable from understanding. In interpretive sociology, the focus is on understanding and interpreting the *meaning of social actions in specific *contexts (in particular, to the social actors involved), as in *symbolic interactionism, *phenomenological sociology, and *ethnomethodology. *See also* INTERPRETIVE CODES; INTERPRETIVE COMMUNITY; INTERPRETIVE REPERTOIRE; INTERPRETIVE TURN. 2. The process of inferring beyond the *literal meaning of a *message or text: 'reading between the lines' with reference to both *textual knowledge and *social knowledge: *see also* COMPREHENSION; CONNOTATION; INFERENCE. 3. In *psychoanalytic theory, the analysis of the *manifest content of dreams in order to reveal unconscious *latent meaning. 4. The application of a *hypothesis, *theory, *schema, or *model to *data, *facts, *information, *messages, *representations, or *events, relating these to existing *knowledge and *frames of reference for the purposes of *categorization, explanation, understanding, and/or *evaluation. *Constructionists and *constructivists argue that descriptive statements, *facts, *representations, and even *perception involve unavoidable interpretation (*see also* PERCEPTUAL CODE; PERCEPTUAL SET; SELECTIVE PERCEPTION; SELECTIVE RECALL; SELECTIVE REPRESENTATION); *realists see such stances as forms of *relativism. 5. The spoken translation of *utterances in a different *language. 6. A distinctive personal style adopted in a particular creative *performance (e.g. of drama or music).

(((⊕))) SEE WEB LINKS

• What makes viewers diverge when interpreting narrative?

interpretive bias *See* ATTENTION.

interpretive codes Although many semiotic *codes can be seen as interpretive codes, this is one way of classifying a major group of codes, alongside *social codes and *textual codes. In this distinction, interpretive codes include *perceptual codes and *ideological codes. Interpretive codes can be seen as forming a basis for *modality judgements, drawing on *textual and *social codes and *knowledge. There is less agreement among semioticians about the status of interpretive codes as semiotic codes than about the other kinds of codes, partly because they are relatively loose and inexplicit (*see also* *hermeneutics).

interpretive community (interpretative community, discourse community) A term introduced by Fish to refer to both *writers and *readers of particular *genres of *texts (but which can be used more widely to refer to those who share any *code). Kuhn used the term 'textual community' to refer to *epistemological communities with shared texts, *interpretations, and beliefs. *Constructivists argue that interpretive communities are involved in the *construction and maintenance of reality within the *ontological domain which defines their concerns (*see* DISCOURSE). The *conventions within the codes employed by such communities become naturalized amongst its members. Individuals belong simultaneously to several interpretive communities. *Compare* EPISTEMIC COMMUNITY; IMAGINED COMMUNITY; VIRTUAL COMMUNITY.

interpretive repertoire For Jonathan Potter (b.1956), a Scottish social psychologist, the *interpretive codes and *textual codes available to those within *interpretive communities which offer them the potential to understand and also, where the code-user has the appropriate *symbolic capital, to produce texts which employ these codes. An interpretive repertoire is part of the symbolic capital of members of the relevant interpretive community. The term is sometimes used synonymously with *discourse.

interpretive turn The growth of social *constructionism within disciplinary discourses in the social sciences in the early 1970s. One of several theoretical 'turning points' identified in the evolution of the social sciences and humanities. Philosophical *realists tend to use this term pejoratively, equating it with (*epistemological) *relativism. *Compare* HISTORIC TURN; LINGUISTIC TURN; RHETORICAL TURN.

interpretivism (interpretive theory) An umbrella term for a range of academic perspectives on the interpretation of social reality and meaning-making, distinguished from scientific *positivism by a focus on understanding rather than prediction and explanation, on *contingency rather than universal laws, and on *reflexivity rather than *objectivism. It includes *phenomenological and *hermeneutic approaches, *ethnomethodology, *symbolic interactionism, social *constructionism, and *social semiotics.

interstitial advert An advertisement that can appear in a web *browser when a user clicks on a *link; it is displayed for a few seconds before the webpage they had selected is loaded.

intersubjectivity 1. The process and product of sharing experiences, *knowledge, understandings, and *expectations with others. A key feature of social *constructionism, *symbolic interactionism, and *phenomenological approaches generally. The existence, nature, and *meaning of things is not entirely up to the individual but subject to social and linguistic constraints within a *culture or *subculture (there has to be some degree of *consensus or communication would be impossible; *see also* LINGUISTIC TURN). The concept of intersubjectivity not only counters the undiluted *subjectivism of extreme philosophical *idealism but also the pure *objectivism of naïve *realism, since the same constraints filter our apprehension of the world. Things and their meanings are intersubjective to the extent that we share common understandings of them. *Cultural identity is experienced through intersubjectivity. *See also* REALITY CONSTRUCTION. **2.** The mutual construction of relationships through shared *subjectivity.

intertextuality The various links in *form and *content which bind any *text to other texts. The semiotic notion of intertextuality introduced by Kristeva is associated primarily with *poststructuralist theorists. It problematizes the idea of a text having boundaries: where does a text begin and end? Although the debts of a text to other texts are seldom acknowledged, texts owe more to other texts than to their own makers. Each text exists in relation to others, and textual *meanings are dependent on such relations (*see also* RELATIONAL MODEL). Texts provide *contexts such as *genres within which other texts may be created and interpreted. Ever-changing contexts generate new meanings. *Compare* INTRATEXTUALITY.

( ) SEE WEB LINKS

- Intertextuality

intertitle Captions and titles that appear as a graphic element cut into a *sequence rather than superimposed over camera *footage. In silent films, dialogue and other *information was communicated in this form.

intervening variable (mediating variable) A factor mediating the relationship between two other factors (*see also* DEPENDENT AND INDEPENDENT VARIABLES). Such a variable is causally situated between them and accounts at least partly for their association. An example would be a study which found that the effect of synthetic voices on *persuasion is mediated by listeners' sense of *social presence. *See also* INDIRECT EFFECTS.

interview **1.** Broadly a 'conversation with a purpose.' **2.** (print journalism) A means of obtaining information for a news story from sources which are generally identified (except for *vox pops, or when the source chooses *anonymity). In television and radio, the interview is recorded and typically presented in the form of *soundbites. If the *entertainment function is primary, the interview may be presented more informally as a conversation, as in a *chat show. **3.** A primarily *qualitative research method in the social sciences that takes the form of either a verbal or written exchange in which a researcher asks an *informant a series of questions, tied to a particular topic or guided by a research question. **Structured interviews** are a formal method of verbal *data-gathering from individuals in which a researcher asks each *respondent exactly the same series of predefined, and usually *closed, questions, as in a survey *questionnaire. These are usually conducted face-to-face or by telephone. This method is very amenable to quantitative analysis but it can involve unconscious *interviewer bias. In **semi-structured interviews** the main questions are written down, although some digressions may be permitted. In **unstructured interviews** the questions are typically not written down but rather are shaped by the development of the conversation. *See also* FOCUS GROUPS; INTERVIEWER BIAS; OPEN AND CLOSED QUESTIONS.

interviewer bias A distortion of response related to the person questioning *informants in research. The interviewer's *expectations or opinions may interfere with their *objectivity or interviewees may react differently to their personality or social background. Both mistrust and over-rapport can affect outcomes. *See also* HALO EFFECT.

intimate distance or zone *See* INTERPERSONAL ZONES.

intimization A trend in journalism where a public figure's private life is considered likely to appeal to the *target audience.

intonation The rise and fall in the *pitch of the voice when someone is speaking. *See also* VOCAL CUE.

intra-action *See* INTRAPERSONAL COMMUNICATION.

intracultural communication *See* INTERCULTURAL COMMUNICATION.

intragroup communication Communication within a small group. *See also* GROUP COMMUNICATION; *compare* INTERGROUP COMMUNICATION; INTERPERSONAL COMMUNICATION.

intranet An interconnected *network of computers that operates according to the same principles as the *internet but is open only to registered users, usually via logins and passwords. Intranets can take the form of a Local Area Network (LAN) or a Wide Area Network (WAN) depending on whether the computers are physically in the same location or spread across different locations.

intrapersonal communication (IC; intra-action) Communication with oneself; dialogical thinking that may or may not be manifested externally (*see also* DIALOGISM). A concept derived from Vygotsky (*see* INNER SPEECH). External manifestations include making private notes, diary-making, drafting and revision of writing, underlining, highlighting, and bookmarking. Even without sharing with others, *externalization provides opportunities for detachment and manipulation that may serve to advance the thinking of the individual. *See also* WRITER-ORIENTED.

intratextuality Internal relations within a *text, in contrast to *intertextuality, which involves 'external' relations with other texts. Within a single *code (e.g. a photographic code) these would be simple *syntagmatic relationships (e.g. the relationship of the image of one person to another within the same photograph). However, a text may involve several codes: a *newspaper photograph, for instance, may have a caption (*see* ANCHORAGE).

intrinsic meaning 1. The meaning of something in and of itself. In relation to the meaning of *texts, this notion is encountered within *formalism, where it is presumed possible to separate a text from its *context and from the *codes which it shares with other texts. However, for many contemporary theorists, a text cannot have a meaning in and of itself: it has no meaning unless someone interprets it, which they do in relation to what they know about texts (*textual knowledge or *textual codes) and what they know about the world (*social knowledge or *social codes), and in relation to the *context. In Saussurean *semiotics, the meaning of a *sign derives from its relation to other signs, without which it would have no meaning: *see also* ARBITRARINESS; RELATIONAL MODEL. **2.** (semantics) The *propositional content of a statement, abstracted from any particular *context of use. **3.** It is sometimes used loosely to refer to what is literally denoted (as in the **dictionary meaning** of a word) or visually depicted: *see also* DENOTATION. **4.** For the German art historian Erwin Panofsky (1892–1968), in relation to artworks it refers to 'those underlying principles which reveal the basic *attitude of a nation, a period, a *class, a religious or philosophical persuasion—unconsciously qualified by one personality and condensed into one work': *see also* ICONOGRAPHY.

introspection A process in which individuals examine their own thoughts and feelings. Where this is used as a method of *data collection it is impossible to judge the accuracy of such 'self-reports', and many mental processes are not accessible to conscious inspection.

introversion [Latin *intro-* 'to the inside'; *vertere* 'to turn') A personality trait in which an individual exhibits more concern with their thoughts and feelings than with social *interaction. The term was introduced to psychology by Jung.

inverted pyramid In news reporting, a pattern of presentation in which the most important elements are reported first (where the story is summarized) with 'the background' reported briefly at the end. This reflects *news values. In traditional practice, *facts are presented in the priority order of who did what, where, when, why, and how. The inverted pyramid structure is argued to make it easier for editors to trim from the end. However, the structure of news stories is seldom this clearcut. In a story based on several sources, each section may echo this overall pattern.

investigative journalism **1.** Journalism that does not merely report an 'official' news agenda (*see* AGENDA SETTING) but researches stories that become newsworthy when brought to the attention of the public. Typically these stories concern ethical wrongdoing such as government or corporate scandals, a famous example being the *Washington Post* reporting of the Watergate scandal which led to the impeachment and resignation of President Richard Nixon in 1974. **2.** A form of populist television journalism where the reporter (typically with hidden camera and microphones) is placed in potentially dangerous situations.

invisibility *See* SYMBOLIC ERASURE.

invisible editing *See* CONTINUITY EDITING.

involvement *See* HIGH AND LOW INVOLVEMENT.

IPC *See* INTERPERSONAL COMMUNICATION.

IPD *See* INTERPERSONAL DISTANCE.

IRC *See* INTERNET RELAY CHAT.

irony Typically, the expression of one's *intended meaning through *language which, taken literally, appears on the surface to express the opposite—usually for humorous effect. The intended meaning is not in the message itself: the audience has to refer to *context cues (for instance, nonverbal *signals) in order to interpret its *modality status (as literal, ironic, or a lie). Where only some members of the audience are able to identify the intended meaning, it can be seen as a form of *narrowcasting. In *rhetoric, it is a *figure of speech and in *semiotics, a kind of double *sign (*see* DOUBLE CODING). Understatement and overstatement can also be ironic. Irony is a characteristic stylistic feature of *postmodernism. *See also* DRAMATIC IRONY.

ISA *See* IDEOLOGICAL STATE APPARATUS.

ISP *See* INTERNET SERVICE PROVIDER.

IT *See* INFORMATION TECHNOLOGY.

italic 1. (**italics, italic script, italic type**) (*typography) The sloping form of a roman *typeface used for special purposes such as emphasis, foreign words, and the titles of books and journals in academic reference lists. 2. (handwriting) A *cursive and slightly slanted style which formed the basis for italic type.

Jakobson's model A linguistic model of *interpersonal communication outlined in 1960 by Jakobson. Drawing on work by Bühler dating from the 1930s, he proposed a model of verbal communication which moved beyond basic *transmission models, highlighting the importance of the *codes and social *contexts involved. He outlines what he regards as the six constitutive factors in any act of verbal communication: 'The addresser sends a message to the addressee. To be operative the message requires a context referred to ('referent' in another, somewhat ambivalent, nomenclature), seizable by the addressee, and either verbal or capable of being verbalized, a code fully, or at least partially, common to the *addresser and addressee (or in other words, to the *encoder and decoder of the message); and finally, a contact, a physical *channel and psychological connection between the addresser and the addressee, enabling both of them to stay in communication.' Jakobson proposes that each of these six factors (addresser, message, context, contact, code, and addressee) determines a different *linguistic function. His model demonstrates that messages and meanings cannot be isolated from contextual factors.

J-curve A graph of the overall percentage of a population that is aware of an *event (on the horizontal axis) in terms of whether they heard it 'through the grapevine' (on the vertical axis): that is, as opposed to having heard it initially through the *mass media. The curve falls at first but then rises markedly higher than the starting point. Bradley S. Greenberg, an American communication theorist, compiled this in 1965 from data charting the *diffusion of news of various events. He identified five types of events in terms of their position on the J-curve, dramatic events being located near the upper end of this curve, where close to 100% of a population is aware of an event and in which more than 50% learned of it through personal contacts rather than through the mass media.

Johari window (JW method) A framework dividing *information about oneself into four quadrants in an overall grid, mapping what other people do and do not know about me against what I know and do not know about myself. These quadrants consist of: open or public information about myself, that which is hidden and known to me alone, that to which I am blind but which others notice, and that which is currently unknown to me or others but which may later become apparent. Self-disclosure enlarges the 'open' area and decreases the others. The solicitation of feedback reduces what I do not know about myself. The term for this disclosure/ *feedback model of self awareness comes from the combination of the names of the concept's two originators: Joe Luft and Harry Ingham, who devised the framework

in 1955. It is often used to assist people to understand and improve their
*interpersonal communication and relationships.

(((⊕))) SEE WEB LINKS

• Johari window

jouissance [French 'enjoyment', connoting *jouir* 'to come' in the sexual
sense] 1. In *psychoanalytic theory, for Lacan, an erotic ecstasy beyond the
Freudian 'pleasure principle', akin to the 'death drive' since entering the *symbolic
order requires its loss, normalizing and regulating pleasure (*plaisir*). The
subsequent lack of *jouissance* leads to a doomed quest for this lost plenitude.
In Kristeva's *feminist theory, Lacan's concept is transformed into *jouissance
féminine*—the feminine libidinal drive repressed by the symbolic order. 2. In
literary and cultural theory, for Barthes, textual bliss in reading which disrupts
*expectations and challenges the reader to participate (which he associates with
*writerly texts) as distinct from textual pleasure (*plaisir*): comfortable reading that
confirms one's cultural assumptions, which he associates with the closed forms
of *readerly texts: *see* CLASSIC REALIST TEXTS.

journalese A pejorative reference to a style of journalistic writing featuring short,
direct sentences and an urgent tone but which is thin on *facts and over-reliant on
*metaphors and clichés.

(((⊕))) SEE WEB LINKS

• BBC news styleguide

journalism 1. Writing about news and current affairs in a range of media
including print, television, radio, and the *internet. 2. A profession in democratic
societies that acts as an intermediary between the public and government,
informing the public about important issues and enabling them to make informed
choices as well as holding politicians and other powerful figures to account for their
actions. This is tied to notions of the *watchdog role of journalism as the *fourth
estate. This position is criticized by critical theorists who argue that journalism's
role is to maintain positions of power: *see* HEGEMONY. 3. Pejoratively, a form of
*entertainment that reports the sensational or lurid aspects of news and also
gossip about celebrities: *see also* SENSATIONALISM.

journalistic autonomy A professional principle among journalists that they
should not be swayed by interested parties, especially if they stand to lose or gain
by a story. This includes criticism or advice from management staff outside of the
profession of journalism: for example, their publisher. *See also* FREEDOM OF THE
PRESS.

journalistic ethics A loose set of ideal principles defining good practice in the
professional reporting of serious news and current affairs. These include *objectivity
and *impartiality, truth and accuracy, protecting the *anonymity of sources, and
responsibility and accountability for both the stories reported and the methods
used to obtain them. *See also* MEDIA ETHICS.

joystick A peripheral interface device for a computer game *console, shaped like
a vertical stick which pivots at the base and allows the user to make smooth

incremental adjustments between two values, unlike a button which is either on or off. Typically joysticks have two axes: forward/backward and left/right and are used to play *videogames or in *simulations (such as flight simulators).

JPEG (Joint Photographic Experts Group, .jpg) The most common *compression standard for still *digital pictures.

jump cut 1. In film or video, an *edit which results in a subject appearing to shift position suddenly in the *frame, which is either the result of breaking the *thirty-degree rule, or a bad match cut. 2. A style of cutting that breaks the conventions of *continuity editing by deliberately joining similar shots together in order to remove moments of redundancy but without masking the discontinuities this creates.

juxtaposition [Latin *juxta* 'next'; French *poser* 'to place'] The act of positioning things next to each other, especially for comparison or contrast (*see also* CONTIGUITY; CO-PRESENCE). Alternatively, an instance of this or the state of being so positioned. John Berger observes that 'The meaning of an image is changed according to what one sees immediately beside it or what comes after it.' As meaning-makers, humankind seems unable to see two juxtaposed images without inferring some connection between them (*see* KULESHOV EFFECT). In film, Eisenstein utilized this phenomenon in his technique of *dialectical montage. *See also* EYELINE MATCH.

JW method *See* JOHARI WINDOW.

kerning In *typography, the adjustment of the space between particular pairs of adjacent characters to optimize their appearance. Not to be confused with **tracking**, which is the adjustment of the spacing evenly between a number of characters.

keyframe 1. In *animation, the drawings that define the start and end of an action: for example, if a figure raises their hand, the first keyframe would be the hand by the figure's side and the next would be the hand fully extended. **Inbetween frames** are *frames that fill in all the points between. 2. In computer *special effects, a set of programmable markers that define a point in a transition between two states so that the computer can generate inbetween frames: *see also* INTERPOLATION.

keyword 1. In *information retrieval, a word that serves as the indexing term for a *topic. 2. In webpages, embedded terms enabling a page to be retrieved by those using these terms in *search engines.

kinemes *See* KINESICS.

kinescope A machine for making a film recording of a video playback. This process is known as **telerecording** and was common practice among broadcasters before videotape machines were developed in the mid 1950s. Recording television pictures on film is a technique that is still used today: for example, when television *archive footage is used in films. *Compare* TELECINE.

kinesics Within the study of *nonverbal communication, a field including bodily movement, *posture, *gesture, *facial expression, and *gaze. Such nonverbal *cues reflect differences in *culture, *gender, and personality and are particularly important in communicating *liking, agreement, and *dominance. The term was coined in 1952 by the American anthropologist Ray Birdwhistell (1918–94), who adopted a linguistic approach to the analysis of *nonverbal communication, identifying basic units of movement called **kinemes**, analogous to *phonemes.

knowledge *See also* SOCIAL KNOWLEDGE; TEXTUAL KNOWLEDGE; *compare* DATA; FACT; INFORMATION. 1. Commonly understood as *information accumulated in the course of a person's life that informs their beliefs as to what is true or false. *General knowledge* is the total of trivial and non-trivial *facts a person can recall: *compare* COMMON SENSE. 2. Stored *information that a person or society draws upon to make sense of a given situation, either in the form of personal or collective memories or externalized in the form of *books and other media stored in libraries. Polanyi distinguishes between **tacit knowledge** acquired in the course of a person's life and *explicit knowledge* acquired through conscious study. **Situated knowledge** refers to contextual understandings—this concept is used to critique *discourses which do not situate their claims in any historical, social, or geographical *context (Haraway calls this the 'god trick' of seeing everything from nowhere). *See also* CONTEXTUALIZATION.

knowledge economy *Compare* INFORMATION ECONOMY. **1. (knowledge-based economy)** The use of *knowledge as the primary tool to produce new economic benefits or maximize existing ones. Unlike industrial economies, knowledge economies focus on intangibles such as *information over raw materials and are therefore motivated by the economics of abundance rather than scarcity. Knowledge industries (computing, media, medicine, etc.) demand people of high intellectual calibre; knowledge workers are educated to a level where they can be autonomous and flexible decision-makers as well as experts in their specialist fields. The term was created by Fritz Machlup (1902–83), an Austrian-American economist, and popularized by the American writer Peter Drucker (1909–2005): *see also* INFORMATION AGE. **2. (economy of knowledge)** The *production and management of knowledge as a product or service.

knowledge gap The difference between the *information rich and poor. The use of this term is associated with the *hypothesis, first proposed by the American communication theorist Phillip J. Tichenor (b.1931), that each new mass medium increases rather than decreases this gap because those with higher levels of income and education have greater *access. *See also* DIGITAL DIVIDE.

knowledge industries Organizations primarily associated with producing or using *data, *information, or *knowledge, and/or with ways of processing, analysing, and presenting these: e.g. academic and educational organizations, research scientists, *market-research companies, those involved in *communication design or *information technology, and, more generally, *content-providers. *Compare* CREATIVE INDUSTRIES; CULTURAL INDUSTRIES.

knowledge/power (Foucault) *See* POWER.

Kuleshov effect **1.** (film) Any *montage sequence in which the relationship of two adjacent *shots appears to be particularly meaningful. In what has come to be referred to as the **Kuleshov** (or **Kuleshov-Pudovkin**) **experiment** (allegedly *c*.1919), the Russian film-makers Kuleshov and Vsevolod Pudovkin (1893–1953) claimed to have assembled a sequence of disconnected shots from library *footage, *intercutting the same shot of the apparently expressionless face of a famous Russian actor with *close-ups of a bowl of steaming soup, a dead woman lying in a coffin, and a little girl playing with a toy bear. Pudovkin wrote that: 'The public raved about the acting . . . They pointed out the heavy pensiveness of his mood over the forgotten soup, were touched and moved by the deep sorrow with which he looked on the dead woman.' Kuleshov concluded that the 'content of the shots in itself is not so important as is the joining of two shots of different content and the method of their connection and their alternation.' We have no proof of the film's existence (it was allegedly destroyed in a fire) or of the experiment having taken place, but even if it were only a 'thought experiment', the concept has proved influential despite the failure of several attempts to replicate it. *See also* DIALECTICAL MONTAGE; JUXTAPOSITION. 2. The phenomenon whereby viewers infer a connection between two adjacent images. 3. The *meaning, *significance, and/or emotional impact ascribed to any such connection. 4. The associative power of *montage. 5. For Bordwell and Thompson, 'any series of shots that *in the absence of an *establishing shot* prompts the spectator to infer a spatial whole on the basis of seeing only portions of the space.'

k

labelling theory (societal reaction theory) The *hypothesis, which originated in sociology in the 1950s, that the social attribution of deviant identities to individuals or groups is a self-fulfilling prophecy leading to the *amplification of deviance. Within this *theory, deviance is regarded as a social construction (*see also* CONSTRUCTIONISM) rather than as an objective property of behaviour deriving from individual psychology or genetic inheritance. Some distinguish **primary deviance**—a violation of *norms prior to labelling—from **secondary deviance**. Labelling theory is closely associated with *symbolic interactionism.

lack 1. In Freudian *psychoanalytic theory, the traumatic discovery of sexual difference in the realization that the mother lacks a penis, inducing castration anxiety in boys. 2. In Lacanian psychoanalytic theory, the child's sense of loss of an illusory wholeness of being on entering the *symbolic order. For Lacan, lack is also the origin of desire. The missing *signifier is constitutive of the *subject. 3. In *poststructuralism, the notion of the incompleteness of all signifying systems.

lacuna (*pl.* lacunae) *Compare* ELLIPSIS. 1. A missing element in a *text. 2. (philosophy) A leap of logic in an *argument. 3. (psychology) Amnesia concerning a specific *event. 4. (translation) A lack of one-to-one equivalence in relation to a word or phrase (a lexical gap).

LAD *See* LANGUAGE ACQUISITION DEVICE.

laissez-faire model *See* MARKET MODEL.

landscape format In photography, painting, and document layout, the orientation of a rectangular viewing *window, *frame, or page so that the width is greater than the height. *Compare* PORTRAIT FORMAT.

language 1. The phenomenon of human symbolic communication, including speech, *writing, and *sign language. In *face-to-face interaction, language is arguably inseparable from *nonverbal communication, often referred to as *body language. Language as a field of study is termed *linguistics. Human language is a conventional system based on the use of words according to a complex system of rules. Linguists regard the faculty of language (sometimes referred to with the French term *langage*) as a defining feature of the human species: other animals are restricted to a particular set of predefined messages. Language is central to human experience, and in *constructionism is seen as constitutive of social reality and *identity. Human language has specific *design features and functions (*see* LINGUISTIC FUNCTIONS). Whereas in *behaviourism language is seen as learned rather than innate, following Chomsky, most linguists argue that we are born with a *knowledge of basic language structures: *see also* DEEP STRUCTURE. 2. The particular system of spoken and written communication used by those within a *speech community, such as Welsh and Arabic. Despite their surface differences, all human languages share certain basic properties, and most linguists argue that *universal grammars underlie them all. Saussure distinguished *langue*, the abstract system underlying a language, from *parole*, instances of its use (*see* LANGUE AND PAROLE). Verbal *signs within a language have a shared *denotation for members of the same linguistic group, acquired (together with many cultural *connotations) through *socialization. Language is central to every *culture. It is an *institution which is independent of any individual user but subject to historical change. Different languages frame reality in different ways—a feature emphasized by Saussure as highlighting the *arbitrariness of linguistic signs—but the extent to which language influences our worldview is a matter of debate (*see* SAPIR-WHORF HYPOTHESIS). Most radically, in *structuralism, language is seen as the agency that produces *subjectivity by *positioning individuals as *subjects. Even without adopting such *linguistic determinism, contemporary cultural theorists reject the notion of language as a neutral medium for 'conveying' *meanings (*see* CONDUIT METAPHOR), seeing it as constitutive of meanings, identities, and relationships in particular social *contexts. *See also* CONSTITUTIVE MODELS; SYMBOLIC INTERACTIONISM. 3. Computer programming systems (contrasted with **natural language**). 4. The *codes used by media such as photography, television, and film: many refer to these, often merely metaphorically, as 'languages' or to 'reading' such media. In *semiotics, the linguistic model led structuralists to seek units of analysis in such media analogous to those used in *linguistics; others have argued that non-linguistic systems of communication lack the double *articulation of human language and cannot be reduced to discrete non-meaningful units analogous to *phonemes. *See also* PICTORIAL COMMUNICATION; VISUAL COMMUNICATION; VISUAL LANGUAGE. 5. Specialized vocabulary and phraseology, such as scientific language, *journalese, and slang. 6. Usage seen as socially inappropriate: 'bad language'. 7. Sometimes a synonym for *animal communication (denied the designation of language by most linguists because such systems lack the combinatory creativity of human language).

language acquisition device (LAD) An innate predisposition in children to acquire the grammatical structure of their mother tongue. This was controversially hypothesized by Chomsky in the 1960s.

language community *See* SPEECH COMMUNITY.

language functions *See* LINGUISTIC FUNCTIONS.

language games An analogy made by Wittgenstein between speaking a language and playing a *game. Different uses of language (e.g. apologies or requests) have different rules which do not exist outside of social practices, and the meaning of words is thus always *context-dependent. *Compare* COMMUNICATION GAME; SPEECH ACT.

language variety *See* REGISTER.

langue and parole Saussure's terms. *Langue* refers to the abstract system of rules and *conventions of a *language—it is independent of, and pre-exists, individual users. *Parole* refers to concrete instances of its use. To Saussure, and to *structuralist semioticians, what matters most are the underlying structures and rules of a semiotic system as a whole rather than specific performances or practices which are merely instances of its use. Applying the notion to semiotic systems in general rather than simply to language, the distinction is one between the semiotic system and its usage in specific *texts and practices. Langue is to parole as *code is to *message. Saussure emphasized the importance of studying the 'language-state' synchronically—as it exists as a relatively stable system during a certain period—rather than diachronically (studying its evolution): *see* DIACHRONIC ANALYSIS; SYNCHRONIC ANALYSIS.

lap dissolve *See* CROSS DISSOLVE.

LA shot *See* LOW-ANGLE SHOT.

Lasswell's model *See* EFFECTS.

late modernity *See* MODERNITY; POSTMODERNITY.

latent image (photography) The image formed when light reacts with the photosensitive chemicals coating a reel of film and fixed in the developing process.

latent meaning (latent content) In *psychoanalytic theory, the hidden, underlying *meanings which can be revealed through the *interpretation of the *manifest content of dreams.

lateral communication (horizontal communication) *Messages and systems of *interaction and *feedback between individuals or departments on the same level in an organization. It is characteristic of an organizational structure termed *organic*, in which control and decision-making is decentralized, and *roles are loosely defined and flexible. *Compare* DOWNWARD COMMUNICATION; UPWARD COMMUNICATION.

lateral integration *See* HORIZONTAL INTEGRATION.

laterality 1. A consistent preference for using one side of the body rather than the other: for instance, having a preferred hand or eye, as in writing or looking through a lens. 2. For hemispheric laterality of the brain, *see* HEMISPHERIC LATERALIZATION.

laws of perceptual organization *See* GESTALT LAWS.

layback In video *post-production, a technique of *insert editing a sound *track onto a tape which already has pictures, or (vice versa) inserting pictures onto a tape that already has sound. Typically, a layback is done to replace a programme's 'guide audio' with fully-mixed sound.

leader The first few centimetres on a spool of film or video tape which are left blank so that when it is threaded onto a take-up spool it has the necessary purchase to pull the film or tape through the projector/recorder.

leading [ledding] In *typography, the space between lines of type.

leading edge *See* BABY BOOMERS.

lead story 1. In *newspaper journalism, the main story on a page. On the front page also known as **splash**. 2. The first item in a news bulletin.

leak *Information, typically of a sensitive or compromising nature, which is passed to the news media.

leakage 1. **(nonverbal leakage)** In *nonverbal communication, unconscious 'expressions' which Goffman referred to as 'given off' through nonverbal *cues (and potentially noticeable to others). 2. **(nonverbal leakage)** The unconscious display of deception through such cues. Psychologists Ekman and Wallace Friesen argue that deceivers attempt to control their behaviour, but that generalized *arousal is often unwittingly exhibited through nonverbal cues. The verbal channel is the most controllable, followed by facial cues; body cues (e.g. clenched hands) and vocal cues (e.g. a shaky voice) are the most likely to reveal deception. 3. In *psychoanalytic theory, the notion that repressed thoughts and feelings may be revealed though dreams and slips of the tongue: *see* PARAPRAXIS.

lean forward or lean back *See* SIT UP OR SIT BACK.

Leavisite Adjective and noun formed from the name of the influential British literary critic F. R. Leavis, typically used as a pejorative reference to an approach to literature and *culture associated by critics with cultural *elitism, *high culture, nostalgia for traditional pre-industrial society, moral judgements, and hostility to *Marxism, 'commercialism', and *mass society. Leavis is also more positively associated with close *textual analysis, though on a *common sense evaluative basis rather than by applying explicit theoretical frameworks. Although disdainful of *popular culture, in 1942 Leavis produced a book for schools (with Denys Thompson) seeking to develop critical awareness through the study of advertisements, *newspapers, and films, which Leavis felt exploited the 'cheapest emotional responses'. The emergence of British *cultural studies, particularly in the work of Williams and Hoggart, is often referred to as **left Leavisism**.

legibility The physical factors in print and *writing which affect ease and efficiency in reading. These relate to matters of *typography, format, reading medium, and *colour. For instance, for *body text, whereas on paper *serif fonts are easier on the eye, *sans serif fonts are favoured for onscreen reading. *Compare* READABILITY.

legitimation (sociology) A term deriving from Weber for the process in which social acceptance is sought for the validity of the authority of a ruling group or the existence of a nation-state. The establishment of **legitimacy** is essential for political stability: without it, there would be a **legitimation crisis**. Marxist theorists have noted the *ideological role of the *mass media in the legitimation of capitalist society through the engineering of *consensus (*see also* MANUFACTURE OF CONSENT).

leitmotif *See* MOTIF.

letterbox format In film and television, horizontal masking of the screen area with black bars across the top and bottom of the picture. Letterboxing preserves the *widescreen composition of feature films when they are shown on television: for example when a film with an *aspect ratio of 2.35:1 is shown on a 16:9 (1.78:1) screen. *See also* ASPECT RATIO; ASPECT RATIO CONVERSION.

levelling and sharpening In retellings of an *event, **levelling** is a selective process by which certain details are unconsciously omitted. Psychological studies by Allport and Leo Postman suggest that retelling tends to make accounts shorter, more concise, more easily grasped and told. **Sharpening** involves the pointing-up of a limited number of details which caught the individual's *attention. Movement is often emphasized or introduced. Items prominent because of their relative size or quantity tend to be retained, as do attention-grabbing labels and familiar *symbols. Explanations may be introduced, especially to produce *closure. Allport and Postman argued that underlying levelling and sharpening is the process of *assimilation. Aspects of a story are sharpened or levelled to make them more consistent with what is seen as the principal *theme, thus making the story more coherent and well-rounded (a good *gestalt). Items relevant to the theme may be imported and those irrelevant to the theme may be omitted. Apparent gaps may be filled and some details may be changed to make them more consistent. *See also* ADDITION; DELETION; SUBSTITUTION; TRANSFORMATION; TRANSPOSITION; *compare* FOREGROUNDING.

lexemes *See* LEXICON.

lexical set *See* COLLOCATION.

lexical words *See* GRAMMATICAL WORDS.

lexicon 1. (*linguistics) The vocabulary of a language (its **lexical items** or **lexemes**), an individual, or a branch of *knowledge. 2. A dictionary.

libel *See* DEFAMATION.

library footage *See* ARCHIVE.

life-space *See* FIELD.

lifestyle 1. (sociology) A concept related to Weber's notion of *status groups reflecting the influence of industrialization and *consumerism on *social identity. 2. (*market research) A characterization of a *target audience in terms of patterns of *taste, *consumption, and aspiration rather than conventional *demographics: *see also* PSYCHOGRAPHICS; SEGMENTATION. 3. (cultural theory) *Postmodern forms of *cultural identity based upon aspects of individual behaviour which are a matter of personal choice, and which distinguish modes of living in late modern consumer society from more traditional 'ways of life'. 4. Loosely, the behaviour and *values of an individual or a *subcultural group (sometimes used pejoratively to refer to 'alternative lifestyles' where these are seen as deviant).

lifestyle format A style of *advertising based on market *segmentation according to the *consumption styles of particular social groups. This began to emerge in the mid 1960s following a phase of *personalization, and has been seen as dominant until the mid 1980s. Such advertisements typically depict *consumption in group *settings on social occasions (entertaining, going out, holidays, relaxing) and product images are presented as emblematic of this *lifestyle. Such formats are particularly associated with alcohol, food, tobacco, and clothing. The term is used by Leiss and his colleagues. *See also* ADVERTISING FORMATS; *compare* DEMASSIFICATION; PERSONALIZED FORMAT; PRODUCT-INFORMATION FORMAT; PRODUCT-SYMBOL FORMAT.

lifestyle television A subgenre of *reality television concerned with consumer-oriented matters of *taste and *style (e.g. *Queer Eye for the Straight Guy*).

lifeworld *See* EVERYDAY LIFE.

lightness A hueless dimension of *colour in relation to a greyscale from black to white. One of the three major psychological dimensions of colour, the others being *hue and *saturation; the psychological counterpart to physical *luminance. Often used synonymously with *brightness.

lightness constancy *See* BRIGHTNESS CONSTANCY.

Likert scale A standard measure of the *attitudes of individuals in relation to a specific *topic. This **attitude scale** is widely used in social science research, consisting of a list of related attitudinal statements which *respondents are asked to rate on a 5-point scale: agree strongly, agree, not sure, disagree, or disagree strongly. The statements represent a mixture of positive and negative attitudes towards the topic, and responses are scored on a 0-4 scale (with the scoring scale reversed for negative statements). *See also* ATTITUDE MEASUREMENT.

liking (interpersonal liking) (psychology) Having a fondness or regard for someone (associated with perceived *similarity to oneself). In relation to social *interaction, liking/disliking (or friendliness/hostility) are terms commonly used to express the degree of warmth or hostility felt towards interactive partners. This is one of the most commonly identified interpersonal *attitudes communicated by *nonverbal behaviour. In the *Yale model, the likeability of the *source is identified as a key factor in the effectiveness of persuasive *messages. *See also* EVALUATION; *compare* AFFILIATION.

limited effects theory (limited effects model) Lazarsfeld's conclusion from *survey research in the 1940s that, contrary to popular assumptions, the *mass media cannot directly change most people's strongly-held *attitudes or opinions. This is usually explained in relation to *selective perception: viewers tend to select and interpret media *messages in accordance with their existing attitudes and beliefs, and their use of the *mass media tends to reinforce these. The limited effects view was later confirmed by Hovland, who demonstrated the importance of many *intervening variables. *See also* ATTITUDINAL EFFECTS; HYPODERMIC MODEL; RECEIVER SELECTIVITY; SELECTIVE EXPOSURE; SELECTIVE INFLUENCE; TWO-STEP FLOW.

linear editing (machine-to-machine editing) Video *editing that is achieved by playing back material on a 'source' machine and recording it on another 'record' machine because videotape cannot be physically cut without creating a picture disturbance. This style of editing is called 'linear' because a video *sequence is built up from beginning to end, one *shot at a time. New material inserted into an existing sequence overwrites existing material, so if a pre-existing sequence needs to be lengthened, all the material after the cut point has to be copied onto a spare tape and copied back again, incurring *generation loss. *Compare* NONLINEAR EDITING.

linear model *See* TRANSMISSION MODELS.

linear narrative A story which may contain stylistic or temporal discontinuities such as *flashbacks, but which is nevertheless conventionally read or told from the beginning to the end, in contrast to an interactive or *hypertext narrative. *Compare* INTERACTIVE FICTION.

linear perspective In two-dimensional visual *representations, the geometrically-based rendering of an illusion of spatial depth in relation to a distant **vanishing point** at which parallel lines converge (*one-point perspective*). The vanishing-point need not be central, or on the horizon, or even within the visible frame. There may also be more than one vanishing-point: *two-point perspective* is seen where a receding surface is not parallel to the *picture plane. The system of 'artificial perspective' was formulated in the Renaissance, although artists have often ignored or 'corrected' the less familiar perspective effects—notably those involved in looking up at a tall building (as have some photographers); this form is depicted in *three-point perspective*. Linear perspective, in strong contrast to the multiple viewpoints of medieval art, is oriented so that the viewer seems to be looking through a **window** with the represented world organized around their visual point of view, a convention which dominated *figurative art until the late 19th century. *Compare* AERIAL PERSPECTIVE; CURVILINEAR PERSPECTIVE; DWINDLING SIZE PERSPECTIVE.

linear timecode (LTC, longtitudinal timecode) A *timecode on videotape in the form of an audio *track. *Compare* VERTICAL INTERVAL TIMECODE.

linguistic determinism A range of views in which our thinking (or worldview) is seen as being determined or shaped by *language—simply by the use of verbal language and/or by the grammatical structures, semantic distinctions, and inbuilt *ontologies within a language. A moderate version is that thinking may be influenced rather than unavoidably determined by language: it is a two-way process, so that the kind of language we use is also influenced by the way we see the world. Critics who are socially oriented emphasize the social *context of language use rather than purely linguistic considerations; any influence is ascribed not to language as such (which would be to reify language) but to usage in particular contexts (*see* LANGUE AND PAROLE) and to particular kinds of *discourse (e.g. a *sociolect). Both *structuralists and *poststructuralists give priority to the determining power of the language system: language patterns our experience

and the *subject is constructed through *discourse. *See also* LINGUISTIC RELATIVISM;
MOULD THEORY; SAPIR-WHORF HYPOTHESIS.

linguistic dualism *See* CLOAK THEORY.

**linguistic functions (language functions, functions of language,
functions)** (*linguistics) The primary communicative roles of language or the
relationships between linguistic *forms and the social *contexts of their use (*see*
CONTEXT OF SITUATION). In the 1930s, Bühler listed the **representational or
referential function** to represent the real world, the **expressive function** to express
the speaker's feelings, and the **appellative or conative function** to appeal to or
influence the hearer. In 1960, Jakobson argued that the dominance of any one of six
factors within an *utterance reflects a different linguistic function: *referential,
*expressive: *conative, *poetic (or aesthetic), *phatic, and *metalingual. In any given
situation one of these factors is 'dominant', and this dominant function influences
the general character of the *message. In Halliday's linguistic typology, the seven
basic functions identified in children's usage are: *heuristic, *imaginative,
*informative, *instrumental, *interactional, *personal, and *regulative. He adds
three adult metafunctions: *ideational, *interpersonal, and *textual. *See also*
COMMUNICATIVE FUNCTIONS; JAKOBSON'S MODEL.

linguistic monism *See* MOULD THEORY.

linguistic relativism (linguistic relativity) The view that every *language
is a unique system of relations and, more radically, that the *phonological,
*grammatical and *semantic distinctions in different languages are completely
arbitrary (*see* ARBITRARINESS). Thus, on the *semantic level, reality is divided up
into arbitrary categories by every language and different languages have different
in-built *ontologies. Concepts may not be translatable (*see* TRANSLATABILITY).
Linguistic relativism emphasizes the *contingency of *signifieds. It is closely
associated with *epistemological *relativism and is a fundamental assumption
involved in the *Sapir-Whorf hypothesis. An opposing viewpoint is that of *linguistic
universalism. *See also* LINGUISTIC DETERMINISM.

linguistics The academic study of *language (often defined as the *scientific* study
of language), the major branches being *phonetics, *phonology, *pragmatics,
*semantics, and *syntax. *See also* CONVERSATION ANALYSIS; CRITICAL
DISCOURSE ANALYSIS; DESIGN FEATURES; DISCOURSE; DISCOURSE ANALYSIS;
ETHNOMETHODOLOGY; GRAMMAR; MORPHOLOGY; PSYCHOLINGUISTICS; RELEVANCE
THEORY; RHETORIC; SAPIR-WHORF HYPOTHESIS; SOCIOLINGUISTICS; SPEECH ACT;
STRUCTURALISM; STYLISTICS; TEXT LINGUISTICS; TRANSFORMATIONAL GRAMMAR.

linguistic turn (communicative turn) A change in emphasis in the *discourse
of the humanities and social sciences reflecting a recognition (beyond the bounds
of *linguistics itself) of the importance of *language in human meaning-making.
The linguistic turn in the humanities came in the 1970s. *See also* CONVERSATION
ANALYSIS; ETHNOMETHODOLOGY; INTERSUBJECTIVITY; STRUCTURALISM; SYMBOLIC
INTERACTIONISM; *compare* RHETORICAL TURN; VISUAL TURN.

link 1. Any connection that exists between two entities: *see also* INTERTEXTUALITY.
2. **(hyperlink)** In *hypertext, an associative element embedded within a
document which directly connects it with another document. In a text document
the link appears as a highlighted word of text; in a photograph as a highlighted
area of the image. *See also* HTML.

lip-sync In film and video, the precision matching of audio and picture
elements when people are shown talking.

listener-oriented communication *See* RECEIVER-ORIENTED
COMMUNICATION.

literacy 1. The ability to read and write, contrasted with **illiteracy**. In looser usage
this also includes basic arithmetical competence. *Compare* MULTIMODALITY; ORACY.
2. **Functional literacy**: a level of minimal competence in reading and writing (and
sometimes also basic arithmetic) essential for daily life and work. 3. Used more
metaphorically for technical competence (e.g. *computer literacy) and/or critical
discrimination (e.g. *media literacy, *news literacy), or even more broadly (e.g.
*cultural literacy, *information literacy, *visual literacy). 4. A feature associated with
cultures depending on the written word, in theoretical opposition to the *orality of
'pre-literate' cultures. The British anthropologist Jack Goody (b.1919) argues that
the *affordances of the written word are a key agent of social change (*see also* GREAT
DIVIDE THEORIES). Literacy is seen by some as enabling logical thinking and
*objectivity. Historical records represented a new form of intergenerational cultural
transmission. The concept of *authorship arose in literate cultures. The British
educationalist Brian Street has criticized orality/literacy great divide theories as
based on an 'autonomous model' of literacy (a form of *media determinism).

literalism 1. A tendency to interpret a verbal expression as if it means no more
than what is made explicit in the form of words used. 2. The stance that the
*meaning of a *text is contained within it and is completely determined by it so that
all the *reader must do is to 'extract' this meaning from the *signs within it. This
stance ignores the importance of 'going beyond the information given' (Bruner)
and limits *comprehension to the *decoding (in the narrowest sense) of textual
properties (without reference to *codes or *contexts).

literal language Verbal expressions which are, or at least intended to 'mean
what they say', and which are purely denotative, in contrast to *figurative language.
This *common-sense notion faces objections that no *text makes sense without
reference to something beyond it (requiring some 'reading between the lines') and
that there can be no *denotation without *connotation. Banishing *metaphor is
an impossible task since it is central to *language.

literal meaning The (supposedly) immanent semantic *content or *message
of a *text: e.g. the **dictionary meaning** of the words within a verbal text; what is
explicitly denoted or depicted. Often as distinguished from figurative or
*metaphoric meaning. *See also* DENOTATION; LITERAL LANGUAGE; MEANING; SENSE.

literary cultures *See* ORAL CULTURES.

literary genres Since classical times, literary forms have been broadly classified into: poetic or lyric (first-person forms), epic or *narrative (in which both *narrators and characters talk), and *drama (in which the characters talk). This relates to the more modern distinction between poetry, *fiction, and drama. More specifically, the classical literary forms were epic, *tragedy, lyric, *comedy, and *satire; modern *genres include the novel, the essay, the biography, and the short story. There are also countless subgenres and *hybrid genres. Frye argues that the four main genres are *comedy, *romance, *tragedy, and *satire. The term **genre fiction** is sometimes used to distinguish popular forms of the novel, such as science fiction, thrillers, detective stories, westerns, historical romances, or love stories from **literary fiction**.

literature review (social sciences) A formal, reflective survey of the most significant and relevant works of published and peer-reviewed academic research on a particular topic, summarizing and discussing their findings and *methodologies in order to reflect the current state of knowledge in the field and the key questions raised. Literature reviews do not themselves present any previously unpublished research. They may be published as review articles in academic journals or as an element in a thesis or dissertation: in the case of the latter, they serve to situate the current study within the *field.

live 1. In television, radio, and on the *internet, any presentation that is broadcast at the same time as it is being produced and so is unedited. **Liveness** is an important characteristic that distinguishes (live) television broadcasts from film showings; and radio broadcasts from audio recordings. 2. The *real-time status of *synchronous communication. 3. A synonym for *immediacy (especially in news), which connotes both topicality and *authenticity, in the sense that there is less opportunity to shape the presentation through the medium by *editing. The American performance theorist Philip Auslander considers liveness to be the *ideological means by which mediated *representations are naturalized. *See also* MEDIATIZATION.

lived experience 1. Personal *knowledge about the world gained through direct, first-hand involvement in everyday *events rather than through *representations constructed by other people (*compare* MEDIATED EXPERIENCE). It may also refer to knowledge of people gained from direct *face-to-face interaction rather than through a technological *medium. 2. In *phenomenology, our situated, immediate, activities and encounters in everyday experience, *prereflexively taken for granted as reality rather than as something perceived or represented: *see also* NATURAL ATTITUDE. 3. From Althusser's *structuralist Marxist perspective, all human activity, which he emphasized is not a *given or pure 'reality', but a 'peculiar relationship to the real' which is 'identical with' *ideology.

live recording A film, television, radio, or internet presentation that is recorded in one continuous session where performers, presenters, or technical staff do not have the option of correcting mistakes. Typically, a live recording may be a repeat of a presentation that was first shown live; however, the decision can sometimes be motivated by creative reasons because of the extra excitement that performing live creates.

loaded language Words or phrases biased towards a view favoured by the person using them. Frequent in the language of *advertising and political *rhetoric. For example, 'I am firm; you are stubborn; he is pig-headed.' *See also* EVALUATION; IDEOLOGICAL BIAS; PROPAGANDA.

localization 1. A form of resistance to *globalization promoting diversity and specialization and opposed to standardization and *homogenization. Localization is often viewed in a dialectical relationship with globalization. *See also* DISEMBEDDING; RE-EMBEDDING. 2. The tailored promotion of products and services by international companies to consumers in particular countries or regions. For example, internationally produced television commercials are overdubbed by actors who talk with regional accents. Products may also be customized to meet the demands of local consumers. For example, refrigerators sold in Spain have more storage for meat, those in France have more storage for vegetables, and those sold in the US are larger because shopping for food is done on a weekly basis.

locutionary act In *speech act theory, Austin's term for the physical *production of a meaningful *utterance, later termed an **utterance act** by Searle. *See also* ILLOCUTIONARY ACT; *compare* PERLOCUTIONARY ACT.

logical appeals *See* RATIONAL APPEALS.

logo (logotype, logogram) 1. An *emblem designed to identify a *brand, sometimes a distinctive rendering of the name (often a trademark). 2. More loosely, any distinctive stylized graphical sign of an organization.

logocentrism *Compare* SCRIPTISM. 1. **(logocentricism)** For Derrida, a Western tendency to build philosophical systems on a *transcendent signified: *see also* ABSENT PRESENCE; DECONSTRUCTION; FOUNDATIONALISM; PHONOCENTRISM. 2. A typically unconscious interpretive *bias which privileges linguistic communication over the revealingly named 'nonverbal' forms of communication and expression, and over unverbalized feelings; logocentrism privileges both the eye and the ear over other sensory modalities such as touch.

long-shot (LS) In photography, film, and television, a standard *shot size which shows all or most of a fairly large subject (for example, a person) and much of the surroundings. Long shots emphasize *context, or contextualize a subject. Some *documentaries with social themes favour keeping people in the longer shots, keeping social circumstances rather than the individual as the focus of attention. *See also* EXTREME LONG-SHOT.

long take A continuous single *shot in a film or television programme, the duration of which exceeds conventional *expectations. These shots can be very complex. Hitchcock's *Rope* (1948) is a famous example of a feature film shot as a series of long *takes. *See also* SHOT DURATION.

long-term effects (cumulative effects) In *theories and research concerning the potential influence of the *mass media on *audiences and/or society, subtle and perhaps indirect consequences only apparent over an extended period of time, as in the so-called slow *drip effect. Schramm's concerns, for instance, included the possibility of 'the gradual building up of pictures of the world from what the mass media choose to report of it; the gradual *homogenization of images and behaviours over large populations, as a result of the universality of the mass media.' Such concerns can be related to the role of the mass media as agents in *socialization, as also in social *expectations theory. However, any such influences are very difficult to prove, and only in stances of extreme *technological determinism would they be treated as extricable from the social processes in which media *production and use are embedded. *See also* AGENDA SETTING; CULTIVATION THEORY; EFFECTS; EFFECTS TRADITION; *compare* SHORT-TERM EFFECTS.

longtitudinal timecode *See* LINEAR TIMECODE.

look *See* GAZE.

looking behaviour *See* GAZE BEHAVIOUR.

looking-glass self A term introduced by Cooley to refer to the dependence of our **social self** or *social identity on our *appearance to others, especially *significant others. Our **self-concept** or **self image**—the ideas and feelings that we have about ourselves—are seen as developing 'reflectively' in response to our *perception and *internalization of how others perceive and evaluate us. This concept is also associated with *symbolic interactionism. *See also* GENERALIZED OTHER; SELF-ESTEEM.

lookism *Bias or discrimination against individuals on the basis of *appearance, often unconscious.

loop gain *See* FEEDBACK.

loose ties *See* WEAK TIES.

lossless (lossy) *See* COMPRESSION.

low-angle shot (LA shot) A photographic composition in which the viewing position is below the subject, giving the impression that the camera is looking up: for example, in a filmed conversation between an adult and a child all the *shots from the child's point of view would be of this kind. Low-angle shots tend to generate a *connotation of high *status or *power. *See also* TILT.

low-contact cultures *Cultures in which people tend to touch each other less often than is usual in most cultures, maintain more *interpersonal distance, face each other more indirectly, have less *eye contact, and speak more quietly. For example, China, Japan, Norway, Sweden, and Finland. *See also* INTERCULTURAL COMMUNICATION; *compare* HIGH-CONTACT CULTURES.

low-context *See also* INTERCULTURAL COMMUNICATION. 1. **Low-context communication**: Edward T. Hall's concept of a particular *communication style in which much of the meaning is (or is intended to be) literal (*see* LITERAL MEANING) and in the explicit *message rather than in the *context: *see also* ELABORATED CODE; EXPLICIT MEANING. 2. **Low-context cultures**: *individualistic cultures (as in the USA and the UK) particularly associated with a low-context communication style. By comparison with *high-context cultures, talk tends to be more important than nonverbal *information; silence tends to be avoided; a personal style is generally preferred to *role-oriented communication; and *sender-oriented communication is predominant.

low culture *See* POPULAR CULTURE.

low involvement *See* HIGH AND LOW INVOLVEMENT.

low-key (photography) A high contrast lighting effect created by the use of a single principal (or key) light to light the scene. Low-key lighting is characteristic of the look of *film noir.

LS *See* LONG SHOT.

LTC *See* LINEAR TIMECODE.

luddite 1. Label applied to English textile workers (named after Ned Ludd) who protested in 1811–16 against the threat to their livelihoods from new industrial technology. 2. A pejorative description of anyone who displays hostility towards *technology: *see also* TECHNOPHOBIA.

ludic [Latin *ludere* 'to play'] 1. An adjective connoting a playfully reflexive text or performance that gently mocks any art regarded as having illusionist presumptions: *see* ILLUSIONISM; REFLEXIVITY. 2. An academic approach to *videogames that resists *narrative framings, characterizing the *form in terms of its nonlinearity, *interactivity, and the goals and *motivations of players.

ludology An approach within *videogame studies emphasizing the *ludic elements of gaming over its *narrative elements.

ludus A type of game that operates according to a specified rule structure. Ludus is distinguished from pure *play (*paidia), because it follows rules and therefore makes demands on the conduct of players (Caillois).

luminance 1. (intensity, physical intensity) The amount of light emitted or reflected by an illuminated surface: a physical dimension creating the psychological visual sensation of *lightness or *brightness. This is one of the three physical properties of light on which *colour vision depends; the other two are *spectral purity and *wavelength. 2. In television technology, the 'brightness' *signal.

lurker A member of a *newsgroup or other online forum who reads messages but does not contribute to the discussion.

McDonaldization A metaphor that links the exploitative logic behind globalized modern culture to the principles and practices of running a fast-food outlet. It is argued that societies worldwide are increasingly homogenized by the application of *Fordism, Taylorism, and *instrumental rationality to the *production of standardized, cheap, but low-quality products or services branded by intensive *advertising (*see also* CULTURAL IMPERIALISM; HOMOGENIZATION). Various businesses, *institutions, and even certain kinds of behaviour have been given the 'Mc' prefix. *USA Today* is known as the McPaper; we also have McDoctors (drive-in clinics), McJobs (poorly-paid work), bland McSex, and (some jibe) pick-and-mix McUniversities. The original term was introduced in 1992 by George Ritzer (b.1930), an American sociologist. The concept can be seen as echoing the concerns of *Frankfurt school *critical theory and the rhetoric of *mass society theory. Critics argue that it underestimates *audience fragmentation, *narrowcasting, and diversity. *Compare* GLOBALIZATION.

machine-to-machine editing *See* LINEAR EDITING.

McLuhanism Any concept deriving from, and/or in the style of, Marshall McLuhan, a Canadian academic who enjoyed international cult status as a media guru in the 1960s. He is best known for his provocative insistence that 'the medium is the message' and for his popularization of the concept of the *global village. 'The medium is the message' had at least four apparent meanings: that the medium shapes its *content (i.e. that the nature of any medium has implications for the kinds of experience which can be best handled with it); that using a medium is important in itself (e.g. watching television or reading books are experiences in themselves regardless of explicit *content); that the message of a medium is the 'impact' it has on society; and that the message of a medium is its transformation of the perceptual habits of its users. McLuhan adopted the stance that communication technologies such as television, radio, *printing, and *writing profoundly transformed both society and 'the human psyche'. Consequently, he is usually regarded as a *technological determinist. The technologies (or media) which he discussed reflected his very broad definition of 'media'. This stance (sometimes known more specifically as *media determinism) can be seen as an application of the same *reductionist approach taken by the *Sapir-Whorf hypothesis to the nature of media in general. Just as Whorf argued that different languages shape our *perception and thinking differently, McLuhan argued that all media do this. For McLuhan, the *neutrality of the medium was a *myth. *See also* HOT AND COOL MEDIA; MEDIA ENVIRONMENT; MEDIUM THEORY; REAR-VIEW MIRROR; SENSE RATIO.

• The official site of Marshall McLuhan

McLurg's Law *See* PROXIMITY.

macro level functions *See* MEDIA FUNCTIONS.

macrosociology (sociology) A level of analysis concerned with *social structures (*institutions or whole societies), or with historical or global processes. Approaches from the perspective of *functionalism and *Marxist theory are examples. *Compare* MICROSOCIOLOGY.

macrostructure *See* DEEP STRUCTURE.

magazine format 1. The standard dimensions for print magazines, typically 28 x 21.5 cm, together with generic *conventions of *language, illustration, and layout, and a diversity of content that represents no single 'authorial' point of view. 2. **(magazine programme)** A television programme with a diverse menu of *content and a formulaic *structure (usually based around current affairs) which are typically anchored by one or more regular hosts. For example, *The One Show* (BBC) in the UK or *Tonight* (NBC) in the US. *See also* ANCHOR.

magic bullet theory *See* HYPODERMIC MODEL.

magic window For the American communication researcher Robert P. Hawkins, 'the degree to which children believe they are viewing either ongoing life or drama.' It is widely noted that very young viewers attribute equal reality to everything on television. In a questionnaire study of 153 children of 4- to 12-years-old (published in 1977), Hawkins confirmed previous research findings that children tend to perceive fictional television as increasingly less real as they grow older. His data reflected a dramatic increase in children's *knowledge in this regard around the age of 8 years; children over 8-years-old rarely thought of television as a magic window on the world, and understood that programmes were made up. This has been a general finding. *See also* CONSTRUCTEDNESS; PERCEIVED REALITY.

mainstreaming A tendency, identified by Gerbner, for television viewing to homogenize opinion among *heavy viewers, increasing the *convergence of views and reducing divergence compared to light viewers.

male chauvinism *See* SEXISM.

male gaze *See also* GAZE. 1. A manner of treating women's bodies as objects to be surveyed, which is associated by *feminists with *hegemonic masculinity, both in everyday social *interaction and in relation to their *representation in visual media: *see also* OBJECTIFICATION. 2. In *film theory, the point of view of a male *spectator reproduced in both the *cinematography and *narrative conventions of cinema, in which men are both the *subject of the gaze and the ones who shape the action and women are the *objects of the gaze and the ones who are shaped by the action. In her *psychoanalytic theory of the male gaze, Mulvey argues that in *classical

Hollywood cinema, the film *spectator oscillates between two forms of looking at the female image: voyeuristic looking involves a controlling gaze; *fetishistic looking involves an obsessive focus on some erotic detail (*see also* VOYEURISM). She claims that these conventions reflect the *values and tastes of patriarchal society.

male norm (male-as-norm) *See also* GENDER BIAS; MARKEDNESS. 1. In relation to *language, the use of masculine terms to stand for gender-inclusive concepts: for example, 'mankind'. *See also* POLITICAL CORRECTNESS. 2. The unconscious employment of one's own gendered perspectives in material intended for both sexes. *Formal features in the visual design of UK higher education websites aimed at both males and females have been found to reflect a bias towards males. In 2005 Gloria Moss and colleagues at the University of Glamorgan Business School found that men preferred straight lines whereas women preferred more rounded forms. Women also liked to see more use of *colour than men, while men liked formal *typography. However, 94% of the British university websites they examined reflected male preferences. Such unintentional imbalances are typically related to under- and over-representation of one sex in particular jobs.

((⊕)) SEE WEB LINKS

• Website design biased to men

M&E (music and effects) Audio *tracks in which dialogue and *voiceover are removed from the final sound *mix. M&Es are used for foreign language versions of films or television programmes or when the *footage is re-edited. *See also* CAPTIONLESS MASTER; FOLEY.

manifest content (manifest meaning) 1. In Freudian *psychoanalytic theory, the elements of a dream consciously and voluntarily recalled by the dreamer (Freud). This material is the product of transformation by *condensation and *displacement. *Compare* LATENT MEANING. 2. In *textual analysis, the *explicit meaning of the text: that which is denoted or directly depicted (*see also* DENOTATION).

manipulative model A set of assumptions underlying the stance of some commentators that the *mass media have an awesome persuasive power over a helplessly passive general public. In a left-wing inflection, this is seen as involving manipulation and mystification by those in political power (or even as a conspiracy). In a right-wing inflection, it is seen leading inevitably towards a lowering of cultural standards and the proliferation of permissive *values. Journalists serve the interests of their paymasters rather than the *public interest. The manipulative model is the polar opposite of the *market model (Cohen and Young). *See also* DOMINANCE MODEL; HYPODERMIC MODEL.

manufacture of consent 1. A phrase originally coined in 1922 by the American journalist Walter Lippmann (1889–1974) to refer to the management of *public opinion, which he felt was necessary for democracy to flourish, since he felt that public opinion was an irrational force. 2. For Herman and Chomsky, the acceptance of government policies by people in the USA on the basis of the partial picture of issues offered by the *mass media, denying them *access to alternative views which would lead them to oppose such policies. They present this as a **propaganda model** in which the mass media select material in relation to the *values of those in power. **3.** The concept found in Gramsci and Althusserian *Marxism, in which the dominant *class sustains its *hegemony through engineering assent: *see also* IDEOLOGICAL STATE APPARATUS. **4.** (sociology) The notion associated with *functionalism that society is dependent upon the engineering of a consensus: *see also* CONSENSUS; LEGITIMATION. **5.** An *allusion to the concept of 'the engineering of consent' defined in 1947, by the Austrian-American public relations pioneer Edward Bernays (1891–1995), as the art of manipulating people without them being aware of it. Bernays, a nephew of Freud, argued that people can be enticed to want things that they do not need if these are linked to their unconscious desires, a notion pursued by Dichter, the 'father of *motivation'.

manuscript **1.** A hand-written book. **2.** A document submitted to a publisher for publication.

many-to-many communication *See* INTERNET.

marcoms *See* MARKETING COMMUNICATIONS.

marginality **1.** (sociology) The state of being partly an insider and partly an outsider. **2.** In cultural and literary theory, a spatial metaphor for subordinated or repressed textual meanings. **3.** The perspective of dissident groups and individuals, which may be interpreted either negatively in terms of alienation or positively in terms of a vantage-point for critique, though by virtue of *marginalization such critiques may gain no hearing within mainstream society.

marginalization (exclusion) (sociology) A spatial metaphor for a process of social exclusion in which individuals or groups are relegated to the fringes of a society, being denied economic, political, and/or symbolic power and pushed towards being 'outsiders'. *See also* MARGINALITY; *compare* DEMARGINALIZATION.

markedness **1.** In *linguistics and *semiotics, the phenomenon, noted by Jakobson, in which one term and/or concept is highlighted as (**markedly**) different from another, as in the words *male/female*, where the former is literally **unmarked** and the latter is linguistically marked by the addition of an initial *fe-*. The unmarked form is typically dominant (e.g. statistically within a text or corpus) and is often used as a generic term while the marked form is used in a more specific sense.
2. (*semiotics) The semantic weighting of concepts as well as terms within *binary oppositions (such as masculinity/femininity). Where terms are conventionally paired, the usual sequence implies a priority: mind/body, public/private, active/passive (*see also* ALIGNMENT). The unmarked term is primary, being given precedence, but at the same time its unmarked *transparency makes it seem to be neutral, normal, and natural (*see also* EXNOMINATION). Unmarked/marked may thus be read as *norm/deviation. When we refer to *nonverbal communication, the very label defines such a mode of communication as secondary. Markedness can thus generate *ideological *connotations. **3.** In *deconstruction, the association of a marked term in an opposition with absence and lack. Derrida demonstrated that

within the oppositional logic of *binarism neither of the terms (or concepts) makes sense without the other. This is what he calls 'the logic of supplementarity': the 'secondary' term which is represented as 'marginal' and external is in fact constitutive of the 'primary' term and essential to it. The unmarked term is defined by what it seeks to suppress. *See also* ABSENT SIGNIFIER. **4.** (*marketing) The explicit labelling of certain products as 'for women' or 'for men', while a very similar product of the same brand (associated with a cultural stereotype with that target group) is left unmarked. For example, many skincare products targeted at women are left unmarked, while other versions are explicitly marked 'for men'; Nike has a primary website that is unmarked, and another called nikewomen.com. **5.** More broadly in cultural theory, the choice of an unconventional form in textual or social practices, which thus 'make a statement'. Conventional, or 'over-coded' texts or practices (which follow a fairly predictable formula) are unmarked whereas those which are unconventional or 'under-coded' are marked. Unmarked forms reflect the *naturalization of dominant cultural *values. **6.** In *socialization, the production of *difference based on the distinction between *norm and deviation (*see also* LABELLING THEORY). Social differentiation is constructed and maintained through the marking of differences. To be marked is to be 'one of them' rather than 'one of us'. **7.** In the history of ideas, the relative weighting given to particular concepts in a particular period. Jakobson observed in 1930 that 'such historico-cultural correlations as life–death, liberty–non-liberty, sin–virtue, holidays–working days, and so on are always confined to relations a–non-a, and . . . it is important to find out for any epoch, group, nation etc. what the marked element is'.

marketing 1. Promoting and selling products or services: *see also* ADVERTISING. **2.** The process of managing the relationship between firms and customers by organizing the demand for and supply of a product or service. This involves identifying *target audiences through research and finding the most effective ways to promote and distribute the product or service. *See also* MICROMARKETING. **3.** The business management discipline concerned with this process.

marketing communications (marcoms) The various ways in which suppliers of goods or services engage in *interaction with their *target audiences. Although this includes *advertising (the most visible form of promotion), the terms are not synonymous.

marketing communications mix The particular selection of media, tools, and techniques used in *marketing communications and how they are integrated in particular campaigns to reach a *target audience.

marketing mix A *marketing strategy traditionally based on the relative weighting given to the *four Ps.

marketing semiotics The use in *marketing of approaches derived from *semiotics, especially in *branding, product *positioning, *targeting, and trend-spotting. *See also* DOMINANT CODE; EMERGENT CODE; RESIDUAL CODE.

((⊕)) SEE WEB LINKS

• *The Semiotics of Advertising*: Goldman et al.

market model (commercial model, free market model, laissez-faire model) A stance of some commentators and journalists that market forces ensure that the *public interest is what determines the coverage of news. The assumptions underlying the market model are that: the media 'gives the public what it wants'; the diversity of *information and opinions in the *mass media minimize the possibilities of manipulation; media power is exaggerated; the public can select or reject media output; and the mass media may reinforce opinions but rarely change them. Within this broad school of thought, the 'social responsibility' position is that the mass media should give the public what it *needs* (rather than *dumbing down or sacrificing quality), while the libertarian position is that it should deliver what the public *wants*. The market model emerged largely as a reaction to its polar opposite—the *manipulative model (Cohen and Young). *See also* PLURALIST MODEL.

market research A systematic process of investigating, collating, and analysing *data on customers or competitors buying and selling a particular product or service. Methods used include *interviews, *focus groups, and *questionnaires. Academic usage in this field favours the term **marketing research** for the investigation of *marketing issues in relation to particular *target audiences, restricting the term **market research** to the investigation of the size of the market for a *brand, product, or service.

Marxist media theory A range of views in which the primary function of the *mass media is regarded as the reproduction of the *status quo (in contrast to liberal *pluralism). In *Marxist theory, the mass media form the arena in which various ideological battles are fought, but in which the *class in control of capital has ultimate control (*see also* CONSCIOUSNESS INDUSTRY; MEDIA HEGEMONY). Media professionals (including those managers who run the media *institutions) consider themselves to be autonomous, but their views reflect those of a controlling elite which determines not just what views are broadcast, but also the perspective from which media debates are framed (*see also* AGENDA SETTING). Audiences may be able to negotiate and contest mass media frameworks (*see also* NEGOTIATED READING; OPPOSITIONAL READING), but they lack ready *access to alternative meaning systems that would enable them to reject them entirely. *See also* DOMINANCE MODEL; FRANKFURT SCHOOL; HEGEMONIC READING; LEGITIMATION; MANUFACTURE OF CONSENT.

(⊕) SEE WEB LINKS
• Marxist media theory

Marxist theory (Marxism) An *ideology or a set of economic, social, and political theories developed from the writings of Marx and Engels. Definitions are hotly debated (Marx himself declared that he was not a Marxist). Most importantly, capitalist society is seen as structured by a dominant *class's exploitation of subordinate classes. A central feature of classical Marxist theory is the *materialist stance that social being determines consciousness. According to this stance, *ideological positions are a function of *class positions, and the *dominant ideology in society is that of its dominant class. There are diverse forms of Marxism. **Classical Marxism** is that which is closest to Marx and Engels. **Orthodox Marxism** (or 'vulgar'

Marxism) is the *dialectical materialism that became the basis of Soviet communism. **Western Marxism** is often referred to as **neo-Marxism**. It represented a philosophical reaction to the *positivism of classical Marxism, in particular *historical and economic determinism. Western Marxism has been particularly important in foregrounding *culture (*see* CULTURAL MATERIALISM). Marxism became a significant influence in European academia from the 1960s. In sociology, it represented a reaction against structural *functionalism, focusing on *conflict rather than *consensus models of society. **Gramscian Marxism** rejects crude materialism, offering a humanist version of Marxism which focuses on human *agency and the struggle for ideological *hegemony. This perspective gave rise to Stuart Hall's notion of *hegemonic, *negotiated, and *oppositional readings. The contrasting *structuralist Marxism of Althusser (**Althusserian Marxism**) peaked in the 1970s. While returning to the 'scientific' materialism of classical Marxism, Althusser rejects its *economism. He insists on the *relative autonomy of the *ideological and cultural superstructure, and even 'the reciprocal action of the superstructure on the base'. *Ideology transforms human beings into *subjects, leading them to see themselves as self-determining agents when they are in fact shaped by ideological processes (*see also* ALWAYS-ALREADY GIVEN; CONSTITUTION OF THE SUBJECT; IDEOLOGICAL STATE APPARATUS; INTERPELLATION). Critics see Althusser's structuralism as an anti-humanistic denial of human *agency and *conflict. The contrast between Althusserian and Gramscian Marxism highlights a divide between *structuralism (or *determinism) and humanism (or voluntarism) within Marxism, as in the broader debate over *structure versus agency in the social sciences. *See also* POST-MARXISM.

masculinism (masculism) A male counterpart to *feminism. Masculists reject the idea of universal patriarchy, arguing that before *feminism most men were as disempowered as most women. However, in the *post-feminist era they argue that men are in a worse position because of the emphasis on women's rights. Like feminism, masculism reflects a number of positions, from the desire for equal rights for men (for example, in cases of child access after divorce), to more militant calls for the total abolition of women's rights.

masculinity *See also* GENDER; GENDER STEREOTYPES; *compare* FEMININITY.
1. In popular usage, characteristics associated with the male *sex. In the conservative discourse of *gender essentialism, masculinity is typically assumed to be universal and unchanging—determined by biological *sex, and an internal facet of *identity. 2. The social *roles, behaviours, and *values culturally prescribed for males in a particular society in a given period (*see also* GENDER). The plural term **masculinities** is often employed as a reminder of a diversity of forms. Masculinities vary across cultures, over historical time, within a culture, and over the life course, though cross-culturally normative expectations include being protective, unemotional, strong, active, dominant, and aggressive. 3. Dominant forms of male *identity in a *culture in a particular period: *see* HEGEMONIC MASCULINITY. 4. A performance of a set of behaviours elicited in *interaction with others in particular situations or institutional *contexts and implicitly negotiated in relation to situational *norms and *expectations regarding masculinity. Here, masculinity is

something that individuals do and the way that they do it, over time. This concept is particularly associated with *symbolic interactionism and *queer theory. **5.** A set of qualities traditionally associated with males but exhibited in varying degrees by both sexes (Bem). **6.** A relational and negative conception of what it means to be a man in terms of being unlike a woman (*see also* DIFFERENCE; OTHERNESS). **7.** Qualities associated with the privileged term (here italicized) in a system of gendered *binary oppositions such as *active*/passive, *mind*/body, *reason*/emotion, *objective*/subjective, *public*/private, *culture*/nature. See also ALIGNMENT; MARKEDNESS. **8.** In *communication styles, a quality associated with *instrumental and *task-oriented communication rather than *expressive or *relational communication. This echoes Parsons' typification of sex roles. **9.** The gendered *connotation of various formal, stylistic, visual, or textural features such as straight (vs curvy), plain (vs fancy or colourful), literal or denotational (vs metaphorical or connotative), hard (vs soft), coarse (vs fine), and heavy (vs light). Notably, masculinity in contemporary Western cultures tends to involve *restricted codes of *colour and clothing by comparison with women.

masculinization **1.** (sociology) A process in which certain social roles or occupations become associated primarily with men, especially if they had been formerly associated with women: *compare* FEMINIZATION. **2.** A historical process in which a phenomenon comes to be culturally gendered as a male domain and/or generates *connotations of *masculinity: e.g. the masculinization of reason or the masculinization of the *public sphere in the 18th century. *See also* GENDERING. **3.** Any perceived tendency for women to behave in ways traditionally more associated with men: for instance, 'butch' lesbians or the former UK Prime Minister Margaret Thatcher. Those drawn to *gender essentialism sometimes fear that female liberation is leading women to behave more like men.

masculism *See* MASCULINISM.

mashup **1.** Broadly, the remixing of existing media content, appropriated and repurposed by *users: *see also* PARTICIPATORY CULTURE; USER-GENERATED CONTENT. **2.** In computer programming, the activity of combining various *application programming interfaces available on the internet in order to create new functionalities, e.g. a website that takes crime statistics for particular areas and displays them on Google maps.

((( ))) SEE WEB LINKS
• What is a mashup?

Maslow's hierarchy of needs (pyramid of needs, motivational hierarchy). A *model of human *motivation developed by Abraham Maslow represented as a pyramid of levels, with the most basic needs at the bottom and the most distinctively human needs at the top. In ascending order, these levels are: physiological (e.g. food and sleep), safety, love/belonging (family, friendship, sex), esteem (e.g. competence and recognition), and self-actualization (to fulfil one's personal potential, e.g. creativity). A topmost level of self-transcendence (spirituality) is sometimes added. Maslow argued that as lower needs are met, individuals seek to satisfy higher needs. He developed the model as a reaction

against *behaviourism, which focuses on rewards. *See also* USES AND
GRATIFICATIONS.

SEE WEB LINKS

• *A Theory of Human Motivation*: Abraham Maslow

mass audience In *mass society theory in the early days of the *mass media, and
in the *rhetoric of both right- and left-wing cultural critics, the pejorative
*representation of mass media *audiences as a vast, undifferentiated collectivity
(*see* MANIPULATIVE MODEL). For Mills, *mass society replaced the *pluralism of
multiple *publics. Contemporary perspectives within both academic disciplines and
the *media industries see audiences in far more differentiated terms (*see* TARGET
AUDIENCE). Furthermore, the size of audiences or *readerships for the same content
in any mass medium has been dramatically reduced with the widespread diffusion
of technological developments such as the *web and satellite broadcasting (*see*
AUDIENCE FRAGMENTATION; DEMASSIFICATION).

mass communication 'One-to-many' messages technologically mediated
through the *mass media, making this a distinctively modern form of
communication. As a form of long-distance communication it has particular
*affordances (*see* DISTANCE COMMUNICATION). In terms of *communicative
functions, its defenders tend to stress *information and *education functions, while
its detractors dwell on *entertainment and *persuasion functions. The dramatic
difference of scale from *interpersonal communication highlights the issue of
potential influence, leading initially to fears about mass manipulation which later
proved to involve an overestimation of media power (*see also* FRANKFURT SCHOOL;
HYPODERMIC MODEL; MANIPULATIVE MODEL). From a sociological perspective a key
difference is its framing within *institutions (*see* MASS MEDIA). To be characterized
as mass communication, widespread *distribution and *access are *necessary
conditions. Issues of *power relations are more significant than in other forms of
communication. As a form of long-distance communication it has particular
*affordances (*see* DISTANCE COMMUNICATION). There is no necessary association
with the pejorative concept of a *mass audience: although the audience is
anonymous and widely dispersed, it is also vastly heterogeneous. While it may be
*live or recorded, it is primarily *asynchronous communication—live two-way
communication through a mass medium occurs only in such special cases as radio
or television phone-ins (which involve broadcast *interpersonal communication).
*Feedback is thus very limited and indirect: it is basically a one-way process. For
Mills in 1956, this was one of the two key sociological characteristics of mass
communication: the other was that relatively few people could be mass
communicators. However, none of these 'limitations' renders audiences passive
(*see* ACTIVE AUDIENCE THEORY; USES AND GRATIFICATIONS). Technologically, mass
communication is conducted through verbal text, graphics, and/or audio-visual
media (e.g. film, television, radio, *newspapers, magazines, etc.). The diversity of
these means (and the need for very different communicative techniques) limits the
usefulness of the term mass communication to a broad umbrella concept.

mass consumption The condition of purchasing and using the standardized
(mass-produced) products created by industrial societies conceived of in terms of

the social patterns that emerge in the analysis of these processes. Modern capitalist society is characterized by mass consumption, which can be seen as a *necessary condition for its existence. It is the basis of *consumer culture. Mass consumption was a particular target of the *Frankfurt school's *critical theory. It was both enabled and required by the mass *production involved in *Fordism; *post-Fordism and *postmodernism have generated a different dynamic. *See also* CONSUMERISM; DEMASSIFICATION.

mass culture 1. Cultural products that are both mass-produced and for *mass audiences. Examples include *mass-media entertainments—films, television programmes, popular books, newspapers, magazines, popular music, leisure goods, household items, clothing, and mechanically-reproduced art. 2. In the affirmative sense, synonymous with *popular culture (the preferred term in *cultural studies and where the focus is on uses rather than *production), although some theorists distinguish it from traditional folk culture because it is oriented toward profit and is organized according to the laws governing *commodity exchange. 3. In the negative sense, a term used from the 1930s to refer to cultural products judged from the perspectives of both *Frankfurt school Marxism (Adorno, Horkheimer, Benjamin) and anti-Marxism (Leavis) to be both trivial and trivializing when compared to serious *high culture (*see also* ELITISM). This can be seen as a privileging of pleasures labelled *aesthetic and the disparagement of those which are 'only *entertainment'. Mass culture is also criticized for its standardization (*see also* BROADCAST CODES; COMMODIFICATION). Since the 1950s, sociologists, joined from the 1980s by *postmodern critics (e.g. Jameson) have taken a more *pluralist view, though some critics see *globalization as leading to *homogenization. 4. That which produces and maintains *hegemony in capitalist societies, allowing the dominant *class to control and pacify the masses. 5. The product of 'the *culture industry' that is analysed in terms of its *commodity form, its psychological effects, and its capitalist *ideology (Adorno, Horkheimer). 6. Sometimes a synonym for *mass society, or more strictly, the *culture of mass society. A monolithic conception of *culture which has been in decline since *post-Fordism, *postmodernism, and the *web: *see also* DEMASSIFICATION; NICHE MARKET; SEGMENTATION.

massification Typically a pejorative reference to the social transformations involved in modernization, in which people are allegedly increasingly treated *en masse* (*see also* HOMOGENIZATION; MASS AUDIENCE). The concept is associated with *mass society theory, where many argue that it leads to weaker family and community ties and to social *fragmentation. It is also associated with the *rhetoric of cultural elites, no doubt reflecting a lessening of their own influence. *Compare* DEMASSIFICATION.

mass market 1. *n.* All the people who can be reached by the transport and *communications infrastructure within a given territory. The concept emerged when industrial methods started producing on a large scale: *see* FORDISM. 2. *n.* Potential purchasers of mass-produced goods who constitute a substantial proportion of the population. 3. *adj.* A pejorative reference to goods made for the 'lowest common denominator'. **Mass marketing** is a monolithic approach to *marketing where consumers and products are treated as homogeneous entities. *Compare* MICROMARKETING; NICHE MARKET.

mass media 1. **(the media)** The various technological means of producing and disseminating *messages and cultural forms (notably *news, *information, *entertainment, and *advertising) to large, widely dispersed, heterogeneous audiences (*see also* MASS COMMUNICATION). In the world today these include *television, *radio, the *cinema, *newspapers, magazines, bestselling books, audio CDs, DVDs, and the *internet. The origins of the mass media are typically traced back to the commercial exploitation of *printing by Gutenberg around 1450, or to early newspapers in the 17th century. 2. Key economic, political, and social *institutions based on producing and disseminating materials using such channels. Typically large-scale organizations concentrated either in the hands of the state, or a public body, or a relatively small number of *media moguls (*see also* MEDIA CONTROLS; MEDIA OWNERSHIP), all being subject to state *regulation and various forms of *censorship. 3. *Ideological forces in these *institutions. These are seen in *Marxist theory as involved in engineering consent in the interests of the dominant *class in capitalist society (*see also* DOMINANT IDEOLOGY; IDEOLOGICAL STATE APPARATUS; LEGITIMATION; MANUFACTURE OF CONSENT). Others have focused on an *agenda setting function. Critics of such stances argue that they fail to account for *conflict and *contradictions within media *institutions, and underestimate the *audience. *See also* ACTIVE AUDIENCE THEORY; DOMINANT READING; NEGOTIATED READING; OPPOSITIONAL READING. 4. From the perspective of *functionalism, media content which serves various functions for society and for individuals: *see also* MEDIA FUNCTIONS; USES AND GRATIFICATIONS. 5. Forms of *mediation between the *public and private spheres, frequently characterized as bringing public issues into the everyday domestic or familial environment and extending the *social knowledge of individuals beyond what is possible in direct *lived experience (within the selective frameworks of media practices). At the same time, *audience fragmentation and the pressures of popularization have led to the media being held responsible by some for diminishing the public sphere and degrading political debate. *See also* DUMBING DOWN; FICTION VALUES; PUBLIC AND PRIVATE SPHERE; STORY MODEL; TABLOIDIZATION. 6. A primary source of *mass culture and shared cultural *imagery; though these are arguably being eroded as a result of increased consumer choice through satellite broadcasting and the web.

mass society **(mass society theory)** A pessimistic view of modern, large-scale, 'atomistic' industrialized urban societies by contrast with traditional 'organic' agrarian communities, typically instancing a loss of unifying *values and beliefs and of restraining *social networks, increasing isolation and alienation, *conformism, political centralization, *impersonal bureaucracy, and the vulnerability of a *mass audience to manipulation (*see also* MANIPULATIVE MODEL; MASSIFICATION). A key function of the *mass media can be seen as sustaining a mass society. As a derogatory term, 'mass society' is also associated with the degradation of cultural forms (as a synonym for *mass culture). Claims such as a lessening of *pluralism, a decline in political participation, a lack of differentiation, and a break-down in family and community ties have been countered. It was a widespread concept immediately before and after World War II (*see* HYPODERMIC MODEL), but it had historical roots in reactions to revolutionary ferment. Some apologists for mass society have championed its greater egalitarianism, mobility, openness, and *consensus.

master 1. An original from which copies are made. 2. The film negative or electromagnetic tape onto which the final assembly of a film, television programme, or piece of music is recorded. 3. **(master shot)** An entire *scene photographed by one camera without *cuts. In film and television, a director will typically choose to film a master *shot first to ensure that a scene has been completely covered. Other angles are then shot to ensure a variety of coverage.

master narratives *See* GRAND NARRATIVES.

masthead (by analogy with the flag at the head of a ship's mast) 1. In popular usage, the title of a *newspaper or magazine displayed at the top of the front page (technically the *flag* or *title*). 2. In newspapers and magazines, part of a page (normally the editorial page) where details of the publication, publisher, and staff are listed. 3. **(header)** On websites, the site title or *logo at the top of a page (often on the left).

match cut In film and video, an *edit that appears to show a seamless action by matching the continuity of its subject while changing the *camera angle: for example, if a person is struggling to get out of a car, cutting from a *close-up at the start of the action to a *mid-shot at the end bridges the temporal gap, although the person's posture and movements must be similar in both shots to avoid a *jump cut. *See also* CONTINUITY EDITING.

materialism 1. In everyday usage, a *value system privileging wealth, possessions and/or bodily pleasures over ethical or philosophical values. This is the antithesis of aestheticism, spirituality, and idealism (in its everyday sense). Also, a typically pejorative reference to such values in individuals, groups, or society. Commonly associated with capitalism. 2. In its broadest philosophical sense, an assertion of the causal primacy of matter over mind (or consciousness); as opposed to philosophical *idealism. Reductionist forms invoke an *ontology in which all reality is material: such claims tend to reduce the explanatory value of the concept. Althusser argued that even *ideology is material. Weaker forms grant a secondary *ontological status to mental phenomena. *Vulgar materialism* is the kind represented by the British writer Samuel Johnson (1709–84) kicking a stone to prove its existence. Some forms emphasize the physical and biological basis of human social being. Materialism rejects *Cartesian dualism and disembodied existence. 3. (*Marxism) The anti-idealist position that the material conditions of existence determine human consciousness, and not vice versa (*see* DIALECTICAL MATERIALISM). More specifically, in historical materialism, the techno-economic basis of the historical evolution of social systems. Even in forms of social and cultural theory not explicitly indebted to Marxist approaches, an emphasis on historical and economic factors indicates this legacy. 4. (cultural theory) An emphasis on such things as the textual *representation of the material conditions of social reality (such as poverty, sickness, and exploitation), the sociocultural and historical contingency of signifying practices, and the specificity and physical properties of media and *signs (suppressed in the *transparency of dominant codes of aesthetic *realism). *Texts themselves are part of the world (*see also* MATERIALITY). The materialist approach to culture is often distinguished by its practitioners from what they characterize as the reduction of substance to *forms and relations in *formalism. *See also* CULTURAL MATERIALISM. 5. In the rhetoric of *postmodernism, despite the fact that many regard it as a form of *idealism, the term is sometimes used to refer to an opposition (as in Derrida) to transcendent explanation: *see* TRANSCENDENT SIGNIFIED.

materiality The material substance of things; in *semiotics, that of the *sign vehicle. While nowadays the *signifier is commonly interpreted as the material (or physical) form of the *sign (something which can be seen, heard, touched, smelt, or tasted), this is more *materialistic than in the *Saussurean model. For Saussure, both the signifier and the *signified were 'form' rather than substance. However, the material form of the sign can itself be a signifier—the same written text might be interpreted somewhat differently depending on whether it was hand-written or word-processed, and it might even generate different *connotations if it were in one *typeface rather than another. So too, whether the text was an 'original' or a 'copy' might affect the sense made of the text (*see* TOKEN)—not everyone would appreciate a photocopied love-letter! The basic material properties of the text may be shaped by the *affordances of the medium employed, which may also generate connotations. Some reflexive aesthetic practices foreground their *textuality—the signs of their *production (the materials and techniques used—thus reducing the *transparency of their style (*see also* REFLEXIVITY). For instance, 'painterly' painters draw our attention to the form and texture of their brushstrokes and to the qualities of the paint. When our prime purpose is instrumental (i.e. when we use the sign, text, or medium as a means to an end) we are seldom conscious of the materiality of the sign, which retreats to transparency as we foreground *content rather than the substance of expression. Within *cultural studies, *cultural materialism emphasizes the materiality of cultural phenomena. References to the materiality of *language allude to its social and conventional character as well as to its manifestation in physical forms (*see also* MEDIA-CENTRICITY).

MCU *See* MEDIUM CLOSE-UP.

meaning [Old English *mænan* 'to have in mind, intend, signify'] *See also* AFFECTIVE MEANING; CONNOTATION; CONTEXTUAL MEANING; DENOTATION; EXPLICIT MEANING; HERMENEUTICS; IDEATIONAL MEANING; IMPLICIT MEANING; INTENDED MEANING; INTRINSIC MEANING; LATENT MEANING; LITERAL MEANING; MANIFEST CONTENT; MEANING-ORIENTED COMMUNICATION; MEANING TRANSFER; METAPHORIC MEANING; PREFERRED READING; REFERENTIALITY; SENSE; SLIPPAGE OF MEANING; SURPLUS MEANING; SYMBOLISM; *compare* SIGNIFICANCE. 1. The (supposedly) immanent semantic *content or *message of a *text; what is explicitly denoted or depicted (*see also* DENOTATION; LITERAL MEANING). This *objectivist framing excludes such factors as socio-historical *context, *authorial intention, readers' purposes, and the *textual and *social codes, *knowledge, or schemata that readers draw on in order to 'go beyond the information given' (Bruner). It does not account for *irony or *figurative language (*see also* LITERAL LANGUAGE). In *linguistics, *semantics is the study of meaning. 2. What is (or seems likely to have been) intended as the preferred *interpretation by the person who produced some specific text or act of communication (*see also* INTENDED MEANING; PREFERRED READING). In aesthetic contexts this has been criticized as the *intentional fallacy, but some assumption of intent has been proposed as a basic *communicative presumption. Grice defines meaning in terms of the intentions of speakers to induce appropriate beliefs in listeners. 3. The conceptual meaning of a *sign: *signified, *interpretant, idea, or thought. *See also* SENSE. 4. What a sign refers to beyond the sign system itself: object, *referent, or *denotation: *see also* REFERENCE. 5. In Saussurean *semiotics, the *signification of purely structural differential relations. The meaning of linguistic *signs is seen in terms of their systemic relation to each other rather than with reference to an extralingual world (*see also* BRACKETING THE REFERENT; RELATIONAL MODEL; STRUCTURALISM). Poststructuralists argue that in this structuralist explanation the stability of meaning is an illusion depending on the clear separation of *langue and parole: they deny any meaning outside of *discourses. *See also* POSTSTRUCTURALISM. 6. The sense that is made of a text or act of communication on a particular occasion and in a particular *context, by one or more interpreters (*see also* INTERPRETATION). In post-Saussurean *semiotics, the denotative and connotative associations and understandings produced as readers decode and interpret signs (whether intentional or not) in relation to *textual (and *social) codes in particular contexts (*see also* CONNOTATION; DENOTATION; JAKOBSON'S MODEL). The contextual dimension frames meaning as relatively dynamic or unstable (*see also* CONTEXT OF SITUATION; PRAGMATICS; SPEECH ACT). This does not imply that a text can mean whatever an individual thinks it means: social *constructionists argue that *interpretations are limited by the extent to which they are able to gain some degree of social *consensus. 7. The subjective attribution of *significance to something (e.g. to an *event). 8. (sociology) The beliefs, *purposes, motives, and reasons of social actors in a social *context that direct their actions towards others; in Weber's social action theory and *symbolic interactionism, social occurrences are explained primarily as the outcome of these meanings.

(⊕) SEE WEB LINKS

• Texts and the construction of meaning

meaning-oriented communication (meaning-centred) 1. (language teaching) A primary focus on, or interest in, what a learner is trying to communicate rather than on the form of words used and their correctness. 2. Communication in which the primary focus is on *content rather than *form, *message rather than *medium or *code, and/or *referential rather than *aesthetic functions. 3. Communication in which the primary focus is on likely intent rather than on *literal meaning. 4. The primary *communication style of informal speech in *individualistic cultures. 5. Communication in which meaning is seen as actively constructed (in particular contrast to *message-oriented communication): the interpretive basis of *interaction models and the constructive basis of *constitutive models.

meaning transfer (*objective correlative) (*advertising) The theory that the close association of a product, *brand, or service with an already positively-evaluated person (*see* ENDORSEMENT) will lead to the transfer of that person's qualities to the brand. In *semiotic terms this involves generating a new *sign by combining two existing ones: the *signifier of the brand becomes combined with the *signified of the person, so that the brand directly signifies their qualities. *See also* APPROPRIATION; JUXTAPOSITION; METAPHOR; *compare* CONDENSATION.

mean world syndrome The belief that the world is a more dangerous place than it actually is because of the disproportionate number of violent acts represented in or publicized by the *mass media. Those most likely to be subject to this are *heavy viewers, especially young children and the elderly, being more dependent on the media as a source of *information (Gerbner). *See also* CULTIVATION THEORY.

mechanical media *See* MEDIUM.

mechanical reproduction The mass *production of identical copies of a *text using technological means (i.e. *printing). The phrase is particularly associated with Benjamin's 1936 essay, 'The Work of Art in the Age of Mechanical Reproduction' (*see* AURA).

((()) SEE WEB LINKS

• The work of art in the age of mechanical reproduction

media *See* MASS MEDIA; MEDIUM.

media aesthetics 1. A field of *theory, research, and practice concerned with the design and analysis of visual and audiovisual materials, particularly in relation to *communicative functions and perceptual processes: *see also* COMMUNICATION DESIGN. 2. The study and appreciation of audiovisual art (e.g. film art). 3. The creative use of the technical *affordances of an expressive or communication medium.

media baron *See* MEDIA MOGUL.

media buying The selection and purchase of *advertising time (television or radio), space (*newspapers or magazines), or 'outdoor space', by **media buyers** or media specialists, primarily seeking cost-effective ways of reaching a specific *target audience in accordance with a media plan (*see* MEDIA PLANNING). This may be undertaken by the media department in an *advertising agency or (increasingly) by independent media buying agencies. *See also* ADVERTISING FORMATS.

media-centricity A pejorative reference to theories or ideas which prioritize the *medium as opposed to other factors, as in McLuhan's 'the medium is the message', which treats *content or sociohistorical *context as secondary (*see* MCLUHANISM). Writing in 2009, Morley argues that *media studies is media-centric in the sense that its current focus is on the 'symbolic realm'—as in the attention given to the virtual dimension, which he characterizes as 'the flow of information' (*see* INFORMATION FLOW). He argues that this is a form of *idealism, and that the balance should be redressed by anchoring the subject in *materialism, with a focus on 'objects, commodities, and persons'.

media consumption 1. An analysis of the relationship between media and their *audiences measured in *circulation figures, viewing amounts, or visitor numbers. 2. A way of measuring media use according to the percentage of disposable income an average person spends on media products. For most of the 20th century, the **relative constancy model** placed this figure at around 3% for most of the developed world. However, this is increasing with the rise of *digital media. 3. Broadly, the use and reception of the mass media by individuals or groups.

media controls Formal government regulation of the mass *media industries and informal self-regulation by the industries themselves. Laws and guidelines influencing the ways in which the media produce, distribute, and/or exhibit materials for audiences (*see* REGULATION). Informal controls include editorial standards, codes of ethics, content *ratings, press councils, and pressure groups.

media culture 1. An increasing awareness of the *mass media or of processes of *mediation as reflected in cultural *discourse: e.g. media sections in *newspapers and mainstream discussions of concepts like *spin. 2. The cultural *contexts, practices, and discourses of those involved in media *production: including journalists, advertisers, film and television professionals, PR agencies—such as London-based media culture of Soho or Shoreditch.

mediacy *See* MEDIA LITERACY.

media dependency theory *See* DEPENDENCY THEORY.

media determinism A synonym for *technological determinism as applied to claims about the 'impact' of *new media technologies on society, *institutions, groups, and/or individuals. The term is often applied to the stance of McLuhan, who made this observation about *printing, for instance: 'Socially, the typographic extension of man brought in nationalism, industrialism, *mass markets, and universal literacy and education' (*see also* MCLUHANISM). Such dramatic generalizations are widely criticized as a *reductionist explanation of complex social changes. Friedrich Kittler (b.1943), a German media theorist, explicitly refers to his own stance, inflected by *poststructuralism, as media determinism.

media ecology 1. A metaphor for the holistic study of media use with particular reference to *context, and especially the interrelationships of a *medium or tool with its users' tasks, *roles, *attitudes, and practices; in contrast to the *reductionism of *media determinism. 2. The concept that the functional relationships of different types of media to each other (and the ways we use them) are continually shifted by the introduction of *new media. 3. The notion of media as environments associated with McLuhan and Neil Postman, who claim that we unconsciously adapt to different media much as animals adapt to different habitats (*see also* MEDIA ENVIRONMENTS; MEDIUM THEORY; *compare* SEMIOSPHERE). 4. Loosely, a synonym for *media culture.

( ) SEE WEB LINKS
• What is media ecology?

media effects *See* EFFECTS.

media environment A metaphorical concept framing the media as environing and invisibly shaping human life. McLuhan commented: '"The medium is the message" means, in terms of the electronic age, that a totally new environment has been created.' *See also* MEDIA ECOLOGY.

media essentialism *See* MEDIA SPECIFICITY.

media ethics Issues of moral principles and standards as applied to the conduct, roles, and *content of the *mass media, in particular *journalistic ethics and *advertising ethics; also the field of study concerned with this topic. In relation to news coverage it includes issues such as *impartiality, *objectivity, *balance, *bias, privacy, and the *public interest. More generally, it also includes *stereotyping, *taste and decency, *obscenity, *freedom of speech, advertising practices such as *product placement, and legal issues such as *defamation. On an institutional level it includes debates over *media ownership and control, *commercialization, accountability, the relation of the media to the political system, issues arising from *regulation (e.g. *censorship) and *deregulation.

media events Exceptional happenings organized with the cooperation of the media by governments, public bodies, or commercial concerns, typically broadcast live across several channels with regular programming suspended to accommodate them. The sociologists Katz and Daniel Dayan (b.1943) identify three forms: firstly, there are 'conquests': associated with an authority, charismatic figure, or major achievement such as the moon landings, climbing Everest, or the running of the four-minute mile. Secondly, 'coronations'; official state events that are celebrations of tradition, such as presidential inaugurations or the crowning, marriages, or funerals of monarchs. And thirdly, 'contests': public trials such as the Oliver North hearings or the O. J. Simpson murder trial. *See also* EVENT; NEWS EVENTS; *compare* PSEUDO-EVENT.

media flows The *diffusion of media content in global markets. Since the 1970s, the global diffusion of American media content has frequently been seen as a kind of *cultural imperialism. It is very much a one-way flow, since only about 2% of US TV programmes are foreign imports (compared to about a third in most countries). Such flows are often more regionalized, based on shared language and cultural affinity. Governments often seek to control media flows as a way of protecting national culture but online media have undermined this cultural *gatekeeper role. *See also* GLOBALIZATION.

media forms (forms of media) A classification of media by type. This may be very general: e.g. visual media, audio media, audiovisual media, print media, and online media; it may also refer more specifically to radio, television, and so on. The term is often used in discussions of media transformation and *hybridization, as in the case of *mobile phones becoming multimedia mobile devices.

media functions 1. The key roles that the *mass media, a particular medium of communication, or specific kinds of media content are seen as playing from the perspective of society **(macro-level functions)**. In sociology within the framework of *functionalism, society is seen as having communication 'needs' of its own. Lasswell in 1948 listed three key media functions: a *surveillance function, a *consensus (or correlation) function, and a *socialization (or transmission) function. Most commentators add a fourth function: *entertainment. 2. The basic human needs which the mass media, a single medium, a media *genre, or specific media content, serve for individuals **(micro-level functions)**. Frameworks vary, but commonly listed are a *diversion (or *entertainment) function, a *social utility function, a *personal identity function, and a *surveillance (or *information) function. *See also* INDIVIDUAL-MEDIA DEPENDENCY; PERSONAL FUNCTIONS; USES AND GRATIFICATIONS.

media grammar 1. A concept drawn from an analogy with *language in relation to patterns structuring *form and *content in a particular medium. 2. In media *production, a set of *conventions, understood as rules, governing how content is presented in a given medium: for example, *film grammar. 3. (*semiotics) A loose reference to *syntagmatic structure in any kind of media *text: *see* SYNTAGM.

media hegemony (media hegemony theory) The theory, derived from Gramscian *Marxism, that an elite controls the *mass media, and that the media promote the *dominant ideology. *See also* CONSCIOUSNESS INDUSTRY; HEGEMONY; MANUFACTURE OF CONSENT. The *audience is not necessarily compliant (*see* DOMINANT READING; NEGOTIATED READING; OPPOSITIONAL READING). 'Corporate media hegemony' refers to the global dominance and influence of powerful commercial mass media organizations and a transnational elite. 'Western media hegemony' refers to a perception that global news media are dominated by *Eurocentric *values and perspectives (*see also* MEDIA IMPERIALISM). Critics argue that ritualistic use of the concept reflects *reification and *determinism and underestimates the contestation highlighted by Gramsci.

media history The historical study of the *mass media pioneered in the 19th century by historians of the press. It is an approach which emphasizes the importance of the specific sociohistorical *contexts within which media technologies evolved, offering the prospect of tracing the role of the media in the making of modern society, and exploring the relationship between social and technological factors from a stance of critical distance. However, the British media researcher James Curran noted in 2002 that 'press and broadcasting historians tend to focus on institutional development, while film historians tend to concentrate on the *content of films—mostly within very limited periods of time.' A focus on media technologies tends towards *technological determinism; rival narratives variously focus on such unifying themes as popular empowerment, elite control, nation-building, and the rise of consumerism (according to political perspectives). Such *grand narratives are rejected by *postmodernists, who stress discontinuities.

media imperialism The alleged US domination of global media markets (primarily those of film and television) based on a dependency relationship with small media companies worldwide, where cheap American imports are purchased in preference to indigenous content. Media imperialism creates conditions of global *homogeneity that are the basis of *cultural imperialism. Proponents of this view point out that all the largest media companies are based in the USA, and the Hollywood film studios directly control *distribution systems in all their principal foreign markets. However, these claims have been strongly criticized because many US media companies are actually owned by foreign conglomerates (e.g. Sony), and many countries also export their media content. For example, Egypt is a major supplier of television programmes for Arab-speaking countries, and Brazilian soap operas or 'telenovelas' are hugely popular in Portuguese- and Spanish-speaking territories all around the world (including in the USA). *See also* MEDIA HEGEMONY.

media industries *See also* CREATIVE INDUSTRIES; *compare* CULTURAL INDUSTRIES. 1. Taken collectively, all the businesses involved with the financing, *production, *distribution, exhibition, and retailing of media products. Media industries comprise independent media *institutions that may be commercially run or not-for-profit concerns. 2. The aspects of the media studied by media economists. Media industries manufacture *entertainment and *informational products often according to a *production-line ethos. The paradigmatic example of this is the Hollywood *studio system. Media industries can be divided into two tiers: large corporations that control the majority of the market and small companies that fight for a share of the remainder. Media industries serve a dual market, selling both to audiences and advertisers, which leads to conflicts of interests. Since the 1980s the trend has been towards more media mergers, creating huge global media corporations like Viacom and Time Warner. 3. The UK media training body, Skillset, divides the creative media industries into ten categories: animation; videogames; film and television facilities; film; *interactive media; corporate and commercials production; photo imaging; print and electronic publishing; radio; television.

(( )) SEE WEB LINKS

• Creative media industries

media law The legislation through which governments regulate the *mass media (*see also* DEREGULATION; REGULATION). It includes issues of *censorship, *copyright, *defamation, broadcast law, and antitrust law. In democracies, media law is seen as a balancing act between two conflicting principles: freedom of expression and constraints laid down in statutes of common law, as in issues of *defamation and the national interest.

(( )) SEE WEB LINKS

• The 1998 Human Rights Act

media literacy (mediacy) 1. *Knowledge, understanding, and experience of various media forms. In some definitions the concept includes *literacy and numeracy. 2. Competence in using various media and the ability to think critically about them. 3. Levels of skill and competence in using media devices.

(( )) SEE WEB LINKS

• Ofcom's definition of 'media literacy'

media logic The dominant processes, established routines, and standardized *formats which *frame and shape the *production of *mass-media content, especially its *representation or *construction of reality, and its manufacture of news (Altheide and Snow). Media logic intersects with commercial logic and political logic—confluences associated with such phenomena as *tabloidization and the *mediatization of politics. Media logic exists wherever *mediation exists. It contributes to the shaping of social order in modern post-industrial cultures.

media mix The use of two or more different media together in an *advertising campaign. *See also* MARKETING COMMUNICATIONS MIX.

media mogul (media baron, media tycoon) A person who has built up, owns, or operates a major media empire and runs it with a distinctive management style, e.g. Rupert Murdoch. In the past, media moguls were industrialists; today they are entrepreneurs. A *crown prince* or *princess* is the son or daughter of a media mogul who inherits the business; e.g. Elisabeth Murdoch (b.1968), an Australian-British media executive, or James Murdoch (b.1972), the British Chief Executive of News Corporation. A *press baron is a mogul whose empire is restricted to *newspaper publishing. *Compare* MOVIE MOGUL.

media organizations *See* INSTITUTIONS.

media ownership The commercial and legal control of interpersonal and mass communication technologies by individuals, corporations, and/or governments. This is not an issue of mere resources since there is also a political dimension to this 'control' which threatens the *pluralism of democratic societies. Corporate mergers and media *convergence therefore prompt debates over media concentration versus pluralism and over the acceptable connotations of control versus regulated stewardship. *See* FOURTH ESTATE; MEDIA MOGUL; PRESS BARON; PUBLIC SERVICE BROADCASTING; PUBLIC SPHERE; REGULATION; *see also* CROSS-MEDIA OWNERSHIP; DIAGONAL INTEGRATION; DIVERSIFICATION; HORIZONTAL INTEGRATION; MARKET MODEL; MEDIA CONTROLS; VERTICAL INTEGRATION.

(⊕) SEE WEB LINKS
• Who owns what?

media phenomenology 1. The utilization of theories and methods from *phenomenology in media research, especially those of Husserl and Heidegger. 2. The study of the media as technologies which are not neutral but which transform both the world and human experience of it by amplifying or reducing phenomena through various transformational structures, as theorized by the American philosopher Don Ihde (b.1934), and others.

media planning The role of a **media planner** in an *advertising agency, ensuring that campaigns reach their *target audiences as effectively as possible through the strategic use of the most appropriate media. Media planning produces a **media schedule** for an advertising campaign, based on objectives for reach, frequency, and impact, and specifying the specific media to be used and the dates when the advertisements are to appear. *See also* EFFECTIVE FREQUENCY; EFFECTIVE REACH; *compare* MEDIA BUYING.

media policy *See also* CROSS-MEDIA OWNERSHIP; DEREGULATION; MEDIA CONTROLS; MEDIA OWNERSHIP; POLITICAL ECONOMY; REGULATION. 1. General principles formally outlined by any organization or group for its relationship to the *mass media (typically focusing on the need for good publicity). 2. At government level, legal frameworks regulating the *mass media as well as a vision of the role of the media more broadly within economic and cultural policy (typically including issues of *national identity). 3. In public debate, a range of issues including: the ownership of media companies (media monopolies, *public service broadcasting, commercial interests); technical aspects (allocating scarce radio frequencies to the military, medical, and media and telecommunications industries, and issues of *convergence—including *identity theft and *surveillance); media content (issues of quality, *taste and decency, and *defamation—set against civil liberties); and issues of *access (ensuring that everyone has access to the media and that minority views are represented).

media power *See* POWER.

media priming A psychological phenomenon whereby media content is seen as providing a prior *frame of reference (a *prime*) within which subsequent related content may be interpreted, as in theories of *agenda setting. Media *genres and *stereotyping are also forms of priming: contextual frameworks which set up certain *expectations. In the rhetoric of the *effects tradition (especially within the *violence debate), **media-priming effects** are short-term attitudinal or behavioural patterns attributed to prior *exposure to related media content. The concept is derived from its usage in cognitive psychology (*see* PRIMING).

media psychology 1. A topic-defined field largely pursued by psychologists studying the *mass media in academic departments other than psychology. It draws on cognitive psychology, social psychology, and developmental psychology. Historically, it has been dominated by laboratory studies of the cognitive and behavioural '*effects' of television and film, but there has been a growing interest in how audiences interpret what they see onscreen. It includes the psychology of particular media, such as the psychology of *advertising and of the *internet. 2. The featuring of psychologists as contributors in the mass media, as in the psychologists' commentaries accompanying the reality TV series *Big Brother*.

(((⊕))) **SEE WEB LINKS**
• APA Division 46

media regulation *See* REGULATION.

media richness A medium's ability to communicate effectively, determined by four factors: its capacity for immediate *feedback, the number of *cues and *channels it utilizes, the degree of *personalization it affords, and its ability to communicate using natural language. The American organizational theorists Richard Daft and Robert Lengel postulated that the purpose of effective communication is to resolve either uncertainty (where there is a lack of *data) or *ambiguity (where there is contradictory data). Rich media can overcome different *frames of reference, clarify ambiguous issues, and change understanding in a timely manner whereas non-rich media require a long time to achieve the same ends, or are incapable of doing so. However, when uncertainty and *ambiguity are low, non-rich media are an effective means of communication. Daft and Lengel's research (conducted in the 1980s) ranked *face-to-face interaction as the richest medium, followed by the telephone, letters, and finally, generic printed messages, e.g. memos. *Compare* SOCIAL PRESENCE.

media schedule *See* MEDIA PLANNING.

media semiotics The study of the *mass media, often associated with the *textual analysis of media *texts and *genres as *sign systems based on the use of *codes which require *encoding and *decoding. References to 'reading' television or film, or to the 'grammar' or 'language' of such media allude to *structuralist semiotic approaches. *See also* SEMIOTICS.

media sociology The study of the *mass media from a social perspective. The media are regarded by sociologists as major social, economic, and political *institutions and important agents of *socialization exercising considerable influence on cultural forms and *imagery. Sociologists stress the social *context of media technologies, and of the *production and use of media content (*see also* SOCIAL DETERMINISM). Media sociology focuses on issues such as media content (e.g. *representation, *bias, *stereotyping); ownership and control (e.g. *censorship, *commercialization, *cross-media ownership, *media controls, *media ownership, *regulation); *ideological influences (e.g. *media hegemony, the *manufacture of consent); issues of democracy (e.g. *agenda-setting, *access, the *information rich and poor); media audiences (e.g. *uses and gratifications, *two-step flow); and *media cultures (e.g. the organizational cultures and occupational practices and routines of *advertising and news). It also explores broad themes such as the implications of the media in relation to *homogenization versus *fragmentation (*see also* CONSENSUS; INTEGRATION; WEAK TIES), or to the shifting and blurring boundaries of the *public and private spheres. Critical media sociology emerged in the *critical theory of the *Frankfurt school. *See also* POLITICAL ECONOMY.

media specificity The issue of the particular technical features and *affordances of different media (and their associated *contexts of use and/or *production), or of the specific qualities of a *text which are related to the medium. The concept is often associated with criticisms of perspectives which do not seem to take sufficient account of differences between, for example, *digital and *analogue photography. The criticism here is that of *reification: the reductive homogenization of 'photography'. However, 'media specificity' can also be a pejorative reference to what is regarded as a form of **media essentialism**, as when a film is criticized as too literary or too theatrical (implying that the use of film should be confined to what it is assumed to be inherently good for). Stances on this issue relate to those on *form and *content: many contemporary theorists would argue that the specificities of form make an important contribution to the generation of meaning.

media studies The academic investigation of the *mass media from perspectives such as *media sociology, *media psychology, *media history, *media semiotics, and *critical discourse analysis. It includes media-specific studies such as television studies, radio studies, and web studies. As an academic degree subject, media studies emerged in the 1970s in the UK, where it is closely associated with *cultural studies; in the USA its concerns are largely represented within the context of *communication studies; it also overlaps with the study of *journalism. It includes the study of the mass media as *institutions, issues of *media ownership and control, media *production, *representation, and *audiences. Cross-media *genres such as *advertising and news are also a key focus. Courses differ in the relative emphasis given to the development of practical media skills. In cultural rhetoric, 'media studies' is frequently used as a pejorative reference to the apparently laughable notion of the media being treated as worthy of serious academic attention; it is caricatured (often, ironically, in the mass media) as a non-academic subject for people seen as incapable of studying anything more demanding. Such views are associated with cultural *elitism, with the mass media being dismissed as *popular culture or *mass culture. A highly selective form of *film studies emerged originally as a separate subject on the basis of an association with high art, and although separate degrees in film studies still exist, the study of film (or at least popular film) is now also widespread within media studies courses.

media system dependency theory *See* DEPENDENCY THEORY.

mediated communication 1. Often a synonym for *mass communication through the *mass media, as distinguished from *interpersonal communication. 2. Interpersonal communication using a technological medium of communication such as a telephone (*see also* COMPUTER-MEDIATED COMMUNICATION). 3. All forms of deliberate communication other than direct *face-to-face interaction based on speech or *sign-language. 4. Indirect *interpersonal communication through a third party: *see also* J-CURVE; TWO-STEP FLOW. 5. Most radically, the mediatedness of all human communication (in the sense that communication always involves a medium, including the medium of *language or *body language).

media theory 1. Broadly, any coherent framework of ideas and concepts for analysing or generating investigable *hypotheses about *mediated communication, including media comparisons and theories of influence and use. Such theories may be further distinguished as sociological (*see* MEDIA SOCIOLOGY), psychological (*see* MEDIA PSYCHOLOGY), *semiotic, *phenomenological, *psychoanalytic, *Marxist, *feminist, *postcolonial, *formalist, *structuralist, *functionalist, and so on (*see also* ACTIVE AUDIENCE THEORY; AGENDA-SETTING; COGNITIVE FILM THEORY; COMMUNICATION THEORY; CULTIVATION THEORY; DEPENDENCY THEORY; DISINHIBITION THEORY; FILM THEORY; RECEPTION THEORY; USES AND GRATIFICATIONS THEORY). *Common-sense notions are sometimes loosely dignified by the term (as in magic bullet 'theory'); approaches seen as inadequately supported by evidence may be dismissed as *grand theory (*see* MCLUHANISM). Critical media theory is associated with the *Frankfurt school: *see also* CRITICAL THEORY. 2. Less generically, a synonym for *medium theory.

mediation [Latin *mediare* 'to go between'] 1. In everyday usage, the intervention of a third party in order to facilitate the resolution of a dispute between two parties. 2. Broadly, being an enabling means or agency for some process or *effect. 3. The transformational processes involved in *perception and recall. This includes *addition, *deletion, *substitution, and *transposition (*see also* LEVELLING AND SHARPENING). Semioticians emphasize the **mediatedness** of experience, arguing that we are always dealing with *signs and *codes, not with an unmediated objective reality. 4. The transformational processes involved in any *representation of reality. This unavoidably involves *framing, selection, *foregrounding, and backgrounding. However, we become so used to *conventions in 'realistic' texts (especially in *indexical audiovisual media) that they seem 'natural' rather than constructed—the *signifieds seem unmediated and the *medium seems *transparent, as when we interpret television or photography as a 'window on the world'. 5. (**mediatization**) Broadly, in communication, the role of any intervening factor in transforming a *message, *meaning, or experience. For instance, *social relations, *power relations, or the *affordances or *biases of a medium (which may select, reduce, or amplify phenomena). For the sociologists Altheide and Snow it is 'the impact of the logic and form of any medium involved in the communication process'. *See also* MEDIA LOGIC. 6. More specifically, the intervening role of the *mass media and journalists in communicating *messages or representing reality to *audiences, which has *ideological implications: *see also* AGENDA-SETTING; BIAS; MEDIA HEGEMONY; MEDIATED COMMUNICATION; NEWS VALUES. 7. In cultural and literary theory, the transformational role of intermediary structures (or *frames) and processes in the *production (and/or reception) of literary and artistic works. 8. In *structuralist theory, the process in which one set of situations in *myth or *narrative is transformed into another. 9. In social science, the role of *intervening variables in *indirect effects.

( ) SEE WEB LINKS

• Processes of mediation

mediatization 1. The increasing importance of the *mass media in society and culture: for example, in politics and sport. Often used pejoratively. *See also* MEDIA CULTURE; MEDIA EVENT. 2. (**mediation, mediation theory**) The influence of *media logic and *format on communication and *content, a factor suggesting the importance of *how* things are communicated: *see also* McLUHANISM; MEDIATION; PUBLICITY MODEL.

media tycoon *See* MEDIA MOGUL.

media usage *See* USES AND GRATIFICATIONS.

media violence *See* VIOLENCE DEBATE.

medium [*pl.* media; Latin *medius* 'middle'] 1. The means or *agency through which communication takes place; often synonymous with *channel. 2. The physical vehicle of expression employed in a *representation, ranging from general categories of artistic or technical forms or modes of expression (e.g. photography) to specific materials, tools, and methods. In linguistic discourse, the term may variously refer to: *language; *speech or *writing (for linguists, the **phonic medium** and the **graphic medium**); or distinctions such as between handwriting and print. In media discourse, it often refers to a specific technical form within *mass communication (whether electronic or *print media) or *interpersonal communication (e.g. *post, *telephone, *computer-mediated communication). Fiske makes a distinction between **presentational media** (the speech and *body language used in face-to-face communicative acts), **representational media** (*texts which can be circulated, such as writing, photographs, advertisements, TV programmes), and **mechanical media** (e.g. telephones, television, film, the *internet, which transmit presentational and representational forms). *Texts are always anchored in the material form of a medium—each having its own *affordances which constrain the *codes which it can support. *McLuhanism draws particular attention to the importance of the medium in its own right. The use of a particular medium can influence the *message: a hand-written letter and a *word-processed circular could carry the same verbal text but generate different *connotations. However, technological *convergence and *postmodernist theorists have blurred distinctions between one medium and another. 3. Most broadly, any substance or process through which reality is apprehended or constructed.

medium close-up (MCU) In photography, film, and television, a standard *shot-size which shows a *foreground subject dominating but not filling the screen. An MCU of a person would show the upper torso and head. In *face-to-face interaction this mimics the *proximity of the *personal zone. *See also* CLOSE-UP.

medium factors *See* CHANNEL FACTORS.

medium long shot (MLS) In photography, film, and television, a standard *shot size in which the *background surroundings are slightly favoured over the *foreground subject in terms of screen area. An MLS of a person would show their head and body above the knees so that much of the surrounding context would also be visible. In *face-to-face interaction this mimics the *proximity of the *social zone. *See also* LONG-SHOT.

medium shot (MS) In photography, film, and television, a standard *shot size in which there is a balance between a *foreground subject and the *background surroundings in terms of screen area. A medium shot of a person would show their head and body above the knees. In *face-to-face interaction this mimics the intimate *proximity of the *social zone.

medium theory (media theory) A mode of analysis focusing on the nature and significance of the specific characteristics of a particular *medium of communication (*see* AFFORDANCES; MODALITY) and on technical, social, and psychological differences between media (*see also* BIAS; CUELESSNESS; IMMEDIACY; NEUTRALITY; PARASOCIAL INTERACTION; PRESENCE; PSYCHOLOGICAL DISTANCE; SOCIAL PRESENCE). Comparisons range from specific media (such as radio vs television) and *types* of media (such as print media vs electronic media), to, most broadly, *mediated communication vs *face-to-face interaction. Despite McLuhan's insistence that 'the medium is the message' (*see* MCLUHANISM), a focus on the medium need not be at the expense of a concern with the implications for *content.

Analysis can be at the micro-level (*see* PERSONAL FUNCTIONS), or at the macro-level (*see* MEDIA FUNCTIONS). The term was coined by Meyrowitz, reflecting the focal concerns of scholars such as Innis, McLuhan, and Ong. *See also* COMMUNICATION TECHNOLOGIES; MEDIA ECOLOGY; MEDIA ENVIRONMENT; MEDIA RICHNESS; MEDIATION; SENSE RATIO; *compare* MEDIA THEORY.

me generation *See also* GENERATION X. 1. Another name for *baby boomers. Some commentators apply the term to the *age cohort born between 1945 and 1964; others to those born between 1970 and 2000. 2. A pejorative description of a group characterized as infantile and selfish, who demand rights but take no responsibility, and who put their own interests before any other consideration. The term alludes to 'the me decade', a coinage of the American author Tom Wolfe (b.1931).

melodrama 1. A sensational *genre in theatre and film, also associated with the style of some popular novels. Victorian melodramas featured exaggerated conflicts between stock *heroes or heroines and villains, evil intrigue, suspense, improbable plot twists, and happy endings. Melodramas highlight moral *values and aim to generate predictable emotional responses from the audience (such as anger or compassion). 2. Loosely synonymous with 'women's film', primarily targeted at women, featuring female protagonists more than any other genre, and appealing to the *emotions. The genre is often the subject of *feminist, *Marxist, and *psychoanalytic theory. Television *soap operas are often melodramas. 3. (*adj.* **melodramatic**) A pejorative term for overemotional or exaggerated effects or behaviour.

membership group *See* REFERENCE GROUP.

meme A hypothetical unit of cultural transmission operating analogously to genes, being capable of self-replication for their own advantage rather than for the benefit of the host individual: for example, a catchy tune or a fashion craze. The term was introduced by the British biologist Richard Dawkins (b.1941). The notion has been criticized by biologists since no evidence of memes has been discovered, and by media theorists (Jenkins) for reviving the discredited *hypodermic model of transmission. *See also* VIRAL MARKETING; VIRAL VIDEO.

memory 1. (psychology) An aspect of *cognition involving the functions of *encoding, storing, and retrieving *information (*see also* AD RETENTION; AIDED RECALL; FORGETTING RATE; MESSAGE DECAY; PRIMACY EFFECT; RECENCY EFFECT; SELECTIVE RECALL; SELECTIVE RETENTION). 2. The hypothesized information storage system in the mind or brain. **Short-term memory (STM)** is memory for information that has been minimally processed (*see* ELABORATION). It is argued to involve limited capacity (famously, for Miller, seven items plus or minus two: a notion with implications for *information design). **Long-term memory (LTM)** is memory for information that has been processed and has become part of an individual's general *knowledge store. **Iconic memory** refers to extremely brief storage of visual and perhaps other *sensory data (*see* AFTER-IMAGE). *Declaratory memory* is conscious memory for communicable information; *procedural memory* is that for how to perform sequences of operations: *see also* DUAL CODING THEORY. 3. Information stored in the mind (in psychology, often used synonymously with *knowledge). **4. (computer memory, memory store)** (computing) Loosely, any device for *data storage and retrieval: *see also* BYTE. **5. Collective memory** refers to ways of framing or representing the past which are shared by a group and central to a sense of *cultural identity, *ethnic identity, *national identity, and so on.

mental imagery *See* VISUAL IMAGERY.

mental representation (representation) *See also* CHUNKING; DUAL CODING THEORY; ENCODING. **1.** In theories of *cognition and *perception based on 'direct realism', a direct mapping of sensory stimuli in the brain. For a semiotician, this would be an *indexical model. *See also* DIRECT PERCEPTION. **2. Mental models:** in psychological theories such as *constructivism, the hypothesized concept that individuals generate internal abstract models of external situations. This is commonly invoked in relation to *visual perception, in which 3D-models of *spatial relations may be posited: e.g. in the work of the British psychologist David Marr (1945–80). It is also used to explain the making of *inferences in the *comprehension of *discourse (*compare* FRAME; SCHEMA). For a semiotician, if such *representations are spatialized and based on resemblance, this would be an *iconic model. **3. Propositional representation (symbolic representation):** a hypothesized *information-processing concept that individuals internally encode information into syntactical structures analogous to those of language: a universal 'language of the mind'. For a semiotician, the *arbitrariness of the symbol system would make this a *symbolic model.

mental set *See* PERCEPTUAL SET.

message Variously, either a *text, its *content, or its *meaning—referents which *literalists tend to conflate (*see also* TRANSMISSION MODELS). In *semiotics, messages are regarded as requiring *encoding and *decoding. As Jakobson argued, understanding messages requires *knowledge of relevant *codes and *contexts: the meaning is not 'in' the message but depends on the application of prior *textual and *social knowledge. Nor can the meaning of a message be reduced to what the *sender intended (as in 'the message of this film . . . '): even when we recognize a *preferred reading we may reject it. As Jeremy Bullmore (b.1929), a British advertising executive, perceptively noted: 'Sometimes we use the word "message" to mean what we put into communication; sometimes to mean what the receiver takes out. And however inconvenient and untidy that may be, we have to realize that these two can be, and indeed almost always are, different. I put in: "I am modest." You take out: "He is conceited."' Even the *medium used may contribute to the meaning of a message: *see* McLUHANISM. In *Jakobson's model of communication messages can have various *linguistic functions: they are not confined to an *information or *referential function.

message decay The corruption of a message over time through the diminishing recall of *information by audiences. A factor in *advertising effectiveness and a key reason for repetition. *See also* AD RETENTION; *compare* WEAROUT.

message factors In *models of communication or *persuasion, specific *variables associated with the characteristics of the message itself that research has identified as among those that can affect its effectiveness. These might include: style, clarity, forcefulness, speed, ordering, amount of material, repetition, number of *arguments, types of *appeal, and extremity of position. *See also* PRIMACY EFFECT; RECENCY EFFECT; YALE MODEL.

message-oriented communication (message-centred)
1. *Communication models framed in terms of the transfer of *messages or *information, or which reduce *meaning to explicit *content (*see also* TRANSMISSION MODELS; *compare* INFORMATIONAL COMMUNICATION). In practice, such formulations are primarily *sender-oriented. 2. Loosely, in communication skills training, a misleading synonym for *meaning-oriented communication.
3. In *linguistics and *semiotics, forms of communication in which the *poetic function is dominant (*see also* LINGUISTIC FUNCTIONS).

messaging The activity of sending an *SMS text message on a *mobile phone, or communication with someone using synchronous online chat software (*see* INSTANT MESSAGING).

metacommunication [Greek *meta* 'beyond, along with'] Communication about communication: a higher-level *framing. Bateson introduced the term as 'the reflection upon or framing of communication that accompanies communication.' *See also* FALSIFIED METACOMMUNICATION; METAMESSAGE; *compare* METALINGUAL FUNCTION.

metalanguage Language used to describe or analyse *language. *Linguistics can be seen as a metalanguage (a 'second-order' language) for describing natural language. Barthes, following Hjelmslev, saw *myth as a metalanguage: a *sign system referring to another sign system. *Structuralism may seem to be an objective metalanguage, but many *poststructuralists argue that this notion is founded on the fallacy that we can step outside language (whereas, as Wittgenstein said, 'the limits of my language are the limits of my world').

metalingual function (metalinguistic or metacommunication function) A *linguistic function in which language is used to refer to itself: for example, 'This is a short sentence.' In *Jakobson's model of linguistic communication this is a key *communicative function which is seen as oriented towards the *code. It can refer to the nature of the *interaction (e.g. to its status as a textual *genre, or more *reflexively to its *constructedness). It is a function distinguishing human from animal language. *Compare* METALANGUAGE.

metamessage An inexplicit commentary *framing the explicit *message of a communicative act, typically reflected in the *manner* of communication and especially in nonverbal *cues (such as tone of voice). It can variously identity the *modality status of the communication, the evaluative stance of the communicator, the *preferred reading, and/or the relationship of the participants (*see* COMMUNICATIVE RELATIONSHIPS). For instance, a message delivered 'tongue in cheek'. *See also* COMMUNICATION STYLE; METACOMMUNICATION.

metanarrative *See* GRAND NARRATIVE.

metaphor [Greek *metaphora* 'transfer, carry over'] **1.** In loose usage, a synonym for *figurative language rather than *literal language, particularly *figures of speech involving association, comparison, or resemblance: *see also* DEAD METAPHOR; MIXED METAPHOR. **2.** In *rhetoric, the most common figure of speech (more strictly, a *trope), in which something is described as if it were something else by virtue of some apparent *similarity, as in the *conduit metaphor in which communication is described as if it consisted of passing parcels. In its narrower sense, metaphor is distinguished from *simile in that the comparison is not flagged by terms such as X 'is like' Y. Metaphor often expresses a relatively abstract concept in terms of a more concrete one. In literary theory, the thing being represented is termed the **tenor** while the concept used to represent it is the **vehicle**—terms introduced by Richards in 1936. For instance, when life is described as a journey, *life* is the tenor and *journey* is the vehicle. The semantic basis of comparison is usually called the **ground**, which in this case might allude to *progress*. Although closely associated with poetic language (where fresh *poetic metaphors* perform a *defamiliarization function), metaphors are not only heavily used in *advertising, but *conventional metaphors* permeate everyday language (*see also* DEAD METAPHOR). George Lakoff and Johnson have argued that *conceptual metaphors* *frame our thinking. While facilitating certain ways of thinking about a phenomenon, a particular metaphor may also inhibit other ways of thinking about it: *see also* SAPIR-WHORF HYPOTHESIS. **3.** In semiotic terms, a form of *analogy which is *iconic in being based on some form of resemblance but also *symbolic (relatively conventional) in its apparent disregard for 'literal' or denotative resemblance. Jakobson represented metaphor and *metonymy as different structural axes, associating metaphor with the *paradigmatic axis (based on substitution) and metonymy with the *syntagmatic axis (based on combination). As a technique, metaphor (or at least poetic metaphor) tends to *foreground itself (the *signifier) rather than what it represents (the *signified): in contrast to *metonymy. Jakobson argued that this underlies the distinction between *romanticism and *realism in literature, art, and film. *See also* PARADIGM; SYNTAGM.

(()) SEE WEB LINKS
• Conceptual metaphor

metaphorical thinking *See* ANALOGICAL THINKING.

metaphoric meaning (**metaphorical** or **figurative meaning**) *See also* FIGURATIVE LANGUAGE; SURPLUS MEANING. **1.** In *semantics, a *meaning which is not intended to be taken literally. **2.** In the *comprehension of *figurative language, the nonliteral purport: what a particular figurative expression is actually intended to signify. The *literal meaning of the message is not the *intended meaning, which has to be inferred. For instance, we might infer that 'film is a mirror' implies that it is a reflection of life. *Deconstructionists challenge the distinction between literal and metaphoric meaning: all language is metaphorical and there is no underlying literal level.

metaphysics of presence *See* DECONSTRUCTION.

metatag In *HTML, a command which contains a brief description of the *content of a webpage and/or a list of *keywords which is not displayed on the page but which is intended for indexing by *search engines.

metathesis *See* TRANSPOSITION.

methodology 1. The philosophical *evaluation of how *knowledge and inquiry are framed within an academic discipline or school of thought: *see also* EPISTEMOLOGY; PARADIGM. 2. **(research methods)** The design of a particular research study: a set of procedures according to which it is undertaken, including techniques of *data gathering and *data analysis (this may involve *quantitative research and/or *qualitative research).

metonymic fallacy In *representation, a tendency for a represented *part* to be taken as an accurate reflection of the *whole* for which it is taken as standing (e.g. a white middle-class woman representing all women). Strictly speaking, this is synecdochic (*see* SYNECDOCHE).

metonymy [Greek 'change of name'] In *rhetoric, a *figure of speech (more strictly a *trope) in which one thing (the **tenor**) is represented by another (the **vehicle**) which is directly related to it or closely associated with it in some way. For instance, 'the press' is a metonym for 'journalists'. Unlike *metaphor, metonymy does not involve a semantic leap, and it can be seen as *foregrounding what it represents (the *signified) and backgrounding itself (the *signifier). Such features lead Jakobson to associate metonymy with aesthetic *realism. However, *poststructuralists insist that metonyms are not based on any intrinsic connection with what they represent, and that *arbitrariness characterizes all figures of speech. Metonymy is often treated as an umbrella term including *synecdoche (based on part-whole relations), though the latter may also be regarded as a separate trope (confining metonymy to more abstract connections such as cause and effect); if separate, these tropes can certainly be seen as related. In semiotic terms, both can be seen as *indexical, and their *interpretation is *context-dependent.

metropolitan bias A criticism made by regional or rural viewers that television programmes feature a disproportionate coverage of items (especially news *events) that take place within urban areas. In the UK, ITV was created as a series of regional companies to counter the perceived metropolitan bias of the BBC towards London.

micro level functions *See* MEDIA FUNCTIONS; PERSONAL FUNCTIONS.

micromarketing Tailoring products and *marketing to particular *target audiences.

microsociology In sociology, a level of analysis concerned with social action, particularly interpersonal *interaction and group behaviour. It explores themes such as the production of *meaning in *face-to-face interaction, the domestic consumption of the media, and occupational routines in news production. *Ethnomethodology and *symbolic interactionism are sociological approaches which focus on this level of analysis. *Compare* MACROSOCIOLOGY.

microstructure *See* SURFACE STRUCTURE.

middle distance In visual images which involve the *representation of spatial depth (originally paintings, but subsequently also photographs), the depicted area between the *foreground and the *background. One of the three *zones of recession lying behind the *picture plane in the visual representation of depth. *See also* PICTORIAL DEPTH CUES.

middle-market newspapers (middle-market tabloids) *Newspapers which are neither *upmarket (primarily *hard news) nor *downmarket (primarily *sensationalist), and which combine *entertainment with more serious news. In the UK, these are the *Daily Mail* and the *Daily Express*, the *target audience being relatively affluent women; in the USA they include the *New York Post* and *USA Today*.

mid-shot (MS) In photography, film, and television, a standard *shot size in which the subject and the *setting occupy roughly equal areas in the *frame. In the case of a person standing, the lower frame passes through the waist. There is space for hand gestures to be seen. This is the most frequently used shot size in filming.

mimesis [Greek 'imitation'] **1.** Broadly, the imitation of life as the goal of art and literature (*see also* FIGURATIVE ART). The **mimetic** purpose in *representation involves an attempt to closely imitate or simulate observable features of an external reality as if this is being experienced directly and without *mediation, and making the absent present (*see* ABSENT PRESENCE). This *illusionist version of **mimetic theory** derives from Aristotle. Mimesis came to be the primary aim of the 19th-century *aesthetic realist movement concerned with the 'accurate' observation and representation of the world in art and literature (*see also* REFLECTIONISM). In literary and aesthetic theory, **mimetic criticism** is that which evaluates works of literature or visual art in terms of the reflection of external reality. **2.** Plato's concept of *showing* (characters talking in their own words) as opposed to *telling* (narrating; *see* DIEGESIS). **3.** Direct imitation in any form of *representation based on resemblance, typically excluding *writing (and sometimes excluding all verbal language, because of its basis in *arbitrariness).

(⊕) SEE WEB LINKS

• Mimesis

mimicry [Greek 'contest'] Games of *competition; one of four game categories introduced by Caillois. *See also* AGON; ALEA; ILINX.

mimic sign *See* ILLUSTRATOR.

mini-series A *prime-time television *series consisting of less than 11 programmes.

minority audiences *Mass media audiences classed as members of a recognized minority (e.g. because of their ethnic background), which historically has been poorly served by mainstream media companies. In the UK, the creation of Channel Four television in the 1980s was intended to address this shortcoming.

mirror phase *See* IMAGINARY.

miscommunication Any *message, or series of messages, the *preferred meaning of which is unwittingly misinterpreted by its *target audience. A common occurrence in *intercultural communication. *Compare* ABERRANT DECODING.

mise-en-abîme (mise-en-abyme) [French 'placing into the abyss'] **1.** The double-mirroring effect created by placing an image within an image and so on, repeating infinitely (**infinite regression**): for example, the album cover of Pink Floyd's *Ummagumma* (1969). This is also known as **Droste effect**. **2.** A reflexive strategy where the content of a medium is the medium itself: for example, Shakespeare's *Hamlet* features a play within a play and Fellini's *8½* (1963) is a film within a film. *See also* REFLEXIVITY. **3.** A formal technique in Western art of placing a small copy of an image inside a larger one.

mise-en-scène [French 'placed on stage'] **1.** In *film theory, the visual composition and *framing of individual *shots. It includes camera position and angle, focus, *setting, sets, costume, and lighting, the pattern of *colour, the relation of people and objects, and movement within the compositional *frame. Some usages exclude *camerawork, but it is always distinguished from *montage. Theorists note that it is an **extracinematic code** since it is not unique to cinema: it was adopted from theatre, where it referred to 'staging'. **2.** In *auteur theory, the distinctive style of particular directors as reflected in the *cinematography.

misinformation The dissemination of false *information, either knowing it to be false (*see* DISINFORMATION), or unknowingly.

misrecognition *See* IMAGINARY.

mix **1.** In audio *post-production and music engineering, the process of combining multiple different channels of recorded or *live sound (audio *tracks), which are fed through a *mixer and/or various effects units so that they can be layered and blended together to create an aesthetically pleasing sound *collage. The person doing the mix dynamically controls or pre-programs the mixer so as to make adjustments of the volume and tonal frequencies of each channel. In digital mixing, sounds are manipulated on a computer and are typically displayed as graphical *events on a *timeline. **2.** Synonymous with a video or audio dissolve: *see* CROSS DISSOLVE. **3.** For marketing usage, *see* MARKETING COMMUNICATIONS MIX; MARKETING MIX; MEDIA MIX.

mixed metaphor A combination of unrelated or incompatible *metaphors in the same *utterance, message, or text: for instance, 'We need to nail this leak!'

mixer (audio mixer, vision mixer, switcher) In audio or video *production and *post-production, a device which can be conceived as a hub to which multiple audio or video *feeds are connected. Each feed is represented by its own dedicated set of controls (buttons, knobs, or faders) on the mixer's interface. By adjusting these controls, the operator can make changes to each feed individually: for example, by applying an effect, or by combining multiple feeds into audio or video collages. The mixer also permits smooth transitions between feeds such as dissolves. *See* MULTICAMERA.

MLS *See* MEDIUM LONG SHOT.

MMOG, MMORPG (massively multiplayer online game or **online role playing game)** A *videogame in the form of a persistent two or three-dimensional graphical *virtual world in which users participate as *avatars, typically going on quests and joining up with teams of other players: examples include *Everquest, World of Warcraft*, and *Eve Online*. *Compare* MUVE.

mobile (mobile phone) A portable telephone using a *cellular radio system, so that users are no longer confined to a fixed spatial location as they were with fixed *telephones based on landlines. In the UK, before 1985 no one had a true mobile; by 2000 over half the population had one, and now almost everyone has one. Mobiles have transcended the conventional functions of voice telephony, incorporating functions such as *SMS text messaging, photography and video-recording, music and video playback, *PDA, and *internet-access (including *email and *web browsing). The mobile has become a key tool for the maintenance of *social networks and the shaping of social identity, especially among adolescents. Ling declares that 'it leads to the sharing of experiences and emotions more immediately than almost any other mediated form of contact, save *face-to-face interaction'. Mobiles have also contributed to the blurring of the *public and private spheres, as in relation to how *co-present others are handled. *See also* GENDERED TECHNOLOGIES; STRONG TIES; WEAK TIES.

mobile communications *See also* CELLULAR RADIO SYSTEM; NOMADIC AUDIENCES; PERSONAL DIGITAL ASSISTANT; TELEWORKING. **1.** Broadly, any communications technology that is portable: for example, a battery-powered television, *WiFi-equipped laptop, cordless landline telephone, or outside broadcasting facility. **2.** A device, network, or service that enables interpersonal communication over a distance between two or more parties: either because the user is mobile and has access to the service in a number of different locations or because the technology is portable and can be carried with the user; i.e. a walkie-talkie radio or *mobile phone.

(()) SEE WEB LINKS

• Mobile communication and mediated ritual

mocap *See* MOTION CAPTURE.

mockumentary A fictionalized *documentary, which can be comic, as in *This Is Spinal Tap* (1984), satirizing the conventions of documentary film-making, or serious, as in the famous radio adaptation of *War of the Worlds* (1938) where the verisimilitude of the documentary form brings an ironic sense of *realism to the presentation. *See also* DOCUMENTARY STYLE.

modality **1. (sensory modality)** A *channel of sensory *perception, such as vision. **2.** A particular *medium, such as speech or writing: *see also* MULTIMODALITY. **3.** In *linguistics (*semantics, *grammar, *stylistics, *text linguistics), the qualification of a statement by some linguistic form indicating a subjective *evaluation of the truth status of its *propositional content or a personal *attitude towards it. For instance, 'You may very well think that...'. **4.** (*semiotics) The reality status accorded to or claimed by a *sign, *text, or *genre. Peirce's classification of signs in terms of the mode of relationship of the *sign vehicle to its *referent reflects their modality—their apparent *transparency in relation to 'reality' (the *symbolic mode, for instance, having low modality). In making sense of a text, its interpreters make 'modality judgements' about it. They assess what are variously described as the plausibility, reliability, credibility, truth, accuracy, or facticity of texts within a given genre as *representations of some recognizable reality. For instance, they assign it to *fact or *fiction, *actuality or acting, *live or recorded, and they assess the possibility or plausibility of the *events depicted or the claims made in it. In doing so, they draw upon their *knowledge of the world (and *social codes) and of the *medium (and *textual codes). Such judgements are made in part with reference to cues within texts which semioticians (following linguists) call **modality markers**, which include features of *form and *content. *See also* ONTOLOGY.

(⊕) SEE WEB LINKS

• Modality and representation

model **1. (theoretical model)** (social science) A formalized specification of a hypothesized set of relationships in a simplified *representation of a system or process; often spatialized in diagrammatic form (as in many *communication models). **2.** Any *representation of one phenomenon by another: for example, an *analogy or *metaphor (e.g. *story model). **3.** Loosely, a synonym for a *theory, a *frame of reference, a set of related conceptual *propositions, or a *paradigm (e.g. *hypodermic model, *reception model). **4.** A computerized simulation of a real-world phenomenon.

modelling (imitation) Copying behaviour. More specifically, the imitation by an individual of some aspect of the behaviour of another person (which they have observed either in real life or onscreen). Imitation is argued to be more likely if the model is powerful and the same sex as the observer. *Social learning theorists such as Bandura argue that this is a key learning process in *socialization (an alternative to *behaviourist theories of *conditioning). *See also* COPYCAT BEHAVIOUR; IDENTIFICATION; ROLE MODEL.

(⊕) SEE WEB LINKS

• Imitation of aggressive models

modelling systems For Lotman, *semiotic structures which can be regarded as *languages insofar as they have basic units combinable by rules and an analogical relation to what they represent. He sees spoken language as a **primary modelling system** and writing as a **secondary modelling system** (a semiotic superstructure) which is built upon it. Since this stance grants primacy to the spoken form, it has been criticized as *phonocentric. The American semiotician and linguist Thomas Sebeok (1920–2001) argues that nonverbal 'language' can be seen as a primary modelling system. Other theorists have extended this notion to *texts in other media, seeing them as secondary modelling systems built out of a primary *language. Cinematic texts, for instance, have sometimes been seen as built upon a primary modelling system of 'graphic language'. However, whether such a 'language' has basic building blocks and what these might be has been hotly disputed.

models of communication *See* COMMUNICATION MODELS.

mode of address In any act of communication, the relationship between *addresser and addressee, which can be inferred from explicit and implicit cues. In relation to *texts, the way in which aspects of the *style, *structure, and/or *content function to *position readers as *subjects (*ideal readers) (e.g. in relation to *class, age, *gender, and *ethnicity). Aspects of this include degrees of directness (*see* DIRECT ADDRESS; INDIRECT ADDRESS) and of *formality, *narrative *point of view, and the *markedness of one form of address compared with another. *See also* COMMUNICATIVE RELATIONSHIPS; ÉNONCIATION; FORMALITY; INTERPELLATION; TEXT-READER RELATIONS.

(⊕) SEE WEB LINKS
• Modes of address

moderator 1. A person who polices an *internet *newsgroup, *chatroom, or *virtual world, ensuring that the rules of conduct (*netiquette) are followed by other members. Moderators can be self-appointed, imposed, or democratically chosen. In some contexts they have powers to temporarily suspend or ban other members. In *MOOs, moderators are called Wizards. 2. In *focus group research the person who facilitates the session.

modernism *See also* MODERNITY; *compare* POSTMODERNISM. 1. (**modernisms**) In literary and cultural theory, a diffuse movement or tendency across the arts in the West which can be traced to the late 19th century, and was at its height from around 1910 to 1930. Some commentators link it to the disillusionment felt after the devastating experience of the First World War. Many argue that the movement persisted until at least the end of the 1960s; others see it as succeeded by *postmodernism after the Second World War (*see also* POSTMODERNITY). Modernism is characterized most broadly by a conscious rejection of tradition and of art as imitation (*see* MIMESIS), and also by a focus on *form rather than content, and by *reflexivity. Initially modernism was associated with the avant-garde, but by definition the avant-garde moves on. Modernism involved considerable cross-fertilization between the arts and between its various forms in different countries. In the visual arts it included Cubism, Dadaism, Surrealism, and Futurism. In painting, modernism typically involved the abandonment of direct *representation or *naturalism. In music it was reflected in the abandonment of melody and harmony in favour of atonality. In architecture it is associated with the Bauhaus school: traditional materials and forms were rejected in favour of functional geometrical forms and new materials (*see* FUNCTIONALISM). In literature, *realism in the novel was replaced by *fragmentation and stream-of-consciousness and free verse became dominant in poetry. Modernist literary works are often complex and difficult, and so are associated by critics with *elitism. In film, modernism is characterized by its reflexivity, anti-illusionism, and *foregrounding of *editing (in strong contrast to *classical Hollywood cinema and its tradition of *continuity editing). 2. A worldview associated with *modernity and the *Enlightenment belief in reason and scientific progress. Modernism variously reflects the influence of Freudian *psychoanalytic theory, *Marxist theory, Darwinism, Nietzschean *relativism, and *structuralism. Some modernist theories are criticized in *postcolonialist theory as involving *Eurocentrism; others are criticized by *feminists as *masculinist. Barthes associates modernism with a plurality of worldviews; some see it as a reaction to (or even *against*) modernity. 3. Conceptions of the self varying from an emphasis on individual *agency in bourgeois individualism and introspective *subjectivity (*see also* PSYCHOANALYTIC THEORY), to an emphasis on the *constitution of the subject in *structuralism.

modernity 1. The condition of being modern. A highly relative concept based on recency and referring loosely to the contemporary age and/or worldviews typically associated with it. 2. **(modern age)** A notion of the present age in terms of a historical rupture with a preceding period. Historically, a conceptualization of the period beginning with the Renaissance and the Reformation in the 15th and 16th centuries, in a periodization of history into ancient, medieval, and modern: a framing which is, however, wholly *Eurocentric. In most current accounts, the no-less Eurocentric concept of a historical epoch inaugurated by the *Enlightenment: markedly anti-traditional (looking to the future rather than the past) and associated with subsequent processes of secularization, the rise of capitalism, urbanization, industrialization, *rationalization, bureaucratization, and the consolidation of the nation-state. Broader conceptions also associate it with the deeper-rooted growth of individualism. Some theorists argue that we have not left modernity but are in **late modernity** (e.g. Giddens); others that we have dwelt in an era of *postmodernity since around 1945, in which case, modernity is the recent past. *See also* MODERNISM. 3. (sociology) A distinction from traditional, pre-industrial societies, modern societies being seen as more fragmented and less homogeneous: *see also* FRAGMENTATION; MODERNIZATION. 4. Technologically, an era of *new media of mass and interpersonal communication, and new modes of transport, available on a mass scale. For McLuhan, the 'electric age' typified by film, television, and the computer.

modernization The processes of becoming modern: primarily the economic, technological, social, institutional, and *ideological changes associated with urbanization, industrialization, *rationalization, and bureaucratization leading to new forms of society in the late 19th and 20th centuries. In sociology, modernization was associated by Durkheim with social differentiation, by the German sociologist Ferdinand Tönnies (1855–1936) with individualization, by Weber with rationalization, by Simmel with *impersonal relations, by Marx with *commodification, by Parsons with structural differentiation, and by the American economist W. W. Rostow (1916–2003) with *mass consumption. It is also closely associated with the growth of *literacy and with social and geographical mobility. *Mass communication and the diffusion of *new media of *interpersonal communication are an integral part of modernization, allowing for decreasing dependence on *face-to-face interaction (*see also* INDIRECT RELATIONSHIPS).

Functionalist sociologists stress the change in *values from traditional societies towards those favouring economic growth (**modernization theory**; *see also* FUNCTIONALISM). Such theories have been widely criticized as based on a Western capitalist model of development (*see also* DEPENDENCY THEORY).

mogul *See* MEDIA MOGUL; MOVIE MOGUL.

monist *See* MOULD THEORY.

monitoring *See* HIGH AND LOW INVOLVEMENT.

monocausal relationship *See* CAUSATION.

monocular cues *See* PICTORIAL DEPTH CUES.

monocular parallax *See* MOTION PARALLAX.

monologic *See* DIALOGIC.

monopoly The situation where one company controls all or a substantial majority of a market. In the UK, the BBC enjoyed a government-enforced monopoly on broadcasting until 1955. *Compare* COMPETITION.

montage [French *monter* 'to assemble'] 1. Most broadly, in European film-making, a synonym for *editing. The process of editing *shots into a *sequence and/or the editing of sequences into the form of a complete film. In *film theory it is distinguished from *mise-en-scène and is regarded as specific to the filmic medium. 2. The use of many short shots to portray action or a sequence of shots representing a condensed series of *events. 3. (**montage editing**) Any film-editing style that represents a contrast to *continuity editing. 4. (**montage sequence**) Any striking sequence of images in a film in which the meaning depends primarily on their *juxtaposition: e.g. the sequence of photographic stills in Pakula's *The Parallax View* (1974). 5. **Soviet** or **thematic montage**: *see* DIALECTICAL MONTAGE. 6. In art and design, an assemblage of cut-out images affixed to a flat surface, typically overlapping. **Collage** is a related form but the cut-outs are not necessarily representational. 7. **Photographic montage**: *see* PHOTOMONTAGE.

MOO *See* MUD OBJECT-ORIENTED.

moral panic (sociology) A social process beginning with the exaggerated *representation in the *mass media of isolated acts of deviant social behaviour (such as mugging, football hooliganism, vandalism, joy-riding, drug abuse, road rage, and child abuse) as a major social crisis of epidemic proportions. The media's sustained coverage of such incidents as a coherent 'story' reflects the use of *sensationalism in the interests of expanding *readerships and *audiences. The *salience of the media coverage (*compare* CULTIVATION THEORY) triggers an over-reaction by *institutions and authorities to counteract the perceived threat, which then tends to circulate role models inspiring those seeking notoriety, stimulating an '*amplification of deviance spiral'. In this framework, deviance is socially constructed. Some argue that governments encourage such scenarios since acting against a common threat can mobilize political support and distract attention from underlying problems. *See also* FOLK DEVILS; LABELLING THEORY; PRIMARY AND SECONDARY DEFINERS.

morpheme A meaningful linguistic unit which cannot be divided into smaller meaningful units (though they are reducible to *phonemes). This may be a complete, irreducible word or any separable component of a word (e.g. a prefix or suffix). *See also* ARTICULATION.

morphology 1. (*linguistics) The study of the internal structure of words: *see also* MORPHEME; *compare* SYNTAX. 2. More generally, the study of the forms of things, as in Propp's *Morphology of the Folktale* (1928): *see also* NARRATOLOGY.

Morse code An early form of electronic communication invented by the American Samuel Morse (1791–1872), in which coded messages were sent along wires in the form of electric pulses which were tapped out letter by letter as a series of tones having two distinct durations, known as dots and dashes.

motif In aesthetic and literary theory, any distinctive recurrent element either within an artwork or *genre, or in the *oeuvre* of an individual. In the case of an internal motif, this performs a unifying function; within a genre, it reflects its *iconography; in the work of an individual, it is *indexical of their *style. Repetition leads a motif to acquire a '*symbolic' significance. Most broadly, motifs may include a *theme, *subject, idea, concept, or device. Visual motifs include images, patterns, figures, forms, objects, shapes, and *colours. Verbal motifs include recurring words, phrases, and poetic images. Narrative motifs include stock characters, situations, incidents, and formulas associated with a genre (*see also* NARRATOLOGY). Filmic motifs include distinctive filmic techniques, such as the use of bullet time in *The Matrix* (1999). Musical motifs (usually called **leitmotifs**) are recurrent musical phrases or variations on a musical theme.

motion blur 1. (photography) Any movement that occurs between the opening and the closing of the camera shutter which results in a blurring of the image. 2. A digital effect added to images to give the impression that they are moving at speed.

motion capture (mocap, performance capture) In digital film and video, a means of recording an actor's movements and *facial expressions so that they can be mapped onto a computer-generated character. An actor performs in the role of the character while wearing a leotard covered in motion detecting sensors. This is how Gollum was created in *The Two Towers* (2001). *Compare* ROTOSCOPE.

motion illusions *See* APPARENT MOTION.

motion parallax (monocular parallax, movement parallax) A monocular cue of visual *depth perception, in which, as the observer moves, nearby objects seem to move rapidly while distant objects appear to move slowly. This is readily observable when looking at the passing scene as one travels on a train.

motion picture *See* FILM.

motivated cut (motivated shot) A *cut to a *shot which can be inferred to be causally related either to the preceding shot or to others in a *sequence: for example, if in the first shot we see a character look out of *frame, and in the second we see a moving car, we can infer that the character is looking at the car. *See also* CAUSATION; CONTINUITY EDITING; *compare* UNMOTIVATED CUT.

motivation 1. The physio-mental forces hypothesized to direct individual behaviour (either those of real individuals or those inferred from depictions of fictional characters). This includes *intrinsic* motivation deriving from the individual (e.g. drives, needs, goals, and desires) and *extrinsic* motivation deriving from external factors (e.g. incentives and sanctions). Motivations for media use are frequently referred to as *uses and gratifications. In *market research contexts, Dichter is referred to as the 'father of motivation'. *See also* CONSUMER BEHAVIOUR; MASLOW'S HIERARCHY OF NEEDS. 2. (**vocabularies of motive**) (sociology) For Mills, the ways in which social actors justify their actions to *significant others in particular social *contexts: *see also* DRAMATURGY; ETHNOMETHODOLOGY; SYMBOLIC INTERACTIONISM. 3. (*semiotics) The extent to which the *signified determines the *signifier: a term used by Saussure, often contrasted with **constraint**. The more a signifier is constrained by the signified, the more 'motivated' the sign is: *iconic signs are highly motivated; *symbolic signs are unmotivated. The less motivated the sign, the more learning of an agreed *code is required.

mould theory The idea that language *moulds* thought rather than simply expressing it. According to the *Sapir-Whorf hypothesis, *content is bound up with linguistic *form, and the use of the *medium contributes to shaping the *meaning. In common usage, we often talk of different verbal formulations 'meaning the same thing', but for those of a Whorfian persuasion, such as Fish, 'it is impossible to mean the same thing in two (or more) different ways' (at least in literary contexts). Reformulating something transforms the ways in which meanings may be made with it, and in this sense, form and content are inseparable. From this so-called **monist** stance words are not merely the 'dress' of thought as they are in *cloak theory. *See also* LINGUISTIC DETERMINISM.

movable type A *printing system based on the use of separate elements to reproduce the individual symbols on a page. This technique was pioneered in China using ceramic pieces in the 11th century; the first movable metal type was produced in Korea in the 13th century, where the first book using this method was printed in 1377. In Europe at this time, wood block printing had only just begun. Around 1450 Gutenberg created his own printing system, using a hand-operated printing press and metal movable type which could produce far more copies than woodblocks, with less deterioration. The use of movable metal type was also a much quicker method than the earlier use of a woodblock for each page. The relatively limited number of Western alphabetical letters made movable type more practicable than it was with thousands of Chinese characters. The Gutenberg Bible of 1455 was one of the first books printed using the new system, and printing subsequently spread rapidly across Europe. Gutenberg's printing system is widely regarded as the most important invention of the second millennium.

(⊕) SEE WEB LINKS
• The Gutenberg Bible

movement parallax *See* MOTION PARALLAX.

movie *See* FILM.

movie mogul The owner of a major film studio, e.g. the American film producer Samuel Goldwyn (1879–1974).

mp3 A *compression format, used to encode digital audio *files, which is claimed to be comparable to CD-quality audio. *See* COMPACT DISC.

MPEG2 (Motion Pictures Expert Group) The digital transmission standard in the UK, USA, Canada, and Australia that can accommodate the characteristics of both *PAL and *NTSC (using H264 compression). The Republic of Ireland uses MPEG4.

MS *See* MEDIUM SHOT; MID-SHOT.

MTV (music television) A cable or satellite television channel and proprietary brand targeting the youth market. It began in the 1980s showing pop music videos interspersed with commercials and either video disc jockeys (VJs) or *idents and *stings. The *channel branding featured a fast *editing style known as **MTV cutting**.

MUD (multi-user domain or **dungeon)** A text-based online *virtual world in which multiple users are connected at the same time to a server (or an array of servers) accessed over the *internet via a client program. MUDs are used for *role play *games and online collaboration.

(⊕) SEE WEB LINKS
• Mudding history and subcultures

MUD object-oriented (MOO, tiny MOO) A *MUD server enhanced with object-oriented programming language, where users can create code to add their own *content—which changes the environment for everyone else.

(⊕) SEE WEB LINKS
• *My Tiny Life*: Julian Dibbell

multi-accentuality The openness of words to more than one *interpretation. A notion advanced by Voloshinov and/or Bakhtin in 1929 in response to the alleged fixity of meaning in Saussure's conception of language. Verbal meanings are subject to historical changes and are a *site of struggle between different social groups in particular sociohistorical *contexts (e.g. in relation to 'black' or 'queer'). Language is never neutral. 'Whenever a sign is present, ideology is present, too.' Dominant groups seek to fix meanings: they seek to decide what constitutes 'extremism', for instance. *Compare* POLYSEMY.

multicamera (multiple-camera) A scene simultaneously photographed by more than one camera. This technique is used extensively in television for filming quiz shows or concerts where the multiple camera *footage is vision-mixed together to produce a main recording along with various other recordings known as 'isos' featuring footage from one or several 'isolated' cameras.

multiculturalism *See* PLURALISM.

multimedia Digital technologies combining various media: for example, video with audio and text options; a buzzword of the 1980s and 1990s when *convergence technologies were a novelty and dedicated media devices such as televisions, radios, and books were the norm. *Compare* MULTIMODALITY.

multimodality (*adj.* **multimodal)** The use of more than one *semiotic mode in meaning-making, communication, and *representation generally, or in a specific situation. Such modes include all forms of verbal, nonverbal, and contextual communication. **Multimodal literacy** refers to awareness and effective use of this range of modalities.

multiplayer A *videogame or videogame option that involves multiple participants, typically using the *internet. *See also* MMOG.

multiple determination *See* OVERDETERMINATION.

multiplexing *See* DIGITAL TRANSMISSION.

multiskilling *See* BI-MEDIA JOURNALISM.

music and effects *See* M&E.

mutual gaze *See* EYE CONTACT.

MUVE (Multi-User Virtual Environment) A persistent two- or three-dimensional graphical *virtual world in which multiple users participate as *avatars. It lacks the goal-orientated structure of a *videogame but retains a *role-playing element: examples include *The Sims Online* and *Second Life*.

myth [Greek *mythos* 'story'] **1.** In popular usage, a widespread belief which is untrue, distorted, *stereotypical, or romanticized, as in 'the myth of the American West'. **2.** (anthropology) A culture-specific allegorical tale or fable accounting for a natural, supernatural, or sociocultural phenomenon, having sacred status in traditional societies. **3.** (*functionalism) Any widespread *narrative encoding cultural *norms and serving to maintain social *cohesion. **4.** (*psychoanalytic theory) *Narratives and dreams reflecting, for Freud, universal psychic conflict (*repression, incest taboo, sibling rivalry, Oedipus complex), and for Jung, *archetypes arising from the 'collective unconscious'. **5.** In the *structuralist anthropology of Lévi-Strauss, a narrative functioning to resolve *contradictions within a culture. He sought to identify universal logical structures underlying these, based on *binary oppositions (e.g. nature/culture, raw/cooked, male/female, good/evil, left/right). In *marketing contexts, this concept has also been applied in *semiotic approaches to *branding. **6.** In the semiotic cultural theory of Barthes, an *ideological form which serves to naturalize major concepts underpinning a worldview within a culture (*see* NATURALIZATION). Myth is seen as a *metalanguage built upon the *orders of signification called *denotation and *connotation and operating within a culture through *codes. An image denoting 'a child' in a context which generates the connotation of innocence would feed into a myth of childhood which functions ideologically to justify dominant assumptions about the status of children in society. *See also* IDEOLOGICAL ANALYSIS.

N

nachträglichkeit *See* DEFERRED ACTION.

naïve realism *See* COMMON SENSE.

narcotization A hypothesized dysfunction of the *mass media (*see also* MEDIA FUNCTIONS) in which mediated *information overload could lead to less social action, superficial involvement, and political apathy. The term 'narcotizing dysfunction' was introduced by Lazarsfeld and Merton in 1948. Subsequent research did not support this hypothesis. The metaphor is often used polemically to allude to television as a drug dulling the critical faculties. *See also* DIVERSION FUNCTION.

narration 1. **(narrating)** Story-telling, or the communicative act or process of relating a sequence of *events or giving an account of a situation, as distinguished from either the *narrative which it produces or from the story. 2. **(narrative)** The way in which a story is told; the strategies used to tell a story (*see also* DISCLOSURE; OBJECTIVE NARRATION; POINT OF VIEW). In relation to *narrative film, Bordwell stresses the *spectator's role (*see also* COGNITIVE FILM THEORY), narration consists of 'the organization of a set of cues for the construction of a story'. 3. A synonym for *narrative form. In modern rhetoric, *discourse that is intended to relate an *event or sequence of events to an audience. One of the four rhetorical modes of discourse identified by Brooks and Warren as fulfilling basic human *communicative purposes. *Compare* ARGUMENT; DESCRIPTION; EXPOSITION. 4. In a story, any element taken to directly represent the voice or thoughts of the *narrator as distinct from other kinds of discourse within the text, such as dialogue. Telling as opposed to showing.

narrative 1. *adj.* Loosely, having the form of a story, as in *narrative film (*see also* NARRATIVITY). The **narrative paradigm** is that narrative is a fundamental way of making sense of experiences. *See also* GRAND NARRATIVES. 2. *n.* Most broadly, a story in any medium: a *representation of a causal or associative 'chain' of real or fictional *events, even without a *narrator—especially a series of related events between which connections are made and which has a recognizable pattern including a beginning, a middle, and an end (*see also* CLASSICAL NARRATIVE STRUCTURE). In the orderly Aristotelian narrative form, causation and goals turn *story (chronological *events: *see also* FABULA) into *plot: events at the beginning cause those in the middle, and events in the middle cause those at the end. The structural study of narratives is termed *narratology. 3. *n.* Conventionally, a story narrated by someone. Narratives are traditionally associated with novels and short stories, but they also include *factual forms such as biography, history, and news reports. The American literary theorist Gerald Prince (b.1942) argues that dramatic performances are *not* narratives, because they are enacted rather than recounted (Plato's distinction between *mimesis and *diegesis). **4.** *n.* A story embodying a *point of view reflecting an actual or implied *narrator. Film theorists have argued that, even if it lacks a narrator, *narrative film involves a form of *narration. Narrative discourse involves not only a story or plot but also narrative devices such as *point of view and *disclosure. **5.** *n.* Sometimes a synonym for *narration.

narrative analysis *See* NARRATOLOGY.

narrative closure **1.** A clear outcome in a *narrative (e.g. the murderer identified, the male lead married to the female lead). **2.** Having a definite and final ending: that which defines a closed narrative form: as opposed to the structural openness of a *soap opera, for instance: *see also* CLOSED FORMS. **3.** The final part of the resolution or dénouement in the structure of a narrative: *see also* CLASSICAL NARRATIVE STRUCTURE. **4.** *Ideological *closure in a narrative as reflected in authorial attempts to govern the *interpretation of *events.

narrative codes **1.** Organizational frameworks for the structural analysis of patterns of *form or *content in *narratives, and from which such narratives are woven: *see also* NARRATOLOGY. **2.** Any of five unifying codes or 'voices' to which, according to Barthes, all of the textual *signifiers in a (*realist) narrative can be analytically assigned as a kind of interpretive network: the *cultural code, the *hermeneutic code, the *proiaretic code, the *semic code, and the *symbolic code.

narrative film (fiction film, feature film) Any film that tells a story, especially those which emphasize the story line and are dramatic.

narrative flow (flow) (*film theory) The continuity of narrative *action* which is interrupted by *spectacle.

narrative grammar A system of formulas underlying the structure of stories. Propp sought to identify a universal grammar of *narrative based on traditional Russian folk tales. *See also* NARRATOLOGY; *compare* STORY GRAMMAR.

narrative structure *See* CLASSICAL NARRATIVE STRUCTURE.

narrative theory *See* NARRATOLOGY.

narrativity *n.* The distinctive quality or features attributed to **narrative forms**.

narratology (narrative theory, narrative analysis) The formal analysis of the structure of *narratives in any medium: a *metalanguage applying a linguistic model and focusing on minimal narrative units (*functions), recurrent *motifs and *roles, and the 'grammar of the plot' (*see* NARRATIVE GRAMMAR). It derives from both *formalism (e.g. Propp) and *structuralism—e.g. Barthes, Greimas, Genette, and the Franco-Bulgarian philosopher Tzvetan Todorov (b.1939). A key influence was that of Lévi-Strauss's structuralist analysis of *myths. *Poststructuralism involves a rejection of the possibility of such a *universal grammar, and various theorists have emphasized the interpretive role of the reader. *See also* FABULA; NARRATIVE CODES.

narrator 1. A person telling a story (*fiction or non-fiction), overtly or covertly: *compare* IMPLIED AUTHOR. 2. In literary fiction, the 'voice' of someone telling the story, which may be the author, an authorial *persona, or a character. The choice is directly related to *point of view. A *third-person point of view is often that of an **omniscient narrator** and tends to connote the authorial voice (*see also* OMNISCIENT POINT OF VIEW). A *first-person point of view is that of a character: often the *hero or heroine. Such narrators may be **obtrusive** or **self-effacing**. 3. In *documentary and educational films, the person delivering a commentary and explanation of *events depicted onscreen: usually presumed to be neutral but well-informed. 4. In *narrative films, a role that is usually only implicit (such narratives often seeming to tell themselves); occasionally overt in an extradiegetic *voiceover—usually as one of the characters.

narrowcast codes The *conventions and frameworks employed in communication aimed at a limited audience. Compared to *broadcast codes they are structurally more complex, less repetitive and predictable, and tend to be more subtle and original. Following Bernstein, Fiske also refers to these as *elaborated codes. Such *codes are not universally shared within a *culture (though they may be widely shared within a *subculture), and in contexts such as *advertising they may be employed in order to reach a particular *target audience.

narrowcasting Special interest programming designed for *niche audiences or for well-educated audiences. *See also* DEMASSIFIED MEDIA; NARROWCAST CODES; *compare* BROADCASTING.

narrowcast media *See* DEMASSIFIED MEDIA.

national identity The public image of an *imagined community (Weber called it a 'community of sentiment'), projecting an illusion of unity reflected symbolically in a flag, a national anthem, and distinctive rituals, and culturally represented in *discourse primarily via historical mythologies and a popular cultural *canon (including *iconic images), narratively constructed and transmitted by social *institutions, in particular the educational system (*see also* CULTURAL LITERACY) and the *mass media (notably in national *news and in *media events). Such *essentialist *representations seek to elicit individual *identification with (and discursive reproduction of) a supposedly shared *identity which claims to transcend other dimensions of identity such as *class and *ethnicity.

National Television Standards Committee *See* NTSC.

natural attitude In the *phenomenological sociology of Schutz, our routine frame of mind in the 'taken-for granted world of *everyday life' where we bracket out the *critical attitude, suspending any philosophical doubts about reality. Synonymous with his phrases 'common-sense thinking' and 'the attitude of everyday life'. The concept originated with Husserl. *See also* COMMON SENSE; PHENOMENOLOGY.

naturalism 1. (*adj.* **naturalistic**) In art and literature, a theory of *representation and a *style based on the detailed depiction or *description of the observable *appearance of things with clinical accuracy and *objectivity and without distortion or stylization. Associated with the artistic goal of mirroring reality and sometimes seen as a form of *illusionism (*see also* MIMESIS). Some see it as a *reductionist form of aesthetic *realism which offers superficial representations of the appearance of things (**verisimilitude**) rather than a deeper, more profound understanding of their nature. Non-naturalistic texts react against naturalistic conventions: for instance, by using the *alienation effect. Regarding TV drama, the British dramatist Dennis Potter (1935–94) declared: 'I don't want to show life exactly as it is. I hope to show a little of what life is about.' 2. **Photographic naturalism (photo-realism)**: the dominant contemporary form of visual naturalism for which *modality judgements tend to be based on standards derived from 35-mm colour photography: *see also* PHOTO-REALISM. 3. For Williams, the *representation of people in their real social environments. 4. The *representation of the role of the 'natural forces' of heredity and environment in shaping the behaviour of characters, as in the novels of Zola which detail the sordid reality of working-class life in the 19th century. 5. In loose usage, a synonym for aesthetic *realism. 6. (**methodological naturalism**) The stance that research in the social sciences should apply scientific methods (e.g. *hypothesis testing) in order to establish generalizable laws about social behaviour—in contrast to interpretive and contextual approaches.

⊕ SEE WEB LINKS

• Naturalism in art

naturalization (naturalizing) The process by which culturally-specific worldviews which are constructed sociohistorically come to be phenomenally experienced by those within a *culture as natural, normal, self-evident *common sense, and are thus taken for granted as universal and immutable, as in the naturalization of *difference (e.g. in *gender essentialism). *Codes which have been naturalized are those which are so widely distributed in a culture and which are learned at such an early age that they appear not to be constructed (*see also* CONSTRUCTEDNESS; TRANSPARENCY). *Myths serve the *ideological function of naturalization—making the cultural seem natural. In Marxist theory, naturalization serves to maintain the ideological *hegemony of the dominant *class (*see also* DOMINANT IDEOLOGY). *Compare* DENATURALIZATION.

natural signs *See* CONVENTIONALITY.

natural sound (actual sound, sound off tape, SOT) In film and video, the audio that is present at the scene and that has been recorded along with the pictures. In contrast to **overdubbed** audio where natural sound is augmented or replaced with other audio in *post-production. *See also* ADR; FOLEY; MIX.

necessary condition In relation to *causation, an essential prerequisite for a specified *effect to occur. It may or may not also be a *sufficient condition. *See also* DETERMINISM.

needs *See* MASLOW'S HIERARCHY OF NEEDS.

negative appeals (*advertising) A persuasive strategy that plays upon the consumer's anxieties and stresses what they would lose by not purchasing the product or service. *See also* ADVERTISING APPEALS; FEAR APPEALS; GUILT APPEALS; *compare* POSITIVE APPEALS.

negotiated reading Within Stuart Hall's *encoding/decoding model, the *interpretation of a *mass media *text by a *decoder who partly shares its *code and broadly accepts the *preferred reading, but sometimes resists and modifies it in a way which reflects their own social position, experiences and interests (local and personal conditions may be seen as exceptions to the general rule)—this position involves *contradictions. *Compare* HEGEMONIC READING; OPPOSITIONAL READING.

neocolonialism *See* POSTCOLONIALISM.

neoformalist film theory An approach to the aesthetic analysis of film based on the work of the Russian *formalists and associated with Kristin Thompson (b.1950), an American film theorist. Neoformalism rejects models of art as *communication, seen (reductively) in terms of *messages passed between *senders and *receivers. Rather, artworks produce pleasure through *defamiliarization that challenges the *spectator's habitual *perceptions of the world. There is no pre-existing method of neoformal analysis: spectators go through certain procedures in understanding films and the ways in which they relate to society. The analysis always involves careful viewing and a constant modification of the two-way interchange between that which the spectator brings to the film and the film's structures as experienced by them. Critics note that this approach focuses on formal and stylistic considerations at the expense of broader cultural, ideological, and institutional issues. *See also* COGNITIVE FILM THEORY.

neo-Marxism *See* MARXIST THEORY.

neophilia A fondness for, or obsession with, novelty and change (exhibited by **neophiles** or **neophiliacs**). It has been suggested that this may be a personality trait. The opposite is **neophobia**. *Compare* TECHNOPHILIA.

net *See* INTERNET.

netiquette A portmanteau word (*net* + *etiquette*). A set of rules governing acceptable behaviour for participants in *chatrooms and other online forums.

network Broadly, an interconnected group of people or objects. *See also* CABLE NETWORK; COMPUTER NETWORKS; DISTRIBUTION; INTERNET; SOCIAL NETWORKS; TELEVISION NETWORK.

network analysis In anthropology, sociology, and political science, a systematic approach analysing interrelation, interdependency, and *interaction within social systems and a theoretical framework for understanding behaviour. Its primary focus is on who is linked to whom, by what forms of linkage, and the behavioural influence of such links. An emphasis on dynamic and *asymmetrical relationships arose in the 1950s as a reaction against the institutional focus of structural *functionalism. *See also* COMMUNICATION NETWORK; CONVERGENCE MODEL; DIFFUSION; RECIPROCITY; SOCIAL NETWORKS; SOCIOGRAM.

network graph *See* SOCIOGRAM.

network society (networked society) An emerging form of society where new *communications technologies have enabled social relationships to form that are no longer geographically bounded. Castells sees networks as being composed of a series of *information nodes, consisting of both organizations and individuals that challenge traditional notions of governance since they cut across or bypass the established organizational structures of civil society. *See also* DISEMBEDDING; GLOBALIZATION; SOCIAL NETWORKS; SPACE OF FLOWS.

⊕ SEE WEB LINKS
• The network society: interview with Manuel Castells

neutrality 1. A journalistic ideal of not taking sides or expressing a personal opinion: *see* BIAS; OBJECTIVITY. 2. **Technological neutrality**: an *instrumentalist notion reflected in the saying that 'a poor worker blames the tools'. However, to theorists such as McLuhan the *medium is not 'neutral' (*see* MCLUHANISM). Each medium or tool has its own *affordances, *biases, and cultural *connotations. In semiotic terms, the *signified may be altered by a change of the medium used for the *sign vehicle: *materiality matters.

New Criticism *See* FORMALISM.

New Historicism *See* CULTURAL MATERIALISM.

new media An umbrella term that first emerged in the 1980s loosely referring to computer-based media. The term applies to a wide range of phenomena and practices: new kinds of textual forms and *entertainment pleasures (*videogames, the *internet, *virtual worlds); new patterns of media *consumption (*convergence, *hypertext, *sit forward and sit back); new ways of representing the world (*blogs, *digitalization, *photoshopping), the self (*avatar, personal homepage), and community (*bulletin boards, *chatrooms, *social networking); new relationships between media producers and consumers (*file sharing, gift economy, *participatory culture, *user-generated content), and new *phenomenological experiences (embodiment, immersion, *presence). New media tend to blur the distinction between *interpersonal and *mass communication (*desktop publishing, *narrowcasting, *public and private spheres); theorists are still debating whether the *mobile phone is a mass medium. The term is regarded as problematic by many because of the ideological implication that 'new' equals 'better' which is *ahistorical because it obscures the fact that all media are new when they are first introduced. However, the term is favoured by others precisely because of its vagueness, as it avoids the *essentialist arguments implicit when the focus is on *ontological form as in the *digital verses *analogue debates, or the promotion of a controversial single key feature such as *interactivity, or a technological framing of the issues as in *computer-mediated communication. Despite a wide consensus about the term's shortcomings, its continued use indicates that there is still an unresolved debate about the nature and impact of new *communication technologies.

(((⊕))) SEE WEB LINKS

- Jon Snow on 'new media'

news In the *mass media, formal reports of *events considered likely to be significant to the *target audience which are normally broadcast or published soon after information about them becomes available. As a *genre in any medium, news is generally expected to be referential and *informational communication reported accurately and without *bias. Nevertheless, certain sectors of news journalism are regularly accused of bias (for instance, right-wing bias in certain *newspapers or on Fox News), and national news outlets invariably adopt a nationalistic stance when the nation is involved in international conflict. *Selective representation is unavoidable, and based on *framing (*see* NEWS FRAMES). Like any form of *representation, news 'manufactures' particular versions of reality rather than being a 'window on the world'. Some sociological research presents news as the product of newsroom routines and as filtered through *gatekeepers. From the journalistic perspective, the selection of items and the prominence and time or space devoted to them is related to inherent *newsworthiness; however, selection is determined by *news values. Some argue that the media are secondary definers, reproducing in news coverage the *ideological *framings of primary definers or dominant groups through their reliance on authoritative sources (*see* PRIMARY AND SECONDARY DEFINERS). Powerful interest groups do seek to influence the agenda when their interests are at stake (*see also* AGENDA SETTING; GLASGOW MEDIA GROUP; MANUFACTURE OF CONSENT). However, audiences are also selective: it was primarily in relation to television news that Stuart Hall developed the concepts of *hegemonic, *negotiated, and *oppositional readings. Although news has always involved turning *events into stories, critics note that commercial pressures lead to an increasing tendency for news to adopt *fiction values, including the newsreader as celebrity (*see also* STORY MODEL; TABLOIDIZATION). More subtly, the genre has been seen as *stereotypically masculine (*see also* INFORMATIONAL COMMUNICATION).

(((⊕))) SEE WEB LINKS

- News media by country

news agency (agency) Any of the organizations such as Reuters, Associated Press, and the Press Association that supply news items and *footage to the world's press, radio, and television, and also news updates for general audiences on the *internet. Critics have argued that news circulated by these agencies is framed within Western perspectives.

news feed Material sent to the headquarters of a news organization from a reporter in the field or from news agencies. *See also* RSS.

news frames The *formats, categories (*see* CATEGORIZATION), and criteria (*see* NEWS VALUES) acting as selective filters, formal *contexts, and modes of informational organization in the reporting of current *events. The *genre itself is framed as *factual (though *fiction values play a part); *see also* STORY MODEL. News coverage by national media is generally framed with reference to categories such as politics, the economy, foreign affairs, domestic affairs, and sport. Within such categories, some events are framed as more *newsworthy than others, as reflected in the time or space devoted to them, and in their ordering. Items may also be informally framed as '*hard news' (with masculine *connotations), or as '*human-interest' stories. In terms of *form rather than content, in television news, newsreaders are accorded a privileged status granted to few others, by virtue of their use of *direct address; this connotes authority. *See also* AGENDA SETTING; FRAMING.

newsgroups (User Network, USENET) A system, first developed in 1979, involving thousands of topic-centred *internet *bulletin boards where people *post and/or reply to messages. *See also* VIRTUAL COMMUNITY.

newsletters *See* ELECTRONIC MAILING LISTS.

newspapers Publications including news, articles, and advertisements, usually issued daily or weekly in printed form, but including web-based versions. In Britain, the first 'news papers' appeared in the 16th century, and the first regular English daily newspaper was the *Daily Courant*, established in 1702. For **newspaper formats,** *see* BERLINER FORMAT; BROADSHEET; TABLOID. *See also* MIDDLE-MARKET NEWSPAPERS.

((⊕)) SEE WEB LINKS
• British Newspapers Online

news values The informal journalistic criteria adopted in the editorial selection, prioritization, and presentation of *events: implicit principles underlying the assessment of *newsworthiness. Drawing on the psychology of *perception, in 1965 Galtung and Ruge proposed eight hypothetical factors likely to influence the selection of reported events in any culture. Such events: match the timescale of the news schedule (unlike long-term trends); are sufficiently consequential to grab the headlines; are open to a clear *interpretation rather than ambiguous; are culturally meaningful; are consonant with normal *expectations; are unanticipated and/or rare; are a continuation of an existing news story; and/or fill a gap in the pattern of news covered. They also suggested four culture-bound factors: events were more likely to become news if they involved elite nations, elite people, a focus on individuals, and/or negative consequences. Journalistic selectivity is not deliberate *bias, but Stuart Hall argues that news values, learned from *socialization into newsroom routines, tend to favour the *status quo. *See also* OBJECTIVITY.

newsworthiness The reportability of an *event by journalists, often unreflexively assumed to be a property inherent in such events or news stories but which is dependent on *news values. Stuart Hall argues that, over time, news actually creates the consensus knowledge by which reporters and the general public recognize newsworthiness.

niche audience A specific *target audience, as opposed to a *mass audience. *See also* NARROWCASTING.

niche market A relatively small market for a specialized product or service, such as a specific demographic group; as opposed to a *mass market. *See also* SEGMENTATION.

noddies (noddy shots UK; nodders US) In television *interviews filmed with one camera, contrived *reaction shots (usually filmed immediately after the interview) that show the interviewer listening or nodding in agreement. *See* CUTAWAY; OVER-THE-SHOULDER SHOT.

nodding *See* HEAD NOD.

node *See* COMMUNICATION NETWORK.

noise 1. In *Shannon and Weaver's model of communication, any unintended changes to the transmitted *signal. This includes distortions of sound or images, radio static, and transmission errors. However, Galtung and Ruge point out that (as with *figure and ground) what is signal and what is noise is not inherent. 2. In *analogue audio, high frequency tape hiss which is an *artefact of the recording process.

noise reduction 1. In analogue audio, a *technology that compressed the recorded *signal before it was laid onto tape and then expanded it again on playback, pushing the high frequency tape hiss beyond the range of human hearing. 2. In digital imaging software, a filter that removes speckles and grain from an image.

nomadic audiences 1. (*cultural studies) A conceptualization of media reception relating to shifting and discontinuous practices rather than to a specific *medium or *genre: a compression of the concept of 'dispersed audiences and nomadic subjects' developed by the American theorist Janice Radway (b.1949). 2. Media users who practise *grazing. 3. Roaming new media users accessing media content in multiple locations using *mobile communication.

nomenclaturism *See* REDUCTIONISM.

non-fiction Prose writing that is *factual or *informational. *Compare* FICTION.

nonlinear editing Computerized film or video *editing systems that manipulate *footage in the form of *data and which involve cutting, adding, and rearranging shots and sequences graphically represented on a *timeline. Traditional film editing is nonlinear because a *shot can be 'spliced' into a sequence by displacing existing material and lengthening its overall duration. However, the term only became widely used in the 1980s, when computerized editing systems started to challenge the dominance of machine-to-machine editing systems used in television and video. *Compare* LINEAR EDITING.

non-programme material (NPM) 1. *Commercials, programme and channel promotional content (such as *teasers and *idents), and public service announcements. The amount of NPM per hour is regulated in most countries and the relative proportions of programme and non-programme material are an issue for consumer *watchdogs. *See also* CLUTTER. 2. Materials generated in a television or radio production but not broadcast, e.g. *rushes and *stock shots.

nonverbal behaviour All bodily acts other than the use of verbal language including, but also often equated with, *nonverbal communication, though sometimes distinguished from this as *unintentional communication (which others include within NVC). Some critics who argue that not all human behaviour is communicative accept that *inferences may be drawn from unencoded acts but suggest that for behaviour to be classed as communicative there must be some degree of shared understanding between those involved (*see also* CODES).

(((⊕))) SEE WEB LINKS

• Nonverbal behaviour

nonverbal bias 1. In *person perception, positive or negative *evaluation influenced by a person's *body language, personal *appearance, or mode of dress. 2. Body language signifying a positive or negative evaluation of someone. For instance, research studies have shown that television *anchors can unconsciously exhibit nonverbal cues reflecting their differential evaluation of political figures, and that such reactions can influence viewers.

nonverbal communication (NVC) 1. Any form of communication other than verbal language (*compare* NONVERBAL BEHAVIOUR). This term can imply that it has a secondary place to verbal communication (*see* LOGOCENTRISM), whereas we communicate more through NVC than through verbal language, mostly without conscious intention. Sometimes it confusingly includes both 'body language' and other nonverbal communication—notably *visual communication (the term *nonverbal behaviour avoids this confusion). It can also include interpersonal *context factors which contribute to meaning-making. 2. **(bodily communication, *body language)** Communication involving bodily *cues (whether intentional or not). Argyle lists eight different nonverbal channels: *facial expression, *gaze, *gesture, *posture, touch, bodily contact, spatial behaviour (*see* PROXEMICS), *appearance, and voice. Popular usage tends to exclude vocal cues, equating nonverbal with nonvocal, but specialists include nonverbal *vocalizations. NVC is usually divided into: *kinesics, *proxemics, *haptics, and *paralanguage. Argyle argues that the four primary functions of NVC are: expressing *emotion, communicating interpersonal *attitudes (*liking, *dominance etc.), presenting personality, and accompanying speech. 3. The study of this topic as an academic subfield of social psychology; also a key topic within *semiotics. Some scholars insist that *nonverbal behaviour cannot be studied independently of verbal behaviour and prefer to frame their studies within the broader term *communication or the narrower one of *face-to-face interaction.

nonverbal language 1. A synonym for *body language. 2. Any system of communication other than speech or writing: for instance, *sign language or *visual language.

nonverbal modifiers Non-linguistic cues in *interpersonal communication which facilitate the *interpretation of messages and moods. In *face-to-face interaction, these are bodily *cues such as *facial expression, *eye contact, and tone of voice; these are often 'given off' unconsciously. In the relative *cuelessness of textual *interaction (as in *messaging systems or *chatrooms), they are deliberately deployed devices such as *emoticons.

nonverbal persuasion The role of non-linguistic factors in communication in influencing audience *attitudes and/or behaviour. In both *interpersonal and *mass communication this includes *body language, interactional style, personal *appearance, and/or mode of dress. In mass communication texts such as advertisements, it also includes *visual imagery, *symbols, and music (*see also* PERIPHERAL ROUTE). *Compare* VISUAL PERSUASION.

norm 1. Broadly, a general (normal) *expectation regarding some phenomenon as distinct from any **deviation** from this: *see also* MARKEDNESS. 2. Statistically, a measure of central tendency with which particular numerical *values can be compared. 3. *See* SOCIAL NORMS.

normative theories (social science) Ways of framing a social phenomenon (such as communication or the *mass media) based on *norms: such as assumptions, *expectations, or prescriptions concerning functions it ought (or ought not) to fulfil (*see also* COMMUNICATIVE FUNCTIONS; MEDIA FUNCTIONS). In relation to the mass media, for instance, they include different *ideological paradigms concerning the relation of the media to the state, as in the traditional Western liberal *pluralist notion of the *free press (*see also* MARKET MODEL; REGULATION). They are also implicit in popular *attitudes to media use, as in widespread notions (and guilty feelings) that 'too much' TV or 'overuse' of the *internet is anti-social, and they underlie notions of what is publicly acceptable in media content. In relation to *language, normative theories seek to prescribe 'correct' usage, or define language in terms of *norm and deviation (as in *literal versus *figurative language).

NPM *See* NON-PROGRAMME MATERIAL.

NTSC US-originated transmission standard for *analogue colour television with a *resolution of 525 lines and a *frame rate of 30 frames per second. *Compare* PAL.

NVC *See* NONVERBAL COMMUNICATION.

object 1. *n.* In everyday usage, something that can be seen and touched. 2. *n.* (psychology) A person, goal, or thing toward which a feeling, *attitude, or action is directed, as in 'she was the object of his attention'; in the distinction between *subject and object, the subject is active and the object is passive. *See also* OBJECTIFICATION. 3. *n.* (philosophy) Something referred to; sometimes restricted to that which is independent of the thinking *subject and external to the mind. In the *Peircean model of the *sign, the *referent or what the sign 'stands for'. The object divides into the *immediate object* (the particular idea that the sign represents) and the *dynamical object* (the reality indicated by that idea of the sign which only becomes known through experiencing the sign in other contexts). Unlike Saussure's abstract *signified, Peirce's triadic model allocates a place for a physical reality which Saussure's model did not feature (though Peirce was not a naïve *realist, and argued that all experience is mediated by signs). The term can refer to abstract concepts and fictional entities as well as to physical objects. 4. *n.* (traditional grammar) A major structural element in a sentence, representing the receiver or goal of an action, as distinct from the *subject; a noun phrase governed by, and normally following, a transitive verb. 5. *n.* (computing) A single element in an object-oriented programming language. 6. *v.* To indicate disagreement.

object constancy *See* PERCEPTUAL CONSTANCY.

objectification (sexual objectification) The dehumanizing reduction of a person (or in *representation, a depiction of a person) to the status of a thing, an anonymous body, or a fetishized body part (*see also* FETISHISM; FRAGMENTATION). *Feminists argue that **female objectification** is a primary mode of women's subjection: in art, film, literature, and life, they are the traditional *objects of the *gaze for heterosexual male *subjects. In psychological **objectification theory** it is argued that as part of *socialization women develop **self-objectification**: learning to see themselves as men see them. Since the mid 1980s, males have also been increasingly objectified in *mass-media contexts such as *advertising.

objective camerawork *Shots filmed from a *third-person point of view. *See also* OBJECTIVE REPRESENTATION; *compare* SUBJECTIVE CAMERAWORK.

objective correlative 1. (literary theory) An image, or 'a set of objects, a situation, a chain of events' calculated to evoke a particular mood or *emotion. The term was popularized in 1919 by the British-American poet T. S. Eliot (1888–1965). 2. For usage in *advertising, *see* MEANING TRANSFER.

objective narration A *narrative style in which the author is self-effacing, passing no comment on characters or *events, and allowing the story to appear to tell itself. Authorial neutrality, however, is impossible, since, for instance, selectivity is unavoidable. *See also* AESTHETIC DISTANCE; PERSONA; POINT OF VIEW.

objective representation (objective camera or **camerawork)** In *documentary-making, a *realist filming style connoting neutrality, typically with eye-level *shots, location sound, and minimal *editing, relying heavily on the *indexical evidentiality of film. *Compare* SUBJECTIVE INTERPRETATION.

objectivism (philosophy) The concept (associated with scientific *methodology) that there is an external world which is independent of our modes of apprehending it, and that it is possible to eliminate *bias and to describe it accurately in terms of verifiable *facts. A form of *epistemological *realism. Philosophers such as Nietzsche and Foucault reject the possibility of *value-free *facts. Even if it were possible in relation to the investigation of physical reality, sociologists argue that the social world cannot be independent of our mode of apprehending it; indeed, *constructionism is built upon the notion of the social reality as constructed. Cognitive, cultural, and linguistic frameworks mediate human experience and reality (*see also* SAPIR-WHORF HYPOTHESIS). This raises the question of whether social research can ever be 'scientific'; for its critics, this condemns such research to *epistemological *relativism.

objectivity 1. **Methodological objectivity**: making and interpreting verifiable observations about the world without researcher *bias: the goal of scientific research based on *objectivism. In social science, many argue that complete objectivity is impossible: for instance, because all research is selective, because *facts are not independent of *theories, and because human *perception is always coloured by subjective *values (*see also* INTERSUBJECTIVITY; SUBJECTIVITY). Anthropological approaches reject the kind of scientific detachment involved in *experiments (*see also* ETHNOGRAPHY). However, social researchers nevertheless seek to minimize *bias, to make their own *values explicit, and to reflect on their influence. 2. **Journalistic objectivity**: in journalism (particularly in *public-service broadcasting), a professional ideal or *norm in *factual reporting involving the related goals of truthfulness, *impartiality, *neutrality, disinterestedness, and the avoidance of conscious bias or distortion (*see also* BALANCE). Most social scientists note, however, that there can be no 'value-free' point of view and *facts are never free of *ideology. Some (particularly Marxists) argue that in the case of news reporting this tends to be the *dominant ideology (*see also* GLASGOW MEDIA GROUP). Outside public-service broadcasting, critics note a right-wing bias in news reporting, as in Fox TV news as well as many *newspapers (*see also* POLITICAL BIAS). *Constructivists note that in television news the *conventions of *realism also serve to connote objectivity (as if the news were unconstructed and simply a window on the world). Selectivity is unavoidable (*see also* NEWS VALUES). *Feminists argue that journalistic objectivity is a *myth reflecting a male *gender bias, being based on the rationalist Cartesian legacy of a dichotomy between the knower and the known. *See also* CARTESIAN DUALISM; SPHERES OF CONSENSUS, LEGITIMATE CONTROVERSY, AND DEVIANCE. 3. **Documentary objectivity**: in *documentary-making, a rhetoric of observational distance and factuality connoted by *realist codes such as that of *objective representation.

oblique angle See CANTED SHOT.

obscenity A legal category that covers *pornographic or violent material considered to be sufficiently extreme to 'deprave and corrupt'. In the UK, the Obscene Publications Act (1959) makes it a punishable offence to distribute, circulate, sell, hire, lend, or give away such material.

observer bias The influence of a researcher's *frame of reference on their observations and *interpretations; in social research, particularly their *expectations and cultural assumptions. Social researchers seek to be reflexive about their own *values (*see also* REFLEXIVITY), although some critics question whether it is possible to step outside one's own cultural framework (*see also* ETHNOCENTRISM).

occlusion (interposition) An important monocular *depth cue in the *visual perception of the world and a *pictorial depth cue and representational *convention in which one object overlaps another, thus indicating that it is in front and closer than the one it partially occludes.

OCR See OPTICAL CHARACTER RECOGNITION.

ocularcentrism (Greek visualism) A perceptual and *epistemological *bias ranking vision over other senses in Western cultures. An example would be a preference for the written word rather than the spoken word (in which case, it would be the opposite of *phonocentrism). Both Plato and Aristotle gave primacy to sight and associated it with reason. We say that 'seeing is believing', 'see for yourself', and 'I'll believe it when I see it with my own eyes'. When we understand we say, 'I see'. We 'see eye to eye' when we agree. We imagine situations 'in the mind's eye'. 'See what I mean?' Commentators such as McLuhan argue that literacy and the printed word have played a key part in the elevation of the eye to such primacy as a way of knowing. *See also* MCLUHANISM; SENSE RATIO; VISUALISM.

ocular convergence See BINOCULAR VISION.

oculesics The study of the communicative role of the eyes in *nonverbal communication (a culturally variable phenomenon). *See also* EYE CONTACT; GAZE.

Oedipal trajectory A simplistic psychoanalytical *interpretation of *classical narrative structure in mainstream cinema, in which (as in many action films) a male *protagonist has to face a crisis, usually resolving it, winning a woman, gaining the approval of a senior male, and achieving *closure. This pattern is argued to enact the Freudian Oedipus complex in which a boy struggles to detach himself from his mother in order to attain a heterosexual masculine identity.

offline *adj.* 1. The condition of not being connected to the *internet: *compare* ONLINE. 2. In the parlance of television *post-production, a programme which is finished in the sense that the creative editorial decisions have been made but which has been edited using non-broadcast quality equipment and so needs to be remade in a *conform and finished off in an *online edit: *see also* EDITING.

offline editing In television *post-production, typically a time-consuming process in which *sequences are assembled from *shots taken from uncut *rushes (or other sources) in order to produce a *final offline cut which is then submitted to a producer or commissioning editor for approval. This is all done at non-broadcast quality to save money. If the cut is approved, an *EDL and *digicut are created which are then used to remake the programme at broadcast quality in a *conform.

omission *See* DELETION.

omniscient point of view *See also* DISCLOSURE; POINT OF VIEW. 1. In written fiction, a traditional *third-person point of view in which the 'godlike' *narrator is usually also the *implied author and thus all-knowing and able to offer or withhold *information about any *events (even those happening simultaneously) and about the actions, *motivations, and unspoken thoughts of any character. Such narrators may be obtrusive (e.g. evaluative) or self-effacing. 2. (film) A mode of *narration in which the audience is shown far more than any single character can see, often from the most informative angles, though film-makers usually selectively withhold information.

180-degree rule *See* CROSSING THE LINE.

one-step flow *See* TWO-STEP FLOW.

one-way communication Message sending in which *feedback or dialogue is minimal or impossible. The term is sometimes applied to the *mass media, especially broadcasting, and also to *downward communication in hierarchical organizations. It is often used pejoratively in relation to a lack of sensitivity to the audience (as in 'preaching'). It usually alludes to *sender-oriented communication and unequal *power relations. It is also often associated with *instrumental or *informational communication. Technically, it also includes *surveillance systems such as security cameras. *See also* ASYMMETRICAL RELATIONSHIPS; *compare* TWO-WAY COMMUNICATION.

online *adj.* 1. Connected to the *internet. 2. In television *post-production, an online *edit, or the product of one: e.g. an online *master. *See also* OFFLINE EDITING.

online communication Any communication that takes place over the *internet. Largely synonymous with *computer-mediated communication.

online community *See* VIRTUAL COMMUNITY.

online editing In television *post-production, typically a final *edit in which effects, *shots, and captions are added to a programme.

onomatopoeia The use of words that, when spoken, seem to resemble a sound associated with what they signify: such as the word 'cuckoo'. In semiotic terms this has been argued to be a rare *iconic use of language, although the use of very different equivalent terms in different languages suggests that a basis in resemblance is less than native-speakers imagine.

ontology *n.* (*adj.* **ontological**) A philosophical term (from metaphysics) referring to assertions or assumptions about the nature of being and reality: about what 'the real world' is. It concerns what Foucault called 'the order of things'—a system of dividing up reality into discrete entities and substances. There are often hierarchical relations within an ontology: certain entities may be assigned prior existence, higher *modality, or some other privileged status. Semantic *oppositions such as between physical and mental or between *form and *content are ontological distinctions. Advancing the theory of ontological relativity, the *Sapir-Whorf hypothesis is that different languages carve up the world differently and have different in-built ontologies, so that some concepts may not be translatable (*see* TRANSLATABILITY). *Realists deny ontological validity to things which they do not regard as part of the external, objective world. For realists, there is an ontological bond between the *signifier and the *signified in representational media which are both *indexical and *iconic (such as photography, film, and television) and which are thus seen as capable of directly reflecting 'things as they are'.

open and closed texts 'Closed texts' tend to encourage a single *interpretation and 'open texts' encourage multiple interpretations. *Informational texts (*foregrounding *content) tend to be more closed and aesthetic texts (foregrounding *form) tend to be more open. Even with texts designed to be closed, interpretation depends ultimately on the *purposes of the reader. Road signs such as 'heavy plant crossing' can be wilfully misinterpreted. Advertisements for upmarket products are often designed to be more open to interpretation, enabling their *target audiences to exercise their *cultural capital. *See also* BROADCAST CODES; CLOSED FORMS; NARRATIVE CLOSURE; NARROWCAST CODES; OPEN FORMS; PREFERRED READING; READERLY; WRITERLY.

open-ended question (open question) *Compare* CLOSED QUESTIONS. 1. In *survey *questionnaires or research *interviews, a question which can be answered freely (in an **open response**) rather than by choosing one of a number of listed options. Such questions are common in *qualitative research. They are more demanding to analyse, but they are less likely to impose a *frame of reference on *respondents. 2. In other settings such as journalistic interviews or discussions, a question which is likely to encourage more than a yes or no answer and which is not a 'leading question' suggesting the answer. 'Why . . . ?' and 'How . . . ?' questions are generally open-ended questions.

open forms Narratives with no structural (or arguably *ideological) *closure. In literary works this is typically a deliberate reaction against the conventions of the *classic realist text. In relation to *mass-media *genres, Tania Modleski (b.1949), an American feminist theorist, argues that the structural openness of *soap operas is an essentially 'feminine' narrative form. Unlike traditional television dramas (e.g. sitcoms) which have a beginning, a middle, and an end, they are *episodic and do not build up towards an ending or *closure of meaning. They delay resolution and make anticipation an end in itself. *See also* OPEN AND CLOSED TEXTS; *compare* CLOSED FORMS; NARRATIVE CLOSURE.

opening shot *See* ESTABLISHING SHOT.

open posture A typically unconscious bodily *posture in which the body tends towards openness—particularly with arms or legs uncrossed. Depending on *context, in social *interaction open postures can signify agreement, an openness to *interaction, and/or the relaxation of a person in an established position of *power or *status. When men's sitting posture exhibits a substantial angle between the upper legs this is sometimes interpreted by *feminist theorists as a *power display, symbolically occupying a large expanse of territory. *Compare* CLOSED POSTURE.

opinion leaders A small number of individuals who exercise a significant influence on other people's ideas through *face-to-face interaction. In *two-step flow theory, they are informal mediators of *mass-media messages to the general public. *See also* DIFFUSION.

opportunity to see *See* REACH.

oppositional reading Within Stuart Hall's *encoding/decoding model, the *interpretation of a *mass-media *text by a *decoder whose social situation places them in a directly oppositional relation to the *dominant code, who understands the *preferred reading but does not share the text's *code and rejects this reading, bringing to bear an alternative *ideological code. This is what is called 'reading against the grain' or a **subversive reading**. *Compare* HEGEMONIC READING; NEGOTIATED READING.

oppositions 1. (*semiotics) Oppositions (typically *binary oppositions) are culturally widespread pairings of concepts (such as male/female and mind/body) that are seen by *structuralist theorists as part of the *deep structure underlying the *surface features of major texts and cultural practices. Oppositions are fundamental in the *structural analysis of such forms. 2. (*semantics) Opposing terms graded on the same dimension that do not exhaust its possibilities (e.g. good–bad, where 'not good' is not necessarily 'bad'); *differences of degree (in some contexts termed **logical contraries**).

optical character recognition (OCR) 1. Pattern recognition software that analyses the shapes of graphical letters in scanned images of text and transforms them into *alphanumeric characters in digital form. 2. A process of turning written text into *digital information that can be displayed and manipulated by a computer.

optical illusion *See* VISUAL ILLUSION.

optical sound A method of encoding *analogue sound on film in the form of a visual pattern one side of the filmstrip. This pattern resembles a series of peaks and troughs which represent loud and quiet sounds. The light from the film projector shines through this pattern onto the surface of a light sensitive diode which converts it into electricity and then into sound.

optics A branch of physics concerned with the study of light and the instruments that process or analyse light waves—particularly lenses and mirrors. *See also* COLOUR; ELECTROMAGNETIC SPECTRUM; EXPOSURE; FOCAL LENGTH; LUMINANCE; SPECTRAL PURITY; WAVELENGTH.

🌐 **SEE WEB LINKS**
• Optics and vision

oracy Fluency in speaking and listening *comprehension, a coinage by analogy with *literacy.

oral communication (oral-aural communication, vocal communication) Human *interaction through the use of speech, or spoken messages. In common usage loosely referred to as *verbal communication, particularly *face-to-face interaction, but more strictly including mediated use of the spoken word (e.g. a telephone conversation), where, in addition to spoken words, there are still also *vocal cues.

oral cultures 1. Societies based on *orality, the term being typically applied to those having no written literature and in which intergenerational cultural transmission of *values, *attitudes, and beliefs is by word of mouth (including through *myths). Theorists such as McLuhan and Ong have stressed fundamental differences between oral and literate cultures (*see* GREAT DIVIDE THEORIES), including different patterns of thought. Critics stressing social and *ideological factors argue that such views are a form of *media determinism. 2. *Subcultures within literate societies which place greater emphasis on the effective use of the speech (and often singing) than on *literacy (as opposed to **literary cultures**).

orality A communicative basis in speech rather than writing; often descriptive of *oral cultures and contrasted with *literacy. This communicative mode is widely romanticized (*see* PHONOCENTRISM). Ong distinguishes between the **primary orality** of preliterate societies and the **secondary orality** of literate societies in which electronic media extend the role of speech beyond *face-to-face interaction, introducing, for instance, *mass audiences.

orders of signification (*semiotics) Barthes' term for structural levels of *signification, *meaning, or *representation in semiotic systems. He adopted the notion from Hjelmslev. The **first order** of signification is that of *denotation: at this level there is a *sign consisting of a *signifier and a *signified. At this denotative level, a picture of a rose signifies the flower. *Connotation is a **second order** of signification (though not secondary in significance) which uses the denotative sign (signifier and signified) as its signifier and attaches to it an additional signified. At this connotative level, the same picture connotes love. Barthes argues that the orders of signification called denotation and connotation combine to produce *ideology in the form of *myth—which has sometimes been described as a third order of signification. Other than for analytical purposes, it is difficult to sustain any clear distinction between these levels.

organizational bias *See* INSTITUTIONAL BIAS.

organizational communication Patterns and processes of formal and informal interpersonal and group *interaction in institutional and business contexts, including administrative and managerial styles; also, this field of study within *communication studies. *See also* DOWNWARD COMMUNICATION; LATERAL COMMUNICATION; SYSTEMS THEORY; UPWARD COMMUNICATION.

orientalism *See* OTHER.

orientation 1. In *face-to-face interaction, the direction in which the head, *gaze, and/or torso of a communicator is facing or angled relative to another participant (broadly, towards or away from them). Where people do not know each other well, leaning forward towards the other person is usually associated with more *liking, higher involvement, or deference. *See also* PERSONAL SPACE; POSTURE. 2. In visual representation, *see* FRONTALITY; LANDSCAPE FORMAT; PORTRAIT FORMAT. 3. In *communication theory and *functionalist media sociology, the functional focus of a communicative act (*see* COMMUNICATIVE FUNCTIONS; CONCEPT-ORIENTED COMMUNICATION; INTERACTION-ORIENTED COMMUNICATION; MEANING-ORIENTED COMMUNICATION; MEDIA FUNCTIONS; MESSAGE-ORIENTED COMMUNICATION; PERSON-ORIENTED COMMUNICATION; PROCESS-ORIENTED COMMUNICATION; RECEIVER-ORIENTED COMMUNICATION; ROLE-ORIENTED COMMUNICATION; SENDER-ORIENTED COMMUNICATION; SOCIO-ORIENTED COMMUNICATION; TASK-ORIENTED COMMUNICATION). *Advertising may be **product-oriented** (*see* PRODUCT-INFORMATION FORMAT) or **user-oriented** (*see* PERSONALIZED FORMAT). A competent professional writer composing a complex text tends to move from a *writer-oriented phase to a *reader-oriented one. 4. (*linguistics) The dominant *linguistic function in an act of communication, or the constituent element in a *communication model which is the focus for a particular function (e.g. the code-oriented *metalingual function in *Jakobson's model). 5. In cross-cultural comparisons, for group-orientation *see* COLLECTIVISTIC CULTURES; for individual-orientation, *see* INDIVIDUALISTIC CULTURES. 6. For value-orientation, *see* VALUES. 7. For sexual orientation, *see* SEXUAL IDENTITY.

orientational metaphors *See* SPATIAL RELATIONS.

orientation shot *See* ESTABLISHING SHOT.

original meaning *See* TEXTUALISM.

orthography The spelling and punctuation system of a *language.

OSS *See* OVER-THE-SHOULDER SHOT.

ostranenie *See* DEFAMILIARIZATION.

other *See also* ALTERITY; DIFFERENCE. 1. A person or group defined as different from oneself or one's own group: the negatively differential basis of *personal or group identity ('me' or 'us' vs 'them'). In *structuralism, a non-self which, by *binary opposition, is constitutive of the *subject. In *poststructuralism, such distinctions are seen as arbitrary. 2. A reference in sociology and *symbolic interactionism to *significant others or *generalized others. 3. In *psychoanalytic theory, for Lacan, the illusory wholeness of the self in the mirror phase; when capitalized, the *lack. In other psychoanalytic discourse, that which is repressed within the self. 4. For Foucault, all those excluded from *power. 5. In *postcolonialism, for Said, the projection by Western cultures onto 'orientals' of qualities opposite and inferior to those which they ascribe to themselves: labelling them irrational, uncivilized, and so on (**orientalism**); part of a *discourse of power enabling control of the colonized subject. This *ideological process has been called **othering**. *See also* EUROCENTRISM; RACISM.

otherness *See* ALTERITY.

OTS (opportunity to see) *See* REACH.

outcome-oriented communication *See* INSTRUMENTAL COMMUNICATION.

out-group *See* IN-GROUP.

out of sync *See* SYNCHRONIZATION.

overcoding The high *redundancy of *broadcast codes associated with structurally simple, formulaic, and repetitive *texts. Overcoding may lead to an overdetermined *reading—to a stronger *preferred reading. *See also* OVERDETERMINATION; *compare* UNDERCODING.

overdetermination 1. **(multiple determination)** A process in which a phenomenon is the result of multiple factors (*see also* CAUSATION). The term is common in *structuralist discourse. 2. In Althusserian *Marxism, the notion that although the structural (economic) base of society determines the (*cultural and *ideological) superstructure it can also be affected by it (*see also* BASE AND SUPERSTRUCTURE). There can be mutual determination or reciprocal relations between 'causes' and 'effects'. 3. For Freud, the multiple meanings or causes of a *symbol in *condensation. 4. In textual *interpretation, the loading of the *preferred reading of a text through *overcoded *broadcast codes and the familiarity of its representational practices.

overdubbing *See* NATURAL SOUND.

overprint colour *See* SECONDARY COLOUR.

over-the-shoulder shot (OVS, OSS) 1. A *shot that shows a person facing the camera on the left- or right-hand side of the *frame and another person with their back to the camera, where only part of their head and shoulders are shown on the other side. 2. Any shot positioned just behind a subject that appears to be looking over their shoulder.

overwrite editing *See* INSERT EDITING.

OVS *See* OVER-THE-SHOULDER SHOT.

paidia An unstructured and undisciplined category of gameplay of the type typically performed by young infants: e.g. leapfrog, hide and seek, and doll-play (Caillois). *Compare* LUDUS.

PAL (Phase Alternate Line) A German-originated colour television standard with a *resolution of 625 lines (576 *active picture) and a *frame rate of 25 frames per second (50 fields), consisting of a black-and-white signal combined with a colour sub-carrier). The advantage the design of PAL has over *NTSC is a means of self-correcting phase errors in the transmission of *colour information.

palmtop computer *See* PERSONAL DIGITAL ASSISTANT.

pan (panning shot) Broadly, any camera movement along an x or y axis that is filmed from a fixed position. In film and video, a dynamic horizontal movement created by turning to the left or right while it is mounted in a fixed position. Insofar as it 'surveys' an area, it can also be termed a **surveying pan**. *See also* FOLLOWING PAN; WHIP PAN; *compare* TILT.

pan and scan A method of showing *widescreen films on 4:3 televisions which involved zooming-in on the picture until it fills the screen and moving this 'zoomed window' from side to side to capture the most important information. *See also* ZOOM.

panopticon [Greek *panoptes* 'all-seeing'] A prison designed by the British philosopher Jeremy Bentham (1748–1832), which took the form of a multi-storey, semicircular building consisting of rows of cells with floor-to-ceiling bars surrounding an inner courtyard, and a guard tower located at its centre. While the prisoners were always visible, the windows of the tower were shielded. Bentham hypothesized that the omnipresent gaze created by the unverifiable presence of the guards would compel the prisoners to good behaviour. Foucault used the panopticon as a *metaphor to describe the subtle methods of control found in modern societies, which internalizes discipline in individuals so that overt coercion is unnecessary. Foucault's theory has influenced *surveillance studies, although it has been criticized as inadequate to the task of describing the full range of modern surveillance practices (*see* DATAVEILLANCE).

(((●))) SEE WEB LINKS

• *The Panopticon*: Jeremy Bentham

paper edit (television) Edit instructions worked out on paper as a list of the start *timecodes and *shot durations of the source material obtained from watching *BITC recordings of the *rushes.

paradigm 1. (*semiotics) A set of associated *signifiers which are all members of some defining category, but in which each signifier is significantly different. Paradigms, along with *syntagms, are the structural forms through which *signs are organized into *codes. In natural language there are grammatical paradigms such as verbs or nouns. In a given context, one member of the paradigm is structurally replaceable with another. The use of one signifier (e.g. a particular item of clothing) rather than another from the same paradigm (e.g. a tee shirt instead of a dress shirt; a baseball cap instead of a top hat) shapes the meaning. **Paradigmatic relations** are the *oppositions and contrasts between the signifiers that belong to the same paradigm from which those used in the text were drawn. **Paradigmatic analysis** is a *structuralist technique which seeks to identify the various paradigms which underlie the *surface structure of a text. This aspect of *structural analysis involves a consideration of the positive or negative *connotations of each signifier (revealed through the *substitution of one signifier for another—the *commutation test), and the identification of 'underlying' thematic paradigms: e.g. *binary oppositions such as public/private. *Compare* SYNTAGM. 2. A set of historically contingent theories, practices, and traditions which functions to guide and protect a set of norms. Kuhn argued that scientists work within certain paradigms that can be compared to *interpretive communities of a specialist kind. The most successful paradigms (e.g. the celestial mechanics of Newton, the evolutionary theory of Darwin) define a stable period in science where a tradition of *knowledge is established and developed. Systematic anomalies may eventually appear which challenge the validity of a paradigm. At first supporters of the paradigm defend it vigorously, but if the challenge is sustained and overwhelming, a period of instability follows. This is only brought to a close when a new paradigm successfully supplants the older one (a 'paradigm shift'). Three successive dominant paradigms in the media *effects tradition were: the 'powerful effects paradigm' from the 1920s to the 1940s (*see* DIRECT EFFECTS; HYPODERMIC MODEL); the *limited effects paradigm from the 1940s to the 1970s; and subsequently the 'cumulative effects paradigm'. *See* CULTIVATION THEORY; DRIP EFFECT; LONG-TERM EFFECTS. 3. Sometimes a synonym for *model, as in **dominance paradigm** (*see* DOMINANCE MODEL) or **difference paradigm** (*see* DIFFERENCE MODEL).

(((●))) SEE WEB LINKS
• Paradigms and syntagms

paradigmatic axis In structuralist *semiotics, an analytical dimension spatialized as a vertical plane representing a set of alternative *signifiers which would be *syntagmatically legitimate in a given structural context. Only one of these can occupy that particular location at any time. Each alternative would signify differently. *See also* PARADIGM; *compare* SYNTAGMATIC AXIS.

paralanguage (paralinguistic features) 1. **(vocalics)** (*speech communication) Meaningful **vocal qualifiers** closely associated with speech, including *vocalizations and 'prosodic features' such as *pitch, rhythm, and loudness, but not including verbal *utterances. The term is sometimes used very loosely as a synonym for all of the meaningful *nonverbal behaviour accompanying speech. The study of paralanguage is called **paralinguistics**. Paralinguistic *cues can provide information about *emotions, *attitudes, personality, and social origins. *See also* PROSODY; VOCAL CUE. **2.** (*written communication) Visual cues serving to modulate the tone of a verbal text or to segment it. Although *phonocentrism often leads written communication to be cast in terms of *cuelessness, it does have paralinguistic features unavailable in speech, such as paragraphs, tables, and illustrations. In printed text, *typography is a paralinguistic feature. The most distinctive paralinguistic features in online communication is the use of *emoticons.

parallel cutting or editing *See* CROSS-CUTTING.

parallel relationships Interactional partnerships in a *dyad that reflect both *complementary and *symmetrical relationships and the *communication styles associated with them. Overall *power or *status is fairly equal, but *dominance and subordination varies situationally. *See also* POWER RELATIONS; RELATIONAL COMMUNICATION.

parapraxis (*colloq.* **Freudian slip**; *pl.* **parapraxes**). Any noticeable mistake in speech ('a slip of the tongue'), writing ('a slip of the pen'), recall, or action. As the joke goes, 'A Freudian slip is like saying one thing, but meaning your mother.' Freud argued that such slips revealed unconscious thoughts and desires that were otherwise repressed.

parasocial interaction (PSI, para-social interaction) A term coined by Horton and Wohl in 1956 to refer to a kind of psychological relationship experienced by members of an audience in their mediated encounters with certain performers in the *mass media, particularly on television. Regular viewers come to feel that they know familiar television personalities almost as friends. **Parasocial relationships** psychologically resemble those of *face-to-face interaction but they are of course mediated and one-sided. On the rare occasions when we encounter celebrities in the street we may smile involuntarily in recognition that we know them but we are obliged to realize that they do not know us. However, onscreen, skilled television presenters foster the illusion of intimacy, a good example in the UK being Paul O'Grady. We are encouraged to feel that what is being said is being directed to us personally. This is assisted by *direct address to the camera. *Chat-show hosts tend to adopt the *conversational style and gestures of an informal face-to-face gathering. The set is often designed to bear some resemblance to a living-room. Skilled hosts blur the line between themselves and the audience— both the studio audience and the audience at home. Guests on the show are treated as a group of close friends. Horton and Wohl stress that parasocial interaction is not like a process of *identification. One-off viewers may choose to be detached, analytical, and even cynical, but regular viewers are more likely to adopt the proffered role.

(((●))) SEE WEB LINKS

• Parasocial interaction: Horton and Wohl

Pareto principle *See* POWER LAW DISTRIBUTION.

parole *See* LANGUE AND PAROLE.

participant observation A mode of *qualitative social research used in *ethnography in which the observer becomes directly involved in the day-to-day activities of the community under study (either covertly or overtly). Researchers follow the example of anthropologists, notably recording direct observations and conducting informal interviews with selected *informants. A primary aim is to understand the subjective worlds of those being studied from their own points of view. This is in strong contrast to the detached mode employed in scientific *experiments. Balancing empathic *subjectivity and impartial *objectivity requires considerable *reflexivity on the part of the observer.

participants In *communication theory and *linguistics, those involved in any act of communication or communicative event. Participant factors include the number involved, *roles (sometimes termed *functions), relationships (including *power relations), and the participants' *encoding and decoding skills (*see also* COMMUNICATIVE FUNCTIONS; COMMUNICATIVE RELATIONSHIPS; RECEIVER SKILLS; SENDER SKILLS). Participant roles include *sender and *receiver or *addresser and addressee (plus sometimes also a separate *source). *Compare* COMMUNICATOR.

participatory culture Activities which transform the experience of media *consumption into the *production of new texts, blurring the boundary between producers and consumers (Jenkins). Before the era of *Web 2.0 this was particularly associated with a global network of fans of *popular culture (e.g. for TV shows such as *Star Trek*) but it has subsequently also become associated with *internet technologies such as YouTube which enable users to appropriate and refashion media content. *See also* MASHUP; USER-GENERATED CONTENT.

(((⊕))) SEE WEB LINKS
• Confronting the challenges of participatory culture

pass-along readers *See* READERSHIP; SECONDARY AUDIENCE.

pathos A quality evoking pity, compassion, or sympathetic sadness. *See also* EMPATHY; SYMPATHY.

pay-per-view (PPV) Cable or satellite television programmes (such as feature films or coverage of sports events) for which subscribers pay individually.

PC 1. *Political correctness. 2. Personal computer.

PDA *See* PERSONAL DIGITAL ASSISTANT.

peak time (UK; **prime time** US). The period on television when the audience is largest; for commercial television, the period when *advertising revenue is highest. On British television, 7 p.m. to 10 p.m.

ped-up or -down In film and video, a *track where the camera moves in a vertical direction (along the y-axis). Ped-up and ped-down *shots involve *motion parallax which creates a feeling of depth, as the relative *occlusion of *foreground and *background elements dynamically changes in the *frame. *Compare* TILT.

peer group *See also* GROUP IDENTIFICATION; PRIMARY AND SECONDARY GROUPS; REFERENCE GROUP; SUBCULTURE. **1.** Any social collectivity in which the members share a common characteristic. **2.** A small group of friends or colleagues with shared interests, activities, and *values. **3.** Individuals belonging to the same age group (especially in childhood and adolescence), especially friends but also members of the same *age cohort within a youth *subculture. **4.** A group of individuals of roughly the same *status.

peer-to-peer network (P2P) A *computer network in which participants make a portion of their resources (such as processing power, disk storage, or *bandwidth) available to others, without the need for central coordination. *See also* BIT TORRENT; FILE SHARING.

Peircean model (*semiotics) Peirce's triadic model of the *sign including the *representamen, the *object, and the *interpretant. *See also* ICONIC; INDEXICAL; SEMIOSIS; SYMBOLIC; *compare* SAUSSUREAN MODEL.

(()) **SEE WEB LINKS**
• Peirce Studies

Peoplemeter A device attached to a television set recording who watches what and when. Viewers identify themselves by pushing buttons.

perceived reality **1.** How real something is perceived as being and the criteria used to evaluate this: e.g. in relation to television, whether it involves actors, whether it is a cartoon, etc. (*see also* MODALITY). In the *effects tradition, typically presented as an *intervening variable in *behaviourist research into relations between onscreen violence and behaviour (especially in relation to children). **2.** In research into children's understanding of the media, an issue which has increasingly revealed the previously underestimated sophistication of children's *modality judgements: *see also* MAGIC WINDOW.

(()) **SEE WEB LINKS**
• Children's understanding of what is 'real' on television

perception (perceiving) **1.** (philosophy) The process of apprehending objects by means of the *senses (a **percept** is something that is perceived). Perception is the conscious awareness of an object or *event. **2.** (psychology) The process or product of organizing and interpreting sensations (*sensory data from external objects or *events) into meaningful patterns. The term also refers to this topic as a field of study within psychology. Perception is distinguished from *sensation: it is an interpretive process—selective, constructive, and evaluative rather than a passive recording of external reality (*see also* CONSTRUCTIVISM; PERCEPTUAL DEFENCE; SALIENCE; SELECTIVE PERCEPTION). Perception is shaped by such factors as contextual and cultural *frames of reference, as well as individual differences, *purposes, and needs (*see also* ATTENTION; BEHOLDER'S SHARE; GESTALT LAWS; INNOCENT EYE; LEVELLING AND SHARPENING; PERCEPTUAL CONSTANCY; PERCEPTUAL SET). It involves both *top-down, hypothesis-driven processes (*see also* SCHEMA

THEORY) and *bottom-up, data-driven processes (*see also* DIRECT PERCEPTION), and has been conceptualized in terms of a *perceptual cycle: *see also* PICTURE PERCEPTION; VISUAL PERCEPTION. **3.** In loose usage, particular ways of understanding a phenomenon (as in 'public perceptions of crime'). **4.** (social psychology) *See* SOCIAL PERCEPTION.

perceptual codes In *semiotic discourse, a fundamental interpretive framework within which human beings construct sensory experience. Some semioticians regard sensory *perception as a *code (*see also* VISUAL SEMIOTICS). Various arguments are encountered, in particular: that *interpretation cannot be separated from *perception; that human perceptual apparatus differs from that of other organisms and so presumably different species inhabit different perceptual realities; and/or that even within the human species, that there are sociocultural, subcultural, and environmental differences in perception. Such perceptual codes must thus be learnt (even if, as the *gestalt psychologists demonstrated, some processes of perceptual *inference seem to be universal). As a semiotic code, perception involves *representation. Unlike most codes, the notion of a perceptual code does not assume *intentional communication (there need be no *sender).

perceptual constancy A psychological mechanism that stabilizes relative shifts in the *appearance of things. *Sensory data is in a continual state of flux and the mind seeks the relative stability necessary for *categorization. *See also* BRIGHTNESS CONSTANCY; COLOUR CONSTANCY; SHAPE CONSTANCY; SIZE CONSTANCY.

perceptual cycle (cyclic model of perception) Neisser's model of *perception as a cyclical process in which *top-down processing and *bottom-up processing drive each other in turn. To be purely data-driven we'd need to be mindless automatons; to be purely theory-driven we'd need to be disembodied dreamers. An active *schema sets up relevant *expectations for a particular *context and if the *sensory data flouts these expectations this may modify the schema or trigger a more relevant one. The basic principle is one of *feedback. *See also* SCHEMA THEORY.

perceptual defence An unconscious process of perceptual distortion under conditions of extremely brief exposure to anomalous or unacceptable objects or *events. Such stimuli may be normalized or not consciously perceived at all. A complementary process is **perceptual vigilance**, which involves heightened sensitivity to threatening events.

perceptual organization (perceptual grouping) The mental grouping of small units within a pattern of sensory stimuli into larger forms. *See also* GESTALT LAWS.

perceptual selectivity *See* SELECTIVE PERCEPTION.

perceptual set (mental set) (psychology) The expectancies or predispositions leading an observer to favour one kind of *interpretation of a pattern of sensory stimuli rather than another. This may be based on contextual *expectations, *frame of reference, recent experience, or current concerns. *See also* ATTENTION.

perceptual vigilance *See* PERCEPTUAL DEFENCE.

performance 1. Artistic enactment for an audience (a dramatic or musical presentation, or some other form of *entertainment). Also, an individual's competence or achievement in such a performance. 2. Most broadly, behaviour: usually overt, observable behaviour, particularly the carrying out of some task, *function, or *role, the adequacy of which can be assessed (e.g. in relation to normal *expectations or competence). In relation to social *interaction, this *dramaturgical metaphor related to *self-presentation is associated with Goffman (*see also* IMPRESSION MANAGEMENT). Related usage includes dynamic framings of *identity, such as in 'the performance of *gender' (*see also* PERFORMATIVITY). The term can also refer to the level of functional adequacy of a product or device or the profitability of an investment. 3. In informal usage, a pejorative reference to a display of exaggerated behaviour. 4. **(linguistic performance)** (*linguistics) A concept introduced in the 1960s by Chomsky, who defined it as 'the actual use of language in concrete situations', seen as secondary to *competence. Later used more widely to refer to the *utterances produced by speakers, including all nonfluencies such as hesitations, false starts, grammatical errors, unfinished sentences, and *parapraxis. *Compare* LANGUE AND PAROLE.

performatives Executive *speech acts: *utterances which do something as well as merely saying something. A performative is not merely a *factual statement, but is in itself an enactment (at least in an appropriate *context): for example, 'I promise . . .'. The term was introduced by Austin and is part of *speech act theory, where performatives are now framed as *illocutionary acts.

performativity In critical and *cultural studies, the concept of *gender as enactive. Drawing on Austin's concept of *performatives, Butler's notion of performativity refers to gender as an ongoing and variable enactment rather than a given *identity (as in *gender essentialism). 'Identity is performatively constituted by the very "expressions" that are said to be its results.' In contrast to the term *performance, *performativity* reflects a rejection of prediscursive identity and a pre-existing subject. Gender identity is a cultural construction produced through repeated *discursive practices. *Queer theory stresses the scope for subversively destabilizing the *binary oppositions of gender, but performativity is not like choosing a costume: it operates in relation to hegemonic *norms for behavioural patterns within a *culture. *See also* DECENTRED SELF.

((⊕)) SEE WEB LINKS

• An interview with Judith Butler

peripheral route In the *Elaboration Likelihood Model (Petty and Cacioppo), a focus on *persuasion using 'peripheral cues' rather than explicit message *content: e.g. *style, *form, *symbolism, *connotations, music, or attractive models. This strategy requires less cognitive effort or *elaboration on the part of *receivers. Its potential influence tends to be short-lived compared with a strategy employing the *central route. *See also* NONVERBAL PERSUASION; VISUAL PERSUASION.

peripheral vision In relation to human eyesight, an area constituting all but the central 2% of the overall field of view around the point of *fixation; it is relatively low resolution and thus offers a less focused image than *foveal vision. As the .

American art historian James Elkins (b.1954) puts it, 'Your eyes don't give you the world like a photograph, crisp from one corner to the other.'

perlocutionary act A *speech act oriented towards the *effects it has on the *addressee (in a particular *context): for instance, communication intended to be persuasive or entertaining. *Nonverbal communication can also have **perlocutionary force**. **Perlocutionary effects** do not necessarily match the addresser's intentions. Contrasted with an *illocutionary act. *Compare* CONATIVE FUNCTION.

persistence of vision 1. A discredited theory explaining the *perception of motion pictures which assumes that an impression of the visual *field (known as an *after-image) either remains on the retina of the eye or is stored by the brain for approximately one twenty-fifth of a second before it decays and is supplanted by the next impression: *see also* APPARENT MOTION; FLICKER FUSION; ICONIC MEMORY; *compare* BETA MOVEMENT; PHI PHENOMENON. 2. A smear effect that is the basis of the impact of firework displays and is produced by the dark-adapted eye which compensates for low light levels by retaining light information over a short period of time. In conditions of bright ambient illumination this effect is lost.

(())) SEE WEB LINKS
• Persistence of vision

persona 1. (*psychoanalytic theory) Jung's concept of a public *role acted out by an individual in relation to social *expectations (as distinct from the private or 'true' self), a concept derived from the masks worn by actors in classical drama: *see also* SELF-PRESENTATION. 2. (literary theory) The assumed identity, role, *alter ego*, or 'second self' adopted by the *narrator or *implied author of a text. Often perceived by readers as the voice of the author—though it may not reflect the author's views at all, as often in *satire (hence the utility of the term to support this distinction).

personal digital assistant (PDA, palmtop computer) A device that offers the combined functionality of a computer and a *mobile phone. *See also* CONVERGENCE; SMARTPHONE.

personal distance *See* INTERPERSONAL ZONES.

personal function Halliday's term for a *linguistic function in which one uses language to express one's *emotions, personality, and 'gut reactions'. For example, 'I hate that!'

personal functions The general micro-level uses that acts of communication, a *medium of communication, or specific kinds of media content can be seen as serving for individuals (not necessarily identical to their conscious *purposes)—as distinct from broader macro-level *social functions. In relation to *mass-media use, such personal functions are usually referred to as *uses and gratifications. Four commonly listed personal functions in using the mass media are: *information, *entertainment, *personal identity, and *social utility. The most widely-noted personal functions of communication in general are: *informational (or *referential), *persuasive (or *conative), and *aesthetic or *entertaining. Each function involves a different *communicative relationship between the participants. Matching functions for the *sender and the *receiver respectively would include: to inform and to understand; to teach and to learn; to persuade and to decide; to entertain and to enjoy. Textual *genres are often presented as serving (or even emerging from) such *communicative functions in particular *contexts. Note that, in relation to the generation of *meaning, idealized *functions (which in a sense are like frozen purposes) are subordinated to the purposes of specific users in particular contexts. People's *communicative purposes do not necessarily match the anticipated functions, so when a text's primary function is to be informative or instructional, this is subordinated to the purposes of receivers—such as when they choose to regard it as primarily entertaining (as in being amused by poor translations of self-assembly furniture instructions). People's purposes, of course, may also be both multiple and highly dynamic. Furthermore, even in the conventionalized contexts of many communicative genres, functions are often combined in various ways, so that an *advertisement may be primarily persuasive, but may also be, to varying degrees, informative, and/or entertaining. Communicative functions have important implications for the relation between *form and *content, so that where the function is *informational, content tends to be *foregrounded, whereas where the function is *aesthetic, form and *style tend to be foregrounded. *See also* INDIVIDUAL-MEDIA DEPENDENCY; LINGUISTIC FUNCTIONS; MEDIA FUNCTIONS.

personal identity *See also* IDENTITY. 1. **(identity)** A *phenomenological sense of oneself as a separate individual being with a distinctive personality and a 'true self' persisting over time; a *self image. 2. (philosophy) The problem of whether 'the same person' can exist over time. 3. The social particulars of an identifiable individual.

personal identity function In relation to general types of use by individuals of the *mass media, a single *medium, a media *genre, or specific *media content, this is usage for purposes such as self-reference, reality exploration, and *value reinforcement. For instance, for adolescents, one unconscious *motivation for watching TV drama may be for models of personal behaviour. *See also* MEDIA FUNCTIONS; USES AND GRATIFICATIONS.

personalization 1. Functionality in media, especially websites, computers, and *mobile phones, that allows users to specify their own display and *content preferences: *see also* USER-GENERATED CONTENT; WEB 2.0. 2. A consumer-oriented style of *advertising: *see* PERSONALIZED FORMAT.

personalized format (user-oriented advertising) A style of *advertising that focuses on what the product could do for the user. From the 1950s, advertisements increasingly played upon people's desires, needs, and wants. Such ads tend to involve *emotional appeals stressing, for instance, romance, warm family relationships, self-improvement, pride of ownership, anxiety about not using the product, or satisfaction in *consumption. A link is often made between the attributes of the people in the ad and their relationship with the product. One variant is the testimonial; another involves a depicted person symbolically standing for the product. The term is used by Leiss and his colleagues. *See also* EGO

APPEALS; MASLOW'S HIERARCHY OF NEEDS; *compare* LIFESTYLE FORMAT; PRODUCT-INFORMATION FORMAT; PRODUCT-SYMBOL FORMAT.

personal space The *interpersonal distances and angles of *orientation that individuals maintain in relation to each other in social *interaction. A boundary regulation mechanism. Different cultural *norms and *contexts can affect these (*see* HIGH-CONTACT CULTURES; LOW-CONTACT CULTURES). The term was coined by the American psychologist Robert Sommer (b.1929), author of a book of the same name, who noted that an individual's personal space is not necessarily like a spherical bubble since people tolerate strangers closer to their sides than directly in front of them. US research has shown that women tend to stand closer to each other than men do, though men adopt women's distance norms when speaking to women. *See also* INTERPERSONAL ZONES; TERRITORIALITY.

personal zone *See* INTERPERSONAL ZONES.

person-oriented communication (person-centred) Term used in communication skills training where the focus is on the *receiver, either positively, as in *receiver-oriented communication or negatively, in problem-solving contexts, where it is suggested that the communication should be 'problem-centred'. Also a *stereotypically feminine *communication style as opposed to *task-oriented communication. *See also* INTERACTION-ORIENTED COMMUNICATION.

person perception 1. (interpersonal perception) An area of study within social psychology: an aspect of *social perception concerned with how people perceive each other (*see also* HALO EFFECT; LIKING; STEREOTYPING). 2. A synonym for *impression formation.

perspective The systematic spatial *representation of any three-dimensional scene on a flat or shallow surface to emulate the view of that scene from a fixed viewpoint. It was a key element in Western representational art from the Renaissance to the late 19th century (*see also* AERIAL PERSPECTIVE; DWINDLING SIZE PERSPECTIVE; TEXTURE GRADIENT). Photography renders perspective automatically (the use of *linear or *curvilinear perspective depends on lens choice); it can sometimes look phenomenally 'unrealistic' because the camera does not have *perceptual constancy.

(⊕) SEE WEB LINKS

• The psychology of perspective

perspectivism *See also* EPISTEMOLOGY; THOMAS THEOREM. 1. Broadly, the stance that the truth of any *knowledge or *fact is tied to a particular *frame of reference (McGuire). 2. (philosophy) A *relativist and anti-objectivist theory (particularly associated with Nietzsche) that there can be radically different views of reality which are incommensurable: *see also* INCOMMENSURABILITY; TRANSLATABILITY. The *Sapir-Whorf hypothesis is a form of perspectivism.

persuasion (persuasive communication) 1. An attempt to induce some change in an *audience's attitudes or behaviour (*see also* ELABORATION LIKELIHOOD MODEL; YALE MODEL). One of the major *communicative functions: *see* PERSUASIVE

FUNCTION. 2. A general classification for forms of *discourse that aim to influence an audience's *attitudes and/or behaviour by appealing to their *emotions and/or their reason. Brooks and Warren distinguish between *argument (using *rational appeals) and persuasion (using *emotional appeals), suggesting that persuasion is almost a fifth type in their list of rhetorical modes of *discourse which meet basic human *communicative purposes. Three key types are religious, political, and commercial. *Compare* ARGUMENT; DESCRIPTION; EXPOSITION; NARRATION.

persuasion models *See* ELABORATION LIKELIHOOD MODEL; YALE MODEL.

persuasive function The communicative goal of influencing the *attitudes and/or behaviour of an *addressee or *audience. One of the primary *communicative functions in both *interpersonal communication (*compare* CONATIVE FUNCTION; PERLOCUTIONARY ACT) and *mass communication (e.g. in *advertising and *political communication). *See also* MEDIA FUNCTIONS; PERSONAL FUNCTIONS; PERSUASION.

phase alternate line *See* PAL.

phatic *See also* INTERACTIONAL COMMUNICATION; LINGUISTIC FUNCTIONS.
1. **(phatic language, phatic communication, phatic communion)** Malinowski's term for speech which functions primarily to develop and maintain *social relationships, in contrast to *informational communication. 2. **Phatic function** in *language: a key linguistic or *communicative function, the role of which is to establish or maintain *social relationships. Chatting about the weather with strangers in a bus queue is an example of phatic communication; *mobile phone text messages between adolescents are often primarily phatic. In *Jakobson's model this function is oriented towards (establishing and maintaining) *contact.

phenomenal 1. Sometimes a synonym for **phenomenological**. 2. **Phenomenal reality** refers to the psychologically subjective '*lived experience' of individuals ('how things seem to me'—which, in the *natural attitude, is typically assumed to be universally shared and equivalent to 'the ways things are').

phenomenology (*adj.* **phenomenological**) *See also* INTERPRETIVISM; MEDIA PHENOMENOLOGY; SUBJECTIVITY. 1. Most broadly, any focus on how things are perceived and experienced. 2. (philosophy) For Husserl, examining and describing one's own intellectual processes introspectively as phenomena appear to consciousness, 'bracketing' out all that is external to consciousness—including preconceptions and external reality. 3. (psychology) An approach focusing on the unique, subjective, mental experiences of the individual in situational *contexts, rather than on behaviour. 4. (sociology) Approaches emphasizing the social construction of reality through everyday *interaction, notably the work of Peter Berger and Luckmann, following the investigation by Schutz of our everyday assumptions (*see also* CONSTRUCTIONISM; CRITICAL ATTITUDE; NATURAL ATTITUDE). Schutz influenced *symbolic interactionism; Berger and Luckmann influenced *conversation analysis and *ethnomethodology.

(((⊕))) SEE WEB LINKS
• The phenomenology of writing by hand

phi phenomenon A kind of *apparent motion seen, for example, when the lights around a theatre marquee sign are illuminated in sequence (at speeds between 60 and 200 Hz), that produces the impression that a shaded area the same size and shape as the lights but the same colour as the background is moving rapidly around the sign. The phi phenomenon, along with *beta movement, have supplanted the *persistence of vision theory as a more plausible explanation of how motion pictures appear to move.

phishing A criminal *internet scam in which a person is duped into revealing personal information (e.g. bank account details) by replying to an official-looking *email or by being directed to a fake website where they are asked to fill out a form. *See also* SPAM.

phoneme (*linguistics) The smallest sound unit in a *language. Meaningless in themselves, phonemes are the building-blocks of *language. Changing one for another changes the meaning of a word, as with /p/ and /b/ in *pat* and *bat*. The English language has only about forty or fifty phonemes but these can be combined to generate hundreds of thousands of words. *See also* ARTICULATION; PHONOLOGY; *compare* MORPHEME.

phonetics A branch of *linguistics concerned with the study of the characteristics, *production, and *perception of speech sounds. *See also* AUDITORY PHONETICS; SPEECH PERCEPTION; SPEECH RECOGNITION; *compare* PHONOLOGY.

phonocentrism 1. A term formulated in 1967 by Derrida describing Plato's privileging of the *immediacy and *proximity of (face-to-face) speech as the only means of obtaining philosophical clarity and truth. 2. More broadly, an interpretive *bias which privileges speech over *writing (and also the oral-aural over the visual, the ear over the eye).

phonology A branch of *linguistics concerned with the study of the sound systems of different *languages. *See also* PHONEME; *compare* PHONETICS.

photograph [Greek 'drawing with light'] A still image of a visible phenomenon in the external world recorded using a *camera through the agency of light. In *semiotic terms, unedited photographic and filmic images are *indexical (based on a direct causal connection) rather than simply *iconic (based on resemblance)— though they can be termed **iconic indexes** (or indices). A photographic image is an index of the effect of light: it is not coincidental that photographs resemble their *referents. The indexical character of photographs encourages interpreters to treat them as 'objective' and *transparent records of 'reality'. In this medium there is less of an obvious gap between the *signifier and its *signified than with non-photographic media. The resemblance is only partial, however. John Berger observed that 'the photograph cannot lie, but . . . the truth it does tell . . . is a limited one.' We need to remind ourselves that a photograph does not simply record and reproduce an *event, but is only one of an infinite number of possible *representations. Representational practices are always involved in selection, composition, lighting, focusing, exposure, processing, and so on. Sontag declared that 'photographs are as much an *interpretation of the world as paintings and

drawings are.' Thus, photographs are 'made' rather than 'taken' (*see also*
PHOTOGRAPHIC CODES).

(⊕) SEE WEB LINKS

• A history of photography

photographic codes In *semiotic discourse, the processes of *transformation
involved in the production of images with a *camera. Supposedly, someone once
handed the artist Picasso a photograph, asking, 'Can't you paint my wife realistically
like this?' The artist replied, 'Is that really what she looks like?' Receiving an
affirmative answer, he declared, 'Then she must be very flat, and quite small.'
Barthes noted that a *photograph *appears* to be 'a message without a *code',
referring to its *indexicality and irreducibility to recombinable elements, but he
went on to argue that the *common-sense notion that it is purely denotative is a
*myth. The British art historian John Tagg (b.1949) adds that 'the *transparency of
the photograph is its most powerful rhetorical device'. Semioticians refer to 'reading
photographs'. Photographic codes include *genre, *camerawork (lens choice,
focus, *aperture, *exposure, camera position), composition (*framing, distance,
*camera angle, lighting), film (quality, type, colour), developing (exposure,
treatments) and printing (paper, size, *cropping). *See also* PICTORIAL CODES;
REPRESENTATIONAL CODES; VISUAL SEMIOTICS.

photographic realism *See* PHOTOREALISM.

photojournalism A photographic *genre characterized by the intention to
communicate information about a topical *event and by the *immediacy of its
images. It has generated many '*iconic' photographs. *See also* DECISIVE MOMENT.

(⊕) SEE WEB LINKS

• Photojournalism

photomontage A photographic image, process, and *genre based on
combining existing photographs from other sources, separated from their original
*contexts: for instance, those produced as anti-Nazi artistic propaganda by the
German artist John Heartfield (1891–1968). The assemblage may be produced
in a computer-graphics package, or by multi-exposure, simultaneous projection,
or physical assembly.

photorealism (photographic realism, super realism, hyper-realism) A
highly detailed and precise artistic representational style of extreme verisimilitude
emulating (or based directly on) sharply-focused photography. It can connote
*impersonality. *See also* NATURALISM.

photoshopping Manipulating a digitized photograph with a computer using
specialist graphics software. The term derives from the name of a proprietary
software package. The relative ease with which an image can be 'photoshopped'
and the sophistication of the results compared to *airbrushing has radicalized the
potential for altering photographic images. However, it has also undermined trust
in the fidelity of photography as an evidential, *indexical medium as expressed
in the old adage that 'the camera never lies'. *See also* DIGITAL.

SEE WEB LINKS
- Photo tampering throughout history

pictogram (pictograph) An *iconic sign in the form of a simplified pictorial
*representation of an object, signifying a closely associated concept: for instance,
the stylized silhouette of a man normally used to signify a public toilet for males.
Such a *sign would signify as intended only to those familiar with the *textual and/or
*social codes on which it draws, when located in a relevant *context. *See also*
WRITING SYSTEMS.

pictorial codes In *semiotic discourse, the artistic *conventions employed in
visual *representation which lead semioticians to refer to such pictures being 'read'
by viewers who are familiar with these conventions. When visual representations
employ *aesthetic codes of *realism, viewers are not conscious of *decoding them
because of the familiarity of their *codes. *See also* PHOTOGRAPHIC CODES; PICTORIAL
DEPTH CUES; PICTORIAL SEMIOTICS; PICTURE PERCEPTION; REPRESENTATIONAL
CODES; TEXTUAL CODES; VISUAL SEMIOTICS.

pictorial communication (graphic communication) The use of images
primarily as *messages. Gombrich argues that 'statements cannot be translated into
images': for instance, as noted by the American film-maker and communication
theorist Sol Worth (1922–77), 'pictures can't say ain't'. Recognition of the *preferred
reading of an image depends on the familiarity of viewers with its *conventions and
*allusions and its relation to the *context of use. Pictorial communication is usually
most effective when used in conjunction with verbal captions as *anchors.
See also PICTOGRAM; VISUAL COMMUNICATION; VISUAL LANGUAGE; VISUAL SEMIOTICS.

pictorial depth cues Any *information in two-dimensional visual
*representations from which three-dimensional *spatial relations can be inferred.
Unlike spatial *perception in the everyday world, only *monocular cues are useful.
These include: *linear perspective, *dwindling size perspective, *aerial perspective,
*texture gradient, *occlusion, *elevation, *familiar size, and highlights and shading
(*see* CHIAROSCURO). *See also* PICTORIAL CODES; PICTURE PERCEPTION.

pictorialism Artistic photography modelled on the *conventions of academic
painting: a carefully composed form of personal expression rather than
spontaneous or *documentary photography. As an anti-mechanistic movement in
photography concerned with photography as a craft (e.g. the texture of the paper
used), it originated in the late 19th century and lasted until the early 20th century,
but its primary concerns remained influential.

pictorial language *See* VISUAL COMMUNICATION; VISUAL LANGUAGE.

pictorial metaphor (visual metaphor) In a visual *representation, juxtaposed
or merged depictions of two different objects or actions designed to encourage
viewers to infer an implicit conceptual link. A visual *trope. Some pictorial
*metaphors are fairly literal visualizations of existing verbal metaphors (such as a
depiction of a storm in a teacup); others are more unconventional, such as an
image of a roll of toilet paper on which the US Bill of Rights is printed. Visual

metaphors are widely used in *advertising, especially for sophisticated *target audiences. *See also* JUXTAPOSITION; MEANING TRANSFER; VISUAL RHETORIC; *compare* KULESHOV EFFECT.

pictorial perception *See* PICTURE PERCEPTION.

pictorial semiotics The study of images, *pictorial codes, and visual media as *sign systems. This includes images in various forms, such as paintings, drawings, photographs, and pictorial advertisements. The field has been dominated by *structuralist analysis which, unlike most *textual analysis, treats texts (in any medium) as part of a system (*see also* STRUCTURALISM). The *linguistic model has involved the application of the *commutation test, but, unlike verbal *language (*see* ARTICULATION), pictorial *representation has proved irreducible to basic, recombinable units which are meaningless in themselves (*see* PICTORIAL COMMUNICATION; VISUAL COMMUNICATION; VISUAL LANGUAGE). *See also* REPRESENTATIONAL CODES; SEMIOTICS; VISUAL SEMIOTICS.

pictorial turn *See* VISUAL TURN.

picture perception (pictorial perception) The processes involved in making sense of visual images. Although some basic perceptual processes may be innate and universal (*see* GESTALT LAWS), pictorial perception draws on the viewer's *knowledge of the world (*see* SOCIAL KNOWLEDGE) and of the *medium and the *conventions employed (*see* TEXTUAL KNOWLEDGE). However 'realistic' a picture is, it requires active *interpretation (*see* BEHOLDER'S SHARE). Although viewers may often broadly agree about what *figurative art depicts or denotes, there is more diversity beyond this 'literal' level. Knowledge of the world is socially variable; the familiarity of the conventions is culturally variable (*see also* HORIZONTAL-VERTICAL ILLUSION). Individual factors are also involved: such as the viewer's *frame of reference. The importance of the viewer's current *purposes has been demonstrated by Yarbus in his use of *eye tracking. In exploring how picture perception works, psychological approaches often apply *schema theory; *pictorial semiotics focuses on the use of *social codes and *textual codes. The *perception of *pictorial depth differs from spatial perception in the everyday three-dimensional world in its reliance on *monocular cues.

picture plane In pictorial analysis, a virtual space corresponding to the surface of a two-dimensional image (such as a painting or a photograph). Since the Renaissance this space within a *frame has been compared to a window on the world: a powerful *metaphor in realist notions of *representation. In *figurative art employing *linear perspective, objects 'facing the viewer' or running horizontally across the picture would be described as 'parallel to the picture plane'. *See also* BACKGROUND; FOREGROUND; FRONTALITY; MIDDLE DISTANCE.

piece-to-camera (PTC) In television news reporting, a *shot where the reporter speaks to the audience directly by looking into the camera lens. *See also* DIRECT ADDRESS.

pillarbox format In film and television, vertical masking of the screen area with bars down the left and right hand sides of the picture. Pillarboxing is less common than *letterboxing but may be used when 4 x 3 pictures are shown on *widescreens such as the 16:9 television format. *Compare* ARCING; *see also* ASPECT RATIO; ASPECT RATIO CONVERSION.

piracy The illegal copying and/or *distribution of media content, including audio, print, video, and computer software. A metaphor that is also applied to a radio station that broadcasts without a licence.

pitch 1. In film and *marketing, the presentation of a proposal or idea to potential investors (*see also* HIGH CONCEPT). 2. A measure of the frequency of vibrations which produce different sound tones. In British English, a raised vocal pitch at the end of an *utterance indicates a question. More generally, lower pitched voices are widely perceived as more authoritative and credible, giving males an advantage. *See also* VOCAL CUE. 3. The up-down rotation (around the side-to-side or x-axis) of a viewpoint (for instance in a 3D-graphical environment such as a *virtual world), as when an aeroplane's nose dips or rises: *see also* ROLL; YAW; *compare* TILT.

pixelation 1. (television) An effect that turns a video picture into a mosaic of squares, which is often used in news programmes and *documentaries to conceal sensitive information such as car number plates. 2. (computer graphics) A mosaic effect, especially when an image is magnified—revealing that it is made of a series of *pixels.

pixels A portmanteau word (*picture* + *element*). *See also* RASTER GRAPHICS; RASTERIZATION. 1. In *digital systems, dots of light which are the smallest elements on computer monitors or video screens. Their *colour depth and size determine the level of detail, or *resolution. *Compare* DPI. 2. In cathode-ray tube televisions, small phosphorescent elements coating the back of the screen which glow when hit by the scanning electron beam.

play 1. In most everyday usage, voluntary engagement in pleasurable activities for enjoyment, diversion, and/or recreation rather than for any 'serious' purpose; not necessarily as part of a *game. *See also* DIVERSION FUNCTION. 2. For the Dutch historian Johan Huizinga (1872–1945), an absorbing activity that constitutes a primary condition of human and animal life which, in its formal characteristics, is non-serious and freely-chosen and exists separated from 'ordinary' reality within a 'magic circle'. 3. For Caillois, a freely-chosen activity that is separate from real life, either by being governed by its own rules or perceived by its players as make-believe and therefore lacking in consequences (*see* AGON; ALEA; ILINX; LUDUS; MIMICRY; PAIDIA). 4. For Brian Sutton-Smith, an ambiguous concept which is not amenable to scientific investigation but can only be understood metaphorically, described in terms of seven 'rhetorics': *progress* (a way for infants to learn and develop); *fate* (taking chances, jeopardizing security, and gambling with destiny); *power* (contests as a way for an individual or group to exert their influence over others); *identity* (fostering a sense of community and team spirit); *imaginary* (creating new *frames of reference and transforming reality); *self* (promoting a sense of personal freedom and happiness); and *frivolity* (indulging in *ludic pleasures for their own sake). 5. A dramatic work, particularly for the stage and for performance before a theatre audience, but also used loosely to refer to a broadcast *drama.

plot *See* FABULA.

pluralism 1. Most broadly, a belief in diversity (e.g. of views, *values, or *interpretations). **Cultural pluralism** (or **multiculturalism**) is the existence of a diversity of *lifestyles or ethnic groups within a society, or a belief in the desirability of such diversity. **Methodological pluralism** is an anti-positivist, anti-objectivist stance favouring multiple models and/or methods of research (e.g. both *qualitative and *quantitative research) in the study of the same phenomenon. Pluralism in the *interpretation of texts and reality also characterizes *postmodernism and *poststructuralism: for instance in the rejection of *grand narratives and of absolute notions of truth. Critics argue that such positions drift towards *relativism.
2. **(liberal pluralism)** In political philosophy, a society (or an *ideological stance on society) in which a diversity of groups share or compete for power and there is no unified and dominant elite. Pluralists argue that in democratic societies *conflicts between competing interests are resolved institutionally, preventing one interest group from prevailing on all issues. **Political and social pluralism**, in contrast to *elitism, is based on horizontal relations between groups rather than vertical *power relations. In its focus on flexible *consensus and *dissensus between social groups, it represents a compromise between *collectivism and individualism. *See also* MARKET MODEL; PLURALIST MODEL.

pluralist model In relation to media power, a liberal *pluralist position in which the *mass media are seen as enjoying significant autonomy from the state, and media professionals are allowed considerable flexibility by the managerial elite. In particular contrast to Marxists, liberal pluralists emphasize the role of the media in promoting *freedom of speech—giving people *access to alternative views. Audiences are seen as more fragmented, able to resist *persuasion, and as more active—being capable of using the media for their own purposes (*see also* ACTIVE AUDIENCE THEORY; AUDIENCE FRAGMENTATION; MARKET MODEL; USES AND GRATIFICATIONS). *Compare* DOMINANCE MODEL.

plurisignation *See* AMBIGUITY.

podcasting A portmanteau term (*i-pod* + *broadcasting*). A means of distributing digital audio content in the form of *data files which can be downloaded from the *internet and played on a home computer, *mp3 audio player, or *smartphone.

poetic function In *Jakobson's model of linguistic communication, a key linguistic or *communicative function which *foregrounds *textual features. Within his model, this function is oriented towards the *message or focused on the message for its own sake (*see also* MESSAGE-ORIENTED COMMUNICATION). In *utterances where the poetic function is dominant (e.g. in literary texts), the language tends to be more 'opaque' than conventional prose in emphasizing the *signifier and *medium (and their *materiality), or the *form, *style, or *code at least as much as any *signified, *content, message, or *referential meaning. Such texts foreground the act and form of expression and undermine any sense of a 'natural' or *transparent connection between a signifier and a *referent. In this sense, where the poetic function dominates, the text is self-referential: form is content and 'the medium [of language] is the message'. The poetic function is generally more metaphorical than metonymic, more connotative than denotative (*see also* CONNOTATION; DENOTATION; METAPHOR; METONYMY). Some later adaptations of Jakobson's model refer to the poetic function as the **formal function** or the **aesthetic function** (so as not to limit it to linguistic contexts). *See also* LINGUISTIC FUNCTIONS.

point-of-audition sound In films and television, *diegetic sound that is perceived by a particular character. The aural equivalent of a *point-of-view shot: e.g. if a person is hiding under blankets the sounds heard by them and the audience are muffled.

point of view The perspective from which a story is told. Written *narratives most often employ third-person point of view ('telling'), but can also use *first-person point of view ('showing') (*see also* DIEGESIS; MIMESIS); a sustained *second-person point of view is very rare in literary forms (but common in such forms as song lyrics). Novels occasionally use more than one point of view or more than one first-person *narrator **(multiple points of view)**. *See also* NARRATOR; OMNISCIENT POINT OF VIEW.

point-of-view shot (POV) In film and television, the visual *representation of the physical viewpoint of a particular character: for example, a shot of a character looking around the room can be followed by a POV shot consisting of a surveying *pan of the room.

point size An Anglo-American unit of *type measurement now used in *desktop publishing. A point is equivalent to 1/72″.

political bias 1. In contexts where *impartiality, *balance, and/or *objectivity are normative (in particular in *public service broadcast *news reporting and political *interviews), a perceived tendency to favour or disfavour a particular political party, candidate, or policy reflected in selection and/or presentation. Such *ideological biases are variously attributed to such factors as government influence, *media ownership, or journalistic affiliations; they may or may not be regarded as involving deliberate manipulation. The standards are variable: *public service broadcasting is generally expected to aspire to higher standards of political impartiality and balance than are privately-owned channels or *newspapers. *Marxists theorists see the *mass media as propagating the *dominant ideology. Others argue that most mainstream Western journalism tends to limit discourse to a relatively narrow range of 'liberal' views. *See also* GLASGOW MEDIA GROUP; MANUFACTURE OF CONSENT. 2. The argument that media of communication differ in the political developments that they facilitate because of their relative accessibility and speed: one of the features which Neil Postman sees as contributing to the *ideological bias of a medium. These factors were also noted by Cooley in 1909. *See also* ACCESS; COMMUNICATION TECHNOLOGIES; DISTANCE COMMUNICATION.

political communication 1. Traditionally, the *production and impact of persuasive political messages, campaigns, and advertising, primarily in the *mass media: *see also* AGENDA SETTING; DOMINANT IDEOLOGY; PROPAGANDA. 2. More broadly, the flow of messages on political matters, both mediated and interpersonal: *see also* MEDIATIZATION; TWO-STEP FLOW. 3. A field within political science and *communication studies concerned with the interaction between political and media *institutions and citizen audiences.

political correctness (PC) A term typically used pejoratively for what is seen as an obsessive avoidance of language or behaviour which might be perceived as offensive or discriminatory; thus 'vertically challenged' is PC for *short*. The conservative popular press often highlight, exaggerate, or even invent examples of 'political correctness gone mad' in order to satirize views othered as the anti-free speech dogma of the political left (*see also* OTHER). The term originally referred to a US campus movement in the 1980s and early 1990s concerned to counter *bias, discrimination, and 'hate speech' arising from *racism, *sexism, and *homophobia.

political economy 1. (classical political economy, classical economics) Originally, 18th-century *Enlightenment theories of economics culminating in the free-market (*laissez-faire*) theories of the British philosopher Adam Smith (1723–90), which emphasized a harmony of interests between classes. Until the 19th century, the name for the academic study of economics (separated as a science in the late 19th century). 2. (**Marxist** or **radical political economy**) For Marx, a 'scientific' critique of capitalist relations of *production, arguing that the state represented the interests of the bourgeoisie, which exploited the working class. The term is also applied to a Marxist approach arising in the 1960s and 1970s, combining sociology and economics and based on historical *materialism. Proponents still see *ideology as subordinate to the economic base: *mass-media content is determined by the economic base of media organizations (*see also* BASE AND SUPERSTRUCTURE). Commercial media are dominated by the need to raise *advertising revenue while public broadcasting is dominated by the need to favour the middle ground and maintain a *consensus. From this perspective *media ownership and control are key issues, especially the concentration of ownership in a global market. The means of producing mass media content are owned and controlled by major corporations such as Time Warner and *media moguls such as Murdoch and the Italian Silvio Berlusconi (b.1936) in the commercial sector or by state-regulated public organizations such as the BBC. Media corporations have the power to generate *target audiences for advertisers. Proponents of the political economy approach to the mass media often define it in opposition to a *cultural studies approach which is seen as concerned with *textual analysis and audience *interpretation at the expense of political and economic factors. *See also* CROSS-MEDIA OWNERSHIP; CULTURE INDUSTRY; DEPENDENCY THEORY; DEREGULATION; MEDIA CONTROLS; MEDIA OWNERSHIP; MEDIA POLICY; REGULATION. 3. A field in political science based on the use of statistical and modelling techniques to test *hypotheses about relationships between the state and the economy (e.g. concerning economic policies and performance).

polysemy (polysemia) (*adj.* polysemic, polysemous) 1. Traditionally, in *linguistics, the capacity of a word to have two or more different senses (*compare* AMBIGUITY). The British comedian Kenneth Williams (1926–88) quipped, 'Is there any such thing as a single entendre?' Sometimes this is restricted to related

meanings, in distinction from **homonymy**. *Context can help to establish the
*preferred meaning. 2. More broadly, in *poststructuralist literary theory,
*linguistics, cultural theory, and *semiotics, an openness to a plurality of meanings
which is seen as a property of all *signs or *texts (*see also* MULTI-ACCENTUALITY).
This is a feature of open (for Barthes, *writerly) texts, and it demonstrates the
importance of active *interpretation by the reader (*see also* ACTIVE AUDIENCE
THEORY). Celeste M. Condit, an American rhetorician (b.1956), suggests that textual
polysemy can usefully be distinguished from interpretive **polyvalence**, in which
audiences agree about the *denotation of a sign or text but differ in their *evaluation
or *interpretation of it.

(⊕) SEE WEB LINKS

• Resonance in advertising rhetoric

polyvocality (polyphony) In contrast to *univocality, the use of multiple voices
as a *narrative mode within a text, typically in order to encourage diverse readings
rather than to promote a *preferred reading. *See also* DIALOGISM.

popular culture (pop culture) 1. Cultural *artefacts or media content produced
for *mass audiences. This equates popular culture with commercial success. The
formal features of *mass-media content may be interpreted in terms of *broadcast
codes. In *critical theory, this is *mass culture: the standardized commercial
products and media texts of the *culture industry, produced for the masses; these
are alleged to reflect the *dominant ideology and to produce *conformity among the
subordinate classes. Commodity culture is distinguished from the *authenticity of
traditional folk culture or from the aesthetic value of *high culture and often
dismissed as 'mere *entertainment'. The *media industries usually argue that they
deliver 'what the public wants'. *See also* COMMODIFICATION; CONSUMER CULTURE;
DUMBING DOWN; ELITISM; FRANKFURT SCHOOL. 2. The *everyday life and/or arts
and *artefacts of 'the people' within a society. The practices and artefacts seen as
reflecting the *tastes and *values of 'ordinary people' (as opposed to the minority
tastes of elite or *high culture). Historically associated with traditional folk
culture (especially *oral culture as distinct from literary culture). British *cultural
studies (e.g. Hoggart) originally defined popular culture as working-class culture.
Contemporary sociology stresses the importance of the diversity of *subcultures
(e.g. black popular culture, teenage popular culture), as distinct from *mass culture.
See also CULTURAL POLITICS. 3. The productive ways in which audiences engage
with the pervasive cultural currency to make it their own, as in *active audience
theory. In the face of the *dominant ideology, resistant audiences are capable of
*oppositional readings, using popular cultural artefacts and *imagery for their own
purposes (*see also* USES AND GRATIFICATIONS). Critics of the subversive audience
approach to popular culture dismiss it as *cultural populism. However, popular
culture clearly plays an important role in relation to the development of *personal
identity, particularly among adolescents. 4. *Mass-media content which seeks to
produce a particular conception of the collective identity of 'the people' within
a society: *see also* IMAGINED COMMUNITY.

popular factual television *See* FACTUAL GENRES.

p

pornography *Representations of sexuality intended to stimulate sexual *arousal, typically consumed by individuals in private (or anonymously in licensed premises). Judged in public as offensive, lacking in artistic or social value, and in some cases as obscene (*see* OBSCENITY). *Feminist definitions focus on representations involving the sexual subordination of women, and tend to make no allowances for redeeming artistic or social *value. Pornography can be 'soft core' or 'hard core', depending on the degree of explicitness, although the boundary lines around such categorizations are continually being redrawn over time. *See also* CENSORSHIP.

portal [Latin *porta* 'gate'] **1. (subject portal)** A website with no original *content of its own which functions as an organizing framework and a hub connecting to online material with a common *theme. **2.** A concept used by the designers of *GUI operating systems and webpages as a *metaphor to make sense of multiple 'windows' though which programs are glimpsed and *users can enter by clicking on the window.

portrait format In photography, painting, and document layout, the orientation of a rectangular viewing *window, *frame, or page so that the height is greater than the width. *Compare* LANDSCAPE FORMAT.

positioning **1.** (*marketing) Establishing a unique *brand identity for a product or service (e.g. a television channel or a magazine) that distinguishes it from comparable rivals. This is consonant with the semiotic principle that signs acquire meaning through their relationship to other signs. *See also* RELATIONAL MODEL. **2.** (social *constructionism) The ways in which individuals negotiate their *identities in everyday *discourse, distinguished from a *role as a more dynamic process enabling multiple intersecting positions. **3. (subject positioning)** (*cultural studies) The process in which members of a *target audience are expected to adopt a *role and mindset in order to make sense of a text (in any medium) in the manner intended. **4.** In nonverbal behaviour: *see* POSTURE. **5.** In filming, the placement of cameras and microphones.

positive appeals (*advertising) A persuasive strategy that stresses what the consumer would gain by purchasing the product or service. *See also* ADVERTISING APPEALS; *compare* NEGATIVE APPEALS.

positivism *Compare* INTERPRETIVISM. **1.** Broadly, a philosophical stance and philosophy of science recognizing as genuine *knowledge only verifiable *facts which can be established through scientific method (the empirical methods of natural science). In social science, it can refer to a search for general laws drawn from direct observation and objective measurement. Positivism was a major influence on *behaviourism. **2. (logical positivism)** (philosophy) A stance that only *propositions verifiable by sensory experience or logic are meaningful. This involves a rejection of metaphysical speculation and a strict separation between *facts and *values. **3.** A pejorative **(anti-positivist** or **post-positivist)** reference to simplistic, unreflexive, empirical research ill-suited to the complexity of social phenomena and human meaning-making.

post 1. *n.* **(posting)** A *message sent to a *newsgroup, discussion list, or *bulletin board: *compare* EMAIL. 2. *n.* **(postal** or **mail service)** The official communications system delivering letters and parcels. The first postal services were established in the early 16th century, but reliable and affordable mail services for ordinary people accompanied the industrial revolution. The advent of email has led to conventional mail being pejoratively referred to as '*snail mail', but physical commodities still require delivery. 3. *v.* To send a message by postal mail or to a *newsgroup, discussion list, or *bulletin board.

postcolonialism (postcolonial theory) (cultural theory) A field of study concerned with the critical analysis of the *ideological impact of Western imperialism and its continuing influence **(neocolonialism)**. 'Post-' does not signify that colonial relations have been overturned. The primary methodology is called **colonial discourse analysis**, which involves the *deconstruction of the *discourses in which colonial relations are constituted, exploring the representational strategies and *subject positions of colonialism. Influenced by Foucault's focus on *power, it is an anti-*Eurocentric investigation of the *representation of *race, *ethnicity, and nationhood and the *marginalization and othering of the colonized. Its exploration of the process of cultural *hybridization reflects an anti-essentialist notion of *identity. It is particularly associated with Said, Bhabha, and Spivak, though the fact that the members of this 'holy trinity' were based in Western universities and drawing on often abstruse *poststructuralism has attracted criticism from those prioritizing the urgent political problems of the formerly colonized. *See also* CULTURAL IDENTITY; ETHNIC IDENTITY; NATIONAL IDENTITY; OTHER.

post-Enlightenment *See* ENLIGHTENMENT.

post-feminism 1. A *discourse popularized by the *mass media in the 1990s reflecting a reaction against the *feminist theories of the 1970s and 1980s, often on the basis that the 'battle of the sexes' is over. In popular *rhetoric, a shift from 'women's lib' to 'girl power'. It is characterized by an (*essentialist) emphasis on *femininity as well as on 'the career woman'. The feminist notion of women as the passive victims of patriarchy is rejected: for instance by the American post-feminists Naomi Wolf (b.1962) and Camille Paglia (b.1947). 2. A postmodern *feminist discourse building upon earlier concerns about patriarchy but extended into other areas such as eco-feminism and *cyberfeminism. It is influenced by *poststructuralism in its rejection of *gender essentialism (e.g. in Butler's engagement with *queer theory).

post-Fordism *Compare* FORDISM. 1. *Production based on relatively small units providing specialized goods or services for segmented markets; closely associated with the decline of the old manufacturing base from the 1960s onwards and the proliferation of new *information technologies. Companies have downsized, often outsourcing parts of the work. 2. A decentralized management style focusing on coordination and facilitation of tasks rather than on control, and emphasizing flexibility. 3. The rise of *consumerism and *lifestyle identities accompanying the decline of *production and *class identities. 4. As applied to cinema, the downsizing of the major studios, the increase of outsourcing and the rise of independent producers and distributors following the demise of the *studio system.

post-industrialism (post-industrial society, post-industrial age) The changes in the form of capitalist societies since the Second World War: a shift from industrial *production to service industries and a '*knowledge economy' in which the basis of power is theoretical *knowledge rather than property, and in which higher education becomes more important. These are seen as characteristic features of *postmodern, 'postcapitalist' society. The term was popularized in a book by Bell in 1973, where he also claimed that while manual jobs would decline, a powerful new professional and technical 'knowledge class' would emerge: a notion which has been widely contested. Ronald Inglehart (b.1934), an American political scientist, has argued that the rise of post-industrialism is generating **postmaterialist** *values. Others have noted that, posited on the basis of technological advances, such arguments involve *technological determinism. *See also* INFORMATION ECONOMY; INFORMATION SOCIETY; INFORMATIZATION; KNOWLEDGE ECONOMY; POSTMODERNITY.

post-Marxism 1. (*post*-Marxism) The development of radical reworkings of *Marxism from the late 1970s, arising in reaction to classical Marxist *materialism, *economism, *historical determinism, anti-humanism, and class *reductionism and influenced by *poststructuralism and *postmodernism, notably in the rejection of *grand narratives (including classical Marxism itself). These emerged in the late 1970s, associated with theorists such as Lyotard, Baudrillard, Foucault, the Argentine political theorist Ernesto Laclau (b.1935), the Belgian political theorist Chantal Mouffe (b.1943), and Stuart Hall. From the 1980s, post-Marxism was increasingly inflected by such cross-currents as *feminism and *postcolonialism. It is an anti-essentialist approach in which *class, society, and history are no longer treated as unitary, universal, pre-discursive categories. Multiple *subject positions are constituted dynamically in *discourse in relation to *class, *gender, race, and nationality. Consequently, there is no uniform class consciousness. Post-Marxist theory has also been influenced by the Gramscian concept of *hegemony. *Ideology and *culture are seen as relatively autonomous of the economic base. *See* BASE AND SUPERSTRUCTURE; CULTURAL MATERIALISM; RELATIVE AUTONOMY.
2. (**post-*Marxism***) Sometimes loosely referring to an abandonment of *Marxism by many former Marxists, particularly after the collapse of Soviet communism in Eastern Europe in 1989–91, when the Marxism which had animated *cultural studies in the 1960s and 1970s was widely disavowed.

postmaterialism *See* POST-INDUSTRIALISM.

postmodernism Where the distinction is maintained, this is widely treated as the *culture of *postmodernity. It often refers loosely to a range of aesthetic trends or stylistic traits emerging in the arts in the post-1945 period in distinction to those of *modernism. However, it is also closely associated with philosophical stances which are variously allied with *poststructuralism, *deconstruction, radical scepticism, and *relativism—with which it shares an anti-foundationalist standpoint (*see also* FOUNDATIONALISM). Ironically postmodernism could almost be defined in terms of resisting definition. Postmodernism does not constitute a unified '*theory' (though many postmodernist theorists grant no access to any reality outside *signification). Nor is there a postmodernist aesthetic 'movement'; postmodernism is highly fragmented and eclectic. However, characteristic features of postmodern texts and practices are the use of *irony and a highly *reflexive *intertextuality—blurring the boundaries of *texts, *genres, and *media and drawing attention to the text's *constructedness and processes of construction. Postmodernism differs from modernism in embracing *popular culture and 'bad taste'. The postmodernist trend is sometimes dated from Lyotard's book, *The Postmodern Condition*, first published in 1979, which characterized postmodernist theory in terms of incredulity towards metanarratives (*see* GRAND NARRATIVES; *see also* POSTMODERNITY).

postmodernity 1. **(postmodern world; postmodern age)** A relational term (*see* MODERNITY) for the social-economic and political transformation of modern advanced industrial capitalism (*see* POST-INDUSTRIALISM; POST-FORDISM). As a historical period its beginnings are traced to various decades from the 1950s to the 1980s. Many theorists interpret it as an intensification of *modernity or capitalism rather than a fundamental break; Giddens prefers the terms **late modernity** or **high modernity**. It is associated with trends such as *globalization (global capitalism), a shift from *production to *consumption, the fragmentation of the *mass market (*see* AUDIENCE FRAGMENTATION), and the decline of the nation-state. 2. A *cultural and *ideological shift from a world of relatively stable *values, beliefs, *theories, and organizational structures to a world of flux, *fragmentation, *ambiguity, and radical scepticism (which critics see as *relativism). Lyotard notes the demise of modernity's *grand narrative of progress (*see also* ENLIGHTENMENT; POSTMODERNISM). Harvey focuses on 'space-time compression' brought about by accelerated transport and *telecommunications. *See also* McLUHANISM.

post-production The work done in film, radio, or television after the raw material making up the programme has been shot or recorded (the *production phase) and before it is shown or *broadcast. This includes *editing, *mixing the sound, and *special effects, as well as creating multiple versions for international markets. *See* ADR; FOLEY; M&E; MASTER; OFFLINE; ONLINE; *compare* PRE-PRODUCTION.

poststructuralism A range of critical stances which developed after, out of, and in relation to *structuralism in the late 1960s and which is associated with 'the *linguistic turn'. Although it is most clearly unified in terms of a reaction against certain features of structuralism, it developed structuralist notions in addition to problematizing many of them. For instance, while Saussure argued for the *arbitrariness of the relationship between the *signifier and the *signified, poststructuralists have taken this notion further, asserting that all signifieds are also signifiers, and that *signification is never final and stable (*see also* DIFFÉRANCE). More radically, many have asserted the total disconnection of the signifier and the signified (*see* EMPTY SIGNIFIER). Such stances involve philosophical *idealism and *epistemological *relativism insofar as they grant no access to any reality outside signification. The primary methodology is *deconstruction, which emphasizes the *indeterminacy of meaning, and the way in which the *dominant ideology seeks to promote the illusion of a *transcendent signified. Like structuralism, poststructuralism is built on the assumption that we are the subjects of *language rather than being simply *instrumental 'users' of it, and poststructuralist thinkers have developed further the notion of 'the constitution of the subject', rejecting the *essentialist notion of the unified self (*see* DECENTRED SELF). Consequently, poststructuralists focus neither on the author nor the reader, but on the act of reading. In terms of *textual analysis, whereas structuralism involves a focus on the text as a self-contained *structure, poststructuralism emphasizes the *intertextuality of *discourse. Poststructuralist *semiotics involves a rejection of Saussure's hopes for semiotics as a systematic 'science' which could reveal some stable, underlying master-system—any such totalizing system would always involve exclusions and *contradictions. For poststructuralists there are no fundamental *deep structures underlying forms in an external world. Poststructuralist theorists include Derrida, Foucault, Lacan, Kristeva, and the later Barthes. Poststructuralism is closely allied with *postmodernism and the terms are sometimes used interchangeably.

post-synchronization *See* SYNCHRONIZATION.

postural echo (postural congruence) In *interpersonal communication, a *similarity or mirroring of body positions and movements between two or more participants. This form of nonverbal adaptation or *accommodation is usually an unconscious signifier of *liking or *affiliation between those of similar *status, though it can sometimes be used more deliberately to attempt to reduce the impression of status differences. *See also* INTERACTIONAL SYNCHRONY; TIE SIGNS.

posture The bodily positions of individuals. Posture is typically studied as an indicator of: degree of attention or involvement; degree of status relative to other interactive partner; degree of *liking for the other person. The study of posture is an aspect of *kinesics. *See also* CLOSED POSTURE; OPEN POSTURE; ORIENTATION.

POV shot *See* POINT-OF-VIEW SHOT.

power 1. ('power to') The ability to achieve a desired outcome. 2. ('power over') For Weber, 'the ability to exert control over people, even against their own will.' If it is accepted as legitimate, based on *status, and requires no direct coercion, it is authority (*see also* LEGITIMATION); *coercive power* is based on *force*. Economic power is based on *class, social power is based on *status, and political power is based on *domination*. 3. A transformative influence attributed to *social structures or *institutions, rather than to individual will. In *Marxist theory, power is a consequence of *class structure. Gramsci argued that power is maintained through *manipulation* in ideological *hegemony. 4. In *functionalism, the capacity to realize common goals in a social system based on a *consensus of *values rather than on coercion or domination (Parsons). This integrationist conception of power as social control or *influence* emphasizes *structure rather than *agency. 5. **(power/knowledge)** For Foucault, a ubiquitous feature of institutionalized *discourses which both constitute and control subjects (rather than something possessed by groups or individuals). Individual subjects internalize the mechanisms of social control (**governmentality**). All social and communicative relations are *power relations. Power and *knowledge are mutually constitutive. **6.** In the psychology of *interpersonal communication, *dominance: *see also* POWER RELATIONS. **7. Media power** refers to the influence attributed to the *mass media over its *audiences (hence 'the *fourth estate'). Research has shown this to be frequently exaggerated (*see* EFFECTS). The term often refers to the use of the media for deliberate persuasive purposes, as in *advertising and political campaigns, but media influences are often indirect (*see* TWO-STEP FLOW), and even unintentional, as in the case of attitudinal influence in *cultivation theory. Media power often refers to subtle *ideological influence (*see also* AGENDA SETTING; MEDIA HEGEMONY).

power distance The degree to which a *culture promotes *status differences among its members: a dimension of cultural variability identified by Hofstede. High power distance cultures are hierarchical and are often also *collectivistic cultures (as in Japan); low power distance cultures are egalitarian and are often also *individualistic cultures (as in the USA and the UK). This is reflected in *nonverbal communication. In high power distance cultures, displays of *emotion (e.g. anger and smiling) are adjusted to status far more than in low power distance cultures. *See also* INTERCULTURAL COMMUNICATION.

power law distribution A mathematical relationship between the frequency and size of an *event, where the frequency increase is inversely proportional to its size increase. For example, the Italian economist Vilfredo Pareto (1848–1923) observed that 80% of the land in Italy was owned by 20% of the population, and from this we get the **Pareto principle** or **80/20 rule**. In the context of social media where *user-generated content is produced by mass participation, the American new-media theorist Clay Shirky (b.1964) predicts that the most contributions will be made by a minority of people, and the most active individual contributor is likely to be twice as active as the second most active.

(⊕) SEE WEB LINKS

• Power laws, weblogs, and inequality

power relations 1. In interpersonal *interaction, the relative *status, *power, and/or *dominance of the participants, reflected in whether *expectations and behaviour are reciprocal, and consequently in *communicative style (*see also* RECIPROCITY). Power relations are a key dimension in *interpersonal communication. *See* ASYMMETRICAL RELATIONSHIPS; COMPLEMENTARY RELATIONSHIPS; PARALLEL RELATIONSHIPS; SYMMETRICAL RELATIONSHIPS. **2.** Relationships of *dominance and subordination between different groups: for instance within stratified social systems or in international relations (e.g. the West vs the rest). **3.** For Foucault, the various patterns of domination and resistance in different social *settings. He insisted that 'There cannot be a society without power relations.'

ppi (pixels per inch) *See* DOTS PER INCH.

PPV *See* PAY-PER-VIEW.

PR *See* PUBLIC RELATIONS.

pragmatic function *See* INTERPERSONAL FUNCTION.

pragmatics 1. (*linguistics) A branch of *semantics concerned with the communicative use and *functions of language in particular social *contexts, especially in conversations: *see also* DISCOURSE ANALYSIS; ILLOCUTIONARY ACT; IMPLICATURE; SPEECH ACT. 2. For Charles W. Morris, a branch of *semiotics concerned with the relation between *signs and their interpreters.

prägnanz [German 'pregnant']. In *gestalt psychology, the grouping of ambiguous sensory stimuli into coherent 'good figures', 'pregnant' with meaning. It is often argued that the simplest *interpretation is the one favoured: this may variously be the one which is perceived as the simplest, is structurally the simplest, has the fewest structural features, is recognized the quickest, is easiest to remember, or is easiest to describe (*see* GESTALT LAWS).

predicate *See* SUBJECT.

pre-emergent forms *See* EMERGENT FORMS.

preferred reading (preferred meaning) A concept used in relation to *texts (typically in *mass-communication *genres) where the *sender of a *message consciously or unconsciously encodes it in ways which function to guide, limit, or control its *interpretation by *receivers. It is not the same as an *intended meaning, since it may embody many assumptions of which even the producers of the discourse were not consciously aware. Stuart Hall originally used the term in relation to television news and current affairs programmes but it has subsequently been applied more widely. Hall tries to address the objections of researchers in the *uses and gratifications field by conceding that although the *interpretation of a text is primarily determined by *audiences, the *encoders of a message are nevertheless more powerful than its *decoders because they also have control over the means of sign *production, or the very *ideological codes that audiences use to form their interpretation of a text. However, Hall has been criticized for appearing to imply that such meanings are invariably encoded in the *dominant code: this stance tends to *reify the *medium and to downplay conflicting tendencies within texts. Sociologists deny that the concept of preferred reading entails *textual determinism since *interpretation involves several possible *reading positions. Just as *reading a text involves an assumption that texts have authors and that authors have intentions, it also requires the assumption that there is likely to be a preferred reading (*see* COMMUNICATIVE PRESUMPTION) and some *inference about what this might be— even if the reader does not accept this reading. *See also* ABERRANT DECODING; CIRCUIT OF COMMUNICATION; ENCODING/DECODING MODEL; HEGEMONIC READING; NEGOTIATED READING; OPEN AND CLOSED TEXTS; OPPOSITIONAL READING.

pre-production The preparatory planning and logistics phase of a film or a radio or television programme before it is shot or recorded. In the wider sense, this includes scripting and financing (*see* PITCH). Once financing has been obtained this includes recruiting *production staff, casting, hiring studio space and *post-production facilities, scouting locations, and *storyboarding. *Compare* POST-PRODUCTION; PRODUCTION.

prereflexive *adj.* 1. Descriptive of an individual's immediate, uncritical reaction to something prior to any conscious *evaluation. For example, when someone knows that they enjoyed a film without knowing why. *Compare* REFLEXIVITY. 2. For Sartre, a state of consciousness prior to reflection that he tries to reconstruct as part of his argument that personal consciousness depends on reflection.

presence *See also* ABSENT PRESENCE; MEDIATION; PARASOCIAL INTERACTION; PRESENCE STUDIES; PSYCHOLOGICAL DISTANCE; SOCIAL PRESENCE; SUSPENSION OF DISBELIEF; TELEPRESENCE; VIRTUAL PRESENCE. 1. Being in a particular place at a particular time: as with *co-present participants in the phenomenological *immediacy of *face-to-face interaction. 2. A powerful *aura associated with someone or something. 3. In *mediated communication or other mediated experiences such as *virtual worlds, a phenomenal experience of 'being there' in which, for a user who is highly involved, the *medium or *technology retreats to *transparency and the experience feels (on some level) unmediated, akin to *face-to-face interaction. It tends to be associated with relatively experienced users of the medium.

presence, metaphysics of *See* DECONSTRUCTION.

presence studies A loose affiliation of computer scientists, engineers, and psychologists concerned with investigating perceptions of being in virtual environments who publish their findings in the MIT journal *Presence: Teleoperators and Virtual Environments. See also* VIRTUAL PRESENCE.

(⊕) **SEE WEB LINKS**
• The concept of presence

presentational media *See* MEDIUM.

press 1. **(printing press)** A method of producing written (or illustrated) texts by applying ink to *movable type or embossed engravings and pressing these onto sheets of paper, initially using a hand-operated press. *Mechanical reproduction (and mass production) via steam-driven presses revolutionized *printing in the 19th century. 2. A generic *metonym for journalists or for any kind of news organization.

press baron A *newspaper proprietor who is perceived as wanting to influence or control what is published. *See also* MEDIA MOGUL.

press release A written statement or news story issued by an organization (e.g. a corporation, government department, political party, pressure group) which is circulated to the media in the hope that it is reported. Typically press releases are written by a **press officer**, a professional journalist who is employed by the organization concerned. *See also* PUBLIC RELATIONS; VIDEO NEWS RELEASE.

prestige *See* STATUS.

price appeals (value appeals) A psychological and rhetorical strategy in *advertising that seeks to persuade consumers that a particular product or service is cheaper or better value for money than its rivals. A *rational appeal; *see also* ADVERTISING APPEALS.

primacy effect (law of primacy, principle of primacy) 1. (cognitive psychology) The tendency in free recall for individuals to be better able to recall the first items in a series than those in the middle. Applying this to persuasive communication would favour 'anticlimax order': *see* CLIMAX; *compare* RECENCY EFFECT. 2. (social psychology) A tendency in *impression formation for first impressions or prior *knowledge of others to dominate our *evaluation of them. 3. In persuasive communication, the *hypothesis that whichever side of an issue is presented first will have a greater influence on the audience. There is evidence both for and against this, suggesting that other factors are more important. *Compare* RECENCY EFFECT.

primacy of the signifier (*semiotics) The prioritization of the form of the sign (the *signifier) over what it signifies (the *signified). This is the basis for the argument that 'reality' or 'the world' is at least partly created by the *language we use—i.e. that the *signified is shaped by the signifier rather than vice versa. Lévi-Strauss emphasized the primacy of the signifier, initially as a strategy for *structural analysis. Poststructuralist theorists such as Lacan, Barthes, Derrida, and Foucault have developed this notion into a *metaphysical presupposition of the priority of the signifier, but its roots can be found in the *bracketing of the referent by Saussure. Critics attack this stance as *idealism. *Compare* SAPIR-WHORF HYPOTHESIS.

primary and secondary definers **Primary definers** are credible individuals and *institutions granted media access to enable their initial *framing of *events which are assumed to be within their area of competence: for instance, experts, official sources, courts, leading politicians, and senior religious figures. The *mass media are **secondary definers**. *See also* AMPLIFICATION OF DEVIANCE; MORAL PANIC.

primary and secondary effects In *effects research, **primary effects** are those which are immediate or more predictable while secondary effects are those which are subsequent or less predictable. **Secondary effects** are distinguished from *indirect effects. The terms do not signify relative importance: a secondary effect could be more important than the primary one.

primary and secondary groups A **primary group** is a small group based largely on long-term *face-to-face interaction, and typically based on *affiliation, such as a family or a friendship group; a **secondary group** is one based on shared goals or interests in which the members are rarely if ever in face-to-face contact with each other, such as a political party or trade union (Cooley). Primary groups are major agents in *socialization; their members tend to share *values and behavioural *norms. **Primary** and **secondary relationships** are those obtaining in primary and secondary groups, respectively. The distinction is not clearcut. *See also* GROUP IDENTIFICATION; PEER GROUP.

primary audience Targeted group for some form of mediated communication, such as for an *advertising campaign or a television channel, defined by *demographics and/or *lifestyle (*see also* TARGET AUDIENCE). *See also* DUAL AUDIENCE; *compare* SECONDARY AUDIENCE.

primary colours (primaries) Pure *colours which cannot be decomposed and which form the basis of other colours. In painting (based on 'the pigment wheel') they are red, yellow, and blue (*see* SUBTRACTIVE COLOUR). In colour *printing (based on 'the process wheel') these are cyan, magenta, and yellow. In theatrical lighting, video, and computer graphics (based on 'the light wheel') they are red, green, and blue, roughly the peak sensitivities of the cones in the human retina (*see* ADDITIVE COLOUR). *Compare* SECONDARY COLOUR.

primary deviance *See* LABELLING THEORY.

primary emotions *See* FACIAL EXPRESSION.

primary involvement *See* HIGH AND LOW INVOLVEMENT.

prime time US term for the night-time period when television audiences are largest: usually from 7 p.m. until midnight. *Compare* PEAK TIME.

priming *See also* MEDIA PRIMING. 1. (cognitive psychology) The triggering of particular *expectations, associations, or memories by a contextual cue (or *prime*): for instance, recognition of the word 'butter' is faster if the word 'bread' has just been used. In *schema theory, an active schema can be seen as a form of priming. The concept is similar to that of *perceptual set. 2. In persuasive communication, providing a prior *context within which subsequent communication will be interpreted.

printing Any automated or mechanical process of reproducing multiple copies of written text, pictures, and/or photographs, through the controlled application of inks or dyes onto a surface, or in the case of photography through chemical reactions. *See also* DESKTOP PUBLISHING; MECHANICAL REPRODUCTION; MOVABLE TYPE; PRESS.

print journalism Published writing on news and current affairs that, along with photographs and *advertising, make up the content of *newspapers, magazines, and other 'paper and ink' periodicals and journals. *Compare* DIGITAL JOURNALISM; ELECTRONIC JOURNALISM.

print media 1. **(print-based media)** Broadly, any written or pictorial form of communication produced mechanically or electronically using *printing, photocopying, or digital methods from which multiple copies can be made through automated processes. 2. More narrowly, any form of 'ink and paper' communication that is not hand-written or hand-typed, including books, circulars, journals, lithographs, memos, magazines, *newspapers, pamphlets, and periodicals.

priorism *See* FOUNDATIONALISM.

private sphere *See* PUBLIC AND PRIVATE SPHERES.

privatization of information (commodification of information) The turning of *information into a *commodity that can be bought and sold rather than being freely available. *See also* INFORMATION ECONOMY.

process model *See* TRANSMISSION MODELS.

process-oriented communication (process-centred) In contexts such as *organizational communication, specialist-client relationships, and conflict management, a *communication style which pays particular attention to *how* an outcome is achieved and/or stresses *interaction (as distinct from purely *instrumental communication). It can be seen as a form of *receiver-oriented communication.

producer In *advertising, film, radio, theatre, and television, a person who oversees a *production from beginning to end and has ultimate responsibility for it, particularly in the areas of logistics and finance. In television, usually the most important member of the crew (above the *director) who is also involved in making many of the creative decisions.

producer choice A controversial policy introduced at the BBC in the 1990s that ran the organization's internal facilities as a market place in which BBC radio and television staff had to compete with outside companies to win contracts from programme *producers.

product-image format *See* PRODUCT-SYMBOL FORMAT.

product-information format (product-oriented advertising) A style of *advertising that focuses primarily on the product and stresses its utility. This includes *description, characteristics, benefits, price, performance, design, and construction. It tends to be text heavy: illustration is primarily used to visualize the product and packaging. This style was dominant in the late 19th and early 20th century but has been in steady decline since then. The term is used by Leiss and his colleagues. *See also* ADVERTISING FORMATS; RATIONAL APPEALS; *compare* DEMASSIFICATION; LIFESTYLE FORMAT; PERSONALIZED FORMAT; PRODUCT-SYMBOL FORMAT.

production 1. Broadly, the generation of a *sign, *text, *utterance, or *message (*see also* TEXTUAL PRODUCTION), often distinguished from reception but in some cases applied even more broadly to the generation of *meaning. 2. The process of making a media product or *text, typically undertaken within the constraints of a fixed time-limit and budget. 3. A moment in the *circuit of communication and *circuit of culture: *compare* CIRCULATION; CONSUMPTION; CULTURAL REPRODUCTION; DISTRIBUTION. 4. A generic term for a media product which is forthcoming or is in the process of being made: *compare* POST-PRODUCTION; PRE-PRODUCTION. 5. The creation or *performance of a pre-existing text associated with a particular director, company, and/or place: e.g. the ill-fated production of *Don Quixote* by the British film-maker Terry Gilliam (b.1940), the National Theatre's production of *Othello*, or the Broadway production of *Cats*.

production company A business that specializes in developing and producing media content (typically films or television programmes) to be commissioned and/or financed by other companies. The production company oversees the entire *production process from *pre-production to *post-production, hiring the staff and facilities. *Compare* DISTRIBUTION; MARKETING.

production still *See* STILL FRAME.

production values A judgement of quality preceded by the adjectives 'high' or 'low', which represents an *evaluation of how much care and money has been spent in the realization of a media product or *text.

productivity (creativity) (*linguistics) The ability to create new *messages by combining existing words (or *signs): one of the *design features of human language, in this case a feature shared with bee dancing, the 'language' of bees (Hockett).

product-oriented advertising *See* PRODUCT-INFORMATION FORMAT.

product placement The promotion of a particular product or brand through its visible inclusion as part of the set or scenery in a film or television *production.

product-symbol format (product-image format) A style of *advertising that tends to feature abstract symbolic associations (e.g. with status, glamour, beauty, or health). The product is depicted within a *context, though typically natural or social *settings operate as a *code rather than a locus of use. Such ads depend on *symbolism, *metaphor, *analogy, *connotation, *allusion, or allegory. This sometimes works by simple *juxtaposition (*see also* MEANING TRANSFER). The term is used by Leiss and his colleagues, who suggest that, although it is still current, the heyday of this style was from around 1925 to 1945. *See also* ADVERTISING FORMATS; EMOTIONAL APPEALS; *compare* DEMASSIFICATION; LIFESTYLE FORMAT; PERSONALIZED FORMAT; PRODUCT-INFORMATION FORMAT.

pro-filmic (pro-filmic event) Everything placed in front of the camera that is then captured on film and so constitutes the film image. *See also* MISE-EN-SCÈNE.

program *See* COMPUTER PROGRAM.

programme 1. In radio and television, a discrete presentation typically lasting half an hour or an hour (in commercial stations interrupted by ad breaks), produced as a stand-alone entity: for example, as an *episode of a *series or as a news bulletin: *compare* NON-PROGRAMME MATERIAL. 2. Up until the 1970s, a term for a broadcast service in the UK, synonymous with *network in the US: for example, the 'National Programme' was a radio service broadcast from London in the 1930s.

programme flow *See* TELEVISION FLOW.

programme schedule A menu of television content for a certain period of viewing: for example, daytime, *prime time, or a forthcoming season. In commercial stations, programme schedules are designed to maximize audience numbers and consequently emphasize entertainment (*see* ENTERTAINMENT FUNCTION). However, the Reithian approach to *public service broadcasting favoured deliberately mixing popular programmes with 'high-minded' content devised to inform and educate audiences (*see* REITHIANISM).

progressive scanning A method of producing television pictures where all of the lines in one *frame of video are displayed in a continuous vertical scan, unlike *interlace scanning where they are divided into two *fields.

progressive segmented frame (PSF) A digital high-definition video format in which both *fields of video are encoded with an image that represents the same instant of time. This creates a *filmic look to the motion of video which, unlike *film mode, does not reduce the vertical *resolution of the image.

proiaretic code (action code, the voice of empirics) The elements relating *events and constructing the *plot in a *realist *narrative. One of five *narrative codes identified by Barthes. *See also* NARRATION.

projection *See* EXTERNALIZATION.

prolepsis *See* FLASHFORWARD.

promotional culture A pejorative term for the permeation of social life by *marketing.

propaganda [Latin 'propagation'] Persuasive mass communication that filters and *frames the issues of the day in a way that strongly favours particular interests; usually those of a government or corporation (*compare* AGENDA SETTING). Also, the intentional manipulation of *public opinion through lies, half-truths, and the selective re-telling of history. *See also* DISINFORMATION; MANUFACTURE OF CONSENT; PUBLIC RELATIONS.

(⊕) SEE WEB LINKS
• *Propaganda*: Edward Bernays

propaganda model *See* MANUFACTURE OF CONSENT.

proposition 1. Loosely, a statement or assertion. 2. In *linguistics (specifically *semantics), the *meaning expressed by a declarative sentence. The same proposition could be expressed by different sentences and in different *languages. Philosophically such propositions (specifically in logic), are either true or false. Gombrich insisted that 'statements cannot be translated into images' and that 'pictures cannot assert', adding that 'language has statements or propositions which can be true or false; *representations cannot. Only statements about representations can be true or false.' 3. (*narratology) One of the network of basic units of meaning to which plots can be reduced (e.g. Hero kills dragon).

propositional meaning *See* IDEATIONAL MEANING.

propositional representation *See* MENTAL REPRESENTATION.

prosody Meaningful vocal variations accompanying speech, including stress or emphasis, *intonation, *pitch variation, pausing, rhythm, tempo, and loudness. *See also* BACK-CHANNEL; DISCOURSE ANALYSIS; VOCAL CUE.

protagonist The leading character in a story, play, or film, usually the *hero or heroine. A character with whom they are engaged in *conflict is the *antagonist.

proxemics A branch of *nonverbal communication concerned with the study of the social and cultural use of *personal space and of spatial issues in *interaction. It explores issues such as *territoriality, crowding, and privacy. The term was coined by Edward T. Hall. *See also* INTERPERSONAL ZONES.

(⊕) SEE WEB LINKS
• Personal space and proxemics

proximity 1. One of the *gestalt laws of *perceptual organization, being the principle that, in visual patterns, features that are close together are grouped together perceptually as units. This principle has a practical application in text design (*see also* GESTALT LAWS). 2. In relation to *news values and *newsworthiness, the factor of closeness, both literal and metaphorical, as a basis for the selection of news items. *Ethnocentrism is evident in Western news coverage in the featuring of countries which are culturally, economically or politically close, regardless of size or proximity. There is a general bias in favour of things 'close to home'. The so-called **McLurg's Law**, named after a legendary British news editor, is that 1 dead Briton is worth 5 dead Frenchmen, 20 dead Egyptians, 500 dead Indians, and 1000 dead Chinese. 3. In *nonverbal communication, physical closeness of interactive partners: proximity is seen as an important cue for *liking. *See also* HIGH-CONTACT CULTURES; INTERPERSONAL DISTANCE; INTERPERSONAL ZONES; LOW-CONTACT CULTURES; PROXEMICS. 4. **Psychological proximity**: *see* PSYCHOLOGICAL DISTANCE.

PSB *See* PUBLIC SERVICE BROADCASTING.

pseudo-communicator *See* COMMUNICATOR.

pseudo-event Boorstin's pejorative term for occurrences staged for the *mass media to report. The production and promotion of such *events makes them more dramatic than spontaneous events. Writing in 1961, Boorstin argued that news is increasingly 'packaged', having become 'news making' rather than 'news gathering' (*see also* FICTION VALUES; STORY MODEL; TABLOIDIZATION). 'Synthetic' celebrities and stars who are 'famous for being famous' are part of the same phenomenon (*compare* PROMOTIONAL CULTURE).

PSF *See* PROGRESSIVE SEGMENTED FRAME.

PSI *See* PARASOCIAL INTERACTION.

psychical distance *See* AESTHETIC DISTANCE.

psychoanalytic theory (psychoanalytical theory) Psychological *models, *hypotheses, and *propositions concerning the unconscious *motivations of human behaviour. Freud, who introduced the term **psychoanalysis**, defined it in 1922 as 'a procedure for the investigation of mental processes which are almost inaccessible in any other way.' Freud argued that unconscious and repressed desires and anxieties could be revealed by skilful *interpretation of the *symbolism and *imagery in dreams, and by extension, in works of art (*see also* CONDENSATION;

DISPLACEMENT; DREAM-WORK; LATENT MEANING; MANIFEST CONTENT; REPRESSION).
Psychoanalytic theory has been most influential in relation to the notion of the
*constitution of the subject, especially gendered *subjectivity (*see also* CINEMATIC
APPARATUS; GAZE), although the Freudian conception of the Oedipus complex has
been repeatedly contested and retheorized (particularly in relation to *feminist
criticisms). Lacan, who saw the unconscious as structured 'like a language' and
dreams as a form of *discourse (*see also* DEEP STRUCTURE; STRUCTURALISM),
emphasizes the role of *language in structuring *subjectivity (*see* SYMBOLIC).
Psychoanalytical theory has been particularly influential in *cultural studies in the
*representation of the subject not as unitary and centred but as fragmented and
riven by inner conflicts (*see also* DECENTRED SELF). In *Marxist theory, *critical
theorists draw on psychoanalytic theory in order to account for subjectivity, while
Althusser uses Lacanian psychoanalysis to explore how *ideology operates (*see*
INTERPELLATION). Psychoanalytic theory has been criticized in particular for
ignoring the social, political, and historical *context and for failing to account for
*class, '*race', and age. *See also* EXTERNALIZATION; FANTASY; FETISHISM; GAZE;
IDENTIFICATION THEORY; IMAGINARY; JOUISSANCE; LACK; OEDIPAL TRAJECTORY;
OVERDETERMINATION; PARAPRAXIS; REAL; SUTURE; VOYEURISM.

psychographics (psychographic segmentation) A portmanteau term
(*psychological + demographics*). (*marketing) The classification of *target audiences
according to psychological rather than *demographic factors: primarily *values,
*attitudes, opinions, interests, personality, and *lifestyles. Often a synonym for
*lifestyles. *See also* SEGMENTATION.

(((⊕))) SEE WEB LINKS
• The VALS™ Survey

psycholinguistics The psychology of *language: a branch of *linguistics and of
psychology concerned with the mental processes involved in linguistic
communication, including language acquisition and the *production and
*comprehension of speech and writing.

psychological distance In *mediated *interpersonal communication, a
*phenomenological feeling of the other person not 'being there' (as opposed to
psychological closeness or **proximity**). Rutter argues that the key difference
between the media used in interpersonal communication is the extent to which they
encourage psychological distance or closeness. This can have various consequences
for *communication styles, depending on other factors, such as tasks, *roles, and
*social relationships. *See also* CUELESSNESS; IMMEDIACY; PRESENCE.

psychological effects 1. Any psychological changes in individuals or groups
attributed to specific causes. 2. In relation to media, psychological influences or
implications of the *mass media or *new media of communication—a focus of
academic media research within the *effects tradition: *see also* ATTITUDINAL
EFFECTS; BEHAVIOURAL EFFECTS; COGNITIVE EFFECTS; MEDIA PRIMING; VIOLENCE
DEBATE; *compare* SOCIAL EFFECTS.

psychologism (psychological reductionism) Typically a pejorative term for the reduction of phenomena to purely psychological explanations. *Compare* SOCIOLOGISM.

PTC *See* PIECE-TO-CAMERA.

P2P *See* PEER-TO-PEER NETWORK.

public access television *See* COMMUNITY BROADCASTING.

public and private spheres 1. In modern sociology, respectively, the realm of politics, public *institutions, and paid employment and the domestic world of the home and family relations. Public life is governed by shared *norms and *values while private life is the realm of the intimate, of *personal identity, and free will (*compare* PRIMARY AND SECONDARY GROUPS). Historians often trace the separation to *modernity, industrialization, urbanization, and the gendered division of labour, though in classical Greece there was also a division between the public world of politics and the private world of family and economic relations. Insofar as they can even be separated, in the discourse of *postmodernism the public and private spheres are not fixed but fluid (*see also* BACK STAGE). Meyrowitz argues that 'electronic media have tended to . . . blur the dividing line between private and public behaviours'. 2. An *ideological dichotomy between domains gendered respectively as male and female, as in 'a woman's place is in the home'. The public sphere is that of adult males; the private sphere is that of women and children. Consequently men tend to be defined by what they do whereas women are associated with nurturing relationships. *Feminists argue that this split is a myth masking women's subordination and perpetuating *gender inequality since both domains are both personal and political. Further *connotations are associated with the public/private split (e.g. culture/nature, production/reproduction, work/consumption, reason/emotion, and instrumentality/expressivity). While in many contexts the public sphere has traditionally been privileged, *romanticism (and especially Rousseau) associated the public sphere with *conformity and falsity and the private sphere with *authenticity and intimacy. *See also* PERSONA. 3. An arena for the open discussion of common concerns and collective social interests (*see also* PUBLIC OPINION). For Habermas, the public sphere derives from the bourgeois salons and pamphleteering of the 18th century. It is 'a network for communicating *information and points of view', and in the modern world the *mass media can be seen as constituting this arena (raising the question of inequalities of *access and *representation). Modern anxieties over the alleged decline of the public sphere and the deterioration of rational discourse about public affairs invariably implicate the mass media (*see also* FICTION VALUES; MEDIATIZATION; STORY MODEL; TABLOIDIZATION), market forces being seen as a major threat to *public interest broadcasting. Giddens argues that the mass media have in fact expanded the public sphere; others that they have transformed the nature of **publicness** though sociologists have long argued that 'the public' does not exist as a singular entity: *see* PUBLICS.

public broadcasting service Any radio or television *institution wholly or partly financed through taxation, grants, or donations, and run by the state or as charities. Such services are typically intended to have a democratic function, independent of government but subject to government regulation seeking to maintain the public service ideal (*see also* PUBLIC SERVICE BROADCASTING; REITHIANISM; SPECTRUM SCARCITY). However, there are pressing commercial and technological challenges to such regimes (*see also* COMMERCIALIZATION). Notable public service broadcasters are the BBC in the UK, ABC in Australia, CBC in Canada (partly funded by advertising), SABC in South Africa, TVNZ and RNZ in New Zealand, and PBS in America.

public distance *See* INTERPERSONAL ZONES.

public domain 1. A category of media *content not subject to *copyright restrictions. 2. A metaphorical area or repository in which *information is placed to which members of the public have unrestricted *access.

publicity model A metaphor for the primary function of the *mass media as being catching and holding *attention (McQuail). This involves more emphasis on *form and technique than on message *content (*see also* MEDIATIZATION). It is a focus which meets the immediate goal of attracting audiences, which, in commercial media, can be sold to advertisers (*see also* AUDIENCE SHARE; RATINGS; REACH). In such media, broadcast programmes, for instance, can be said to exist to support commercials. The publicity factor can thus be seen as underlying the competitiveness of the media. The audience is seen as relatively passive, seeking diversion or entertainment (*see* DIVERSION FUNCTION; ENTERTAINMENT FUNCTION). The goal of attracting audiences has led to the accusation of the dominance of *fiction values (*see also* STORY MODEL; TABLOIDIZATION). In *ideological framings, this also facilitates *agenda setting. *Compare* DOMINANCE MODEL; MANIPULATIVE MODEL; RECEPTION MODEL; RITUAL MODEL; TRANSMISSION MODELS.

publicity stunt An *event contrived so that it is reported in the media. *See also* PSEUDO-EVENT.

public journalism *See* CIVIC JOURNALISM.

public opinion Views about issues or *events of social concern that are expressed openly at a particular time by a significant percentage of the population, as distinct from the private opinions of individuals or those expressed within small circles. Since the advent of 'opinion polls', the term is widely taken to refer to the results of *surveys. In theories of political liberalism, public opinion is seen as involving free debate leading to the possibility of a rational *consensus (*see also* PUBLIC AND PRIVATE SPHERES). Critics argue that it can be manipulated by governments and powerful *institutions (*see also* DOMINANCE MODEL; DOMINANT IDEOLOGY; MANIPULATIVE MODEL; MANUFACTURE OF CONSENT; MEDIA HEGEMONY). The *mass media play a key role in the dissemination (and filtering) of views and many argue that they are central in generating a consensus (*see also* AGENDA SETTING; GATEKEEPERS; IMAGINED COMMUNITY; NEWS VALUES; SPIRAL OF SILENCE). However, this tends to homogenize media content (*see* PLURALIST MODEL) and underestimate the active interpretive role of audiences (*see* ACTIVE AUDIENCE THEORY; ENCODING/DECODING MODEL; RECEIVER SELECTIVITY; *see also*

J-CURVE; TWO-STEP FLOW). Despite popular usage, public opinion does not reflect a general consensus. In democratic societies there are multiple opinions and *publics. On any controversial issue, public opinion is divided between several alternative and inconsistent viewpoints.

(())) SEE WEB LINKS

• *Public Opinion*: Walter Lippmann

public relations (PR) 1. Any enterprise seeking to generate free media coverage (forfeiting the control over the message that is offered by *advertising). 2. Creating, *framing, and/or shaping news stories to favour the interests of those who are represented: *see also* SPIN.

publics (sociology) Loose, transitory, and heterogeneous social collectivities (not normally termed 'groups') unified by shared interest in particular public *events or issues (*see also* EPISTEMIC COMMUNITY). The members of such collectivities may not necessarily have any direct contact with each other and may be personally unknown to each other. In this sense, any public issue or event has its own public as long as that issue is a matter of widespread public interest, and 'the public' does not exist. *See also* PUBLIC AND PRIVATE SPHERES; PUBLIC OPINION.

public service broadcasting (PSB) Any broadcasting regime with the ideal of giving priority to the interests of the general public rather than commercial interests, often framed as giving the public what it *needs* rather than what it *wants*, offering a forum for disseminating *information within the public sphere (*see also* BALANCED PROGRAMMING; PUBLIC AND PRIVATE SPHERES; PUBLIC BROADCASTING SERVICE; *compare* MARKET MODEL). In such conceptions, PSB is seen as having a democratic function (*see also* ACCESS), *information and *education being more important than *entertainment, and the quality of programme content being a high priority (*see also* QUALITY TELEVISION; REITHIANISM). It also makes a major contribution to shaping a sense of *national identity (*see also* IMAGINED COMMUNITY). PSB has been increasingly eroded by commercial pressures, and some argue that it is no longer a tenable model (*see also* AUDIENCE FRAGMENTATION; COMMERCIALIZATION; DUMBING DOWN; FICTION VALUES; SPECTRUM SCARCITY). In the UK, the Broadcasting Act of 1954 led to the break-up of the BBC monopoly and to Independent Television (*see* DUOPOLY), the Broadcasting Act of 1982 recognized the needs of *minority audiences and led to Channel 4, and those of 1990 and 1996 accommodated the 'free market economics' of satellite television and digital broadcasting (*see also* DEREGULATION).

publishing The activity of mass producing and disseminating *information either via the medium of print, or electronically on the *internet.

pull-down (3:2 pull-down) A method used to transfer film running at 24 frames per second via a *telecine for transmission on *NTSC television systems running at 30 frames per second. The first *frame of film occupies three television *fields; the next, two fields, and so on.

pull focus A technique in *cinematography of shifting focus between two subjects placed at different distances in front of the camera and filmed using a long lens that restricts the *depth of field. The result is that one subject goes out of focus as the other comes sharply into focus. This creates a shifting of emphasis: for example between two characters. *Compare* SELECTIVE FOCUS.

pulse, pulseband *See* DIGITAL TRANSMISSION.

punctum (*pl.* **puncta**) [Latin 'puncture' or 'wound'] A term used by Barthes to refer to an incidental but personally poignant detail in a photograph which 'pierces' or 'pricks' a particular viewer, constituting a private meaning unrelated to any cultural *code.

pupil dilation The expansion of the opening in the iris of the eye. Pupil dilation is involuntary, and usually merely an adjustment to darker conditions, but it can also communicate emotional *arousal (*see also* LEAKAGE). Even with photographs, viewers express more interest in an attractive model when the pupils are retouched to appear larger. In *face-to-face interaction this kind of nonverbal *signal is neither deliberately intended nor consciously noticed, so if we count it as an act of communication then it reminds us that neither of these is a necessary condition for communication.

purity *See* SPECTRAL PURITY.

purposes 1. Broadly, the intentions, aims, or goals of an individual which motivate their behaviour on any particular occasion (*see also* COMMUNICATIVE PURPOSES). Some psychologists reject the concept altogether (*see also* BEHAVIOURISM). In sociology, especially in social *action theory and *symbolic interactionism, purposes, along with beliefs, are a key focus of attention in understanding the behaviour of social actors. *See also* USES AND GRATIFICATIONS. 2. Loosely, broad categories of use or social functionality for a tool or medium. In social science, this is normally termed a *function (e.g. *media functions, *linguistic functions)—except in the rhetoric of *technological determinism where *technologies may be treated as if they have purposes of their own.

qualifiers (*linguistics) Words and phrases that signify uncertainty or tentativeness, used to soften the impact of *utterances or to avert negative reactions. For instance, 'perhaps', 'probably', 'possibly', 'maybe', 'seems'. It is often argued that women tend to use qualifiers more than men, and their use is seen as *stereotypically feminine, although any such differences are dependent on *context and mitigated by age (*see also* GENDERLECT). Often used synonymously with hedges (*see also* HEDGING).

qualitative research (qualitative analysis) Methods of investigating phenomena which do not involve the collection and analysis of numerical *data. Any interpretive method which focuses on understanding *meanings. This typically includes *phenomenology, *psychoanalytic theory, *critical theory, *semiotics, *hermeneutics, *discourse analysis, *conversation analysis, *focus groups, *interviews, *symbolic interactionism, *ethnomethodology, *participant observation, and *ethnography. Positivistic critics see such methods as 'soft', unscientific, and of no value beyond the formulation of *hypotheses. Some regard qualitative and quantitative methodologies as *epistemologically incompatible; however, there need be no necessary contradiction in employing both methods in the same research study. *Compare* QUANTITATIVE RESEARCH.

quality press *See* BROADSHEET.

quality television *See also* CULTURAL CAPITAL; NARROWCAST CODES; *compare* DUMBING DOWN; FICTION VALUES; STORY MODEL; TABLOIDIZATION; TASTE. 1. For television academics in the UK, a notion associated with the Reithian values of *public service broadcasting delivering impartial news reporting and educational documentaries or traditional high-cultural forms like theatre, art, and literature targeting middle-class audiences: *see also* REITHIANISM. 2. Negatively, an oxymoron, particularly in comparison to popular commercial television. Robert J. Thompson, an American media theorist (b.1959) claimed that quality TV is best defined by what it is not: it is not standard television content. 3. For cultural critics, an evaluative judgement focusing on *textual features and relating a programme's perceived pedigree, prestige, and cultural influence to other high culture forms. Such judgements vary over time and across cultures.

quantitative research (quantitative analysis) Methods of investigating phenomena which involve the collection and analysis of numerical *data. Such methods are particularly associated with *surveys and *experiments. *Compare* QUALITATIVE RESEARCH.

quantization In *digitization, the process of mapping a continuous stream of *data such as an *analogue signal into a series of discrete points. A quantize error is the amount a value has to be rounded up or down in order to be quantized.

queer theory A critical discourse developed in the 1990s in order to deconstruct (or 'to queer') sexuality and *gender in the wake of gay *identity politics, which had tended to rely on *strategic essentialism. Opposed to gender essentialism, queer theorists see sexuality as a discursive *social construction, fluid, plural, and continually negotiated rather than a natural, fixed, core identity. 'The *representation of gender is its construction,' declares the Italian-American feminist theorist Teresa de Lauretis, who coined the term 'queer theory' in 1990. Butler, seeking to destabilize binary oppositions such as gay/straight, introduced the key concept of *performativity. Queer theorists *foreground those who do not neatly fit into conventional categories, such as bisexuals, transvestites, transgendered people, and transsexuals. Existing movements which have been significant influences are *feminism and *poststructuralism (particularly the methodology of *deconstruction). Foucault's influence has also been of central importance, particularly his argument that homosexuality (and indeed heterosexuality) as an identity emerged only in the late 19th century. Queer theory has itself been a significant influence on cultural and literary theory, *postcolonialism, and sociology, and 'queering' is now applied also to the 'boundaries' of academic disciplines.

questionnaire A document designed to be completed by selected *respondents, containing a list of questions—some eliciting *demographic information, others pertaining to a particular research topic. Questionnaires are widely used in marketing *surveys and also a standard method of *data-gathering in the social sciences, where they include an ethical disclaimer (*see* INFORMED CONSENT). *See also* ATTITUDE MEASUREMENT; CLOSED QUESTIONS; CONSENT FORM; OPEN-ENDED QUESTION; QUANTITATIVE RESEARCH.

QWERTY The standard configuration of letters on English-language computer keyboards, alluding to the initial letter sequence. This layout has persisted even though it was originally devised in the late 19th century to reduce the jamming of adjacent typewriter keys.

race A classification of human beings into distinct groups according to supposedly 'natural' biological differences related to genetic inheritance (such as skin colour or facial features). Scientifically discredited since the 1950s, the concept often features in *common-sense discourse. Race is thus *ideologically established as a fundamental and essential *identity (*see also* BIOLOGICAL ESSENTIALISM), and differences in *values, aptitudes, behaviour, and personality are subsequently 'explained' by race (*see also* BIOLOGICAL DETERMINISM). However, all human beings belong to the same species. The anti-essentialist view is that race does not explain differences: it is the result of the creation of differences through *representation. In social science and *cultural studies, race is seen as a cultural, discursive, and performative construction rather than a natural or objective *fact: the terms *ethnicity and ethnic group are usually preferred; where the term is used (as for instance, when social actors themselves employ the term), it is often placed within inverted commas. In the UK, immigrants from the Indian subcontinent are called black, but in the USA this term is reserved for those of African descent. What counts as 'race' has changed throughout the history of the concept. 'Race' is a fiction, but it is still a potent concept (or a 'necessary fiction') in some people's narratives of experience. *Strategic essentialism is a part of *identity politics. Differences of perspective are revealing: in the USA, blacks are far more likely than whites to see race as a central issue.

racial stereotypes Generalizations about the shared characteristics of a particular group, supposedly based on the biological basis of *race but actually based on perceived cultural differences from a dominant culture. Such generalizations lead to the *racist assumption that any individual who is a member of a particular 'race' must have characteristics which are part of that racial stereotype. The *mass media frequently draw upon such stereotypes as a convenient shorthand but regardless of intention, as agents of *socialization, they tend to reinforce them as *common sense. There can be no depiction of what any group is 'really like', but it is possible to broaden the range of ways in which *representations are constructed and to focus more often on specificities rather than generalizations. *See also* ETHNIC STEREOTYPES; OTHER; STEREOTYPING.

racism Prejudiced *attitudes, ideologies, practices, or policies based on an irrational belief in the inherent inferiority of those seen as belonging to other *races (*see also* ETHNOCENTRISM; EUROCENTRISM). It involves 'othering' in terms of specific negative *stereotypes of *racial difference, as well as the *exnomination of the definers. It reflects ignorance, dislike, hatred, or fear, and serves to privilege one group while justifying the exclusion, subordination, or exploitation of others.

Racism is not a monolithic and unchanging phenomenon and some commentators prefer to refer to **racisms** (e.g. the different forms it takes in the UK and the USA). It may be overt or covert, conscious or unintentional, individual, cultural, or institutional (*see also* INSTITUTIONAL BIAS). Racism has been argued to depend less on intentions than on consequences. *See also* ESSENTIALISM; EUROCENTRISM; EXOTICISM; HATE STARE; OTHER.

radical media or press *See* ALTERNATIVE MEDIA.

radio 1. The first electronic mass medium of communication, involving an audio *signal broadcast wirelessly in the form of *radio waves from a high-power *transmitter to a low-power *receiver **(radio set)**. Radio shares many of its representational and institutional characteristics with *television. *See also* LIVE; RADIO GENRES. 2. A means of *interpersonal communication over short distances which uses transmitter/receiver devices that use a low-power *half-duplex radio *signal.

radio genres The kinds of programming that make up radio broadcasts. Most commonly, music interspersed with DJ chat. *Genres such as *soap operas and quiz shows were pioneered by radio; others include situation comedies, sketch shows, serials, *plays, concerts, *documentaries, talk shows, sports reports, and news bulletins.

radio waves The part of the *electromagnetic spectrum characterized by longer *wavelengths, which have the ability to pass through solid objects and are therefore used as a transmission medium for radio, television, *mobile phones, and *WiFi applications. The Institute of Electrical and Electronics Engineers (IEEE) defines radio waves as those having a wavelength of 1000 kilometres to 1 millimetre. More commonly these are measured as in cycles per second, or hertz. AM radio uses wavelengths of (300 KHz to 30 MHz). FM radio and some TV signals use frequencies in the range of 30 to 300 MHz, which are known collectively as **very high frequency (VHF)**. TV, mobile phone, WiFi, and Bluetooth signals are in the **ultra high frequency (UHF)** range of 300–3000 MHz. These are at the very edge of the radio spectrum and because of the gradated nature of electromagnetic radiation, they may also be characterized as belonging to the microwave spectrum. At higher frequencies than radio waves, signals tend to get disrupted or even blocked by atmospheric disturbances. *See also* ELECTROMAGNETIC SPECTRUM; SPECTRUM SCARCITY.

(()) SEE WEB LINKS

• IEEE definition of radio waves

raster graphics (bitmap graphics) A *digital image format in which picture information is reproduced by 'gridding' an image and assigning a colour value to each square of the grid like a mosaic. The level of detail is determined by the number of squares (*resolution) and by the number of colours assigned to each square (*colour depth). The 'blockiness' of the overall image may be reduced by employing *anti-aliasing techniques. *Compare* VECTOR GRAPHICS; *see also* DPI.

rasterization [Latin *rastrum* 'rake', specifically, the lines left in the soil by a rake] **1.** A process of producing a picture on a television screen or computer monitor by dividing up the picture information into a series of hundreds or thousands of different coloured lines or squares, in an analogous way to an artist creating a mosaic picture out of hundreds of different coloured tiles. **2. Raster scan:** the pattern of horizontal lines that make up the pictures on a television set. **3.** (computer graphics) A method of *encoding picture information and mapping it onto a grid consisting of thousands of small squares of light called *pixels.

ratings (audience ratings) *See also* AUDIENCE MEASUREMENT. **1.** An independent measure of the relative popularity of particular television or radio programmes in terms of the number of viewers and the *audience share (based on a representative audience sample). In *media buying, a rating is the percentage of a particular *demographic group constituting the audience for a specific TV or radio programme on average per minute; accumulated ratings are called **gross rating points** (GRP), used to calculate *reach and frequency. Ratings are particularly important for commercial broadcasters, who charge more for advertisement slots during high-rated programmes. **2.** Weekly tables of the most popular television programmes in rank order made available for the general public (e.g. in listings magazines). **3. (appreciation index)** Audience scores relating to their *evaluation of the relative quality of particular radio or television programmes. **4. Rating systems** for classifying films according to their suitability for audiences: *see* CERTIFICATION.

rational appeals (logical appeals) In persuasive communication such as *advertising and political communication, rhetorical strategies based on *information or *argument (*see also* PRODUCT-INFORMATION FORMAT). In advertising, this includes *utilitarian appeals, *price appeals, and *value appeals. These may stress a product's attributes (feature appeals) or practical benefits (e.g. convenience, economy, performance, efficiency, efficacy, reliability, or durability). They may also involve comparisons with competitors. Advertisers' choices between emotional and rational appeals are influenced by whether the product or service is seen as being likely to entail high or low cognitive involvement (*see also* CENTRAL ROUTE; ELABORATION; ELABORATION LIKELIHOOD MODEL). Products such as computers are amenable to rational appeals. *See also* ADVERTISING APPEALS; HIGH AND LOW INVOLVEMENT; *compare* EMOTIONAL APPEALS.

rationalization **1.** A psychological *defence mechanism whereby an individual retrospectively justifies their actions by inventing a plausible logical explanation, repressing the true *motivation. **2.** (sociology) For Weber, the master process whereby *everyday life and *interpersonal relations in modern capitalist society are transformed by the application of the 'iron cage' of *instrumental rationality. Weber saw bureaucratic regulation, creeping managerialism, and government *surveillance as increasingly restricting individuality (*compare* FORDISM). This perspective influenced the *Frankfurt school; while agreeing with the general condemnation of narrowly instrumental reason, Habermas retains an *Enlightenment faith in reason.

reach (audience reach) *See also* AUDIENCE MEASUREMENT. 1. (broadcasting) Daily, weekly, quarterly, or yearly estimates of the total number of viewers or listeners for a television channel or a radio station. Broadcasters pay particular attention to the overall pattern of rises and falls in such figures, particularly on a yearly basis. The full dataset includes *demographic subsets. 2. For *newspapers and magazines, variously, the number of copies sold (*see* AUDITED CIRCULATION) or an estimate of the number of actual readers (publications may be passed around). These figures include demographic subsets. 3. Either the estimated number of people or households using the *internet or of those who have internet *access (sometimes indicating regularity and/or *demographics). 4. (*advertising) The percentage of the *target audience exposed at least once to a specific ad over a period (normally four weeks). This is combined with **frequency**: the average number of times that the target audience has the **opportunity to see (OTS)** the ad. These two figures are then multiplied to produce **gross rating points (GRP)** representing the value of a broadcast slot or publication space (*see also* EFFECTIVE REACH). 5. Sometimes simply a shorthand reference to reaching as many people as possible: e.g. 'Minister Tells BBC: Go For Audience Reach, Not Just Share'. *See also* AUDIENCE SHARE.

reaction shot In film and video, typically but not exclusively a *close-up of a person (or any other entity capable of emoting) responding to an ongoing or recently completed action, *event, or situation. Such *shots tend to be used as *cutaways but they also communicate information about the meaning and context of a scene. For example, a fight has a different meaning if the reaction is one of laughter rather than horror, but this also depends upon whose reaction is depicted.

readability The relative ease of *comprehension of written texts in relation to perceived levels of difficulty in *content and written *style. *Compare* LEGIBILITY.

reader Any individual *decoder or interpreter of a *message or *text: a real reader as distinct from an *implied reader.

readerly (readable) An English rendering of Barthes' use of the word *lisible* (literally 'legible'), a term he applied to *realist texts that he saw as undemanding of the reader, employing familiar *conventions or *codes and thus 'closed' rather than open to diverse *interpretations (*see also* BROADCAST CODES; CLASSIC REALIST TEXTS; CLOSED FORMS; NARRATIVE CLOSURE), in contrast with those which are *writerly. However, as Barthes' own analysis of Balzac's story *Sarrasine* shows, rather than being an inherent quality of a particular text, it depends at least partly on the way in which it is read. *Compare* OPEN AND CLOSED TEXTS.

reader-oriented 1. In the process of written composition, a stage at which the *style and *structure of a text is subordinated to the needs of the reader rather than to those of the writer; also drafts of a text which reflect this feature. For instance, compared to an earlier *writer-oriented phase, a reader-oriented text might include more *signposting. 2. **Reader-oriented theory**: *see* READER-RESPONSE THEORY; RECEPTION THEORY.

reader-response theory (reader-response criticism, reader-oriented or audience-oriented theory or criticism) In literary and cultural theory, various approaches since the late 1960s exploring the role of the reader as an active participant in making sense of texts (*see also* ACTIVE AUDIENCE THEORY; BEHOLDER'S SHARE). Reader-response theorists reject *textual determinism: they do not assume that meaning resides within the text (in contrast to *formalists; *see also* AFFECTIVE FALLACY), or that meaning is determined by *authorial intention (*see also* INTENTIONAL FALLACY). Some see such readings as 'guided' by the text (e.g. Fish, Iser, Booth); *subjectivists draw on *psychoanalytic theory, seeing readings as driven by deep psychological needs—e.g. the **transactive criticism** of the American literary critic Norman Holland (b.1927), emphasizing the 'identity theme'. Reader-response theory is *phenomenological in its location of *meaning in the act of *reading. Iser's approach is based on the idea that a text contains 'gaps' which a reader has to fill in subjectively, but the text sets limits to this creative role (*see also* IMPLIED READER). Some texts set more limits than others (*see also* CLOSED FORMS; OPEN AND CLOSED TEXTS; OPEN FORMS; READERLY; WRITERLY). *Structuralist theories emphasize that the reader has to draw upon relevant *codes in order to make sense of texts (*see also* ABERRANT DECODING; READING POSITIONS). In the late 1970s Fish argued that readers draw on reading strategies shared with particular *interpretive communities (this more social rather than individual focus tends to be called reader-oriented theory, though Fish refers to his own approach as **affective stylistics**). Literary theories tend to focus on ideal readers, ignoring both actual individuals and *subjectivity (e.g. gendered ways of reading); they also tend to focus on *cognitive processes. A related approach focusing on the historical context as an influence on readers' *interpretations is termed *reception theory. For empirical approaches in social science, *see* AUDIENCE RESEARCH. *See also* HEGEMONIC READING; NEGOTIATED READING; OPPOSITIONAL READING.

readership Those who read a particular publication (e.g. an issue of a *newspaper or magazine), regardless of whether they purchased a copy: non-purchasers being **pass-along readers** (*see* SECONDARY AUDIENCE). In the case of periodicals, this is likely to be far higher than the *audited circulation.

(((●))) SEE WEB LINKS
• National Readership Survey

reading The process of making sense of a *text. While the term 'reading' appears to be *graphocentric and *logocentric beyond its application to written verbal texts, it is applied more broadly in *semiotics to texts in any *medium. Semioticians refer to 'reading' visual media such as photographs, television, and film: this is intended to emphasize that, however *transparent such *representations may seem to be, viewers actively interpret them with reference to *textual codes and *social codes. *See also* ACTIVE AUDIENCE THEORY; BEHOLDER'S SHARE; COMPREHENSION; DECODING ABILITY; HEGEMONIC READING; INTERPRETATION; INTERPRETIVE CODE; NEGOTIATED READING; OPPOSITIONAL READING; PREFERRED READING; RECEIVER SKILLS; RECEPTION STUDIES; RECEPTION THEORY.

reading against the grain *See* OPPOSITIONAL READING.

reading direction The sequential flow of the writing system of a particular language (e.g. for English this is left to right; for Arabic or Hebrew it is right to left). Linguists Ting Ting Chan and Benjamin Bergen (2004) have offered experimental evidence that 'the location where a *writing system starts is where speakers attend first in their visual *field'. Other factors play a part of course: for most people the right hemisphere is dominant for visuo-spatial tasks, giving an attentional bias to the left visual field (*see also* HEMISPHERIC LATERALIZATION). The pattern of the *saccade varies depending on what the brain needs to know (*see also* EYE MOVEMENTS). However, Wölfflin argues that Westerners tend to read pictures from left to right. In European art, movement tends to enter from the left, and photographic manuals often recommend this direction of action. Before-and-after formats follow this pattern and even within a single *frame, figures 'facing the future' face right. Several theorists have argued that Westerners tend to identify with figures on the left, seeing it as 'our' side. In Windows Messenger, users invariably initiate a virtual hug by choosing a right-facing *emoticon. In cultures where the reading direction is right to left, these principles are reversed, as can be seen by looking at cartoon strips versioned for Western readers. *See also* DIAGONALITY; FLIPPED IMAGE; GLANCE CURVE.

(((⊕))) **SEE WEB LINKS**

• Writing direction influences spatial cognition

reading positions *See* HEGEMONIC READING; NEGOTIATED READING; OPPOSITIONAL READING.

real 1. *adj.* Actual rather than imaginary; physical rather than mental; objective rather than subjective. 2. *adj.* Empirical, as opposed to theoretical. 3. *n.* In the *psychoanalytic theory of Lacan, 'the Real' is a primal, homogeneous realm where there is no absence, loss, or *lack. Here, the infant has no centre of *identity and experiences no clear boundaries between itself and the external world. It is not what we understand as 'reality' because it cannot be known: it is excluded from the *symbolic (it resists *representation) and from the *imaginary (it is unimaginable).

realism 1. In everyday usage, a *common-sense recognition of practical realities (often contrasted with *idealism). 2. (**aesthetic realism**, sometimes synonymous with *naturalism or *illusionism) The usage of this term varies in relation to the aesthetic movements, theoretical frameworks, and media with which it is associated—so there are many different 'realisms', though a common realist goal is 'to show things as they really are'. Realism tends to be defined in opposition to other terms (especially *romanticism, *idealization, artifice, abstraction, *stylization). Realist art purports to represent without transformation a world existing prior to, and independently of, the act of *representation (*see also* MIMESIS). 'Realistic' texts even in media such as photography, film, and television involve representational *codes which are historically and culturally variable but which are experienced as natural (*see also* NATURALIZATION). Familiarity (from repetition) leads experienced viewers of such media to take these codes for granted, so that they retreat to *transparency (*see* PHOTOGRAPHIC CODES). Realism involves an *instrumental view of the *medium as a neutral means of representing reality. Realist representational practices tend to mask the processes involved in producing texts, as if they were unmediated *slices of life 'untouched by human hand' (*see also* CLASSIC REALIST TEXT; MEDIATION). Aesthetic realism leaves a compelling sense that 'the camera never lies', that television is a 'window on the world' and so on. **Anti-realist** *aesthetics involves the principle that 'progressive' texts should reflexively foreground their own construction, their own processes of *signification. *See also* REFLEXIVITY; *compare* NATURALISM. **3. Psychological realism:** the perceived coherence and plausibility of characters and their *motivations within narratives. In everyday usage 'realistic' *representations are those which are interpreted as being in some sense 'true to life'. **4. (philosophical realism)** A philosophical (specifically *epistemological) stance on 'what is real?' For those drawn towards philosophical realism, an objective and knowable reality exists indisputably 'outside' us and independently of our means of apprehending it—there are well-defined objects in the world which have inherent properties and fixed relations to each other at any instant. Realists usually acknowledge that 'social reality' is more subjective than 'physical reality' (which is seen as objective). They argue that truth (in the form of *facts) can be generated by testing beliefs or theories against external reality, which involves physical constraints on the *idealism of reality as a purely mental construction. Naïve realists assume the possibility of *direct perception of the world. Realism involves an assumption that the accurate *description of reality is possible. It is reflected in the routine assumptions of *common sense. Marxist *materialism is a version of *epistemological realism. *See also* CRITICAL REALISM; OBJECTIVISM.

reality construction While *common sense suggests that reality exists prior to, and outside *signification (*see also* REALISM), according to *constructionists (who refer to the **construction of reality**), 'reality has authors' and what we experience as reality is a set of *codes which represent the world; realities are made, not given or 'discovered'. 'Reality' is constructed in *representations. Some semioticians, following Barthes, refer to reality as an 'effect' of the sign. Many pluralize the term or bracket it with quotation marks to emphasize their rejection of the *realist notion of a single, objective, knowable, external reality. Not all realities are equal, and texts are *sites of struggle in which realities are contested. Everyday *interaction functions as **reality maintenance** (*see also* REFLEXIVITY). *See also* PHENOMENOLOGY.

reality television *See also* DOCUSOAP; FICTION VALUES; LIFESTYLE TELEVISION. **1.** A *hybrid genre combining *fly-on-the-wall *documentary, quiz show, and popularity contest which involves television broadcasts supported by *internet content such as webpages and streamed media in which selected members of the public spend time together in the same location. Notable examples include *Big Brother* and *Survivor*, which first aired in the UK in 1992 and 1997 respectively. **2.** Broadly, any *documentary programme from the 1990s onwards which is designed primarily to entertain rather than inform.

real motion *See* APPARENT MOTION.

real-time **1.** *Events perceived as happening within the ordinary timeframe experienced by people in their everyday lives. **2.** A perceptual timeframe where a computer's processing time is expressed as synchronous with the hours, minutes, and seconds experienced by a human operator. Real-time computing permits dynamic interaction with the computer, as opposed to periods where the computer's performance is either too fast or too slow for this kind of seamless operation to take place: e.g. when the computer is performing billions of calculations a second, or when it is rendering a large file.

rearrangement *See* TRANSPOSITION.

rear-view mirror *See also* McLUHANISM; MEDIA ECOLOGY. **1.** Broadly, the notion that we drive into the future looking backwards, and consequently the present cannot be revealed until it has become yesterday. **2.** A *metaphor employed by McLuhan to refer to the tendency to *frame new technologies in terms of those from the recent past: for example, the telephone was first called the 'talking telegraph'.

receiver **1.** In the simplest *transmission models of communication (in which a *sender transmits a *message to a receiver), a person who receives the message, or more broadly the *audience for the message. This is the most common meaning of references to receivers in communication contexts (listeners, readers, viewers). Sometimes distinguished from addressee on the basis that the receiver is not necessarily the intended *reader. The term is often criticized for connoting passivity. *See* ACTIVE AUDIENCE THEORY; *see also* ADDRESSER AND ADDRESSEE; RECEPTION THEORY; SENDER/RECEIVER. **2.** In *Shannon and Weaver's model of communication (1949), the element which changes the transmitted *signal into a message that it forwards to the *destination. Weaver notes that in *speech communication the receiver would be the ear 'and the associated eighth nerve' of the listener. In subsequent *information theory, whatever converts a physical signal into a usable form. **3.** (*communications technology) A device that detects and decodes an electromagnetic *signal sent from a *transmitter which is modulated to carry encoded *information: e.g. a telephone, a radio, or a television set (*see also* DECODER).

receiver bias *See* RECEIVER SELECTIVITY.

receiver factors In *models of communication or *persuasion, specific *variables associated with the receiver(s) that research has identified as among those that can affect the effectiveness of the *message. These might include: age, sex, level of education, *self-esteem, resistance to persuasion, level of involvement, incentives for participation, and so on. For instance, those most vulnerable to persuasion are those with low *self-esteem; an existing deep involvement with an issue **(ego involvement)** makes people less vulnerable to persuasion unless the *argument is consistent with the individual's current position (*see also* SELECTIVE EXPOSURE). *See also* AUDIENCE FACTORS; DECODING ABILITY; RECEIVER SKILLS; YALE MODEL.

receiver-oriented communication (receiver-centred) Communication which takes account of *receiver factors and makes allowances for their *frame of reference (*compare* SENDER-ORIENTED COMMUNICATION). Sometimes called *interaction-oriented communication and in *speech communication, **listener-oriented communication**. *See also* CONATIVE FUNCTION.

receiver selectivity (receiver bias, screening) The attentional filtering of message *content or *information by audiences according to perceptual and interpretive *biases. In *informational communication, for instance, the most important factor is that individuals favour information which they perceive as being important to them: that is, reflecting its personal relevance to their interests, priorities, and current concerns (*see also* ATTENTION; ELABORATION; SURVEILLANCE FUNCTION). In relation to people's processing of news items, the American political scientist Doris Graber (b.1923) notes that other key factors include emotional appeal, human interest, societal importance, and job relevance, while key reasons for rejecting items are disturbingness, remoteness (*see* PROXIMITY), and complexity. Receiver selectivity is sometimes subdivided into *selective exposure, *selective attention, *selective perception, and *selective recall.

receiver skills (decoder skills) The abilities of individuals to interpret verbal and *nonverbal communication (involving listening, *reading, and/or viewing). These range from simple *comprehension to *empathy, and include the ability to infer the *preferred reading of nonliteral messages and to detect deception. The American psychologist Judith A. Hall found that, in relation to *decoding nonverbal cues, women tend to be more accurate and faster than men, particularly in relation to facial cues. *See also* COMMUNICATION COMPETENCE; DECODING ABILITY; *compare* SENDER SKILLS.

recency effect (law of recency, principle of recency) 1. (cognitive psychology) The tendency in free recall for individuals to be better able to recall the last items in a series or the tendency to remember better *information that was more recently learned. Applying this to persuasive communication would favour 'climax order'. However, the effect is not consistent: for instance, it can be negated by distractions between presentation and recall. *Compare* PRIMACY EFFECT. 2. (social psychology) A tendency in *impression formation a tendency under some circumstances for later *information about people to supplant earlier information. This is less common than the *primacy effect.

reception *See* AUDIENCE.

reception model A conceptualization of the *mass media (or of media research) in terms of the active role of *audiences in meaning-making (McQuail), or more broadly in terms of the uses to which they put the media (*see also* USES AND GRATIFICATIONS). An overemphasis on the audience's interpretive role is seen by critics as a form of *cultural populism. *See also* ACTIVE AUDIENCE THEORY; *compare* PUBLICITY MODEL; RITUAL MODEL; TRANSMISSION MODELS.

reception studies *Compare* RECEPTION THEORY. 1. Loosely, a synonym for *audience studies, *reader-response theory, or *reception theory. 2. (*film theory) An approach associated with the work of the American cultural theorist Janet Staiger (b.1946), involving the analysis of the meaning of individual films in relation to the various historical *discourses that circulated at the time of their release, such as reviews by fans and critics, news articles, and promotional interviews with stars and production staff.

reception theory *Compare* RECEPTION STUDIES. **1.** [German *Rezeptionsästhetik* 'reception aesthetics'] (literary theory) Jauss's historically-oriented approach in which the *interpretation of texts is seen as dependent on the reading public's *horizon of expectations in a given period. The interpretation of texts thus changes over time (*see also* AESTHETIC DISTANCE). The term is also often applied to the work of Iser and more broadly to the European tradition as distinct from North American theorists. *Compare* HERMENEUTICS. **2. (audience reception theory)** More generally, any theory of how audiences interpret *texts, such as *active audience theory and *reader-response theory, as distinct from *textual analysis. **3.** (*film theory) A term sometimes applied to interpretive (especially psychoanalytical) frameworks concerning cinematic *spectatorship, as distinct from empirical studies of audience members: *see* CINEMATIC APPARATUS; GAZE THEORY; SPECTATOR; SUTURE.

reciprocity **1.** In *functionalism and *exchange theory, the basis of most social *interaction in mutual give-and-take: a *norm of responding in ways which are similar in kind in **reciprocal relationships** (with **reciprocal roles** and **reciprocal behaviour**) and without which communication would break down. It can also be seen as a means of reflecting and constructing *social relations and *social identity through bonding and differentiation. *See also* COMMUNICATION NETWORK; NETWORK ANALYSIS; SOCIAL NETWORK; SOCIOGRAM; SYMMETRICAL RELATIONSHIPS; *compare* ASYMMETRICAL RELATIONSHIPS. **2.** In relation to social systems, the interdependence of parts of the system, as distinguished from the degree of functional autonomy of these parts: *see also* FUNCTIONALISM. **3. (reciprocity of perspectives)** In *interpersonal communication, for the American sociologist Aaron Cicourel (b.1928), the extent to which the participants share taken-for-granted *common-sense assumptions about the *framing of a particular communicative situation. *See also* CONVERGENCE MODEL; ETHNOMETHODOLOGY; FRAME OF REFERENCE; SYMBOLIC INTERACTIONISM; THOMAS THEOREM.

recontextualization **1.** Taking something from its usual *context and resituating it in an unfamiliar *context. As an aesthetic practice, this is characteristic of surrealism, where it serves the function of 'making the familiar strange and the strange familiar', in the words of Novalis, otherwise known as Friedrich von Hardenberg (1772–1801), a German poet. *See* ESTRANGEMENT. **2.** Applying a concept associated with or developed in one context to other situations. **3.** A technique used in visual and sound collage (e.g. in music), and in *photomontage, all of which can also be seen as a form of *bricolage. Some examples of musical collage have generated *copyright controversies (e.g. Negativland's *U2*). **4.** The process in which any *representation changes the *meaning of what it ostensibly merely re-presents by reframing it in a different context: notable examples include *mass-media news coverage and advertisements: *see also* FRAMING.

(((⊕))) SEE WEB LINKS

• Negativland interviews U2's 'The Edge'

recording (RX in television *post-production**)** Broadly, any activity which converts transient *information into a more enduring form, or the product of this activity (a storage medium such as a stone tablet, scroll, book, photograph, film, vinyl disc, audio or video tape, CD, DVD, etc.). Separating the material from its makers enables it to be distributed, published, or broadcast (*see also* WRITING). *See also* ELECTRONIC RECORDING.

recuperation *See* INCORPORATION.

recursive communication theory The stance of Klaus Krippendorff, a German-American communication theorist (b.1932), that *communication can only be studied from the perspective of the *discourse produced by it. *Compare* CONSTITUTIVE MODELS.

redtop (red top tabloid) In Britain, a *tabloid *newspaper, named after the colour of the *masthead. In terms of *communicative functions, the redtops generally focus more on the *entertainment function than on the *information function.

reductionism (reductivism) The reduction of explanatory factors involved in some phenomenon to a single primary function or cause. For instance, **nomenclaturism** reduces *language to the purely *referential function of naming things; *technological determinism reduces social change to a single cause; *transmission models of communication reduce *meaning to *content. It is typically a negative term (though *structuralist analysts use deliberate reduction). *Realists criticize what they see as the reduction of reality by *conventionalists to nothing more than *signifying practices. *Materialists criticize *formalism as an *idealist reduction of referential content and material substance to abstract systems, but materialists are also accused by their critics of being reductionist. Disciplinary perspectives are often attacked as reductionist: sociologists tend to criticize *psychologism (reduction to individual psychology) while psychologists tend to criticize *sociologism (*social determinism). Some other 'isms' which have been criticized as reductionist include *economism (economic determinism), biographism (reduction of textual meaning to authorial biography), and *communicationism.

redundancy In *information theory, the percentage of a *message or *text which could be eliminated without loss of *information. Up to 50% of the letters in most conventional written prose messages could be randomly removed and the original could still be reconstructed by a native speaker of that language because of contextual cues such as *semantics, *syntax, and *morphology, all of which function to reduce uncertainty: such messages have a redundancy of 50%. Texts using *broadcast codes have a high degree of redundancy—being structurally simple and repetitive (*overcoded). In *perception, there is always more *sensory data than we need to be aware of—we don't need to see much to fill in the gaps. In communication generally, redundancy helps to compensate for *noise. Such redundancy facilitates *selective perception. *Compare* OVERDETERMINATION.

re-embedding (sociology) New forms of *social relations, communities, and politics (*see* GLOCALIZATION) arising alongside a decline in traditional forms of social *cohesion (Giddens). *Compare* EMBEDDING.

reference *See* REFERENTIALITY.

reference group 1. In sociology and social psychology, any social collectivity functioning as a *frame of reference in relation to which an individual evaluates their actions and circumstances or which influences their behaviour and *attitudes. It may or may not also be a **membership group** to which the individual belongs (a *peer group). It may include aspirational, negative, and even imaginary reference groups. *See also* GENERALIZED OTHER; GROUP IDENTIFICATION; IN-GROUP.
2. **(consumer group)** (*marketing) A category of consumers which an individual identifies with, respects, or aspires to join, or of which they are already a member and which influences their *attitudes and behaviour. These may constitute a *target audience.

referent (*semiotics) What the *sign 'stands for' outside the sign system. In the *Peircean model of the sign this is called the *object. In the *Saussurean model of the sign a referent in the world is not explicitly or directly featured—only the *signified—a concept in the mind. This is sometimes referred to as *bracketing the referent. Note that referents can include ideas, *events, and material objects. Anti-*realist theorists reject the concreteness of referents, regarding them as products of *language.

referential code *See* CULTURAL CODE.

referential communication *See* INFORMATIONAL COMMUNICATION.

referential fallacy (referential illusion) (*semiotics) The assumption that it is either a *necessary condition of a *sign that the *signifier has a *referent (in particular, a *material object in the world), or that the *meaning of a sign lies purely in its referent. Such assumptions are flawed because many signifiers do not have referents (e.g. a connective such as 'and' in *language). The existence of a sign is no guarantee of the existence in the world of a corresponding referent. The reference in texts is primarily—*poststructuralists say that it can only be—to other *texts (*see* INTERTEXTUALITY) rather than to the world. The fallacy is reflected in judgements that the (referential) *Peircean model of the sign is superior to the *Saussurean model.

referential framings *See* FRAMING.

referential function (for Bühler, the **representative function)** A key linguistic or *communicative function, the role of which is to impart *information. In *Jakobson's model of linguistic communication this function is oriented towards the *context or *referent. *See also* INFORMATIONAL COMMUNICATION; LINGUISTIC FUNCTIONS; REFERENTIALITY; *compare* INFORMATION FUNCTION.

referentiality (referential meaning) 1. Reference to the external world (rather than to oneself, to *language, or to a *text). In language this is exemplified in *description; in visual media, depiction. *See also* DENOTATION. 2. The issue of what is being referred to.

referential language *See* INFORMATIONAL COMMUNICATION.

reflectance *See* COLOUR.

reflectionism (reflection theory) The notion that a *representation in any *medium reflects, or ought to reflect, 'the way things are' in everyday reality. It is based on the *metaphor of the mirror: the goal of art, as Hamlet observes, is 'to hold... a mirror up to nature'. Certainly, from a *phenomenological perspective, people do seek, and psychologically seem to need, reflections in the media of people like themselves, of familiar experiences, and of their world (*see also* PERSONAL IDENTITY FUNCTION). The concern of *constructionist critics is to avoid the assumption of naïve *realism that reality is wholly independent of, and pre-existing, its representation rather than as in any way *constructed* by it. On this basis, reflectionism is often dismissed as a fallacious assumption in relation to fictional *literary genres. However, this does not invalidate a concern for examining relationships between the world and its representations. For instance, the reflectionist *rhetoric of accuracy and distortion is wholly understandable in evaluating news coverage (if at times naïve about *news values). Reflectionist assumptions are unavoidably embedded in criticisms of *stereotyping; more loosely, they figure also in the stance that the *mass media reflect dominant contemporary *values. Here the concern is not the extent to which 'reality' is 'reflected' in a representation, but *whose* realities or values are represented and whose are erased. *See also* MAGIC WINDOW; MIMETIC THEORY.

reflectivity–impulsivity (reflection–impulsivity) (psychology) A *cognitive style in problem-solving related to whether the individual tends to make quick decisions or instead weighs up alternatives before deciding. This was identified in 1958 by the American psychologist Jerome Kagan (b.1929).

reflexiveness (*linguistics) The feature of language whereby it can be used to refer to, or describe, itself, as in 'This is a sentence'. One of the key *design features of human *language identified by Hockett. *See also* METALINGUAL FUNCTION.

reflexivity 1. A process of self-consciousness where an individual subject or group becomes the object of its own scrutiny, sometimes called **self-reflexivity**: *see also* PREREFLEXIVE. 2. An aesthetic practice which *foregrounds the signs of a text's *production (the materials and techniques used)—thus reducing the *transparency of its *style. Anti-realist aesthetics (for example, Brechtian theatre) involves the principle that texts should reflexively foreground their own construction (*see also* ALIENATION EFFECT). *Postmodernism often involves a highly reflexive *intertextuality. 3. (*ethnomethodology) The concept that routine conversations create the situations to which they refer, and that it is through such means that social reality is created and sustained: *see* CONVERSATION ANALYSIS. 4. Media reflexivity can be at the level of the text or at the level of the mediated subject. In the former the medium becomes part of the presentation: the opening *shot of a *news programme often takes the form of a *long-shot which shows the cameras and lighting equipment in the *studio. Self-consciousness on behalf of the televised subject (for example, in a celebrity interview) can create a reflexive effect in an otherwise *naturalistic presentation.

register (discourse genre) In *linguistics (specifically *sociolinguistics and *stylistics), any particular variety of a *language (**language variety**) defined according to the situation of use. It concerns issues of appropriateness in relation to stylistic and *formal features and degrees of *formality. The extent of an individual's repertoire of registers is a feature of their *communicative competence. The choice of an appropriate register is based on *subject matter or domain, *linguistic function, medium, social *context, and relationships between the participants (*see also* COMMUNICATIVE RELATIONSHIPS). In relation to the *mass media, examples would include *journalese and the language of *advertising.

regulation Control and supervision of organizations exercised by external authorities through the application of rules. As for **media regulation** (or *media controls), government regulation of *mass-media organizations is one form: it includes direct government intervention and the actions of government-appointed regulators such as Ofcom in the UK and the Federal Communications Commission (FCC) in the USA. The other form of *media control is self-regulation within the *media industries (e.g. in the UK by the Press Complaints Commission and the Advertising Standards Authority). The extent of political control varies from country to country, ranging across a spectrum from authoritarian regimes (such as those of the Nazis and fascists in World War II), through more paternalistic regimes such as those in the former European communist countries (with mostly state-owned media), via those favouring social responsibility (as in Western liberal democracies), to hypothetical libertarian regimes subject only to market forces. In Western democracies, regulation is justified on the basis of the *public interest and the protection of the consumer. Government regulation is typically seen as taking the form of the imposition of restrictions, but it can also include measures designed to stimulate domestic *production, diversity of *content, public benefit, or programme quality. It can be divided into *economic* regulation, *technical* regulation, and *content* regulation. *Ideological and moral factors shape media content. The mass media are seen as essential to the free flow of *information within a democracy, offering adequate *access for all citizens to a range of alternative views (*see also* MARKET MODEL). The coverage of news and current affairs in *public service broadcasting (though not in newspapers) is expected to be impartial (*see also* BALANCE; BIAS; IMPARTIALITY; OBJECTIVITY). However, where such *expectations are breached, regulatory transparency is essential since actions perceived as involving state intervention constitute a threat to the goal of media neutrality. For the regulation of media content, *see* CENSORSHIP; COPYRIGHT; DEFAMATION. Economic regulation relates to issues of ownership and *competition. Issues such as licensing fees, concentration of ownership, and *cross-media ownership have generated political debate. Technical regulation relates to issues such as *spectrum scarcity. *See also* DEREGULATION; MEDIA CONTROLS; MEDIA OWNERSHIP; MEDIA POLICY; POLITICAL ECONOMY; PUBLIC SERVICE BROADCASTING.

regulative uses (Lull) *See* STRUCTURAL USES.

regulators In *nonverbal communication, visual or audible *signals functioning to regulate the flow of speech in conversational *turn-taking. These include *head nods, *posture shifts, and *eye contact, and they are culturally variable. One of five types of nonverbal acts according to Ekman and Wallace Friesen (the others being *adaptors, *affect displays, *emblems, and *illustrators).

regulatory function (regulative function) Halliday's term for a *linguistic function in which one uses language to influence the behaviour of others or to control events. For example, 'Do as you're told!'

reification 1. The treatment of a relatively abstract *signified (e.g. technology, mind, or self) as if it were a single, bounded, undifferentiated, fixed, and unchanging thing, the essential nature of which could be taken for granted (*see* ESSENTIALISM). It is a *representational practice which functions to establish the self-evident reality of the concept in question, treating it as if it has the *ontological status of a specific physical thing in an objective *material world. Reification suppresses the human intervention involved in the defining process as if the *signifier were *neutral and had been an integral part of a pre-existing thing in the world. Reification makes no allowance for the cultural and *ideological frameworks which produced the signifier. Just because we have a word for something such as the self or the mind does not make it a 'real' entity, and yet the widespread and routine use of a signifier can appear to validate the existence of the signified as a taken-for-granted thing in itself. *Perception itself may unavoidably involve reification. *Technological determinists are often criticized for reifying technology in general or a particular *medium such as television or the computer. Reification is a difficult charge to avoid, since any use of linguistic *categorization (including words such as 'society' or 'culture') could be attacked as reification. 2. (*Marxist theory) The conversion of the *subject to an *object, as when the worker becomes a *commodity: *see also* COMMODITY FETISHISM.

reinforcement *See* CONDITIONING.

reinscription In cultural and literary theory, the re-establishment of an existing concept in a different *form or *context from its conventional one but without any radical transformation. A *transgressive* reinscription would subvert the concept (*see* TRANSGRESSION).

Reithianism A vision of *public service broadcasting associated with the Scotsman John Reith (1889–1971), who became managing director of the BBC in 1923 and declared that it should aim to inform, educate, and entertain (very much in that order). For him, PSB was based on four principles: firstly, it should be protected from commercial pressures; secondly, it should serve the whole nation, not just urban centres; thirdly, it should be under the control of a single unified body; and fourthly, it should be a *monopoly. *See also* PUBLIC BROADCASTING SERVICE; QUALITY TELEVISION; *compare* COMMERCIALIZATION; FICTION VALUES.

relational communication 1. (**relationship-oriented** or **-centred**) In *interpersonal communication, a *communication style or an act of communication in which the primary focus, or a key aspect, is the relationship between the participants (*see also* COMMUNICATIVE RELATIONSHIPS). Particularly in *intercultural communication, a normative style or focus associated with *collectivistic cultures and typically contrasted with *task-oriented communication (*see also* ROLE-ORIENTED COMMUNICATION). *Gender stereotypes often frame relational communication primarily as a *feminine style (*compare* EXPRESSIVE COMMUNICATION; INFORMATIONAL COMMUNICATION; INSTRUMENTAL COMMUNICATION). *Constitutive models stress the role of communication in the dynamic construction and maintenance of relationships. *See also* RELATIONAL MODEL. 2. In communication research, a field concerned with the study of verbal and *nonverbal communication in personal relationships. *See also* ASYMMETRICAL RELATIONSHIPS; COMMUNICATIVE RELATIONSHIPS; COMPLEMENTARY RELATIONSHIPS; PARALLEL RELATIONSHIPS; POWER RELATIONS; SYMMETRICAL RELATIONSHIPS; *compare* CONVERSATION ANALYSIS; CRITICAL DISCOURSE ANALYSIS. 3. Sometimes a synonym for a *relational model of communication.

relational editing *See* ASSOCIATIVE EDITING.

relational meaning *See* DIFFERENCE.

relational message A *message expressing a *social relationship between the communicators. *See also* RELATIONAL COMMUNICATION; *compare* CONTENT MESSAGE.

relational model 1. (transactional models, transactive models, transactional communication) A nonlinear framing of *communication as a process geared to mutual understanding and influence in the *context of the relationships between the participants (*see also* CONVERGENCE MODEL; POWER RELATIONS; RELATIONAL COMMUNICATION), in particular contrast to linear *transmission models. Writing in 1974, Schramm argues that normative *expectations regarding the *function of the relationship (*see* COMMUNICATIVE FUNCTIONS; COMMUNICATIVE PURPOSES; COMMUNICATIVE RELATIONSHIPS) determine the *roles played by the participants, and that *performances are governed by an implicit *contract. Social psychologists stress the involuntary behavioural coordination involved (rather than individual *purposes), and see relationships as dynamic systems—a conceptualization which strains the *affordances of the static spatial representation of such models. Within the *constitutive model, relational forms (relationships) and processes (patterns of communicative acts) can be seen as mutually constitutive. *See also* COMMUNICATION MODELS; RECURSIVE COMMUNICATION THEORY; SYSTEMS THEORY; *compare* COMMUNICATION GAME; INTERACTION MODEL. 2. (*semiotics) Saussure's conception of *meaning as dependent on the relation between *signs. A word makes sense as part of a formal, generalized and abstract system of *language rather than having an inherent *value in and of itself or an intrinsic (extralinguistic) relationship to a *referent in the world (*see also* ARBITRARINESS). Language, for Saussure, is a system of functional *differences and *oppositions. *Advertising furnishes a good example of this notion, since what matters is *positioning a product is not the relationship of advertising *signifiers to real-world *referents, but the differentiation of each sign from the others to which it is related. Saussure's concept of the relational identity of signs is at the heart of *structuralism. *See also* BRACKETING THE REFERENT; SAUSSUREAN MODEL.

relational uses The various ways in which individuals make use of *television for purposes of social *interaction (Lull). This includes: facilitating communication, constructing opportunities for *affiliation and avoidance, as a social learning resource, and demonstrating competence or *dominance. *See also* SOCIAL FUNCTIONS; USES AND GRATIFICATIONS; *compare* STRUCTURAL USES.

relationship-centred or -oriented communication *See* RELATIONAL COMMUNICATION.

relative arbitrariness (relative conventionality) (*semiotics) The concept that the relationship between the *signifier and the *signified (or *referent) varies in its degree of *arbitrariness or *conventionality from being wholly arbitrary (*symbolic, as in language), through being based on some resemblance (*iconic, as in paintings), to being directly or causally connected (*indexical, as in photographs). Although Saussure did refer to relative arbitrariness, it is a concept primarily associated with Peirce; resemblance and direct connection are incompatible with *bracketing the referent.

relative autonomy 1. In Althusserian *Marxist theory, the relative independence of the 'superstructure' of society (including *ideology and *culture) from the economic (or techno-economic) 'base' (in contrast to the stance in classical *Marxism that the latter determines the former—a stance similar to that of *technological determinism). Indeed, Althusser referred also to 'the reciprocal action of the superstructure on the base', a stance reflected in *cultural materialism. He insisted that the economic 'base' is determinant only in the 'last instance'. *See also* BASE AND SUPERSTRUCTURE. 2. In the context of *semiotics, the *Saussurean model of the *sign assumes the relative autonomy of *language in relation to reality (it does not directly feature a real-world *referent); there is no essential bond between words and things. In a semiotic system with double *articulation (as in verbal language) the levels of the *signifier and of the *signified are relatively autonomous. The signifier and the signified in a sign are autonomous to the extent that their relationship is *arbitrary (commentators also speak of *relative arbitrariness or 'relative conventionality').

relative size *See* DWINDLING SIZE PERSPECTIVE.

relativism (epistemological relativism) Frequently either a pejorative term used by critics of *constructionism (notably *realists, for whom it may refer to any *epistemological stance other than realism) or by constructionists themselves referring to a position whereby 'anything goes' with which they do not want to be associated. Critics associate relativism with an extreme *idealism or nihilism denying the existence of a real material world—which it does not necessarily entail. Since few theorists choose to label themselves relativists it is difficult to define the term adequately. One characterization is the stance that there are numerous alternative versions of reality which can only be assessed in relation to each other and not in relation to any absolute, fixed, and universal truth, reality, *meaning,

*knowledge, or certainty (*see also* PERSPECTIVISM). Such categories are
*contingent—temporary, provisional, and dependent on *context and
circumstances. Any defence of absolutes tends to be denounced as metaphysics.
There can be no '*value-free' *facts. Relativism is an anti-essentialist position.
The semiotic stance which problematizes 'reality' and emphasizes *mediation
and representational *convention in the form of *codes is criticized as relativism
(or extreme *conventionalism) by those veering towards *realism. Such critics
often object to what they see as a sidelining of referential concerns which are
foundational in realist discourse—such as truth, *facts, accuracy, *objectivity, *bias,
and distortion. Even in relation to the *interpretation of a *text, the stance that
*meaning depends on how *readers interpret it rather than residing within the text
has been criticized by *literalists as relativism (*see* AFFECTIVE FALLACY).

relevance theory (*linguistics) A theory of *pragmatics based on the principle
that it is a *necessary condition for communication that all *utterances are
presumed to relate to contextual assumptions (*see also* CONTEXT OF SITUATION).
Relevance theory was developed by the linguists Dan Sperber (b.1942) and Deirdre
Wilson in the 1980s as an **inferential model** based on inferring a *preferred
meaning, which they argue is an alternative to 'the *code model*' based on *decoding
a shared *code. *See also* INFERENCE; *compare* COGNITIVE FILM THEORY.

remediation 1. The *representation of one *medium in another, which operates
on a number of levels: for example, a *shot of a painting in a film or a film's
cinematography employing a painterly aesthetic. For Bolter and Richard Grusin,
American new media theorists, remediation is a defining characteristic of all *new
media. *See also* HYPERMEDIA; IMMEDIACY. 2. The process by which *new media are
developed to represent more fully human perceptual and communicational
faculties: for example, stereo is an improvement on mono sound because humans
have two ears. Proposed by the American media theorist Paul Levinson (b.1947).
3. The processes by which humans compensate for the unforeseen consequences of
their technological innovation. For example, the problem of not being able to see
through a wall is solved by a window and the problem of the window destroying
privacy is solved by blinds (Levinson).

reportage The retelling of newsworthy *events to those who did not witness
them first-hand: i.e. the content of all news and current affairs media.

representamen One of the three elements of the *Peircean model of the *sign,
referring to the form which the sign takes (not necessarily material). When it refers
to a non-material form it is comparable to Saussure's *signifier whereas when it
refers to material form it is what some commentators refer to as the *sign vehicle.
See also INTERPRETANT; OBJECT.

representation [Latin *repraesentare* 'to make present or manifest'] 1. Depicting
or 'making present' something which is absent (e.g. people, places, *events, or
abstractions) in a different form: as in paintings, photographs, films, or *language,
rather than as a *replica. *See also* DESCRIPTION; *compare* ABSENT PRESENCE. 2. The
function of a *sign or *symbol of 'standing for' that to which it refers (its *referent).
3. The various processes of *production involved in generating representational

texts in any medium, including the *mass media (e.g. the filming, *editing, and *broadcasting of a television *documentary). Such framings of the concept privilege *authorial intention. *See also* AUTEUR THEORY; AUTHORIAL DETERMINISM; SENDER-ORIENTED COMMUNICATION. 4. A text (in any medium) which is the *product* of such processes, usually regarded as amenable to *textual analysis ('a representation'). 5. *What* is explicitly or literally described, depicted, or denoted in a *sign, *text, or *discourse in any *medium as distinct from its *symbolic meaning, *metaphoric meaning, or *connotations: its manifest referential *content, as in 'a representation of . . .' *See also* MIMESIS; NATURALISM; REFERENTIALITY. 6. *How* (in what ways) something is depicted. However 'realistic' texts may seem to be, they involve some form of *transformation. Representations are unavoidably selective (none can ever 'show the whole picture'), and within a limited *frame, some things are *foregrounded and others backgrounded: *see also* FRAMING; GENERIC REPRESENTATION; SELECTIVE REPRESENTATION; STYLIZATION. In *factual genres in the *mass media, critics understandably focus on issues such as truth, accuracy, *bias, and *distortion (*see also* REFLECTIONISM), or on whose realities are being represented and whose are being denied. *See also* DOMINANT IDEOLOGY; MANIPULATIVE MODEL; STEREOTYPING; SYMBOLIC ERASURE. 7. The relation of a *sign or *text in any medium to its *referent. In *reflectionist framings, the *transparent *re*-presentation, reflection, *recording, transcription, or reproduction of a pre-existing reality (*see also* IMAGINARY SIGNIFIER; MIMESIS; REALISM). In *constructionist framings, the *transformation of particular social realities, *subjectivities, or *identities in processes which are ostensibly merely *re*-presentations (*see also* CONSTITUTIVE MODELS; INTERPELLATION; REALITY CONSTRUCTION). Some *postmodern theorists avoid the term representation completely because the *epistemological assumptions of *realism seem to be embedded within it. 8. A cycle of processes of textual and meaning production *and* reception situated in a particular sociohistorical *context (*see also* CIRCUIT OF COMMUNICATION; CIRCUIT OF CULTURE). This includes the active processes in which *audiences engage in the *interpretation of texts (*see also* ACTIVE AUDIENCE THEORY; BEHOLDER'S SHARE; PICTURE PERCEPTION). *Semiotics highlights *representational codes which need to be decoded (*see also* ENCODING/DECODING MODEL; PHOTOGRAPHIC CODES; PICTORIAL CODES; REALISM), and related to a relevant *context (*see also* JAKOBSON'S MODEL). 9. (*narratology) *Showing* as distinct from *telling* (*narration). 10. **(mental representation)** The process and product of encoding perceptual experience in the mind: *see* DUAL CODING THEORY; GESTALT LAWS; MENTAL REPRESENTATION; PERCEPTUAL CODES; SELECTIVE PERCEPTION; SELECTIVE RETENTION. 11. A relationship in which one person (a representative) acting on behalf of another (as in law), or a political principle in which one person acts, in some sense, on behalf of a group of people, normally having been chosen by them to do so (as in representative democracies). 12. In *quantitative research, the principle of a (representative) cross-section reflecting, in relevant ways, a larger population: *see also* SAMPLING.

representational art *See* FIGURATIVE ART.

representational code A *textual code in any medium which recognizably depicts or describes a *referent, whether factual or fictional, plausible or implausible. Texts employing representational codes which are perceived as 'realistic' (especially in film and television) can be experienced as if they were recordings or direct reproductions of reality rather than as *representations in the form of *codes: this is partly a function of the *familiarity* of such codes. *See also* CONSTRUCTEDNESS; MAGIC WINDOW; PHOTOGRAPHIC CODES; PICTORIAL CODES; REALISM; SUSPENSION OF DISBELIEF.

representational function *See* INFORMATIVE FUNCTION.

representationalism (representationism, representative theory, representative realism, indirect realism) A philosophical theory of *perception in which the mind is argued to apprehend objective material reality through internal *mental representations constructed from immediate sense data from which the corresponding existence of objects in the physical world can be inferred. *See also* EPISTEMOLOGY.

representational media *See* MEDIUM.

representative function *See* REFERENTIAL FUNCTION.

repression 1. (*psychoanalytic theory) The principal unconscious *defence mechanism, in which memories or impulses which would induce anxiety or guilt are excluded from consciousness. Such feelings persist in the unconscious and return in the symbolic form of dreams (*see* CONDENSATION; DISPLACEMENT), *parapraxis, and so on (often referred to as 'the return of the repressed'). 2. The political imposition of restrictions on an individual or group's *freedom of speech or action.

reproduction *See* CULTURAL REPRODUCTION; MECHANICAL REPRODUCTION.

repurposing Using in one *medium the *content originally produced for another medium.

residual code A synonym for Williams's concept of a *residual form. Adopted as a concept in *marketing fashion trend-spotting. *See also* DOMINANT CODE; *compare* EMERGENT CODE.

residual forms (residual formations) Williams's term for one of three categories of cultural forms or *codes that coexist within a society at any particular moment in history, the residual form reflecting previously dominant cultural *institutions, traditions, *styles, movements, social forces, *values, practices, and *identities that are in decline and have lost their cultural legitimacy, but which, unlike **archaic forms,** still persist. Residual cultures express enduring *structures of feeling that have come to be neglected, ignored, marginalized, denied, opposed, or repressed by the dominant culture. *See also* CULTURAL MATERIALISM; DOMINANT FORMS; EMERGENT FORMS.

resistive readings *See* NEGOTIATED READING; OPPOSITIONAL READING; SAVVY CONSUMER.

resolution 1. In digital images, the number of *pixels per inch (ppi) on a screen or printable dots per inch (*dpi). The standard screen resolution is 72 ppi. 2. (*television) The number of horizontal lines: for example, *PAL has a resolution of 625 lines, *NTSC has 525 lines, and HDTV has 1 080 lines: *see* HIGH DEFINITION TELEVISION. 3. In digital audio, the sound quality determined by number of samples and the audio bit depth. CD audio is sampled 441 000 times a second (44.1 kHz). 4. (*narrative) *See* CLASSICAL NARRATIVE STRUCTURE; DÉNOUEMENT.

respondent A person replying to questions in a *survey or *interview. In social science, usually in formal *questionnaires or *structured interviews. *Compare* INFORMANT.

restricted code 1. Within linguistic **deficit theory,** the relatively informal, concrete, and *context-bound (*indexical) linguistic patterns to which (in the 1960s) Bernstein argued the working class is confined, disadvantaging them in the schooling system (*see also* HIGH-CONTEXT; IMPLICIT MEANING; *compare* ELABORATED CODE). Deficit theory has been widely contested by linguists: these *codes have never been proven to be *sociolects. 2. (cultural theory) Any of the formulas which Fiske suggests are employed in *popular culture texts aimed at a wide audience: *see* BROADCAST CODES.

retention *See* AD RETENTION.

retinal disparity (binocular disparity) The difference in optical perspective between the two retinal images, which acts as a binocular *depth cue. *See also* BINOCULAR VISION.

retinal images *See* VISUAL IMAGERY.

reverse cut *See* CROSSING THE LINE.

reverse shot *See* OVER-THE-SHOULDER SHOT.

reverted image *See* FLIPPED IMAGE.

RGB (red, green, blue) 1. An *additive colour model derived from three *primary colours which reproduces a broad array of the spectrum and is used in video graphic array (VGA) computer monitors and electronic cameras: *see also* COLOUR; PIXELS; *compare* COMPONENT; COMPOSITE. 2. In the physiology of human vision, 'red', 'green', and 'blue' are loose terms for three different types of visual receptor cones in the retina with peak sensitivities to particular ranges of *wavelengths within the visible band of the *electromagnetic spectrum. The sensitivities of these differently specialized cones (and consequently their ability to absorb light) actually overlap.

rheme *See* THEME.

rhetoric 1. The art of *persuasion and the techniques of effective expression, traditionally primarily in oratory, but also in written composition; additionally, the study of this topic. 'Modern rhetoric' has concerned itself more broadly with effective communication and the poststructuralist 'new rhetoric' has focused on the rhetorical construction of all *discourse. Classical rhetoric is *receiver-oriented insofar as it is concerned with influencing *audiences using both *rational and *emotional appeals. The traditional subdivisions were: invention (the construction of valid *arguments), disposition (arrangement), expression, *memory, and delivery. Rhetoricians catalogued the various *figures of speech: rhetoric is particularly concerned with the relation between *metaphoric and *literal meaning and between *form and *content. *See also* VISUAL RHETORIC. 2. In loose usage, a pejorative term for insubstantial or even deceptive language, as in 'mere rhetoric' and 'empty rhetoric', a usage underestimating the unavoidably figurative basis of *language. 3. The specific kind of *discourse employed in a particular domain, with its own distinctive features and implicit *ideological functions, as in 'the rhetoric of nationalism' in the popular press.

((⊕)) SEE WEB LINKS

• Figures of rhetoric in advertising language

rhetorical turn (discursive turn) A change in emphasis in the *discourse of the humanities and social sciences reflecting a recognition (outside the academic field of *rhetoric itself) that rhetorical forms are deeply and unavoidably involved in the shaping of realities. *Form and *content are inseparable; *language is not a neutral medium and our choice of words matters. To say that a glass is 'half empty' is not the same as saying that it is 'half full'. It has been distinguished from the *linguistic turn primarily through its stronger anti-objectivism and its emphasis on the loadedness of language (*see also* LOADED LANGUAGE). A book entitled *The Rhetorical Turn* by the American communication theorist Herbert W. Simons (b.1939) was published in 1990.

rhizome A complex botanical metaphor developed by Deleuze and Guattari for a non-hierarchical organizing structure based on a horizontal root that grows through the soil sprouting new plants. The rhizome is an alternative to a tree-like structure, because its radical asymmetry, random distribution, and interconnectedness means that it cannot be understood in terms of *binary oppositions; consequently it resists *categorization and *structural analysis. Distributed networks like the *internet and nonlinear writing systems like *hypertext are rhizomatic. *See also* BOTTOM-UP PROCESSING; EMERGENCE.

rich media *See* MEDIA RICHNESS.

rising action *See* FREYTAG'S PYRAMID.

ritual interaction A standardized form of social interpersonal *interaction (either face-to-face or mediated), a primary function of which is to develop and maintain social *cohesion and solidarity, sustaining *social relationships and their definitions of reality. Durkheim (focusing on public *events) and Goffman (focusing on the routines of everyday interpersonal *interaction, or social *episodes) saw ritualized *face-to-face interaction as a catalyst for social *cohesion. Ling argues that this also applies to mediated interaction, including *interpersonal communication via *mobile phones. *See also* ETHNOMETHODOLOGY; INTERACTION RITUALS; INTERCHANGE; PHATIC FUNCTION.

ritual interchange *See* INTERCHANGE.

ritual model (expressive model) A *metaphor for the primary function of the *mass media as the *representation or celebration of shared understandings, *values, and beliefs. It is based on a conceptualization of *communication by the American communication theorist James Carey (1935–2006). Such communication is seen as drawing upon a common pool of cultural *imagery, *symbolism, and *codes, bringing together those for whom these are familiar features of their *cultural identity. Audiences are in this sense participants rather than *receivers or spectators. It is seen as *expressive communication for the pleasures of *performance rather than as *instrumental or *informational communication, although it has the unifying *social function of maintaining society over time (*see* IMAGINED COMMUNITY). *See also* INTEGRATION; SOCIALIZATION FUNCTION; *compare* PUBLICITY MODEL; RECEPTION MODEL; TRANSMISSION MODELS.

role 1. **(social roles)** In sociology and social psychology, a relatively predictable pattern of individual behaviour adapted to the social *expectations associated with a particular social position, *status, situation, or relationship: for instance, a parental role (*see also* COMMUNICATIVE RELATIONSHIPS; RELATIONAL COMMUNICATION). In several theories, including *Frankfurt school perspectives, the *mass media are seen as playing a part in the reproduction of social roles. Whereas in the **role theory** of *functionalist sociology the emphasis is on the place of roles in the *social structure and their determination by *social norms, in social psychology roles are seen as part of a dynamic process of *interaction (*see also* ROLE PLAYING; ROLE TAKING). Roles are related (*see also* RECIPROCITY) and are the building blocks of *institutions and social systems. Individuals have multiple roles (a **role set**) and this can lead to **role conflict** or **role strain**: *see also* GENDER ROLES. 2. (*narratology) Basic *functions performed by an actor or character: for instance, the *hero or heroine, or the villain.

role distance The relative subjective detachment of an individual from a *role they are playing that enables them to improvise. In contrast to the relatively deterministic conception of *roles in *functionalism, from this *dramaturgical perspective there is always scope for improvisation in social *roles. The individual's *performance projects a particular impression of the self. The concept derives from Goffman (1956). *Compare* HABITUS.

role model A real person or a fictional character whose behaviour, *attitudes, and/or *values are seen by individuals as worthy of imitation or emulation: in social learning theory, this is seen as a major mode of *socialization. The *mass media constitute a major source of such models. *See also* MODELLING; REFERENCE GROUP; SIGNIFICANT OTHER.

role-oriented communication (role-centred) A *communication style that emphasizes the social *roles of the participants. *Interaction tends to be formal or even ritualistic. This style is common in *high-context cultures. *See also* COMMUNICATIVE RELATIONSHIPS; RELATIONAL COMMUNICATION.

role playing *See also* DRAMATURGY. 1. Playing a part, as in a *play, or adopting the *role of another person in a role-playing exercise or *game. 2. Adapting one's patterns of behaviour to conform to *expectations in some social position, situation, or relationship.

role taking (social psychology) The dynamic process of imaginatively adopting the perspective of others in *interaction in order to adjust one's own *role behaviour to this **(role making)**. In contrast to the conception of roles within *functionalism, in *symbolic interactionism, interaction can modify or create roles. For Mead, role taking is central in the development of the self.

roll The clockwise or anti-clockwise rotation (around the front-to-back, or z-axis) of a viewpoint (for instance in a 3D-graphical environment such as a *virtual world). *See also* PITCH; YAW; *compare* CANTED SHOT.

rolling news (24-hour news) (television) The style of presentation of a dedicated news channel (such as CNN and Al Jazeera) which typically consists of a format of continuous news coverage involving a mix of traditional studio-based presentation with news *anchors talking to correspondents in the field (voiced over or intercut with live or roughly edited *footage) and studio-based interviews and discussions. Short news bulletins every 15 minutes punctuate this content and news teams prepare for longer news programmes, typically at the top of each hour, in which new material, such as updated news reports, is introduced into the mix. In extraordinary circumstances (e.g. the aftermath of 11 September 2001) many regular television channels also adopt these conventions.

romance 1. *n.* In contemporary usage, a popular literary and *film genre, designed primarily for a female *target audience, with a plot revolving around love, and often seen as a form of *escapism. Medieval romances included the Arthurian tales, and by the late 18th century romances had become associated with improbable plots and high-blown language. Romance is one of Frye's four main *literary genres: *see also* COMEDY; SATIRE; TRAGEDY. 2. *adj.* A family of *languages derived from Latin: French, Italian, Spanish, Portuguese, and Romanian. 3. A personal relationship involving both emotional and sexual attraction.

romanticism 1. A Western artistic movement (*c.*1780–1850) in which artworks are primarily expressive. It is variously associated with the *values such as individuality, creativity, imagination, originality, spontaneity, organicism, *emotion, *subjectivity, nature, and the unconscious. It represents a direct contrast to both (neo-)*classicism and *realism. 2. (philosophy) A movement which emerged with Rousseau, for whom civilization represented the corruption of the essential goodness of humankind, and who consequently idealized nature, childhood, and primal cultures. More broadly, it was associated with an emphasis on individual *identity and freedom.

rotoscope In film and television *special effects, a technique in which the movements of live actors are filmed and their outlines traced *frame by frame either to create *travelling mattes or to become the basis of the movement of animated characters. *Compare* MOTION CAPTURE.

rough cut In film and video *editing, an *edit or first assembly of *shots which approximates the look of the finished scene but typically needs more work: the equivalent of a first draft. *Compare* FINAL CUT.

RSS (Really Simple Syndication; RSS feed) An automated subscription service which *emails text-based updates from a website to registered users. *Compare* NEWS FEED.

running order A chronological list of the items and their timings that makes up the content of a radio or television programme. For *live broadcasts, it is the production assistant's job to ensure that the presenters adhere to the running order. Later items are dropped if certain items overrun.

rushes 1. Unedited videotape or film reels shot for a particular project. 2. Broadly, any source material that is used in an *edit.

RX *See* RECORDING.

saccade (saccadic eye movement) A rapid, unconscious movement of the eyes from one *fixation point to another. These take place approximately three times per second and reflect the brain's search for the *data it needs for its current purposes. If we were conscious of our rapid eye movements the world would seem highly unstable and confusing. *See also* EYE MOVEMENTS.

salience (perceptual salience, salience effects) In *perception and cognition, what stands out most prominently. This may involve both *bottom-up processes driven by *sensory data, and *top-down processes driven by individual factors. All things being equal, our *attention is drawn to intense stimuli such as bright lights, loud noises, saturated *colours, and rapid motion. However, salience effects can also be less universal and physical and more individual and contextual. Top-down cognitive, emotional, and *motivational factors include *knowledge, task, mood, concerns, needs, *values, *biases, and *expectations. We notice whatever is most relevant to our current *frame of reference. Our attention is also drawn to anything that dramatically flouts our expectations. *See also* FIELD DEPENDENCE AND INDEPENDENCE; FIGURE AND GROUND; FOREGROUNDING.

sampling 1. In research and statistics, the process of selecting individuals from a larger population: a **sample** designed to be representative in relevant respects as a basis for *inferences about the larger population. **Sample size** refers to the number of people selected. *See also* CONVENIENCE SAMPLE; DATA-GATHERING. 2. The act of *digitizing sound information in a computer or **sampler**—a keyboard instrument which pitch-shifts sampled sounds to create musical intervals: *see also* BRICOLAGE; COPYRIGHT; MASHUP.

sans serif A *font family of *typefaces in which the main strokes are of consistent thickness and lack terminal 'tails' (*serifs).

Sapir-Whorf hypothesis (Whorfianism, Whorfian hypothesis) Broadly, the belief that people who speak different *languages perceive and think about the world quite differently, their worldviews being shaped or determined by the language of their *culture (a notion rejected by *social determinists and by *realists). The stance is loosely derived from the theories of Benjamin Lee Whorf and his teacher Edward Sapir in the 1930s, though subsequent interpretations often bear little relation to their actual claims. In its most extreme version the *hypothesis can be described as relating two associated principles: *linguistic determinism and *linguistic relativism. While few linguists would accept the hypothesis in its strong, extreme, or deterministic form, many now accept a weak, more moderate, or limited Whorfianism, namely that the ways in which we see the world may be influenced to some extent by the kind of language we use. *See also* MOULD THEORY.

SEE WEB LINKS
• The Sapir-Whorf hypothesis

satellite broadcasting The transmission of television and radio from *communications satellites in geo-stationary orbit to Earth-based receivers. **Satellite television** can target individual nations (e.g. Sky in the UK) or international audiences (e.g. CNN or Al Jazeera). *See also* BROADCASTING; *compare* TERRESTRIAL BROADCASTING.

satire A *genre in literature, film, and other media which is used to deflate, ridicule, and censure the perceived folly or immorality of what is represented. Tools include *irony, sarcasm, wit, caricature, exaggeration, distortion, and parody. Satire invites the audience's moral indignation. One of Frye's four main *literary genres (*see also* COMEDY; ROMANCE; TRAGEDY).

saturation (*colour theory) The subjective psychological experience of the apparent colourfulness or vividness of a colour relative to a grey of the same *brightness (the perceived quantity of *hue in a stimulus). One of the three major psychological dimensions of *colour, the others being *brightness and *hue. The corresponding physical dimension is *spectral purity.

Saussurean model In *semiotics and *linguistics, Ferdinand de Saussure's dyadic model of the *sign consisting of the *signifier and the *signified. *See also* ARBITRARINESS; BRACKETING THE REFERENT; DIFFERENCE; LANGUE AND PAROLE; SIGNIFICATION; STRUCTURALISM; SYNCHRONIC ANALYSIS; VALUE; *compare* PEIRCEAN MODEL.

saving face *See* FACE-SAVING.

savvy consumer A category of media-literate consumers who are knowledgeable about *marketing and *targeting, cynical about *advertising, and who can see through traditional sales *pitches. Critics argue that there is a 'con' involved in making audiences *feel* savvy and sceptical. *See also* CONSUMER CULTURE.

scenario 1. Most broadly, an outline of a possible *sequence of *events. 2. A brief written outline of a *screenplay, or the screenplay itself. 3. (*schema theory) A synonym for a mental *script.

scene 1. The physical location and *setting of an incident in real life or *fiction. 2. In a *narrative, a *sequence of actions in a single location and a single period of time; one of a series which together constitute the *plot. Traditionally, in *drama, a subdivision of an act. 3. In Burke's *dramaturgical theory, the *context of an act: where and when it takes place.

sceptical viewers *See* SAVVY CONSUMER.

scheduling *See* MEDIA PLANNING; PROGRAMME SCHEDULE.

schema (*pl.* **schemata, schemas**) **(cognitive schema)** A mental semantic framework or *representation built up from prior *knowledge and experience that serves to guide our search for *data in relevant *contexts and which may in turn be modified by the actual data encountered (*see also* PERCEPTUAL CYCLE). In *perception, schemata assist *interpretation but *assimilation can also lead to distortion (*see* LEVELLING AND SHARPENING). Schemata facilitate *cognitive processes such as the generation of *inferences and *hypotheses. They are invoked both in relation to *events in *everyday life and in relation to *texts in any *medium. *See also* SCRIPT; TOP-DOWN PROCESSING.

schema theory A psychological theory, stemming from cognitive science, in which the *interpretation of the world and of texts is seen as involving the application of relevant *social and *textual schemata (*see also* SCHEMA; SCRIPT). This simplifies reality, setting up *expectations about what is probable in relation to particular *contexts. Schema theory is consistent with the notion of both *perception and recall as constructive and selective *cognitive processes (*see also* CONSTRUCTIVISM; PERCEPTUAL CYCLE; SELECTIVE PERCEPTION). *Compare* PRIMING.

((SEE WEB LINKS

• Schema theory and the interpretation of television programmes

scheme *See* FIGURE OF SPEECH.

scientific attitude *See* CRITICAL ATTITUDE.

scopophilia **(scopic drive)** Pleasure in looking; in Freudian *psychoanalytic theory, an infantile instinct. In relation to the dominance of the *male gaze in *classical Hollywood cinema, Mulvey refers to scopophilia as the pleasure involved in looking at other people's bodies as (particularly, erotic) objects without being seen either by those on screen or by other members of the audience. Mulvey argues that cinema viewing conditions facilitate both the voyeuristic process of the *objectification of female characters and also the narcissistic process of *identification with an ideal ego seen on the screen. *See also* MALE GAZE; VOYEURISM; *compare* FETISHISM.

screening 1. A showing of a film or video *production to an audience; usage includes previews of films and commercials. 2. (*perception) Filtering out some stimuli or *data (*see also* ATTENTION). In the related usage of communication, *see* RECEIVER SELECTIVITY. 3. (*psychoanalytical theory) Anything which functions to defend someone from becoming aware of the *latent meaning of a symbol, dream, or *event. 4. **(call screening)** Checking the identity of phone callers before deciding whether to accept a call. This challenges the *sender-oriented relationship of caller to called (*see* TELEPHONE), and is enabled by a built-in feature of *mobile phones. 5. (research) The preselection of a subset of participants or instances for a study or test, **screening out** others.

screenplay **(film script)** A written document in a standard format that tells the story of a film through dialogue and stage directions.

screen time The running time of a film as compared to the timespan of the story: for example, the story of *Citizen Kane* (1941) that presents sixty years in the life of Charles Foster Kane in a screen time of just under two hours. *See also* FABULA.

script 1. *n.* The written text of a play, broadcast, or film (*see* SCENARIO; SCREENPLAY); *v.* to produce such a text. 2. *n.* **(scenario)** (*schema theory) A kind of *schema representing a shared social understanding of a familiar, *stereotypical, and predictable *event or sequence of events and associated *roles (*compare* DRAMATURGY). Scripts can be applied both to *everyday life (*social schemata) and to *narratives in various media (*textual schemata). Scripts help us to 'go beyond the information given' by making assumptions about what is usual in the situations they apply to, allowing us to make *inferences about aspects of the situation which are inexplicit: *see also* SOCIAL COGNITION. 3. *n.* Handwriting as opposed to *printing, and a *font family in which typefaces resemble handwriting. 4. *n.* In *internet computing, a simple program executed within a web server.

scriptible *See* WRITERLY.

scriptism (graphocentrism) A *bias in which writing is privileged over speech. In many literate cultures, text has a higher status than speech: written language is often seen as the standard. McLuhan, using a coinage of the Irish author James Joyce (1882–1941), referred to 'ABCEDmindedness'—an *unconscious bias which he regarded as 'the psychological effect of *literacy'. It reflects a scriptist bias to refer, as many scholars do, to 'oral literature', or to any semiotic systems, written or not, as a *text. Scriptism is closely associated with *ocularcentrism. Ong comments that 'Because we have by today so deeply interiorized writing, made it so much a part of ourselves . . . we find it difficult to consider writing to be a *technology.' *Compare* LOGOCENTRISM; PHONOCENTRISM.

scrolling The activity of reading or browsing through material displayed on a computer screen which, even when it is paginated, is displayed as if mounted on a vertical roller, so that it moves up or down: thus resembling a scroll rather than a book.

search engine Software that identifies and retrieves relevant *content on the *internet pertaining to specific *keywords entered by a user.

secondary audience 1. A *demographic group to which an *advertising *message appeals beyond its *primary audience: *see also* DUAL AUDIENCE. 2. An audience thought likely to influence the behaviour of the *target audience. 3. **(pass-along readers)** Those who read but did not purchase a particular magazine or a particular issue of it.

secondary colour *Compare* PRIMARY COLOURS. 1. In *subtractive colouring (as in painting), any of the three *colours produced by mixing pairs of *primary colours: green (blue and yellow), orange (red and yellow), and violet (red and blue). 2. **(overprint colour)** (*printing) A colour produced by overprinting two *primary colours: red (magenta and yellow), green (cyan and yellow), and blue (magenta and cyan). 3. In *additive colouring (as with TV and computer screens), a colour produced by mixing two *primary colours: cyan (green and blue), yellow (red and green), and magenta (red and blue).

secondary definers *See* PRIMARY AND SECONDARY DEFINERS.

secondary deviance *See* LABELLING THEORY.

secondary effects *See* PRIMARY AND SECONDARY EFFECTS.

secondary groups *See* PRIMARY AND SECONDARY GROUPS.

secondary involvement *See* HIGH AND LOW INVOLVEMENT.

second-person point of view (second-person narration) A form of *narration in which the reader, viewer, or listener is directly addressed (sometimes explicitly as 'you'). The second-person *point of view is rare in literary fiction and films but it is common in advertisements, television programmes with presenters, practical handbooks and guides, *role-playing *games, and musical lyrics. *See also* DIRECT ADDRESS; *compare* FIRST-PERSON POINT OF VIEW; THIRD-PERSON POINT OF VIEW.

segmentation The division of a market into separate groupings of consumers, based on *consumption patterns, *demographics, or *lifestyles. *See also* AUDIENCE FRAGMENTATION; DEMOGRAPHIC VARIABLES; GEOGRAPHIC SEGMENTATION; NICHE MARKET; PSYCHOGRAPHICS; TARGET AUDIENCE.

selection, axis of A *structuralist term for the 'vertical' axis in the analysis of a textual structure: the plane of the *paradigm (Jakobson). *Compare* COMBINATION, AXIS OF.

selective attention (psychology) A general tendency for human beings to focus on only some of the *sensory data or *information available to them at any given time. We cannot attend to everything: **selective inattention** (also called **perceptual defence**) is unavoidable. Selectivity is a key feature of *attention; it is based on *salience, which is generally conceptualized as a mental 'filter'. *See also* COCKTAIL PARTY EFFECT; SELECTIVE PERCEPTION.

selective distortion (*marketing) A tendency to interpret *information in ways which reinforce existing *attitudes or beliefs. In communication research, the preferred term is *selective exposure. *Compare* SELECTIVE ATTENTION; SELECTIVE RETENTION.

selective exposure A tendency for people both consciously and unconsciously to seek out material that supports their existing *attitudes and opinions and to actively avoid material that challenges their views. More broadly, audiences may seek congruence with their predispositions, including any aspect of their *identity. Some psychologists have argued that individuals selectively screen out *information to avoid *cognitive dissonance. The concept derives from US *mass-media research in the early 1960s, where it supported theories of *limited effects and the rejection of the *hypodermic model. In *interpersonal communication it is reflected in **selective listening**. *See also* RECEIVER SELECTIVITY; *compare* SELECTIVE DISTORTION.

selective focus (differential focus) (photography) The use of a limited *depth of field in order to focus sharply on a particular object while everything else is out of focus. This serves to *foreground that object and to direct the viewer's *attention to it.

selective influence (selective influence theory) In mass-communication *effects research, the theory that rather than the *mass media having direct and uniform effects on *audiences, audience *attention, *interpretation, recall, and (cognitive, affective, and behavioural) responses to messages are influenced by the cognitive differences, *subcultural identities, and *social relationships of individuals. In 1938, a radio dramatization of *The War of the Worlds* included simulated news bulletins which caused a minor panic among listeners in the USA who tuned in part-way through the broadcast, leading them to believe that Martians were indeed landing on Earth. However, the American psychologist Hadley Cantril (1906–69) demonstrated that those who were not fooled drew both on *textual knowledge to identify the genre as science fiction, and on *social knowledge in checking for external evidence. *See also* LIMITED EFFECTS THEORY; RECEIVER SELECTIVITY.

selective listening *See* SELECTIVE EXPOSURE.

selective perception (perceptual selectivity) A feature of human *perception in which we *foreground certain *sensory data and *background the rest (*see also* SELECTIVE ATTENTION). As Gombrich noted in relation to visual perception, 'We can focus on something in our field of vision, but never on everything ... To see at all, we must isolate and select.' There is usually massive *redundancy in sensory data and we can easily fill in the gaps (*see also* CLOSURE). The selectivity of perception is primarily driven by the current *purposes and needs of the individual (*see also* PERCEPTUAL SET; SALIENCE; *compare* SELECTIVE EXPOSURE). In the service of such *motivation, several universal processes have a transformative (not merely a 'filtering') influence: *addition, *deletion, *substitution, *transposition (*see also* ASSIMILATION; LEVELLING AND SHARPENING). *See also* ATTENTION.

(((⊕))) SEE WEB LINKS
• *They Saw a Game: a Case Study* by Albert Hastorf and Hadley Cantril

selective recall The unconscious distortions involved in human recollection. As with *selective perception (from which it is difficult to separate recall), several standardizing processes have a transformative function: *addition, *deletion, *substitution, *transposition (*see also* ASSIMILATION; LEVELLING AND SHARPENING).

selective reception *See* RECEIVER SELECTIVITY.

selective representation The transformative processes and products involved in the ostensibly objective, *factual, and *informational reporting or depiction of phenomena in *texts or *discourse in any medium. These may variously be conscious or unconscious and include: *addition, *deletion, *substitution, *transposition, as well as *framing, *foregrounding, and *backgrounding. They can be seen as key factors in relation to issues of representational *bias such as *stereotyping and *symbolic erasure. Although the apparent passivity of the underlying filter *metaphor underplays active *agency and tends to imply unavoidability, greater alertness to such processes among relevant professionals could, of course, help to reduce *bias in *factual genres. *See also* REPRESENTATION.

selective retention The human tendency to remember *messages that are consistent with the individual's existing *attitudes and beliefs. *Compare* SELECTIVE EXPOSURE; SELECTIVE RECALL.

selective sound In *sound design, emphasizing particular sounds over others because they are significant for the *narrative: for example, amplifying the sound of a character's heartbeat to communicate tension.

self-concept *See* LOOKING-GLASS SELF.

self-esteem (self-evaluation) The extent to which individuals value or respect themselves (termed high or low self-esteem). Self-evaluation is based primarily on such factors as: how we believe others evaluate us (*see* LOOKING-GLASS SELF); how we compare ourselves with others, especially *significant others whom we perceive as similar to ourselves in some way (**social comparisons**); and how we interpret our own behaviour (**self perception**). It may also depend on the *status of social groups to which one belongs (*see* SOCIAL IDENTITY).

self-esteem appeals *See* EGO APPEALS.

self-fulfilling prophecy *See* THOMAS THEOREM.

self-image *See* LOOKING-GLASS SELF.

self-monitoring An individual's sensitivity and adjustability to social and interpersonal *cues and contextual *expectations as reflected in their *self-presentation and *expressive behaviour (termed high or low self-monitoring).

self-perception *See* SELF-ESTEEM.

self-presentation A form of *impression management reflecting conscious or unconscious control by individuals of the impressions that their social *performances are creating in particular *contexts of *interaction (situated *social identity). A *dramaturgical concept of *role playing introduced by Goffman. *See also* PERSONA; SELF-MONITORING.

self-serving bias 1. Any tendency to interpret *events in ways that favour the interpreter. 2. (**defensive attribution**) (psychology) A tendency for individuals to attribute their own successes to personal strengths (such as talent) and their failures to external circumstances (such as bad luck).

self-touch In *nonverbal communication, a conscious or unconscious *gesture involving an individual contacting their own body: for instance, touching their hair, temple, nose, chin, or ear with a hand or finger. Some are conscious acts of self-grooming; others are deliberate gestures, such as putting a finger to the lips. Many are less deliberate gestures not consciously intended to communicate but which can be emotionally expressive. Sometimes self-touch seems to play a part in assisting concentration. Other forms include nervous mannerisms (such as wringing one's hands or biting one's lip). Some of those performed publicly allude to what they signify, such as partially covering the eyes or ears (as if closing communicative channels) or touching the forehead (as if reacting to a headache): self-touching is more uninhibited in private. Some public self-touching seeks to conceal feelings (as in covering the face). An increased rate of self-touching can variously suggest anxiety, stress, deception, guilt, suspicion, or hostility. Picking and scratching can reflect displaced aggression (*see* DISPLACEMENT ACTIVITIES). As relics of earlier behavioural adaptations they are called *adaptors or **self-adaptors**. Some signify self-comfort through emulating contact by others: as in hugging one's own shoulders. Some self-touching is mediated by objects (such as chewing a pencil). Children and women tend to engage in more self-touching than men do.

semantic code *See* SEMIC CODE.

semantic differential A technique developed by Osgood and colleagues for mapping the various *connotations or *affective meanings *phenomenologically evoked in individuals by particular cultural phenomena. Osgood's semantic differential scale employs a series of seven-point bipolar rating scales. The three key factors underlying connotations are argued to be *activity* (e.g. active–passive, fast–slow), *potency* (e.g. strong–weak, heavy–light), and *evaluation* (e.g. good–bad, beautiful–ugly).

semantics 1. Most broadly, the study of *meaning: *see also* SENSE; REFERENCE. 2. A branch of *linguistics concerned with the meaning of words and sentences, distinguished from the study of *syntax or *phonology, and traditionally also from *pragmatics—though contemporary theorists stressing the dependence of meaning on *context have argued that semantics can only be understood in terms of pragmatics. *See also* AFFECTIVE MEANING; AMBIGUITY; CONNOTATION; DENOTATION; IDEATIONAL MEANING; POLYSEMY; *compare* GENERAL SEMANTICS. 3. (philosophy) The study of logical principles determining whether *propositions are true or false. 4. (*semiotics) The study of the meaning of *signs, and of the relationship of *sign vehicles to *referents. 5. In informal pejorative usage (as in 'that's just semantics'), *arguments seen as based on 'playing word games'.

semantic web Berners-Lee's vision of the future *World Wide Web as an intelligent provider, in which software agents analyse, interpret, and tailor *information to meet the needs of specific users.

semic code (semantic code, the voice of the person) The elements in a *narrative relating to characters, *settings, objects, or *themes. One of five *narrative codes identified by Barthes.

semiology [French *sémiologie*] 1. The study of *signs, more commonly termed *semiotics. 2. The study of signs by those within the Saussurean (*linguistic) tradition (e.g. Barthes and Lévi-Strauss). 3. Semiotic *textual analysis.

semiosis 1. Broadly, the process of thinking or meaning-making as we experience it. For semioticians, this involves an exchange of *signs whereby one thought prompts another and then another in a continuous chain of associations. 2. For Peirce, the process of thinking in *signs, which in his terminology can be described as a process of perceiving a *representamen, which calls to mind an *object through the actions of an *interpretant, which itself functions as another representamen calling to mind another object through the actions of another interpretant—and so on and so forth, potentially indefinitely. *See* UNLIMITED SEMIOSIS.

semiosphere For Lotman, 'the whole semiotic space of the culture in question'—a semiotic ecology in which different languages and media interact (*see also* MEDIA ECOLOGY).

semiotic 1. Adjectival form of the noun *semiotics. 2. *n.* **(semeiotic)** A rendering of a reference made in 1690 to *semeiotikê* (or 'the doctrine of signs') by the English philosopher John Locke (1632–1704)—the first explicit mention of *semiotics as a branch of philosophy. 3. *n.* **(semeiotic)** For Peirce, the 'formal doctrine of signs' (which he saw as closely related to logic), deriving the term from its use by Locke. 4. *n.* For Kristeva, a modality of the signifying process distinguished from, and existing in a dialectical relation with, the *symbolic. Semiotic processes are pre-symbolic and are seen as unregulated, *transgressive, instinctual, and maternal.

semiotic economy The infinite use of finite elements. The structural feature of double *articulation within a *semiotic system allows an infinite number of meaningful combinations to be generated using a small number of low-level units. This key *design feature is held to be the basis of the productivity and creative economy of verbal *language. The English language has only about 40 or 50 elements of second articulation (*phonemes) but these can generate hundreds of thousands of language *signs.

semiotic model *See* ENCODING/DECODING MODEL.

semiotics 1. The study of *signs (both verbal and nonverbal). Semiotics is widely assumed to be purely a *structuralist method of *textual analysis, but it is much more broadly concerned with how things signify and with *representational practices and systems (in the form of *codes). Different traditions in modern semiotic theory derive from the *Saussurean and *Peircean models of the sign, though in modern cultural and media theory the influence of Jakobson and Eco can be seen as bridging these traditions. Consequently, while the Saussurean terms *signifier and *signified are better known than the terms used in the Peircean model, the latter's modes of relationship are widely adopted. *See* ICONIC; INDEXICAL; SYMBOLIC; *see also* MARKETING SEMIOTICS; MEDIA SEMIOTICS; PICTORIAL SEMIOTICS; SOCIAL SEMIOTICS; VISUAL SEMIOTICS. 2. As distinct from *semiology, studies within the Peircean tradition or philosophically-oriented (rather than linguistically-oriented) approaches.

(⊕) SEE WEB LINKS

• Semiotics for beginners

semiotic square A spatial *representation of the logical relations of a semantic category. Greimas introduced the semiotic square as a means of mapping the logical conjunctions and disjunctions relating key semantic features in a *text. If we begin by drawing a horizontal line linking two familiarly paired terms such as 'beautiful' and 'ugly', we turn this into a semiotic square by making this the upper line of a square in which the two other logical possibilities—'not ugly' and 'not beautiful'—occupy the lower corners. The semiotic square reminds us that this is not simply a *binary opposition because something which is not beautiful is not necessarily ugly and that something which is not ugly is not necessarily beautiful. Occupying a position within such a framework invests a sign with meanings. The semiotic square can be used to highlight 'hidden' underlying *themes in a text or practice.

semiotic triangle (triadic model) Any three-part *representation of relations within the *sign, shown as a triangle. In a generic form, left to right on the base, the points include the *sign vehicle as the first element and the *sense as the second, with the *referent at the apex as the third. Genuine triads involve *mediation: here the referent is related to the sign vehicle via the mediation of the sense; consequently the baseline is usually represented as a dotted line. In the version produced in 1923 by Richards and the philosopher Charles Ogden (1889–1957), the terms are: symbol, thought or reference, and referent. *Compare* PEIRCEAN MODEL.

sender In *transmission models of *communication, the *source of a *message to the *receiver(s). In such models the message is seen as owned as well as originated by the sender, who is also thought of as directing the act of communication and determining the *meaning (or at least the *preferred meaning)—though *see also* INTENTIONAL FALLACY. It is not always clear who the sender is. For instance, in an advertisement, the sender may, from different points of view be: the advertiser whose product is being advertised, the *advertising agency which produced the ad, or a celebrity endorsing the product. In a literary text, the *narrator as well as the *author could be seen as a sender. The sender is not always even aware of sending, as in meanings 'given off' by *body language. *See also* SENDER-ORIENTED COMMUNICATION; SENDER/RECEIVER; *compare* COMMUNICATOR.

sender factors (sender variables) In *models of communication or *persuasion, specific *variables associated with the *sender of a *message that research has identified as among those that can affect its effectiveness. In research within the *Yale model, these are referred to as *source factors. *See also* CHANNEL FACTORS; CONTEXT FACTORS; MESSAGE FACTORS.

sender-oriented communication (sender-centred, source-oriented) *See also* EXPRESSIVE FUNCTION; *compare* INTERACTION-ORIENTED COMMUNICATION. 1. Communication in which the primary focus is on the purposes of the *sender and which tends to ignore *receiver factors (*compare* RECEIVER-ORIENTED COMMUNICATION). This is a common feature of bureaucratic and managerial *downward communication that alienates many of their audiences. It is typically associated with *asymmetrical relationships in which the sender is dominant and the receiver is subordinate and dependent. Such communication is within the framework set by the sender; the receiver must adjust to it. 2. An inherent feature of *transmission models of communication, in which the primary focus is on the sender's *instrumental intentions and how effectively these can be achieved—rather than on communication as a dialogue or *interaction. **3.** Often used pejoratively in contexts where communication skills trainers are trying to persuade senders to be more *receiver-oriented. As an evangelist put it, 'You can't just say what *you* want to say, in the way that *you* want to say it. You have to figure out how to express your message in terms that your *audience* will understand and relate to'. **4.** The dominant *communicative style favoured in *individualistic cultures.

sender/receiver Within *transmission models of communication (and in the *conduit metaphor), the *participants in acts of communication (communication being presented as a linear process of sending *messages to a *receiver). A *sender is the originator of a *message on a particular occasion; *receivers are their *audience on this occasion (in *synchronous interpersonal communication these roles are usually switchable and in normal everyday conversation between equals they shift constantly). These terms are often preferred to speaker/listener, writer/reader, and so on because they apply to diverse *media. A perceived *similarity of the sender to the receiver can be a key factor in the effectiveness of persuasive communication. *Compare* ADDRESSER AND ADDRESSEE; ENCODING/DECODING MODEL.

sender skills (sending skills, encoder skills) In *transmission models of communication, the competence of individuals in effectively communicating their *intended meanings to *target audiences, verbally and/or nonverbally, in a given *medium and situational *context. In *encoding/decoding models this would include utilizing *codes that are shared with the *target audience. Sender skills are often reductively conceived in terms of *instrumental communication. In relation to *affective or *expressive communication, expressive people tend to be extraverts (*see* EXTRAVERSION) and to be good at *self-monitoring. In *nonverbal communication, women tend to have better *encoding skills than men. *See also* SENDER; *compare* COMMUNICATION COMPETENCE; RECEIVER SKILLS.

sensation As conventionally distinguished from *perception, sensation is the initial physiological process of detecting an immediate external sensory stimulus prior to its *interpretation and *categorization. Such a distinction is purely analytical: many psychologists contend that any experience involves interpretation.

sensationalism In the *mass media, a tendency in the reporting of *events to dramatize and exaggerate in order to attract *attention and increase *circulation or *audience share. Often associated with *dumbing down. *See also* FICTION VALUES; INFOTAINMENT; STORY MODEL; TABLOIDIZATION.

sense 1. Loosely, *meaning. **2.** A distinct meaning of a word or expression as defined in a dictionary. **3.** (*semiotics) The conceptual meaning of a sign; in the *Saussurean model, the *signified; in the *Peircean model, the *interpretant: *see also* SEMIOTIC TRIANGLE; *compare* REFERENCE. **4.** A subjective category of sensory impressions: a sensory *modality (traditionally, sight, hearing, touch, taste, or smell).

sense ratio McLuhan's *metaphor for the relative dominance of the various human senses within the human 'sensorium'. He argued that different media extend different senses, and their 'interiorization' transforms mental processes. He *phonocentrically romanticized *oral cultures, and saw *writing and *printing as having led to an *ocularcentrism which disrupted what he saw as the natural balance of the senses. He also saw electronic media as restoring this balance by 'stimulating all the senses simultaneously'. *See also* MCLUHANISM.

sensitization Within the media *effects tradition, a *hypothesis involving a sort of reverse *modelling whereby television viewers react so strongly to some extreme example of realistic violence that they are less likely to imitate it. Where viewing of violence is 'light', sensitization may be more likely than *desensitization. *See also* VIOLENCE DEBATE.

sensory data (sense data) The physical effects of the external world on our subjective *senses (raw sensory stimuli) which are selectively filtered through *attention. In *constructivist theory, these are the basic building blocks of our perceptual experience; for *positivism, they are the only valid basis of *knowledge. *See also* BOTTOM-UP PROCESSING.

sequence 1. In film and video *editing, a series of *shots or *scenes that have been edited together: *see also* MONTAGE. 2. (*semiotics) A temporal *syntagm. 3. (*narratology) A series of related *events or *propositions, or the overall narrative structure: *see also* CLASSICAL NARRATIVE STRUCTURE; FREYTAG'S PYRAMID.

serial On television or radio, a drama *series consisting of sequential *episodes of an ongoing *narrative shown in a regular time slot: for instance, a *soap opera.

serialization Presenting or adapting a *narrative so that the story is told over a finite number of discrete *episodes. *See also* DRAMATIZATION.

series On television or radio, an ongoing *drama in which the main characters and format remain the same from programme to programme but each *episode is a self-contained plot (unlike a *serial). *See also* MINI-SERIES.

serif A *font family of *typefaces in which the main strokes have terminal strokes (serifs), normally at the top and bottom. The four main types of serif are bracketed (e.g. Times New Roman), hairline (e.g. Bodoni), slab (e.g. Rockwell), and wedge (e.g. Latin fonts). *Compare* SANS SERIF.

servomechanism *See* FEEDBACK.

SET *See* EXCHANGE THEORY.

setting 1. The historical period and geographical region forming the backdrop for a *narrative in any medium. 2. The *context of a particular social *episode in *everyday life: *see also* CONTEXT OF SITUATION. 3. The background for a depicted *figure or *subject in a visual representation: *see also* GROUND. 4. One of three key elements in *advertising formats, the others being product and person.

set-top box *See* DIGITAL TELEVISION.

setup In film and video *production, a way of defining an individual *shot that stresses the preparation involved. In feature films this includes positioning the camera and actors (who must be appropriately costumed and made up), dressing the set, adjusting the lighting and sound, etc. Set ups that are not filmed are called rehearsals; when the camera is running they are *takes.

sex 1. The classification of individuals as male or female on the basis of biological characteristics, as distinct from the cultural category of *gender. Poststructuralist theorists have argued that the distinction between sex and gender is based on an untenable *binary opposition of nature vs culture. Even the binary of male vs female is problematized by those who are intersexed, transsexual, or surgically reassigned. 2. Sexual activity, often *stereotypically gendered into active and passive *roles.

sex differences *See* GENDER DIFFERENCES; SEXUAL DIFFERENCE.

sexism *See also* HETEROSEXISM. 1. Individual *attitudes, beliefs, and/or behaviour reflecting prejudice against people on the basis of their biological *sex and/or *gender roles, typically that of males against females on the basis of their supposed inherent inferiority (a form of *gender essentialism). **Male chauvinism** refers to the open expression of sexism by males (*see also* STEREOTYPING). The term dates from the 1970s. 2. Social or institutional practices perceived as devaluing, denigrating, or discriminating against one sex (again typically women); *see also* INSTITUTIONAL BIAS. Examples include the depiction of women as sex objects (*see* OBJECTIFICATION), *gender stereotypes in the *mass media (including the *representation of *gender roles), and the use of the *male norm in *language. *See also* POLITICAL CORRECTNESS.

sex object *See* OBJECTIFICATION.

sex roles *See* GENDER ROLES.

sex or sex role stereotypes *See* GENDER STEREOTYPES.

sexual difference (sex differences) The notion that there are inherent differences between males and females beyond the biological ones (a form of *gender essentialism). It is found both in male *sexism and in separatist forms of *feminism. The everyday use of the phrase 'the opposite sex' reflects the apparent naturalness of the concept of the sexes being 'opposites'. However, there are no opposites in nature. There is no universal category of 'men' and 'women' or universal '*opposition' between them which is the same in every culture. Oft-cited psychological differences such as in relation to spatial skills or field dependence involve statistical overlaps rather than distinct differences between males and females: *see also* FIELD DEPENDENCE AND INDEPENDENCE. *Compare* GENDER DIFFERENCES.

sexual identity (sex identity) 1. The biological *sex with which a person identifies, or is identified: *see also* GENDER IDENTITY. 2. **(sexual orientation)** An individual's sexual preference or orientation as heterosexual, homosexual, or bisexual as part of their sense of *identity. Foucault and others have argued that homosexuality as a basis for identity ('being homosexual'), as opposed to engaging in sexual activities with those of the same sex, is historically a very recent one: the term 'homosexual' was first devised only in 1869.

SFX *See* SPECIAL EFFECTS.

shallow focus *See* DEEP FOCUS.

Shannon and Weaver's model The most well-known and influential formal model of communication, developed in 1949 by Claude Shannon and Warren Weaver (*see* COMMUNICATION MODELS). It is a *transmission model consisting of five elements: an *information *source, which produces a message; a *transmitter, which encodes the message into *signals; a *channel, to which signals are adapted for transmission; a *receiver, which decodes (reconstructs) the message from the signal; a *destination, where the message arrives. A sixth element, *noise, is a dysfunctional factor: any interference with the message travelling along the channel (such as static on the telephone or radio) which may lead to the signal received being different from that sent. For the telephone the channel is a wire, the signal is an electrical current in it, and the transmitter and receiver are the telephone handsets. Noise would include crackling from the wire. In face-to-face conversation, my mouth is the transmitter, the signal is the sound waves, and your ear is the receiver; noise would include any distraction you might experience as I speak. It is a very linear model; unlike later models it does not even include a *feedback loop. Shannon and Weaver were mathematicians, and Shannon worked for Bell Telephone Laboratories. This work proved valuable for communication engineers in dealing with such issues as the capacity of various communication channels in *bits per second, thus contributing to computer science. It led to very useful work on *redundancy in language, and in making *information measurable it gave birth to the mathematical study of *information theory. Consequently it is hardly surprising that Shannon and Weaver's model is information-centred rather than meaning-centred, but this points to its limitations as a general model of human communication.

(⊕) SEE WEB LINKS

• A Mathematical Theory of Communication

shape constancy (form constancy) A psychological mechanism that dampens our consciousness of apparent changes in the shapes of things from different angles. In the cinema, even if we are seated at one side rather than centrally, this mechanism ensures that we quickly adapt. *See also* PERCEPTUAL CONSTANCIES.

sharpening *See* LEVELLING AND SHARPENING.

shifters 1. Term adopted by Jakobson from the Danish linguist Otto Jespersen (1860–1943) for *indexical symbols in *language—grammatical units with a deictic character (such as personal pronouns), which can be decoded only by reference to the specific situational *context of particular *messages: time, place, *addresser and addressee. *See also* DEIXIS. 2. More broadly, any *sign having a *referent which can be determined only in relation to the situational context of its use.

shooting ratio In film and television, the amount of material filmed as *rushes compared to the amount which ends up in the finished presentation: typically 5:1 for *dramas and 20:1 for *documentaries, although these figures can vary considerably.

shooting script The version of the *screenplay that is used as a guide during filming, which may be subject to ongoing revisions.

short-term effects In *theories and research concerning the potential influence of the *mass media on audiences and/or society, minimally delayed and direct consequences of media use. Alleged *effects often included in this category include imitation (*see* MODELLING), *arousal, fear, *disinhibition, *desensitization, *catharsis, and *attitude change. *Compare* LIMITED EFFECTS THEORY; LONG-TERM EFFECTS.

shot *See also* TAKE. 1. In film and television, a sequence of continuous action unedited and terminated by a *cut (or other *transition). The shot is the basic unit from which scenes or programmes are constructed. However, as an analytical unit the shot can sometimes be problematic: in Hitchcock's *Rope* (1948), each shot (or take) lasts up to ten minutes. In such cases shots may need to be broken down according to camera movement within the shot. Further analytical problems are posed by **shots-within-shots,** as in Buster Keaton's *Sherlock Jr.* (1924), where we see a film within a film. Shots are classified in various ways, in particular: by *camera angle, by *shot size, by camera movement (e.g. *pan, *track), by the number of people in frame (e.g. *two-shot), by function (*establishing shot, *general view, *master shot, *noddies, *point-of-view shot, *reaction shot), by *shot duration, by location (*EXT, *INT), by special techniques (e.g. *deep focus), by position (*over-the-shoulder shot), by juxtaposition (*reverse shot), and by source (*stock shot) (*see also* MISE-EN-SCÈNE). 2. **(take)** In film and television, a single uninterrupted run of the camera and the unedited film *footage that this produces.

shot duration The length of time that a particular *shot lasts. *See also* CUTTING RATE; CUTTING RHYTHM; LONG TAKE.

shot/reverse-shot In film, a standard way of representing a conversation taking place between two people that consists of cutting between *over-the-shoulder shots featuring each person. *See also* SUTURE.

shot size In photography and film, how much of a subject is visible within a *frame. *See also* BIG CLOSE-UP; CLOSE-UP; EXTREME LONG-SHOT; LONG-SHOT; MID-SHOT; WIDE SHOT.

shot summary (shot-by-shot summary) A detailed breakdown and *description of all the *shots which comprise a particular *sequence in a film or television programme, or a complete summary of the shots in an *advertisement. This is primarily denotative (*see* DENOTATION), consisting of numbered summaries for each shot, which may include thumbnail screen stills or simple sketches representing the shots, *shot durations, *shot sizes, *camerawork, *transitions, and brief descriptive summaries, which may include dialogue and references to *sound effects or musical lyrics.

sign 1. (*semiotics) A meaningful unit which is interpreted as 'standing for' something other than itself. Signs are found in the physical form of words, images, sounds, acts, or objects (this physical form is sometimes known as the *sign vehicle). Signs have no *intrinsic meaning and become signs only when sign-users invest them with meaning with reference to a recognized *code. The two main models of the sign are the *Saussurean model and the *Peircean model: *see also* CONVENTIONAL SIGN; NATURAL SIGN. 2. An *advertisement located in a public space.

((⊕)) SEE WEB LINKS

• Signs

signage Public and corporate signs, including roadsigns and commercial display signs.

signal 1. A beam of electromagnetic energy (typically radio waves, microwaves, or visible light) which is the *medium of transmission for radio, television, mobile phone, and *computer-mediated communication. A **carrier signal** is a sine wave of regular height and length the amplitude or frequency of which is modulated to encode either *digital or *analogue information. 2. In *Shannon and Weaver's model of communication, the physical form into which the *transmitter changes the *message in order to send it via the communication *channel. In telephony this is a varying electrical current; in face-to-face conversation it is the varying sound pressure in the air. The signal can be distorted by *noise. 3. Distinguished by some theorists from *symbols as a kind of *natural sign: e.g. by the German philosopher Ernst Cassirer (1874–1945) and the American philosopher Susanne Langer (1895–1985). 4. (*social signals) In *nonverbal communication, any specific bodily *cue which communicates, consciously or unconsciously, such as eyebrow-raising or pupil dilation. Unlike *utterances, nonverbal signals are sent continuously and simultaneously.

signal-to-noise ratio 1. A measure of the capacity of a recording or transmission medium to carry a usable *signal which exists below a threshold where the *signal starts to distort and above a threshold where it becomes indistinguishable from background *noise: e.g. the tape hiss of audio recordings: *see also* SHANNON AND WEAVER'S MODEL. 2. Loosely, the amount of wanted *information as compared with the amount of unwanted information in a given communication (*see also* REDUNDANCY).

significance 1. The subjective *value, personal relevance, or perceived *motivation seen by an individual or group as underlying particular *messages or acts by others, as distinct from any explicit *meaning or stated *purpose. 2. (*hermeneutics) A reader's relation of a particular text to their own experiences, beliefs, and *values, as distinct from the author's *intended meaning. 3. The broader social or historical importance of some *event or *artefact. 4. (**statistical significance**) A measure of the improbability of some result having occurred by chance. The smaller the 'p value', the less likely that the result is due to chance, and the more statistically significant it is.

significant other 1. Any individual adopted as a *role model by another individual, and who influences their *values, *norms, behaviour, and self-image. The concept is particularly associated with Mead and the American psychiatrist Harry Stack Sullivan (1892–1949). *See also* LOOKING-GLASS SELF; SOCIALIZATION; *compare* GENERALIZED OTHER. 2. Colloquially, someone with whom one is romantically involved, or one's life-partner.

signification 1. The defining function of *signs (i.e. that they signify, or 'stand for' something other than themselves). 2. The process of signifying (*semiosis). 3. What is *signified; *meaning or *intended meaning: *see also* ORDERS OF SIGNIFICATION. 4. The reference of *language (or any sign system) to reality: *see also* REFERENTIALITY. 5. The relationship between the *sign vehicle and the *referent: *see* ICONIC; INDEXICAL; SYMBOLIC. 6. Signs as part of an overall semiotic system. 7. A *representation.

signified 1. *n.* [French *signifié*] In *linguistics and *semiotics, the mental concept represented by the *signifier in the *Saussurean model of the *sign. In *bracketing the referent, Saussure does not exclude the indirect reference of signs to physical objects in the world as well as to abstract concepts and fictional entities, but the signified is not itself a *referent in the world (in contrast to Peirce's *object). The term is often used more broadly to refer to what the *signifier 'stands for'. 2. Simple past and past participle of *verb* **to signify**: that which is meant, indicated, or symbolized. *See also* SIGNIFICATION.

signifier [French *signifiant*] In the Saussurean tradition, the *form which a *sign takes. For Saussure himself, in relation to linguistic signs, this meant a non-material form of the spoken word—'a sound-image' ('the psychological imprint of the sound, the impression it makes on our senses'). Subsequently, it has invariably been treated as the material (or physical) form of the sign—something which can be seen, heard, felt, smelt or tasted (also called the *sign vehicle). For Saussure, this is one of the two parts of the *sign (*compare* SIGNIFIED). *See also* PRIMACY OF THE SIGNIFIER; SAUSSUREAN MODEL.

signifying practice Signifying practices are the meaning-making behaviours in which people engage (including the *production and *reading of *texts) following particular *conventions or rules of construction and *interpretation. Social semioticians focus on signifying practices in specific sociocultural *contexts—on parole rather than langue (*see also* LANGUE AND PAROLE), and tend towards *diachronic rather than *synchronic analysis—in contrast to *structuralist semioticians who focus on the formal structure of sign systems. *Realists criticize what they see as the reduction of reality by *conventionalists to nothing more than signifying practices.

sign language (gestural language) *See also* NONVERBAL LANGUAGE. 1. **(sign)** *Visual languages of *gesture learned as a primary *language, notably those used by the deaf, e.g. British Sign Language (BSL), American Sign Language (ASL). 2. Gestural systems used as an alternative to speech, such as that used by Plains Indians of North America. 3. Occupational gesture *codes, e.g. the 'tic-tac' code used on British racecourses to communicate the betting odds. 4. Manual language systems representing an existing *language, e.g. fingerspelling (used in association with sign languages for the deaf) and signed forms of spoken language.

signposting In text design, structuring a document or webpage clearly, logically, and consistently in order to make it easily navigable for the reader. This includes using sections, headings and subheadings, cross-references (or *hyperlinks), and lists. *See also* CHUNKING.

sign system (*semiotics) Usually synonymous with a *code and/or *language.

sign vehicle The physical or material form of the *sign (e.g. words, images, sounds, acts, or objects). For some commentators this means the same as the *signifier (which for Saussure did not refer to material form). The Peircean equivalent is the *representamen: the form which the sign takes, but even for Peirce this was not necessarily a material form. Note that the specific material form used (e.g. a word written in one typeface rather than another) may generate *connotations of its own. *See also* SEMIOTIC TRIANGLE.

similarity 1. One of the *gestalt laws of *perceptual organization, being the principle that, in visual patterns, features that look similar are grouped together perceptually as units. This principle has a practical application in text design. 2. (*semiotics) The basis of *iconicity in resemblance. 3. In *social learning theory, the degree to which an individual perceives someone to resemble themselves in some key respect(s)—a factor which can influence the likelihood of *modelling. 4. (*communication theory) The extent to which an audience member perceives the *source of a message to be like themselves in some way—a *source factor which can influence the persuasive effectiveness of the *message. 5. **(similarity attraction hypothesis)** (social psychology) The idea that we like people who are similar to ourselves in certain respects.

simile A *figure of speech (specifically a *trope) in which one thing is explicitly compared with something else of a different kind using the words 'as' or 'like', as in 'Television is like a mirror'. *Compare* METAPHOR.

simplex A transmission system that is only active in one direction, which means that the *transmitter and the *receiver cannot swap roles. Broadcast television is a simplex system. *See also* FULL-DUPLEX; HALF-DUPLEX.

simulacrum (*pl.* **simulacra)** Baudrillard's term (borrowed from Plato) for a 'copy without an original'—the main form in which we encounter *texts in *postmodern culture. More broadly, he used the term to refer to a *representation which has no *referent in everyday reality, such as a *virtual world created on a computer. He declared in *Simulations* (1983) that 'Henceforth, it is the map that precedes the territory...The map engenders the territory.' *See also* HYPERREALITY; VIRTUAL REALITY; *compare* PSEUDO-EVENT.

simulation A dynamic *model of a system that represents its structural elements and functional relations as processes taking place over time. Simulations are constructed to model a particular portion of reality, which has been theoretically identified by investigators as a system composed of related units that behave in a certain way. If the simulation is accurate, it will provide these investigators with information about the real states of the system. Simulations are related to certain kinds of *games in that they are both explorations through *play, but they differ in the degree of formality/informality in which they are applied and the accuracy/ tentativeness of their relationship towards the systems they model. *See also* SIMULACRA.

simulcast 1. *v.* To broadcast a programme simultaneously on two or more *channels or media. 2. *n.* A programme thus broadcast.

site of struggle (site) 1. A discursive domain (e.g. *class, *gender, religion, or ethnicity) in which dominant *discourses compete for ideological *hegemony in an endless quest to fix *meaning. This conception derives from Gramsci's notion of *ideology as a site of struggle. 2. In *poststructuralist discourse, any situational or textual *context in which *meanings and/or *identities are constructed, negotiated, and contested (*see also* HEGEMONIC READING; NEGOTIATED READING; OPPOSITIONAL READING). The *mass media constitute a site of struggle in relation to both their *content and selective *access.

situatedness 1. The dependence of *meaning (and/or *identity) on the specifics of particular sociohistorical, geographical, and cultural *contexts, social and *power relations, and philosophical and *ideological frameworks, within which the multiple perspectives of social actors are dynamically constructed, negotiated, and contested. Such approaches are often perceived by *realists as radical *relativism. *See also* CONTEXTUALIZATION. 2. **Social situatedness**: the notion that the development of individual intelligence is dependent on its embedding in a social (and cultural) *context. It derives from the work of Vygotsky in the 1920s.

sit up or sit back (lean forward, lean back) A phrase that alludes to a popular conceptualization of watching television as a passive, reactive, and relaxing activity and of using computers or the *internet as more active, interactive, and demanding. This tends to underestimate the demands of television viewing (*see also* ACTIVE AUDIENCE THEORY) and the growth in computer-based entertainment, although it may still reflect the initial attitudes with which many people approach these two modes. *See also* HIGH AND LOW INVOLVEMENT.

size constancy The psychological dampening down of dramatic size changes. Our retinal image of a person approaching us would double in size as they halved the distance between us, but we are rarely aware of this. *See also* PERCEPTUAL CONSTANCY.

sjuzhet *See* FABULA.

slander *See* DEFAMATION.

sleeper effect A phenomenon whereby when a viewpoint from a high-credibility *source is followed by another from a low-credibility source, the persuasive advantage of the former diminishes over time and, after its *source is forgotten, the latter counter-intuitively becomes as persuasive as the original message. This was a controversial finding of studies by Hovland and others from the Yale school. *See also* SOURCE CREDIBILITY; YALE MODEL.

slice of life [French *tranche de vie*] A term originally applied to 'realistic' writers such as Zola, implying that such work presented episodes of *everyday life as if it were an unmediated recording. For instance, dialogue might bear a striking resemblance to real-life conversations, or the *frame of the work (such as the last page of the novel, the final curtain onstage, or the picture *frame of a painting) might seem to cut across ongoing action like a photographic snapshot.

slippage of meaning (the sliding signified) In contrast to the stability of the relationship between *signifier and *signified in Saussure's *structuralist conception of *language, as Lacan puts it, there is 'an incessant sliding of the signified under the signifier': a signifier leads only to another signifier, never to a signified. For Derrida, there is thus an inherent *indeterminacy of meaning (*see* DIFFÉRANCE). However, sanity and communication depend on at least the provisional illusion of the stability of meaning. Lacan argues that there are anchoring points (*points de capiton*) in a discourse which make *interpretation possible, albeit retrospectively. *See also* DECONSTRUCTION; FREEPLAY; TRANSCENDENT SIGNIFIED; UNLIMITED SEMIOSIS.

slips of the tongue *See* PARAPRAXIS.

slow motion (motion pictures) The effect of slowing down the motion of a photographed subject which can be achieved by playing back the film or videotape at a slower *frame rate than normal, or by photographing the subject at a higher frame rate and playing it back at normal speed—the latter method being preferable because it creates a smoother motion.

smallness One of the *gestalt laws of *perceptual organization, being the principle that, in visual patterns, smaller areas tend to be seen as figures against a larger background. *See also* FIGURE AND GROUND.

small talk Polite, informal conversation about nothing of any particular importance. A form of *discourse often *stereotypically associated by men with women's talk (men's talk thus being an unmarked form; *see also* MARKEDNESS). Malinowski argues that the function of such discourse is phatic (*see* PHATIC COMMUNICATION).

smart mob People who use mobile communication technologies to act in concert even if they don't know each other. *See also* SOCIAL MEDIA; *compare* FLASH MOB.

smartphone A device that typically combines the functions of a *mobile phone, *mp3 music- and video-player, camera, and portable computer with *internet access.

smiley *See* EMOTICON.

SMS (Short Message Service) A short *message sent from a *mobile phone. Also called a **text message**. Such messages tend to be *telegraphic in style: closer to speech than to formal writing. Texting is particularly popular among teenagers and young adults, especially females, and it is frequently primarily *phatic in function.

snail mail In *internet parlance, a colloquial term for the traditional letter and/or the postal service that delivers them (typically contrasted with the speed of *email). The analogy was first made in the 1840s, when the comparison was with *telegraphy. *See also* POST.

SNS *See* SOCIAL NETWORKING SITE.

soap opera (soap) A regularly broadcast television or radio *drama *serial of indefinite duration with multiple plotlines and a regular cast of characters, typically involving a depiction of the problems of *everyday life in a specific setting using the formal *conventions of *realism. The *genre emerged on American radio in the 1930s, owing its name to the original sponsorship by major soap powder companies and to its perceived overdramatization. The content varies from the fantasy lifestyles of the fabulously rich in the glossy American productions *Dallas* (1978–91) and *Dynasty* (1981–89) to the everyday lives of ordinary people in the long-running British productions *Coronation Street* (1960–) and *EastEnders* (1985–) and the Australian *Neighbours* (1985–) and *Home and Away* (1988–). Soap operas generally appeal to a predominantly female audience (the ratio of females to males in current British soap audiences tends to be about 60:40), arguably because they usually offer for possible *identification a wider range of different female characters than other *genres. *See also* DOCUSOAP; OPEN FORMS.

social acceptance appeals In persuasive communication, particularly in *advertising, a rhetorical strategy which plays on the audience's desire to gain the approval of others. It is an *emotional appeal to a common personal *value which is particularly important in *collectivistic cultures, to more conservative consumers, and to teenagers seeking *peer group acceptance. It plays on the desire for recognition, status, respect, *affiliation, and belonging, and the desire to avoid embarrassment or rejection. It is widely used in advertisements for products such as deodorants. Its use in advertisements for alcohol or cigarettes is prohibited in *advertising codes of ethics in many countries. *See also* ADVERTISING APPEALS.

social behaviour *See* INTERACTION.

social capital A resource consisting of interpersonal and *social relationships upon which individuals draw and to which they contribute. Unlike *cultural capital and *economic capital, this is a resource of a social group rather than of an individual. It supports social *cohesion and is in tension with individualism. However, *access to such resources is restricted to those within the same social or professional group. The American political scientist Robert Putnam (b.1941) argues that in the USA there has been a general decline in social capital and social solidarity, associated with an increase in individualism.

social codes (*semiotics) Interpretive frameworks representing the world as it is understood within a *culture or *subculture. These are drawn upon in making sense not only of the world, but also of any *representations of it. Much of this is *tacit knowledge. Social codes include unwritten codes such as bodily codes and behavioural codes. While all semiotic codes are in a broad sense social codes (being based on social *conventions), social codes can also be seen as forming a major group of codes, alongside *textual codes and *interpretive codes. *See also* COMMON SENSE; CONVERSATIONAL CURRENCY; CULTURAL LITERACY; DRAMATURGY; FACE-WORK; FOLK PSYCHOLOGY; FRAME; INTERACTION RITUALS; RITUAL INTERACTION; SOCIAL KNOWLEDGE; *compare* SOCIAL SCHEMATA.

social cognition The processing of social *information by individuals and its potential influence on social behaviour; the study of this field within social psychology. *See also* COGNITION; IMPRESSION FORMATION; PERSON PERCEPTION; SCRIPT; SOCIAL PERCEPTION; STEREOTYPING.

social comparisons *See* SELF-ESTEEM.

social construction or constructionism *See* CONSTRUCTIONISM.

social determinism 1. (***cultural determinism, social shaping**) In *theories of the relationship between society and *technology or *media, a stance which asserts the primacy of social (and political) factors rather than the autonomous influence of the *medium (whether this is *language or a technology). Social determinists reject the causal priority given to language by *linguistic determinists and to technology by *technological determinists. Those who emphasize social determination focus on such issues as the circumstances of *production, modes of use, *values, *purposes, skill, *style, choice, control, and *access rather than on the *structure of the text or *code or the technical features of the *medium. Like any strong *determinism, extreme social determinism is a form of *reductionism. An extreme social determinist position relating to the decoding of texts (more specifically, *audience determinism) would reduce individual decodings to a direct consequence of social *class position. A more moderate stance would stress that access to different codes is influenced by social position. *Structuralist *semiotics tends to be allied with *textual determinism and is criticized for ignoring social determination. *Compare* SOCIOLOGISM. 2. (**environmental determinism**) In the nature vs nurture debate, the stance that the social and physical environment, or nurture, is the stronger factor. *Compare* BIOLOGICAL DETERMINISM.

social distance *See* INTERPERSONAL ZONES.

social effects *Compare* PSYCHOLOGICAL EFFECTS. 1. Any social changes attributed to specific causes: *see also* SOCIAL DETERMINISM. 2. In relation to media, social influences or implications of the *mass media or *new media of communication—one focus of academic media research and theory within the *effects tradition. McLuhan's notion that 'the medium is the message' refers in part to the social 'impact' of new media. For instance, in relation to the historical advent of *printing, McLuhan argued deterministically that 'socially, the typographic extension of man brought in nationalism, industrialism, *mass markets, and universal literacy and education'. *See also* MEDIA DETERMINISM.

social functions The general roles that communicative acts, or a *medium of communication, can be seen as serving for society as a whole as opposed to simply for individuals. The most widely-listed social functions of communication or of the *mass media include *surveillance, *consensus, and *socialization (derived from Lasswell). Schramm adds *entertainment (which he also lists as a *personal function). *See also* COMMUNICATIVE FUNCTIONS; LINGUISTIC FUNCTIONS; MEDIA FUNCTIONS; REGULATIVE USES; SOCIAL UTILITY FUNCTION; STRUCTURAL USES; *compare* PERSONAL FUNCTIONS.

social grade *See* CLASS.

social identification *See* GROUP IDENTIFICATION.

social identity *See also* GROUP IDENTIFICATION; IDENTITY; IN-GROUP.
1. Broadly, an individual's self-definition in relation to others: *see also* LOOKING-GLASS SELF. 2. (social psychology) Those ideas that we have about ourselves which are based on our membership of major social categories (such as nationality, *ethnicity, *sex, religion) and which contribute to the formation of our *self-concept*. These are the '*in-groups' to which we belong. The Polish-British psychologist Henri Tajfel (1919–82) argued that within such groups members maintain a positive self-concept by distinguishing themselves from the negatively-defined 'out-group', which is the root of prejudice.

social integration function *See* SOCIAL UTILITY FUNCTION.

socialization 1. **(enculturation)** Broadly, both formal and informal processes by which individuals adapt to the behavioural *norms and *values in a culture and learn to perform established social *roles. A distinction is often made between *primary* socialization—learning *attitudes, *values, and appropriate individual behaviour, largely through family and schooling in childhood, and *secondary* socialization—learning by youths and adults of appropriate group behaviour, e.g. in occupational socialization. *See also* INTERNALIZATION. 2. The deliberate induction of individuals by social agencies into dominant *norms and *values in that *culture. This narrower conception ignores the importance of the *mass media and *peer groups in socialization (e.g. in **gender socialization**—the learning of behaviour and *attitudes considered appropriate for one's own *sex). 3. A specific *communicative function or *media function from a social rather than an individual perspective: *see* SOCIALIZATION FUNCTION.

socialization function (transmission function) One of the roles that the *mass media, a particular *medium, or specific kinds of media *content, are seen as playing from the perspective of society (macro-level functions): in this case, the transmission (across time and among groups) of values, the social heritage, and normative models of behaviour within a *culture. For Lasswell in 1948 this was one of the three key functions of social *communication (the others being the *surveillance function and the *consensus function). Schramm suggests that it is comparable to an *educational function for individuals. There is little doubt that the mass media are important agents of *socialization. *See also* IMAGINED COMMUNITY; MEDIA FUNCTIONS; RITUAL MODEL; *compare* TRADITIONAL TRANSMISSION.

social knowledge Understanding of reality and the world and cultural *knowledge of *social codes and situational *contexts, including *common sense, *folk psychology, *cultural literacy, and familiarity with social *roles and *communicative purposes. Such knowledge is of course essential for making sense of everyday *events; additionally, along with *textual knowledge, it is an essential resource for inferring the *preferred meaning of *texts (which themselves extend social knowledge). It is acquired through *socialization and *lived experience, much being *tacit knowledge. In *schema theory it is seen as mentally represented in *social schemata. *See also* CONVERSATIONAL CURRENCY; DRAMATURGY; FACE-WORK; FRAME; INTERACTION RITUALS; RITUAL INTERACTION; *compare* SOCIAL CODES.

social learning theory A theory that behaviour is learned by observation, *identification, and imitation, sometimes assisted by reinforcement (not necessarily direct reinforcement). For instance, sex-typed behaviour is seen as learned from observing, identifying with, and imitating same-sex models (both at home and in the *mass media), together with reinforcement for sex-appropriate behaviour from *significant others. Bandura argued that reinforcement is not necessary for *modelling.

social media A broad category or *genre of communications media which occasion or enable social *interaction among groups of people, whether they are known to each other or strangers, localized in the same place or geographically dispersed. It includes *new media such as *newsgroups, *MMOGs, and *social networking sites. Such media can be thought of metaphorically as virtual meeting places which function to occasion the exchange of media content among users who are both producers and consumers. Social media have also become adopted as a significant marketing tool. *See also* INTERACTIVITY; USER-GENERATED CONTENT; WEB 2.0.

social networking site (SNS; social network site) *See also* SOCIAL MEDIA; SOCIOGRAM. 1. A website, such as Facebook or MySpace, enabling individual users to create personal profiles linked to those of their online contacts. Such sites are widely used as marketing tools. 2. In a more restricted sense, a website designed primarily for individual users to develop their own personal *user-generated content around their existing offline *social networks, and in which the focus is on people rather than *topics.

social networks Patterns of *interpersonal relationships among individuals based on *face-to-face interaction and/or *mediated communication. The concept of social networks was introduced by Radcliffe-Brown in 1940. Such networks (based on links rather than individuals) emerge from *interaction and can cut across and influence *institutions; they can also shape individual behaviour. In sociology and anthropology, kinship and friendship networks have been a key focus; the advent of the internet has stimulated the concept of *network societies. *See also* COHESION; COMMUNICATION NETWORKS; DIFFUSION; EXCHANGE THEORY; GROUP COMMUNICATION; GROUP IDENTIFICATION; INFORMATION FLOW; IN-GROUP; NETWORK ANALYSIS; PEER GROUP; PRIMARY AND SECONDARY GROUPS; REFERENCE GROUP; SOCIAL STRUCTURE; SOCIOGRAM; STRONG TIES; TWO-STEP FLOW; WEAK TIES; *compare* SPACE OF FLOWS.

social norms (norms) (sociology) Common standards within a social group regarding socially acceptable or appropriate behaviour in particular social situations, the breach of which has social consequences. The strength of these norms varies from loose *expectations to unwritten rules. Norms (such as those for social *roles) are internalized in *socialization. *Functionalists emphasize that society, its *institutions, and social order depend on social norms, but within a society different social groups also have their own norms. Compliant behaviour is termed *normative* but the existence of social norms does not prevent them from being frequently violated. *Ethnomethodologists and *symbolic interactionists emphasize the contestation of norms, and *Marxists stress the role of coercion rather than normative *consensus. For other uses of the term, *see* NORM.

social perception 1. (social psychology) The processes involved in the apprehension, *evaluation, and *interpretation of ourselves and others: an aspect of *social cognition. *See also* HALO EFFECT; IMPRESSION FORMATION; PERSON PERCEPTION; REFERENCE GROUP; SELF-PERCEPTION; STEREOTYPING. 2. The social determinants of *perception: *see also* EXPECTATIONS; PERCEPTION; PRIMACY; PRIMING; SALIENCE.

social presence A subjective or phenomenal quality attributed to a *medium related to the sensory *channels which it supports. Media differ in their degree of social presence and this is argued to be a factor in determining the ways in which individuals use them in *interaction since the choice of medium affects the nature of the *interaction. In 1976, the British psychologists John Short, Ederyn Williams, and Bruce Christie ranked face-to-face communication as having the most social presence, followed by *CCTV, the telephone (including speaker-phones and audio conferencing systems), and finally business letters. Media with high social presence are able to communicate *facial expression, direction of *gaze, *posture, dress, and nonverbal vocal *cues, which represent the *presence of another person (*see also* PSYCHOLOGICAL DISTANCE). However, it is not true that media with high social presence are simply better, for those with low social presence are better suited to *task-oriented purposes where the sense of presence is not an issue. *See also* CUELESSNESS; *compare* MEDIA RICHNESS.

social realism Visual art or literature depicting subjects of social concern using realistic representational techniques as a form of left-wing protest against injustices such as poverty or social deprivation. *See also* CLASSIC REALISM; EMOTIONAL REALISM; REALISM.

social relations (social relationships) Persistent reciprocal *interaction between individuals, enabling the development of shared *expectations.

social schemata Hypothetical mental templates that help individuals to make sense of new experiences with reference to *expectations established by previous *lived experience of the everyday social and perceptual world. *See also* SCHEMA THEORY; SOCIAL KNOWLEDGE; *compare* SOCIAL CODES.

social semiotics 1. The study of *signifying practices in specific sociocultural *contexts. Saussure wrote of *semiotics as 'a science that studies the life of signs within society', but social semiotics reverses the *structuralist priorities regarding *langue and parole. Signs do not exist without interpreters, and semiotic *codes are social *conventions. 2. The *semiotic analysis of *social codes and phenomena (e.g. *nonverbal communication) as distinguished from the *textual analysis of *textual codes.

social shaping *See* SOCIAL DETERMINISM.

social signals Argyle's term for nonverbal *cues in social *interaction.

social situation All of the social factors influencing individual behaviour or experience in a specific *context of *interaction at a particular time. *See also* CONTEXT OF SITUATION.

social structure The fundamental and relatively enduring framework of social *institutions, *roles, *statuses, and *norms constituting the interrelated elements of society at a particular time. Sometimes distinguished from *processes* and frequently determinatively opposed to *agency. A key issue is the extent to which social structure depends on *consensus or coercion. *See also* BASE AND SUPERSTRUCTURE; FUNCTIONALISM; SOCIAL NETWORKS; STRUCTURE.

social text In *structuralism and *poststructuralism, a textualist *metaphor for culture as a system of *signs within which *meanings and realities are produced and interpreted; in interpretive social analysis, culture and the social world may thus be seen as a *text which is amenable to being read for deep meanings or deconstructed—as in the work of Kristeva or the American anthropologist Clifford Geertz (1926-2006). The conception of social phenomena such as *gender, *ethnicity, or *class as texts rather than as *givens enables *ideological analysis in terms of alternatives to the *dominant reading which seeks to establish them as natural categories (*see also* NEGOTIATED READING; OPPOSITIONAL READING). The notion of social reality as authored is seen by its critics as *relativism. *Deconstruction dissolves the *ontological distinction between text and *context, between *representation and world. Derrida's declaration that 'there is nothing outside the text' enrages *literalists.

social ties *See* STRONG TIES; WEAK TIES.

social utility function (social integration function) In relation to general types of use by individuals of the *mass media, a single *medium, a media *genre, or specific media *content, this is usage which strengthens our contact with others in our society. This is argued to derive from a need of individuals for *affiliation. Examples include using the mass media as *conversational currency, going on a date at the cinema, using the radio or TV as environmental background (*see also* STRUCTURAL USES), and relating to characters or presenters onscreen (*see* PARASOCIAL RELATIONSHIPS). *See also* IMAGINED COMMUNITY; MEDIA FUNCTIONS; USES AND GRATIFICATIONS.

social zone *See* INTERPERSONAL ZONES.

societal reaction theory *See* LABELLING THEORY.

sociocentricity *See* SOCIAL DETERMINISM.

sociogram (network graph) (sociology) A diagrammatic representation of patterns of social relations between individuals: for instance, a friendship network (who is friends with whom). This *sociometric* (social measurement) technique reveals isolates, cliques, and 'bridges'. *Social networking sites can be seen as dynamic sociograms. *See also* COMMUNICATION NETWORK; NETWORK ANALYSIS; RECIPROCITY; SOCIAL NETWORKS.

sociolect (*sociolinguistics) The distinctive ways in which *language is used by members of a particular social group. In semiotic terms it can refer more broadly to *subcodes shared by members of such groups. *Compare* DIALECT; GENDERLECT; IDIOLECT.

sociolinguistics The study of language in relation to social *contexts, *social relationships, and cultural factors (such as *class, *gender, and *ethnicity). *See also* ACCOMMODATION; CODE-SWITCHING; COMMUNICATIVE COMPETENCE; CONTEXT OF SITUATION; CONVERSATION ANALYSIS; DIALECT; DISCOURSE ANALYSIS; ELABORATED CODE; ETHNOMETHODOLOGY; GENDERLECT; LINGUISTIC RELATIVITY; REGISTER; RESTRICTED CODE; SOCIOLECT; SPEECH COMMUNITY.

sociologism (sociological reductionism) Typically a pejorative term for the reduction of phenomena to purely sociological explanations. *See also* REDUCTIONISM; SOCIAL DETERMINISM; *compare* PSYCHOLOGISM.

socio-oriented communication A style of family communication and media use, identified by Lull, that involves: an emphasis on harmonious *social relations and the feelings of others; children being encouraged to get along with other family members and friends, to give way in arguments, to avoid controversy, to repress anger, and to stay away from trouble; parental control, verbal and restrictive punishment; high levels of total TV viewing (*see* HEAVY VIEWERS) but low news consumption. *Compare* INTERACTION-ORIENTED COMMUNICATION.

soft focus In photography and *cinematography, a blurring of the image created by filters, rather than an out of focus *shot. Soft focus is considered to be flattering because it obscures, blemishes, and creates a pleasing glow around the subject.

soft news *Mass-media journalistic features that are *not* *factual reports of *newsworthy *events—examples being entertainment and leisure stories. There is a *stereotypical *connotation of *femininity. *See also* ENTERTAINMENT FUNCTION; FICTION VALUES; STORY MODEL; *compare* HARD NEWS.

soft sell In *advertising, the use of a subtle sales message, typically employing *emotional appeals and *imagery to generate positive associations for a brand rather than seeking immediate sales. Its focus is not on *information or product benefits. *See also* PERIPHERAL ROUTE; *compare* HARD SELL.

software Coded instructions in the form of programs that perform certain tasks using a computer's hardware. Software includes a computer's operating system and all its applications (colloquially, **apps**). These are written in *source code* (a programming language such as Java or C++) and are then converted by a compiler program into *binary. **'Software studies'** refers to the academic exploration of how software tools frame the cultural representation of digital *data in conventions of *information retrieval, visualization, *knowledge creation, and the understanding of *new media.

(⊕) SEE WEB LINKS

• Software takes command

solipsism *See* IDEALISM.

SOT (sound off tape) *See* NATURAL SOUND.

sound bed In audiovisual *editing, either using a pre-existing piece of audio (e.g. a music *track), or cutting together audio material from *rushes (e.g. selected quotations) to create a coherent audio track which structures the subsequent editing of pictures.

soundbite A brief quote lifted out of, or assembled from, a longer statement. Soundbites have become a mainstay of news and current affairs reporting. Those in the public eye (notably politicians) have become adept at tailoring their statements to feature soundbites. Neil Postman argues this has a detrimental effect on political *discourse as more complex *arguments and nuances are lost.

soundbite journalism The technique of reporting highly editorialized versions of news or current affairs stories that are presented as simplified summaries.

sound bridge In film or television, sound that either continues over a *cut or starts before a cut, having the effect of counteracting the abruptness of the visual *transition. *See also* ASYNCHRONOUS SOUND.

sound design Broadly, the technical and creative process that goes into creating a sound *mix. In film and television this includes combining *diegetic and non-diegetic sounds and music effects to enhance the impact and meaning of the visuals. Many of the elements that combine in the final mix have to be sourced or created in *post-production. *See also* AUDITORY PERSPECTIVE.

sound effects Any non-diegetic sounds other than music or dialogue. These tend to be added in *post-production. *Compare* DIEGETIC SOUND.

sound mixing *See* MIX.

sound off tape *See* NATURAL SOUND.

sound perception *See* AUDITORY PERCEPTION.

sound perspective (auditory perspective, aural perspective) 1. In filming, a convention whereby sounds heard by the audience reflect the relative distances of their apparent sources in three-dimensional space. In a *long-shot, sounds in the *background would be quieter than those in the *foreground. However, the sound perspective is often kept constant in a cut sequence even when *shot sizes change. 2. In sound recording, the apparent distance from the listener of a sound in a *mix, based on aural cues such as volume, frequency, echo, timbre, and reverberation.

In stereo recordings depth effects can also be created by *panning and phase reversal.

source 1. **(information source)** In *Shannon and Weaver's model, the point of origin of a *message. For example, in *speech communication, the source would be the speaker (*see also* AUTHOR; SOURCE FACTORS). 2. In the *mass media, the perceived origin of a *message. In *advertisements, where a model or actor is a spokesperson for the product in the ad, they count as a source: *compare* SENDER. 3. A person from whom a journalist obtains *information for a news story. The mass media are often criticized for over-reliance on official sources. 4. In *linear editing, the playback as opposed to the 'record' machine.

source factors (source variables, sender factors or **variables)** The terminology used in some models of *communication or *persuasion for specific *variables associated with the *source (or perceived source) of a *message that research has identified as among those that can affect its effectiveness. In research within the *Yale model, **source credibility** has been shown to be particularly important. For instance, persuasion is most effective when the source is seen as knowledgeable, trustworthy, powerful, and attractive. The more we like someone, the more we are likely to be persuaded by them—especially if we identify with them. We are likely to respond positively to messages from a source we perceive as similar to ourselves (*see* IDENTIFICATION; SIMILARITY). *See also* SENDER FACTORS.

source-oriented communication *See* SENDER-ORIENTED COMMUNICATION.

Soviet montage *See* DIALECTICAL MONTAGE.

space of flows The spatial logic of networking which is organized around connections, in contrast to the **space of places** where the special logic is organized around localities (Castells). In a *network society, dynamic flows of people, *information, and money, circulate between nodes which form associations that are increasingly independent of specific local *contexts. However, the notion of place still has meaning among groups and organizations (*see also* VIRTUAL COMMUNITY; *compare* SOCIAL NETWORK).

space perception *See* SPATIAL PERCEPTION.

space-time compression *See* TIME-SPACE COMPRESSION.

spam Unsolicited *emails, which constitute the vast majority of all the emails sent. Named by Joel Furr (b.1967) after a Monty Python comedy sketch where every item of a café menu included the processed luncheon meat known as Spam.

(⊕) SEE WEB LINKS

• Spam reaches 30-year anniversary

spatial behaviour *See* PROXEMICS.

spatial perception (space perception) The apprehension and *interpretation of physical, experiential, and/or pictorial space, including the *spatial relations between objects, and movement. Psychologically, individuals differ in their spatial skills, such as the mental rotation of objects and spatial orientation. Oft-cited references to males tending to demonstrate better spatial skills than females involve statistical overlaps rather than distinct differences between the sexes. *See also* BINOCULAR VISION; DEPTH PERCEPTION; INTERPERSONAL ZONES; MOTION PARALLAX; PERSONAL SPACE; PICTORIAL DEPTH CUES; VISUAL PERCEPTION.

spatial relations Relative distances, orientations, and angles between the viewer and the viewed, or between parts of a visual representation, such as: above/below, in front/behind, close/distant, left/right, north/south/east/west, and inside/outside (or centre/periphery). Such structural relationships are not semantically neutral. Lakoff and Johnson have shown how fundamental **orientational metaphors** are routinely linked to key concepts in a *culture. 'Up' (or higher) is often positively valorized compared with 'down' (or lower) (*see* CAMERA ANGLE; ELEVATION); *reading direction can be linked to the signification of left and right in visual representation (*see* FLIPPED IMAGE). *See also* DIAGONALITY; FRONTALITY; MISE-EN-SCÈNE; OCCLUSION; ORIENTATION; PICTORIAL DEPTH CUES; PROXIMITY; SHOT SIZE; SPATIAL PERCEPTION; SYNTAGM; ZONES OF RECESSION.

spatial zones *See* INTERPERSONAL ZONES.

special effects (SFX, visual effects) *See also* GREEN SCREEN; MOTION CAPTURE; ROTOSCOPE; TRAVELLING MATTE. 1. In film and television, either trick *shots designed to deceive the viewer—for example, the digital matte paintings that represented the buildings of ancient Rome in *Gladiator* (2000)—or the creation of fantastic spectacles such as the digital realization of the alien planet Pandora in *Avatar* (2009). Special effects can be mechanical or optical, although since the 1990s more and more have been achieved digitally. 2. A specialist job in film *production and *post-production that creates *shots which are too expensive, dangerous, or impossible to achieve 'in camera'. 'Visual effects' is a more accurate term since such shots involve specialist film-making departments whereas audio effects tend to be created as a part of a film's *sound design.

spectacle [Latin *spectaculum* 'public show'] 1. A public *performance, *media event, or epic film produced on a grand scale and with impressive visual effects. 2. For Mulvey, one of the two primary formal components of mainstream film, the other being *action* (*see* NARRATIVE FLOW). Spectacle is a freezing of the flow of action, frequently featuring the erotic depiction of 'woman as image' by the objectifying *male gaze. 3. For the French philosopher Guy Debord (1931–94), writing in the 1960s, the 'society of the spectacle' is a cultural obsession with *appearances and the *image: *mass consumption and electronic media have created a society of *spectators and inauthentic experience: *compare* AESTHETICIZATION; HYPERREALITY.

spectacularization The process of producing a *representation in the form of a major *spectacle: for instance, television commercials with extravagant budgets and visual effects, as in many of those produced by established or aspiring film *directors.

spectator 1. A person who watches and listens to a public *performance or sporting *event, usually with reference to those attending rather than the *viewers of broadcast coverage. A common *connotation is that spectators watch without actively participating (which neglects emotional and cognitive involvement). **2. (film spectator)** In *psychoanalytical and *structuralist *film theory, a relatively passive viewing *subject constituted through the adoption of an ideal '*subject position' anticipated by the filmic text. This phenomenon is commonly referred to as cinematic **spectatorship**: *see also* CINEMATIC APPARATUS; IDEAL READER; INTERPELLATION; POSITIONING; SUTURE; VIEWING SUBJECTS. **3.** In *cognitive film theory, a viewer engaged in the active interpretation of a film: *see also* ACTIVE AUDIENCE THEORY. **4.** An individual viewer of a film: an actual member of a *film audience, usually in the specific social *context of a cinema. This is normal usage in empirical studies of film audiences.

spectral purity (purity) A physical dimension of light in which the fewer wavelengths the greater purity; it corresponds to the psychological dimension of *saturation. This is one of the three physical properties of light on which *colour vision depends; the other two are *luminance and *wavelength.

spectrum scarcity The conception of radio frequencies as a finite and limited resource that needs to be managed carefully. The part of the *electromagnetic spectrum that is suitable as a transmission medium constitutes only a narrow band of frequencies. These must be shared among the military, the emergency services, as well as the radio and television services. Consequently, in the UK, it was seen as imperative that the licensing of these frequencies should be subject to government *regulation and control lest the transmission of radio signals fell into a 'chaos of the ether'. *See also* PUBLIC SERVICE BROADCASTING.

speech act (*pragmatics) Goal-directed actions performed with words in *interpersonal communication, defined primarily with reference to the speaker's intentions and the effects on the listener(s). The term was introduced by Austin and is also associated with Searle in an analytical approach called **speech act theory**. Some regard speech acts as the basic units of *discourse. The term is frequently used synonymously with *illocutionary act. *See also* DISCOURSE ANALYSIS; LOCUTIONARY ACT; PERFORMATIVES; PERLOCUTIONARY ACT; *compare* CONVERSATION ANALYSIS.

speech circuit [French *circuit de la parole*] Saussure's cyclical and symmetrical *model of oral *interpersonal communication, originally published in 1915, famously represented in the form of two facing heads with what look like telephone wires slung between them and connecting their brains, mouths, and ears. Unlike most *transmission models, it has directional arrows indicating not only *feedback but the equal participation of both participants. It is *sender-oriented insofar as *comprehension on the part of the listener is presented as a kind of mirror of the speaker's initial process of expressing a thought. The textual commentary refers only briefly to the speaker's use of 'the *code provided by the *language' (a code which is assumed to be shared), but at each end of the process in the diagram there is a *representation of a process of mental decoding or encoding to or from the 'sound pattern' (or *signifier) and the concept (or *signified). The concept of *codes,

and of *encoding/decoding was to become central to *structuralist *semiotics.
See also SAUSSUREAN MODEL.

speech communication The study of human spoken *interaction.
Undergraduate programmes, widespread in the USA, usually include *interpersonal
communication, *group communication, *organizational communication, and
*rhetoric (or persuasive communication). Institutional programmes typically
emphasize communication skills and effectiveness more broadly, and hence
often also include *written communication, *intercultural communication, and
*mediated communication. Research programmes include the investigation of
issues such as the contextual *functions of *oral communication and the
development of *speech recognition systems.

speech community (language community) Any group of people sharing
a common *language or language variety.

speech perception The process in which listeners hear vocal sounds and
recognize and comprehend linguistic units within the *acoustic flow. *See also*
AUDITORY PERCEPTION; COCKTAIL PARTY EFFECT; PHONETICS; PHONOLOGY.

speech recognition 1. **(word recognition)** In *speech perception, the initial
*cognitive processes involved in decoding vocal sounds: *see also* PHONETICS.
2. **(automatic speech recognition** or **computer speech recognition)** The use
of computer software to convert human speech into written text, or to respond to
voice commands.

spheres of consensus, legitimate controversy, and deviance A
conception of journalistic *objectivity proposed in 1986 by Daniel Hallin, an
American communication theorist, in his analysis of the US reporting of the
Vietnam War that sees it as a negotiation between three *ideological provinces. The
sphere of consensus is a province of implicit agreement wherein journalists
present the 'official line' as the only correct point of view. The **sphere of legitimate
controversy** is a province of objectivity wherein issues can be debated among
different parties representing a plurality of views. The **sphere of deviance** is a
province excluding or ridiculing those whose views are considered to be too radical,
irresponsible, or even dangerous to be given a fair hearing. *See also* IMPARTIALITY.

spin (*public relations) Selectively creating *narratives and *frames for *events so
that those particular definitions of situations are privileged which best serve the
client's interests. Often a pejorative term. *See also* BIAS; BURYING; FRAMING;
PROPAGANDA; SOUND BITE; THOMAS THEOREM.

spin doctor A press relations specialist whose role is to manage *mass-media
coverage of those whose interests they represent, especially a political adviser
responsible for news management. Alastair Campbell (b.1957) became famous as
spin doctor for British Prime Minister Tony Blair's administration between 1994
and 2003.

spiral of silence The theory that media reports of *public opinion tend to
reflect the majority view, since those in the minority tend to be less vocal, expressing

their opinions only when they seem consonant with those of the majority. In a spiral process, media coverage reinforces the majority view.

splice In film or audio *editing, the act of joining two cut pieces of film or audio tape together, or the product of this process (*see also* CUT). This process is still necessary: film is a mechanical technology and even films which have been edited digitally need to be cut and spliced together at some point to create a master print for *distribution.

splice in *See* INSERT EDITING.

split track Audio *tracks used to record different information: for example, a mono *mix on track one and music and effects (*see* M&E) on track two.

sponsorship An arrangement whereby all or part of the funding of a media product or *production is provided by a commercial company as a form of *advertising.

spyware A portmanteau term (*spying + software*). Computer or *internet software that covertly gathers *information about the activities of the users of a particular computer (e.g. recording all the addresses of all the internet sites they visit, or the keystrokes they use) for the benefit of commercial companies, governments, or law enforcement agencies. Such software may be embedded in the code of webpages. *See also* SURVEILLANCE.

standard ratio *See* ASPECT RATIO.

star 1. Broadly, any well-known and idolized film, television, or stage performer; **stardom** refers to having the status of a star. 2. (film) Broadly an appellation given to any element of a film identified as its primary box office draw: this is usually a charismatic actor, although it can apply to *directors, *producers, and even *special effects. 3. For Dyer, not so much a real person but a discursive construction made up of *signs that communicate particular meanings to audiences: Marilyn Monroe, John Wayne, and Tom Cruise are all real people of course, but we cannot be certain that their actual personalities bear any relation to their onscreen or offscreen *personas, which are both heavily stage-managed and manipulated by the media.

star system An exploitative method of managing the lives as well as the careers of a studio's top performers. In *classical Hollywood cinema, stars were contracted with a certain studio and were given a quota of films per year in which to appear. Charismatic performers were contracted as young men and women and groomed by the studio so that they represented certain *personas for audiences (e.g. romantic lead, tough guy, ingénue, vamp). Their offscreen lives were also strictly controlled, compelling gay actors such as Rock Hudson to enter into arranged marriages.

station identification *See* IDENT.

status 1. (social status) A defined position in a social system: what someone is, or their position in relation to others (e.g. child, parent, wife, mother, teacher). 2. An individual's relative rank within a hierarchy (distinguished from *class by Weber). 3. The behavioural *expectations for an established *role (for which it is sometimes a synonym). 4. **(prestige)** An *evaluation of an individual's social esteem by others. 5. **(status set)** Loosely, the combined statuses of an individual (sometimes regarded as related to social *class).

status quo The existing social, economic, and/or political system or the current *power relations.

status symbols Colloquial term for visible *signs by which individuals display a special or elevated social position.

stereopsis *See* BINOCULAR VISION.

stereotyping A form of inaccurate, *value-laden *representation and *categorization reflecting fixed, preconceived beliefs and *expectations based on exaggerated and oversimplified generalizations about the supposedly inherent traits of an entire social group. Such essentializing beliefs are shared within a *reference group and resistant to *factual evidence. It typically refers to the prejudice of *negative* stereotyping, though it can also include positive representation. It is widely encountered in *mass-media texts, where it tends to reflect culturally dominant representations (*see also* SYMBOLIC WORLD). *See also* BIAS; CLASS STEREOTYPES; ETHNIC STEREOTYPES; ESSENTIALISM; EXOTICISM; FOLK DEVILS; GENDER STEREOTYPES; HOMOPHOBIA; LABELLING; LEVELLING AND SHARPENING; OTHER; PRIMING; RACIAL STEREOTYPES; RACISM; SELECTIVE REPRESENTATION; SEXISM; TOLERANCE OF AMBIGUITY; TYPECASTING; TYPIFICATION.

still frame 1. An effect where the motion of film or video appears to freeze, which is achieved by producing multiple duplications of the same frame. 2. A photograph taken from an isolated *frame of film or video. This is not the same as a **production still,** which is a still photograph taken on set or on location for promotional purposes.

sting In radio and television, *channel or programme branding that consists of short impactful *sequences of images and/or music and sound effects used as a form of punctuation between programmes or separating items within programmes.

stock shot Generic film or video *footage which appears in a motion picture which has not been shot for that production, but rather has been purchased from a company specializing in the production of such footage, or from an *archive.

story *See* FABULA.

storyboard In film and television, a visualization device which represents complex *sequences in the form of a series of illustrations like a comic strip.

story grammar A system of formal rules describing the underlying structure and sequence of units in a particular kind of text (based on folktales), as distinct from a **story schema,** which is a mental framework of *expectations for such texts, based on experience, gathered from reading, of the regularities previously encountered in other examples. This concept is that of the American psychologist Jean M. Mandler.

story model In relation to journalism, a characterization of its primary purpose being to make *events meaningful for the audience by framing these as entertaining or aesthetically satisfying *narratives which they can relate to their own lives: a narrative model as distinct from an **information model** which focuses on the provision of *facts. The concept derives from a distinction made in 1926 by Mead in relation to *newspapers. It is loosely related to the distinction between *soft news and *hard news. *See also* FICTION VALUES; INFOTAINMENT; NEWS FRAMES; TABLOIDIZATION; *compare* PUBLICITY MODEL.

strapline 1. (*marketing) A slogan attached to a *brand name. 2. In a *newspaper or magazine, a subsidiary heading.

strategic anti-essentialism The adoption (and adaption) by one cultural group of a cultural form drawn from a different *culture, typically in order to resist an imposed *cultural identity. The concept derives from the American cultural theorist George Lipsitz (b.1947). *See also* APPROPRIATION; *compare* STRATEGIC ESSENTIALISM.

strategic essentialism A political tactic employed by a minority group acting on the basis of a shared *identity in the public arena in the interests of unity during a struggle for equal rights. The term was coined by Spivak and has been influential in *feminism, *queer theory, and *postcolonial theory. *Compare* ESSENTIALISM; STRATEGIC ANTI-ESSENTIALISM.

streaming Digital *distribution of audio or video material in *real-time (or as close to real-time as the technological constraints allow). Also called **webcasting**.

striping (blacking) Formatting a videotape by recording continuous black and silence for the duration of the tape, so that it can be used for *insert editing. *See also* CONTROL TRACK.

stroboscopic movement *See* BETA MOVEMENT.

strong ties Intimate *social relationships with family members, lovers, friends—an *in-group—as distinct from loose or *weak ties with other members of society. Strong ties involve frequent contact, affection, *similarity or like-mindedness, and a sense of obligation, and tend to be seen as offering tangible psychological support. It is often assumed that they also depend heavily on *face-to-face interaction, but Ling observes that the *mobile phone is particularly supportive of contact within in-groups, making its members constantly accessible to each other and enabling the immediate sharing of experiences and *emotions.

structural analysis The identification of a relational framework underlying the surface features of particular kinds of *texts (*genres) or cultural practices. In *structuralism, there are two structural axes: that of the *syntagm and that of the *paradigm. *See also* DEEP STRUCTURE; STRUCTURE; SURFACE STRUCTURE; TEXTUAL ANALYSIS.

structural determinism 1. In classical *Marxist theory, the subordination of the social 'superstructure' to the techno-economic 'base': *see* BASE AND SUPERSTRUCTURE; *see also* ECONOMISM. 2. The stance that the pre-given *structure of some signifying system—such as *language or any kind of textual system—determines the *subjectivity (or at least behaviour) of individuals who are subjected to it. Althusser was a structural determinist in this sense (*see* INTERPELLATION). This anti-humanist position contrasts with perspectives stressing the role of human *agency.

structural functionalism *See* FUNCTIONALISM.

structuralism Approaches to linguistic, psychological, and sociocultural phenomena as formal systems of relations in which universal principles, laws, or rules are seen as underlying the surface patterns of particular instances (*see also* DEEP STRUCTURE; LANGUE AND PAROLE; SURFACE FEATURES). Cultural variation is seen as secondary. The system is seen as a unitary whole which is greater than the sum of its parts (*compare* FUNCTIONALISM). Typically, structuralist theorists see this as an objective, scientific approach. Saussure was a pioneer of linguistic structuralism (*see also* SAUSSUREAN MODEL; SYNCHRONIC ANALYSIS). Subsequent structuralists frame *sign systems as *languages—as with Lévi-Strauss and myth, kinship rules, and totemism, Lacan and the unconscious, and Barthes and Greimas and the 'grammar' of narrative. The search for underlying semantic *oppositions is characteristic of *structural analysis (*see also* BINARY OPPOSITIONS). Priority is given to the power of the language system in determining *subjectivity (a principle shared by *poststructuralists). Structuralist *textual analysis is *synchronic, seeking to delineate the *codes underlying the *production and *interpretation of texts by comparing those within the same *genre and identifying invariant constituent units. The analysis of specific texts seeks to break down larger, more abstract units into 'minimal significant units' by means of the *commutation test, then groups these units by membership of *paradigms and identifies the *syntagmatic relations which link the units. 2. (social psychology) Theories emphasizing data-driven processes in *social perception (*see* BOTTOM-UP PROCESSING), as opposed to *constructivist theories, which emphasize theory-driven processes (*see* TOP-DOWN PROCESSING).

((⊕)) SEE WEB LINKS

• Structuralism

structural uses In relation to the functions of *television for its users, for Lull, these are environmental and regulative uses as distinct from *relational uses. He lists as **environmental uses** background sound, companionship, and entertainment, and as **regulative uses** (behavioural regulation) the punctuation and structuring of time and activities and the patterning of talk. *See also* ENTERTAINMENT FUNCTION; SOCIAL FUNCTIONS; USES AND GRATIFICATIONS.

structure 1. An organizing pattern, overall design, composition, or system of formal relations between spatial and/or temporal features in a *text in any *medium, or the relationship between its parts. For example, in narrative *genres, narrative structure (*see* CLASSICAL NARRATIVE STRUCTURE). In *structuralist *semiotics, formal structural relations between *textual features are termed *syntagms. 2. Conceptual relations (such as thematic *binary oppositions) identified by *structural analysis as underlying the *surface features of a *text or *code: *see also* DEEP STRUCTURE. 3. (*linguistics) The double *articulation of human *language. 4. (*Marxist sociology) The *articulation of *base and superstructure in a social formation, 'structured in *dominance'. 5. (sociology) *See* SOCIAL STRUCTURE. Thematically in sociological *discourse, a fundamental *opposition with *agency representing the extent to which human actions are determined by *social structures: *see also* STRUCTURAL DETERMINISM.

structures of feeling Distinctive *values and ways of organizing experience shared by a generation within a *culture and reflected in common patterns and conventions in certain artistic forms and social practices in a particular historical period. The concept evolves in the writings of Raymond Williams. *See also* CULTURAL MATERIALISM; DOMINANT FORM; EMERGENT FORM; RESIDUAL FORM.

studio system *See also* AUTEUR THEORY; CLASSICAL HOLLYWOOD CINEMA; FORDISM; HORIZONTAL INTEGRATION; MEDIA OWNERSHIP; STAR SYSTEM; VERTICAL INTEGRATION. 1. From the 1920s, a collection of commercial companies based in Hollywood and New York and including Metro Goldwyn Meyer, Paramount, Warner Brothers, and 20th Century Fox, that regarded films primarily as moneymaking products and controlled every aspect of their financing, *production, *marketing, *distribution, and exhibition. In *The Hollywood Studio System* (1986), Douglas Gomery, an American film historian, claims that the studio system was based on a business model first developed in the 1910s by the controller of Paramount, Adolph Zukor (1873–1976). 2. A standardized approach to mass-producing films, such as dividing the film-making process into specialist departments and controlling *stars and technicians by keeping them under exclusive contracts.

style 1. Broadly, in relation to *texts or artworks in any *medium, the particular way in which something is represented or communicated (the manner of *representation) as distinct from its *content, *subject, or *literal meaning. The separation of style from content is often argued to be impossible except as an analytical convenience. It refers to textual, as distinct from structural *form: to the way in which the materials are manipulated. It can vary according to *medium, *genre, *context, and historical period. Stylistic features may be *foregrounded, as in poetic language or *expressive communication, or backgrounded (and intended to be *transparent) as in the codes of aesthetic *realism or in *instrumental communication. *Compare* FORM. 2. In literary criticism and *linguistics, any distinctive patterns of language use. These may be phonological, syntactic, lexical (diction), or rhetorical (*imagery). *See also* CLOAK THEORY; CONNOTATION; FIGURATIVE LANGUAGE; IDIOLECT; IMAGERY; LEXICON; PHONOLOGY; REGISTER; STYLISTICS; SYNTAX. 3. Shared patterns in the *codes and *signifying practices of a subcultural group which signify cultural *identity and *difference: for instance, the counter-hegemonic practices of youth *subcultures identified by the British cultural theorist Dick Hebdige (b.1951). *See also* BRICOLAGE; COMMUNICATION STYLE; LIFESTYLE.

stylistics In *linguistics and literary criticism, the study of *styles of language use (both written and spoken) in particular *contexts: for instance, the study of language use in *genres such as advertisements. *See also* CONVERSATIONAL

ANALYSIS; CRITICAL DISCOURSE ANALYSIS; DISCOURSE ANALYSIS; FIGURATIVE
LANGUAGE; FOREGROUNDING; IDIOLECT; REGISTER; RHETORIC; TEXT LINGUISTICS.

stylization (*adj.* **stylized**) Figurative visual *representation seeking to typify its
*referent through simplification, exaggeration, or *idealization rather than to
represent unique characteristics through *naturalism. *See also* FIGURATIVE ART;
GENERIC REPRESENTATION; STYLE.

subcode 1. (*semiotics) For Metz, specific signifying systems representing
alternative (*paradigmatic) choices within an overall *code, such as a particular
*style of lighting or *editing within the general cinematic codes of lighting or editing.
This can include particular aesthetic styles in any medium (such as *romanticism or
*realism). For Eco, *connotation could be seen as a subcode insofar as it is built on
'a more basic one'. 2. (*linguistics) For Jakobson, any of the recognized varieties of
language which together form a network constituting the overarching code of a
language, and between which users switch (*see also* CODE-SWITCHING). Each is
linked to appropriate *contexts or *functions: *see also* CONTEXT OF SITUATION;
REGISTER. 3. A cultural form or *communication style shared by the members of a
subcultural group. Members of any *culture have access to multiple subcodes.

subculture The shared system of *values, *norms, *beliefs, and *lifestyles of a
substantial minority within a wider host *culture: for instance, youth culture, gang
culture, ethnic groups, gay culture, religious groups, and occupational groups.
Those which represent a reaction against mainstream culture are sometimes
termed **countercultures**. In *postmodernity, social *fragmentation and diversity has
arguably led to subcultures becoming more culturally significant than the
supposedly dominant culture.

subject 1. What is denoted, depicted, or referred to, or the topic of a *discourse or
a study: *see also* CONTENT; DENOTATION; REFERENTIALITY; REPRESENTATION. 2. In
loose usage, an individual person, a human being, or social actor. 3. **(Cartesian
subject)** (modern philosophy) The knower or self as distinct from the known or
*object: *see also* CARTESIAN DUALISM; REFERENT. 4. **(grammatical subject)**
Typically, in a clause or sentence, the performer of an action (the **agent**), in the form
of a noun phrase (*compare* THEME), as distinct from the **predicate** (which makes
some assertion or denial about the subject). 5. (cultural theory) The active,
dominant, or initiating agent as opposed to the passive, subordinated, or receptive
*object of the agent's actions or desires: *see also* MALE GAZE. 6. In *structuralist
*psychoanalytic theory and Althusserian *Marxist theory, an identity or sense of
selfhood socially constructed by dominant sociocultural and *ideological processes
(e.g. in terms of categories such as *class, age, *gender, and *ethnicity). The notion
of the (discursive) *positioning of the subject refers to the *constitution
(construction) of the subject through *discourse (a form of *linguistic determinism).
For the linguist Benveniste the subject has no existence outside specific discursive
moments, being constantly reconstructed through *discourse. For Althusser, the
subject is an effect of *ideology (*see also* INTERPELLATION); for Foucault, the subject
is an effect of *power relations. *Poststructuralist theorists critique the concept of
the unified subject: people have multiple and shifting identities (*see* DECENTRED

SELF). This represents a strong contrast to the liberal humanist *Enlightenment concept of the individual as a rational, self-determining agent with an enduring identity, as in the notion of *authorship. *See also* AGENCY; ESSENTIALISM; SUBJECT-POSITION. **7. (research subject)** (psychology) A participant in a research study, especially in an *experiment. **8.** (political theory) The citizen: a subject of the state.

subjective camerawork In television and film, the use of the camera to show us *events as if from a particular participant's visual *point of view (encouraging viewers to identify with that person's way of seeing events or even to feel like an eyewitness to the events themselves). Such *camerawork is typically hand-held. Unlike *point-of-view shots, which can function in isolation to augment a *sequence containing *objective camerawork, subjective camerawork represents exclusively what a particular person is seeing. It can include *reaction shots of the person whose point of view is being represented (although these are filmed in *close-up so as to exclude other *context cues). *See also* FIRST-PERSON POINT OF VIEW.

subjective narration or point of view *See* FIRST-PERSON POINT OF VIEW.

subjectivism Any theory in which a phenomenon is seen as dependent on human ideas or beliefs. For instance, ethical *relativism or *ontological *idealism.

subjectivity *Compare* INTERSUBJECTIVITY. **1.** Selfhood, or the self-conscious awareness of the individual. In cultural theory, this is often seen as a concept which is historically modern in Western culture (*see also* ENLIGHTENMENT). *Structuralists and classical Marxists see subjectivity as a process of *structural determinism (*see* SUBJECT). For Foucault, subjectivity is the product of *discourse: *see also* IDENTITY POLITICS. **2.** The particular personal perspectives of individuals (privileged, for instance, in *romanticism, *hermeneutics, and *phenomenology); typically contrasted by positivists with *objectivity on the basis that it is inherently biased by personal *values.

subject position In theories of textual *positioning, a role which a reader is obliged by the *structure and *codes of a text to adopt in order to understand the *preferred meaning (*see also* IDEAL READER; IDENTIFICATION). For some, the power of the *mass media resides in their ability to position the *subject in such a way that media *representations are taken to be reflections of everyday reality. Contemporary theorists contend that there may be several alternative (even contradictory) subject positions from which a text may make sense, and these are not necessarily built into the text itself (or intended).

subliminal message A visual and/or auditory message hidden from conscious *perception within a conventional message in any medium. It is designed to be below the liminal point or threshold level of conscious perception but allegedly subconsciously perceptible, such as a single *frame in a film. Experiments in using this technique in *advertising and propaganda have not demonstrated any significant *behavioural effects on audiences.

submissiveness *See* DOMINANCE.

subplot A storyline secondary to the main plot in a *narrative or *drama.

substance *See* FORM.

substitution 1. One of the four logical ways in which *perception, *memory, or *representation can perform a significant *transformation of its source material. Substitution involves replacing some feature from an original stimulus with another which was not. An example of this being done very consciously is the *commutation test. *See also* ADDITION; DELETION; TRANSPOSITION. 2. (*rhetoric) *Immutatio*, one of Quintilian's four types of rhetorical *figures of speech involving deviation (*mutatio*): in this case, the substitution of elements, e.g. *metaphor, *metonymy.

subtext Underlying any *text, *utterance, or action, a *meaning, *theme, or viewpoint interpreted as being implied, backgrounded, hidden, repressed, or unconscious rather than explicit or *foregrounded. *See also* CONNOTATION; HIDDEN AGENDA; *compare* PERIPHERAL ROUTE.

subtitle In film and video, a caption that appears in the lower third of the screen, providing a simultaneous translation of foreign language dialogue or a text version for the hearing impaired. *See also* CLOSED CAPTIONING.

subtractive colour The process of mixing pigments together. Blending these lets more light be absorbed and less reflected (hence 'subtractive'). With pigment, yellow and magenta produce red, yellow and cyan produce green, and cyan and magenta produce blue. *See also* COLOUR; *compare* ADDITIVE COLOUR.

subversive reading *See* OPPOSITIONAL READING.

subvertising A campaigning technique whereby politically motivated short films or eye-catching images are created to resemble *advertisements but whose purpose is to stigmatize *brands and raise consumer consciousness about the corporate strategies behind them. *See also* CULTURE JAMMING.

sufficient condition In relation to *causation, a circumstance which is adequate on its own to produce a specified *effect. It may also be a *necessary condition or alternatively a different condition may also be a sufficient condition for the same *event to occur. *See also* CAUSATION; DETERMINISM.

sujzet *See* FABULA.

super realism *See* PHOTOREALISM.

superstructure *See* BASE AND SUPERSTRUCTURE.

surface structure 1. (*linguistics) The formal syntactic patterns observable in sentences and seen as deriving from an underlying *deep structure. This concept was introduced by Chomsky in the 1960s; later he argued that this also applied to the semantic representation. *See also* SYNTAX; TRANSFORMATIONAL GRAMMAR. 2. **(surface features, microstructure)** (*structuralist theory) The explicit formal patterns observable in *texts, *narratives, dreams, or cultural practices, underlying which a fundamental *deep structure is argued to exist (and from which surface structures arise through *transformation). *Poststructuralists deny that there are stable underlying structures.

surfing 1. The activity of browsing the *internet: *see also* FLÂNEUR. 2. **(channel surfing)** *See* CHANNEL HOPPING.

surplus meaning Signification beyond the *literal level: beyond that which is explicitly denoted or depicted, as in a pun (*see* ALLUSION; CONNOTATION; HIDDEN AGENDA; IMAGERY; IMPLICIT MEANING; IRONY; LATENT MEANING; METAPHOR; METAPHORIC MEANING; SUBTEXT; SYMBOLISM). This is subjective and related to the openness of a *text to *interpretation (*see also* OPEN AND CLOSED TEXTS; READERLY; WRITERLY). Surplus meaning is avoided in *instrumental communication and *informational texts; *expressive communication and *aesthetic texts tend to depend on it, as in literature and art; *advertising also often exploits it. *See also* ORDERS OF SIGNIFICATION.

surroundedness One of the *gestalt laws of *perceptual organization, being the principle that, in visual patterns, areas that can be seen as surrounded by others tend to be seen as figures (*see also* FIGURE AND GROUND).

surround sound Audio systems designed for cinemas (but also available for the home) featuring either five or seven separate audio channels directed at speakers mounted all around the auditorium.

surveillance [French 'to watch over'] 1. Social technologies of *power which include any covert and/or overt techniques and tools used by governments and other organizations to identify, track, and monitor other people through direct or mediated observation, and by gaining access to their personal data. *See also* CCTV; DATA MINING; PANOPTICON; TOTAL INFORMATION AWARENESS. 2. For Lasswell, a key function of *mass communication: *see* SURVEILLANCE FUNCTION.

surveillance function 1. The role of circulating *information and news: one of the most important general roles that the *mass media, a particular medium, or *factual media *genres, can be seen as serving for society as a whole. It is one of the three functions of social communication listed by Lasswell in 1948, the other two being the *consensus function and the *socialization function. *See also* FUNCTIONALISM; MEDIA FUNCTIONS. 2. In relation to general types of use by individuals of the *mass media, a single medium, a media *genre, or specific media *content, this is an *informational function, referring to usage for the purpose of information-seeking. This includes both keeping up with news of current events and increasing general *social knowledge. It is not confined to the context of *genres associated primarily with information (*see* FACTUAL GENRES). This is seen as addressing an individual's cognitive needs: *see also* USES AND GRATIFICATIONS.

surveillance society A society which routinely monitors the lives of its citizens for the purposes of administration and control. According to David Lyon, a Canadian sociologist, in *The Electronic Eye* (1994), a society in which *surveillance practices begin to touch upon every aspect of the everyday lives of its citizens. Computer technologies have led to an intensification of these practices: consequently an *information society is arguably also a surveillance society.

survey A method of systematic investigation in which a group of people is polled for views on a particular topic. *See also* DEMOGRAPHICS; QUESTIONNAIRE.

suspension of disbelief The concept that to become emotionally involved in a narrative, audiences must react as if the characters are real and the *events are happening now, even though they know it is 'only a story'. 'The willing suspension of disbelief for the moment' was how the British poet Coleridge phrased it in 1817, with reference to the audiences for literary works. Schramm argues that this is a general *expectation for all entertainment (*see also* ENTERTAINMENT FUNCTION): we are 'prepared to go along with a story or a spoof or a good joke, to identify and agonize with a character who never lived . . . to have a certain empathy with fictional characters, to go along with the conventions of films or broadcasts.'

suture Literally, surgical stitching. In *psychoanalytic *film theory, a *metaphor for the 'stitching' of a *spectator into the narrative illusion, notably through the use of the *shot/*reverse shot technique (which makes the spectator alternately the *subject and *object of the look). *See also* CINEMATIC APPARATUS; CONTINUITY EDITING; IMAGINARY.

switcher *See* MIXER.

symbol 1. Most broadly, in non-semiotic usage, anything that is understood to stand for or represent something else (*see also* REPRESENTATION). In *semiotics, this is termed a *sign. 2. More specifically, in common usage, a standardized image, mark, or object representing an abstract concept. 3. (*semiotics) A *sign in which the relationship between the *sign vehicle and the *referent is arbitrary or conventional: *see also* ARBITRARINESS; CONVENTION; SYMBOLIC; *compare* ICONIC; INDEXICAL. 4. (*psychoanalytic theory) Dream images, words, or behaviour representing in some disguised form 'the return of the repressed': that being an unconscious desire, impulse, or need. In this context, there is usually some basis in resemblance (which in semiotics would make it *iconic): for instance, a 'phallic symbol' can be anything longer than it is wide (*see also* CONDENSATION; DISPLACEMENT; PARAPRAXIS). 5. In relation to films, literature, and art, any object, character, action, *event, *scene, or *setting, the existing cultural *connotations or the current *context of which lead audiences to infer that such a sign has a particular resonance and represents something beyond itself. Such symbols are distinguishable from *metaphors in that what they signify is left open to the reader's *interpretation: *compare* MOTIF.

symbolic 1. *adj.* Appertaining to a *symbol in any of its senses. 2. *adj.* (*semiotics) A mode of relationship in a *sign between a *sign vehicle and its *referent in which the vehicle does not resemble the *referent but which is arbitrary or purely conventional—so that the relationship must be learnt (e.g. the word 'stop', a red traffic light, a national flag, a number); *see also* ARBITRARINESS; CONVENTION. The symbolic mode, the *iconic mode, and the *indexical mode are concepts in the *Peircean model of the sign, where they represent relationships between the *representamen and the *object. Where the relation is solely symbolic, the sign may be referred to as a *symbol; however, most signs involve more than one mode. **Symbolicity** is the noun for the quality of being symbolic: *compare* ICONIC;

INDEXICAL. **3.** *n.* **(symbolic order)** 'The Symbolic' is Lacan's term for the phase when the child gains mastery within the public realm of verbal *language—when a degree of individuality and autonomy is surrendered to the constraints of linguistic conventions and the Self becomes a more fluid and ambiguous relational *signifier rather than a relatively fixed entity. Lacan declares that 'it is the world of words that creates the world of things'; language creates reality as we know it. However, it also represents a *lack: the loss of our pre-symbolic mode of being, since the *real cannot be captured in words (*see also* ABSENT PRESENCE). *Structuralists focus on the symbolic order rather than the *imaginary, seeing language as determining *subjectivity. *Compare* IMAGINARY. **4.** *n.* For Kristeva, a modality of the signifying process distinguished from, and existing in a dialectical relation with, the *semiotic. Symbolic processes in this sense are seen as rational, transcendental, and paternal.

symbolic annihilation *See* SYMBOLIC ERASURE.

symbolic capital The communicative repertoire of an individual or group, which is related in part to educational background. Bourdieu outlined various interrelated kinds of 'capital'—economic, cultural, social, and symbolic. In semiotic terms, symbolic capital reflects differential *access to, and deployment of, particular *codes. *See also* CULTURAL CAPITAL; HABITUS; SOCIAL CAPITAL.

symbolic code (the voice of symbol) The elements in a *narrative generating *meaning through the use of *symbols and *oppositions (Barthes). *See also* NARRATIVE CODES.

symbolic erasure (symbolic annihilation, invisibility) The under-representation of members of a particular social group within a *medium, *genre, or *text (or in particular social *roles or *contexts within these). For instance, the invisibility of homosexuality onscreen under the *Hays Code until the 1960s. *See also* MALE NORM; VISIBILITY.

symbolic gestures *See* EMBLEMS.

symbolic interactionism (interactionism, symbolic interaction theory) In social psychology and sociology, the *microsocial study of the dynamic negotiation of meanings and constitution of social realities by social actors through their use and *interpretation of *signs in processes of social *interaction within specific situational *contexts. The term was coined in 1937 by the American sociologist Herbert Blumer (1900-87) and the concept was significantly influenced by the ideas of Mead, for whom language is central in the formation of mind, self, and society. In contrast to *functionalism and *behaviourism, symbolic interactionists stress active and constructive *interpretation and negotiation by human agents rather than the *structural determinism of human actions and *identity. Society is seen as pluralistic and conflictual. Individuals are regarded as developing their view of self from the perceived *expectations of *significant others. The favoured research methodology involves *ethnography and *participant observation. *See also* CONSTITUTIVE MODELS; CONSTRUCTIONISM; DRAMATURGY; FRAME OF REFERENCE; FRAMING; IMPRESSION MANAGEMENT; INTERACTION MODEL; INTERCHANGE; INTERPRETIVISM; INTERSUBJECTIVITY; LABELLING THEORY; LOOKING-GLASS SELF; QUALITATIVE

RESEARCH; RITUAL INTERACTION; ROLES; THOMAS THEOREM; *compare*
CONSTRUCTIVISM; CONVERSATION ANALYSIS; ETHNOMETHODOLOGY;
PHENOMENOLOGY; SOCIAL COGNITION.

symbolic representation 1. Sometimes a synonym for human *language,
typically alluding to the relation between words and the *referents for which they
stand having no necessary basis in resemblance: *see also* ARBITRARINESS; SYMBOLIC.
2. The process of *mental representation, involving the *encoding of *knowledge in
abstract forms: *see also* SYMBOLIZATION.

symbolic violence 1. Bourdieu's term for the imposition on subordinated
groups by the dominant *class of an *ideology which legitimates and naturalizes the
*status quo: *see also* DOMINANT IDEOLOGY; *compare* INTERPELLATION. 2. For
Gerbner, the *representation of physical violence in any *medium, though his
own concern is *television, where such representations are seen as influencing the
assumptions of *heavy viewers about social reality: *see* CULTIVATION THEORY.
'Symbolic violence . . . is a show of force and demonstration of power' showing 'who
can get away with what against whom.' It functions as an instrument of social
control that tends to maintain the existing social order: *see also* VIOLENCE DEBATE.

symbolic world The everyday world as selectively represented and constructed
on *television (across different *factual and fictional *genres) within which Gerbner
argues that *heavy viewers live (in the sense that it dominates their mental picture
of the real world). It is a world, for instance, in which violence prevails and power
is largely in the hands of middle-aged white males while other groups are
symbolically erased or grossly under-represented and stereotyped (*see* CULTIVATION
THEORY; SYMBOLIC ERASURE). While such *representations do not represent
*demographic realities, they arguably reflect dominant cultural *values.

symbolism (symbolic meaning) The use (or perceived use) of *symbols to
represent ideas or qualities. *See also* COLOUR SYMBOLISM; CONDENSATION;
PRODUCT-SYMBOL FORMAT; RITUAL MODEL; SURPLUS MEANING; SYMBOL; SYMBOLIC;
VISUAL PERSUASION; VISUAL RHETORIC.

symbolization 1. The process of *encoding an abstract *representation of
something. 2. (social learning theory) Being able to use words and images to
think about behaviour. 3. (*psychoanalytic theory) A *defence mechanism whereby
an unconscious desire, impulse, or need is represented as something else in
dream images, or in words or actions: *see also* CONDENSATION; DISPLACEMENT;
DREAM-WORK; PARAPRAXIS.

symmetrical relationships (symmetrical roles) *See also* POWER RELATIONS;
RELATIONAL COMMUNICATION. 1. Interactional partnerships in a *dyad based on
relative equality of *status and/or *power and employing *communication styles
that reflect this (Watzlawick). *Expectations and behaviour are reciprocal (*see*
RECIPROCITY). Differences are minimized and the behaviour of one person tends
to mirror the other. These relationships may reflect *affiliation but they can become
competitive: *compare* ASYMMETRICAL RELATIONSHIPS. 2. More broadly,
communicational arrangements on occasions when the roles of *sender and

*receiver are reversible, and there is constant *feedback: *see also* TWO-WAY COMMUNICATION.

symmetry One of the *gestalt laws of *perceptual organization, whereby in visual patterns, symmetrical areas tend to be seen as figures against asymmetrical backgrounds. *See also* FIGURE AND GROUND.

sympathy A sense of fellow-feeling evoked by a particular person, creature, or even an inanimate object to which we attribute *emotions—either directly observed in the world, or represented in any medium (such as in a novel or a film), in which the observer, reader, or listener is closely in accord with their state of mind and emotions (sometimes referred to as emotional *identification). If you feel sorry for a character in a film you are experiencing sympathy, but if you are so terrified that you flinch when they do, you are experiencing *empathy. Brecht's use of the *alienation effect is intended to inhibit both sympathy and *empathy on the part of the audience towards the protagonists in order to encourage a critical attitude towards the represented social realities.

synchronic analysis The study of a system (a *language or a *code) as if it were frozen at one moment in time. *Structuralist *semiotics focuses on synchronic rather than *diachronic analysis and is criticized for ignoring *historicity. *Compare* DIACHRONIC ANALYSIS.

synchronization (sync) 1. Broadly, any process that aligns a number of separate temporal sources so that they run in unison. Such sources are considered to be 'in sync,' but if they drift out of alignment they are 'out of sync.' 2. **(post-synchronization)** In film or video *post-production, the process of taking separate moving images and sound recorded at the same event and matching them together. In *editing parlance, **sync** is any picture source that has synchronized sound—most typically *footage of speaking subjects.

synchronous communication *Interaction in which participants can communicate in *real-time—without significant delays. This feature ties together the *presence or absence of the *producer(s) of the *text and the technical features of the *medium. Synchronous communication is usually *interpersonal communication.

synchronous sound In audiovisual media, sound cues that are exactly aligned to picture cues, primarily so that the words people speak match their mouth movements. *Compare* ASYNCHRONOUS SOUND.

synecdoche (*rhetoric) A *trope or *figure of speech involving the substitution of part for whole, genus for species, or vice versa. For instance, 'get your butt over here!' (presumably accompanied by the rest of their body). Some theorists do not distinguish synecdoche from *metonymy.

syntactics For Charles W. Morris, a branch of *semiotics concerned with the study of the structural relations between *signs. He divides semiotics into three branches: syntactics, *semantics, and *pragmatics.

syntagm (*adj.* **syntagmatic**) (*semiotics) An orderly combination of interacting *signifiers which forms a meaningful whole (sometimes called a 'chain'). In language, a sentence, for instance, is a syntagm of words. **Syntagmatic relations** are the various ways in which constituent units within the same text may be structurally related to each other. A signifier enters into syntagmatic relations with other signifiers of the same structural level within the same text. Syntagmatic relationships exist both between signifiers and between *signifieds. Relationships between signifiers can be either *sequential* (e.g. in film and television *narrative sequences), or *spatial* (e.g. *montage in posters and photographs; *see also* SPATIAL RELATIONS). Relationships between signifieds are conceptual relationships (such as *argument). Syntagms are created by the linking of signifiers from *paradigm sets which are chosen on the basis of whether they are conventionally regarded as appropriate or may be required by some syntactic rule system (e.g. *grammar). **Syntagmatic analysis** is a *structuralist technique which seeks to establish the *surface structure of a text and the relationships between its parts. The study of syntagmatic relations reveals the rules or *conventions underlying the *production and *interpretation of texts. *Compare* PARADIGM.

syntagmatic axis (*structuralist *semiotics) An analytical dimension spatialized as a horizontal plane representing a combination of related *signifiers within a *text. This is typically thought of as a sequence (in a menu, the syntagmatic axis might be starter–main course–dessert), but it can also refer to co-present signifiers (such as 'meat and two veg'). *See also* SYNTAGM; *compare* PARADIGMATIC AXIS.

syntax [Greek 'together-arrangement'] The grammatical relations between words, phrases, and/or clauses within sentences (and the study of this within *linguistics). One of the two fields within the study of *grammar; the other being *morphology. *Compare* SYNTACTICS.

systemic bias *See* INSTITUTIONAL BIAS.

systems theory An interdisciplinary approach that analyses structures as interrelated webs of interacting parts performing particular *functions. *See also* BOTTOM-UP PROCESSING; COMMUNICATION NETWORK; CYBERNETICS; DEEP STRUCTURE; EMERGENCE; FORMALISM; FUNCTIONALISM; MEDIA DEPENDENCY; ORGANIZATIONAL COMMUNICATION; STRUCTURALISM.

syuzhet *See* FABULA.

tabloid 1. A *newspaper format with a page size approximately half that of *broadsheets: *see also* REDTOPS; *compare* BERLINER FORMAT. 2. *adj.* **(tabloidese)** Pejorative term for a *downmarket style of journalism that is populist and/or sensationalist.

tabloidization A contemporary shift of focus in journalism away from *hard news and serious *factual *information and toward *soft news and *entertainment. The term is associated with the rhetoric of *dumbing down. *See also* FICTION VALUES; INFOTAINMENT; STORY MODEL.

tacit knowledge 1. The informal understandings of individuals (especially their *social knowledge) which they have not verbalized and of which they may not even be aware, but which they may be inferred to know (notably from their behaviour). This includes what they need to know or assume in order to produce and make sense of messages (*social and *textual knowledge). Tacit knowledge is distinguished from explicit or formal *knowledge and the term is sometimes used synonymously with *common sense, in the sense of taken-for-granted knowledge. The concept is important in *phenomenological sociology and *ethnomethodology. It derives from Polanyi, who declared that 'We can know more than we can tell.' 2. More specifically for Polanyi, our general awareness and holistic understanding which provide a background framework facilitating our deliberate focus of *attention on specific phenomena. He sees such informal 'personal knowledge' as the foundation of all *knowledge.

tactile communication *See* HAPTICS; TOUCH.

tag 1. In *HTML, a function written between angle brackets <>, applied to an element sandwiched between it and an 'end tag'—written thus: </>. For example, to display in a browser the word 'new' in italics, the code used would be: <i>new</i>. *See also* METATAG. 2. Labelling an online media document (photograph, video, written text, etc.) with a descriptive *keyword which is a means of indexing the document for online searches: *see also* TAG CLOUD.

tag cloud A visual cluster of words representing the frequency of the *tags attached by readers to a *text. **Word clouds** indicate the frequency of words within the text of a book or a *blog (normally lexical words rather than *grammatical words) as a quick indication of the *content. In both cases relative frequency is reflected in the *font sizes used to depict the words.

tag line *See* BYLINE.

tag questions (tag) Question phrases at the end of statements, e.g. 'He will be there, won't he?'

take In film *production, a *set up that is being filmed, as opposed to a rehearsal. A take is a continuous *shot that commences when directors shout 'action' and lasts until they call 'cut'. Multiple takes can be recorded until the *director is satisfied with the results.

talking head 1. Originally, in the parlance of television production staff, a name for any person, other than the presenter who appears in vision in an interview situation without an interviewer being present and offers opinions or recounts events for the benefit of the viewer. Often used in a pejorative sense because the use of such commentators in a visual medium suggests an over-reliance on 'telling' rather than 'showing'. 2. In a narrower sense, an expert or 'pundit' who appears on a news or current affairs programme in order to voice an opinion.

talk radio Radio stations that do not play music, but typically feature DJ-led discussions on topical issues or current events where members of the public phone in with their opinions.

talk show *See* CHAT SHOW.

target audience (target market) The selected segment of a total population to whom a *text, *message, or product is primarily directed (*see also* NICHE AUDIENCE; PRIMARY AUDIENCE; *compare* SECONDARY AUDIENCE). In *marketing, *segmentation is usually on the basis of *demographic variables, *geographic segmentation, and/or *psychographics or *lifestyles (*see also* MICROMARKETING; REFERENCE GROUP). *See also* AUDIENCE FRAGMENTATION; NARROWCASTING; POSITIONING.

target factors *See* DESTINATION.

targeting (*advertising) Choosing the *medium (and space or timeslot) which will expose the *message to the largest percentage of the *target audience. *See also* SEGMENTATION.

task-oriented communication (task-centred) A *communication style characterized by being *instrumental or goal-oriented and often associated with *individualistic cultures. Often contrasted with an *interaction-oriented, *person-oriented, or *receiver-oriented style. *See also* CUELESSNESS.

taste 1. The *sensation, *perception, and discrimination of flavours detected in the mouth. 2. Traditionally, the ability of an individual to 'appreciate' that which is regarded as beautiful or well-crafted and the tendency to exhibit this in patterns of *consumption. While Kant saw taste as based on transcendent criteria, it is highly culturally-specific (*see also* AESTHETICS). Often referred to as a trait that can be 'cultivated', Bourdieu argues that taste is a form of *cultural capital which serves to naturalize *class differences. 3. A relational hierarchy of cultural forms reflecting and serving to maintain social distinctions. This is based on *aesthetic criteria established over time by the dominant class, exalting the endorsed *canon as the only true art, and systematically denigrating popular *entertainment. High art is positioned at a rarefied distance from the primary drives which are associated by the upper class with the working class. *See also* HIGH CULTURE; POPULAR CULTURE. 4. For Bourdieu, the particular cultural choices and patterns of *consumption of any member of society in relation not only to the arts but also to everyday lifestyle issues such as clothing, hairstyles, sport, and food. All of these for him result from the set of dispositions that he terms the *habitus.

taxonomy *See* CATEGORIZATION.

Taylorism *See* FORDISM.

teaser A fragment or *montage of a film or of a television or radio programme intended to entice audience members to want to watch or listen to the subsequent production.

technological determinism The stance that new technologies are the primary cause of major social and historical changes at the macrosocial level of social structure and processes and/or subtle but profound social and psychological influences at the microsocial level of the regular use of particular kinds of tools. Whatever the specific technological 'revolution' may be, technological determinists (both optimistic and pessimistic) present it as a dramatic and inevitable driving force, the 'impact' of which will lead to deep and 'far-reaching' *effects or consequences. Technology is presented as autonomous. Technological determinism is often associated with a belief in the *neutrality of technology, but is sometimes linked with the notion of the non-neutrality of technology in the form of the stance that we cannot merely use technology without also, to some extent, being used by it. Very broad claims about the impact of technology are open to the criticism of *reification. Where technological determinism focuses on *communications media in particular it is sometimes referred to as *media determinism. A moderate version of technological determinism is that our regular use of particular tools or media may have subtle influences on us, but that it is the social *context of use which is crucial. The term was coined by Veblen. *Compare* LINGUISTIC DETERMINISM.

(⊕) SEE WEB LINKS

• Technological or media determinism

technology [Greek *tekhné* 'art, craft'] 1. In the modern era, the practical application of scientific *knowledge, especially for productive (e.g. industrial) purposes. 2. Tool-using and/or tool-making: traditionally regarded as a distinctively human skill, though there are examples of other animals using existing objects as tools. 3. Any physical apparatus used to generate material culture. In common usage this refers to tools and machines and often also to products created with these. It includes communication technologies and technological media. In more specialist usage it can (as in Plato) include writing but not speech (a factor in *phonocentrism). Every tool or *medium has particular *affordances. 4. Any means by which human beings act on their environment or seek to transcend bodily limitations. This can include *language (not just writing). For Foucault, 'technologies of the self' are the techniques employed by individuals to transform themselves: *compare* IMPRESSION MANAGEMENT. 5. For McLuhan, the 'extensions of man': 'all human tools and technologies are direct extensions either of the human body or of our senses'. He saw new *communication technologies as changing our environment (*see also* MEDIA ECOLOGY) and as having a transformative influence on both society and the human psyche: *see also* SENSE RATIOS. **6.** For the French philosopher and sociologist Jacques Ellul (1912–94), *technique*: all rational methods of doing things (skills, methods, procedures, routines). In particular, the means-end thinking of *instrumentalism. *Frankfurt school *critical theory sees instrumental rationality as an *ideology. **7.** For Heidegger, a fundamental 'enframing' through which we initially discover the world using that which is 'ready-to-hand', and which we treat as the means to realize certain ends. He warns that when a technological enframing becomes our dominant mode of being, we risk seeing the world as a mere resource for exploitation. **8.** (sociology) All productive practices, including hand-working. Technology is seen as a social product including all of the tools, *knowledge, techniques, and systems of organization involved in material *production. *Social determinism sees technology as shaped by society rather than the other way round. *Compare* TECHNOLOGICAL DETERMINISM. **9.** (*Marxist theory) The means of *production in a given historical period, seen as a key factor in determining *social structure: *see also* BASE AND SUPERSTRUCTURE.

technophilia Enthusiasm for new technologies. The opposite of *technophobia. *See also* NEOPHILIA; TECHNOROMANTICISM.

technophobia Fear or dislike of new technologies, especially computer-based technologies. The opposite of *technophilia. Ever since Mary Shelley's *Frankenstein* in 1818, our recurrent fears about technology have been regularly reflected in speculative fiction and films: the fear of knowing too much, the fear of losing control, the fear of losing our souls, and the fear of supplantation. *See also* LUDDITE.

(((◉))) SEE WEB LINKS
• Imagining futures, dramatizing fears

technoromanticism Typically a pejorative term for a naïve faith in *technology as supportive of the ideals of *romanticism (particularly in relation to creativity and the ideal of an organic community). As distinct from the term **technorationalism**, used pejoratively by *Frankfurt school *critical theorists to refer to reductive *instrumentalism. *See also* NEOPHILIA; TECHNOPHILIA.

telecine 1. A machine for making a video recording of a reel of motion picture film. The telecine machine scans a film negative or positive and converts it to a video *signal or a digital *data file. *Compare* KINESCOPE. **2. (TK)** The process of transferring film to video. Today this is almost always done to transfer *rushes shot on film for television *documentaries, *dramas, and music videos. In the UK, before telecine machines the transfer from film to video was achieved by projecting the film on a screen speeded up to 25 frames per second and filming it with a video camera.

telecommunication (telecommunications) The technical systems enabling the electronic transmission and reception of *data or *messages over a distance in *analogue or *digital form via radio signals, wires, or fibre optic cables. The technologies include *telegraphy, the *telephone system (both fixed and mobile), radio and television *broadcasting systems, the *internet (*broadband or other), and local area networks. The term also refers to the associated industries. *See also* DISTANCE COMMUNICATION.

teleconferencing *See* VIDEOCONFERENCING.

telegenic (of a person) Looking good on *television. *See also* LOOKISM.

telegram A short *message delivered in text-form by the postal system but sent and received using *telegraphy. The service was discontinued in 1982 in the UK.

telegraphy [Greek 'distance writing'] (*adj.* **telegraphic**) The first electrical technology of communication that, from the 1830s, allowed *messages to be sent over great distances using a device called a **telegraph**. These were sent along wires as electrical pulses in the form of *Morse code. As Meyrowitz observes, 'Communication and travel were once synonymous . . . The invention of the telegraph caused the first break between information movement and physical movement.' *See also* DISTANCE COMMUNICATION.

telematics A portmanteau term (*telecommunication* + *informatics*). Broadly, communicating at a distance using computers. In a narrower sense, the phenomenal experience of such communication (*see* TELEPRESENCE). A **telematic society** or **culture** is one in which the computer is the primary medium of communication. *See also* CYBERSPACE; EMAIL; SURFING; VIRTUAL REALITY.

telephone [Greek 'far'+ 'voice'] A voice communication device including a microphone which converts sound vibrations into an electrical *signal so that individuals can communicate over distances, unlike *radio using a *full-duplex signal enabling both parties to talk and be heard simultaneously. On 14 February 1876 Alexander Graham Bell filed an application with the US Patent Office for an 'electric-speaking telephone'. Henry M. Boettinger (b.1924), a former assistant vice-president of AT&T, observes that 'the telephone was the first device to allow the spirit of a person expressed in his own voice to carry its message without directly transporting his body.' The first British telephone exchange was opened in 1879, with 7 or 8 subscribers in the City of London; telephones became widespread only after the Second World War. There is an *asymmetrical relationship between the caller and the called, and telephone conversations tend to be *sender-oriented. The *mobile phone has dramatically extended the flexibility of telephony. *See also* GENDERED TECHNOLOGIES.

(((⊕))) SEE WEB LINKS

• Using the telephone

telepresence The psychological phenomenon of feeling present at a location physically distant from one's actual location created through human operators working closely with robotic technologies employing high quality sensory feedback. The concept was proposed in 1980 by the American computer scientist Marvin Minsky (b.1927).

SEE WEB LINKS

• Minsky's telepresence article

telerecording *See* KINESCOPE.

teletext Information accessible on *analogue television sets which consisted of pages of text and crude illustrations created in *ASCII, embedded into the *vertical interval of a television *signal. Digital teletext brought more capacity and *interactivity to the system (*see* INTERACTIVE TELEVISION).

television (TV) [Greek *telé* 'far'+ Latin *visio* 'seeing'] **1.** An electronic *technology enabling the encoding and decoding of 'moving images' and synchronized sounds, together with their unidirectional, instantaneous, long-distance transmission and reception as modulated electrical *signals either sent through cable or broadcast through the airwaves (*see also* BROADCASTING; CABLE TELEVISION; RADIO WAVES; SATELLITE BROADCASTING; TERRESTRIAL BROADCASTING). The technology was developed in the late 19th and early 20th century. **2.** The *mass communications *medium for audiovisual *broadcasting. As a broadcasting medium it has much in common with *radio, from which it inherited key genres (*see* RADIO GENRES; TELEVISION GENRES). As an audiovisual medium it tends to be distinguished from *cinema primarily in relation to: the 'small screen', domestic reception, relatively low viewer involvement, and the greater *attentional role of sound. The domesticity of the medium influences the preferred *mode of address. *See* DIRECT ADDRESS; DOMESTIC COMMUNICATION TECHNOLOGIES; GLANCE; HIGH AND LOW INVOLVEMENT; PARASOCIAL INTERACTION; TELEVISION FLOW; TELEVISION VIEWING STYLES. **3.** The live or recorded audiovisual broadcasts produced for, and transmitted by, this medium (*see* COMMERCIALS; IDENT; PROGRAMME; TELEVISION GENRES). The first regular broadcasts in the UK and US began in the 1930s, though broadcasting was not widespread until the 1950s. By the 1970s critical *television studies had begun to subject this output to *textual analysis. The vast reach of television and the tendency for TV news to be treated as a 'window on the world' generated *ideological analysis (*see also* DOMINANT IDEOLOGY; MANIPULATIVE MODEL; MANUFACTURE OF CONSENT; MEDIA HEGEMONY). Subsequently, in *cultural studies attention turned to diversity of *interpretation in television *audiences: *see also* ACTIVE AUDIENCE THEORY; ENCODING/DECODING MODEL. **4.** An industry concerned with producing and transmitting audiovisual broadcasts, regulated in varying ways by governments (*see* PUBLIC SERVICE BROADCASTING; REGULATION), and subject to commercial pressures in retaining and increasing *audiences (*see also* COMMERCIALIZATION; POLITICAL ECONOMY). **5. (TV set** or **receiver)** An electronic device and domestic consumer *entertainment product with a screen and sound system for receiving and reproducing moving images and sounds sourced either remotely from broadcasts or cable, or locally: e.g. from *DVD (*see also* BROWN GOODS; TELEVISION RECEPTION). In the UK and the USA, about 99% of the population own at least one television set. **6.** Commercially, a major advertising medium for delivering *target audiences to advertisers, both nationally and regionally, by time of day (*see also* COMMERCIALS). It has high levels of *reach and impact compared to other advertising media (*see also* MEDIA BUYING). However, TV advertising is highly intrusive (unrequested): *see also* ZAPPING; ZIPPING. **7.** A major cultural *institution closely associated with shifting leisure patterns, the concept of the *global village, and with the perpetuation of *consumerism (*see also* TELEVISION CULTURE; TELEVISUAL REALITY). In the UK watching TV now accounts for more time than all other leisure pursuits combined, and the medium has been seen as fulfilling multiple functions (*see also* MEDIA FUNCTIONS; RELATIONAL USES; STRUCTURAL USES; TELEVISION VIEWING PATTERNS; USES AND GRATIFICATIONS). It has traditionally been argued to be a unifying experience (particularly at the national level), though many see this as undermined by the increased diversity of channels. *See also* AUDIENCE FRAGMENTATION; IMAGINED COMMUNITY; PUBLIC AND PRIVATE SPHERES; SOCIALIZATION FUNCTION.

(⊕) SEE WEB LINKS

• British television history

television channel *See also* CHANNEL. 1. The frequency band of the *electromagnetic spectrum that is licensed to particular television stations. 2. A television station with its own *brand identity that produces its own *content (*see* PROGRAMME) or buys it in from other providers.

television culture *Compare* FILM CULTURE. 1. The sociocultural functions of the medium of television: especially, its contribution to *socialization through circulating shared *imagery, frameworks, and *norms (*see also* CULTURAL REPRODUCTION; MEDIA FUNCTIONS). Also, the relative prominence of television within a culture, particularly as reflected in the prevalence of television imagery (including images of television as well as images from television). 2. The sociocultural contextualization of television *production and/or reception which distinguishes it from other media. For instance, the social *context and domestic politics of reception which distinguish television from cinema. *See also* GLANCE; TELEVISION FLOW. 3. Domestically-produced television programming distinguished from that of other nations: for instance, within the discourse of *national identity: *see also* CREATIVE INDUSTRIES; IMAGINED COMMUNITY. 4. A pejorative term dismissing the cultural worth of television *content and *style, connoting negative framings of *popular culture, *fiction values, *dumbing down, *homogenization, and so on. 5. Sociologically, the occupational communities and shared *codes of those employed in the various television industries.

television flow (flow, programme flow) The viewer's *perception of the output of broadcast television as a continuous blur of *imagery and sounds rather than as a discrete progression of identifiable programmes clearly bracketed by *advertising breaks. Williams contends that what distinguishes television from other cultural forms such as books, plays, and concerts is that it does not present an ordered menu of content. From this perspective, it makes sense to say that we are 'watching television' rather than watching a particular programme. *See also* McLUHANISM.

television genres Different types of programme and non-programme material broadcast on television and having distinctive *textual features, *subjects, *functions, *audiences, *text-reader relationships, and modes of involvement (*see also* HIGH AND LOW INVOLVEMENT; TELEVISION VIEWING STYLES; USES AND

GRATIFICATIONS). Such *genres provide an interpretive *frame of reference, in particular influencing the *expectations of viewers (*see also* TEXTUAL SCHEMATA). They may be *factual genres, *fiction, or hybrids of these modalities (e.g. *docusoaps, *docudrama). Those most broadly recognized include *news programmes, *commercials, weather forecasts, *soap operas, sitcoms, *chat shows, game shows, variety shows, *reality TV, medical dramas, crime shows, popular music shows, sports programmes, and religious programmes. Many television genres were inherited from radio (*see* RADIO GENRES). *See also* HYBRID GENRES; SERIAL; SERIES.

(⊕) SEE WEB LINKS

• Television genres, themes, and formats (BFI)

television network 1. A group of television companies that share the same medium of transmission, e.g. a cable network, a satellite network. 2. A model for television *distribution in which a central programme-maker provides content for affiliates: other television stations which enter into a contractual agreement with the *content provider. *See also* TELEVISION CHANNEL.

television reality *See* TELEVISUAL REALITY.

television reception 1. A *signal in the form of *radio waves received via an aerial (or via cable or broadband) or microwave signals received via a satellite dish, which are subsequently decoded into moving pictures and audio by circuitry inside a television set or a set-top box. 2. The perceived quality of the received television *signal. 3. The ways in which television is used and the *interpretation of TV content by viewers in particular *contexts: *see also* ACTIVE AUDIENCE THEORY; GLANCE; HEAVY VIEWERS; HIGH AND LOW INVOLVEMENT; PARASOCIAL INTERACTION; RELATIONAL USES; SIT UP OR SIT BACK; SOCIAL USES; STRUCTURAL USES; TELEVISION FLOW; USES AND GRATIFICATIONS.

television studies The academic study of television, institutionally situated within *media studies, *cultural studies, or *mass communication, or allied with *film studies. The most common approaches include *textual analysis, *audience research, *political economy, and historical and sociological studies. *See also* GLASGOW MEDIA GROUP; USES AND GRATIFICATIONS.

television viewing patterns *Data on what is watched, when, how, and for how long, by various TV audience segments over a specified period. *Segmentation is frequently based on age, *sex, social *class, and/or *ethnicity. It may also distinguish between categories of viewers based on average amounts of viewing: light viewers (watching less than 2 hours per day), medium viewers (watching 2-4 hours), or *heavy viewers. Viewing is frequently classified by programme genre (*see also* TELEVISION GENRES), *channel, or daypart (e.g. *peak time). The study of such patterns can involve the keeping of viewing diaries. Traditional viewing patterns related to time of day have been argued to have been eroded by *audience fragmentation, media *convergence, and the online availability of TV on demand. *See also* AUDIENCE MEASUREMENT; TELEVISION VIEWING STYLES.

television viewing styles Modes of *interaction by individuals with *television in particular viewing contexts, including the viewer's relative focus on TV compared to simultaneous activities, degree of *attention to the screen, and levels of involvement with TV content. This is sometimes referred to in terms of **emotional involvement** or **critical detachment** (*see* HIGH AND LOW INVOLVEMENT). Some researchers have identified differences in viewing styles which relate to *gender stereotypes, such as an instrumental or goal-directed style among males and a relationship-oriented style among females (*compare* EXPRESSIVE COMMUNICATION; INSTRUMENTAL COMMUNICATION). This is reflected in observations such as that women are more likely to talk as they watch. In household contexts, the tendency for men to exercise more control over what they watch suggests the basis of such *performances of *gender in *power rather than *sex (*see also* PERFORMATIVITY). *See also* CHANNEL SURFING; GLANCE; GRAZING; PARASOCIAL INTERACTION; SIT UP OR SIT BACK; TELEVISION VIEWING PATTERNS; ZAPPING; ZIPPING.

television violence *See* VIOLENCE DEBATE.

televisualism (*adj.* **televisual**) The incorporation into another *medium of any *style or *content that is distinctively associated with *television: for example, a football *videogame which features instant replays. *Compare* CINEMATIC; FILMIC.

televisual reality Life, personalities, and the world represented and constructed on the television screen, especially when boundaries between TV and the everyday world are blurred and when TV is phenomenally experienced as an enhanced reality, when that which is most like TV is most real, or when the reality in which people live is framed by the *symbolic world of TV (*see* CULTIVATION THEORY). A form of *mediated experience distinguished from *lived experience of the social and material world. Sometimes used synonymously with *reality TV, often pejoratively.

teleworking The utilization of *computer-mediated communications technologies like mobile telecommunications and the *internet so that a worker is not tied to a specific location such as an office but can work wherever there is suitable *connectivity.

tenor *See* METAPHOR; METONYMY.

terrestrial broadcasting Earth-based transmission of radio and television, as distinguished from *satellite broadcasting. *See also* BROADCASTING.

territoriality 1. The behavioural ways in which individuals make claims to temporary or enduring ownership of spatial zones or objects. This can communicate (for instance) aggression, *dominance, intimacy, *affiliation, or diplomacy. Dominance, for example, is commonly signified by the control of more territory than others. Males tend to occupy more space than females do (for instance, in the legs apart seating posture). Goffman includes in his 'territories of the self', *personal space (*see also* INTERPERSONAL ZONES; PROXEMICS) and **possessional territory**: 'any set of objects that can be identified with the self and arrayed around the body wherever it is'. Such items include personal effects that can be deployed as territorial **markers** (e.g. bagging seats), or objects over which control is exercised temporarily, such as television sets, radios, and magazines. Phenomenally, over-close *proximity, unwanted touch (*see* HAPTICS), and sustained *gaze can be experienced as a territorial violation, though the limits are socioculturally variable. Territoriality is found throughout the animal kingdom, but the related and distinctively human concept of privacy is a historically modern idea reflected in the design of houses from the 18th century onwards: *see also* PUBLIC AND PRIVATE SPHERES. 2. For Deleuze and Guattari, a restriction of the free flow of individual desire imposed by an *institution such as the family or the state.

tertiary involvement *See* HIGH AND LOW INVOLVEMENT.

text [Latin *texere* 'to weave'] 1. Loosely, something written, typed, or printed. 2. A *message. 3. A complete piece of writing which is the focus for literary analysis, such as a poem or a novel. 4. (*linguistics) Any continuous stretch of *discourse having linguistic *coherence and semantic *cohesion, especially in written form, but including speech and *sign language in specific *contexts. Often also defined in terms of having a particular *communicative function (*see also* GENRE). Spoken forms can include not only monologues but also conversations or interviews. 5. The precise words used in a particular printed work (as distinct from interpretive factors 'outside' the text). By extension, any discursive artwork (especially literary works and films) regarded by literalists as containing authoritative evidence about what is meant: as in 'refer to the text' (*see also* INTENTIONAL FALLACY). Such a concept makes no allowance for *comprehension and *interpretation requiring readers to draw on both *textual and social codes. It excludes any *subtext. In *formalism, the primary focus is on close *textual analysis: *see also* EXEGESIS; LEAVISITE. 6. In *structuralist literary theory, a conceptualization of any literary creation as a product of the social institution of writing (*écriture*), actively generated by the reader in the process of interpretation guided by relevant *codes and *conventions (*see also* ACTIVE AUDIENCE THEORY; OPEN AND CLOSED TEXTS; READERLY; WRITERLY; *compare* READER-RESPONSE THEORY); a manifestation of *language which transcends any particular work or single *author (*see also* INTERTEXTUALITY). This is distinguished from a **work**: a bounded material object consisting of printed pages. 7. In *semiotics and cultural theory, any set of *signs which can be read for *meaning: this can include films, television and radio programmes, advertisements, paintings, and photographs (*see also* TEXTUAL ANALYSIS). To some *structuralists, the world is *social text. Although the term appears to privilege written texts (seeming *graphocentric and *logocentric), it applies to any form (including images, sounds, gestures and so on). Communicative texts are constructed and interpreted with reference to the *codes and *conventions associated with a *genre and in a particular *medium of communication. Texts are the product of *signifying practices and processes of *representation and *position both their makers and their readers. 8. A recording in any *medium which can be circulated and exists independently of its *author(s) (and users); in this sense the term excludes unrecorded speech. 9. In any written or printed text, the main body of a work (historically, the original words of the author) as distinct from surrounding material (such as illustrations, indexes, or appendices). *Poststructuralists see texts as unbounded: is the title part of the text? **10.** Same as *text message. **11.** (computing) *Data in the form of *alphanumeric characters. **12.** A book which is prescribed reading for a course of study; a textbook. **13.** A *theme or *topic, especially if religious.

text-audience relations *See* TEXT-READER RELATIONS.

text linguistics [German *Textlinguistik*] A sub-branch of *linguistics concerned with the study of *texts. This includes *textuality and the classification of texts by *genre in terms of their *textual features. Particular concerns include text *structure (*see also* COHERENCE; COHESION) and the social *functions of texts. *Compare* DISCOURSE ANALYSIS; STYLISTICS.

text message *See* SMS.

text-picture ratio *See* WORD-IMAGE RELATIONS.

text-reader relations (text-audience relations) The participatory *roles and relationships of the *addresser and addressee for a *text in any *medium. This often includes narrator–audience and writer–reader (or producer–user) relations and is often formulated as **writer-text-reader relations**. Stuart Hall's *encoding-decoding model of *mass communication broke away from dominant *sender-receiver *transmission models by allowing for the reader's contestation of the *preferred meaning (*see also* DOMINANT READING; NEGOTIATED READING; OPPOSITIONAL READING). Traditional text-reader relations are also transgressed when a textual format allows readers to contribute to shaping the text, as in *interactive fiction or computer games (*see* ERGODIC). Different *genres involve different communicative *contracts or sets of *expectations for producer–audience relationships. *Informational texts *foregrounding *content offer less scope for *interpretation than aesthetic texts foregrounding *form. *See also* ACTIVE AUDIENCE THEORY; MODE OF ADDRESS; OPEN AND CLOSED TEXTS; POINT OF VIEW; READERLY; WRITERLY; *compare* COMMUNICATIVE RELATIONSHIPS.

text-to-speech A computer software program that uses speech synthesizer technology to vocalize text written in a word processor program or other application.

textual analysis In media, film, and *cultural studies, the academic study of *texts in any *medium, using methods such as *structuralist *semiotic analysis, *content analysis, or *discourse analysis. Purely *formalist research focusing on the *text as a source of *meaning is often criticized for neglecting reception factors, on the basis that meaning is ultimately determined by the *reader (within the constraints of textual evidence and subject to sustainability within *interpretive communities). *See also* FORMAL FEATURES; STYLISTICS; *compare* TEXT LINGUISTICS.

textual codes (*semiotics) Interpretive frameworks representing our *knowledge of *texts, *genres, and *media, and their *conventions of *form, *style, and *content within a *culture or *subculture. These are drawn upon in both *production and *interpretation. Textual codes include scientific and *aesthetic codes, *genre, rhetorical and stylistic codes, and *mass-media codes. While many semiotic codes are treated by some semioticians as 'textual' codes (*see* SOCIAL TEXT), this can be seen as forming one major group of *codes, alongside *social codes and *interpretive codes. *See also* ADVERTISING CODES; ADVERTISING FORMATS; BROADCAST CODES; ENCODING/DECODING MODEL; FILM GENRES; NARRATIVE CODES; NARROWCAST CODES; PHOTOGRAPHIC CODES; PICTORIAL CODES; RADIO GENRES; READING; REALISM; REPRESENTATIONAL CODES; STORY GRAMMAR; STYLE; TELEVISION GENRES; *compare* TEXTUAL KNOWLEDGE; TEXTUAL SCHEMATA.

textual community *See* INTERPRETIVE COMMUNITY.

textual determinism The stance that the *form and *content of a *text determine how it is decoded. Critics of this stance argue that *decoders may bring to the text *codes of their own which may not match those used by the *encoder(s), and which may shape their decoding of it. *See also* AUTHORIAL DETERMINISM; LITERALISM; *compare* ABERRANT DECODING; AUDIENCE DETERMINISM; ENCODING/ DECODING MODEL; NEGOTIATED READING; OPPOSITIONAL READING.

textual features Distinctive formal (particularly stylistic and structural) aspects of an *utterance, *text, or artwork in any *medium. The focal concern of *textual analysis (especially within *formalism). *See also* FORM; FORMAL FEATURES; RHETORIC; STRUCTURE; STYLE; STYLISTICS; TEXT LINGUISTICS; TEXTUALITY.

textual function Halliday's term for a *linguistic function in which *language makes reference to itself and encompasses both *given and new *information. This is presented as one of three essential metafunctions reflected in all adult language usage (*compare* IDEATIONAL FUNCTION; INTERPERSONAL FUNCTION).

textualism 1. The *interpretation of a written *text based on establishing its original meaning—the *sense that the precise wording used was commonly understood to have at the time it was published. Primarily associated with statutory *interpretation (in US legal contexts) and with Biblical *exegesis. *See also* EXEGESIS; MEANING; *compare* HERMENEUTICS; RECEPTION THEORY. 2. **(strong textualism)** A pejorative reference to the *poststructuralist stance that everything is textual: *see also* SOCIAL TEXT.

textuality 1. **(texture)** (literary theory) A *formalist concept in New Criticism referring to the unique particularity of the expressive verbal *surface features in a work (such as *imagery and *connotations), as distinct from its *structure, *argument, or *meaning. 2. (*linguistics) The properties defining *texts as distinct from other types of linguistic units (such as words or clauses): primarily, *coherence and *cohesion. 3. (*poststructuralist *discourse) The inescapable writtenness of social reality: *see also* SOCIAL TEXT; TEXTUALISM; *compare* CONSTRUCTIONISM.

textual knowledge Familiarity with a range of *media, *genres, and *textual codes and *conventions of *form and *content. Along with *social knowledge, it is an essential resource for inferring the *preferred meaning of *texts in their *reading and *interpretation. In *schema theory it is seen as mentally represented in *textual schemata. *See also* ADVERTISING CODES; AESTHETIC CODES; BROADCAST CODES; CONVERSATIONAL CURRENCY; FILM GENRES; LITERARY GENRES; NARRATIVE CODES; NARROWCAST CODES; PHOTOGRAPHIC CODES; PICTORIAL CODES; RADIO

GENRES; READING; REALISM; REPRESENTATIONAL CODES; STORY GRAMMAR; TACIT
KNOWLEDGE; TELEVISION GENRES; TEXTUAL CODES.

textual poaching The subversive *appropriation of *mass-media texts (or of
characters within them) by fans for their own pleasure. The concept has been
popularized by Jenkins, but the term was originated by de Certeau. *See also*
ACTIVE AUDIENCE THEORY; BRICOLAGE; FANDOM.

textual production The process of producing a *text in any *medium. This is
traditionally associated with a linear model in which, depending on the medium,
subsequent steps in the communicative sequence initiated by this act consist of
textual reproduction, *distribution, and *consumption (or reception). However,
textual *production can be seen as part of a *circuit of communication.

textual schemata Mental templates that help individuals to make sense of the
*form and *content of new textual experiences, so that *reading and *interpretation
involves reference to *expectations established by previous experience of *media,
*texts, and *genres. *See also* ADVERTISING FORMATS; FILM GENRES; LITERARY GENRES;
RADIO GENRES; SCHEMA THEORY; TELEVISION GENRES; *compare* SOCIAL SCHEMATA;
STORY GRAMMAR; TEXTUAL CODES; TEXTUAL KNOWLEDGE.

texture gradient An important monocular *depth cue in the *visual perception
of the world and a *pictorial depth cue and representational *convention in
which the size, spacing, and fineness of detail of similar elements decreases in
proportion to the distance from the observer. A form of *perspective. *Compare*
DWINDLING SIZE PERSPECTIVE.

TG *See* TRANSFORMATIONAL GRAMMAR.

thematic montage *See* DIALECTICAL MONTAGE.

theme (*adj.* **thematic**) 1. (literary theory) The central, dominant, or unifying idea
in a *text (or several texts), or a standpoint on the *subject, implicit or explicit, which
is reflected in recurrent *motifs, *imagery, and/or *symbols. 2. More loosely, the
general *topic of a text or group of texts. 3. In *discourse analysis and systemic-
functional *linguistics, the part of a sentence that indicates the *topic: what the
*utterance is about. This is often the initial element. The **rheme** is the semantically
important part of an utterance communicating *information relating to the theme.
Some theorists also refer to an intervening part (e.g. a verb) as a **transition** or a
transitional element. For example, in 'The medium is the message', 'The medium'
is the theme, 'is the message' is the rheme, though some would list 'is' as the
transition. The distinction is sometimes related to the concepts of *given and new.

theory 1. In natural science and social science, a set of formal, testable
*hypotheses or *propositions designed to explain some phenomenon: *see also*
MODEL. 2. More loosely, any systematic explanatory *framing of a phenomenon: for
instance, *psychoanalytic theory or *symbolic interactionism. 3. A pejorative
reference to speculation as opposed to *fact: **theoretical** rather than empirical
approaches. *See also* GRAND THEORY. 4. General principles as distinct from *practice*
or practical activities within some domain. Often used pejoratively by

practitioners of some skill to refer to academic study. A pragmatic distinction between theory and practice is widespread in film and media-studies courses.

theory-driven processing *See* TOP-DOWN PROCESSING.

third-person effects The supposedly dramatic impact of *mass media on people other than those reporting this phenomenon. For instance, most consumers agree that *advertising works, but never on them. Many blame onscreen violence for violent behaviour on the streets, but this never affects anyone they know. This reflects an ironic impact of the media on their own judgements.

third-person point of view (third-person narration) In literary *fiction, the most common mode of *narration in which the *narrator acts as a non-participating observer of the represented *events. Often an *omniscient point of view, though sometimes reflecting restricted *knowledge (a limited *point of view) and sometimes limited reliability; usually such narrators are self-effacing rather than intrusive commentators. In academic writing, third-person narration has traditionally been regarded as more 'objective' and '*transparent' than first-person narration; contemporary critics note that this style obscures authorial *agency—*facts and *events appear to 'speak for themselves'. *Compare* FIRST-PERSON POINT OF VIEW; OBJECTIVE CAMERAWORK; SECOND-PERSON POINT OF VIEW.

third place 1. Community meeting spaces such as cafés, pubs, and village halls which are neither domestic nor work spaces. The concept was proposed by the American sociologist Ray Oldenburg (b.1932). 2. In the context of *videogames a *virtual space which is neither an actual space nor a dream space.

thirty-degree rule Film and video editing guidance which suggests that the camera must shift at least thirty degrees when cutting between two *shots of the same subject (which are also of a similar sizes); otherwise the *edit will be perceived as a *jump cut. *See also* CROSSING THE LINE.

Thomas theorem (Thomas axiom) A concept formulated by the American sociologist William Isaac Thomas (1863–1967) that '"*facts" do not have a uniform existence apart from the persons who observe and interpret them. Rather, the "real" facts are the ways in which different people come into and define situations'. Famously, as he and his research assistant and wife Dorothy Swaine Thomas (1899–1977) put it in 1928, 'If men define situations as real, they are real in their consequences'. Such a 'subjective' **definition of the situation** by a social actor, group, or *subculture is what Merton came to call a **self-fulfilling prophecy** (as in cases of 'mind over matter'). It is at the heart of *symbolic interactionism. *See also* CONSTRUCTIONISM; FRAME OF REFERENCE; FRAMING; PERSPECTIVISM.

threads 1. In *bulletin boards and *newsgroups, a means of collating individual *posts that is built into the software in which the replies to a particular *message are listed below the original one , usually with indented left-hand margins. 2. A display of threaded *posts. A collection of individual posts that are replies to an initial message.

Three Act Structure *See* CLASSICAL NARRATIVE STRUCTURE.

360-degree commissioning (television) A demand from broadcasters that new programming should be 'multiplatform,' or designed to be integrated with other *interactive media content which is made available at the same time across the *internet, on *mobile phones, and as a part of interactive television services. *See also* CONVERGENCE.

3:2 pull-down *See* PULL-DOWN.

TIA *See* TOTAL INFORMATION AWARENESS.

tie signs Nonverbal *signals or verbal signs constituting public displays of a personal bond between two individuals. Most obviously, these can take the form of close *proximity and *orientation, sustained body-contact, shared *facial expressions, *postures, *gestures, and/or verbal exchanges. They can reflect relationships ranging from casual to very intimate. The term was coined by Desmond Morris in 1977. *See also* HAPTICS; POSTURAL ECHO; PROXEMICS.

tilt (film and television) A dynamic vertical *camera movement created by angling up or down a camera which is mounted in a fixed position. Tilts do not involve *motion parallax. *See also* HIGH-ANGLE; LOW-ANGLE; *compare* PED-UP OR -DOWN.

timecode In professional video recording formats, a dedicated audio or video *track that identifies each *frame according to a chronological counter that is divided into hours, minutes, seconds, and *frames. *See also* BURNT-IN TIMECODE; LINEAR TIMECODE; VERTICAL INTERVAL TIMECODE; *compare* EDGE NUMBERS.

timeline A chronological display of an edited *sequence, divided vertically into separate audio and/or video *tracks onto which graphical *representations of the material which is being edited are displayed. A timeline exists in its own 'window,' and is part of the interface of a computer-based *nonlinear editing system.

timeshifting (time-shift viewing) The domestic practice of recording TV programmes so they can be watched at times other than their scheduled broadcast slot.

time-space compression The notion of a 'shrinking world,' conceived as existing without boundaries in a continual present which is a consequence of the logic of late capitalism enabled by modern communications and transport technologies. Harvey sees this as a challenging, exciting, stressful, and sometimes deeply troubling experience. *See also* FUTURE SHOCK; GLOBALIZATION; GLOBAL VILLAGE.

tiny MOO *See* MUD OBJECT-ORIENTATED.

titleless master *See* CAPTIONLESS MASTER.

TK An abbreviation for *telecine or a label signifying that a tape has been through a *grading process.

token A particular instance of some generic form (a **type**). In *linguistics, each individual example of the occurrence of a particular word (sometimes including its inflections or variants). In the sentence, 'rose is a rose is a rose', there are three types (*rose*, *is*, *a*) and three tokens of the word *rose*. The *medium used may determine whether a *text (e.g. a painting) is a type which is its own sole token (unique original) or simply one token amongst many of its type (a *copy without an original), e.g. a printed reproduction of that painting. The **type-token ratio** refers to how many *different* words there are in a text in relation to the total wordcount.

tokenism (*adj.* **tokenistic**) The recruitment or *representation of a small number of members of an under-represented group when this action is negatively perceived (especially by members of such groups) as ritualistic *political correctness or strategic public *impression management.

tolerance of ambiguity A *cognitive style representing the degree to which an individual is comfortable with situations or stimuli which lack a single clear and regular pattern or an obviously correct *interpretation. In *perception and recall this is reflected in the extent to which they tend to transform irregular configurations into standardized forms. We all tend to standardize like this to some extent, but those who are more intolerant of *ambiguity show a stronger tendency to do this. Some features of such intolerance include a strong preference for: *symmetry, regularity, familiarity, simple dichotomies, black-and-white solutions, rapid *closure, *stereotyping, and compartmentalization. Contexts in which rational analysis has a high status (such as scientific research) tend to discourage ambiguity; contexts in which individual *interpretation is prominent (such as the arts) tend to show more acceptance of it. *See also* ASSIMILATION; LEVELLING AND SHARPENING.

top-down communication *See* DOWNWARD COMMUNICATION.

top-down processing (**theory-driven processing, hypothesis-led processing**) A mode of *perception (or a phase in a *perceptual cycle) in which *schemata or *hypotheses set up prior *expectations which drive the search for *data. This is the dominant mode when you are convinced, on the basis of limited data, that you have seen a friend, just before *bottom-up processing comes into play, alerting you to inconsistent data as you realize that it is a total stranger. Also, an analogous mode of *inference. *Compare* BOTTOM-UP PROCESSING.

topic 1. The *subject of a *text or *discourse. 2. (classification) A *theme or heading within a subject. 3. (*linguistics) Part of a sentence indicating what the sentence is about: *see also* GIVEN; *compare* THEME. 4. In traditional *rhetoric, any standard *argument or set piece used in speeches.

total information awareness (TIA) A massive *surveillance programme which aimed to identify potential terrorists through compiling detailed records of the activities of millions of suspects. TIA was proposed in 2001 by the US government under the auspices of the Pentagon and rejected by Congress in 2002.

touch *See* HAPTICS.

track 1. (**tracking shot**) (film and video) A dynamic *shot that moves horizontally along an x-, y-, or z-axis (**track left, right, in,** or **out**) which is created by moving the camera rather than by a *pan, *tilt, or *zoom. Tracking involves *motion parallax, which creates a feeling of depth, as *foreground elements change dynamically in the *frame to occlude or reveal *background elements. *Compare* PAN. **2.** In audio and video recordings, a particular area on the surface of electromagnetic tape where dedicated audio or video information is written and read. **3.** A way of conceiving of individual channels of information as separate entities represented in the form of dials, meters, buttons etc., which allow an operator to manipulate them separately: for example, on an audio *mixer, to adjust the overall balance of the individual elements involved in a sound *mix. In graphical displays such as in *nonlinear editing systems, individual channels of information are represented in a *timeline.

tracking 1. (film and video) *See* TRACK. **2.** (typography) *See* KERNING.

track laying In film and video *post-production, the preparatory work that is done before a sound *mix that involves assembling all the sounds that are needed for the mix, mapping them to separate *tracks and cueing them so that they occur at the right time in the mix or ensuring that they are synchronized with the pictures. *See also* SYNCHRONIZATION.

traditional transmission (*linguistics) The feature of language whereby it is learned in social groups. Traditional transmission was identified by Hockett as a key *design feature of human language: in this case, one that does not appear to be shared by the communication systems of other species. *Compare* SOCIALIZATION FUNCTION.

tragedy A serious *drama with an unhappy ending involving the downfall of the *protagonist. One of Frye's four main literary *genres, the others being *comedy, *romance, and *satire. For Aristotle, this involved *catharsis, and a **tragic flaw** on the part of the hero: 'Pity is aroused by unmerited misfortune, fear by the misfortune of a man like ourselves' (*see also* IDENTIFICATION).

trailing edge *See* BABY BOOMERS.

transactional communication or model *See* RELATIONAL MODEL.

transactive criticism *See* READER-RESPONSE THEORY.

transactive models *See* RELATIONAL MODEL.

transcendent signified (transcendental signified) For Derrida, the illusion of an ultimate *referent at the heart of a signifying system which is portrayed as 'absolute and irreducible', stable, timeless, and *transparent—as if it were independent of and prior to that system. He argued that dominant *ideological *discourse relies on this *metaphysical foundation. All other *signifieds within the signifying system are subordinate to this final meaning to which they point. Derrida noted that this privileged signified is subject to historical change, so that Neo-Platonism focused on 'the Monad', Christianity focused on God, Romanticism focused on consciousness, and so on. Without such a foundational term to provide *closure for meaning, every signified functions as a *signifier in an endless play of *signification. *See also* FOUNDATIONALISM.

transcoding 1. Translation between *languages or *codes or between levels within a language or code (*see also* CODE-SWITCHING). *Structuralists argue that some kind of translation is unavoidable in human communication. Lévi-Strauss declared that 'understanding consists in the reduction of one type of reality to another'. Greimas observed that '*signification is . . . nothing but . . . *transposition from one level of language to another, from one language to a different language, and meaning is nothing but the possibility of such transcoding'. *See also* TRANSLATABILITY. 2. (computing) Conversion of files by software from one format to another. This can involve lossy *compression.

transformation 1. Most broadly, a change from one form to another. 2. The tendency toward standardization involved in *perception, recall, and *representation: *see also* ADDITION; ASSIMILATION; DELETION; LEVELLING AND SHARPENING; SELECTIVE PERCEPTION; SELECTIVE RECALL; SUBSTITUTION; TRANSPOSITION. 3. (*linguistics) A rule-driven process converting patterns from one structural form to another: *see* TRANSFORMATIONAL GRAMMAR. 4. In *structuralist cultural theory the analogous notion, found in Lévi-Strauss, that new structural patterns within a culture are generated from existing ones through formal **transformational rules** based on systematic *similarities, equivalences, or parallels, or alternatively, symmetrical inversions. The patterns on different levels of a structure (e.g. within a *myth) or in different structures (e.g. in different myths) are seen as logical transformations of each other. Rules of transformation enable the analyst to reduce a complex structure to some more basic constituent units. Lévi-Strauss claimed that the structure of relations underlying the practices of one particular culture is a transformation of other possible structures belonging to a universal set. Structures can be transformed by a systematic change in structural relationships. By applying transformation rules the analyst could reconstruct a whole structure from a fragment and later stages from earlier ones. *See also* ADDITION; DELETION; SUBSTITUTION; TRANSPOSITION.

transformational grammar (TG) (*linguistics) A *grammar in which different structural levels are related by *transformation rules. In the 1960s, Chomsky argued that the syntactical *surface structure of sentences within a language could be generated from underlying *deep structures via the application of a limited set of rules.

transgression 1. Flagrant violation of rules, *codes, or *conventions, as in 'code transgressive' art which breaks *genre conventions, generates new *hybrid genres, or even appears to break out of existing genres. 2. (*poststructuralist theory) Challenging and breaking down conventional categories and ways of *framing phenomena, as in *queer theory, which seeks to destabilize *gender: *see also* DECONSTRUCTION.

transition 1. In film *editing, any of the techniques used to change from one *shot to another, by far the most common being a simple *cut (*see also* CROSS DISSOLVE; FADE-IN; FADE-OUT; WIPE). In *semiotics, the set of alternative transitions constitutes a *paradigm, and within the dominant *codes of *continuity editing the paradigmatic choice of anything other than the 'unmarked' cut makes the transition salient and meaningful: *see also* MARKEDNESS. 2. In historical periodization, the evolution from one historical period or era to another, as opposed to the revolutions implied in *great divide theories. 3. (*discourse analysis) *See* THEME.

translatability Capability of conversion into, or expression in, another *language, *form, or *medium. Linguistic *universalists argue that we can say whatever we want to say in any language, and that whatever we say in one language can always be translated into another. For *linguistic relativists translation between one language and another is at the very least, problematic, and sometimes impossible (*see also* INCOMMENSURABILITY; PERSPECTIVISM). Some commentators also apply this to the 'translation' of unverbalized thought into language. Even within a single language, some suggest that any reformulation of words has implications for *meaning, however subtle: it is impossible to say exactly the same thing in different words; reformulating something transforms the ways in which meanings may be made with it, and in this sense, *form and *content are inseparable and the use of the *medium contributes to shaping the meaning. In the context of the written word, the untranslatability claim is generally regarded as strongest in the expressive arts and weakest in the case of formal scientific papers. Within the literary domain, untranslatability is favoured in romantic literary theory, for whom the connotative meanings of words are crucial (*see also* CONNOTATION; ROMANTICISM). The formalist New Criticism in literary theory also condemns 'the heresy of paraphrase' (*see also* FORMALISM). Logocentric theorists argue that pictorial texts can generally be translated into language but that linguistic texts can seldom be translated into pictorial forms (*see also* LOGOCENTRISM; PICTORIAL COMMUNICATION). Benveniste argued that the first principle of semiotic systems is that they are not synonymous: we cannot say the same thing in systems based on different units: we cannot directly translate from one medium or *code to another without transforming meaning (*see also* TRANSCODING).

transmission function *See* SOCIALIZATION FUNCTION.

transmission models (**transmissive** or **process models**) 1. (**linear models**) Any *common-sense (but highly-*reductionist) conceptions of *communication, framing it in terms of a *sender transmitting or 'conveying' a *message or *information to a *receiver (a one-way process). Everyday references to communication are often based on this *conduit metaphor (as in references to 'delivering the curriculum'). Transmission is also the basis for *Shannon and Weaver's model of communication. Such models have been widely criticized because they ignore key factors such as *social and *textual codes, *contexts (primarily situations), *medium, *communicative functions, and *communicative relationships. They reduce *meaning to *informational *content, treat reception as passive, and are *sender-oriented. Many transmission models, especially in relation to *mass communication, add that the act of communication has some kind of *effect on receivers: an asymmetrical framing. *See also* COMMUNICATION MODELS; HYPODERMIC MODEL. 2. More broadly (e.g. when contrasted with *constitutive or *meaning-oriented models), all *message-oriented models of communication—whether these are linear models or circular *interaction models. 3. A metaphor for the primary function of the *mass media being the *instrumental one of relaying

messages (the media as messengers). McQuail sees as prototypical a version
outlined by the American communication theorists Bruce H. Westley and Malcolm
S. MacLean in 1957, in which messages are selected primarily in terms of what is
popular with the audience, making this process dependent on *feedback. The
media are thus regarded as relatively neutral, a notion consonant with the *market
model. This takes no account of the biases of *selective representation (*see also*
NEWS VALUES; NEWSWORTHINESS) or of pressures from market forces or dominant
groups: *compare* PUBLICITY MODEL; RECEPTION MODEL; RITUAL MODEL.

(⊕) SEE WEB LINKS
• Transmission model

transmitter 1. A device that generates or amplifies an electromagnetic *signal
which is modulated to carry *information: *see* ANALOGUE; DIGITAL; MOBILE PHONE;
RADIO WAVES. 2. In *Shannon and Weaver's model of communication (1949), that
which changes a *message from a *source into a *signal sent over a communication
*channel. For example, in *speech communication, Weaver tells us that the
transmitter would be the speaker's voice.

transparency 1. The way in which a familiar *medium, tool, or technique
retreats to invisibility through repeated use for competent users, who focus instead
on their *purposes: *see also* NEUTRALITY. 2. The apparent invisibility to readers of
the *constructedness of a *text (especially a *mass-media text) when it employs
familiar *conventions or *codes. Particular *media and *genre conventions become
so familiar through everyday usage that they come to seem simply 'natural' (*see also*
NATURALIZATION). When a *medium is treated *instrumentally as purely a means to
an end, its mediation becomes transparent (and its *materiality is minimized). The
importance accorded to transparency varies in relation to genre and *function:
*poetic language tends to be more opaque than conventional prose. In *realistic
texts, the authorial goal is for the medium, codes, and *signs to be discounted by
readers as transparent and for the makers of the text to be invisible. Semioticians
have sought to demonstrate that the apparent transparency of even the most
'realistic' *signifier, text, genre, or medium is illusory, since *representational codes
are always involved. *See also* CLASSIC REALIST TEXT; *compare* MARKEDNESS.

transposition 1. One of the four logical ways in which *perception, *memory, or
*description/depiction can perform a significant structural *transformation of its
source material. Transposition involves changing the spatial or sequential
relationship of elements. For instance, in trying to recall a scene, an eye-witness
might unconsciously and innocently 'normalize' a 'disordered' sequence of *events.
See also ADDITION; DELETION; SUBSTITUTION; TRANSFORMATION. 2. (*rhetoric)
Transmutatio, one of Quintilian's four types of rhetorical *figures of speech
involving deviation (*mutatio*): in this case, the rearrangement or permutation of
elements, e.g. inversion or **metathesis,** as in an Australian judge's comment about
feminists: 'If I had my way with Germaine Greer's followers, I would put them all
behind bras.'

travelling matte In film, a *special effect where a subject is filmed against
a blue or green background (*see* GREEN SCREEN) in order to generate an opaque

mask (or matte) which exactly matches their movements so that the subject can then be superimposed over a separately filmed background and not appear to be semi-transparent. In television and video this is called *chroma keying or **colour separation overlay**.

treatment In the *media industries, an outline of a film, programme, or series which describes its key elements before a *script is written and enables *producers to assess its viability. *See also* HIGH CONCEPT; PITCH.

trending topics *See* HASH TAG.

triad *See* DYAD.

triadic model *See* SEMIOTIC TRIANGLE.

trimming In film and video *editing, the procedure of adjusting the beginning and end *cuts of a particular *shot in relation to the preceding or following *footage, or adding to or taking away from the overall duration of a *sequence. In traditional film editing, the strips of film that are cut out of a sequence are called **trims**. These are saved in labelled containers called 'bins' in case they need to be cut back into a sequence at a later time; hence trimming is the process of adding or removing them.

troll A member of a *newsgroup or other online forum who deliberately *posts misinformed or provocative messages in order to goad other members into posting hostile replies, thereby initiating a flame war. *See also* DISCLOSURE; FLAMING; *compare* GRIEFER.

trompe-l'œil *See* ILLUSIONISM.

tropes Rhetorical *figures of speech that can be found not just in written and spoken language but in all forms of communication. Traditionally the four 'master tropes' are regarded as being: *metaphor, *metonymy, *synecdoche, and *irony. Tropes use words (or other *signifiers) in *senses beyond their *literal meaning.

truth to feeling *See* EMOTIONAL REALISM.

Turing test A pragmatic method devised by Alan Turing (1912–54), a British mathematician, for judging the 'intelligence' of computers. A person is shown into a room furnished with only a chair and a terminal and is asked to type their own choice of questions in order to determine whether the verbal responses displayed on the screen come from a computer or another human being. If after five minutes the interrogator cannot decide, the computer (or more specifically its programming) has passed the Turing test.

turn-denying In conversational *turn-taking, declining the turn when it is offered by remaining silent, through the use of vocal *back-channels (e.g. 'uh-huh', 'mm-hmm', 'yeah'), or through nonverbal *signals (*gaze avoidance and aversion, relaxed *posture, *head nods and shakes, or smiles). *See also* REGULATORS.

turning point *See* CRISIS.

turn-maintaining (turn-suppressing) In conversational *turn-taking, preventing another person from speaking through the use of audible *signals (increased volume and tempo, *filled pauses, decreased frequency and duration of silent pauses, or audible inhalation) and/or visible signals (continued gesticulation, gazing away from the listener, 'stop' *emblems, or touching the listener). *See also* REGULATORS.

turn-requesting In conversational *turn-taking, indicating a desire to speak. This is done through audible *signals (audible inhalation, simultaneous speech, rapidly repeated vocal *back-channel cues) and/or visible signals (open mouth, raised index finger, forward lean, gazing at speaker, quickened *head nods). *See also* REGULATORS.

turn-taking (conversation turn-taking) A system of rules, of which users are largely unconscious, that helps to ensure smooth transfers of initiative in interpersonal *speech communication. It is based mainly on *nonverbal behavioural *cues. Visual cues include direction of *gaze, *eye contact, *gesture, *posture, head and body movement, and *facial expression. Audible cues include volume, *pitch, tempo, pauses, silence, inhalation, and vocal *back-channels. *See also* REGULATORS; TURN-DENYING; TURN-MAINTAINING; TURN-REQUESTING; TURN-SUPPRESSING; TURN-YIELDING.

turn-yielding In conversational *turn-taking, indicating that you are finished and that the other person may start talking. This involves using audible *signals (decreased volume, slowed tempo, dropped *pitch for declaratives, raised pitch for interrogatives, or extended silent pause) and/or visible signals (cessation of *illustrators, long gaze at listener, or eyebrow raising). *See also* REGULATORS.

24-hour news *See* ROLLING NEWS.

two-shot In film *camerawork, a *shot in which two subjects are shown together: for example, an interviewer and interviewee, or two characters having a conversation. *See also* NODDIES; REVERSE SHOT.

two-step flow A *hypothesis that the *mass media do not have direct *effects on the general public but rather that persuasive media *content is mediated to wider audiences by *opinion leaders, so that media influence is filtered through *interpersonal communication via *social networks. This conceptualization reflected a strong contrast to **one-step flow** theory: the direct, powerful, immediate effects assumed in the *hypodermic model. The concept was outlined by Lazarsfeld and colleagues in 1944, and further developed by Katz and Lazarsfeld in 1955. The phenomenon has arguably been reduced as *access to the media has increased. *See also* DIFFUSION; GATEKEEPERS.

two-way communication Any *interaction involving dialogue. Associated with *interpersonal communication as opposed to *mass communication. *See also* SYMMETRICAL RELATIONSHIPS; UPWARD COMMUNICATION; *compare* ONE-WAY COMMUNICATION.

TX In broadcasting and television *post-production, an abbreviation for **transmission**: for example, a tape of a programme to be broadcast is known as a 'TX master'. *See also* MASTER.

type 1. *n.* A category of people or things sharing some characteristics. 2. *n.* (*linguistics) *See* TOKEN. 3. *n.* (*typography) Printed characters or letters (originally a single unit). 4. *v.* To write using a keyboard.

typecasting 1. Casting an actor or actress repeatedly in the same kind of *role because of their *appearance and their familiarity to audiences in such roles. 2. *Stereotyping someone.

typeface (*typography) An *alphabet of any size designed for reproduction, including different weights (e.g. bold), but excluding variations such as italic. Typefaces can be broadly classified by appearance into Roman, Blackletter (or Gothic), and Celtic types. Those most commonly used today are Roman types, which have four subcategories: *serif, *sans-serif, *cursive, and ornamental (*compare* FONT FAMILY). *See also* TYPOGRAPHY.

typeface personality The dominant *connotations of the use of a particular *font (which can be inflected by the *context). Fonts are commonly regarded by typographers as having certain connotational dimensions, such as formal/casual, friendly/serious, warm/cool, and traditional/modern. These can be seen as reflecting different *text-reader relations. Designers often use *serif fonts to reinforce a classic, formal, or authoritative visual identity and *sans serif fonts to create a clean, modern one. Certain qualities of fonts can generate *gender connotations. For instance, curvy or rounded forms (including *script fonts and *italic) are seen as more feminine, and straighter, more upright forms as more masculine. The same pattern is associated with lighter and thinner forms (and those with varying stroke thicknesses) as distinct from bolder forms (and those with more uniform stroke thickness).

((()) SEE WEB LINKS

• EsperFonto

type family *See* FONT FAMILY.

type font A complete set of any one size and style of a particular *typeface.

type-token ratio *See* TOKEN.

typification (sociology) The use of *social schemata based on typical features rather than unique instances, guiding our behavioural *expectations in particular situations. These are based on mediated *information as well as *lived experience. Also, the process by which we construct a mental picture of the social world on this basis. *See also* STEREOTYPING.

typography 1. The art and process of designing typeset material, including the choice of *fonts (*see also* TYPEFACE PERSONALITY), *legibility, *leading, *kerning, layout, and the use of *white space. 2. Loosely, the appearance of printed texts.

U

UCC (user-created content) *See* USER-GENERATED CONTENT.

UGC *See* USER-GENERATED CONTENT.

UHF (ultra high frequency) *See* RADIO WAVES.

unaided recall *See* AIDED RECALL.

unconscious bias Any distortion of experience by an observer or reporter of which they are not themselves aware. This includes the processes of unintentional selectivity and transformation involved in *perception, recall, *representation, and *interpretation (*see also* ADDITION; ASSIMILATION; DELETION; HALO EFFECT; LEVELLING AND SHARPENING; LOOKISM; NONVERBAL BIAS; PERCEPTUAL DEFENCE; PERCEPTUAL SET; RECEIVER SELECTIVITY; SALIENCE; SELECTIVE ATTENTION; SELECTIVE DISTORTION; SELECTIVE EXPOSURE; SELECTIVE PERCEPTION; SELECTIVE RECALL; SELECTIVE REPRESENTATION; SELECTIVE RETENTION; STEREOTYPING; SUBSTITUTION; TRANSPOSITION; TYPIFICATION). It also includes the influence of sociocultural frameworks on an observer or reporter, the cultural familiarity of which renders them transparent to them (*see also* ETHNOCENTRISM; GENDER BIAS; INTERVIEWER BIAS; MALE NORM; NEWS VALUES; OBSERVER BIAS; OCULARCENTRISM; PHONOCENTRISM; PROXIMITY; SCRIPTISM). *See also* BIAS.

undecidability *See* INDETERMINACY.

undercoding The low *redundancy of narrowcast *codes in *texts which are code-transgressive and structurally complex. A quality associated with artworks. *See also* NARROWCASTING; TRANSGRESSION; *compare* OVERCODING.

underground media or press *See* ALTERNATIVE MEDIA.

under-representation *See* SYMBOLIC ERASURE.

uniform resource locator (URL) A unique *internet address that carries encoded *information about a document's type and location.

unintentional communication *Compare* INTENTIONAL COMMUNICATION.
1. Meanings 'given off' (Goffman) by an individual's *body language through nonverbal *leakage, or unconsciously signified by their *appearance, dress, or behaviour, including whatever may be noticeable by its absence in a particular *context (*see also* ANALOGIC COMMUNICATION). As Watzlawick observed, 'one cannot *not* communicate', regardless of whether an observer's *inferences are

warranted. 2. Meanings within a *text discernible by an audience but of which the author was not aware: *see also* INTENTIONAL FALLACY. 3. *See* MISCOMMUNICATION.

unique selling proposition (USP) The particular benefits that a product, *brand, or service offers to consumers which differentiate it from its rivals in the marketplace.

universal grammar A hypothetical set of basic linguistic rules and parameters with which, according to Chomsky, all human beings are born.

universalism 1. **(cognitive universalism)** The *structuralist notion, found in Lévi-Strauss and analogous to Chomsky's notion of *transformational grammar, that all human beings unconsciously impose structure on the world through the same fundamental mental categories: *see also* BINARY OPPOSITION; DEEP STRUCTURE; TRANSFORMATION. 2. **(linguistic universalism)** The view that, while languages vary in their *surface structure, every language is based on the same underlying universal structure or laws (*see also* UNIVERSAL GRAMMAR). In contrast to *linguistic relativists, universalists argue that we can say whatever we want to say in any *language, and that whatever we say in one language can always be translated into another: *see also* TRANSLATABILITY.

universe of discourse The entire system of concepts forming a *frame of reference within a particular domain or *discourse. For instance, 'the world of advertising' within which a particular discourse is framed. *See also* INTERPRETIVE COMMUNITY.

univocality In contrast to *polyvocality, the use of a single voice as a *narrative mode within a *text. Univocal texts offer a *preferred reading of what they represent. By obscuring *agency, this mode of *narration, in association with *third-person point of view, tends to be associated with the apparently 'unauthored' *transparency of *realism. Univocality contributes to *closure by suppressing *contradiction.

unlimited semiosis The term coined by Eco to refer to the way in which, for Peirce (via the *interpretant), for Barthes (via *connotation), for Derrida (via *freeplay), and for Lacan (via 'the sliding signified'; *see* SLIPPAGE OF MEANING), the *signified is endlessly commutable—functioning in its turn as a *signifier for a further signified. In contrast, while Saussure established the general principle that *signs always relate to other signs (*see* RELATIONAL MODEL), within his *structuralist model the relationship between *signifier and *signified is portrayed as stable and predictable. *See also* DIFFERENCE.

upmarket A *target audience with higher-than-average socioeconomic demographics for the relevant population. Also known as **upscale**. *Compare* DOWNMARKET.

upward communication (bottom-up communication) Message-sending, *information flow, and *feedback within organizational hierarchies from subordinates to superiors (e.g. employee to management). *See also* ORGANIZATIONAL COMMUNICATION; SYSTEMS THEORY. *Compare* DOWNWARD COMMUNICATION; LATERAL COMMUNICATION; TWO-WAY COMMUNICATION.

URL *See* UNIFORM RESOURCE LOCATOR.

usability An approach to the design of technological *interfaces which attempts to make them intuitive and easy to use. Usability can be applied to any technology but it is specifically associated with web design through the work of Jakob Nielsen (b.1957), a Danish web-usability theorist.

(((())) SEE WEB LINKS
• Jakob Nielsen's website

USENET *See* NEWSGROUPS.

user A generic term for someone who uses any form of *interactive software, including webpages and *videogames. In traditional *communication models, the user occupies the role of the *receiver (*see also* AUDIENCE; CONSUMER; SPECTATOR; VIEWER). Critics of the term argue that it implies that the users of traditional media are necessarily passive. *Compare* ACTIVE AUDIENCE.

user bits *See* BURNT-IN TIMECODE.

user-generated content (UGC, user-created content, UCC) *See also* PARTICIPATORY CULTURE. 1. Online material that is either originated or appropriated and refashioned by amateur producers and accessible to general users of the *internet. 2. Broadly, any material produced by the audience or users of a medium: for example, amateur *footage of news events.

user network *See* NEWSGROUPS.

user-oriented advertising *See* PERSONALIZED FORMAT.

uses and gratifications A *functionalist approach to the *mass media framed in terms of people's *motivations and needs—concerned, in other words, with *why* people use the media rather than with media *effects on people: *see* ENTERTAINMENT FUNCTION; INFORMATION FUNCTION; MASLOW'S HIERARCHY OF NEEDS; PERSONAL IDENTITY FUNCTION; SOCIAL UTILITY FUNCTION. Gratifications can be obtained from a medium's *content (e.g. watching a specific programme), from familiarity with a *genre within the medium (e.g. watching soap operas), from general exposure to the *medium (e.g. watching TV), and from the social *context in which it is used (e.g. watching TV with the family). *See also* INDIVIDUAL-MEDIA DEPENDENCY; MEDIA FUNCTIONS; RELATIONAL USES; STRUCTURAL USES; *compare* ACTIVE AUDIENCE THEORY; RECEPTION THEORY.

(((())) SEE WEB LINKS
• Why do people watch television?

use value *See* COMMODIFICATION; COMMODITY.

USP *See* UNIQUE SELLING PROPOSITION.

utilitarian appeal (utility appeal) (*advertising) A psychological and rhetorical strategy which emphasizes the benefit of some product or service in terms of its practical functionality. This is a *rational appeal rather than an *emotional one. *See also* ADVERTISING APPEALS; HIGH AND LOW INVOLVEMENT.

utterance Any uninterrupted stretch of speech (or sometimes writing) produced by an individual on a particular occasion. Utterances alternate (*see also* INTERCHANGE), unlike nonverbal *signals.

u

valorization Loosely, the attribution of *value, but more specifically in *semiotics its attribution to members of *binary oppositions, where one *signifier (and *signified) is unmarked (and *positively* valorized) while the other is marked (and *negatively* valorized). Valorization is involved in processes of *naturalization while *devalorization* (or *revalorization*) is involved in the *deconstruction of the *ideological assumptions built into oppositional frameworks (a process of *denaturalization). *See also* MARKEDNESS.

value *See also* EVALUATION; FICTION VALUES; INSTRUMENTAL VALUES; NEWS VALUES; PRODUCTION VALUES. *n.* 1. A judgement of the relative desirability, usefulness, or worth of something within a given *culture which is frequently treated as if it were an absolute quality intrinsic to the object (*see also* RELATIVISM). This is reflected, for instance, in distinctions between the products of *high culture and *popular culture. 2. **(social value, cultural value)** An abstract principle widely shared within a particular culture, acting as a behavioural and evaluative ideal and internalized in *socialization. Values constitute the basis on which people rank things in relation to each other. *Functionalism stresses the importance of shared values for the maintenance of social order, social *integration, and social *cohesion (*see also* CONSENSUS; NORM). Values differ between cultures (e.g. Western, Islamic, and Asian values); historically, they are argued to have shifted during modernization, industrialization, and post-industrialization (e.g. capitalist societies having become more secular, less traditional, and more materialistic). Collectively, cultural values constitute a **value system**. 3. **(value-orientation, value system)** (*attitude research) An organizing principle held by an individual about appropriate or ethical behaviour; such values are regarded as deeper than *attitudes. 4. **(economic value)** (economics) The price of something as determined by supply and demand. 5. A subjective judgement of worth in relation to price: *see also* PRICE APPEALS. 6. For **use value** and **exchange value** in *Marxist theory, *see* COMMODIFICATION; COMMODITY. 7. For Saussure, meaning as the relation of a word (or *sign) to others within the signifying system as a whole. He distinguished the value of a sign from its *signification or *referential meaning. For him, language is a relational system of values and a sign does not have an absolute value in itself (*see also* DIFFERENCE; RELATIONAL MODEL). Words in different languages can have equivalent referential meanings but different values since they belong to different networks of associations. 8. **(value judgement)** (*epistemology) A subjective *bias deriving from what many theorists (such as *constructionists and *Marxists) regard as the unavoidable involvement of *evaluation in *perception and *interpretation and the impossibility of neutral observers. *See also* FRAME OF REFERENCE; IDEOLOGICAL BIAS; IDEOLOGY; IMPARTIALITY; INTERVIEWER BIAS; OBJECTIVITY; OBSERVER BIAS; SELECTIVE PERCEPTION. **9.** In statistics and mathematics, a quantity represented by a number (a **numerical value),** or (additionally in computing) the content of a *variable: not necessarily numerical, e.g. true or false.

value appeals *See* PRICE APPEALS.

vanishing point *See* LINEAR PERSPECTIVE.

variable 1. *adj.* Changeable or situationally different (as in 'culturally variable'). **2.** *n.* A measurable trait differing from one instance to another (as distinct from a *constant*). **3.** *n.* Items of *data to which *values are assigned. **4.** *n.* (social science) A categorical abstraction such as *race or *class seen as a differentiating attribute of individuals: *see also* DEMOGRAPHIC VARIABLES. **5.** *n.* A measurable factor which is either *continuous* and quantitative (such as age; *see also* ANALOGUE) or *discrete* and categorical (such as sex; *see also* DIGITAL). **6.** *n.* In research *experiments, a factor that changes or can be changed: *see also* CAUSATION; CORRELATION; DEPENDENT AND INDEPENDENT VARIABLES; INTERVENING VARIABLE.

VCR *See* VIDEOCASSETTE RECORDER.

vector graphics Computer graphics using mathematical formulae to produce images by mapping coordinates, specifying *colours, and drawing lines and curves (known as **vectors**). This results in a smaller file size than *raster graphics. This system is used in web animation formats such as Flash.

vehicle 1. (literary) *See* METAPHOR; METONYMY. **2.** (*semiotics) *See* SIGN VEHICLE.

verbal bias *See* LOGOCENTRISM.

verbal communication Human *interaction through the use of words, or *messages in linguistic form. Colloquial usage refers to speech (*oral communication), especially face-to-face, but academic usage includes mediated forms, written communication, and sometimes *sign language. Logically, as distinguished from *nonverbal communication, though in much communication these are complementary modes.

verisimilitude *See* NATURALISM.

vertical integration Strategic acquisitions and new ventures by companies with integrated management and *production and a *production-oriented focus. The motives are to achieve *economies of scale and to control each stage of production. This may involve a company gaining control of its suppliers (**backward integration**) or of its outlets (**forward integration**). Vertical integration (of *production, *distribution, and exhibition) characterized the movie industry in the *studio system era. *See also* DIVERSIFICATION; HORIZONTAL INTEGRATION; MEDIA OWNERSHIP; *compare* DIAGONAL INTEGRATION; HORIZONTAL INTEGRATION.

vertical interval The area at the top of a television image that does not contain picture information. In *PAL the first 25 lines of the screen represent the vertical interval. In the early days of television, these lines were needed to stabilize the picture. As the technology improved, the vertical interval was used by television engineers for various functions like carrying *vertical interval timecode and *closed caption information, and services such as *teletext. *Compare* ACTIVE PICTURE.

vertical interval timecode (VITC) *Timecode information encoded along with the video *signal, which typically appears in the UK as a series of white dashes recorded onto TV lines 19 and 21 in the *vertical interval of a television image. The advantage VITC has over *linear timecode (LTC) is that it can display usable *timecode information when a videotape is either completely still or moving very slowly. The disadvantages are that VITC becomes unreadable when the picture breaks up: for example, when it is rewound at high speed, and because VITC is part of the video signal, it cannot be changed or inserted without re-recording the video.

vertical ownership Ownership of the means of both supply and *distribution. *See also* VERTICAL INTEGRATION.

VHF (very high frequency) *See* RADIO WAVES.

VHS (video home system) The first mainstream video-recording technology for the home (along with Betamax) which used cassette tapes to store television programmes and also became a popular format for viewing rented films. *See* ELECTRONIC RECORDING; TIMESHIFTING; VIDEO NASTIES.

video 1. Broadly, any *analogue or *digital technology that produces still or moving pictures electronically including: television, *camcorders, CCTV, high definition cinema formats, and *internet movie file formats. 2. A system of electronically capturing, storing, transmitting, and reproducing moving or still images. Analogue video technologies include *PAL or *NTSC *television, and *VHS, while digital video includes *DVD, *MPEG-2, and *streamed media: *see also* FIELD.

video blog *See* VLOG.

videocassette recorder (VCR, videotape recorder, video recorder) A device which records a video *signal onto electromagnetic tape. Various formats of VCRs have been developed over the years including *VHS, Beta SP, Digibeta, and D5.

videoconferencing Simultaneous visual and auditory communication involving multiple participants (**conferencing**) at a distance (**teleconferencing** is purely auditory). When computer-based, also called **computer conferencing.**

videogame A computer-based *game involving a single player or any number of players. What is considered to be a videogame covers a broad spectrum ranging from simple games played on *mobile phones to vast and persistent online *virtual worlds.

videogame genres Types of *videogames that both borrow generic *conventions from other media, especially film (e.g. science fiction, gangster, horror, and war) but also focus on the activity of the player (e.g. 'beat 'em up', driving, first-person shooter, *role play, 'shoot 'em up', *simulation, and sports) which all imply different modes of engagement. There are also many *hybrid genres: for example, the *Grand Theft Auto* series combines a driving *game with 'beat 'em up' and 'shoot 'em up', set within a world of gangsters and petty criminals. *See also* FIRST-PERSON POINT OF VIEW; GENRE; INTERACTIVE FICTION; MMOG.

videogame studies (game studies) A fledgling field within the humanities that studies *videogames as well as other forms of *play as important cultural phenomena, rather than as causes of moral harm. *See* ERGODIC; LUDOLOGY; NARRATIVE; *compare* EFFECTS TRADITION.

((()) SEE WEB LINKS
• Game Studies

videogame violence *See* VIOLENCE DEBATE.

Video Home System *See* VHS.

video nasties *VHS video releases of horror films that caused a *moral panic in the UK and led to the introduction of the Video Recordings Act in 1984. *See also* CENSORSHIP; VIOLENCE DEBATE.

video news release (VNR; electronic press kit, EPK) A compilation of *broadcast quality (*news or *current affairs) *footage and *interviews without *voiceovers, captions, or other *branding elements. This is intended to be used as a 'kit of parts' by other news outlets to produce their own version of the stories. Electronic press kits tend to be associated with *entertainment and promotion; video news releases with *hard news and current affairs. They are licensed or given away by advertisers, governments, non-governmental organizations (such as single-issue pressure groups), and PR companies. They have been criticized for influencing news agendas (*see also* AGENDA SETTING).

((()) SEE WEB LINKS
• Supplying VNRs to the BBC

video-on-demand (VOD) Video services, such as the BBC iPlayer and YouTube, which contain a selection of pre-recorded programmes for viewers to watch at a time of their choosing rather than at their scheduled broadcast time. *Compare* TIMESHIFTING.

video streaming A technology which, in theory, allows large video files on the *internet to dynamically load and play without the user experiencing any delay. In practice users may experience some delay as the file is loading or 'buffering'. *See also* STREAMING.

videotape (VT) Plastic tape coated with a ferromagnetic material which stores a video *signal through electromagnetism. *See also* ELECTRONIC RECORDING.

videotape recorder *See* VIDEOCASSETTE RECORDER.

viewer 1. A person who looks at something: *see also* BEHOLDER'S SHARE; PICTURE PERCEPTION; VISUAL PERCEPTION. 2. An individual member of the television *audience; in *film theory the term *spectator is favoured: *see also* GLANCE; HEAVY VIEWERS; TELEVISION VIEWING PATTERNS; TELEVISION VIEWING STYLES.

viewing context *See* CONTEXT OF RECEPTION.

viewing figures *See* AUDIENCE MEASUREMENT.

viewing styles *See* TELEVISION VIEWING STYLES.

viewing subjects In theories of the *gaze (especially in *film theory), the *subjectivity of those looking at a visual *representation that is argued to be constituted through a process of *interpellation into particular kinds of *subject position. *See also* SPECTATOR.

violence debate The popular controversy or *moral panic about whether or to what extent the depiction of violence in the *mass media, or a particular medium (such as *cartoon violence, *video nasties, violent films, and 'shoot'em up' *videogames), can be held responsible for violent behaviour, associated closely with the issue of the *censorship of violent media *content. The research evidence is complex, contradictory, and inconclusive, but the *hypodermic model of *direct effects has long been discredited. *See also* AROUSAL; BEHAVIOURAL EFFECTS; CATHARSIS; CONTAGION EFFECT; COPYCAT BEHAVIOUR; CULTIVATION THEORY; DESENSITIZATION; DISINHIBITION THEORY; EFFECTS; EFFECTS TRADITION; MEAN WORLD SYNDROME; MEDIA PRIMING; MODELLING; SENSITIZATION; SYMBOLIC VIOLENCE; THIRD-PERSON EFFECTS.

viral marketing (viral advertising) A *marketing strategy which makes attractive content available online in the hope that it will spread among users: for example, every *email sent using Hotmail in the 1990s contained information about how users could get their own free Hotmail account.

viral video An *internet video that becomes hugely popular in a very short time through amplified word of mouth, whereby users recommend it to others using online communication tools. Likening the spread of such media to a virus suggests that users have no choice in the matter and the concept has been criticized as reinvigorating the discredited *hypodermic model.

(()) SEE WEB LINKS
• If it doesn't spread, it's dead

virtual audiences In *computer-mediated communication, all those individuals and groups who access the *internet and receive (and send) *messages using it. This includes the use of *email, *instant messaging systems, *chatrooms, electronic distribution lists, *newsgroups, electronic *bulletin boards, *virtual worlds, and the World Wide Web. Notably different from *mass audiences in being driven by shared interests (*see also* EPISTEMIC COMMUNITY; NARROWCASTING) and in the potential *interactivity involved. In relation to *interpersonal communication, virtual audiences are also distinguished by their potential *anonymity.

virtual community A social aggregation that emerges online when people communicate with each other in a public forum for long enough, and with enough human feeling, that they form meaningful personal bonds (Rheingold). *See also*

EPISTEMIC COMMUNITY; IMAGINED COMMUNITY; INTERPRETIVE COMMUNITY; ONLINE COMMUNITY.

SEE WEB LINKS

• *Virtual Community*: Howard Rheingold

virtual ethnography A *methodology outlined in 2000 by Christine Hine, a British media researcher, involving *participant observation of cultural activities mediated by *information and communications technologies, on the *internet or in *virtual worlds.

virtuality The wide-ranging presence of the virtual in *culture. For example, virtual money transactions where no real wealth is exchanged and the *virtual space in which a telephone conversation is held (Rutter).

virtual presence The sensation of being in an interactive computer-generated *simulation of an environment, associated with *virtual reality technologies. *See also* PRESENCE STUDIES; TELEMATICS.

virtual reality 1. An interface that allows a person to interact directly with virtual objects in a three-dimensional computer-generated world. Typically a user would wear a head-mounted display, headphones, and force-feedback gloves. 2. A medium that creates a sense of *virtual presence through simultaneous visual, aural, and haptic stimuli, which is designed to make participants feel that they are in another place, by substituting their normal sensory input with *information produced by a computer. *See also* CYBERSPACE; TELEPRESENCE.

virtual space 1. A perceived representational space created by computer graphics software that employs a Cartesian coordinate system consisting of X, Y, and Z axes: *see* VIRTUAL REALITY; VIRTUAL WORLD. 2. A metaphorical way of conceptualizing the *interactions that 'take place' over a computer network: *see* CYBERSPACE.

virtual world A three-dimensional computer-generated environment that can be explored either from the *first-person point of view of an embodied participant (*see* VIRTUAL REALITY) or in the form of an *avatar.

visibility 1. In sexual *identity politics, the issue of making non-normative *gender identities more public in *everyday life and in media *content. As distinct from (relative) invisibility. *See also* HAYS CODE; SYMBOLIC ERASURE. 2. The increasing publicness of various phenomena which were formerly more private and not generally open to the public gaze: *see also* PUBLIC AND PRIVATE SPHERES. 3. The global openness to public view of people and *events, primarily due to television and the *internet: *see also* GLOBAL VILLAGE.

vision mixer *See* MIXER.

visual anthropology A branch of social anthropology (closely related to visual sociology) concerned with the social significance of visual and spatial practices (including *proxemics), and the use of visual media (particularly photography and film) in the study of *culture. *See also* ETHNOGRAPHY; VISUAL CULTURE.

visual cognition *See* VISUAL INFORMATION PROCESSING.

visual communication The generation and *interpretation of *messages and *connotations in visual forms, particularly still and moving images but also *body language (especially *gestures and *facial expression, but also *proximity, *orientation, and *posture) and non-linguistic forms in written texts (such as *typography and *emoticons). These are very often used in close association with verbal language (*see also* ANCHORAGE). Pictures can be informative and evocative, but there is academic debate about whether or not an image can communicate a *proposition (or make a statement); notably, many theorists argue that pictures cannot express a negative. The term also refers to this topic as a field of academic study. *See also* COMMUNICATION DESIGN; PICTORIAL COMMUNICATION; VISUAL LANGUAGE; VISUAL PERCEPTION; VISUAL RHETORIC; VISUAL SEMIOTICS.

(⊕) SEE WEB LINKS
• *Studying Visual Communication*: Sol Worth

visual consumption Visually-oriented *consumer behaviour, such as window-shopping, watching music videos, web-*surfing, and taking snapshots. *See also* AESTHETICIZATION; CONSUMER CULTURE; FLÂNEUR; GAZE; IMAGE; LOOKISM; MALE GAZE; SAVVY CONSUMER; SPECTACLE; SPECTACULARIZATION; TELEGENIC; USES AND GRATIFICATIONS; VISUAL CULTURE; VISUAL IMPERATIVE; VISUALISM; VISUAL MERCHANDIZING; VISUAL TURN; VOYEURISM.

visual culture Visual forms and practices within a society, including those of *everyday life, *popular culture, and *high culture, together with the processes of *production and *consumption or reception associated with them. This includes all visual media (visual art, photography, film, television, posters, etc.). *See also* AESTHETICIZATION; CODES OF LOOKING; FLÂNEUR; GAZE; OCULARCENTRISM; PICTURE PERCEPTION; SPECTACULARIZATION; SURVEILLANCE; VISUAL ANTHROPOLOGY; VISUAL CONSUMPTION; VISUAL IMPERATIVE; VISUALISM; VISUALITY; VISUAL MERCHANDIZING; VISUAL PRACTICES; VISUAL SEMIOTICS.

(⊕) SEE WEB LINKS
• History of visual communication

visual effects *See* SPECIAL EFFECTS.

visual grammar (visual syntax) Meaningful structural relationships between images in a sequence (as in a film or a comic strip), or between formal elements within a single image in any medium (as in the relationship between different parts of a webpage). *See also* COMMUNICATION DESIGN; FILM GRAMMAR; INFORMATION DESIGN; PICTORIAL SEMIOTICS; SYNTAGM; VISUAL SEMIOTICS.

visual illusion (optical illusion) Any anomaly in which a visual stimulus becomes systematically distorted in the process of *perception. Some of these are universal phenomena; others are culturally variable (for instance, those related to familiarity with *linear perspective). Their existence counters the notion that *visual perception is a passive process. *See also* APPARENT MOTION; HORIZONTAL–VERTICAL ILLUSION.

(⊕) SEE WEB LINKS

• Optical illusions and visual phenomena

visual imagery 1. Any depiction of things in a visual medium. 2. **(retinal images)** In *perception, the constantly fluctuating pattern of light projected onto the retina by the lens of the eye corresponding point-by-point (though inverted and reversed) to an external stimulus to which we have no direct access. 3. (psychology) An analogical *mental representation of a sensory stimulus (which is not currently physically present and which is constructed from *memory and imagination. **Mental imagery** is not limited to visual stimuli. 4. (literary criticism) Descriptive language that evokes a picture in the reader's mind: *see* IMAGERY. 5. A synonym for *visual rhetoric.

visual imperative The notion that the visual dimension of *culture is becoming increasingly dominant, and that *spectacle and display are dominating cultural forms. *See also* AESTHETICIZATION; IMAGE; OCULARCENTRISM; SPECTACULARIZATION; VISUAL CONSUMPTION; VISUAL CULTURE; VISUALISM; VISUAL TURN.

visual information processing **(visual cognition)** The various *cognitive processes involved in interpreting visual data (including *attention, *encoding, and decoding). The psychologist Gregory notes that 'We are so familiar with seeing that it takes a leap of imagination to realize that there are problems to be solved.' *See also* COGNITION; COGNITIVE FILM THEORY; GESTALT LAWS; INDIRECT PERCEPTION; MENTAL REPRESENTATION; PERCEPTION; PERCEPTUAL CYCLE; PICTURE PERCEPTION; PRIMING; SCHEMA THEORY; SELECTIVE PERCEPTION; TOP-DOWN PROCESSES; VISUAL PERCEPTION.

visualism 1. Most broadly, a *bias in favour of that which can be seen. 2. For **Greek visualism,** *see* OCULARCENTRISM. 3. **(hegemonic visualism)** The dominance of *postmodern culture by visual media, stimulated by new technologies of image *production and dissemination: *see also* AESTHETICIZATION; IMAGE; SPECTACLE; SPECTACULARIZATION; SURVEILLANCE; VISUAL IMPERATIVE.

visuality 1. The condition of visualness. 2. Vision as a social construction and/or the social world as a visual construction: *see also* CONSTRUCTIONISM. 3. A system of visual meanings transcending particular *artefacts: *see also* VISUAL CULTURE; VISUAL PRACTICES. 4. In Foucauldian discourse, the role of vision within an *epistemological regime: in its ascendancy, the objectifying and subjectifying power of vision within the 'scopic' regime of *modernity, based on *optics, *linear perspective, and Cartesian rationality: *see also* GAZE; OCULARCENTRISM; SPECTACLE; SURVEILLANCE. 5. The relation between seeing, knowing, visual *representation, and power. 6. A synonym for *visualism.

visual language 1. Loosely, any signifying system or visual *code in which a set of standard images is used as the sole or primary means of communicating concepts (as in the care symbols stitched into clothes). The use of the term '*language' is metaphorical where the system cannot be reduced to basic, recombinable units which are meaningless in themselves. *See* ARTICULATION; PICTORIAL COMMUNICATION; VISUAL COMMUNICATION; *see also* NONVERBAL LANGUAGE; PICTOGRAM; PICTORIAL SEMIOTICS; VISUAL GRAMMAR. 2. Any *texts demonstrating a communicative dependence on the use of words, images, and shapes to reinforce each other, as in flatpack furniture assembly guides: *see also* ANCHORAGE; COMMUNICATION DESIGN; INFORMATION DESIGN.

visual literacy The ability to read, understand, interpret, critically evaluate, use, and produce *messages in visual forms. The semioticians Gunther Kress (b.1940) and Theo van Leeuwen (b.1947) contend that 'In terms of . . . visual literacy, education produces illiterates.' *See also* BEHOLDER'S SHARE; LITERACY; PICTORIAL COMMUNICATION; READING; VISUAL COMMUNICATION; VISUAL LANGUAGE.

visual merchandizing The design and implementation of visual presentation and displays in commercial environments in order to promote products, services, or *brands through the coordinated use of space, light, and *colour. *See also* COMMUNICATION DESIGN; VISUAL CONSUMPTION; VISUAL PERSUASION.

visual metaphor *See* PICTORIAL METAPHOR.

visual perception The dynamic psychological and psychophysical processes involved in the selection, organization, and *interpretation of patterns in the ever-changing configurations of light on the retina, and in relating these to other perceptual information and to previous experience and *knowledge. *See also* ATTENTION; EYE MOVEMENTS; FIGURE AND GROUND; GESTALT LAWS; PERCEPTION; PERCEPTUAL CONSTANCIES; PERCEPTUAL CYCLE; PICTURE PERCEPTION; SACCADE; SELECTIVE PERCEPTION; VISUAL INFORMATION PROCESSING.

(((⊕))) SEE WEB LINKS
• Visual perception

visual persuasion The use of images to influence people's *attitudes and/or behaviour: for instance, through *meaning transfer, implied claims, *emotional appeals, *connotation, *pictorial metaphor, and visual *symbolism. This is a common strategy in *advertising, *political communication, and *propaganda. Persuasive *texts are occasionally wholly wordless (assuming the viewer's familiarity with the *codes) but there is usually some verbal *anchorage. *See also* COMMUNICATION DESIGN; INFORMATION DESIGN; PERIPHERAL ROUTE; PERSUASION; PICTORIAL COMMUNICATION; SUBLIMINAL MESSAGE; VISUAL COMMUNICATION; VISUAL LANGUAGE; VISUAL RHETORIC; *compare* NONVERBAL PERSUASION.

visual pleasure *See* SCOPOPHILIA.

visual practices The various ways in which images of any kind are produced and interpreted in specific sociocultural *contexts. *See also* VISUAL ANTHROPOLOGY; VISUAL COMMUNICATION; VISUAL CULTURE.

visual rhetoric 1. The purposive use of *symbolic visual, spatial, and/or spatio-temporal forms to communicate with an *audience, as distinct from purely *expressive communication: *see also* COMMUNICATION DESIGN; INFORMATION DESIGN; VISUAL COMMUNICATION; VISUAL LITERACY. 2. Persuasive *imagery and *symbolism in visual media and the cultural practices involved in its construction, use, and *interpretation: *see also* PERSUASION; VISUAL CULTURE; VISUAL GRAMMAR; VISUAL IMAGERY; VISUAL LANGUAGE; VISUAL METAPHOR; VISUAL PRACTICES. 3. An interdisciplinary field of academic study in which *rhetoric provides a theoretical framework for the analysis of the communicative uses of visual *artefacts or of the role of the visual dimension in *texts: *see also* COMMUNICATION DESIGN; INFORMATION DESIGN; RHETORIC; RHETORICAL TURN; VISUAL COMMUNICATION; VISUAL TURN.

( ) SEE WEB LINKS

• Visual rhetoric

visual semiotics The systematic study of the use of visual *signs and *codes in the *production and/or *interpretation of *texts and in processes of *representation in any *medium or *genre, and sometimes also of the role of *perceptual codes in *visual perception. *Structuralist analysis often employs the concept of *visual language. *See also* AESTHETIC CODES; PHOTOGRAPHIC CODES; PICTORIAL SEMIOTICS; PICTURE PERCEPTION; REPRESENTATIONAL CODES; SEMIOTICS; TEXTUAL CODES; VISUAL COMMUNICATION; VISUAL GRAMMAR; VISUAL SYNTAX.

visual syntax *See* VISUAL GRAMMAR.

visual turn (pictorial turn) A shift in emphasis in the humanities and social sciences toward an increasing concern with the importance of the visible. It is usually seen as having gained prominence in the 1990s and as having succeeded the *linguistic turn. *Compare* VISUAL CULTURE; VISUAL IMPERATIVE.

VITC *See* VERTICAL INTERVAL TIMECODE.

vlog (video blog) An online video featuring a person expressing an opinion about some *topic. *See also* BLOG.

VNR *See* VIDEO NEWS RELEASE.

VO *See* VOICEOVER.

vocal/auditory channel *See* AURAL/ORAL CHANNEL.

vocal communication *See* ORAL COMMUNICATION.

vocal cue Any meaningful variation in the sound of the voice during talk. These include: **vocal qualifiers** (rate, rhythm, duration, *pitch, tone, *articulation, loudness, pauses); *vocalizations; and **vocal characterizers** (laughing, crying, yawning, coughing, and so on). A sarcastic *intonation can mark an *utterance as ironic. Vocal cues signify *dominance, trustworthiness, dynamism, likeableness, and competence more effectively than *facial expression. Louder, faster, and deeper voices are associated with *dominance. *See also* BACK-CHANNEL; FILLED PAUSES; PARALANGUAGE; PROSODY.

vocalics *See* PARALANGUAGE.

vocalization 1. Human *production of nonverbal sounds (**vocal segregates**) using the voice, such as 'um' and 'ah': *see also* FILLED PAUSES; PARALANGUAGE; VOCAL CUE. 2. More broadly, the use of the voice to produce words or other sounds.

vocal qualifiers *See* PARALANGUAGE; VOCAL CUE.

vocal segregates *See* VOCALIZATION.

VOD *See* VIDEO-ON-DEMAND.

voiceover (VO) Spoken *narration accompanying film or video images in which the person speaking is not depicted.

voter apathy A perceived lack of engagement in the political process in Western democracies, evidenced by low voter turnouts at general elections. Neil Postman blames this on the '*dumbing down' of the media—a view contested by Brian McNair (b. 1959), a British sociologist.

vox pop [Latin *vox populi* 'voice of the people'] (journalism) An *interview with a member of the public canvassed for their opinion, typically in the street.

voyeurism [French 'looker'] An obsessive practice in which an individual (usually male) gains gratification from observing others as sexual objects without themselves being observed. Regarded in *psychoanalytic theory as an active role, compared with its passive opposite: **exhibitionism**. *See also* GAZE; MALE GAZE; OBJECTIFICATION; SCOPOPHILIA; *compare* FETISHISM.

VR *See* VIRTUAL REALITY.

VT *See* VIDEOTAPE.

v

WAP (Wireless Application Protocol) The first service that displayed webpages on *mobile phones.

warm colours *See* COLOUR TEMPERATURE.

watchdog 1. A function of the news media in democratic societies to expose and criticize perceived abuses of political power: *see also* FOURTH ESTATE. 2. A form of *advocacy journalism that scrutinizes the actions of public figures and *institutions and exposes any wrongdoing. 3. Groups or individuals whose investigations focus on biases in the *mass media.

watershed (television) A time after which programmes which contain adult themes, nudity, strong violence, or 'bad language' may be shown. In the UK this is 9 p.m.

wavelength *See also* ELECTROMAGNETIC SPECTRUM. 1. In *colour *perception, visible light reflected from surfaces in the visual *field: a physical factor primarily responsible for the psychological perception of *hue. This is one of the physical properties of light on which colour vision depends; the other two are *spectral purity and *luminance. 2. In radio and television transmission, the length of a single oscillation of a *signal wave measured as frequency (hertz) in terms of the number of waves that can be counted every second.

weak ties (loose ties) *Social relationships which are not close or intimate, as distinct from *strong ties. Weak ties are argued to involve infrequent contact, superficial bonds, and a narrow scope. Some associate them with online relationships, but remarkably strong ties sometimes develop in *virtual communities, and can be an antidote to isolation. Some sociologists argue that social *cohesion and the public sphere depend on the maintenance of weak ties. Mark Granovetter (b.1943), an American sociologist, argues that weak ties provide individuals with *access to more people, and more importantly a more diverse range of people and ideas, since they are often less similar to ourselves than in strong ties. Diffuse links can thus aid the *diffusion of *information and ideas. Ling suggests that the *mobile phone (which is supportive of strong personal ties) may be hostile to weak ties insofar as its public use reduces our involvement in the immediate public sphere. *See also* PUBLIC AND PRIVATE SPHERE.

(⊕) SEE WEB LINKS

• Granovetter's theory of the strength of weak ties

wearout The declining effectiveness of an advertisement or a campaign associated with increased *exposure: a repetition effect that leads to consumer boredom or irritation. An issue of *advertising effectiveness. *See also* AD RETENTION; FORGETTING RATE; MESSAGE DECAY.

web *See* WORLD WIDE WEB.

web browser *See* BROWSER.

webcam 1. A remotely-operated camera transmitting still images to the web which periodically updates images of anything from coffee machines to the surface of Mars. 2. Computer hardware and software enabling users to record video of themselves and upload it to the *internet or to engage in videochats (e.g. via an *instant messaging system).

webcasting A portmanteau term (*web* + *broadcasting*). The transmission of live or pre-recorded audio or video content that is *streamed over the web at a specific time. *See also* STREAMING; VIDEO STREAMING.

weblog *See* BLOG.

Web 2.0 The web seen as a platform for participation in which the consumer is also a producer. This was enabled by multiple software applications that supported *user-generated content. The term 'Web 2.0' was coined in 2003 by Tim O'Reilly (b.1954) and Dale Dougherty of O'Reilly Media as a *marketing response to the *dot-com crash of 2000–02. It is intended to be seen in contrast to a selective framing of 'Web 1.0', which characterized the web of the 1990s primarily as a source of *information delivered through the *browser, perpetuating the model of *production and *consumption associated with other *mass media.

(⊕) SEE WEB LINKS
• What is Web 2.0?

webzine 1. Broadly any *internet magazine: *see also* E-ZINE. 2. More narrowly, online magazines that do not have print counterparts but which are produced by traditional publishing houses: for example, Slate.com, which is currently owned by the Washington Post Company.

Westernization The spread of cultural values associated with Western Europe and their impact on other cultures. *See also* CULTURAL IMPERIALISM; DISNEYFICATION; ENLIGHTENMENT; ethnocentrism; McDONALDIZATION; MODERNITY; POSTCOLONIALISM.

whip pan In filming, a very fast *pan that results in a horizontal blurring. Cutting between two whip pans creates a stylized *transition between *shots that is frequently used in martial arts movies. *Compare* CRASH ZOOM.

white balance A camera setting which adjusts the *colour balance to compensate for the different lighting conditions present in indoor and outdoor shooting.

white goods A category of domestic electrical consumer goods including home-laundry appliances, refrigeration equipment, cooking appliances, microwave ovens, and dishwashers. Though these goods are now found in a variety of *colours, the concept persists. In contrast to *brown goods, they have traditionally been marketed to females with a primary focus on *appearance. *See also* GENDERED TECHNOLOGIES.

whiteness In dominant Western *discourse, an unmarked and naturalized category: an invisible, normative, non-colour positioned as neutral. Used in particular in the often unconscious construction of racial otherness but also more widely associated with positive cultural *connotations in contrast to blackness. *See also* COLOUR; DIFFERENCE; ETHNOCENTRISM; EUROCENTRISM; EXNOMINATION; MARKEDNESS; NATURALIZATION; OTHER; RACISM.

white space In a design or layout, blank, unused areas containing no text or images. For relevant *target audiences a sense of spaciousness in print or webpage design (as with the related use of physical space in *visual merchandising) can variously generate *connotations such as *upmarket, feminine, or sophisticated, in contrast to 'busy' designs (*see* CLUTTER).

Whorfian hypothesis, Whorfianism *See* SAPIR-WHORF HYPOTHESIS.

widescreen A general category of *aspect ratios, initially encompassing a range of cinema formats but now including television, in which the horizontal axis is significantly longer than the 4 x 3 dimensions of the *Academy aperture. *See also* LETTERBOX.

(⊕) SEE WEB LINKS

• Demonstrations of widescreen presentations

wide shot (WS) In photography and filming, loosely synonymous with *long shot because such shots often involve the use of a wide angle lens which creates a large *depth of field where both *foreground and *background elements are in focus.

WiFi A local area network that uses radio *signals to transmit and receive *data over short distances. The term WiFi is a brand name for the IEEE 802 standard of data transmission. It alludes to Hi-Fi (high fidelity audio).

wiki [Hawaiian 'fast'] Website software that enables multiple users to collaborate in order to create webpages. *See also* USER-GENERATED CONTENT.

wild sound (wild track) (film and television) Any unsynchronized sound that is added to a mix. *See also* SYNCHRONIZATION; TRACK.

willing suspension of disbelief *See* SUSPENSION OF DISBELIEF.

window *See* GRAPHICAL USER INTERFACE; LINEAR PERSPECTIVE; MAGIC WINDOW; REALISM.

wipe 1. *n.* (film and video) Any of a variety of optical *transitions in the form of a line or shape that sweeps across the screen. The relative infrequency of its use makes it a *marked transition compared to a *cut. 2. *v.* To erase a recording on magnetic tape.

wireless 1. *Radio waves as a medium of transmission for a *radio, *television, or *data *signal: *see also* WiFi. 2. Anachronistic name for a domestic radio receiver and metonym for the medium of radio: *see also* REAR-VIEW MIRROR.

withholding information *See* DISCLOSURE.

word cloud *See* TAG CLOUD.

word-image relations 1. **(text-picture ratio)** The ratio of words to images in terms of the area occupied (e.g. on a page). In *newspapers, this has traditionally been a key *signifier—a high proportion of pictures usually signifies a more downmarket publication. 2. The nature of the association between a co-present image and text: for instance, the relation of *anchorage between a *newspaper photograph and its caption. This is problematic in cases such as the famous 1936 painting *La trahison des images* (*The Treachery of Images*) by the Belgian surrealist René Magritte (1898–1967), which depicts a smoker's pipe and includes the sentence 'Ceci n'est pas un pipe' (This is not a pipe).

word processor 1. Software used for the manipulation of text documents, including formatting and spelling checks. 2. A dedicated hardware device sold in the 1970s that is regarded as a precursor to the personal computer.

word recognition *See* SPEECH RECOGNITION.

World Wide Web (the web, WWW, W3) 1. A vast repository of multimedia *information accessible on the *internet which is linked together through *hypertext. 2. A collection of software developed in 1989 by Berners-Lee to run over the internet consisting of webpages written in *hypertext mark-up language (HTML) and stored in directories as websites. Each webpage has its own unique address or 'universal resource locator' or URL. These are stored on networked computers known as servers which are accessed using 'hypertext transfer protocol' (HTTP) and read using a *browser. The World Wide Web is often mistakenly assumed to be synonymous with the *internet, but the internet preceded the web by two decades.

writerly An English rendering of Barthes' use of the word *scriptible*. He applied the term to texts that he saw as (desirably) demanding of the reader: polysemic, intertextual, full of *connotations, code-transgressive, and thus 'open' to active *interpretation: for example, he identified the short story *Sarrasine* by Honoré de Balzac as a writerly text (*see also* INTERTEXTUALITY; NARROWCAST CODES; OPEN AND CLOSED TEXTS; POLYSEMY). Such texts tend to be *reflexive. As Barthes himself demonstrates, 'writerly' may apply as much to a way of reading as to the text itself. *See also* INDETERMINACY; JOUISSANCE; *compare* READERLY.

w

writer-oriented In the process of written composition, a developmental stage at which the style and structure of a text primarily serves the needs of the writer (e.g. clarifying and organizing ideas) and makes few concessions to the needs

of other readers; also drafts of a text which reflect this feature. *See also*
INTRAPERSONAL COMMUNICATION; *compare* READER-ORIENTED.

writing 1. A *medium which carries *language in the form of visible marks and
from which *messages can be constructed and recorded with variable durability
(from sky-writing to headstones). It is not adequately conceptualized as a
transcription of speech since it has formal features and functions of its own. Its
*affordances compared with speech include: spatial configurability, which enables
the use of forms such as tables; physical separability from its author, enabling
dissemination (*see also* DISTANCE COMMUNICATION); durability, enabling historical
records; and a technological status, involving special equipment and skills, which
necessitates deliberate learning and teaching (*see also* LITERACY). Compared to
speech, writing is commonly seen as a secondary system (*see* PHONOCENTRISM), but
it can also be seen (as in *deconstruction) as primary (*see* SCRIPTISM), as well as
an equal but different form of language (*see also* MODELLING SYSTEMS). Although
images have many of the same *affordances as writing, it is usually argued that
of the two forms, only writing can be used to make unambiguous statements
(especially representing negatives, tense, or absence), and that communicative
visual forms often require the *anchorage of a written caption. *See also* PICTORIAL
COMMUNICATION; VISUAL COMMUNICATION; VISUAL LANGUAGE. 2. The activity or
process of producing written messages. Functions range from the instrumental
one of recording or communicating ideas to the constitutive *intrapersonal
communication of 'discovering' meaning: as Graham Wallas (1858–1932), a British
psychologist, put it, 'How do I know what I think until I see what I say?' 3. The
product of the process of writing, typing, or *printing: a written *text, ranging
from a *writer-oriented scribble to a reader-oriented novel. 4. Sometimes
specifically handwriting, often with *connotations such as individuality and
informality: *see also* SCRIPT.

writing systems The particular modes of linguistic *representation within
which verbal texts are graphically constructed and recorded. Most broadly, they can
be divided into those which are *phonological* (as with most modern forms), in which
the written symbols, signs, or *graphemes are related to the sounds of the spoken
form, and those which are not (as in the early history of writing); *see also*
PHONOLOGY. Phonological systems are either *syllabic* or *alphabetic*, and represent
sounds rather than meanings. In syllabic systems, the 'syllabograms' represent
individual spoken syllables (as in the Japanese *katakana* syllabary); in alphabetic
systems, the 'phonograms' or letters represent *phonemes with varying
degrees of regularity (English being very irregular; Spanish being very regular).
Non-phonological systems are either: *pictographic*, where the pictograms or
pictographs resemble real-world entities (*see also* ICONIC); *ideographic*, where the
ideograms or ideographs represent either real-world entities or abstract concepts in
a more conventionalized way; or *logographic*, where the logograms or logographs
represent words (as in Chinese and in the derivative Japanese *kanji*). In practice,
most writing systems involve a combination of modes. **Cuneiform** is a form of
writing (originally pictographic) using wedge-shaped marks to represent both
phonological and non-phonological languages; **hieroglyphic** is a form of

pictography, where the signs, or hieroglyphs, include ideograms, phonograms, and also determinatives, which indicate different senses of otherwise identical signs. Media theorists such as Innis, McLuhan, and Ong have argued that different writing systems have different social and/or psychological implications (a form of *media determinism).

( ) SEE WEB LINKS

• Writing systems

written communication Verbal messages primarily in the form of *writing (usually hand-written, typed, or printed) but which can also include images and other graphical elements. One of the two modes of communication through *language, the other being *oral communication. This includes *synchronous communication (such as *instant messaging), *asynchronous communication (such as postal mail and *email), and forms which blur the boundaries (such as *SMS text messages).

WS *See* WIDE SHOT.

w

XCU *See* BIG CLOSE-UP.

XLS *See* EXTREME LONG-SHOT.

Yale model 1. A model of *persuasion associated with a school of social psychologists at Yale University in New Haven, Connecticut: *see* HIERARCHY OF EFFECTS. 2. An approach within the *effects tradition to researching persuasive communication developed from the early 1950s. It seeks to identify basic causal factors underlying differences in the effectiveness of persuasive communication in 'opinion change'. *See also* CHANNEL FACTORS; DESTINATION; MESSAGE FACTORS; RECEIVER FACTORS; SOURCE FACTORS.

yaw The side-to-side rotation (around the vertical, or y-axis) of a viewpoint (for instance in a 3D-graphical environment such as a *virtual world). *See also* PITCH; ROLL; *compare* PAN.

zapping The practice among television viewers of rapidly changing from one *channel to another using a remote control device, especially during commercial breaks (*compare* ZIPPING). Some commentators see this as characteristically *postmodern in breaking up linearity, or subversively anti-capitalist. It can also refer to muting the audio during commercials. *See also* ACTIVE AUDIENCE THEORY; CHANNEL HOPPING; GRAZING.

zine *See* E-ZINE.

zipping Fast-forwarding through commercials on recorded media during playback. *Compare* ZAPPING.

zones of recession In visual images which involve the *representation of spatial depth, three general categories of distance from the viewer: *foreground, *middle distance, and *background. *See also* PICTURE PLANE.

zoning Regionalizing advertisements within cable systems or networks.

zoom (film and video) A *shot that appears to move towards or away from an object so that it grows or shrinks in the *frame. Zooms are created through the camera lens and shot from a fixed camera position and do not involve *motion parallax. *Compare* TRACK.

zoosemiotics *See* ANIMAL COMMUNICATION.

Biographical Notes

This list of brief biographical details was compiled to reduce repetition in entries. It is not intended as a list of key figures in the field, although it includes many whose ideas have had some influence within it. The use of bold indicates that the person has a web link. To access these web links go to www.oup.com/uk/reference/resources/media and select 'appendix web links' in the resources section. You will then be able to click straight through to the websites.

Aarseth, Espen (b.1965) Norwegian literary/videogame theorist.

Adorno, Theodor (1903–69) German philosopher and cultural theorist.

Allport, Gordon (1897–1967) American psychologist.

Altheide, David (b.1945) American sociologist.

Althusser, Louis (1918–90) French philosopher.

Argyle, Michael (1925–2002) British psychologist.

Aristotle (384–322 BC) Greek philosopher.

Austin, John L. (1911–60) British philosopher.

Bakhtin, Mikhail M. (1895–1975) Russian philosopher and literary theorist.

Ball-Rokeach, Sandra (b.1941) American media system theorist.

Bandura, Albert (b.1925) American psychologist.

Barthes, Roland (1915–80) French literary and cultural theorist.

Bateson, Gregory (1904–80) British-American anthropologist and cyberneticist.

Baudrillard, Jean (1929–2007) French cultural theorist, sociologist, and philosopher.

Baudry, Jean-Louis (b.1930) French film critic.

Beardsley, Monroe C. (1915–85) American philosopher.

Bell, Daniel (b.1919) American sociologist.

Bem, Sandra L. (b.1944) American psychologist.

Benjamin, Walter (1892–1940) German philosopher.

Benveniste, Émile (1902–76) Syrian-French linguist.

Berger, John (b.1926) British art critic and writer.

Berger, Peter (b.1929) Austrian-American sociologist.

Berkowitz, Leonard (b.1926) American psychologist.

Berners-Lee, Tim (b.1955) British computer scientist.

Bernstein, Basil (1924–2000) British sociologist and linguist.

Bhabha, Homi K. (b.1949) Indian postcolonial theorist.

Bolter, Jay David (b.1951) American new media theorist.

Boorstin, Daniel J. (1914–2004) American historian.

Booth, Wayne C. (1921–2005) American literary critic.

Bordwell, David (b.1947) American film theorist.

Bourdieu, Pierre (1930–2002) French sociologist.

Brecht, Bertolt (1898–1956) German playwright and theatre director.

Brooks, Cleanth (1906–94) American literary critic.

Bruner, Jerome (b.1915) American psychologist.

Bühler, Karl (1879–1963) German psychologist.

Burke, Kenneth (1897–1993) American literary theorist.

Butler, Judith (b.1956) American philosopher.

Cacioppo, John T. (b.1951) American psychologist.

Caillois, Roger (1913–78) French intellectual.

Castells, Manuel (b.1942) Spanish sociologist.

Certeau, Michel de (1925–86) French cultural theorist.

Chomsky, Noam (b.1928) American linguist and political activist.

Cohen, Stanley (b.1942) South African-British sociologist and criminologist.

Cooley, Charles H. (1864–1929) American sociologist.

DeFleur, Melvin L. (b.1923) American mass communication theorist.

Deleuze, Gilles (1925–95) French philosopher.

Derrida, Jacques (1930–2004) Algerian-French philosopher.

Dichter, Ernest (1907–91) American psychologist.

Dilthey, Wilhelm (1833–1911) German philosopher.

Durkheim, Émile (1858–1917) French sociologist.

Dyer, Richard (b.1945) British film historian.

Eco, Umberto (b.1932) Italian novelist and semiotician.

Eisenstein, Sergei (1898–1948) Soviet film director and film theorist.

Ekman, Paul (b.1934) American psychologist.

Engels, Friedrich (1820–95) German political theorist.

Fairclough, Norman (b.1941) British linguist.

Firth, John Rupert (1890–1960) British linguist.

Fish, Stanley (b.1938) American literary theorist.

Fiske, John (b.1939) British-American media scholar.

Foucault, Michel (1926–84) French philosopher and historian of ideas.

Freud, Sigmund (1856–1939) Austrian psychiatrist.

Frye, Northrop (1912–91) Canadian literary theorist.

Galtung, Johan (b.1930) Norwegian sociologist.

Genette, Gérard (b.1930) French literary theorist.

Gerbner, George (1919–2005) American communication theorist and researcher.

Gibson, James J. (1904–79) American psychologist.

Gibson, William (b.1948) American-Canadian novelist.

Giddens, Anthony (b.1938) British sociologist.

Goffman, Erving (1922–82) American-based Canadian sociologist.

Gombrich, Ernst (1909–2001) Austrian-born British art historian.

Gramsci, Antonio (1891–1937) Italian philosopher.

Gregory, Richard L. (1923–2010) British psychologist.

Greimas, Algirdas Julien (1917–1992) Lithuanian linguist and semiotician.

Grice, H. Paul (1913–1988) British-American philosopher.

Guattari, Félix (1930–92) French philosopher and psychotherapist.

Guiraud, Pierre (1912–82) French linguist.

Gutenberg, Johann (*c*.1400–*c*.1468) German inventor of the printing press.

Habermas, Jürgen (b.1929) German sociologist and philosopher.

Hall, Edward T. (1914–2009) American anthropologist and cross-cultural researcher.

Hall, Stuart (b.1932) Jamaican-British sociologist and cultural theorist.

Halliday, Michael A. K. (b.1925) British-Australian linguist.

Haraway, Donna (b.1944) American philosopher.

Harvey, David (b.1935) British-American geographer and social theorist.

Heidegger, Martin (1889–1976) German philosopher.

Henley, Nancy M. (b.1934) American psychologist.

Herman, Edward S. (b.1925) American political economist.

Hirsch, E. D. (b.1928) American literary critic.

Hitchcock, Alfred (1899–1980) British filmmaker.

Hjelmslev, Louis (1899–1965) Danish linguist.

Hockett, Charles F. (1916–2000) American linguist.

Hofstede, Geert (b.1928) Dutch cultural theorist.

Hoggart, Richard (b.1918) British cultural theorist.

Horkheimer, Max (1895–1973) German philosopher and cultural theorist.

Horton, Donald (b.1910) American psychologist.

Hovland, Carl I. (1912–61) American psychologist.

Husserl, Edmund (1859–1938) German philosopher.

Hymes, Dell (b.1927) American linguist.

Innis, Harold Adams (1894–1952) Canadian political theorist.

Iser, Wolfgang (1926–2007) German literary scholar.

Jakobson, Roman (1896–1982) Russian-American linguist.

Jameson, Fredric (b.1934) American literary critic.

Jauss, Hans Robert (1921–97) German literary theorist.

Jenkins, Henry (b.1958) American media theorist.

Johnson, Mark L. (b.1949) American philosopher.

Jung, Carl (1875–1961) Swiss psychiatrist.

Kant, Immanuel (1724–1804) German philosopher.

Katz, Elihu (b.1926) American sociologist.

King, Martin Luther Jr. (1929–68), American clergyman and civil rights leader.

Koffka, Kurt (1886–1941) German psychologist.

Köhler, Wolfgang (1887–1967) German-American psychologist.

Kristeva, Julia (b.1941) Bulgarian-French philosopher, literary critic, and psychoanalyst.

Kuhn, Thomas S. (1922–96) American historian of science.

Kuleshov, Lev (1899–1970) Soviet filmmaker and film theorist.

Lacan, Jacques (1901–81) French psychoanalyst.

Lakoff, George P. (b.1941) American linguist.

Lasswell, Harold (1902–78) American political scientist and communication theorist.

Lazarsfeld, Paul (1901–76) Austrian-American sociologist.

Leavis, Frank R. (1895–1978) British literary critic.

Leiss, William (b.1939) American communication theorist.

Lévi-Strauss, Claude (1908–2009) French anthropologist.

Ling, Rich (b.1954) American telecommunications researcher.

Livingstone, Sonia (b.1960) British psychologist.

Lotman, Yuri (1922–93) Russian semiotician.

Luckmann, Thomas (b.1927) Slovenian-born German sociologist.

Lull, James (b.1950) American media researcher.

Lyotard, Jean-François (1924–98) French philosopher.

MacCabe, Colin (b.1949) British literary and film theorist.

Maccoby, Eleanor E. (b.1917), American psychologist.

McGuire, William J. (1925–2007) American psychologist.

McLuhan, Marshall (1911–80) Canadian literary scholar.

McQuail, Denis (b.1935) British sociologist.

Malinowski, Bronisław (1884–1942) Polish anthropologist.

Marcuse, Herbert (1898–1979) German philosopher.

Marx, Karl (1818–83) German political theorist.

Maslow, Abraham (1908–70) American psychologist.

Mead, George Herbert (1863–1931) American philosopher, sociologist, and psychologist.

Merton, Robert K. (1910–2003) American sociologist.

Metz, Christian (1931–93) French film theorist.

Meyrowitz, Joshua (b.1949) American media theorist.

Miller, George A. (b.1926) American psychologist.

Mills, C. Wright (1916–62) American sociologist.

Morley, David (b.1947) British sociologist.

Morris, Charles W. (1903–79) American semiotician.

Morris, Desmond (b.1928) British zoologist and ethologist.

Mulvey, Laura (b.1941) British film theorist.

Murdoch, Rupert (b.1931) Australian-American media mogul.

Neisser, Ulric (b.1928) American psychologist.

Nietzsche, Friedrich (1844–1900) German philosopher.

Ong, Walter J. (1912–2003) American literary theorist.

Osgood, Charles E. (1916–91) American psychologist.

Parsons, Talcott (1902–79) American sociologist.

Peirce, Charles Sanders (1839–1914) American philosopher and logician.

Petty, Richard E. (b.1951) American psychologist.

Piaget, Jean (1896–1980) Swiss psychologist.

Plato (429–347 BC) Greek philosopher.

Polanyi, Michael (1891–1976) Hungarian philosopher.

Postman, Leo (1918–2004) Russian-American psychologist.

Postman, Neil (1931–2003) American media theorist and cultural critic.

Propp, Vladimir (1895–1970) Russian literary theorist.

Quintilian, or Marcus Fabius Quintilianus (c.35–c.100) Roman rhetorician.

Radcliffe-Brown, Alfred R. (1881–1955) British anthropologist.

Rheingold, Howard (b.1947) American writer on new media.

Robertson, Roland (b.1938) British sociologist.

Rock, Irvin (1922–95) American psychologist.

Rousseau, Jean-Jacques (1712–78) French philosopher.

Ruge, Mari Holmboe (b.1934) Norwegian political scientist.

Rutter, Derek R. (b.1946) British psychologist.

Said, Edward (1935–2003) Palestinian-American cultural theorist.

Sapir, Edward (1884–1939) American linguist.

Sartre, Jean-Paul (1905–80) French philosopher and writer.

Saussure, Ferdinand de (1857–1913) Swiss linguist.

Schleiermacher, Friedrich (1768–1834) German philosopher.

Schramm, Wilbur (1907–87) American communication theorist.

Schutz, Alfred (1899–1959) Austrian-American philosopher.

Searle, John R. (b.1932) American philosopher.

Shannon, Claude (1916–2001) American electronic engineer and mathematician.

Shklovsky, Viktor (1893–1984) Russian writer.

Simmel, Georg (1858–1918) German sociologist.

Snow, Robert P. (b.1937) American sociologist.

Sontag, Susan (1933–2004) American philosopher and literary theorist.

Spencer, Herbert (1820–1903) British sociologist and philosopher.

Spivak, Gayatri Chakravorty (b.1942) Indian literary critic.

Tannen, Deborah (b.1945) American linguist.

Thompson, Kristin (b.1950) American film theorist.

Toffler, Alvin (b.1928) American futurologist.

Veblen, Thorstein (1857–1929) Norwegian-American sociologist and economist.

Voloshinov, Valentin (1895–1936) Russian linguist.

Vygotsky, Lev (1896–1934) Soviet psychologist.

Warren, Robert Penn (1905–89) American poet, novelist, and literary critic.

Watzlawick, Paul (1921–2007) Austrian-American psychologist and communication theorist.

Weaver, Warren (1894–1978) American scientist and mathematician.

Weber, Max (1864–1920) German sociologist and political economist.

Wertheimer, Max (1880–1943) German psychologist.

Whorf, Benjamin Lee (1897–1941) American linguist.

Williams, Raymond (1921–88) British cultural theorist, critic, and novelist.

Wimsatt, William K. (1907–75) American literary theorist and critic.

Wittgenstein, Ludwig (1889–1951) Austrian-British philosopher.

Wohl, Richard (1921–1957) American psychologist.

Wölfflin, Heinrich (1864–1945) Swiss art historian.

Yarbus, Alfred L. (b.1914) Russian psychologist.

Young, Jock (b.1942) British criminologist.

Zola, Emile (1840–1902) French novelist.

Further Reading

General

Burke, Peter and Asa Briggs (2010) *A Social History of the Media: From Gutenberg to the Internet* (3rd edition). Cambridge: Polity.

Chandler, Daniel (2007) *Semiotics: The Basics* (2nd edition). Abingdon: Routledge.

Crowley, David and Paul Heyer (2006) *Communication in History: Technology, Culture, Society* (5th edition). Upper Saddle River, NJ: Pearson.

Ellis, Andrew and Geoffrey Beattie (1986) *The Psychology of Language and Communication*. Hove: Lawrence Erlbaum.

Finnegan, Ruth (2002) *Communicating: The Multiple Modes of Human Interconnection*. Abingdon: Routledge.

Fiske, John (1990) *Introduction to Communication Studies*. Abingdon: Routledge.

Giles, David (2003) *Media Psychology*. Abingdon: Routledge.

Hall, Stuart (ed.) (1997) *Representation: Cultural Representations and Signifying Practices*. London: Sage/Open University.

Martin, Judith N., Thomas K. Nakayama, and Lisa A. Flores (eds) (2002) *Readings in Intercultural Communication: Experiences and Contexts* (2nd edition). Boston, MA: McGraw Hill.

Rogers, William (2007) *Persuasion: Messages, Receivers, and Contexts*. Lanham, MD: Rowman & Littlefield.

Schirato, Tony and Susan Yell (2000) *Communication and Culture: An Introduction*. London: Sage.

Wetherell, Margaret, Stephanie Taylor, and Simeon J. Yates (eds) (2001) *Discourse Theory and Practice: A Reader*. London: Sage/Open University.

Interpersonal communication

Argyle, Michael (1994) *The Psychology of Interpersonal Behaviour* (5th edition). London: Penguin.

Hall, Judith and Mark L. Knapp (2005) *Nonverbal Communication in Human Interaction*. Belmont, CA: Wadsworth.

Hargie, Owen D. W. (ed.) (2006) *The Handbook of Communication Skills*. Abingdon: Routledge.

Henley, Nancy (1987) *Body Politics: Power, Sex and Nonverbal Communication*. New York: Simon and Schuster.

Horst, Heather and Daniel Miller (2006) *The Cell Phone: An Anthropology of Communication*. Oxford: Berg.

Ling, Rich (2004) *The Mobile Connection: The Cell Phone's Impact on Society*. Amsterdam: Morgan Kaufmann.

Mass Communication

Butler, Jeremy G. (2002) *Television: Critical Methods and Applications* (2nd edition). Mahwah, NJ: Lawrence Erlbaum.

Cohen, Stan and Jock Young (eds) (1981) *The Manufacture of News: Social Problems, Deviance and the Mass Media*. Beverly Hills, CA: Sage.

Cook, Guy (2001) *The Discourse of Advertising* (2nd edition). Abingdon: Routledge.

Creeber, Glen (ed.) (2008) *The Television Genre Book* (2nd edition). London: Palgrave Macmillan/BFI.

Crissell, Andrew (2002) *An Introductory History of British Broadcasting* (2nd Edition). Abingdon: Routledge.

Curran, James and Jean Seaton (2009) *Power Without Responsibility: Press, Broadcasting and the Internet in Britain* (7th edition). Abingdon: Routledge.

Fennis, Bob M. and Wolfgang Stroebe (2010) *The Psychology of Advertising*. Hove: Psychology Press.

Goldman, Robert (1992) *Reading Ads Socially*. Abingdon: Routledge.

Graber, Doris (1993) *Processing the News: How People Tame the Information Tide* (2nd edition). Langham, MD: University of America Press.

Hartley, John (1982) *Understanding News*. Abingdon: Routledge.

Leiss, William, Stephen Kline, Sut Jhally, and Jacquelline Botterill (2005) *Social Communication in Advertising: Consumption in the Mediated Marketplace* (3rd edition). Abingdon: Routledge.

Livingstone, Sonia (1998) *Making Sense of Television* (2nd edition). Abingdon: Routledge.

McQuail, Denis (2010) *McQuail's Mass Communication Theory* (6th edition). London: Sage.

Newton, Julianne H. (2001) *The Burden of Visual Truth: The Role of Photojournalism in Mediating Reality*. Mahwah, NJ: Lawrence Erlbaum.

Schramm, Wilbur and Donald F. Roberts (1974) *The Process and Effects of Mass Communication* (2nd edition). Urbana, IL: University of Illinois Press.

Seiter, Ellen (1999) *Television and New Media Audiences*. Oxford: Oxford University Press.

Tumber, Howard (ed.) (1999) *News: A Reader*. Oxford: Oxford University Press.

New Media

Egenfeldt-Nielsen, Simon, Jonas Heide Smith, and Susana Pajares Tosca (2008) *Understanding Video Games: The Essential Introduction*. Abingdon: Routledge.

Joinson, Adam N. (2003) *Understanding the Psychology of Internet Behaviour: Virtual Worlds, Real Lives*. Basingstoke: Palgrave Macmillan.

Lister, Martin, Jon Dovey, Seth Giddings, Kieran Kelly, and Iain Grant (2009) *New Media: A Critical Introduction* (2nd edition). Abingdon: Routledge.

Thurlow, Crispin, Alice Tomic, and Laura Lengel (2004) *Computer Mediated Communication: An Introduction to Social Interaction Online*. London: Sage.

Wood, Andrew F. and Matthew J. Smith (2001) *Online Communication*. Hillsdale, NJ: Lawrence Erlbaum.

Visual communication

Alvarado, Manuel, Edward Buscombe and Richard Collins (eds) (2001) *Representation and Photography: A Screen Education Reader*. Basingstoke: Palgrave.

Barnard, Malcolm (2005) *Graphic Design as Communication*. Abingdon: Routledge.

Berger, Arthur Asa (2007) *Seeing is Believing: An Introduction to Visual Communication*. New York: McGraw-Hill

Kress, Gunther and Theo Van Leeuwen (2006) *Reading Images: The Grammar of Visual Design*. Abingdon: Routledge.

Messaris, Paul (1997) *Visual Persuasion: The Role of Images in Advertising*. Thousand Oaks: Sage.

Rutter, Derek R. (1984) *Looking and Seeing: The Role of Visual Communication in Social Interaction*. Chichester: John Wiley.

Smith, Ken, Sandra Moriarty, Gretchen Barbatsis, and Keith Kenney (eds) (2005) *Handbook of Visual Communication: Theory, Methods and Media*. Mahwah, NJ: Lawrence Erlbaum.

Tagg, John (1988) *The Burden of Representation: Essays on Photographies and Histories*. London: Macmillan.

Worth, Sol (1981) *Studying Visual Communication*. Philadelphia, PA: University of Pennsylvania Press.